THE OXFORD ANTHOLOGY OF
AUSTRALIAN LITERATURE

THE OXFORD ANTHOLOGY OF
AUSTRALIAN
LITERATURE

Edited by Leonie Kramer and Adrian Mitchell

Melbourne
OXFORD UNIVERSITY PRESS
Oxford   Auckland   New York

OXFORD UNIVERSITY PRESS

Oxford London New York Toronto
Delhi Bombay Calcutta Madras Karachi
Kuala Lumpur Singapore Hong Kong Tokyo
Nairobi Dar es Salaam Cape Town
Melbourne Auckland
and associates in
Beirut Berlin Ibadan Mexico City Nicosia

National Library of Australia
Cataloguing-in-Publication data:

The Oxford anthology of Australian literature.

Includes index.
ISBN 0 19 554477 3
ISBN 0 19 554476 5 (pbk.)
1. Australian literature. I. Kramer, Leonie, 1924- .
II. Mitchell, Adrian, 1941- .

A820.8

OXFORD is a trademark of Oxford University Press

Designed by Jan Schmoeger
Typeset by Asco Trade Typesetting Limited
Printed by Kings Time
Published by Oxford University Press, 7 Bowen Crescent, Melbourne

Cover illustration
Tom Roberts   Australian 1856–1931   *Evening When the Quiet East*
Flushes Faintly at the Sun's Last Look, oil on canvas, 50.8 × 76.2 cm.
Reproduced by permission of the National Gallery of Victoria.

CONTENTS

IV: Contemporary Writing

ACKNOWLEDGEMENTS

The editors wish to thank the copyright-holders for permission to use the following material:

Arthur Adams: 'The Australian' from *Collected Verse*, Whitcombe & Tombs. Glenda Adams: 'A Snake Down Under' from *The Hottest Night of the Century*, Angus & Robertson; 'The Mothers have Curly Hair', *Bulletin*, 1981, permission of the author. Robert Adamson: 'The River' from *Cross the Border*, Prism Books, permission of the author. Thea Astley: 'Hunting the Wild Pineapple' from *Hunting the Wild Pineapple*, Thomas Nelson Australia, permission of the author. Murray Bail: 'The Drover's Wife' from *Contemporary Portraits and Other Stories*, University of Queensland Press; permission to use photograph of Sir Russell Drysdale's painting *The Drover's Wife* from Lady Drysdale. C.E.W. Bean: extracts from *On the Wool Track*, Angus & Robertson. Bruce Beaver: 'Sittings by Appointment Only' from *Open at Random*, South Head Press; 'Flying' from *As it Was*, University of Queensland Press, permission of the author. John Blight: poems from *A Beachcomber's Diary*, Angus & Robertson. Martin Boyd: 'The Light on the Sea' from *Much Else in Italy*, Macmillan; 'Expatriate' from *Day of My Delight*, Lansdowne Press; permission from Curtis Brown (Aust.). W.A.J. Boyd: 'The Swagsman' from *Old Colonials*, Sydney University Press. Vincent Buckley: poems from *Selected Poems*, Angus & Robertson. Charles Buckmaster: 'Wilpena Pound' from *The Lost Forest*, Prism Books, permission from Robert Adamson. David Campbell: 'Tree in a Landscape', from *The Man in the Honeysuckle*; other poems from *Selected Poems*, both Angus & Robertson. Peter Carey: 'A Windmill in the West' from *The Fat Man in History*, University of Queensland Press. Hal Colebatch: 'The Last Grammarians' from *In Breaking Waves*, Hawthorn Press; 'Walking home from work', *Bulletin*, 1980, permission of the author. Peter Cowan: 'The Tractor' from *The Empty Street: Stories*, Angus & Robertson. Bruce Dawe: poems from *Sometimes Gladness: Bruce Dawe. Collected Poems 1954–1978*, Longman Cheshire. Rosemary Dobson: 'Translations under the Trees', 'At the Coast' from *The Continuance of Poetry: 12 Poems for David Campbell*, Brindabella Press; other poems from *Selected Poems*, Angus & Robertson, permission from Curtis Brown (Aust.).

Michael Dransfield: 'bum's rush', 'a difficult patriotism' from *Streets of the Long Voyage*; 'And No Bird Sings' from *Voyage into Solitude*, both University of Queensland Press. Robert D. FitzGerald: 'The Always Beginning' from *Product*; other poems from *Forty Years' Poems*, both Angus & Robertson. Mary Gilmore: 'She Was a Scented Land' from *Old Days, Old Ways*; 'Old Botany Bay' from *The Singing Tree*; 'The Waradgery Tribe', 'Nurse No Long Grief' from *The Passionate Heart and Other Poems*, all Angus & Robertson. Peter Goldsworthy: 'Brickie' from *Readings From Ecclesiastes*, Angus & Robertson. Jamie Grant: 'Farmer Picking Mushrooms', *Poetry Australia*, 1977, permission of the author. Robert Gray: poems from *Creek Water Journal*, University of Queensland Press. John Griffin: poems from *A Waltz on Stones*, Makar Press, permission of the author. William Grono: 'The Way We Live Now', *Westerly*, 1969, permission of the author. Elizabeth Harrower: 'The Beautiful Climate' from *Modern Australian Writing*, ed. Geoffrey Dutton, Fontana, permission of the author. J.S. Harry: 'Between the Sand Dunes and the Cattle' from *Hold, for a Little While, and Turn Gently*, Island Press; 'Time in a Pelican's Wing', *Southerly*, 1980, permission of the author. Kevin Hart: poems from *The Lines of the Hand: Poems 1976–1979*, Angus & Robertson. William Hart-Smith: poems from *Selected Poems*, Angus & Robertson. Gwen Harwood: 'Thoughts Before Sunrise' from *The Lion's Bride*; other poems from *Selected Poems*, both Angus & Robertson. Nicholas Hasluck: poems from *Anchor and Other Poems*, Fremantle Arts Centre Press, permission of the author. Shirley Hazzard: 'Nothing in Excess' from *People in Glass Houses*, Macmillan, permission of the author. Rachel Henning: extracts from *The Letters of Rachel Henning*, ed. David Adams, Angus & Robertson. Harry Heseltine: 'Australian Image: The Literary Heritage', *Meanjin*, 1962, permission of the author. Dorothy Hewett: poems from *Windmill Country*, Overland Press, permission of the author. A.D. Hope: 'Standards in Australian Literature' from *Australian Literary Criticism*, ed. Grahame Johnston, Oxford University Press, permission from Curtis Brown (Aust.); poems from *Collected Poems 1930–1970*, Angus & Robertson. Antigone Kefala: 'The Peanut Vendor' from *The Alien*, Makar Press; 'Heraklion' from *Thirsty Weather*, Outback Press, permission of the author. Alister Kershaw: 'The Last Expatriate', *Australian Letters*, 1958, permission of the author. Alec King: 'Contemporary Australian Poetry' repr. from *The Writer in Australia*, ed. John Barnes, Oxford University Press. Peter Kocan: 'Lost Causes', *Poetry Australia*, 1978, permission of the author; other poems from *Armistice*, Angus & Robertson. Christopher Koch: 'The Radio Men' from *The Doubleman*, a novel in progress, permission of the author. David Lake: 'To Horace' repr. from *Recent Queensland Poetry*, ed. Greg McCart, Refulgence Publishers, permission of the author. Eve Langley: 'Australia' repr.

from *A Book of Australian Verse*, ed. Judith Wright, Oxford University Press. Geoffrey Lehmann: poems from *A Voyage of Lions*, Angus & Robertson. Morris Lurie: 'Rappaport Lays an Egg' from *Inside the Wardrobe*, Outback Press, permission of the author. James McAuley: 'Book of Hours' from *poems 1970–1976: Time Given*, Brindabella Press; 'Music Late at Night' from *Music Late at Night*; other poems from *Collected Poems 1936–1970*; 'The Grinning Mirror', Sections 3 & 4, from *The End of Modernity*, all Angus & Robertson. Shane McCauley: 'Beached Whales', 'Two-Up School, Anzac Day', *Quadrant*, 1983, permission of the author. Hugh McCrae: 'Evening', 'Earth' from *The Best Poems of Hugh McCrae*, ed. R.G. Howarth, Angus & Robertson; 'Memories' from *Satyrs and Sunlight*, Thomas Lothian, 2nd ed., permission from Lady Huntly Cowper. Nan McDonald: poems from *Selected Poems*, Angus & Robertson. Roger McDonald: poems from *Airship*, University of Queensland Press. Dorothea Mackellar: 'My Country' from *The Poems of Dorothea Mackellar*, Rigby, permission from Curtis Brown (Aust.). Kenneth Mackenzie: poems from *The Poems of Kenneth Mackenzie*, ed. E. Jones and G. Little, Angus & Robertson. David Malouf: 'On refusing an all risk insurance policy' from *Bicycle*; 'Reading Horace Outside Sydney, 1970', 'Report from Champagne Country' from *Neighbours in a Thicket*; 'For Two Children: Lelo and Alex Tesei' from *First Things Last*, all University of Queensland Press. John Manifold: 'Incognito' from *Op 8: Poems 1961–1969*; other poems from *Collected Verse*, both University of Queensland Press. Frederic Manning: poems from *Eidola*, John Murray (Publishers) Ltd. Alan Moorehead: 'Botany Bay' from *The Fatal Impact*, Hamish Hamilton Ltd., permission from the estate of Alan Moorehead. Frank Moorhouse: 'The Commune Does Not Want You' from *Tales of Mystery and Romance*, Angus & Robertson. John Morrison: 'Dog-Box' from *North Wind*, Penguin Books Australia, permission of the author. Walter Murdoch: 'My Bush Fire', 'On Pioneering' from *Selections From Walter Murdoch*, Angus & Robertson. Les A. Murray: poems from *The Vernacular Republic: Poems 1961–1981*, Angus & Robertson. John Shaw Neilson: poems from *The Poems of Shaw Neilson*, ed. A.R. Chisholm, Angus & Robertson. Barry Oakley: 'Scanlan' from *The Great God Mogadon and Other Plays*, University of Queensland Press. Desmond O'Grady: 'The Importance of Being Henry' from *Valid for All Countries*, University of Queensland Press. Geoff Page: 'Bondi Afternoon, 1915 (Elioth Gruner)', 'Smalltown Memorials' from *Smalltown Memorials*, University of Queensland Press; 'Streeton' from *Cassandra Paddocks*, Angus & Robertson. Vance Palmer: 'The Rainbow Bird' from *The Rainbow Bird and Other Stories*, ed. A. Edwards, Angus & Robertson. A.B. Paterson: poems from *The Collected Verse of A.B. Paterson*, Angus & Robertson. Grace Perry: 'Girl at the Piano' from *Frozen Section*,

Edwards & Shaw; 'Route 31' from *Black Swans at Berrima*; 'House at Beecroft' from *Journal of a Surgeon's Wife and Other Poems*, both South Head Press, permission of the author. Hal Porter: 'Country Town' from *Hal Porter: Selected Stories*, ed. Leonie Kramer; 'Brett' from *Fredo Fuss Love Life*, both Angus & Robertson. Peter Porter: poems from *Collected Poems*, Oxford University Press. Katharine Susannah Prichard: 'The Cooboo' repr. from *An Australian Storybook*, ed. Nettie Palmer, Angus & Robertson. Roderic Quinn: 'Noon on the Barrier Ranges' from *Poems*, Angus & Robertson. Jennifer Rankin: 'Cliffs' from *Earth Hold*, Secker & Warburg. Henry Handel Richardson: 'The Bathe' from *The Adventures of Cuffy Mahony & Other Stories*, Angus & Robertson. Roland Robinson: poems from *Deep Well*, Edwards & Shaw. Judith Rodriguez: 'nu-plastik fanfare red' from *nu-plastik fanfare red*; 'Family' from *Mudcrab at Gambaro's*, both University of Queensland Press. J.R. Rowland: poems from *The Feast of Ancestors*, Angus & Robertson. Steele Rudd: 'A Kangaroo Hunt from Shingle Hut' from *On Our Selection*, Angus & Robertson. Thomas Shapcott: 'Shabbytown fugue' from *Begin with Walking*, University of Queensland Press. R.A. Simpson: poems from *Selected Poems*, University of Queensland Press, permission of the author. Kenneth Slessor: poems from *Selected Poems*, Angus & Robertson. Vivian Smith: poems from *Tide Country*, Angus & Robertson. Christina Stead: 'The Boy', *Meanjin*, 1973, permission from the estate of Christina Stead. P.R. Stephensen: 'The Foundations of Culture in Australia', Section 3, repr. from *The Writer in Australia*, ed. John Barnes, Oxford University Press. Douglas Stewart: poems from *Selected Poems*, Angus & Robertson. Harold Stewart: 'The Leaf-Maker' from *Phoenix Wings: Poems 1940–6*, Angus & Robertson; 'Sailing Down the Bay of Ise' from *The Exiled Immortal*, Brindabella Press; both poems revised by and printed with permission of the author. Randolph Stow: 'Raw Material', *Westerly*, 1961; poems from *Outrider: Poems 1956–1962*, Macdonald & Co., permission from Richard Scott Simon Ltd. Andrew Taylor: 'Norwinch Sleeping' from *The Cat's Chin and Ears: A Bestiary*, Angus & Robertson; other poems from *The Cool Change*, University of Queensland Press. Richard Tipping: poems from *Domestic Hardcore*, University of Queensland Press. Chris Wallace-Crabbe: 'The Wild Colonial Puzzler' from *The Foundations of Joy*; other poems from *Selected Poems*, both Angus & Robertson. Francis Webb: poems from *Francis Webb: Collected Poems*, Angus & Robertson. Patrick White: 'The Prodigal Son', *Australian Letters*, 1958; 'Willy-Wagtails by Moonlight' from *The Burnt Ones*, Eyre & Spottiswoode, permission from Curtis Brown (Aust.). Michael Wilding: 'Another Day on a Selection' from *Pacific Highway*, Hale & Iremonger, permission of the author. Judith Wright: poems from *Collected Poems 1940–1970*, Angus & Robertson. Fay Zwicky: 'Summer Pogrom' repr. from *The Golden*

Apples of the Sun, ed. Chris Wallace-Crabbe, Melbourne University Press; 'Identity' from *Kaddish*, University of Queensland Press, permission of the author.

We have been unable to trace or contact the holders of copyright for the following material. Robert Hughes: 'The Intellectual in Australia' repr. from *Australian Writing Today*, ed. Charles Higham, Penguin. Rex Ingamells: poems from *Selected Poems*, Georgian House; extract from *Conditional Culture* repr. from *The Writer in Australia*, ed. John Barnes, Oxford University Press. Nettie Palmer: extracts from *Fourteen Years: Extracts from a Private Journal 1925–1939*, Meanjin Press.

We gratefully acknowledge the patient assistance, over a long period, of Mrs Betty Briggs.

The Russell Drysdale painting, *The Drover's Wife*, on p. 542 is reproduced by kind permission of Lady Russell Drysdale.

INTRODUCTION

The purpose of this anthology is to represent the range of Australian writing in prose and verse from the end of the eighteenth century to the present day. In making this selection our principal consideration has been the quality of the writing. We hope to have shown that the work of the early writers has more than historical interest, though their achievement is limited in various ways by the conditions under which they wrote.

A secondary consideration has been to document the continuity of Australian writing. Though in terms of the established literatures of the world Australian literature has a very short history, it is possible to identify a sense of tradition, especially in the writing of the last forty years. One can detect recurrent attitudes, preoccupations, and ambitions from the early nineteenth century to the present day; and there is significant evidence of modern writers acknowledging a debt to their predecessors, either by direct reference, or by imitation of their example.

Critics and commentators on Australian writing have frequently, and understandably, anticipated or actually discovered signs of its growth to maturity. The analogy between human development and literary change has never been a satisfactory one; it poses considerable problems for the critic of an emergent literature, by both expecting and finding too much too soon. In expressing scepticism about the value of the analogy, we are also expressing the hope that this selection provides for a variety of possible interpretations of Australian literary history.

Whenever possible we have avoided extracting passages. We have had to make exceptions in the case of general prose. Major novelists such as Henry Handel Richardson, Boyd, White and others are represented only by short works, or, in Boyd's case, extracts from non-fictional prose. We have not included long poems with the exception of Harpur's *The Creek of the Four Graves*, but in the note to Section III we refer to the importance of long poems in that period.

In the final section—Contemporary Writing—our principle of selection has been slightly varied to allow us to include a large number of individual authors. This section, therefore, offers not a strict selection of the work of the last decade, but a sample which indicates its quantity and range.

1

Within each section the order is chronological, though with a margin of tolerance to permit occasionally what seem to us interesting juxtapositions, or to establish significant points of emphasis.

Readers of *The Oxford History of Australian Literature* will find the anthology a useful accompaniment to that text. In turn the *History* provides bibliographical detail and a critical commentary which will enable readers to extend their reading in the subject.

I : THE BEGINNING TO 1918

Commentary

The original inhabitants of Australia—the Aborigines—have a long oral tradition, much of which has now been transcribed and translated. Throughout the colonial period little was known or understood of Aboriginal culture. The history of writing in Australia therefore begins with European settlement.

The more interesting writing in the early years is mainly in the form of letters, diaries, memoirs, journals and reports; and while it is not strictly literary in intention, it forms the basis of much fiction and poetry of later times. The early poetry is heavily dependent on eighteenth-century models, and these were appropriate enough for the occasional verse that the times required. Imitation does not in itself necessarily inhibit the creative imagination, but the early poets were at best minor versifiers, whose work has more historical than literary interest.

There are recurring preoccupations—with hardships of the early settlement, differences between the antipodes and England, the sense of distance and isolation, the mysteries of the unexplored regions and the excitements of discovery and hopes for the future. The mixed emotions of excitement and apprehension, hope and despair, belief in the future and nostalgia for the past emerge later in more complex responses to the experience of living in Australia. Australia was still technically a collection of British colonies and the literature reflects many of the cultural dispositions literary historians call Victorian.

Towards the end of the nineteenth century many of the positive expectations of the people were expressed in a growing perception of common ideals, culminating in Federation in 1901. Urban growth did not displace admiration for the values of pioneering and the bush life; and egalitarianism, social democracy and nationalism were strongly promoted. Joseph Furphy's novel *Such is Life* (1903) celebrates some of the sentiments of the period in which it was set, the 1880s.

This section ends with the First World War, which gave rise in Australia to the legend of the ANZACS. The war did not at once produce any significant literature, but it seems to have shown Australians to themselves for the first time. In particular, the qualities of courage and idealism exhibited at Gallipoli created, in spite of the military failure of the campaign, a strong sense of national pride. Contemporary writers and film-makers have found this a rich source of material.

So, in 130 years, the Commonwealth evolved from its origins as a penal settlement in the remote antipodes to a federation of states, joined not only constitutionally but in a remarkable unity of interests and purpose which defines the national spirit; and in the discussions of the basis of federation and in its first significant test as a nation, it caught a glimpse of its own strengths.

Watkin Tench   (1758?–1833)

Prose writer. Born and educated in England; in Australia
1788–1792.

from THE SETTLEMENT AT PORT JACKSON

1.

Monday, April II, 1791. At twenty minutes before seven o'clock,
we started from the governor's house at Rose Hill, and steered for a
short time nearly in a north-east direction, after which we turned to
north 34° west, and steadily pursued that course until a quarter before four o'clock, when we halted for the night. The country for the
first two miles, while we walked to the north-east, was good, full of
grass, and without rock or underwood; afterwards it grew very bad,
being full of steep barren rocks, over which we were compelled to
clamber for seven miles, when it changed to a plain country,
apparently very sterile, and with very little grass in it, which rendered walking easy. Our fatigue in the morning had, however, been
so oppressive, that one of the party *knocked up*. And had not a
soldier, as strong as a pack-horse, undertaken to carry his knapsack,
in addition to his own, we must either have sent him back, or have
stopped at a place for the night which did not afford water. Our two
natives carried each his pack, but its weight was inconsiderable,
most of their provisions being in the knapsacks of the soldiers and
gamekeepers. We expected to have derived from them much information relating to the country; as no one doubted that they were
acquainted with every part of it between the sea-coast and the river
Hawkesbury. We hoped also to have witnessed their manner of living in the woods, and the resources they rely upon in their journies.
Nothing, however, of this sort had yet occurred, except their examining some trees, to see if they could discover on the bark any
marks of the claws of squirrels and opossums, which they said
would shew whether any of those animals were hidden among the
leaves and branches. They walked stoutly, appeared but little fatigued, and maintained their spirits admirably, laughing to excess
when any of us either tripped or stumbled; misfortunes which much
seldomer fell to their lot than to ours. At a very short distance from
Rose Hill, we found that they were in a country unknown to them;
so that the farther they went, the more dependent on us they became, being absolute strangers inland. To convey to their under-
standings the intention of our journey, was impossible. For,
perhaps, no words could unfold to an Indian, the motives of curiosity, which induce men to encounter labour, fatigue, and pain, when
they might remain in repose at home, with a sufficiency of food.—

We asked Colbee the name of the people who live inland, and he called them Boò-roo-ber-on-gal; and said, they were bad; whence we conjectured, that they sometimes war with those on the sea coast, by whom they were undoubtedly driven up the country from the fishing ground, that it might not be overstocked: the weaker here, as in every other country, giving way to the stronger. We asked how they lived. He said, on birds and animals, having no fish. Their laziness appeared strongly when we halted; for they refused to draw water, or to cleave wood to make a fire; but as soon as it was kindled (having first well stuffed themselves), they lay down before it and fell asleep. About an hour after sunset, as we were chatting by the fire side, and preparing to go to rest, we heard voices at a little distance in the wood. Our natives catched the sound instantaneously, and bidding us be silent, listened attentively to the quarter whence it had proceeded. In a few minutes we heard the voices plainly; and wishing exceedingly to open a communication with this tribe, we begged our natives to call to them, and bid them to come to us, to assure them of good treatment, and that they should have something given them to eat. Colbee no longer hesitated, but gave them the signal of invitation, in a loud hollow cry. After some whooping, and shouting, on both sides, a man, with a lighted stick in his hand, advanced near enough to converse with us. The first words, which we could distinctly understand were, 'I am Colbee, of the tribe of Càd-i-gal.' The stranger replied, 'I am Bèr-ee-wan, of the tribe of Boo-roo-ber-on-gal.' Boladeree informed him also of his name, and that we were white men and friends, who would give him something to eat. Still he seemed irresolute. Colbee therefore advanced to him, took him by the hand, and led him to us. By the light of the moon, we were introduced to this gentleman, all our names being repeated in form by our two masters of the ceremonies, who said that we were Englishmen, and *Bùd-yee-ree* (good), that we came from the sea coast, and that we were travelling inland. Bereewan seemed to be a man about thirty years old, differing in no respect from his countrymen with whom we were acquainted. He came to us unarmed, having left his spears at a little distance. After a long conversation with his countrymen, and having received some provisions, he departed highly satisfied.

Tuesday, April 12th, 1791. Started this morning at half past six o'clock, and in two hours reached the river. The whole of the country we passed was poor, and the soil within a mile of the river changed to a coarse deep sand, which I have invariably found to compose its banks, in every part, without exception, that I ever saw. The stream at this place is about three hundred and fifty feet wide; the water pure and excellent to the taste; the banks are about twenty feet high, and covered with trees, many of which had been evidently bent by the force of the current, in the direction which it runs, and some of them contained rubbish and drift wood in their branches, at least forty-five feet above the level of the stream. We saw many ducks, and killed one, which Colbee swam for. No new production among the shrubs growing here was found: we were acquainted with them all. Our natives had evidently never seen this river before: they stared at it with surprise, and talked to each other. Their total ignorance of the country, and of the direction in which they had walked, appeared, when they were asked which way Rose Hill lay; for they pointed almost oppositely to it. Of our compass they had taken early notice, and had talked much to each other about it: they comprehended its use; and called it "Nàà-Mòro," literally, "To see the way";—a more significant or expressive term cannot be found.

April, 1791. Supposing ourselves to be higher on the stream than Richmond Hill, we agreed to trace downward, or to the right hand.—In tracing, we kept as close to the bank of the river, as the innumerable impediments to walking which grow upon it, would allow. We found the country low and swampy: came to a native fire-place, at which were some small fish-bones: soon after we saw a native, but he ran away immediately. Having walked nearly three miles we were stopped by a creek which we could neither ford, or fall a tree across: we were therefore obliged to coast it, in hope to find a passing place, or to reach its head. At four o'clock we halted for the night, on the bank of the creek.—Our natives continued to hold out stoutly. The hindrances to walking by the river side, which plagued and entangled us so much, seemed not to be heeded by them, and they wound through them with ease; but to us they were intolerably tiresome. Our perplexities afforded them an inexhaustible fund of merriment and derision:—did the sufferer, stung at once with nettles and ridicule, and shaken nigh to death by his fall, use any angry expression to them, they retorted in a moment, by calling him by every opprobrious name which their language affords.— Boladerree destroyed a native hut to-day very wantonly, before we could prevent him. On being asked why he did so, he answered, that the inhabitants inland were bad; though no longer since than last night, when Bereewan had departed, they were loud in their praise. But now they had reverted to their first opinion:—so fickle and transient are their motives of love and hatred.

2.

But not to multiply arguments on a subject, where demonstration (at least to me) is incontestable, I shall close by expressing my firm belief, that the Indians of New South Wales acknowledge the existence of a superintending deity. Of their ideas of the origin and duration of his existence; of his power and capacity; of his benignity or maleficence; or of their own emanation from him, I pretend not to speak. I have often, in common with others, tried to gain information from them on this head; but we were always repulsed by obstacles, which we could neither pass by, or surmount. Mr Dawes attempted to teach Abaroo some of our notions of religion, and hoped that she would thereby be induced to communicate hers in return. But her levity, and love of play, in a great measure defeated his efforts; although every thing he did learn from her, served to confirm what is here advanced. It may be remarked, that when they attended at church with us (which was a common practice) they always preserved profound silence and decency, as if conscious that some religious ceremony on our side was performing.

The question of, whether they believe in the immortality of the soul, will take up very little time to answer. They are universally fearful of spirits. They call a spirit, *Mawn*: they often scruple to approach a corpse, saying that the *mawn* will seize them, and that it fastens upon them in the night when asleep. When asked where their deceased friends are, they always point to the skies. To believe in after existence is to confess the immortality of some part of being. To enquire whether they assign a *limited* period to such future state would be superfluous: this is one of the subtleties of speculation, which a savage may be supposed not to have considered, without impeachment either of his sagacity or happiness.

Their manner of interring the dead has been amply described. It is certain that instead of burying they sometimes burn the corpse; but the cause of distinction we know not. A dead body, covered by a canoe, at whose side a sword and shield were placed in state, was once discovered. All that we could learn about this important personage was, that he was a *Gwee-a-gal*, (one of the tribe of Gweea) and a celebrated warrior.

To appreciate their general powers of mind is difficult. Ignorance, prejudice, the force of habit, continually interfere to prevent dispassionate judgment. I have heard men so unreasonable, as to exclaim at the stupidity of these people, for not comprehending what a small share of reflection would have taught them they ought not to have expected. And others again I have heard so sanguine in their admiration, as to extol for proofs of elevated genius what the commonest abilities were capable of executing.

If they be considered as a nation, whose general advancement and acquisitions are to be weighed, they certainly rank very low, even in the scale of savages. They may perhaps dispute the right of precedency with the Hottentots, or the shivering tribes who inhabit the shores of Magellan. But how inferior do they show when compared with the subtle African; the patient watchful American; or the elegant timid islander of the South Seas. Though suffering from the vicissitudes of their climate,—strangers to cloathing: tho' feeling the sharpness of hunger, and knowing the precariousness of supply from that element on whose stores they principally depend, ignorant of cultivating the earth,—a less enlightened state we shall exclaim can hardly exist.

But if from general view we descend to particular inspection, and examine individually the persons who compose this community, they will certainly rise in estimation. In the narrative part of this work, I have endeavoured rather to detail information, than to deduce conclusions; leaving to the reader the exercise of his own judgment. The behaviour of Arabanoo, of Baneelon, of Colbee, and many others, is copiously described; and assuredly he who shall make just allowance for uninstructed nature, will hardly accuse any of those persons of stupidity, or deficiency of apprehension.

To offer my own opinion on the subject, I do not hesitate to declare, that the natives of New South Wales possess a considerable portion of that acumen, or sharpness of intellect, which bespeaks genius. All savages hate toil, and place happiness in inaction: and neither the arts of civilized life can be practised, or the advantages of it felt, without application and labour. Hence they resist knowledge, and the adoption of manners and customs, differing from their own. The progress of reason is not only slow, but mechanical.—*"De toutes les instructions propres à l'homme, celle qu'il acquiert le plus tard, et le plus difficilement, est la raison même."* The tranquil indifference, and uninquiring eye, with which they surveyed our works of art, have often, in my hearing, been stigmatized as proofs of stupidity, and want of reflection. But surely we should discriminate between ignorance and defect of understanding. The truth was, they often neither comprehended the design, nor conceived the utility of such works: but on subjects in any degree familiarized to their ideas, they generally testified not only acuteness of discernment, but a large portion of good sense. I have always thought that the distinctions they shewed in their estimate of us, on first entering into our society, strongly displayed the latter quality:—when they were led into our respective houses, at once to be astonished and awed by our superiority, their attention was directly turned to objects with which they were acquainted. They passed without rapture or emotion, our numerous artifices and contrivances: but when they saw a collection of weapons of war, or of the skins of animals and birds, they never failed to exclaim, and to confer with each other on the subject. The master of that house became the object of their regard, as they concluded he must be either a renowned warrior, or an expert hunter. Our surgeons grew into their esteem from a like cause. In a very early stage of intercourse, several natives were present at the amputation of a leg: when they first penetrated the intention of the operator, they were confounded; not believing it possible that such an operation could be performed without loss of life; and they called aloud to him to desist: but when they saw the torrent of blood stopped, the vessels taken up, and the stump dressed, their horror and alarm yielded to astonishment and admiration, which they expressed by the loudest tokens.—If these instances bespeak not nature and good sense, I have yet to learn the meaning of the terms.

If it be asked why the same intelligent spirit which led them to contemplate and applaud the success of the sportsman, and the skill of the surgeon, did not equally excite them to meditate on the labours of the builder, and the ploughman; I can only answer, that what we see in its remote cause, is always more feebly felt, than that which presents to our immediate grasp, both its origin and effect.

Their leading good and bad qualities I shall concisely touch upon.—Of their intrepidity no doubt can exist: their levity, their fickleness, their passionate extravagance of character, cannot be defended. They are indeed sudden and quick in quarrel; but if their resentment be easily roused, their thirst of revenge is not implacable.—Their honesty, when tempted by novelty, is not unimpeachable; but in their own society, there is good reason to believe, that few breaches of it occur.—It were well if similar praise coud be given to their veracity: but truth they neither prize nor practice. When they wish to deceive, they scruple not to utter the grossest and most hardened lies. Their attachment and gratitude to those among us, whom they have professed to love, have always remained inviolable, unless effaced by resentment, from sudden provocation; then, like all other Indians, the impulse of the moment is alone regarded by them.

BARRON FIELD   (1786–1846)

Poet, prose writer. Born and educated in London; was in Australia 1817–1824.

from JOURNAL OF AN EXCURSION ACROSS THE BLUE MOUNTAINS OF NEW SOUTH WALES, OCTOBER, 1822

Monday, 7th October, 1822.

This spring month is the fittest to make this excursion in. The winter nights are too cold, and the summer days too hot. In the autumn the flowers are not in bloom.

The difficulties of the travel commence at Emu Ford over the river Nepean, a branch of the Hawkesbury. Crossing this stream is always a work of such time and trouble, and sometimes of such difficulty and danger that the traveller should send forward his cart or baggage-horses, to overcome it, half a day before he rides or rows through it himself. The ferry is the property of government, who have hitherto delayed either to provide a punt themselves or to suffer the stock-holders of the colony to build one by subscription. The consequences are frequent losses of cattle in swimming, and injury of sheep in boating, over. Although the river was not un-usually high, we were obliged to unload our cart before it could be drawn through the ford; and thus lost several hours in transporting the baggage by one small boat, and in reloading the cart.

On the banks of the Nepean, I saw almost the only deciduous native tree in the territory, namely, the white cedar (melia azedar-ach), the common bead-tree of India, beautiful in itself, and congen-ial to me from that singularity. All the other indigenous trees and shrubs, that I have seen, are evergreens; the eternal eucalyptus, with its white bark and its scanty tin-like foliage, or the dark casuarina tall, and exocarpus funeral; all as unpicturesque as the shrubs and flowers are beautiful:—the various, justly called proteaceous, bank-sia, and the hesperidean mimosa, the exquisite epacris, the curious grevillea, xanthorrhoea, the sceptre of Flora, telopea the magni-ficent, and thysanotus the lovely. New South Wales is a perpetual flower garden, but there is not a single scene in it of which a painter could make a landscape, without greatly disguising the true charac-ter of the trees. They have no lateral boughs, and cast no masses of shade; but, in return, it is to this circumstance, which causes so little vegetable putrefaction, that the healthiness of the climate is mainly to be attributed. "A part of their economy (says Mr Brown the botanist), which contributes somewhat to the peculiar character of the Australian forests, is, that the leaves both of the eucalyptus and acacia, by far the most common genera in Terra Australis, and, if taken together, and considered with respect to the mass of vegetable matter they contain (calculated from the size, as well as the number of individuals), nearly equal to all the other plants of that country, are vertical, or present their margin and not either surface towards the stem, both surfaces having consequently the same relation to light." Can this circumstance be partly the cause of their un-picturesqueness—of the monotony of their leaf? Or is it merely their evergreenness? "In the Indies (says Linnæus) almost all the trees are evergreen, and have broad leaves; but in our cold regions, most trees cast their foliage every year, and such as do not, bear acerose, that is, narrow and acute, leaves. If they were broader, the snow which falls during the winter would collect among them, and break the branches by its weight. Their great slenderness prevents any such effect, and allows the snow to pass between them." But snow is not unknown to the eucalypti and acaciæ of New Holland; and may not the verticalness of the broad leaves of some of them answer the same snow-diverting purpose as the acerose-leavedness of European evergreens? Yet the foliage of the eucalypti is always scanty; that of the acaciæ acerose; and the snow of Australia is apt to melt. Be this as it may, no tree, to my taste, can be beautiful that is not deciduous. What can a painter do with one cold olive-green? There is a dry harshness about the perennial leaf, that does not savour of humanity in my eyes. There is no flesh and blood in it: it is not of us, and is nothing to us. Dryden says of the laurel:

From winter winds it suffers no decay;
For ever fresh and fair, and every month is May.

Now it may be the fault of the cold climate in which I was bred, but this is just what I complain of in an evergreen. "For ever fresh," is a contradiction in terms; what is "for ever fair" is never fair; and without January, in my mind, there can be no May. All the dearest allegories of human life are bound up in the infant and slender green of spring, the dark redundance of summer, and the sere and yellow leaf of autumn. These are as essential to the poet as emblems, as they are to the painter as picturesque objects; and the common consent and immemorial custom of European poetry have made the change of seasons, and its effect upon vegetation, a part, as it were, of our very nature. I can therefore hold no fellowship with Australian foliage, but will cleave to the British oak through all the bareness of winter. It is a dear sight to an European to see his young compatriot trees in an Indian climate, telling of their native country by the fall of their leaf, and, in due time, becoming a spring unto themselves, although no winter has passed over them, just as their fellow-countrymen keep Christmas though in the hottest weather, and, with fresh fruits about them, affect the fare and sometimes the fire-side of old England. "New Holland (says Sir James Smith) seems no very beautiful or picturesque country, such as is likely to form, or to inspire, a poet. Indeed the dregs of the community, which we have poured upon its shores, must probably subside and purge themselves, before any thing like a poet, or a disinterested lover of nature, can arise from so foul a source. There seems, however, to be no transition of seasons in the climate itself, to excite hope, or to expand the heart and fancy."

Yet let me do justice to the evergreens of New Holland. It is to the scantiness of their foliage that the grazier owes the dry wholesomeness of the native grasses, however thin; and it is to the undecaying and aromatic, myrtaceous, perennial leaf that the colonists attribute the healthiness of their climate. No miasmata come from the marshes or fallen leaves of Australian forests. Intermittent fevers are unknown here. An opinion has obtained in North America that evergreens increase cold. In New South Wales the cold is found to be increased by clearing the land of them, although they certainly retain the night air so long in the valleys, that the hills are warmer than those in the winter. In the summer the hills are cooler from the sea breeze. I should therefore say, build on a hill. The climate of New South Wales is becoming generally cooler, as the colony gets cleared of timber. While I am comparing the trees of America and Australia, it is important to agriculture that I should mention that the stumps of the eucalypti, from the quantity of gum they contain, do not rot in the ground soon after the trees have been cut down, as those of the American and Norfolk Island timbers do.

They must be grubbed up, or burnt out by piling the surrounding sods over them, like a kiln.

At Emu Plains or Island (for it is sometimes insulated by the washings of the mountains, when the Nepean is flooded) there is a government agricultural establishment of 350 men and a few women, with a good brick house for the superintendent, and wooden huts for the convict labourers. Here are grown for the benefit of the crown, wheat, maize and tobacco; but experience everywhere proves the loss at which government raises its own supplies. These plains are not naturally cleared; but they will soon be free from stumps by the labour of these convicts, and will then leave a rich tract of arable land for favoured grantees.

It is this river, whether we call it Hawkesbury or Nepean, that is the Nile of Botany Bay; for the land on its banks owes its fertility to the floods which come down from the Blue Mountains, and which have been known to swell the waters nearly a hundred feet above their usual level; and as these floods are uncertain and often destructive of the growing crops, I once thought that government (if it is to farm at all) had better have kept the whole of this precarious garden in its own hands; since it is only public foresight that would provide against the loss of a harvest, and only public wealth that could support it. After the flood of 1817, the government ration was reduced from eleven to three pounds of wheat per week; but since that period so much wheat has been grown in the fine districts of Appin and Airds, and in the island of Van Diemen's Land, that the colony is now almost independent of these flood-farmers; and they are yearly going out of fashion, for the benefit of the state. Nothing can be more uncertain than the heavy rains of the climate. Sometimes (but not of late years) the country is worse afflicted with long droughts, in which the woods take fire and consume the grass, and the cattle have perished for want of water. Often do the rains descend, and the floods come, when the Hawkesbury corn is in the ground, and the colony has sometimes suffered from the improvidence of these farmers, in not building their wheat stacks out of the reach of the devouring waters. The extraordinary fertility of these flooded lands, which have borne a crop of wheat and a crop of maize in each year for the last five-and-twenty years, has naturally induced their tenants to rely too much upon this lubberland sort of farming, just as the inhabitants of Vesuvius cannot be induced to abandon that mountain after a lava-flood from its volcano, and see nothing in present ruin but the prospect of future riches. "So the Ohio (says Mr Birkbeck), with its annual overflowing, is unable to wash away the inhabitants of Shawnee Town." But it is surely impolitic to grant away such precarious and hotbed lands. In so indifferent a general soil as that of New South Wales, a better system of agriculture should be taught; and what encouragement is given to the general farmer to bedew his land with the sweat of his brow, when he sees that of his idle neighbour on the banks of the river irrigated by the flood, and producing as good a crop, with no other labour than that of hoeing and strewing? It is only upon the chance of the flood's devouring, instead of feeding, that the general farmer can calculate for occasional remuneration; and when this calamity happens, the river farmer, whose rapid gains induce him as rapidly to spend, is found entirely unprovided, and his whole district is reduced to subscription and beggary. This, in itself, is not one of the least of the political evils of such a system. It is an encouragement to future improvidence, and fosters a disposition too literally to take no thought of the morrow, but to consider and imitate the gigantic lily (doryanthes excelsa)—a disposition which must be supposed to be already too natural among the small settlers, who have emerged from the conditions of convicts. Another good reason against granting away this land, and suffering it to be cleared, is, that the floods wash the fallen timber into the channel of the river, and obstruct the navigation. The removal of the trees from its banks has not only contributed to choke the river by their falling in, but has occasioned derelictions on one side and alluvions on the other.

But we shall never get our cart up Lapstone Hill at this rate; and it is so steep and long, that we were obliged to shift our baggage twice in ascending it, notwithstanding Governor Macquarie's Government and General Order of the 10th of June, 1815, says, that "the facility of the ascent to Spring Wood excited surprise, and is certainly not well calculated to give the traveller a just idea of the difficulties he has afterwards to encounter." I found Lapstone Hill as difficult as any in the journey, except Mount York; and we did not reach Spring Wood (twelve miles and a half from the river), where alone there is a space enough in the forest to encamp upon, till after 9 o'clock at night. There is little or no grass here, and the timber consists principally of those species of eucalyptus called by the colonists stringy and iron-bark. Here is stationed an acting corporal's party of the 48th regiment, in a small barrack.

WILLIAM WOOLLS (1814–1893)

Poet, prose writer. Born and educated in England; came to Australia
in 1832.

THE COUNTRY

Beatus ille qui procul negotiis

Happy the man from business free,
As ancient mortals used to be,
Who, far from Sydney's dusty ways,
In sweet retirement spends his days,
And cultivates the fertile soil
Which once confess'd his father's toil.
The drum and fife ne'er break his sleep,
Nor cannons roaring o'er the deep,
Nor does the Colonel's dreaded corps
With sticks and stones assail his door.
He cares not with the great to dine,
And taste Sir———'s sparkling wine;
Or on the weary Jury sit
And shake his sides at———'s wit;
But—happy man—he gently twines
Around the fence his tender vines,
And as the older boughs decay,
He lops the useless load away.
Now in the valley he surveys
His wandering herds of cattle graze,
And sheep unnumber'd pour along,
Urged by the dog's discordant tongue.
Train'd by his care, the opening flower
With fragrant perfumes fills the bower,
And luscious fruits of purple dye
At every step delight his eye.
Sometimes at ease supinely laid
Beneath acacias' pleasing shade,
Where gliding streamlets steal along
He listens to the warbler's song;
Or sleeps the sultry hour away
Till soothing zephyrs cool the day.
When on the distant mountains' height
The wonted blue is capt with white,
And wintery breezes blow again,
With chilling fierceness o'er the plain,
Then, at full speed, the sportive horse
Leads forth his master to the course.

Where the swift hounds with joy pursue,
The emu and the kangaroo —
Then, sallying forth, with murderous aim,
He fills his spacious bag with game,
While far and near the woods resound,
As numerous victims strew the ground.
But if a chaste and virtuous wife,
Crown all the pleasures of his life,
And, ever smiling, ever gay,
Drive all the cares of time away,
Who—happy thus—would stoop to prove
The pains and aches of wanton love,
And view the fair ones o'er and o'er
When Marshall's vessels reach the shore?
Behold she brings the home-made wine,
Press'd from the clusters of his vine,
And cheese and butter, and a hoard
Of unbought dainties for her lord,
Anxious alone in all her toil,
To win from him a favouring smile.
And who amidst such joys as these,
Would long for foreign luxuries —
The crusty port, the bright champaign,
Or cordials wafted o'er the main?
At silent eve he joys to view
The flocks their homeward course pursue,
And see the labouring oxen bow
Their languid necks beneath the plough,
While as the twilight fades away,
And night succeeds the passing day,
He views the stars and planets move,
In silent harmony above.
Rapt from the earth, he fain would fly,
Far from the glance of mortal eye,
And leave his prison-house of clay,
For the bright scenes of endless day.
The merchant said, and swiftly he
Resolved to sell his property,
And, far from Sydney's dusty ways,
In sweet retirement spend his days;
But whilst he counts his thousands o'er,
And calculates his goods in store,
His greedy feelings soon revive,
And still in town he vows to live.

HENRY PARKES (1815–1896)

Poet, editor, politician. Born in England; had little schooling; came
to Australia in 1839.

SOLITUDE

Where the mocking lyre-bird calls
To its mate among the falls
Of the mountain streams that play,
Each adown its tortuous way,
When the dewy-fingered even
Veils the narrow'd glimpse of Heaven:
Where the morning re-illumes
Gullies full of ferny plumes,
And a woof of radiance weaves
Through high-hanging vaults of leaves;
There, 'mid giant turpentines,
Groups of climbing, clustering vines,
Rocks that stand like sentinels,
Guarding Nature's citadels;
Lowly flowering shrubs that grace
With their beauty all the place—
There I love to wander lonely,
With my dog companion only;
There indulge unworldly moods
In the mountain solitudes;
Far from all the gilded strife
Of our boasted 'social life',
Contemplating, spirit-free,
The majestic company
Grandly marching through the ages—
Heroes, martyrs, bards, and sages—
They who bravely suffered long,
By their struggles waxing strong,
For the freedom of the mind,
For the rights of humankind!
   Oh, for some awakening cause,
Where we face eternal laws,
Where we dare not turn aside,
Where the souls of men are tried—
Something of the nobler strife
Which consumes the dross of life,
To unite to truer aim,
To exalt to loftier fame!
Leave behind the bats and balls,
Leave the racers in the stalls,

Leave the cards forever shuffled,
Leave the yacht on seas unruffled,
Leave the haunts of pampered ease,
Leave your dull festivities!—
Better far the savage glen,
Fitter school for earnest men!

EDWARD WILLSON LANDOR   (1811–1878)

Prose writer, journalist, editor. Born and educated in England;
came to Australia in 1841.

WOODMAN'S POINT

from THE BUSHMAN; OR LIFE IN A NEW COUNTRY

There is a pleasant ride along the shore from Fremantle to a little
bay about seven miles distant, one side of which, covered with lofty
trees, runs far into the sea, and is called Woodman's Point. The sea
in this part appears to be only a few miles broad; Garden-island
forming the opposite shore, the southern extremity of which seems
almost to join Cape Perron, and thus presents the appearance of a
vast bay. Not long ago, the blackened remains of a small house, or
hovel, were to be seen on the verge of the wood, facing towards
Cape Perron. Around it might be distinguished the traces of a garden of considerable extent; a few stunted vines still continued
annually to put forth the appearance of verdure, which served only
to tempt the appetite of the stray cattle that wandered down to this
solitary spot. A large bed of geraniums had extended itself across
the path which used to lead to the door of the house; and their
varied and beautiful flowers, rejoicing in this congenial climate, gave
additional melancholy to the scene. It was evident those plants had
been reared, and tended, and prized for their beauty; they had once
been carefully cultured, pruned, and watered—now they were left
to bloom or to die, as accident permitted. Near to this bed of geraniums, but apart and solitary, untouched even by weeds, of which
there were only few in that sandy soil, grew an English rose-tree. Its
long, unpruned boughs straggled wildly on the ground. It looked
the picture of desolation and despair. A few imperfect flowers occasionally peeped forth, but knew only a short and precarious existence, for the shrub being no longer sheltered behind the house, was
now exposed to the daily violence of the sea-breeze.

This widowed rose, deprived of the hand which had tended it so
carefully, and of the heart which its beauty had gladdened, seemed
now in its careless desolation awaiting the hour when it should die.

It really looked, with its drooping boughs, its torn blossoms, and its brown leaves, rustling and sighing to the breeze, like a sentient being mourning without hope. Those who have never lived in exile from their native land, can have no idea of the feelings with which a lonely colonist, long separated from all the associations of home, would regard a solitary plant which so peculiarly calls up home memories. Pardon us, good reader, this appearance of sentiment; you who will read these lines in Old England—that land which we must ever think of with pardonable emotion—will evince but little sympathy with us, who necessarily feel some fond regard for the Mother from whom we are parted, and are naturally drawn towards the inanimate things by which we are reminded of her. There is in this colony of Western Australia a single daisy root; and never was the most costly hot-house plant in England so highly prized as this humble little exile. The fortunate possessor pays it far more attention than he bestows upon any of the gorgeous flowers that bloom about it; and those who visit his garden of rare plants find nothing there that fills them with so profound a feeling of interest as the meek and lowly flower which recalls to their memories the pleasant pastures of Old England.

But to return to the ruins of Woodman's Point. This plot of land, now so neglected and forlorn, was once the blooming garden of a very singular old man, who owed his support to the vegetables which it produced, and to the fish that he caught from the little cobble which danced at anchor in the bay, whenever the weather permitted the fisherman to exercise his art. No one knew his history, but his conversation and deportment told you that he was of gentle birth, and had been well educated. His manners were particularly amiable and retiring, and every one who visited the solitary old man came away impressed with a melancholy interest in his fate.

He always welcomed a visitor with gentle pleasure, and seemed glad of the opportunity of showing his crops of vegetables and the flowers in which he delighted.

The rose-tree never failed to arrest his steps for a moment. He had brought it himself from England as a cutting, and there was evidently some history attached to it; but he never shared his confidence with any one; and the history of the rose-tree, like his own, was never revealed.

There was only one point on which he betrayed any feeling of pride—and that was his name. No one else would perhaps have been so proud of it, but he himself ever seemed to regard it with veneration.

He called himself Anthony Elisha Simson; and never failed to make you observe that his patronymic was spelt without a "*p.*"

Nothing irritated him so much as to receive a note addressed, "A. E. Simpson, Esq."

The Simsons, he would assure you, were an old family in the northern counties of England, and traced back their genealogy to the Conquest; whereas the Simpsons were of quite a different, and doubtless inferior origin. Nothing more than this did he ever relate concerning his family or his personal history.

He arrived in the colony a few years after its foundation, without any other effects than what were contained in a portmanteau and carpet-bag, and with only a few sovereigns in his purse. Without associating himself with any one, he early fixed upon the spot where he afterwards built his house, and established his permanent abode. Here he began to make his garden, and did not disdain to earn a few shillings occasionally by cutting firewood for a man who supplied Fremantle with that necessary article. It was this occupation that caused the settlers, who knew nothing more of him, to give him the title of "The Woodman"—a name which soon attached to the locality.

After he had been some time in the colony, Mr Simson began to express great impatience for the arrival of letters from England. Whenever a vessel arrived at the port, he would put on his old shooting-coat, and walk along the shore to Fremantle, where, after having inquired in vain at the post-office, he would purchase a pound of tea, and then return home again.

Years went by. Every time that a vessel arrived, poor Simson would hurry to Fremantle. He would watch, with eyes of ill-repressed eagerness, the mail carried to the post-office in boxes and large sacks. Surely amid that multitude of letters there must be one for him! Patiently would he wait for hours at the window, whilst the postmaster and his assistants sorted the letters; and when he had received the usual answer to his inquiry, he would return to his abode with down-cast looks.

As time passed on he grew more fretful and impatient. Receiving no intelligence from England, he seemed to be anxious to return thither. He would drop expressions which led his visitors (generally government officers who called upon him in their rides) to believe he would depart from the colony were he rich enough to pay his passage, or were he not restrained by some other powerful motive.

His mind ran altogether upon the Old Country, and it was with reluctance that he planted the vegetables and cured the fish which were essential to his support.

For many hours during the day he used to be seen standing fixed as a sentinel on the low rock which formed the extremity of the ridge called after himself—the Woodman's Point—and looking *homewards*.

Doubtless, thought was busy within him—the thought of all he had left or acted there. None had written to him; none remembered or perhaps wished to remember him. But home was in his heart, even whilst he felt there was no longer a home for him. A restless anxiety preyed upon his mind, and he grew thin and feeble; but still whenever a sail was seen coming round the north end of Rottnest, and approaching the port, he would seize his staff, and set out upon his long journey to Fremantle to inquire if there were, at last, a letter awaiting him.

May we imagine the growing despair in the heart of this poor old exile, as life seemed ebbing away, and yet there came no news, no hope to him from home? Frequently he wrote himself, but always to the same address—that of a broker, it was supposed, in Throgmorton-street. But no answer was ever returned. Had he no children—no friends?

Naturally weak-minded, he had now grown almost imbecile; but his manners were still so gentle, and every thing about him seemed to betoken so amiable and so resigned a spirit, that those who visited him could scarcely part again without tears. As he grew more feeble in body, he became more anxious to receive a letter from home; he expected that every one who approached his dwelling was the bearer of the intelligence so long hoped for in vain; and he would hasten to greet him at the gate with eager looks and flushed cheeks—again only to be disappointed.

At length it was with difficulty that he tottered to the Point, to look for a vessel which might bring him news. Although no ship had arrived since he last sent to the post-office, he would urge his visitor, though with hesitating earnestness, to be so good as to call there on his return, and ascertain if by chance a letter were not awaiting him. He said he felt that his hour was approaching, but he could not bear to think of setting out on that long journey without having once heard from home. Sometimes he muttered, as it were to himself, that treachery had been practised against him, and he would go and expose it; but he never allowed himself to indulge long in this strain. Sometimes he would try to raise money enough by drawing bills to pay his passage, but no one would advance anything upon them.

Daily he became more feeble, and men began to talk of sending him a nurse. The last visitor who beheld him alive, found him seated in the chair which he had himself constructed, and appearing less depressed than usual. He said he expected soon to receive news from home, and smiled with child-like glee. His friend helped him to walk as far as the rose-tree, which was then putting forth its buds. "Promise," said the old man, laying his trembling hand upon the other's arm, "promise that when I am gone you will come and see them in full blow? Promise! you will make me happy."

The next day they sent a lad from Fremantle to attend upon him. The boy found him seated in his chair. He was dead. A mound of earth at the foot of a mahogany-tree, still marks the spot where he was buried. Those *friends* at home who neglected or repulsed him when living, may by chance meet with this record from the hand of a stranger—but it will not move them; nor need it now.

ROBERT LOWE   (1811–1892)

Poet, politician. Born and educated in England; was in Australia 1842–1850.

TWO SATIRES ON THE GLADSTONE COLONY

1

How blessed the land where Barney's gentle sway
Spontaneous felons joyfully obey;
Where twelve bright bayonets only can suffice
To check the wild exuberance of vice!
Where thieves shall work at trades with none to buy,
And stores unguarded pass unrifled by;
Strong in their new-found rectitude of soul,
Tame without law, and good without control!

Bless'd land! what mightly words thy future hides!
What zigzag road shall climb thy mountain sides!
Where travellers shall view with proud disdain
The shorter path across the neighbouring plain!

What harbours bristling with unsounded reefs
Shall shield the Navies of thy future chiefs!
What aqueducts shall bear thy river's bed,
Free from the modern heresy of lead,
To slake some parched city's thirst profound,
Built ere a single water-hole was found!

In that blest region sure 'twill natural seem
To bridge the dry and ford the turbid stream,
And each invention there will meet success,
Which makes the labour more and produce less.
Windmills in swamps and water-wheels on high,
This shall the stream eschew and that the sky;
The sail shall steam, the oar the sail disgrace,
Oars change to paddles, paddles poles replace,
Till one by one each art and science fall,
And Barney's intellect is all in all.

2

Here Barney landed—memorable spot,
Which Mitchell never from the map shall blot—
Leaving his steamer stranded on a bank,
Regardless if the sailors swam or sank.

Obeying Nature's most esteemed command—
Self-preservation—here did Barney stand.
What did he there? The venerable man!
He came an embryo city's birth to plan;
Wiser than Solomon, when first he traced
Tadmor and Balbec, cities of the waste.

For six long hours he did the search pursue—
For six long hours—and then he thirsty grew;
Back to the rescued steamer did he steer,
Drew the loud cork and quaffed the foaming beer;
Then ate his dinner with tremendous gust
And with champagne relieved his throat adust;
Fished for his brother flatfish from the stern,
And thus, victorious, did to Sydney turn!

Weep not, my Barney! tremble not, my Brown!
Nor dread abatement of your high renown;
What though the Commissariat growl to pay
Your steamer's hire at thirty pounds a day;
What though your city on the northern shore
Remain as much a phantom as before;
Though people ask you for their *quo* a *quid*,
And say: "Twas ever thus that Barney did.
Thus did he build a quay beneath the tide—
Thus scoop a basin where no ship can ride—
Thus carry roads on lowlands and o'er highlands—
Thus spoil our harbour—thus blow up our islands.'

Weep not, my friends! Who knows, or who can tell
How well yourselves he served, and us, how well?
Oh! had some fever with its breath of flame
Blighted heroic Barney's stalwart frame;
Or had some savage, ignorant and dull,
Spiked the electric battery of his skull,
Then had our cup of woe indeed been full.
But now, let envy howl, let faction groan,
Yet, Barney! yet we have thee all our own.
Critics may cavil, governors may chafe,
We've lost a thousand pounds—but Barney's safe!

ON THE DEATH OF RICHARD WINDEYER

(Extract from a Parliamentary address)

The more we observe of that most admirable, contemptible,
wonderful, anomalous being, man, the more we are satisfied that he
is as much the slave of custom and habit as the meanest animal of

creation. Man in a colony is simply a money-making creature. From morn till night, all the year round, his faculties are strained up to and concentrated upon that one object. He has no time for anything else. No time to love, no time to hate, no time to rejoice, no time to mourn. He does not seem even to heap up riches that he may enjoy them. He does not buy books, pictures, busts, or laboratories, or any other means of strictly rational pleasure for the sake of rational pleasure, but he makes money that he may *have* it, and enable his wife, perhaps by piquant dinners and stylish equipage, to excite the envy, hatred, malice and uncharitableness of her neighbours. Life to the money-making colonist is truly a battle; a great fight which he unceasingly carries on in order that he may win a joyless fortune and at last die respectably—with assets.

Hence it is that in New South Wales we are never put out of our way by sudden deaths or unexpected bereavements of friends and relations. Whilst we are all laying about us right and left for the purpose of effecting our own advancement, we as little turn aside from our own absorbing pursuits when we find a man down, as we should do at a Waterloo or in an earthquake. We bury each other with about as much emotion as we feel when we dine with each other, perhaps frequently with more pleasure. This is a remarkable fact. We should probably regard it as philosophy and stoicism if we did not know it to be acquired insensibility.

We have been betrayed into this slight opening-up of an old vein of thought in us by a recent event, which ought not to be without interest to those who feel or profess to feel an interest in the condition of New South Wales. A man of many remarkable qualities of mind and character, of singular industry, energy, and general ability, and favourably distinguished from the mass in a variety of ways, has very lately been removed from among us by death. Richard Windeyer has passed from time into eternity with little more notice or observation than is usually paid to the memory of the least interesting individual who has paid the debt of nature. We have heard one or two persons express surprise at this. We, however, so far from participating in such a feeling, should have felt surprise had it been otherwise. It would have slightly disturbed our conviction of the indifferency of colonial human nature, and shaken the theory which we have above faintly adumbrated to the reader.

We have never been willing, and we believe we are unable, to acquire this insensibility. We would not for more gold than we could tell give up the delight we can always feel in the contemplation of a great character. When our hope and confidence in human goodness and honesty wax faint within us, a thought of such men as Hampden and Washington will purge away the perilous stuff which weighs upon our heart, and put us again upon tolerant terms with our own nature. It is for this reason that we believe it to be good— not merely as a tribute of respect to the departed, but as a means of encouraging men towards unselfish aims and objects—to notice and

discuss the merits of every man, who, having done or attempted
something for the benefit of his race, has left his life to us, as a
portion of human history which may be studied for the benefit of
the survivors. The season too for such a notice is advantageous.
Death is a great soberiser of the more volatile and thoughtless part
of us. The mind expatiates with a thoughtful awe in the void which
death has made. We discuss but the memory and the image of the
man whom so lately we saw and heard in all the alert intelligence of
this apparently immortal life. What is he? Where is he? What is he
doing now? It is truly a mighty change, to take place in one second
of time—that change from life to death which makes such questions
necessary. Whatever he is, wherever he is, whatever he may be
doing, we shall soon, very soon all of us, go to the knowledge of it,
as God shall please. So let us, whilst we are permitted, sometimes
close our ledgers and cast aside our briefs, and think of this un-
shunnable destiny that awaits us a little onward. Thus shall we grow
familiar with it, and when our hour is come, we shall go hence with
decency and with composure.

FREDERICK SINNETT   (1830–1866)

Journalist. Born in England; came to Australia in 1849.

from THE FICTION FIELDS OF AUSTRALIA

Man can no more do without works of fiction than he can do without clothing, and, indeed, not so well; for, where climate is propi-
tious, and manners simple, people often manage to loiter down the
road of life without any of the 'lendings' that Lear cast away from
him; yet, nevertheless, with nothing between the blue heaven and
their polished skins, they will gather in a circle round some dusky
orator or vocalist, as his imagination bodies forth the forms of
things unknown, to the entertainment and elevation of his hearers.
To amend our first proposition, then, works of fiction being more
necessary, and universally disseminated, than clothing, they still resemble clothing in this, that they take different shapes and fashions
in different ages. In the days of Chaucer—

> First warbler, whose sweet breath
>   Preluded those melodious bursts that fill
> The spacious times of great Elizabeth
>   With sounds that echo still—

didactic and descriptive poetry was almost the only recognized
vehicle of fiction. Then came the bursts that Chaucer preluded; and

in Shakespeare's days the dramatic form prevailed over all others. For some time afterwards every kind of feeling and thought found its expression in miscellaneous verse; and (though he was, of course, not the first novelist) Fielding, probably, set the fashion of that literary garment of the imagination, which has since been almost exclusively worn—the novel.

In the shape of novels, then, civilized man, at the present day, receives the greater part of the fictitious clothing necessary to cover the nakedness of his mind; and our present inquiry is into the feasibility of obtaining the material for this sort of manufacture from Australian soil. We are not, of course, questioning the practicability of writing novels in Australia. Thackeray might have begun *The Newcomes* in Kensington, and finished the book in Melbourne, as well as on the Continent. Our inquiry is into the feasibility of writing Australian novels; or, to use other words, into the suitability of Australian life and scenery for the novel writers' purpose; and, secondly, into the right manner of their treatment.

A reference to the second topic almost forestalls the necessity of our stating the distinct conviction by which we are possessed, that genuine Australian novels are possible; and, as a corollary from their being possible, it follows, with apparent obviousness, that they are desirable, inasmuch as it is desirable that the production of things necessary or comfortable to humanity should be multiplied and increased.

First, however, we must deal with the possibility; for, it has been our lot to fall in with men, by no means altogether given over to stupidity, who deem, what Signor Raffaello calls, 'this bullock-drivers' country' to present a field, not by any process whatsoever to be tilled and cultivated so as to produce novels, for some ages to come. The real reason, we take it, why our incredulous acquaintances arrived at the opinion they expressed, is, that such cultivation has not yet prospered to any remarkable extent; and that it is always difficult to believe in the possibility of anything of which there is no existing example and type. But, as this particular reason for disbelief is one which, while it has much actual weight over men's minds, is not often openly advanced, some more specific and respectable arguments were required, and, accordingly, were soon forthcoming.

In the first place, then, it is alleged against Australia that it is a new country, and, as Pitt said, when charged with juvenility, 'this is an accusation which I can neither palliate nor deny'. Unless we go into the Aboriginal market for 'associations', there is not a single local one, of a century old, to be obtained in Australia; and, setting apart Mr Fawkner's pre-Adamite recollections of Colonel Collins, there is not an association in Victoria mellowed by so much as a poor score of years. It must be granted, then, that we are quite debarred from all the interest to be extracted from any kind of archaeological accessories. No storied windows, richly dight, cast a dim, religious light over any Australian premises. There are no ruins for that rare old plant, the ivy green, to creep over and make his dainty meal of. No Australian author can hope to extricate his hero or heroine, however pressing the emergency may be, by means of a spring panel and a subterranean passage, or such like relics of feudal barons, and refuges of modern novelists, and the offspring of their imagination. There may be plenty of dilapidated buildings, but not one, the dilapidation of which is sufficiently venerable by age, to tempt the wandering footsteps of the most arrant parvenu of a ghost that ever walked by night. It must be admitted that Mrs Radcliffe's genius would be quite thrown away here; and we must reconcile ourselves to the conviction that the foundations of a second *Castle of Otranto* can hardly be laid in Australia during our time. Though the corporation may leave Collins Street quite dark enough for the purpose, it is much too dirty to permit any novelist (having a due regard to her sex) to ask the White Lady of Avenel, or a single one of her female connections, to pass that way.

Even if we survive these losses, the sins of youth continue to beset us. No one old enough for a hero can say,

I remember, I remember the house where I was born,

apropos of a Victorian dwelling. The antiquity of the United States quite puts us to shame; and it is darkly hinted that there is not so much as a 'house with seven gables' between Portland and Cape Howe.

Mr Horne, in his papers on dramatic art, observed very truly, that one does not go to the theatre (or the novel) for a facsimile of nature. If you want that you can see nature itself in the street or next door. You go to get larger and more comprehensive views of nature than your own genius enables you to take for yourself, through the medium of art. In the volume of Shakespeare's plays, for example, is compacted more of nature than one man in a million perceives in a life's intercourse with the world. Shakespeare, like all the kings of fiction, was a great condenser. We are not detained by him, except occasionally, and for subsidiary artistic purposes, with mere gossip about the momentary affairs of the men and women brought upon the scene. A verbatim report of a common evening's conversation would fill a book, and the greater part of what would be reported would be quite uninteresting, uninstructive, and unconducive to the purposes of art. The author of genius leaves no apparent gaps in the discourse; and brings about in the reader's mind a half-illusion that he is listening to a complete and unstrained dialogue; whereas, in fact, the speeches are so concise, and in such sequence, that we only have the essence of any possible conversation. Conversation is one of the essential processes of the writer of fiction, whatever form he may adopt—otherwise the description of years of life would take years to read.

Now, in the old world, we are accustomed to this kind of conversation; to conversations not reported verbatim, but artistically.

From Shakespeare downwards hundreds of authors have performed this service with admirable general fidelity; and have, at the same time, with artistic skill, concealed the evidences of their own labor as effectually as the sculptor does, in whose smooth and finished marble no mark of the chisel is to be discerned. This much, which is entirely due to the manner of the narrative, we have suffered ourselves to believe an attribute of the matter; and, because daily life, which is not much more prosaic on one part of the earth's surface than on another, has been, in the old world, so often and so admirably converted to the purposes of art, we fancy it to be peculiarly adapted to those purposes. Here we have not been accustomed to see nature through the medium of art, but directly; and though, to the eye of genius, 'the earth and every common sight' possesses a 'glory and a freshness', and needs no abridgement or coloring, yet to possess such powers of perception is the privilege only of one among thousands. The great mass of mankind can only hope to catch glimpses of the glory of 'every common sight', when genius holds it up for them in the right light. This genius has not yet done for Australian nature. Most of us have had more than enough of positive Australian dialogue, but we have never read an Australian dialogue artistically reported. We have heard squatter, and bullock-driver, and digger, talk, and we think it would be very uninteresting, no doubt; and a verbatim report of the conversation of Brown, Jones, and Robinson, in the old world, would be equally uninteresting, but we know by experience that genius can report it so as to be interesting—yet to leave it the conversation of Brown, Jones, and Robinson still. The first genius that performs similar service in Australia will dissipate our incredulity, as to this matter, for ever.

It is not to be assumed that, if the life going on about us seems somewhat slow and tedious, the picture of it must be equally so; for the picture is microcosmic, and does not reproduce the life itself, but a compact and comprehensive likeness of it, that enables us to see, in a few minutes, and in true perspective, the scenes which, in actual existence, we plod through only in the course of years. It is, however, superfluous to deal theoretically with the objection, that fiction cannot properly deal with things close upon the foreground of our observation, because it is destroyed by experience. European novelists, during one period, thought that their works acquired an extra charm by dealing chiefly with distant times and places. Scott's genius invested distant times and places with such interest that people began to fancy such distance an essential of such interest. Dickens, on the contrary, by his genius, suddenly awoke London to a perception of the artistic uses that could be made of everyday London life; and men, in the constant habit of having their boots cleaned at Borough inns, were startled to find how the 'boots' at a Borough inn might be a Sam Weller. Thackeray has, perhaps, gone still farther in selecting his characters from the precise time and circle of his readers. From his pages many old *habitués* of clubs first acquire a true understanding of club life, and the majority of his admirers are, perhaps, most delighted with seeing their own experiences reproduced to them by this master-mind, with the exquisite and seemingly intuitive sense which belongs to him—of the manner in which true art makes keenly pleasurable the contemplation of what, in its absolute shape, we tire of every day of our lives. The most successful and delightful novels of the present day are so invariably those which deal with immediately surrounding circumstances, both of time and place, that we shall not discuss farther the second objection we have noticed. A somewhat cognate objection— that of the smallness of the community among which the scenes of Australian novels must at present be necessarily laid—we shall deal with hereafter.

The first is—that details of time and place are to the novel writer what costume is to the painter. Your hack artists, who, year after year, go 'fossicking' for artistic nuggets in such rich but exhausted claims as the Vicar of Wakefield and Don Quixote, and who present the Royal Academy every May with their views of how Moses looked when he brought back the gross of green spectacles, and how Sancho twirled in the air when he was tossed in the blanket, or, when aiming at the truth historical, condemn Edward's wife to suck his wounds through all time, and Alfred to neglect everlasting cakes in a perpetual neat-herd's cottage, are unable to construct a picture out of nature's own materials; they can only copy the microcosmic pictures of others. Some there be, even, who are more undisguisedly the painters of costume, and whose pictures merely stand in the place of a *Belle Assemblée* to a bygone generation. These are great in the peculiarities of armours and doublets, and tell us, with the nicest accuracy, how the barons and John *dressed*—when he signed the great charter—and nothing more. But the true artist, whether he work with brush or pen, deals with nature, and with human feelings and human passions; and the question of clothing is considered for the sake of accuracy and unity, and as an accident, not as an essential.

With respect to feelings and passions, then, which of them is there excluded from Australian soil? Certainly not that master passion which is the fiction writers' most constant theme.

> All thoughts, all passions, all delights,
> That ever move this mortal frame,
> Are but the ministers of love,
> And feed his sacred flame.

'Love rules the court, the camp, the grove,' and Australians as effectually as dwellers in old countries; and all the joys and sorrows of that emotion—which wise people, aged sixty and upwards, and other non-combatants in Cupid's warfare, laugh at and long for— are present for the novelist to deal with, as he tells, in some new form, the oft-told tale of which mankind never tires. Nay, the very fact that numberless lovers are here separated from their loves, should suggest a thousand various stories and situations, peculiar, in their details, to the soil, and yet dealing with a cosmopolitan and universal interest.

Is the opposite feeling of hate banished from Australia? We could contentedly give up the possibility of Australian novels for the assurance that we resided in such a Utopia. Alas! that such a perfect reality cannot be obtained by the sacrifice of so much novelists' capital.

Is avarice extinct among us? Most emphatically, No! And with the presence of avarice, we have that of all the schemes, and plots, and wiles, with which the avaricious man ministers to his fault. The rapid turns and changes of this place give, indeed, peculiarly free scope for developing the romance of money-making; and it is not to be overlooked that the desire to make money has good as well as bad phases. Novelists would not have been true to their vocation of giving 'a picture in little' of the world as it really is, if they did not, at the present time, cause the plots of their stories very often to turn upon pecuniary failures and successes. Money means command over almost all external things and resources, and is left out of consideration only by those old romancists whose knightly heroes were comfortably provided with whatever their authors thought good for them without the vulgar and mundane necessity of what we call 'making money'—a slow and unromantic process, quite incompatible with their gallant and adventurous lives. Novel heroes now no longer have their occasions supplied out of treasure chambers bursting open to a potent 'open sesame'. We deal with money in a more business-like way. We fight for it in the chancery court as plaintiff in the great case of Jarndyce and Jarndyce—we lose it in the Bundelcund bank—uncle John muddles away the property of Mr Caxton, senior; and hero Pisistratus has even to find his way out to this very country of Australia to retrieve the family fortunes. Novel heroes must not expect, in these days, to lead lives of perfect freedom from pecuniary difficulties and embarrassments, any more than other people. They enjoy, as it is, an unfair advantage in the certainty they have of making fortunes in the long run. To judge, however, by the spirit that authors have recently been evincing, there is no security for the poor fellows being left in possession of even this advantage much longer.

A novelist, indeed, can invest more people with the desire to make money than he can even bring the passion of love to bear upon;—for, with respect to money-makers, the means and ends are alike infinitely various, and susceptible of being adapted to every possible age and character. Ralph Nickleby, and his nephew Nicholas, had, in common, the wish to make money, but the wish in the one was associated with all that was base, and mean, and sordid, in the other with the best and noblest hopes and desires. There is no source of interest connected with money-making of which the Australian novelist cannot avail himself. The means and the motives are at his own command, and he can make us watch the process with every feeling, from that of perfect sympathy to perfect scorn, according to the genius and skill with which those means and motives are conceived and portrayed. At the same time, he can make his tale thoroughly Australian. The events may be true and natural to this place, while impossible for any other. We need not labour to show that the same truth holds good of the feelings and passions. We have here 'the same organs, dimensions, senses,' as the good folks in Europe. 'If you tickle us, do we not laugh? If you prick us, do we not bleed?' Human nature being the same, the true requisites of the novelist are to be found in one place as well as in another. Australia offers fresh scenery, fresh costumes, and fresh machinery, new as to its details—great advantages, to those that know how to use them—and, for the rest, presents a field neither better nor worse than most others, in which people love, and hate, and hope, and fear, and strive, and are disappointed, and succeed, and plot, and scheme, and work out their destinies, and obey the good and evil impulses of their infinitely various natures.

One word as to scenery. Many worthy people thought railways would put an end to romance in England. The new police act, it was conceived by others, would be equally destructive to the raw material of novels. The romance of robbery, some imagined, ended when robbers ceased to wear gold-laced coats and jack boots, and to do their business on horse-back. The genius of fiction, however, can accommodate herself to greater changes than these, and remains just as fresh and as blooming under circumstances that make people, unacquainted with the invulnerable hardiness of her constitution, predict her immediate decline and death. For our part we hold that there is comparatively little in the circumstance, and almost all in the genius that handles it; but those who believe in mounted robbers, and mourn over the introduction of railways, should feel that in Australia the novelists' golden age is revived. When Waverley travelled up from London, to visit his northern cousins, the Osbaldistones, he went on horseback, and took a fortnight over the journey—that is the way we manage here to this very day. There was a great deal of 'sticking-up' then, and there; and there is here, and now. Sir William of Deloraine had to swim the stream that it would have spoiled a magnificent description for him to have crossed by a cast-iron bridge, as he would do in the reign of Victoria; but in the colony which bears her name, the Central Road Board cannot be accused of having destroyed the romance of the watercourses. How, in the name of gas-pipes and rural police, is a traveller to be lost and benighted in England nowadays. Here he can be placed in that unpleasant but interesting predicament, without violating, in the least, the laws of perfect probability. Look at a railway map of England, and see where

> Now spurs the lated traveller apace
> To gain the timely inn.

He has no control over the iron-horse that whirls him along, and when he gets to the terminus he gains the timely inn in a Hansom cab. Here the description applies with precise accuracy. In short, the natural and external circumstances of Australia partake much more of what we used to call romance than those of England, but we refuse to claim any advantage on this score, and content ourselves with reasserting that those who know how to deal with it can extract almost as much out of one set of circumstances as out of another, wherever the human heart throbs and human society exists.

We explain the absence of any really first-class Australian novels simply by a reference to the mathematical doctrine of probabilities. It is only once in many years that there steps forth from among the many millions of the British people a novelist able to break up new ground, and describe phases and conditions of life undescribed before. The great mass of those that load the circulating library shelves

> Remodel models rather than the life.

They only sing the same old song over again, 'with variations'. Like most painters, they fancy that they are imitating nature when they are only imitating pictures of nature previously painted. Just as hack orators can only quote from quotations, so hack novelists can only deal with such scenes and characters as have been put upon the stage before. Give them a set of circumstances, for the mode of handling which, for novelistic purposes, they have no precedent, and they know not what to make of it. Show them an actual living man, some type of whom is not to be found in already existing novels, and they can make no use of the material at all. They pass him as they pass thousands of good human materials every day without recognizing their worth. When the real genius has once laid hold of the new material, however, and shown them how to mould him to the purposes of art, they can 'remodel the model' *ad infinitum*, so much easier is it to steal out of books than to accept the gifts of nature.

Well, then, we argue, if only now and then out of the population of all England there arises a novelist capable of breaking up fresh ground, it is not to be wondered at that no such man has yet risen here. Geniuses are like tortoiseshell tom-cats—not impossible, only rare. Every ten years one is born unto Great Britain, but probably none exists in Australia, and a reason precisely analogous to this makes it improbable that we have at present among us any one capable of doing justice to Australian materials of fiction. There are not cats enough in Australia to entitle us to a tortoiseshell tom yet, according to the doctrine of averages.

We have to confess that we labour under the same disadvantages as afflict the hacks and copyists, and we cannot, therefore, point out how the great untouched Australian quarry is to be rightly worked. Only as we roam about the motley streets, or ride through the silent bush, we have just sense enough to feel that, when the capable eye comes to look upon them, all these rude amorphous materials may be arranged in form of the highest and most artistic beauty. The recorders are tuneless only because there is no one who knows how to play upon them; in the right hands they will 'discourse most eloquent music'.

But if we have not the genius to say how the quarry is to be worked—if we had, we should work it instead of talking about it—we are able to see certain peculiar defects in the attempts that have hitherto been made at Australian novel writing, and one or two of these we will here point out.

In the first place we may remark that most Australian stories are *too* Australian, and, instead of human life, we have only local 'manners and customs' portrayed in them. The *dramatis personae* are not people with characters and passions, but lay figures, so constructed, and placed in such attitudes, as to display the costumes of the place and period. The few Australian novels which have been written are too apt to be books of travels in disguise. The authors are but voyagers sailing under the false colors of novelists, and you might as well call the illustrations to Cook's voyages (depicting 'natives of Nootka sound', 'war dance among the Sandwich Islanders,' etc.) pictures, as such works novels. They have their uses, doubtless, and are not to be despised, but they are, at best, works of simple instruction as to matters of fact, rather than works of art. If we were asked what was the first requisite of a novel, we should say human character. The second—human character. The third—human character. Even plot and incident comes afterwards and the mere question of costume and local coloring after plot and incident. In most Australian stories the order is reversed, and Australian customs are predominant. We must be careful not to be misunderstood here, or we might be supposed to say, what would be contrary to the whole tenor of our writing, and to imply that beau ideal Australian novels would only differ in trivial and minor things from any other novels. Let us, then, illustrate what we mean by an example, and let us take the exquisite scene (from *The Antiquary*) in old Mucklebackit's cottage.

That scene could have been laid nowhere else but in the dwelling of a fisherman upon the Scottish coast. Nowhere else could the characters and incidents have developed themselves in that form. Grief for a son's loss is, indeed, not an emotion confined to one time and place; and such grief Scott could have brought before us in palace or hovel, as he pleased; but the novelist has to show us the same human feelings and passions working under various circumstances and modified by them. Now, in the scene we speak of, all local circumstances—all local coloring—sound and striking as they are, are subordinated to this purpose. Everything else is merely accessory to the display of human character and passion; but human characters and passions are affected and changed by such accessory circumstances; and, thus, while the relative importance of the elements of fiction remains unaltered, the change in the lesser implies change in the greater, and the combined whole is new, and full of new interest. We have not space to extract the scene here, but, if the reader take sufficient interest in this kind of speculation, let him open *The Antiquary* and read the description again, and, perhaps, he will apprehend us better. If not, he will not regret reading it again for its own sake.

Now, in the kind of novel we want to see written, but do not expect to read for some time, we want to see a picture of universal human life and passion, but represented as modified by Australian externals. The description of all these externals must then be truthful and complete, but subordinated to the larger purposes of fiction.

In further illustration of the defect we allude to let us consider what a London story would be, if written in the spirit, and after the fashion, of most Australian stories. The *dramatis personae* would walk the stage merely to illustrate, in their acts, the habits and peculiarities of London. The work would be a sort of amalgam of *The Great Metropolis*, *The Book of Trades*, *The Strangers' Guide to London*, and *The Police Reports*. We should learn how different classes of people spend the twenty-four hours—how they live, and what they live upon. We should learn the manner in which policemen arrange their beats, and the system according to which cab fares are regulated. We should learn that there are butchers in Whitechapel, and noblemen in Mayfair. We should learn how London dairymen water their milk, and London bakers get up in the small hours to knead their dough with their heels,—but we should have no true novel, or work of art or genius. We should have a picture, not of human life, as modified by London externals, but of some London externals alone.

We had intended, in this paper, to have reviewed some of the best Australian stories that have yet been published, but these general remarks have extended to such a length that we must postpone the fulfilment of this intention until next month. In the meantime we content ourselves with the concluding remark, that real genius is ever able to draw its inspiration from the rills that run at its own feet, and without travelling to Helicon—that everywhere nature has new beauties and truths for the eye and mind that know how to perceive and grasp them—and that, when we complain of her sterility, we should rather humbly confess our own.

The fault is ours, if, in this fresh and vast country, peopled with men of all characters, and degrees, and nations, in which all human feelings and emotions are astir, in which the pulse of existence beats with almost feverish speed, we regard the whole scene as tame and prosaic, and able to furnish the materials for no books but ledgers. What should we have made of such far more barren places as have given up hidden treasures, and been made bright and beautiful for all generations, at the touch of such genius as his, for example,

Who trod in glory and in joy,
Following his plough along the mountain side?

RICHARD ROWE   ('Peter 'Possum') (1828–1879)

Journalist, poet. Born in Wales; in Australia 1853–1858.

SUNDAY AFTERNOON

from PETER 'POSSUM'S PORTFOLIO

I feel like a bird in a cage, left without groundsel, seed and water, when masonry forms my horizon on a Sunday afternoon.

In wet weather the damp streets, with their closed shops and towering walls, look like huge graving-docks; in fine, they are monotonous canals of stagnant sunshine. Their Pompeian stillness—unbroken, save by the rattle of an occasional omnibus, and the hoarse croaking of its driver and shrill treble of its cad, ejaculating in amœbean contest "Glebe! Glebe! New*town*! New*town*! Barwan Park!" "Wool'm'loo! 'm'loo!" "Padding*tun*!"— oppresses me, congests my brain. The weariness of all the busy week, gathered into one overwhelming feeling of *ennui*, seems to be brooding in the atmosphere of dust; and when the bells begin to ring for church, you miss their morning's silvery sound of joy, their evening's softer sound of peace. *Ding-dong, ding-dong*, in dull, metallic tones, without a single touch of poetry, is all they say.

Disregarding their drowsy call to drowsy prayer—afternoon-service to me is always suggestive of undigested pudding on the part of both priest and people—I make a point of joining one of the many throngs that pour out from all sides of Sydney, like swarming bees, on Sunday afternoon. Let me sketch a few of my companions.

Look at those servant-girls with their year's wages on their backs—chaotic heaps of discordant colours—masses of jumbled rainbow; so that a tulip-bed in all its glory is not arrayed like one of these. Like red harvest-moons shining through cloud-wreaths, their round, ruddy faces literally blaze with robust, rude health out of their feathers, flowers and gauze. Their podgy hands seem bursting from their coverings, like overripe gooseberries. Delicate French gloves and glittering bracelets hardly harmonise with raw-beef wrists.

Contrast the little milliner—her pale face flushing into sea-shell pink in the fresh breeze. Her dress, probably , has not cost a tithe of the value of Bridget's; but which looks the more like a lady? Of course, I don't blame poor Bridget for her costly and yet clumsy splendour—she knows no better; but I read in the pretty little milliner a pretty little lesson on the benefit of taste.

There goes a shop-boy, smoking and gorgeously attired, and mounted on a hired or borrowed hack. He fondly imagines that he is the focus of hundreds of admiring eyes, and that all who gaze on him consider him a squatter. Alas! his seat bewrayeth him; squatters don't ride like that. The few who do look at him, take him for a tailor.

A pair of lovers: "She," as the old music-books say , with a face a perfect flower-garden of smiles; "He," all awkward and confused. Why on earth should *the man* always be ashamed of being in love? It is the poor woman that commits the folly.

A family group: *Paterfamilias*, a German baker of bland but spooney aspect; he smiles incessantly upon his little English wife, and punctuates her rapid flow of words with the assenting *Ja!* or the emphatic *Nein*! He nurses two of the children, moreover; and very curious it is to behold the bland and spooney aspect of the father's face repeated in the countenances of those young Teutons.

Suppose we embark in one of the crowded craft that wave their smoke-burgees, and scarcely less sooty flags, over holiday-makers bound for Parramatta, Cremorne, Watson's Bay, or Manly Beach. What comical collections of humanity the good folks are—intensely conscious, for the most part, of their "Sunday clothes," glossy and wrinkled silk and broadcloth winking, as it were, in the unwonted blaze to which they are exposed—reminiscences of press and drawers suffusing with a bashful blush the immaculate purity of their hebdomodal resurrection. How solemnly the good people take their pleasure—in the orthodox, ponderous manner of Britons, on whatever shore their fate may cast them. Grave they look, as if going to a funeral. The very actors yonder, in abnormal hats—escaped, for a brief respite, from the week-long atmosphere of orange-peel and gas—succumb to the prevailing sentiment, take their key-note from the dominant tone of the circumambient lugubrious glee; and, cigar in mouth,—

With shorn cheeks pale against its ruddy glow,—they cluster around the funnel, as though they would keep themselves in countenance by its example, whilst doing anything so dissipated as smoking. A serious silence reigns from stem to stern, unbroken save when the steersman turns his quid, emitting its mahogany-hued juice upon the sun-scorched deck with a splash that sounds like that of "the first of a thunder-shower," in the awful hush.

Such mournful merrymakers become tiresome after a bit; so leaving them, as Elia says of the Egyptian hermits, to "enjoy one another's want of conversation," let us look around.

The flags of all nations flash like splendid meteors athwart the sapphire sky, and boats with snowy sails fly like sea-birds over the blue waters. Now we pass a huge emigrant-ship, alive with passengers, gazing anxiously over the bulwarks at their 'promised land;" and anon a tiny, anchored yacht, that seems to be fretting for freedom, as it pulls at its tether like little Barbara Lewthwaite's lamb, and then, finding the effort vain, swims round and round its buoy in a pretty little pet of impatient, impotent anger.

We may well be proud of our harbour. Lovely are its deep, indenting waters; covered with dancing dimples, swathed in sheets of gold; rolling in emerald green, heaving in violet blue; blushing beneath the parting gaze of the setting sun, or looking up to him pale and trembling in the morn, when all night long the thunder has pealed and echoed through the dark. Still, although a gem of the first *water*, Port Jackson would certainly be all the better for a brighter setting.

Like a mighty army of Huns in never-ending march, the gloomy trees sweep down from the far distance to the melancholy shore. Here and there, it is true, the sombre mass is enlivened by a break that beams in cultivated beauty and tells of the sweet charities of Home; but even on its enlivener the black bush casts a shadow from its superfluity of shade. The islands, too, that, clad in *verdure*— waving with the foliage of more favoured lands—*might* be so beautiful, remind one now, as they gaze drearily upon their doubles in the reflecting waters, of widows in old mourning, embrowned by the dust and heat of many a weary day, hanging over their mirrors in half-hopeless longing for the time when they may cast aside their rusty weeds. Pinchgut is free from the "sad-coloured" raiment; but Pinchgut decorated with a tower like a gigantic hat—a monstrously magnified drab Mountcastle—doth not add greatly to the harbour's picturesque.

Now let us land on the North Shore, and wander through the fragrant forest—not so ugly when one is in it, and can discriminate the hues that blend into a pall of gloom when seen from a distance; let us roam through its silent solitudes sprinkled with many a holy, happy nunnery of flowers, until we come to St Leonard's churchyard. "Rejoice, Oh, young man, in thy youth!" has hitherto been the summer-breeze's song; the rest of the text it murmurs, like a solemn refrain, as it rustles in the waving grass above the graves.

In the "Deaths"—calmly chronicled in that little tablet above the programme of the day's bustle and merry-making—there is an appeal that catches every eye, and dims for a moment its kindling fires of revelry or greed. Another of Time's waves has dashed its spray upon the shore. We all of us take, perforce, an interest in Death, because it is our common doom. The *loneliness* of deaths out here adds a peculiar melancholy to these records. Far from the old familiar places, the old familiar faces, we drop unheeded as the yellow leaves silently falling in the quiet autumn air, and rot like them unnoticed in the ground. How many a one for whom Love across the sea has looked and longed in vain lies in our graveyards! Those despairing mothers' and sisters' appeals for tidings of So-and-so, who sailed from such a place, in this ship or the other, "and has not since been heard of," make the third column of the *Herald* a very pathetic one to me. I am afraid the tidings are but seldom gained, or if gained, are very seldom glad. Disappointment, Dissipation, Desperation, Death, keep a firm grip upon their victims. Not once in a hundred times is the missing son or brother found: when found, perhaps, it would have been better for the peace of those who sought him, that he should have remained lost to them in knowledge as in life. A foul, festered heart, contrasted with the pure, bright spirit that those who seek the lost one loved, is but a dreary resurrection after long, weary years of brow-wrinkling, eye-dimming, heart-breaking, anxiety.

I ought, perhaps, to apologise for preaching: my excuse for my sermon must be that I have been writing on—Sunday Afternoon.

Charles Harpur   (1813–1868)

Poet. Born in N.S.W.; little formal education.

THE CREEK OF THE FOUR GRAVES

Part I

I verse a Settler's tale of olden times—
One told me by our sage friend, Egremont;
Who then went forth, meetly equipt, with four
Of his most trusty and adventurous men
Into the wilderness,—went forth to seek
New streams and wider pastures for his fast
Augmenting flocks and herds. On foot were all,
For horses then were beasts of too great price
To be much ventured upon mountain routes,
And over wild wolds clouded up with brush,
And cut with marshes, perilously pathless.

So went they forth at dawn: and now the sun
That rose behind them as they journeyed out,
Was firing with his nether rim a range
Of unknown mountains that, like rampires, towered
Full in their front, and his last glances fell
Into the gloomy forest's eastern glades
In golden masses, transiently, or flashed

Down on the windings of a nameless Creek,
That noiseless ran betwixt the pioneers
And those new Apennines;—ran, shaded up
With boughs of the wild willow, hanging mixed
From either bank, or duskily befringed
With upward tapering, feathery swamp-oaks—
The sylvan eyelash always of remote
Australian waters, whether gleaming still
In lake or pool, or bickering along
Between the marges of some eager stream.

Before them, thus extended, wilder grew
The scene each moment—beautifully wilder!
For when the sun was all but sunk below
Those barrier mountains,—in the breeze that o'er
Their rough enormous backs deep fleeced with wood
Came whispering down, the wide upslanting sea
Of fanning leaves in the descending rays
Danced interdazzlingly, as if the trees
That bore them, were all thrilling,—tingling all
Even to the roots for very happiness:
So prompted from within, so sentient, seemed
The bright quick motion—wildly beautiful.

But when the sun had wholly disappeared
Behind those mountains—O what words, what hues
Might paint the wild magnificence of view
That opened westward! Out extending, lo,
The heights rose crowding, with their summits all
Dissolving, as it seemed, and partly lost
In the exceeding radiancy aloft;
And thus transfigured, for awhile they stood
Like a great company of Archeons, crowned
With burning diadems, and tented o'er
With canopies of purple and of gold!

Here halting wearied, now the sun was set,
Our travellers kindled for their first night's camp
The brisk and crackling fire, which also looked
A wilder creature than 'twas elsewhere wont,
Because of the surrounding savageness.
And soon in cannikins the tea was made,
Fragrant and strong; long fresh-sliced rashers then
Impaled on whittled skewers, were deftly broiled
On the live embers, and when done, transferred
To quadrants from an ample damper cut,
Their only trenchers,—soon to be dispatched
With all the savoury morsels they sustained,
By the keen tooth of healthful appetite.

And as they supped, birds of new shape and plume,
And wild strange voice, nestward repairing by,
Oft took their wonder; or betwixt the gaps
In the ascending forest growths they saw
Perched on the bare abutments of those mountains,
Where haply yet some lingering gleam fell through,
The wallaroo look forth: till eastward all
The view had wasted into formless gloom,
Night's front; and westward, the high massing woods
Steeped in a swart but mellowed Indian beauty—
A deep dusk loveliness,—lay ridged and heaped
Only the more distinctly for their darkness
Against the twilight heaven—a cloudless depth
Yet luminous from the sunset's fading splendor;
And thus awhile, in the lit dusk, they seemed
To hang like mighty pictures of themselves
In the still chambers of some vaster world.

The silent business of their supper done,
The Echoes of the solitary place,
Came as in sylvan wonder wide about
To hear, and imitate tentatively,
Strange voices moulding a strange speech, as then
Within the pleasant purlieus of the fire
Lifted in glee—but to be hushed erelong,
As with the night in kindred darkness came
O'er the adventurers, each and all, some sense—
Some vague-felt intimation from without,
Of danger, lurking in its forest lairs.

But nerved by habit, and all settled soon
About the well-built fire, whose nimble tongues
Sent up continually a strenuous roar
Of fierce delight, and from their fuming pipes
Full charged and fragrant with the Indian weed,
Drawing rude comfort,—typed without, as 'twere,
By tiny clouds over their several heads
Quietly curling upward;—thus disposed
Within the pleasant firelight, grave discourse
Of their peculiar business brought to each
A steadier mood, that reached into the night.

The simple subject to their minds at length
Fully discussed, their couches they prepared
Of rushes, and the long green tresses pulled
Down from the boughs of the wild willows near.
Then four, as pre-arranged, stretched out their limbs
Under the dark arms of the forest trees
That mixed aloft, high in the starry air,

In arcs and leafy domes whose crossing curves
And roof-like features,—blurring as they ran
Into some denser intergrowth of sprays,—
Were seen in mass traces out against the clear
Wide gaze of heaven; and trustful of the watch
Kept near them by their thoughtful Master, soon
Drowsing away, forgetful of their toil,
And of the perilous vast wilderness
That lay around them like a spectral world,
Slept, breathing deep;—whilst all things there as well
Showed slumbrous,—yea, the circling forest trees,
Their foremost boles carved from a crowded mass
Less visible, by the watchfire's bladed gleams,
As quick and spicular, from the broad red ring
Of its more constant light they ran in spurts
Far out and under the umbrageous dark;
And even the shaded and enormous mountains,
Their bluff brows glooming through the stirless air,
Looked in their quiet solemnly asleep:
Yea, thence surveyed, the Universe might have seemed
Coiled in vast rest,—only that one dim cloud,
Diffused and shapen like a mighty spider,
Crept as with scrawling legs along the sky;
And that the stars, in their bright orders, still
Cluster by cluster glowingly revealed
As this slow cloud moved on,—high over all,—
Looked wakeful—yea, looked thoughtful in their peace.

Part II

Meanwhile the cloudless eastern heaven had grown
More and more luminous—and now the Moon
Up from behind a giant hill was seen
Conglobing, till—a mighty mass—she brought
Her under border level with its cone,
As thereon it were resting: when, behold
A wonder! Instantly that cone's whole bulk
Erewhile so dark, seemed inwardly a-glow
With her instilled irradiance; while the trees
That fringed its outline,—their huge statures dwarfed
By distance into brambles, and yet all
Clearly defined against her ample orb,—
Out of its very disc appeared to swell
In shadowy relief, as they had been
All sculptured from its substance as she rose.

Thus o'er that dark height her great orb conglobed,
Till her full light, in silvery sequence still

Cascading forth from ridgy slope to slope,
Like the dropt foldings of a lucent veil,
Chased mass by mass the broken darkness down
Into the dense-brushed valleys, where it crouched,
And shrank, and struggled, like a dragon doubt
Glooming some lonely spirit that doth still
Resist the Truth with obstinate shifts and shows,
Though shining out of heaven, and from defect
Winning a triumph that might else not be.

There standing in his lone watch, Egremont
On all this solemn beauty of the world,
Looked out, yet wakeful; for sweet thoughts of home
And all the sacred charities it held,
Ingathered to his heart, as by some nice
And subtle interfusion that connects
The loved and cherished (then the most, perhaps,
When absent, or when passed, or even when *lost*)
With all serene and beautiful and bright
And lasting things of Nature. So then thought
The musing Egremont: when suddenly—hark!
A bough crackt loudly in a neighboring brake,
And drew at once, as with a 'larum, all
His spirits thitherward in wild surmise.

But summoning caution, and back stepping close
Against the shade-side of a bending gum,
With a strange horror gathering to his heart,
As if his blood were charged with insect life
And writhed along in clots, he stilled himself,
Listening long and heedfully, with head
Bent forward sideways, till his held breath grew
A pang, and his ears rung. But Silence there
Had recomposed her ruffled wings, and now
Brooded it seemed even stillier than before,
Deep nested in the darkness: so that he
Unmasking from the cold shade, grew erelong
More reassured from wishing to be so,
And to muse Memory's suspended mood,
Though with an effort, quietly recurred.

But there again—crack upon crack! And hark!
O Heaven! have Hell's worst fiends burst howling up
Into the death-doom'd world? Or whence, if not
From diabolic rage, could surge a yell
So horrible as that which now affrights
The shuddering dark! Ah! Beings as fell are near!
Yea, Beings, in their dread inherited hate
And deadly enmity, as vengeful, come

In vengeance! For behold, from the long grass
And nearer brakes, a semi-belt of stript
And painted Savages divulge at once
Their bounding forms!—full in the flaring light
Thrown outward by the fire, that roused and lapped
The rounding darkness with its ruddy tongues
More fiercely than before,—as though even *it*
Had felt the sudden shock the air received
From their dire cries, so terrible to hear!

A moment in wild agitation seen
Thus, as they bounded up, on then they came
Closing, with weapons brandished high, and so
Rushed in upon the sleepers! three of whom
But started, and then weltered prone beneath
The first fell blow dealt down on each by three
Of the most stalwart of their pitiless foes!
But One again, and yet again, heaved up—
Up to his knees, under the crushing strokes
Of huge-clubbed nulla-nullas, till his own
Warm blood was blinding him! For he was one
Who had with Misery nearly all his days
Lived lonely, and who therefore, in his soul,
Did hunger after hope, and thirst for what
Hope still had promised him,—some taste at least
Of human good however long deferred,
And now he could not, even in dying, loose
His hold on life's poor chances of to-morrow—
Could not but so dispute the terrible fact
Of death, even in Death's presence! Strange it is:
Yet oft 'tis seen that Fortune's pampered child
Consents to his untimely power with less
Reluctance, less despair, than does the wretch
Who hath been ever blown about the world
The straw-like sport of Fate's most bitter blasts,
Vagrant and tieless;—ever still in him
The craving spirit thus grieves unto itself:

'I never yet was happy—never yet
Tasted unmixed enjoyment, and I would
Yet pass on the bright Earth that I have loved
Some season, though most brief, of happiness;
So should I walk thence forward to my grave,
Wherever in her green maternal breast
It might await me, more than now prepared
To house me in its gloom,—resigned at heart,
Subjected to its certainty and soothed
Even by the consciousness of having shaped
Some personal good in being;—strong myself,

And strengthening others. But to have lived long years
Of wasted breath, because of woe and want,
And disappointed hope,—and now, at last,
To die thus desolate, is horrible!'

And feeling thus through many foregone moods
Whose lines had in the temper of his soul
All mixed, and formed *one* habit,—that poor man,
Though the black shadows of untimely death,
Inevitably, under every stroke,
But thickened more and more,—against them still
Upstruggled, nor would cease: until one last
Tremendous blow, dealt down upon his head
As if in mercy , gave him to the dust
With all his many woes and frustrate hope.

Struck through with a cold horror, Egremont,
Standing apart,—yea, standing as it were
In marble effigy, saw this, saw all!
And when outthawing from his frozen heart
His blood again rushed tingling—with a leap
Awaking from the ghastly trance which there
Had bound him, as with chill petrific bonds,
He raised from instinct more than conscious thought
His death-charged tube, and at that murderous crew
Firing! saw one fall ox-like to the earth;—
Then turned and fled. Fast fled he, but as fast
His deadly foes went thronging on his track!
Fast! for in full pursuit, behind him yelled
Wild men whose wild speech hath no word for *mercy*!
And as he fled, the forest beasts as well,
In general terror, through the brakes a-head
Crashed scattering, or with maddening speed athwart
His course came frequent. On—still on he flies—
Flies for dear life! and still behind him hears
Nearer and nearer, the so rapid dig
Of many feet,—nearer and nearer still.

Part III

So went the chase! And now what should he do?
Abruptly turning, the wild Creek lay right
Before him! But no time was there for thought:
So on he kept, and from a bulging rock
That beaked the bank like a bare promontory,
Plunging right forth and shooting feet-first down,
Sunk to his middle in the flashing stream—
In which the imaged stars seemed all at once

To burst like rockets into one wide blaze
Of interwrithing light. Then wading through
The ruffled waters, forth he sprang and siezed
A stake-like root that from the opponent bank
Protruded, and round which his earnest fear
Did clench his cold hand like a clamp of steel,
A moment,—till as swiftly thence he swung
His dripping form aloft, and up the dark
O'erjutting ledge went clambering in the blind
And breathless haste of one who flies for life:
When in its face—O verily our God
Hath those in his peculiar care for whom
The daily prayers of spotless Womanhood
And helpless Infancy, are offered up!—
When in its face a cavity he felt,
The upper earth of which in one rude mass
Was held fast bound by the enwoven roots
Of two old trees,—and which, beneath the mould,
Just o'er the clammy vacancy below,
Twisted and lapped like knotted snakes, and made
A natural loft-work. Under this he crept,
Just as the dark forms of his hunters thronged
The bulging rock whence he before had plunged.

Duskily visible, thereon a space
They paused to mark what bent his course might take
Over the farther bank, thereby intent
To hold upon the chase, which way soe'er
It might incline, more surely. But no form
Amongst the moveless fringe of fern was seen
To shoot up from its outline,—up and forth
Into the moonlight that lay bright beyond
In torn and shapeless blocks, amid the boles
And mixing shadows of the taller trees,
All standing now in the keen radiance there
So ghostly still, as in a solemn trance.
But nothing in the silent prospect stirred—
No fugitive apparition in the view
Rose, as they stared in fierce expectancy:
Wherefore they augured that their prey was yet
Somewhere between,—and the whole group with that
Plunged forward, till the fretted current boiled
Amongst their crowding trunks from bank to bank;
And searching thus the stream across, and then
Lengthwise, along the ledges,—combing down
Still, as they went, with dripping fingers, cold
And cruel as inquisitive, each clump
Of long flagged swamp-grass where it flourished high,—

The whole dark line passed slowly, man by man,
Athwart the cavity—so fearfully near,
That as they waded by the Fugitive
Felt the strong odor of their wetted skins
Pass with them, trailing as their bodies moved
Stealthily on,--coming with each, and going.

But their keen search was keen in vain. And now
Those wild men marvelled,—till, in consultation,
There grouped in dark knots standing in the stream
That glimmered past them, moaning as it went,
His vanishment, so passing strange it seemed,
They coupled with the mystery of some crude
Old fable of their race; and fear-struck all,
And silent, then withdrew. And when the sound
Of their receding steps had from his ear
Died off, as back to the stormed Camp again
They hurried to despoil the yet warm dead,
Our Friend slid forth, and springing up the bank,
Renewed his flight, nor rested from it, till
He gained the welcoming shelter of his Home.

Return we for a moment to the scene
Of recent death. There the late flaring fire
Now smouldered, for its brands were strewn about,
And four stark corpses plundered to the skin
And brutally mutilated, seemed to stare
With frozen eyeballs up into the pale
Round visage of the Moon, who, high in heaven,
With all her stars, in golden bevies, gazed
As peacefully down as on a bridal there
Of the warm Living—not, alas! on them
Who kept in ghastly silence through the night
Untimely spousals with a desert death.

O God! and thus this lovely world hath been
Accursed for ever by the bloody deeds
Of its prime Creature—Man. Erring or wise,
Savage or civilised, still hath he made
This glorious residence, the Earth, a Hell
Of wrong and robbery and untimely death!
Some dread Intelligence opposed to Good
Did, of a surety , over all the earth
Spread out from Eden—or it were not so!

For see the bright beholding Moon, and all
The radiant Host of Heaven, evince no touch
Of sympathy with Man's wild violence;—
Only evince in their calm course, their part
In that original unity of Love,

Which, like the soul that dwelleth in a harp,
Under God's hand, in the beginning, chimed
The sabbath concord of the Universe;
And look on a gay clique of maidens, met
In village tryst, and interwhirling all
In glad Arcadian dances on the green—
Or on a hermit, in his vigils long,
Seen kneeling at the doorway of his cell—
Or on a monster battle-field where lie
In sweltering heaps, the dead and dying both,
On the cold gory ground,—as they that night
Looked in bright peace, down on the doomful Forest.

Afterwards there, for many changeful years,
Within a glade that sloped into the bank
Of that wild mountain Creek—midway within,
In partial record of a terrible hour
Of human agony and loss extreme,
Four grassy mounds stretched lengthwise side by side,
Startled the wanderer;—four long grassy mounds
Bestrewn with leaves, and withered spraylets, stript
By the loud wintry wingéd gales that roamed
Those solitudes, from the old trees which there
Moaned the same leafy dirges that had caught
The heed of dying Ages: these were all;
And thence the place was long by travellers called
The Creek of the Four Graves. Such was the Tale
Egremont told us of the wild old times.

A STORM IN THE MOUNTAINS

Part I

A lonely Boy, far venturing from his home
Out on the half-wild herd's dim tracks I roam:
A lonely Truant, numbering years eleven,
'Mid rock-browed mountains heaping up to heaven!
Here huge-piled ledges, ribbing outward, stare
Down into haggard chasms; onward, there,
The vast backed ridges are all rent in jags,
Or hunched with cones, or pinnacled with crags.
A rude peculiar world, the prospect lies
Bounded in circuit by the bending skies.

Now at some stone tank scooped out by the shocks
Of rain-floods plunging from the upper rocks,
Whose liquid disc, in its undimpled rest,
Glows like a mighty gem, brooching the mountain's breast,

I drink, and muse,—or mark the wide spread herd,
Or list the tinkling of the dingle-bird;
And now tow'rds some wild-hanging shade I stray,
To shun the bright oppression of the day:
For round each crag, and o'er each bosky swell,
The fierce refracted heat flares visible—
Lambently restless, like the dazzling hem
Of some else-viewless veil held trembling over them.

A change is felt—a change that yet reveals
A something only that mere instinct feels,
Why congregate the swallows in the air,
And northward, then in rapid flight repair?
At once unsettled, and all roaming slow
With heads declined, why do the oxen low?
With sudden dwelling din, remote, yet harsh,
Why roar the bull-frogs in the tea-tree marsh?
Why cease the locusts to throng up in flight,
And clap their gay wings in the fervent light?
Why climb they, bodingly demure, instead,
The tallest spear-grass to the bending head?
Instinctively along the sultry sky,
I turn a listless, yet enquiring eye;
And mark that now, with a most gradual pace,
A solemn trance creams gradual o'er its face;
Slow, but inevitable—wide about
On all hands from the South effusing out:
Yon clouds that late were laboring past the sun,
Reached by its sure arrest, one after one,

Come to a heavy halt;—as travellers see
In the wide wilderness of Abraby,
Some pilgrim horde at even, band by band,
Halting amid the grey interminable sand.
Thence down descending, its dull slumbrous weight
Sullenly settles on the mountain's great
Upheaving heads, until the airs that played
About their rugged temples—all are laid:
While drawing nearer far off heights appear,
As in a dream's wild prospect—strangely near!
Till into wood resolves their robe of blue,
And the grey crags come bluffly into view.
—Such are the signs and tokens that presage
A Summer Hurricane's forthcoming rage.

At length the South sends out her cloudy heaps,
And up the glens a dusky dimness creeps.
The birds, late warbling in the hanging green
Of steep-set brakes, seek now some safer screen,—

Skimming in silence o'er the ominous scene.
The herd in doubt no longer wanders wide,
But, fast ingathering, throngs yon mountain's side,
Whose echoes, surging to its tramp, might seem
The muttered troubles of some Titan's dream.

Fast the dim legions of the mustering Storm
Throng denser, or protruding columns form;
While splashing forward from their cloudy lair,
Convolving flames, like scouting dragons, glare:
Low thunders follow, laboring up the sky;
And as forerunning blasts go blaring by,
At once the Forest, with a mighty stir,
Bows, as in homage to the Thunderer!

Hark! from the dingoes' blood-polluded dens,
In the gloom-hidden chasms of the glens,
Long fitful howls wail up; and in the blast
Strange hissing whispers seem to huddle past;
As if the dread stir had aroused from sleep
Weird Spirits, cloistered in yon cavy steep,
(On which, in the grim Past, some Cain's offence
Hath haply outraged Heaven!)—and who, from thence
Wrapt in the boding vapours, rose amain
To wanton in the wild-willed Hurricane!

The glow of day is quenched—expunged the sun
By cloud on cloud dark-rolling [into] one
Tremendous mass of latent thunder—spread
Wide out, and over every mountain's head,
Whose sable bosom, as the storm-blast sweeps
Its surface, heaves into enormous heaps,
And seems a pendent ocean to the view,
With weltering whale-like forms all hugely roughen'd through.

Yet see in the Storm's front, as void of dread,
How sails yon Eagle like a black flag spread
Before it—coming! On his wide wings weighed,
Hardly he seems to move, from hence surveyed;
When, far aloft, a bulging mass of gloom
That bends out o'er him, bloating as with doom,
Grows frightfully luminous! Short stops his flight!
His dark form shrivels in the blasting light!
And then as follows a sharp thunderous sound,
Falls whizzing, stone-like, lifeless to the ground!

Part II

Now like a shudder at great Nature's heart
The turmoil grows. Now Wonder, with a start,

Marks where, right overhead, wild Thor careers,
Girt with black Horrors and wide-flaming Fears!
Arriving thunders, mustering on his path,
Swell more and more the roarings of his wrath,
As out in widening circles they extend—
And then—at once—in utter silence end.

Portentous silence! Time keeps breathing past—
Yet it continues! May this marvel last?
This wild weird silence in the midst of gloom
So manifestly big with latent doom?
Tingles the boding ear; and up the glens
Instinctive dread comes howling from the wild-dogs' dens.

Terrific Vision! Heaven's great ceiling splits,
And a vast globe of writhing fire emits,
Which, flanking out in one continuous stream,
Spans the black concave like a burning beam,
A moment;—then, from end to end, it shakes
With a quick motion—and in thunder breaks!
Peal rolled on peal! while heralding the sound,
As each concussion thrills the solid ground,
Fierce glares coil snake-like round the rocky wens
Of the *red* hills, or hiss into the glens;
Or thick through heaven like flaming falchions swarm,
Cleaving the teeming cisterns of the Storm,
From which rain-torrents, (searching every gash)
Split by the blast, come sheeting, with a dash
Most multitudinous—down through the trees,
And 'gainst the smoking crags that beetle over these!

On yon grey Peak, with rock-encrusted roots,
The seeming Patriarch of the Wood upshoots,
In whose proud-spreading top's imperial height,
The mountain Eagle loveth most to 'light:
Now dimly seen through the tempestuous air,
His form seems harrowed by a mad despair,
As with his ponderous arms uplifted high,
He wrestles with the Storm and threshes at the sky!
But not for long. Up in the lurid air,
A swift red bolt is heard to hurtle there—
A dread crash follows—and the Peak is bare!
Huge fragments, hurrying from its shattered cone,
Wide in the murky air aré seen alone—
Huge shapeless fragments round about it cast,
Like crude-wing'd, mad-limbed Monsters squandering in the blast!

The duskness thickens! With despairing cry
From shattering boughs the rain-drenched parrots fly!

Loose rocks wash rumbling from the mountains round,
And half the forest strews the smoking ground!
Stemm'd by the wet crags the blasts wilder moan,
And the caves labor with a ghostlier groan!
Resistless torrents down the gorges flow
With knasshing clamours harshening as they go;
And where from craggy bluffs their volumes leap,
Bear with them—down, in many a whirling heap,
Those sylvan wrecks that littered late the path
Of the loud Hurricane's all-trampling wrath;
While to their dread percussions inward sent,
The hearts of the great hills beat with astonishment!

Strange darings seize me, witnessing this strife
Of Nature; while, as heedless of my life,
I stand exposed. And does some destined charm
Hold me secure from elemental harm,
That in the mighty riot I may find
How through all being works the light of Mind?
Yea, through the strikingly external see
My novel Soul's divulging energy!
Spirit transmuting into forms of thought
What but for its cognition were *as nought*!
Soul wildly drawn abroad—a Protean force
Clothing with higher life the Tempest in its course.

The Storm is Past. Yet booming on afar
Is heard the rattling of Thor's thunder-car,
And that low muffled moaning, as of grief,
Which follows, with a wood-sigh wide and brief.
The clouds break up. The sun's forth bursting rays
Clothe the wet landscape with a spangling blaze.
The birds begin to sing a lively strain,
And merry echoes ring it o'er again.
The clustered herd is spreading out to graze,
Though lessening torrents still a hundred ways
Flash downward, and from many a tanky ledge
A mantling gush comes quick and shining o'er the edge.

'Tis evening; and the torrents' furious flow
Hath now subsided in the lake below.
O'er all the freshened scene no sound is heard,
Save the short twitter of some busied bird,
Or a faint rustle caused amongst the trees
By wasting fragments of a broken breeze.
Round with a heightened buoyancy I stroll,
And a new happiness o'erflows my soul,

As from some cause beyond the reach of thought,
And which this notion has within me wrought
Through instinct only, that the Storm to day,
Hath haply purged some pestilence away,
Whose sultry venom in all nature's ways
Would else have lurked for many doomful days:
And hence, even 'mid the sylvan carnage spread
O'er every turn in the wild paths I tread,
Full many a flowery nook and sunny brow
Presents some pleasantness unmarked till now.

Thus, when the elements of social life
Burst with a soul-quake into mortal strife,
Some prophet feeling, we know not from whence,
Doth moralise the agony; and thence
Wished Peace, returning, like a bird of calm,
Brings to the wounded world a doubly-valued balm.

A MIDSUMMER NOON IN
THE AUSTRALIAN FOREST

Not a bird disturbs the air,
There is quiet everywhere;
Over plains and over woods
What a mighty stillness broods.

Even the grasshoppers keep
Where the coolest shadows sleep;
Even the busy ants are found
Resting in their pebbled mound;
Even the locust clingeth now
In silence to the barky bough:
And over hills and over plains
Quiet, vast and slumbrous, reigns.

Only there's a drowsy humming
From yon warm lagoon slow coming:
'Tis the dragon-hornet—see!
All bedaubed resplendently
With yellow on a tawny ground—
Each rich spot nor square nor round,
But rudely heart-shaped, as it were
The blurred and hasty impress there,
Of a vermeil-crusted seal
Dusted o'er with golden meal:
Only there's a droning where
Yon bright beetle gleams the air—

Gleams it in its droning flight
With a slanting track of light,
Till rising in the sunshine higher,
Its shards flame out like gems on fire.

Every other thing is still,
Save the ever wakeful rill,
Whose cool murmur only throws
A cooler comfort round Repose;
Or some ripple in the sea
Of leafy boughs, where, lazily,
Tired Summer, in her forest bower
Turning with the noontide hour,
Heaves a slumbrous breath, ere she
Once more slumbers peacefully.

O 'tis easeful here to lie
Hidden from Noon's scorching eye,
In this grassy cool recess
Musing thus of Quietness.

DAWN AND SUNRISE IN
THE SNOWY MOUNTAINS

A few thin strips of fleecy clouds lie long
And motionless above the eastern steeps,
Like shreds of silver lace: till suddenly,
Out from the flushing centre to the ends
On either hand, their lustrous layers become
Dipt all in crimson streaked with pink and gold;
And then, at last, are edged as with a band
Of crystal fire. And now, even long before
The Sun himself is seen, off tow'rds the west
A range of mighty summits, more and more,
Blaze, each like a huge cresset, in the keen
Clear atmosphere. As if the Spirit of Light,
Advancing swiftly thence, and eastward still,
Kept kindling them in quick succession;—till
The universal company of cones
And pyramidal peaks, stand burning all
With rosy fires, like a wide ranging circ
Of God-great altars,—and even so announce
The Sun that now, with a vast flash, is seen
Pushing his rim above yon central height.

Rachel Biddulph Henning   (1826–1914)

Letter writer. Born in England; came to Australia in 1854.

from THE LETTERS OF RACHEL HENNING

1.

The shearers, nine in number, have a cook of their own and buy their own extra rations, everything except flour, beef, tea and sugar. They pay a man about £2 a week to cook for them while they are shearing. Christmas Eve, yesterday, was signalized by a chase and capture on the station. One of the shepherds came in the night before and said that his hut, which is near the road, had been robbed, while he was out with his sheep, and his blankets, clothes and rations stolen. Biddulph gave him some more blankets. Yesterday afternoon Julian came in in a state of great excitement to say that the man who had stolen the things had just passed the station, and that the shepherd had recognized the blankets he was carrying.

Biddulph mounted Julian's horse and went off through the bush at a gallop. Pat, Mr Palmer's man, followed, also on horse-back, and everybody else on the station ran.

Biddulph presently came back with the culprit mounted on Pat's horse. He conducted him up to the stockyard, and the whole of the property was found in his possession. Moreover, he had borrowed Pat's horse the day before, promising to leave it at Exmoor, where he said his own horse was left, and then had ridden it on past the station evidently with the intention of stealing it.

Biddulph said he could not have the trouble and expense of sending him to Port Denison in custody, 110 miles, and afterwards appearing against him at Rockhampton, 370 miles off. So he had him then and there tied up to a tree and soundly flogged, Pat, who is a stout Irishman, being the executioner; and he bestowed two dozen with hearty goodwill, stimulated by the remembrance of his wrongs about the horse.

Justice being administered in this summary manner, Biddulph gave the man some rations that he might not be obliged to rob any more shepherds at stations and sent him off, at the same time warning the shepherds all down the road to look after their huts.

2.

About a month ago a Mr Digby started on foot from Port Denison—he was coming up this way by the high road, but he unfortunately took a "short cut", lost himself and was out for fourteen days with nothing to eat but the gum which oozes out of the trees. I cannot think how he lived so long. He was found by some bushmen and brought to Mr Paterson's, a station about thirty miles from here. He has been there more than a fortnight, and every care has been taken of him, but they say he cannot recover, as he has been so weakened by want of food that he cannot keep down anything but liquids.

One of the shepherds who went out to the Flinders with Biddulph's sheep returned here a short time ago, and he told us that, having one day lost himself in the bush with his flock, he came upon the body of a man lying under a tree. The blacks had evidently found it, but instead of disturbing and robbing it they had laid a piece of bark over the head and another over the feet and left. He took the news on to the next station, Mr Henry's, and was told that a week or two before, a riderless horse with all the usual accoutrements of saddle, blankets, etc., had found its way in to the station; and by the books and clothes rolled up in the blankets it was evidently a gentleman's "swag".

The shepherd did not know whether they found out his name or not. It seems always to me a terrible end to be "lost in the bush". I had rather hear of anyone being killed by the blacks at once.

3.

Since I last wrote to you the station has been enlivened by an elopement. During the absence of Alick (the black boy who fought so valiantly on the Flinders), Billy, the other station blackboy, ran away with Biddy, the wife of the aforesaid Alick. Alick came back the next day, and his rage was great when he found out his loss, especially as they had taken all his property with them, and particularly 35s. which comprised his worldly wealth and which he kept tied up in an old sock.

He picked out a formidable "waddy" and set out in pursuit, vowing vengeance. In the meantime Billy and Biddy, finding running away not quite so pleasant as they had expected, came back the third day in a very penitent state of mind. The nights were very cold just then. They had had "nothing to eat but cold water", and Biddy said "I believe mine cry good deal, cry all day." Billy fled to the Two Mile station to be out of the way of Alick's wrath. Biddy was obliged to abide it, but he was persuaded not to give her the beating he promised, and which she certainly deserved, and in a few days they became good friends, especially as he recovered the precious 35s.

Since that Alick has been ill and Biddy has made her peace by carefully attending him. He caught cold and had a sort of chest attack, and used to lie in his hut and groan and cough and yell alternately. Biddy came down one morning. "I believe that fellow dead," she said. We went up to see after him and found him all right enough, only coughing. Annie called into the gunyah "Are you better, Alick?" "No," he shouted very loud. "I'm dead."

However, he did not die, and next day Mr Hedgeland prescribed a mustard plaster for his cough. So one was made, and then Mr Hedgeland took it up to Biddy and told her how to put it on, and to wash the place with a little warm water when it came off. About twenty minutes after, he went up to see after his patient, and he found Alick lying outside his hut groaning and shivering without a rag on him (it was a cold day).

Alick looked the picture of hopeless resignation. "What have you been doing to Alick?" Mr Hedgeland asked. "I believe I washed that fellow all over," Biddy said with a doleful face. "And where is the mustard plaster?" "Pudding inside long of hut," she said, and there was the plaster carefully rolled up and put away in a corner, and if Mr Hedgeland had not gone up when he did I think it very probable she would have made him eat it as the second part of the prescription.

Of course, Alick caught a worse cold than ever, but he is better now, and consumes quantities of mutton broth and cornflour. I hope he will be well soon, for we are very short of horses. They have all betaken themselves to distant parts of the run, and no one can find them like a blackboy.

MARCUS CLARKE   (1846–1881)

Novelist, short story writer, essayist, journalist. Born and educated in London; came to Australia in 1863.

PREFACE TO GORDON'S POEMS

The poems of Gordon have an interest beyond the mere personal one which his friends attach to his name. Written, as they were, at odd times and leisure moments of a stirring and adventurous life, it is not to be wondered at if they are unequal or unfinished. The astonishment of those who knew the man, and can gauge the capacity of this city to foster poetic instinct, is, that such work was ever produced here at all. Intensely nervous, and feeling much of that shame at the exercise of the higher intelligence which besets those who are known to be renowned in field sports, Gordon produced his poems shyly, scribbled them on scraps of paper, and sent them anonymously to magazines. It was not until he discovered one morning that everybody knew a couplet or two of 'How We Beat the Favourite' that he consented to forego his anonymity and appear in the unsuspected character of a versemaker. The success of his republished 'collected' poems gave him courage, and the unreserved praise which greeted *Bush Ballads* should have urged him to forget or to conquer those evil promptings which, unhappily, brought about his untimely death.

Adam Lindsay Gordon was the son of an officer in the English army, and was educated at Woolwich, in order that he might follow the profession of his family. At the time when he was a cadet there was no sign of either of the two great wars which were about to call forth the strength of English arms, and, like many other men of his day, he quitted his prospects of service, and emigrated. He went to South Australia and started as a sheep farmer. His efforts were attended with failure. He lost his capital, and, owning nothing but a love for horsemanship and a head full of Browning and Shelley, plunged into the varied life which gold-mining, 'overlanding,' and cattle-driving affords. From this experience he emerged to light in Melbourne as the best amateur steeplechase rider in the colonies. The victory he won for Major Baker in 1868, when he rode Babbler for the Cup Steeplechase, made him popular, and the almost simultaneous publication of his last volume of poems gave him welcome entrance to the houses of all who had pretensions to literary taste. The reputation of the book spread to England, and Major Whyte-Melville did not disdain to place the lines of the dashing Australian author at the head of his own dashing descriptions of sporting scenery. Unhappily, the melancholy which Gordon's friends had with pain observed increased daily, and in the full flood of his success, with congratulations pouring upon him from every side, he was found dead in the heather near his home with a bullet from his own rifle in his brain.

I do not purpose to criticize the volumes which these few lines of preface introduce to the reader. The influence of Browning and of Swinburne upon the writer's taste is plain. There is plainly visible also, however, a keen sense for natural beauty and a manly admiration for healthy living. If in 'Ashtaroth' and 'Bellona' we recognize the swing of a familiar metre, in such poems as the 'Sick Stockrider' we perceive the genuine poetic instinct united to a very clear perception of the loveliness of duty and of labour.

'Twas merry in the glowing morn, among the gleaming grass,
　To wander as we've wandered many a mile,
And blow the cool tobacco cloud, and watch the white wreaths pass,
　Sitting loosely in the saddle all the while;
'Twas merry 'mid the blackwoods, when we spied the station roofs,
　To wheel the wild scrub cattle at the yard,
With a running fire of stockwhips, and a fiery run of hoofs,
　Oh! the hardest day was never then too hard!

Aye! we had a glorious gallop after 'Starlight' and his gang,
　When they bolted from Sylvester's on the flat;
How the sun-dried reed-beds crackled, how the flint-strewn ranges
　To the strokes of 'Mountaineer' and 'Acrobat';　　　　　　[rang
Hard behind them in the timber, harder still across the heath,
　Close behind them through the tea-tree scrub we dash'd;
And the golden-tinted fern leaves, how they rustled underneath!
　And the honeysuckle osiers, how they crash'd!

This is genuine. There is no 'poetic evolution from the depths of internal consciousness' here. The writer has ridden his ride as well as written it.

The student of these unpretending volumes will be repaid for his labour. He will find in them something very like the beginnings of a national school of Australian poetry. In historic Europe, where every rood of ground is hallowed in legend and in song, the least imaginative can find food for sad and sweet reflection. When strolling at noon down an English country lane, lounging at sunset by some ruined chapel on the margin of an Irish lake, or watching the mists of morning unveil Ben Lomond, we feel all the charm which springs from association with the past. Soothed, saddened, and cheered by turns, we partake of the varied moods which belong not so much to ourselves as to the dead men who, in old days, sung, suffered, or conquered in the scenes which we survey. But this our native or adopted land has no past, no story. No poet speaks to us. Do we need a poet to interpret Nature's teachings, we must look into our own hearts, if perchance we may find a poet there.

What is the dominant note of Australian scenery? That which is the dominant note of Edgar Allan Poe's poetry—Weird Melancholy. A poem like 'L'Allegro' could never be written by an Australian. It is too airy, too sweet, too freshly happy. The Australian mountain forests are funereal, secret, stern. Their solitude is desolation. They seem to stifle, in their black gorges, a story of sullen despair. No tender sentiment is nourished in their shade. In other lands the dying year is mourned, the falling leaves drop lightly on his bier. In the Australian forests no leaves fall. The savage winds shout among the rock clefts. From the melancholy gum strips of white bark hang and rustle. The very animal life of these frowning hills is either grotesque or ghostly. Great grey kangaroos hop noiselessly over the coarse grass. Flights of white cockatoos stream out, shrieking like evil souls. The sun suddenly sinks, and the mopokes burst out into horrible peals of semi-human laughter. The natives aver that, when night comes, from out the bottomless depth of some lagoon the Bunyip rises, and, in form like monstrous sea-calf, drags his loathsome length from out the ooze. From a corner of the silent forest rises a dismal chant, and around a fire dance natives painted like skeletons. All is fear-inspiring and gloomy. No bright fancies are linked with the memories of the mountains. Hopeless explorers have named them out of their sufferings—Mount Misery, Mount Dreadful, Mount Despair. As when among sylvan scenes in places

> Made green with the running of rivers,
> And gracious with temperate air,

the soul is soothed and satisfied, so, placed before the frightful grandeur of these barren hills, it drinks in their sentiment of defiant ferocity, and is steeped in bitterness.

Australia has rightly been named the Land of the Dawning. Wrapped in the mist of early morning, her history looms vague and gigantic. The lonely horseman riding between the moonlight and the day sees vast shadows creeping across the shelterless and silent plains, hears strange noises in the primeval forest, where flourishes a vegetation long dead in other lands, and feels, despite his fortune, that the trim utilitarian civilization which bred him shrinks into insignificance beside the contemptuous grandeur of forest and ranges coeval with an age in which European scientists have cradled his own race.

There is a poem in every form of tree or flower, but the poetry which lives in the trees and flowers of Australia differs from those of other countries. Europe is the home of knightly songs, of bright deeds and clear morning thought. Asia sinks beneath the weighty recollections of her past magnificence, as the Suttee sinks, jewel-burdened, upon the corpse of dead grandeur, destructive even in its death. America swiftly hurries on her way, rapid, glittering, insatiable even as one of her own giant waterfalls. From the jungles of Africa, and the creeper-tangled groves of the islands of the South, arise, from the glowing hearts of a thousand flowers, heavy and intoxicating odours—the Upas-poison which dwells in barbaric sensuality. In Australia alone is to be found the Grotesque, the Weird, the strange scribblings of nature learning how to write. Some see no beauty in our trees without shade, our flowers without perfume, our birds who cannot fly, and our beasts who have not yet learned to walk on all fours. But the dweller in the wilderness acknowledges the subtle charm of this fantastic land of monstrosities. He becomes familiar with the beauty of loneliness. Whispered to by the myriad tongues of the wilderness, he learns the language of the barren and the uncouth, and can read the hieroglyphs of haggard gum-trees, blown into odd shapes, distorted with fierce hot winds, or cramped with cold nights, when the Southern Cross freezes in a cloudless sky of icy blue. The phantasmagoria of that wild dream-land termed the Bush interprets itself, and the Poet of our desolation begins to comprehend why free Esau loved his heritage of desert sand better than all the bountiful richness of Egypt.

ADAM LINDSAY GORDON   (1833–1870)

Poet. Born at Fayal, Azores; educated in England; came to Australia in 1853.

A DEDICATION

To the author of 'Holmby House'

They are rhymes rudely strung with intent less
        Of sound than of words,
In lands where bright blossoms are scentless,
        And songless bright birds;
Where, with fire and fierce drought on her tresses,
Insatiable Summer oppresses
Sere woodlands and sad wildernesses,
        And faint flocks and herds.

Where in dreariest days, when all dews end,
        And all winds are warm,
Wild winter's large floodgates are loosen'd,
        And floods, freed by storm
From broken-up fountain heads, dash on
Dry deserts with long pent-up passion—
Here rhyme was first framed without fashion,
        Song shaped without form.

Whence gather'd?—The locust's glad chirrup
        May furnish a stave.
The ring of a rowel and stirrup,
        The wash of a wave,
The chaunt of the marsh frog in rushes
That chimes through the pauses and hushes
Of nightfall, the torrent that gushes,
        The tempests that rave.

In the deep'ning of dawn, when it dapples
        The dusk of the sky,
With streaks like the redd'ning of apples,
        The ripening of rye,—
To eastward, when cluster by cluster,
Dim stars and dull planets, that muster,
Wax wan in a world of white lustre
        That spreads far and high.

In the gathering of night gloom o'er-head, in
        The still silent change,
All fire-flusht when forest trees redden
        On slopes of the range,

When the gnarled knotted trunks Eucalyptian
Seem carved like weird columns Egyptian
With curious device, quaint inscription,
          And hieroglyph strange.

In the Spring, when the wattle gold trembles
          'Twixt shadow and shine,
When each dew-laden air draught resembles
          A long draught of wine,
When the skyline's blue burnisht resistance
Makes deeper the dreamiest distance,
Some song in all hearts hath existence,—
          Such songs have been mine.

They came in all guises, some vivid
          To clasp and to keep,
Some sudden and swift as the livid
          Blue thunder flame's leap.
This swept through the first breath of clover
With memories renew'd to the rover—
That flasht while the black horse turn'd over
          Before the long sleep.

To you (having cunning to colour
          A page with your pen,
That through dull days, and nights even duller,
          Long years ago ten,
Fair pictures in fever afforded)
I send these rude staves, roughly worded
By one in whose brain stands recorded
          As clear now as then,

'The great rush of grey "Northern water",
          The green ridge of bank,
The "sorrel" with curved sweep of quarter
          Curl'd close to clean flank,
The Royalist saddle fast squarely,
And, where the bright uplands stretch fairly,
Behind, beyond pistol shot barely,
          The Roundheaded rank—

—'A long launch, with clinging of muscles,
          And clenching of teeth
The loose doublet ripples and rustles!
          The swirl shoots beneath!'—
Enough.—In return for your garland—
In lieu of the flowers from your far land—
Take wild growth of dreamland or star land,
          Take weeds for your wreath.

Yet rhyme had not fail'd me for reason,
          Nor reason for rhyme,
Sweet Song! had I sought you in season,
          And found you in time.
You beckon in your bright beauty yonder,
And I, waxing fainter yet fonder,
Now weary too soon when I wander—
          Now fall when I climb.

It matters but little in the long run,
          The weak have some right,
Some share, in the race that the strong run,
          The fight the strong fight.
If words that are worthless go westward,
Yet the worst word shall be as the best word,
In the day when all riot sweeps restward,
          In darkness or light.

THE SICK STOCKRIDER

Hold hard, Ned! lift me down once more, and lay me in the shade;
    Old man, you've had your work cut out to guide
Both horses, and to hold me in the saddle when I sway'd,
    All through the hot, slow, sleepy, silent ride;
The dawn at 'Moorabinda' was a mist rack dull and dense,
    The sunrise was a sullen sluggish lamp;
I was dozing in the gateway at Arbuthnot's bound'ry fence,
    I was dreaming on the Limestone cattle camp;
We crossed the creek at Carricksford, and sharply through the haze,
    And suddenly the sun shot flaming forth;
To southward lay 'Katâwa' with the sandpeaks all ablaze
    And the flush'd fields of Glen Lomond lay to north—
Now westward winds the bridle path that leads to Lindisfarm,
    And yonder looms the double-headed bluff;
From the far side of the first hill, when the skies are clear and calm,
    You can see Sylvester's woolshed fair enough.
Five miles we used to call it from our homestead to the place
    Where the big tree spans the roadway like an arch;
'Twas here we ran the dingo down that gave us such a chase
    Eight years ago—or was it nine?—last March.

'Twas merry in the glowing morn, among the gleaming grass,
    To wander as we've wander'd many a mile,
And blow the cool tobacco cloud, and watch the white wreaths pass,
    Sitting loosely in the saddle all the while;
'Twas merry 'mid the blackwoods when we spied the station roofs,
    To wheel the wild scrub cattle at the yard,

With a running fire of stockwhips and a fiery run of hoofs,
  Oh! the hardest day was never then too hard!

Ay! we had a glorious gallop after 'Starlight' and his gang,
  When they bolted from Sylvester's on the flat;
How the sun-dried reed-beds crackled, how the flint-strewn ranges
    rang
  To the strokes of 'Mountaineer' and 'Acrobat';
Hard behind them in the timber, harder still across the heath,
  Close beside them through the tea-tree scrub we dash'd;
And the golden-tinted fern leaves, how they rustled underneath!
  And the honeysuckle osiers, how they crash'd!

We led the hunt throughout, Ned, on the chestnut and the grey,
  And the troopers were three hundred yards behind,
While we emptied our six-shooters on the bushrangers at bay,
  In the creek with stunted box-tree for a blind!

There you grappled with the leader, man to man and horse to horse,
  And you roll'd together when the chestnut rear'd;
He blaz'd away and missed you in that shallow watercourse—
  A narrow shave—his powder singed your beard!

In these hours when life is ebbing, how those days when life was
    young
  Come back to us—how clearly I recall
Even the yarns Jack Hall invented, and the songs Jem Roper sung,
  And where are now Jem Roper and Jack Hall?

Ay! nearly all our comrades of the old colonial school,
  Our ancient boon companions, Ned, are gone;
Hard livers for the most part, somewhat reckless as a rule,
  It seems that you and I are left alone.

There was Hughes, who got in trouble through that business with
    the cards,
  It matters little what became of him,
But a steer ripp'd up MacPherson in the Cooraminta yards,
  And Sullivan was drown'd at Sink-or-swim,
And Mostyn—poor Frank Mostyn—died at last a fearful wreck,
  In 'the horrors' at the Upper Wandinong,
And Carisbrook the rider at the Horsefall broke his neck,
  Faith! the wonder was he saved his neck so long!

Ah! those days and nights we squandered at the Logans'; in the
    Glen—
  The Logans, man and wife, have long been dead,
Elsie's tallest girl seems taller than your little Elsie then,
  And Ethel is a woman grown and wed.

I've had my share of pastime, and I've done my share of toil,
  And life is short—the longest life a span—

I care not now to tarry for the corn or for the oil,
  Or for the wine that maketh glad the heart of man;
For good undone and gifts misspent and resolutions vain,
  'Tis somewhat late to trouble. This I know,
I should live the same life over, if I had to live again;
  And the chances are I go where most men go.

The deep blue skies wax dusky and the tall green trees grow dim,
  The sward beneath me seems to heave and fall,
And sickly, smoky shadows through the sleepy sunlight swim,
  And on the very sun's face weave their pall.
Let me slumber in the hollow where the wattle blossoms wave,
  With never stone or rail to fence my bed;
Should the sturdy station children pull the bush flowers on my
    grave,
  I may chance to hear them romping overhead.

I don't suppose I shall, though, for I feel like sleeping sound,
  That sleep they say is doubtful. True; but yet
At least it makes no difference to the dead man underground
  What the living men remember or forget.
Enigmas that perplex us in the world's unequal strife
  The future may ignore or may reveal,
YET SOME, AS WEAK AS WATER, NED! TO MAKE THE BEST OF LIFE,
  Have been, TO FACE THE WORST, AS TRUE AS STEEL.

HENRY KENDALL   (1839–1882)
Poet, journalist. Born in N.S.W.; little formal education.

PREFATORY SONNETS

I

I purposed once to take my pen and write
  Not songs like some tormented and awry
  With Passion, but a cunning harmony
Of words and music caught from glen and height,
And lucid colours born of woodland light,
  And shining places where the sea-streams lie;
But this was when the heat of youth glowed white,
  And since I've put the faded purpose by.
I have no faultless fruits to offer you
  Who read this book; but certain syllables
  Herein are borrowed from unfooted dells
And secret hollows dear to noontide dew;

And these at least, though far between and few,
   May catch the sense like subtle forest spells.

II

So take these kindly, even though there be
   Some notes that unto other lyres belong:
   Stray echoes from the elder sons of Song;
And think how from its neighbouring, native sea
The pensive shell doth borrow melody.
   I would not do the lordly masters wrong,
   By filching fair words from the shining throng
Whose music haunts me, as the wind a tree!
   Lo, when a stranger, in soft Syrian glooms
Shot through with sunset, treads the cedar dells,
And hears the breezy ring of elfin bells
   Far down by where the white-haired cataract booms,
He, faint with sweetness caught from forest smells,
   Bears thence, unwitting, plunder of perfumes.

DEDICATION—TO A MOUNTAIN

To thee, O Father of the stately peaks,
Above me in the loftier light—to thee,
Imperial brother of those awful hills
Whose feet are set in splendid spheres of flame,
Whose heads are where the gods are, and whose sides
Of strength are belted round with all the zones
Of all the world, I dedicate these songs.
And, if within the compass of this book,
There lives and glows *one* verse in which there beats
The pulse of wind and torrent—if *one* line
Is here that like a running water sounds,
And seems an echo from the lands of leaf,
Be sure that line is thine. Here in this home
Away from men and books and all the schools,
I take thee for my Teacher. In thy voice
Of deathless majesty, I, kneeling, hear
God's grand authentic gospel! Year by year,
The great sublime cantata of thy storm
Strikes through my spirit—fills it with a life
Of startling beauty! Thou my Bible art
With holy leaves of rock, and flower, and tree,
And moss, and shining runnel. From each page
That helps to make thy awful Volume, I
Have learned a noble lesson. In the psalm
Of thy grave winds, and in the liturgy

Of singing waters, lo! my soul has heard
The higher worship; and from thee indeed
The broad foundations of a finer hope
Were gathered in; and thou hast lifted up
The blind horizon for a larger faith!
Moreover, walking in exalted woods
Of naked glory—in the green and gold
Of forest sunshine—I have paused like one
With all the life transfigured; and a flood
Of light ineffable has made me feel
As felt the grand old prophets caught away
By flames of inspiration; but the words
Sufficient for the story of my Dream
Are far too splendid for poor human lips!
But thou to whom I turn with reverent eyes—
O stately Father whose majestic face
Shines far above the zone of wind and cloud
Where high dominion of the morning is—
Thou hast the Song complete of which my songs
Are pallid adumbrations! Certain sounds
Of strong authentic sorrow in this book
May have the sob of upland torrents—these,
And only these, may touch the great World's heart;
For lo! they are the issues of that Grief
Which makes a man more human, and his life
More like that frank exalted life of thine.
But in these pages there are other tones
In which thy large superior voice is not—
Through which no beauty that resembles thine
Has ever shone. *These* are the broken words
Of blind occasions when the World has come
Between me and my Dream. No song is here
Of mighty compass; for my singing robes
I've worn in stolen moments. All my days
Have been the days of a laborious life;
And ever on my struggling soul has burned
The fierce heat of this hurried sphere. But thou
To whose fair majesty I dedicate
My book of rhymes—thou hast the perfect rest
Which makes the heaven of the highest gods!
To thee the noises of this violent time
Are far faint whispers; and, from age to age,
Within the world and yet apart from it
Thou standest! Round thy lordly capes the sea
Rolls on with a superb indifference
For ever: in thy deep green gracious glens
The silver fountains sing for ever. Far
Above dim ghosts of waters in the caves,

The royal robe of morning on thy head
Abides for ever! evermore the wind
Is thy august companion; and thy peers
Are cloud, and thunder, and the face sublime
Of blue midheaven! On thy awful brow
Is Deity; and in that voice of thine
There is the great imperial utterance
Of God for ever; and thy feet are set
Where evermore, through all the days and years,
There rolls the grand hymn of the deathless wave.

MOSS ON A WALL

Dim dreams it hath of singing ways,
   Of far-off woodland water-heads,
And shining ends of April days
   Amongst the yellow runnel beds.

Stoop closer to the ruined wall,
   Wherein the wilful wilding sleeps,
As if its home were waterfall
   By dripping clefts and shadowy steeps!

A little waif, whose beauty takes
   A touching tone, because it dwells
So far away from mountain lakes,
   And lily leaves, and lightning fells.

Deep hidden in delicious floss
   It nestles, sister, from the heat:
A gracious growth of tender moss,
   Whose nights are soft, whose days are sweet.

Swift gleams across its petals run,
   With winds that hum a pleasant tune:
Serene surprises of the sun,
   And whispers from the lips of Noon.

The evening-coloured apple-trees
   Are faint with July's frosty breath;
But lo, this stranger getteth ease
   And shines amidst the strays of Death!

And at the turning of the year,
   When August wanders in the cold,
The raiment of the nursling here
   Is rich with green and glad with gold.

O, friend of mine, to one whose eyes
   Are vext because of alien things,

For ever in the wall moss lies
    The peace of hills and hidden springs.

From faithless lips and fickle lights
    The tired pilgrim sets his face,
And thinketh here of sounds and sights
    In many a lovely forest-place.

And when by sudden fits and starts
    The sunset on the moss doth burn,
He often dreams, and lo, the marts
    And streets are changed to dells of fern!

For, let me say, the wilding placed
    By hands unseen amongst these stones,
Restores a Past by Time effaced,
    Lost loves and long-forgotten tones!

As sometimes songs and scenes of old
    Come faintly unto you and me,
When winds are wailing in the cold,
    And rains are sobbing on the sea.

BELL-BIRDS

By channels of coolness the echoes are calling,
And down the dim gorges I hear the creek falling:
It lives in the mountain where moss and the sedges
Touch with their beauty the banks and the ledges.
Through breaks of the cedar and sycamore bowers
Struggles the light that is love to the flowers;
And, softer than slumber, and sweeter than singing,
The notes of the bell-birds are running and ringing.

The silver-voiced bell-birds, the darlings of daytime!
They sing in September their songs of the May-time;
When shadows wax strong, and the thunder-bolts hurtle,
They hide with their fear in the leaves of the myrtle;
When rain and the sunbeams shine mingled together,
They start up like fairies that follow fair weather;
And straightway the hues of their feathers unfolden
Are the green and the purple, the blue and the golden.

October, the maiden of bright yellow tresses,
Loiters for love in these cool wildernesses;
Loiters, knee-deep, in the grasses, to listen,
Where dripping rocks gleam and the leafy pools glisten:
Then is the time when the water-moons splendid
Break with their gold, and are scattered or blended

Over the creeks, till the woodlands have warning
Of songs of the bell-bird and wings of the Morning.

Welcome as waters unkissed by the summers
Are the voices of bell-birds to thirsty far-comers.
When fiery December sets foot in the forest,
And the need of the wayfarer presses the sorest,
Pent in the ridges for ever and ever
The bell-birds direct him to spring and to river,
With ring and with ripple, like runnels whose torrents
Are toned by the pebbles and leaves in the currents.

Often I sit, looking back to a childhood,
Mixt with the sights and the sounds of the wildwood,
Longing for power and the sweetness to fashion
Lyrics with beats like the heart-beats of Passion;—
Songs interwoven of lights and of laughters
Borrowed from bell-birds in far forest-rafters;
So I might keep in the city and alleys
The beauty and strength of the deep mountain valleys:
Charming to slumber the pain of my losses
With glimpses of creeks and a vision of mosses.

ORARA
(THE GLEN OF ARRAWATTA)

A sky of wind! And while these fitful gusts
Are beating round the windows in the cold,
With sullen sobs of rain, behold I shape
A Settler's story of the wild old times:
One told by campfires when the station drays
Were housed and hidden, forty years ago;
While swarthy drivers smoked their pipes, and drew,
And crowded round the friendly beaming flame
That lured the dingo howling from his cave
And brought sharp sudden feet about the brakes.

A tale of Love and Death! And shall I say
A tale of Love in Death; for all the patient eyes
That gathered darkness, watching for a son
And lover, never dreaming of the fate—
The fearful fate he met alone, unknown,
Within the ruthless Australasian wastes?

For in a far-off sultry summer rimmed
With thunder-cloud and red with forest fires,
All day, by ways uncouth and ledges rude,
The wild men held upon a stranger's trail

Which ran against the rivers and athwart
The gorges of the deep blue western hills.

And when a cloudy sunset, like the flame
In windy evenings on the Plains of Thirst
Beyond the dead banks of the far Barcoo,
Lay heavy down the topmost peaks, they came
With pent-in breath and stealthy steps, and crouched
Like snakes amongst the tussocks, till the Night
Had covered face from face and thrown the gloom
Of many shadows on the front of things.

There, in the shelter of a nameless Glen
Fenced round by cedars and the tangled growths
Of blackwood, stained with brown and shot with grey,
The jaded white man built his fire, and turned
His horse adrift amongst the water-pools
That trickled underneath the yellow leaves
And made a pleasant murmur, like the brooks
Of England through the sweet autumnal noons.

Then, after he had slaked his thirst, and used
The forest fare, for which a healthful day
Of mountain-life had brought a zest, he took
His axe, and shaped with boughs and wattle-forks
A wurley, fashioned like a bushman's roof:
The door brought out athwart the strenuous flame:
The back thatched in against a rising wind.

And while the sturdy hatchet filled the clifts
With sounds unknown, the immemorial haunts
Of echoes sent their lonely dwellers forth
Which lived a life of wonder: flying round
And round the glen—what time the kangaroo
Leapt from his lair and huddled with the bats—
Far-scattering down the wildly-startled fells.

Then came the doleful owl; and evermore
The bleak morass gave out the bittern's call;
The plover's cry: and many a fitful wail
Of chilly omen, falling on the ear
Like those cold flaws of wind that come and go
An hour before the break of day.

Anon
The stranger held from toil, and, settling down,
He drew rough solace from his well-filled pipe
And smoked into the night: revolving there
The primal questions of a squatter's life;
For in the flats, a short day's journey past
His present camp, his station yards were kept

With many a lodge and paddock jutting forth
Across the heart of unnamed prairie-lands,
Now loud with bleating and the cattle bells
And misty with the hutfire's daily smoke.
Widespreading flats, and western spurs of hills
That dipped to plains of dim perpetual blue;
Bold summits set against the thunder-heaps;
And slopes be-hacked and crushed by battling kine!
Where now the furious tumult of their feet
Gives back the dust and up from glen and brake
Evokes fierce clamour, and becomes indeed
A token of the squatter's daring life,
Which growing inland—growing year by year—
Doth set us thinking in these latter days.
And makes one ponder of the lonely lands
Beyond the lonely tracks of Burke and Wills;
Where, when the wandering Stuart fixed his camps
In central wastes afar from any home
Or haunt of man, and in the changeless midst
Of sullen deserts and the footless miles
Of sultry silence, all the ways about
Grew strangely vocal, and a marvellous noise
Became the wonder of the waxing glooms.

Now after Darkness, like a mighty spell
Amongst the hills and dim dispeopled dells,
Had brought a stillness to the soul of things,
It came to pass that, from the secret depths
Of dripping gorges, many a runnel-voice
Came, mellowed with the silence, and remained
About the caves, a sweet though alien sound:
Now rising ever, like a fervent flute
In moony evenings, when the theme is love:
Now falling, as ye hear the Sunday bells
While hastening fieldward from the gleaming town.

Then fell a softer mood; and Memory paused
With faithful Love, amidst the sainted shrines
Of Youth and Passion in the valleys past
Of dear delights which never grow again.
And if the stranger (who had left behind
Far anxious homesteads in a wave-swept isle
To face a fierce sea-circle day by day,
And hear at night the dark Atlantic's moan)
Now took a hope and planned a swift return,
With wealth and health and with a youth unspent,
To those sweet ones that stayed with Want at home,
Say *who* shall blame him—though the years are long,
And Life is hard, and waiting makes the heart grow old?

Thus passed the time until the Moon serene
Stood over high dominion like a dream
Of Peace: within the white-transfigured woods;
And o'er the vast dew-dripping wilderness
Of slopes illumined with her silent fires.
Then, far beyond the home of pale red leaves
And silver sluices and the shining stems
Of runnel-blooms, the dreamy wanderer saw,
The wilder for the vision of the moon,
Stark desolations and a waste of plain
All smit by flame and broken with the storms:
Black ghosts of trees, and sapless trunks that stood
Harsh hollow channels of the fiery noise
Which ran from bole to bole a year before,
And grew with ruin, and was like, indeed,
The roar of mighty winds with wintering streams
That foam about the limits of the land
And mix their swiftness with the flying seas.

Now when the man had turned his face about
To take his rest, behold the gem-like eyes
Of ambushed wild things stared from bole and brake
With dumb amaze and faint-recurring glance
And fear anon that drove them down the brush;
While from his den the dingo, like a scout
In sheltered ways, crept out and cowered near
To sniff the tokens of the stranger's feast
And marvel at the shadows of the flame.

But, under screen of glittering leaf and vine,
The man grew silent, and a fitful sleep
Veiled all the strange surroundings; and, while Night
In white mid-heaven shone with star by star,
A swift wild spirit from the sphere of Dreams
Slid down and took the weary wanderer's soul
Far back, away from wood and singing stream
To where the Past with all its varied hues
Of beam and shadow rose and lived again.
Yea, when the subtle spectre waved its wand,
The shining life that left the body saw
The vivid features of a bygone storm:
Fierce horns of land and gleaming crescents shot
With fire-like foam; and bends of moaning bay
Sad with the cry of shipwreck, and the cry
Of strong sea-eagle hunting for the drowned.
Ah! then before the mourning spirit's view
Passed bold New Zealand girt with lordly hills
That live with highest thunder and the snow
And speak with God and Morning in the flame,

And, where the teeth of reef by reef shone out
In straits of roaring water, lo, the hull
Of ruined vessel reeling in the surf
Was seen in that weird dream; and then there came
A hand of change that drew the sea away
And hushed the lips of tempest: then the soul
Beheld an English meadow starred with flowers
And cool with deep green grasses where the kine
Stand dreaming in a tender April sun.
And, past a border fragment with the breath
Of Sussex blooms, the life outside the flesh
Saw at a leafy window one who sat
In all the glory of her golden hair
With sweet blue eyes that strained towards the wave
At watch for him whose step in Northern zones
On Northern lawns was never heard again.

So came and went the visions till a voice
Of beauty sang the soul into its shell
And lulled its life into a perfect sleep.
Thereafter grew the wind; and chafing depths
In distant waters sent a troubled cry
Across the slumb'rous Forest; and the chill
Of coming rain was on the stranger's brow
When, flat as reptiles hutted in the scrub,
A deadly crescent crawled to where he lay—
A band of fierce fantastic savages
That, starting naked round the faded fire,
With sudden spears and swift terrific yells,
Came bounding wildly at the white man's head,
And faced him, staring like a dream of Hell!
Here let me pass! I would not stay to tell
Of hopeless struggles under crushing blows;
Of how the surging fiends with thickening strokes
Howled round the Stranger till they drained his strength;
How Love and Life stood face to face with Hate
And Death; and then how Death was left alone
With Night and Silence in the sobbing rains.

Ah! while within the folds of dumb dank hills
Of dark Orara lined with wailing oaks
The dying traveller moaned a touching prayer,
The greyhaired fathers of a Saxon home
Sat by their Saxon fire, what time the board
Was stacked with generous fare of meat and drink;
And these white elders talked into the night
With cheerful voices of the sturdy son
Who left their thresholds seven years before,
And crossed the seas, and under other skies

Found Fortune's fruit; and now was on his way
(So thought the fathers) to his friends again.

But after many moons, the searchers found
The body mouldering in the mouldering dell
Amidst the fungi and the bleaching leaves,
And buried it; and raised a stony mound
Which took the mosses: then the place became
The haunt of fearful legends, and the lair
Of bats and adders.

                    There he lies and sleeps
From year to year: in soft Australian nights;
And through the furnaced noons; and in the times
Of wind and wet! yet never mourner comes
To drop upon that grave the Christian's tear
Or pluck the foul dank weeds of death away.
But while the English Autumn filled her lap
With faded gold, and while the reapers cooled
Their flame-red faces in the clover grass,
They looked for him at home; and when the frost
Had made a silence in the morning lanes,
And cooped the farmers by December fires,
They looked for him at home: and through the days
Which brought about the million-coloured Spring
With moon-like splendours in the garden plots,
They looked for him at home: while Summer danced,
A shining singer through the tasselled corn,
They looked for him at home. From sun to sun
They waited. Season after season went,
And Memory wept upon the lonely moors
And Hope grew voiceless, and the watchers passed,
Like shadows, one by one, away.

                              And he,
Whose fate was hidden under forest leaves,
And in the darkness of untrodden dells,
Became a marvel. Often by the hearths
In winter nights, and when the wind was wild
Outside the casements, children heard the tale
Of how he left their native vales behind
(Where he had been a child himself) to shape
New fortunes for his father's fallen house;
Of how he struggled—how his name became,
By fine devotion and unselfish zeal,
A name of beauty in a selfish land;
And then, of how the aching hours went by
With patient listeners praying for the step

Which never crossed the floor again. So passed
The tale to children; but the bitter end
Remained a wonder, like the unknown grave
Alone with God and Silence in the hills.

ADA CAMBRIDGE (1844–1926)

Novelist, poet, hymn writer. Born in England; came to Australia in
1870.

PRACTISING THE ANTHEM

A summer wind blows through the open porch,
    And, 'neath the rustling eaves,
A summer light of moonrise, calm and pale,
    Shines through a vale of leaves.

The soft gusts bring a scent of summer flowers,
    Fresh with the falling dew,
And round the doorway, glimmering white as snow,
    The tender petals strew.

Clear through the silence, from a reedy pool
    The curlew's whistle thrills;
A lonely mopoke sorrowfully cries
    From the far-folding hills.

O lovely night, and yet so sad and strange!
    My fingers touch the key;
And down the empty church my Christmas song
    Goes ringing, glad and free.

Each sweet note knocks at dreaming memory's door,
    And memory wakes in pain;
The spectral faces she had turn'd away
    Come crowding in again.

The air seems full of music all around—
    I know not what I hear,
The multitudinous echoes of the past,
    Or these few voices near.

Ah me! the dim aisle vaguely widens out,
    I see me stand therein;
A glory of grey sculpture takes the light
    A winter morn brings in.

No more I smell the fragrant jessamine flowers
  That flake a moonlit floor;
The rustling night-breeze and the open porch
  I hear and see no more.

Great solemn windows, down a long, long nave
  Their shadow'd rainbows fling;
Dark Purbeck shafts, with hoary capitals,
  In carven archways spring.

And overhead the throbbing organ waves
  Roll in one mighty sea,
Bearing the song the herald angels sang
  Of Christ's nativity.

Dear hands touch mine beneath the open book,
  Sweet eyes look in my face,—
They smile, they melt in darkness; I am snatch'd
  From my familiar place.

The summer night-wind blows upon my tears;
  Its flowery scent is pain.
O cold, white day! O noble minster—when
  May I come back again?

To hear the angels' anthem shake the air,
  Where never discord jars,—
The Christmas carols in the windy street,
  Under the frosty stars;

The dream-like falling from the still, grey skies,
  With falling flakes of snow,
Of mellow chimes from old cathedral bells,
  Solemn and sweet and slow.

To hear loved footsteps beating time with mine
  Along the churchyard path,—
To see that ring of faces once again
  Drawn round the blazing hearth.

When may I come? O Lord, when may I go?
  Nay, I must wait Thy will.
Give patience, Lord, and in Thine own best way
  My hopes and prayers fulfil.

FALLEN

For want of bread to eat and clothes to wear—
  Because work failed and streets were deep in snow,
  And this meant food and fire—she fell so low,
Sinning for dear life's sake, in sheer despair.

Or, because life was else so bald and bare,
   The natural woman in her craved to know
   The warmth of passion—as pale buds to blow
And feel the noonday sun and fertile air.

And who condemns? She who, for vulgar gain
   And in cold blood, and not for love or need,
     Has sold her body to more vile disgrace—
     The prosperous matron, with her comely face—
   Wife by the law, but prostitute in deed,
In whose gross wedlock womanhood is slain.

'AUSTRALIE' (Emilie Heron) (1845–1890)

Essayist, poet, journalist. Born in Sydney; educated privately.

FROM THE CLYDE TO BRAIDWOOD

A winter morn. The blue Clyde river winds
'Mid sombre slopes, reflecting in clear depths
The tree-clad banks or grassy meadow flats
Now white with hoary frost, each jewell'd blade
With myriad crystals glistening in the sun.

Thus smiles the Vale of Clyde, as through the air
So keen and fresh three travellers upward ride
Toward the Braidwood heights. Quickly they pass
The rustic dwellings on the hamlet's verge,
Winding sometimes beside the glassy depths
Of Nelligen Creek, where with the murmuring bass
Of running water sounds the sighing wail
Of dark swamp-oaks, that shiver on each bank;
Then winding through a shady-bower'd lane,
With flickering streaks of sunlight beaming through
The feathery leaves and pendant tassels green
Of bright mimosa, whose wee furry balls
Promise to greet with golden glow of joy
The coming spring-tide.

               Now a barren length
Of tall straight eucalyptus, till again
A babbling voice is heard, and through green banks
Of emerald fern and mossy boulder rocks,
The Currawong dances o'er a pebbly bed,
In rippling clearness, or with cresting foam
Splashes and leaps in snowy cascade steps.
Then every feature changes—up and down,

O'er endless ranges like great waves of earth,
Each weary steed must climb, e'en like a ship
Now rising high upon some billowy ridge
But to plunge down to mount once more, again
And still again.

                    Naught on the road to see
Save sullen trees, white arm'd, with naked trunks,
And hanging bark, like tatter'd clothes thrown off,
An undergrowth of glossy zamia palms
Bearing their winter store of coral fruit,
And here and there some early clematis,
Like starry jasmine, or a purple wreath
Of dark kennedea, blooming o'er their time,
As if in pity they would add one joy
Unto the barren landscape.

                    But at last
A clearer point is reach'd, and all around
The loftier ranges loom in contour blue,
With indigo shadows and light veiling mist
Rising from steaming valleys. Straight in front
Towers the Sugarloaf, pyramidal King
Of Braidwood peaks.

                  Impossible it seems
To scale that nature-rampart, but where man
Would go he must and will; so hewn from out
The mountain's side, in gradual ascent
Of league and half of engineering skill
There winds the Weber Pass.

                  A glorious ride!
Fresher and clearer grows the breezy air,
Lighter and freer beats the quickening pulse
As each fair height is gain'd. Stern, strong, above
Rises the wall of mountain; far beneath,
In sheer precipitancy, gullies deep
Gloom in dark shadow, on their shelter'd breast
Cherishing wealth of leafage richly dight
With tropic hues of green.

                  No sound is heard
Save the deep soughing of the wind amid
The swaying leaves and harp-like stems, so like
A mighty breathing of great mother earth,
That half they seem to see her bosom heave
With each pulsation as she living sleeps.
And now and then to cadence of these throbs
There drops the bell-bird's knell, the coach-whip's crack,

The wonga-pigeon's coo, or echoing notes
Of lyre-tail'd pheasants in their own rich tones,
Mocking the song of every forest bird.

Higher the travellers rise—at every turn
Gaining through avenued vista some new glimpse
Of undulating hills, the Pigeon-house
Standing against the sky like eyrie nest
Of some great dove or eagle. On each side
Of rock-hewn road, the fern trees cluster green,
Now and then lighted by a silver star
Of white immortelle flower, or overhung
By crimson peals of bright epacris bells.

Another bend, a shelter'd deepening rift,
And in the mountain's very heart they plunge—
So dark the shade, the sun is lost to view.
Great silver wattles tremble o'er the path,
Which overlooks a glen—one varying mass
Of exquisite foliage, full-green sassafras,
The bright-leaf'd myrtle, dark-hued Kurrajong
And lavender, musk-plant, scenting all the air,
Entwined with clematis or bignonia vines,
And raspberry tendrils hung with scarlet fruit.

The riders pause some moments, gazing down,
Then upward look. Far as the peeping sky
The dell-like gully yawns into the heights;
A tiny cascade drips o'er mossy rocks,
And through an aisle of over-arching trees,
Whose stems are dight with lichen, creeping vines,
A line of sunlight pierces, lighting up
A wealth of fern trees; filling every nook
With glorious circles of voluptuous green,
Such as, unview'd, once clothed the silent earth
Long milliards past in Carboniferous Age.

A mighty nature-rockery! Each spot
Of fertile ground is rich with endless joys
Of leaf and fern; now here a velvet moss,
And there a broad asplenium's shining frond
With red-black veinings or a hart's-tongue point,
Contrasting with a pale-hued tender brake
Or creeping lion's-foot. See where the hand
Of ruthless man hath cleft the rock each wound
Is hidden by thick verdure, leaving not
One unclothed spot, save on the yellow road.

Reluctant the travellers leave the luscious shade
To mount once more. But now another joy—

An open view is here! Before them spreads
A waving field of ranges, purple grey,
In haze of distance with black lines of shade
Marking the valleys, bounded by a line
Of ocean-blue, o'er whose horizon verge
The morning mist-cloud hangs. The distant bay
Is clear defined. The headland's dark arms stretch
(Each finger-point white-lit with dashing foam)
In azure circlet, studded with rugged isles—
A picturesque trio, whose gold rock sides glow
In noonday sunlight, and round which the surf
Gleams like a silvery girdle.

              The grand Pass
Is traversed now, the inland plateau reach'd,
The last sweet glimpse of violet peaks is lost,
An upland rocky stream is pass'd, and naught
But same same gum-trees vex the wearied eye
Till Braidwood plain is reach'd

              A township like
All others, with its houses, church, and school—
Bare, bald, prosaic—no quaint wild tower,
Nor ancient hall to add poetic touch,
As in the dear old land—no legend old
Adds softening beauty to the Buddawong Peak,
Or near-home ranges with too barbarous names.
But everything is cold, new, new, too new
To foster poesy; and famish'd thought
Looks back with longing to the mountain dream.

BODALLA

A glimpse of England amid Australian hills

   Amid the range that nears the southern coast
Bodalla lies—a smiling valley green;
So green, that to home-loving eyes it seems
E'en like a quiet dream of England hid
And nestled in the wild Australian hills.
There gleam the still blue lake and winding stream,
The golden corn-fields and the sunny slope;
While here and there are cottage homes and farms,
With browsing herds in clover pastures fed;
And furrow'd land o'er which the plough has pass'd,
In winter readiness for English seed,
That here, unconscious of an alien soil,
With old-world freshness still will spring and grow.

The very air of all this peaceful land
Is soft and still, for sheltering mountains rise,
And, glooming blue and dark with varying shade,
Shut out the blighting winds, that restless blow
Yet cannot pass the tree-clad ramparts high;
While all the moisture steaming from the earth,
Held in, though rising, turns to dewy mist
And veils th' enclosing hills in sweet revenge;
Thus softly soothing all their rugged lines,
Deep'ning their shadows—adding richer glow.

And through alluvial flats the Tuross winds;
At first a serpentining silver stream,
But widening with blue waters to the sea
And overhung by blossoming wattles green;
Or like a liquid pathway glancing broad
Between a solemn avenue of oaks—
Swamp-oaks, with fibrous fir-like leaves, that droop
Till dark reflections quiver in the deeps,
And thro' whose chords the gentlest wind will sigh
With soft Æolian sounds, that lull the soul,
Yet stir its depths with longings vague and sweet.

A happy vale! that any man might love
To call his own and cherish to his heart!
See, in the midst, upon a rising slope
Beneath the shelter of the Bumbo Mount,
There gleams the homestead—gabled cottage white,
With creeping vines and garden flowers bright;
While on one side stand gold-brown stacks of hay,
The dairy and surroundings of the farm,
The clustering village of the workers' homes,
The quick steam-engine and the blacksmith's forge,
Then in the front, o'er mignonetted beds,
The eye looks on a meadow rich and broad,
Its glistening tints in double greenness shown
And thrown out by the fringing ranges dark;
While round the fields the bending river flows
And almost makes an island of the spot,
Which seems so English-like, that we could look
And half believe ourselves again at home,
Or think this were a memory, taking form,
A reminiscence sweet, or waking dream!

Ah, Comerang! shall I picture thee at morn,
While still the valley sleeps in robe of mist.
And lowing cows of varied hue and form
Thro' frosty fields are driven to the sheds,
Where childish milkmaids, rosy-faced and bright,
With skilful hands press out the creamy milk?

Or shall I paint thee in the golden hues
Of evening light—which, e'er the sun has set,
Floods all the fields with tinted radiance soft
And glances bright through lengthening shadows deep;
While in the west the purpling mountains glow,
Or faintly redden with a parting blush,
As day's king, ling'ring o'er his last good night,
Illumes the heights o'er which his glory sinks?

Nay, there is still a sweeter, holier time!
The sacred stillness of the Sunday morn,
When all the sounds of industry have ceased,
And labour's garments for a while put off,
The people answer to the echoing bell
That calls them to the work of prayer and praise.
Now, like a family gather'd in the hall—
The homestead hall with church-like hangings deck'd,
They listen to the words, and pray the prayers
That thousand brethren e'en are lifting up
In distant churches at the self-same hour;
And music sweet and joyous hymns resound,
In men's deep bass and children's voices high,
Rising, thro' country air so pure and still,
To the Great Father of the fruitful earth.

WILLIAM ALEXANDER JENYNS BOYD ('Old Chum')   (1842–1928)

Journalist. Born in France; educated in Switzerland, France and Italy; came to Australia in 1860.

THE SWAGSMAN

from OLD COLONIALS

> —I saw within my head,
> A gray and gap-toothed man as lean as death,
> Who slowly rode across a wither'd heath,
> And lighted at a ruin'd inn, and said—
> TENNYSON—*Vision of Sin.*

IF Mr Tennyson had been to Australia, I should have said that his type for the "Vision of Sin" was the Australian swagsman.

Now, every foot traveller in Australia carries what is known as a "swag," *i.e.*, a pack or load, which varies in size and contents from a tin pannikin to eighty pounds weight of blankets, clothing and provisions. But if I were to denominate every man who carries a swag a swagsman, I should feel that I was doing a gross injustice to the great army of hard-working men who for multifarious reasons are daily, weekly, and yearly journeying across that Tom Tiddler's ground of the labour-seeking population known as the "bush."

No, I should be unjust if I were to class all these under one head as swagsmen.

My swagsman is a creature generally "gray, gap-toothed and lean;" though sometimes he may be a man in what ought to be the prime of life. But what swagsman ever remembered that glorious period in his existence when all his lately-dormant energies were aroused with a consciousness of power and strength, when to will was to do, and when obstacles and difficulties in the path of life only arose to be removed by indomitable perseverance? Such a period of life belongs not to the true swagsman.

He is too lazy to work; he is too mean to mix with other men. He is insolent when chance gives him the opportunity to be anything but cringing and hypocritical. He is a thief by inclination, and a liar of the most stupendous magnitude. He tramps across the country ostensibly looking for work, and at the same time praying Heaven that he may not find it. In his person he is filthy; his clothes are merely the cast-off apparel of some nobler individual of the *genus homo*. If you ever had the curiosity to know the contents of his swag, and were possessed of sufficient temerity to handle the seething, fetid, ragged blanket which represented that peculiar baggage, you would probably discover that it contained either nothing, or else a few nondescript rags, or even empty bottles.

It seems that, no matter to what depth of degradation a man may have fallen, he still has some lingering sense of pride. Even the debased creature under notice feels that, though he may own few or none of this world's goods, still he must make a show of being the possessor of something. To walk up to a house in the bush and crave a night's lodging, without giving evidence of being prepared to roll up in a blanket of his own, would give rise to suspicion, and possibly denial. Our swagsman, therefore, bulges out his tattered remains of a blanket with anything he can lay his hands on—rags, grass, and even empty bottles.

Idleness being the mainspring of the journeys of the swagsman (*anglicè*, tramp), it is not to be supposed that he acts without some method; and the method is one which ensures the necessary food and lodging, at the same time that it obviates all necessity for exertion on his part.

Let us follow yonder shambling figure, sneaking along as the evening shadows steal o'er the settler's homestead. He casts furtive glances on all sides; he is on the look-out for anything lying about, a saddle, a whip, a bridle, anything which he may lay thieving hands on and convert into cash, by the process of transfer to some shanty-keeper as unscrupulous as he is himself. Now he has arrived at the door. His wits and his appetite are sharpened, as a vision is afforded him through the half-open door of a well-spread table and a comfortable fire.

"Want a night's lodging."

"Well, come in. Bring your swag on to the verandah. How far have you come?"

Now is the time for the swagsman to concoct his "yarn." He must be consistent, and he must also have a knowledge of the locality, of the neighbourhood, and of the work going on in the district. This information he readily procures at his last resting-place, and by using it judiciously he obtains what he requires. Work? Oh, dear no! supper, bed and breakfast. Work is only for such poor, mean-spirited fellows as think they should earn their own living. Work, indeed! What are the rich for? Isn't it to support the poor? Isn't the swagsman poor? Then hasn't he a right to a share of the good things which others possess. Work? Not while he has a leg to carry him, or a shred of his greasy blanket remains. He has had a long tramp to-day. He was working at so-and-so's station, fencing. (There is no fencing going on at this station; 'cute swagsman has noticed this.) When the job was finished, he wasn't wanted, so he left that morning to try elsewhere for something to do.

"Well, get some supper, and we'll see what's to be done. I haven't got any fencing wanting doing." (Bless your innocence, squatter, swagsman knew that without your telling him.)

Swagsman is very sorry. He's good at fencing. Was working for years at nothing else. But perhaps something would turn up in the morning to keep him from tramping over the country.

So saying, he rolls up before the fire, and admiring his own tact in securing his supper and breakfast, with a night's shelter, applies his distorted faculties, not to wooing the drowsy god, but to deciding on the best means of escaping from a probable offer of honest labour, which it is the business of his life to shun.

At last his deep breathing announces that sleep has over-powered him; but long before daylight arrives to arouse the household to renewed activity, our swagsman, who has surreptitiously provided himself with sufficient food during the last night's supper to serve him as a breakfast, rises from his lair and, there being no doors to unlock, silently makes his way out of the house. The dogs look up sleepily as he steps off the verandah, but recognizing the guest of their master, utter no warning growl. He gains the paddock fence, and is soon lost among the trees. Most probably he has taken some token of remembrance with him, in the shape of a bridle, pistol, or even a pair of green hide hobbles. So he wanders on and on, crawling from station to station, ever seeking, never finding, and never wishing for the work which would render him a useful member of society. He is a social pest, an incubus on the settler, the abhorrence of the real worker. He may truly be said to have, in a great measure, been the means of destroying the confidence of the employer in the employed. Before the swagsman became known a traveller in search of employment was always sure of a hospitable reception at the hands of the squatter. I have lived on a station where it was invariably the custom to serve out two men's rations weekly for the benefit of travellers. All this is now done away with in the more settled parts of the colonies. Travellers have to provide themselves with their own food, and if they run short on the road they must purchase from the squatter as they would at an ordinary store.

It is singular how fond these men are of a lonely life. They are never known to have an associate in their wanderings, probably from a knowledge of the fact that "two of a trade never agree." I have just been told of one of these travellers who walked the whole way from the neighbourhood of Rockhampton to the far north of Queensland, begging his way from homestead to homestead, and at last, weary and done up, tired nature compelled him to stop for a few days at a northern station, where he was offered employment as cook. As soon as he was strong enough he started off, to go whither he knew not, and after long wandering he was lost sight of, and probably perished, either at the hands of the blacks, or by starvation.

It is only a peculiar state of civilization which can give birth to such characters as the swagsman. The bush settlers are given to unbounded hospitality. No traveller ever arrived at the house of one of these pioneers of civilization without being made cordially welcome; and at far out-stations, where visits of strangers are as infrequent as angels' visits are said to be, it is with regret that the stranger is allowed to depart, particularly if he be of the right sort, i.e., one who will give a helping hand when required, and who is a lively companion at the camp fire. I have travelled some thousands of miles both in Queensland, New South Wales, and Victoria, on foot and horseback, in buggy, dray and waggon, and have ever met the same kindly feeling. I remember once being attacked with fever and ague during a wet season in the north of Queensland. I left my camp and made my way to a station some forty miles off. Never shall I forget the care bestowed upon me there. I was tended as if I were in the midst of my own family. The wet season was nearly over, and rations, or at any event luxuries, were getting scarce at the station, and I have every reason to believe that I consumed the only bottle of port and the last of several little extra comforts which this hospitable family had left. No thought rose in their minds that they would themselves be deprived of these things till the roads were dry enough to admit of the passage of drays. A stranger was ill, and the supplies were ungrudgingly brought forth. If this should ever find its way to that station, the hospitable owners will doubtless recognize the writer, and accept his gratitude.

To return to my theme. Taking advantage of this state of things, idle, dissipated vagabonds, who had—if ever they had done work in their lives—been dismissed from every employment as worthless;

fellows who had squandered whatever means they might once have possessed in drink and debauchery, set themselves to the task of compelling the honest community to support them; and so successful were they in imposing on the credulity and good nature of the dwellers in the bush, that the country became infested with these scoundrels to such an extent that men were obliged in self-defence to forbear hospitality, or only extend it to those of whom they had some knowledge, or who were vouched for as honest by a neighbour. During the late great rush to the Palmer gold-field, I happened to be on a journey in that direction. I then met men travelling away to the new El Dorado with absolutely no more provision against weather, blacks, and hunger, than a pint pot and a walking stick. They depended entirely upon the squatters to support them. One of these men on arriving at the last station, two hundred miles from the diggings, inquired if any provisions were obtainable on this latter portion of the road. On being replied to in the negative, he begged a few provisions, and actually started on the back track. He had travelled nearly twelve hundred miles, only to travel back without reaching his destination; but it mattered little to him, so long as he could, leech-like, gorge himself at the expense of the squatters whom he honoured with his visits. Others plunged into this wilderness of two hundred miles trusting to luck, "to roll through," as they expressed it.

Here is an incident which occurred on a cattle station I visited. A gaunt, hungry-looking, fever and ague stricken wretch walked into the squatter's room one day, and demanded something to eat. He made a very plausible story. He had lost his horse, which had bolted from him, and all his clothes and provisions and money were gone. His appearance certainly excited compassion. The squatter provided him with all he needed, and the man, with blessings on his lips, departed. That evening a man who was working on the station was benighted, as he was returning home after having been away at a neighbouring station. He fell in with a camp of men, who were laughing over a good story, and it appeared that the very man who had been so kindly treated by the squatter was boasting of how he had frightened old F——into giving him rations, by showing a pistol and threatening to blow his brains out.

This fellow was a true swagsman. I could multiply instances of the mean, sneaking doings of these ruffians, but enough has been said. Happily the type is on the decrease, and probably the swagsman and the blackfellow will be simultaneously extinguished.

As the train from Ipswich to Oxley was speeding on its way on Tuesday afternoon, between Goodna and Oxley, the passengers were surprised to find it brought suddenly to a stand-still at a point where no station existed. The cause was discovered to be that the driver had noticed some object lying across the line ahead of him, and had consequently put down his brakes and stopped the train.

The obstacle proved to be an elderly man, *apparently a swagsman*, who was lying with his body across the rails. On being accosted, and the reason of his extraordinary situation demanded, he briefly explained that he was desirous of having his head—to which, by anticipation, he applied a gory epithet—cut off. The man was at once taken into the train and guarded in a second-class carriage, and will no doubt be afforded an opportunity of further explaining himself before the proper authorities—*Queenslander*, February 13, 1875.

MARY HANNAY FOOTT   (1846–1918)

Poet. Born in Glasgow; came to Australia in 1853; educated in Melbourne.

WHERE THE PELICAN BUILDS

The horses were ready, the rails were down,
    But the riders lingered still—
        One had a parting word to say,
    And one had his pipe to fill.
Then they mounted, one with a granted prayer,
    And one with a grief unguessed.
        'We are going,' they said, as they rode away—
    'Where the pelican builds her nest!'

They had told us of pastures wide and green,
    To be sought past the sunset's glow;
        Of rifts in the ranges by opal lit;
    And gold 'neath the river's flow.
And thirst and hunger were banished words
    When they spoke of that unknown West;
        No drought they dreaded, no flood they feared,
    Where the pelican builds her nest!

The creek at the ford was but fetlock deep
    When we watched them crossing there;
        The rains have replenished it thrice since then,
    And thrice has the rock lain bare.
But the waters of Hope have flowed and fled,
    And never from blue hill's breast
        Come back—by the sun and the sands devoured—
    Where the pelican builds her nest!

IN TIME OF DROUGHT

The river of God is full of water—Psalm

The rushes are black by the river bed,
    And the sheep and the cattle stand
Wistful-eyed, where the waters were,
    In a waste of gravel and sand;
Or pass o'er their dying and dead to slake
    Their thirst at the slimy pool.
Shall they pine and perish in pangs of drought,
    While Thy river, O God, is full!

The fields are furrowed, the seed is sown,
    But no dews from the heavens are shed;
And where shall the grain for the harvest be?
    And how shall the poor be fed?
In waterless gullies they winnow the earth,
    New-turned by the miner's tool;
And the wayfarer faints 'neath his lightened load—
    Yet the river of God is full.

FRANCIS WILLIAM LAUDERDALE ADAMS   (1862–1893)

Essayist, poet, novelist, short story writer, playwright. Born in Malta; educated in England; came to Australia in 1884; returned to England in 1889.

MELBOURNE, AND HER CIVILIZATION, AS THEY STRIKE AN ENGLISHMAN

from AUSTRALIAN ESSAYS

It is difficult to speak of Melbourne fitly. The judgment of neither native nor foreigner can escape the influence of the phenomenal aspect of the city. Not fifty years ago its first child, Batman's, was born; not forty, it was a city; a little over thirty, it was the metropolis of a colony; and now (as the inscription on Batman's grave tells us) "*Circumspice!*" To natives their Melbourne is, and is only, "the magnificent city, classed by Sir George Bowen as the ninth in the world," "one of the wonders of the world." They cannot criticise, they can only praise it. To a foreigner, however, who, with all respect and admiration for the excellencies of the Melbourne of to-day as compared with the Melbourne of half-a-century ago, has travelled and seen and read, and cares very little for glorifying the *amour-*

propre of this class or of that, and very much for really arriving at some more or less accurate idea of the significance of this city and its civilization; to such a man, I say, the native melodies in the style of "Rule Britannia" which he hears everywhere and at all times are distasteful. Nay, he may possibly have at last to guard himself against the opposite extreme, and hold off depreciation with the one hand as he does laudation with the other!

The first thing, I think, that strikes a man who knows the three great modern cities of the world—London, Paris, New York—and is walking observingly about Melbourne is, that Melbourne is made up of curious elements. There is something of London in her, something of Paris, something of New York, and something of her own. Here is an attraction to start with. Melbourne has, what might be called, the *metropolitan tone*. The look on the faces of her inhabitants is the *metropolitan look*. These people live quickly: such as life presents itself to them, they know it: as far as they can see, they have no prejudices. "I was born in Melbourne," said the wife of a small bootmaker to me once, "I was born in Melbourne, and I went to Tasmania for a bit, but I soon came back again. *I like to be in a place where they go ahead.*" The wife of a small bootmaker, you see, has the *metropolitan tone*, the *metropolitan look* about her; she sees that there is a greater pleasure in life than sitting under your vine and your fig-tree; she likes to be in a place where they go ahead. And she is a type of her city. Melbourne likes to "go ahead." Look at her public buildings, her New Law Courts not finished yet, her Town Hall, her Hospital, her Library, her Houses of Parliament, and above all her Banks! Nay, and she has become desirous of a fleet and has established a "Naval Torpedo Corps" with seven electricians. All this is well, very well. Melbourne, I say, lives quickly: such as life presents itself to her, she knows it: as far as she can see, she has no prejudices.

As far as she can see.—The limitation is important. The real question is, *how* far can she see? how far does her civilization answer the requirements of a really fine civilization? what scope in it is there (as Mr Arnold would say) for the satisfaction of the claims of conduct, of intellect and knowledge, of beauty and manners? Now in order the better to answer this question, let us think for a moment what are the chief elements that have operated and are still operating in this Melbourne and her civilization.

This is an English colony: it springs, as its poet Gordon (of whom there will presently be something to be remarked) says, in large capitals, it springs from "*the Anglo-Saxon race ... the Norman blood.*" Well, if there is one quality which distinguishes this race, this blood, it is its determined strength. Wherever we have gone, whatever we have done, we have gone and we have done with all our heart and soul. We have made small, if any, attempt to conciliate others. Either they have had to give way before, or adapt themselves to us. India, America, Australia, they all bear witness to our determined, our pitiless strength. What is the state of the weaker nations that opposed us there? In America and Australia they are perishing off the face of the earth; even in New Zealand, where the aborigines are a really fine and noble race, we are, it seems, swiftly destroying them. In India, whose climate is too extreme for us ever to make it a colony in the sense that America and Australia are colonies; in India, since we could neither make the aborigines give way, nor make them adapt themselves to us, we have simply let them alone. They do not understand us, nor we them. Of late, it is true, an interest in them, in their religion and literature, has been springing up, but what a strange aspect do we, the lords of India for some hundred and thirty years, present! "In my own experience among Englishmen," says an Indian scholar writing to the *Times* in 1874, "I have found no general indifference to India, but I have found a Cimmerian darkness about the manners and habits of my countrymen, an almost poetical description of our customs, and a conception no less wild and startling than the vagaries of Mandeville and Marco Polo concerning our religion." Do we want any further testimony than this to the determined, the pitiless strength of "the Anglo-Saxon race ... the Norman blood?"

Well, and how does all this concern Australia in general and Melbourne in particular? It concerns them in this way, that the civilization of Australia, of Melbourne, is an Anglo-Saxon civilization, a civilization of the Norman blood, and that, with all the good attendant on such a civilization, there is also all the evil. All? Well, I will not say all, for that would be to contradict one of the first and chief statements I made about her, namely that "as far as she can see Melbourne has no prejudices," a statement which I could not make of England. *"This our native or adopted land,"* says an intelligent Australian critic, the late Mr Marcus Clarke, *"has no past, no story. No poet speaks to us."* "No," we might add, *"and (thus far happily for you) neither, as far as you can see, does any direct preacher of prejudice."* And here, as I take it, we have put our finger upon what is at once the strength and the weakness of this civilization.

Let us consider it for a moment. The Australians have no prejudice about an endowed Church, as we English have, and hence they have, what we have not, religious liberty. As far as I can make out, there is no reason why the wife of a clergyman of the Church of England should in this colony look down upon the wife of a dissenting minister as her social inferior, and this is, on the whole, I think, well, for it tends to break up the notion of caste that exists between the two sects; it tends, I mean, to their mutual benefit, to the interchange of the church's sense of "the beauty of holiness" with the chapel's sense of the passion of holiness. Here, then, you are better off than we. On the other hand, you have no prejudice, as we at last have, against Protection, and consequently you go on benefiting a class at the expense of the community in a manner that can only, I think, be defined as short-sighted and foolish. Here we are better off than you. Again, however, you have not the prejudice that we have against the intervention of the State. You have nationalized your railways, and are attempting, as much as possible, to nationalize your land. You are beginning to see that a land tax, at any given rate of annual value, would be (as Mr Fawcett puts it) "a valuable national resource, which might be utilized in rendering, unnecessary the imposition of many taxes which will otherwise have to be imposed." Here you are better off than we, better off both in fortune and general speculation. Again, you have not yet arrived at Federalism, and what a waste of time and all time's products is implied in the want of central unity! Now the first and third of these instances show the strength that is in this civilization, and the second shows a portion of the weakness, at present only a small portion, but, unless vigorous measures are resorted to and soon, this Protection will become the great evil that it is in America. There is just the same cry there as here: "Protect the native industries until they are strong enough to stand alone"—as if an industry that has once been protected will ever care to stand alone again until it is compelled to! as if a class benefited at the expense of the community will ever give up its benefit until the community takes it away again!

On one of the first afternoons I spent in Melbourne, I remember strolling into a well-known book-mart, the bookmart "at the sign of the rainbow." I was interested both in the books and the people who were looking at or buying them. Here I found, almost at the London prices (for we get our twopence or threepence in the shilling on books now in London), all, or almost all, of the average London books of the day. The popular scientific, theological, and even literary books were to hand, somewhat cast into the shade, it is true, by a profusion of cheap English novels and journals, but still they were to hand. And who were the people that were buying them? The people of the dominant class, the middle-class. I began to enquire at what rate the popular, scientific, and even literary books were selling. Fairly, was the answer. "And how do Gordon's poems sell?" "*Oh they sell well*," was the answer, "*he's the only poet we've turned out.*"

This pleased me, it made me think that the "go-ahead" element in Victorian and Melbourne life had gone ahead in this direction also. If, in a similar book-mart in Falmouth (say), I had asked how the poems of Charles Kingsley were selling, it is a question whether much more than the name would have been recognized. And yet the middle-class here is as, and perhaps more, badly—more appallingly badly—off for a higher education than the English provincial middle class is. Whence comes it, then, that a poet like Gordon with the cheer and charge of our chivalry in him, with his sad "trust and only trust," and his

> "weary longings and yearnings
> for the mystical better things:"

whence comes it that he is a popular poet here? Let him answer us English for himself and Melbourne:

> "You are slow, very slow, in discerning
> that book-lore and wisdom are twain:"

Yes, indeed, to Melbourne, such as life presents itself to her, she knows it, and, what is more, she knows that she knows it, and her self-knowledge gives her a contempt for the pedantry of the old world. Walk about in her streets, look at her private buildings, these banks of hers, for instance, and you will see this. They *mean* something, they *express* something: they do not (as Mr Arnold said of our British Belgravian architecture) "only express the impotence of the artist to express anything." They express a certain sense of movement, of progress, of conscious power. They say: "Some thirty years ago the first gold nuggets made their entry into William Street. Well, many more nuggets have followed, and wealth of other sorts has followed the nuggets, and we express that wealth—we express movement, progress, conscious power.—*Is that, now, what your English banks express?*" And we can only say that it is not, that our English banks express something quite different; something, if deeper, slower; if stronger, more clumsy.

But the matter does not end here. When we took the instance of the books and the people "at the sign of the rainbow," we took also the abode itself of the rainbow; when we took the best of the private buildings, we took also the others. Many of them are hideous enough, we know; this is what Americans, English, and Australians have in common, this inevitable brand of their civilization, of their determined, their pitiless strength. The same horrible "pot hat," "frock coat," and the rest, are to be found in London, in Calcutta, in New York, in Melbourne.

Let us sum up. "The Anglo-Saxon race, the Norman blood:" a colony made of this: a city into whose hands wealth and its power is suddenly phenomenally cast: a general sense of movement, of progress, of conscious power. This, I say, is Melbourne—Melbourne with its fine public buildings and tendency towards banality, with its hideous houses and tendency towards anarchy. And Melbourne is, after all, the Melbournians. Alas, then, how will this city and its civilization stand the test of a really fine city and fine civilization? how far will they answer the requirements of such a civilization? what scope is there in them for the satisfaction of the claims of conduct, of intellect and knowledge, of beauty, and manners?

Of the first I have only to say that, so far as I can see, its claims are satisfied, satisfied as well as in a large city, and in a city of the above-mentioned composition, they can be. But of the second, of the claims of intellect and knowledge, what enormous room for improvement there is! What a splendid field for culture lies in this middle-class that makes a popular poet of Adam Lindsay Gordon!

It tempts one to prophesy that, given a higher education for this middle-class, and fifty—forty—thirty years to work it through a generation, and it will leave the English middle-class as far behind in intellect and knowledge as, at the present moment, it is left behind by the middle-class, or rather the one great educated upper-class, of France.

There is still the other claim, that of beauty and manners. And it is here that your Australian, your Melbourne civilization is, I think, most wanting, is most weak; it is here that one feels the terrible need of "a past, a story, a poet to speak to you." With the Library are a sculpture gallery and a picture gallery. What an arrangement in them both! In the sculpture gallery "are to be seen," we are told, "admirably executed casts of ancient and modern sculpture, from the best European sources, copies of the Elgin marbles from the British Museum, and other productions from the European Continent." Yes, and Summers stands side by side with Michaelangelo! And poor busts of Moore and Goethe come between Antinous and the Louvre Apollo the Lizard slayer! But this, it may be said, is after all only an affair of an individual, the arranger. Not altogether so. If an audience thinks that a thing is done badly, they express their opinion, and the failure has to vanish. And how large a portion of the audience of Melbourne city, pray, is of opinion that quite half of its architecture is a failure, is hideous, is worthy only, as architecture, of abhorrence? how many are shocked by the atrocity of the Medical College building at the University? how many feel that Bourke Street, taken as a whole, is simply an insult to good taste?

"Yes, all this," it is said, "may be true, as abstract theory, but it is at present quite out of the sphere of practical application. You would talk of Federalism, and here is our good ex-Premier of New South Wales, Sir Henry Parkes, making it the subject of a farewell denunciation. 'I venture to say now,' says Sir Henry Parkes, 'here amongst you what I said when I had an opportunity in London, what I ventured to say to Lord Derby himself, that this federation scheme must prove a failure.' You talk of Free-trade and here is what an intelligent writer in the *Argus* says *apropos* of 'the promised tariff negotiations with Tasmania.' 'In America,' he says, 'there is no difficulty in inducing the States to see that, whatever may be their policy as regards the outside world, they should interchange as between each other in order that they may stand on as broad a base as possible, but we can only speculate on the existence of such a national spirit here.'—These facts, my good sir," it is said, "as indicative of the amount of opposition that the nation feels to the ideas of Free-trade and Federalism, are not encouraging."—They are not, let us admit it at once, but there are others which are; others, some of which we have been considering, and, above and beyond everything, there is one invaluable and in the end irresistible ally of these ideas: there is *the Tendency of the Age—the*

Time-Spirit, as Goethe calls it. Things move more quickly now than they used to do: ideas, the modern ideas, are permeating the masses swiftly and thoroughly and universally. We cannot tell, we can only speculate as to what another fifty—forty—thirty years will actually bring forth.

Free-trade—Federalism—Higher Education, they all go together. The necessities of life are cheap here, wonderfully cheap; a man can get a dinner here for sixpence that he could not get in England for twice or thrice the amount. "There are not," says the *Australasian Schoolmaster,* the organ of the State Schools, "there are not many under-fed children in the Australian [as there are in the English] schools." But the luxuries of life (and let us remember that what we call the luxuries of life are, after all, necessities; they are the things which go to make up our civilization, the things which make us feel that there is a greater pleasure in life than sitting under your vine and your fig-tree, whatever Mr George may have to say to the contrary)—the luxuries of life, I say, are dear here, very dear, owing to, what I must be permitted to call, an exorbitant tariff, and, consequently, the money that would be spent in fostering a higher ideal of life, in preparing the way for a national higher education, is spent on these luxuries, and the claims of intellect and knowledge, and of beauty and manners, have to suffer for it. Here is your Mr Marcus Clarke, for instance, talking grimly, not to say bitterly, of "the capacity of this city to foster poetic instinct," of his "astonishment that such work" as Gordon's "was ever produced here." He is astonished, you see, that the claims of intellect and knowledge, and of beauty and manners are enough satisfied in this city to produce a talent of this sort; he is astonished, because he does not see that there is an element in this city which, in its way, is making for at any rate the intellect and knowledge—an element which is a product, not of England but of Australia; a general sense of movement, of progress, of conscious power.

Free-trade—Federalism—Higher Education, they all, I say, go together; but if one is more important than the other, then it is the last. Improvement, real improvement, must always be from within outwards, not from without inwards. All abiding good comes, as it has been well said, by evolution not by revolution. "Our chief, our gravest want in this country at present," says Arnold, " our *unum necessarium,* is a middle-class, homogeneous, intelligent, civilized brought up in good public schools, and on the first plane." How true is this of Australia too, of Melbourne! There are State schools for the lower-class, but what is there for the great upper educated class of the nation? The voluntary schools, the "private adventure schools." And what sort of education do *they* supply either in England or here? "The voluntary schools," says a happy shallow man in some Publishers' circular I lit on the other day, "the voluntary schools of the country" [of England] "have reached the highest degree of efficiency." This, to those who have taken the trouble to study the question, not to say to have considerable absolute experience in the English voluntary schools—this is intelligence as surprising as it ought to be gratifying. To such men, the idea they had arrived at of the English voluntary schools was somewhat different; their idea being that these schools were, both socially and intellectually, the most inadequate that fall to the lot of any middle class among the civilized nations of Europe. "Comprehend," says Arnold to us Englishmen, and he might as well be saying it to you Australians, "comprehend that middle-class education—the higher education, as we have put it, of the great upper educated class—is a great democratic reform, of the truest, surest, safest description."

"But there are many difficulties to be overcome—so many, that we doubt these abstract theories to be at present within the sphere of practical application. There is such a mass of opposition to the idea of Federalism. And, as for the idea of Free-trade, we can only speculate on the existence of a national spirit here. The thinking public is quite content with its State schools for the lower class, and cares little or nothing about State schools and a higher education for the upper class. They are much more interested in the religious questions of the day—the Catholic attitude, the conflict between Mr Strong and his Presbytery on the subject of Religious Liberalism or Latitudinarianism, as you may please to call it, etcetera, etcerera, etcetera."—All this is so, let us admit it at once, but it does not discourage us. We know, or think we know (which is, after all, almost the same thing), that these three questions—Free-trade, Federalism, Higher Education—are the three great, the three vital questions for Australia, for Melbourne. We know that, sooner or later, they will have to be properly considered and decided upon, and that, if Melbourne is to keep the place which she now holds as the leading city, intellectually and commercially, of Australia, they will have to be decided upon in that way which conforms with "the intelligible law of things," with the *Tendency of the Age*, with the *Time-Spirit*. For this is the one invaluable and, in the end, irresistible ally of Progress—of Progress onward and upward.

BARCROFT BOAKE   (1866–1892)

Poet. Born and educated in Sydney.

WHERE THE DEAD MEN LIE

Out on the wastes of the Never Never—
    That's where the dead men lie!
There where the heat-waves dance for ever—
    That's where the dead men lie!
That's where the Earth's loved sons are keeping
Endless tryst: not the west wind sweeping
Feverish pinions can wake their sleeping—
    Out where the dead men lie!

Where brown Summer and Death have mated—
    That's where the dead men die!
Loving with fiery lust unsated—
    That's where the dead men lie!
Out where the grinning skulls bleach whitely
Under the saltbush sparkling brightly;
Out where the wild dogs chorus nightly—
    That's where the dead men lie!

Deep in the yellow, flowing river—
    That's where the dead men lie!
Under the banks where the shadows quiver—
    That's where the dead men lie!
Where the platypus twists and doubles,
Leaving a train of tiny bubbles;
Rid at last of their earthly troubles—
    That's where the dead men lie!

East and backward pale faces turning—
    That's how the dead men lie!
Gaunt arms stretch with a voiceless yearning—
    That's how the dead men lie!
Oft in the fragrant bush of nooning
Hearing again their mother's crooning,
Wrapt for aye in a dreamful swooning—
    That's how the dead men lie!

Only the hand of Night can free them—
    That's when the dead men fly!
Only the frightened cattle see them—
    See the dead men go by!
Cloven hoofs beating out one measure,
Bidding the stockmen know no leisure—
That's when the dead men take their pleasure!
    That's when the dead men fly!

Ask, too, the never-sleeping drover:
    He sees the dead pass by;
Hearing them call to their friends—the plover,
    Hearing the dead men cry;
Seeing their faces stealing, stealing,
Hearing their laughter, pealing, pealing,
Watching their grey forms wheeling, wheeling
    Round where the cattle lie!

Strangled by thirst and fierce privation—
    That's how the dead men die!
Out on Moneygrub's farthest station—
    That's how the dead men die!
Hard-faced greybeards, youngsters callow;
Some mounds cared for, some left fallow;
Some deep down, yet others shallow;
    Some having but the sky.

Moneygrub, as he sips his claret,
    Looks with complacent eye
Down at his watch-chain, eighteen carat—
    There, in his club, hard by:
Recks not that every link is stamped with
Names of the men whose limbs are cramped with
Too long lying in grave-mould, cramped with
    Death where the dead men lie.

'STEELE RUDD'   (Arthur Hoey Davis) (1868–1935)

Novelist, short story writer. Born in Queensland; had little
schooling.

A KANGAROO HUNT FROM SHINGLE HUT

from ON OUR SELECTION

We always looked forward to Sundays. It was our day of sport.
Once, I remember, we thought it would never come. We longed
restlessly for it, and the more we longed the more it seemed to
linger.

A meeting of selectors had been held, war declared against the
marsupial, and a hunt on a grand scale arranged for this particular
Sabbath. Of course, those in the neighbourhood hunted the kangaroo every Sunday, but "on their own," and always on foot, which
had its fatigues. This was to be a raid *en masse* and on horseback.
The whole countryside was to assemble at Shingle Hut and proceed
thence. It assembled, and what a collection! Such a crowd! such

gear! such a tame lot of horses! and *such* a motley swarm of lean, lank, lame kangaroo-dogs!

We were not ready. The crowd sat on their horses and waited at the slip-rails. Dogs trooped into the yard by the dozen. One pounced on a fowl, another lamed the pig, a trio put the cat up a peach-tree, one with a thirst mounted the water-cask and looked down it, while the bulk of the brutes trotted inside and disputed with Mother who should open the safe.

Dad loosed our three, and pleased they were to feel themselves free. They had been chained up all the week, with scarcely anything to eat. Dad didn't believe in too much feeding. He had had wide experience in dogs and coursing at Home on his grandfather's large estates, and always found them fleetest when empty. *Ours* ought to have been as fleet as locomotives.

Dave, showing a neat seat, rode out of the yard on Bess, fresh and fat and fit to run for a kingdom. They waited for Dad. He was standing beside *his* mount—Farmer, the plough-horse, who was arrayed in winkers with greenhide reins, and an old saddle with only one flap. He was holding an earnest argument with Joe.... Still the crowd waited. Still Dad and Joe argued the point.... There was a murmur and a movement and much merriment. Dad was coming; so was Joe—perched behind him, "double bank," rapidly wiping the tears from his eyes with his knuckles.

Hooray! They were off. Paddy Maloney and Dave took the lead, heading for kangaroo country along the foot of Dead Man's Mountain and through Smith's paddock, where there was a low wire fence to negotiate. Paddy spread his coat over it and jumped his mare across. He was a horseman, was Pat. The others twisted a stick in the wires, and proceeded carefully to lead their horses over. When it came to Farmer's turn he hesitated. Dad coaxed him. Slowly he put one leg across, as if feeling his way, and paused again. Joe was on his back behind the saddle. Dad tugged hard at the winkers. Farmer was inclined to withdraw his leg. Dad was determined not to let him. Farmer's heel got caught against the wire, and he began to pull back and grunt. So did Dad. Both pulled hard. Anderson and old Brown ran to Dad's assistance. The trio planted their heels in the ground and leaned back. Joe became afraid. He clutched at the saddle and cried, "Let me off!" "Stick to him!" said Paddy Maloney, hopping over the fence. "Stick to him!" He kicked Farmer what he afterwards called "a sollicker on the tail". Again he kicked him. Still Farmer strained and hung back. Once more he let him have it. Then, off flew the winkers, and over went Dad and Anderson and old Brown, and down rolled Joe and Farmer on the other side of the fence. The others leant against their horses and laughed the laugh of their lives. "Worse 'n a lot of d...d jackasses," Dad was heard to say. They caught Farmer and led him to the fence again. He jumped it, and rose feet higher than he had any need to, and had not old Brown dodged him just when he did he would be a dead man now.

A little further on the huntsmen sighted a mob of kangaroos. Joy and excitement. A mob? It was a swarm! Away they hopped. Off scrambled the dogs, and off flew Paddy Maloney and Dave—the rest followed anyhow, and at varying speeds.

That all those dogs should have selected and followed the same kangaroo was sad and humiliating. And such a waif of a thing, too! Still, they stuck to it. For more than a mile, down a slope, the weedy marsupial outpaced them, but when it came to the hill the daylight between rapidly began to lessen. A few seconds more and all would have been over, but a straggling, stupid old ewe, belonging to an unneighbourly squatter, darted up from the shade of a tree right in the way of Maloney's Brindle, who was leading. Brindle always preferred mutton to marsupial, so he let the latter slide and secured the ewe. The death scene was most imposing. The ground around was strewn with small tufts of white wool. There was a complete circle of eager, wriggling dogs—all jammed together, heads down, and tails elevated. Not a scrap of the ewe was visible. Paddy Maloney jumped down and proceeded to batter the brutes vigorously with a waddy. As the others arrived they joined him. The dogs were hungry, and fought for every inch of the sheep. Those not laid out were pulled away, and when old Brown had dragged the last one off by the hind-legs, all that was left of that ewe was four feet and some skin.

Dad shook his head and looked grave—so did Anderson. After a short rest they decided to divide into parties and work the ridges. A start was made. Dad's contingent—consisting of himself and Joe, Paddy Maloney, Anderson, old Brown, and several others—started a mob. This time the dogs separated and scampered off in all directions. In quick time Brown's black slut bailed up an "old man" full of fight. Nothing was more desirable. He was a monster, a king kangaroo; and as he raised himself to his full height on his toes and tail he looked formidable—a grand and majestic demon of the bush. The slut made no attempt to tackle him; she stood off with her tongue out. Several small dogs belonging to Anderson barked energetically at him, even venturing occasionally to run behind and bite his tail. But, further than grabbing them in his arms and embracing them, he took no notice. There he towered, his head back and chest well out, awaiting the horsemen. They came, shouting and hooraying. He faced them defiantly. Anderson, aglow with excitement, dismounted and aimed a lump of rock at his head, which laid out one of the little dogs. They pelted him with sticks and stones till their arms were tired, but they might just as well have pelted a dead cow. Paddy Maloney took out his stirrup. "Look out!" he cried. They looked out. Then, galloping up, he swung the iron at the marsupial and nearly knocked his horse's eye out.

Dad was disgusted. He and Joe approached the enemy on Farmer. Dad carried a short stick. The old man looked him straight in
the face. Dad poked the stick at him. He promptly grabbed hold of
it, and a piece of Dad's hand as well. Farmer had not been in many
battles—no Defence Force man ever owned him. He threw up his
head and snorted, and commenced a retreat. The kangaroo followed
him up and seized Dad by the shirt. Joe evinced signs of timidity.
He lost faith in Dad, and, half jumping, half falling, he landed on the
ground, and set out speedily for a tree. Dad lost the stick, and in
attempting to brain the brute with his fist he overbalanced and fell
out of the saddle. He struggled to his feet and clutched his antago-
nist affectionately by both paws—standing well away. Backwards
and forwards and round and round they moved. "Use your knife!"
Anderson called out, getting farther away himself. But Dad dared
not relax his grip. Paddy Maloney ran behind the brute several times
to lay him out with a waddy, but each time he turned and fled
before striking the blow. Dad thought to force matters, and began
kicking his assailant vigorously in the stomach. Such dull, heavy
thuds! The kangaroo retaliated, putting Dad on the defensive. Dad
displayed remarkable suppleness about the hips. At last the brute
fixed his deadly toe in Dad's belt.

It was an anxious moment, but the belt broke, and Dad breathed
freely again. He was acting entirely on the defensive, but an awful
consciousness of impending misfortune assailed him. His belt was
gone, and his trousers began to slip—slip—slip! He called wildly to
the others for God's sake to do something. They helped with
advice. He yelled "Curs!" and "Cowards!" back at them. Still, as he
danced around with his strange and ungainly partner, his trousers
kept slipping—slipping! For the fiftieth time and more he glanced
eagerly over his shoulder for some haven of safety. None was near.
And then—oh, horror!—down *they* slid calmly and noiselessly.
Poor Dad! He was at a disadvantage; his leg work was hampered.
He was hobbled. Could he only get free of them altogether! But he
couldn't—his feet were large. He took a lesson from the foe and
jumped—jumped this way and that way, and round about, while
large drops of sweat rolled off him. The small dogs displayed renewed and ridiculous ferocity, often mistaking Dad for the marsupial. At last Dad became exhausted—there was no spring left in
him. Once he nearly went down. Twice he tripped. He staggered
again—down he was going—down—down—and down he fell! But
at the same moment, and, as though they had dropped from the
clouds, Brindle and five or six other dogs pounced on the "old
man." The rest may be imagined.

Dad lay on the ground to recover his wind, and when he mounted
Farmer again and silently turned for home, Paddy Maloney was
triumphantly seated on the carcass of the fallen enemy, exultingly
explaining how he missed the brute's head with the stirrup-iron,
and claiming the tail.

ANDREW BARTON PATERSON   ('The Banjo') (1864–1941)

Poet, journalist. Born in N.S.W.; educated in Sydney.

THE MAN FROM SNOWY RIVER

There was movement at the station, for the word had passed around
   That the colt from old Regret had got away,
And had joined the wild bush horses—he was worth a thousand
     pound,
   So all the cracks had gathered to the fray.
All the tried and noted riders from the stations near and far
   Had mustered at the homestead overnight,
For the bushmen love hard riding where the wild bush horses are,
   And the stock-horse snuffs the battle with delight.

There was Harrison, who made his pile when Pardon won the cup,
   The old man with his hair as white as snow;
But few could ride beside him when his blood was fairly up—
   He would go wherever horse and man could go.
And Clancy of the Overflow came down to lend a hand,
   No better horseman ever held the reins;
For never horse could throw him while the saddle-girths would
     stand—
   He learnt to ride while droving on the plains.

And one was there, a stripling on a small and weedy beast;
   He was something like a racehorse undersized,
With a touch of Timor pony—three parts thoroughbred at least—
   And such as are by mountain horsemen prized.
He was hard and tough and wiry—just the sort that won't say die—
   There was courage in his quick impatient tread;
And he bore the badge of gameness in his bright and fiery eye,
   And the proud and lofty carriage of his head.

But still so slight and weedy, one would doubt his power to stay,
   And the old man said, "That horse will never do
For a long and tiring gallop—lad, you'd better stop away,
   Those hills are far too rough for such as you."
So he waited, sad and wistful—only Clancy stood his friend—
   "I think we ought to let him come," he said;
"I warrant he'll be with us when he's wanted at the end,
   For both his horse and he are mountain bred.

"He hails from Snowy River, up by Kosciusko's side,
   Where the hills are twice as steep and twice as rough;
Where a horse's hoofs strike firelight from the flint stones every
     stride,
   The man that holds his own is good enough.

And the Snowy River riders on the mountains make their home,
　Where the river runs those giant hills between;
I have seen full many horsemen since I first commenced to roam,
　But nowhere yet such horsemen have I seen."

So he went; they found the horses by the big mimosa clump,
　They raced away towards the mountain's brow,
And the old man gave his orders, "Boys, go at them from the jump,
　No use to try for fancy riding now.
And, Clancy, you must wheel them, try and wheel them to the
　　right.
　Ride boldly, lad, and never fear the spills,
For never yet was rider that could keep the mob in sight,
　If once they gain the shelter of those hills."

So Clancy rode to wheel them—he was racing on the wing
　Where the best and boldest riders take their place,
And he raced his stock-horse past them, and he made the ranges
　　ring
　With the stockwhip, as he met them face to face.
Then they halted for a moment, while he swung the dreaded lash,
　But they saw their well-loved mountain full in view,
And they charged beneath the stockwhip with a sharp and sudden
　　dash,
　And off into the mountain scrub they flew.

Then fast the horsemen followed, where the gorges deep and black
　Resounded to the thunder of their tread,
And the stockwhips woke the echoes and they fiercely answered
　　back
　From cliffs and crags that beetled overhead.
And upward, ever upward, the wild horses held their way,
　Where mountain ash and kurrajong grew wide;
And the old man muttered fiercely, "We may bid the mob good day,
　No man can hold them down the other side."

When they reached the mountain's summit, even Clancy took a
　　pull—
　It well might make the boldest hold their breath;
The wild hop scrub grew thickly, and the hidden ground was full
　Of wombat holes, and any slip was death.
But the man from Snowy River let the pony have his head,
　And he swung his stockwhip round and gave a cheer,
And he raced him down the mountain like a torrent down its bed,
　While the others stood and watched in very fear.

He sent the flint-stones flying, but the pony kept his feet,
　He cleared the fallen timber in his stride,
And the man from Snowy River never shifted in his seat—
　It was grand to see that mountain horseman ride.

Through the stringy barks and saplings, on the rough and broken
     ground,
   Down the hillside at a racing pace he went;
And he never drew the bridle till he landed safe and sound
   At the bottom of that terrible descent.

He was right among the horses as they climbed the farther hill,
   And the watchers on the mountain, standing mute,
Saw him ply the stockwhip fiercely; he was right among them still,
   As he raced across the clearing in pursuit.
Then they lost him for a moment, where two mountain gullies met
   In the ranges— but a final glimpse reveals
On a dim and distant hillside the wild horses racing yet,
   With the man from Snowy River at their heels.

And he ran them single-handed till their sides were white with
     foam;
   He followed like a bloodhound on their track,
Till they halted, cowed and beaten; then he turned their heads for
     home,
   And alone and unassisted brought them back.
But his hardy mountain pony he could scarcely raise a trot,
   He was blood from hip to shoulder from the spur;
But his pluck was still undaunted, and his courage fiery hot,
   For never yet was mountain horse a cur.

And down by Kosciusko, where the pine-clad ridges raise
   Their torn and rugged battlements on high,
Where the air is clear as crystal, and the white stars fairly blaze
   At midnight in the cold and frosty sky,
And where around the Overflow the reed-beds sweep and sway
   To the breezes, and the rolling plains are wide,
The Man from Snowy River is a household word today,
   And the stockmen tell the story of his ride.

CLANCY OF THE OVERFLOW

I had written him a letter which I had, for want of better
   Knowledge, sent to where I met him down the Lachlan years ago;
He was shearing when I knew him, so I sent the letter to him,
   Just on spec, addressed as follows, "Clancy, of The Overflow."

And an answer came directed in a writing unexpected
   (And I think the same was written with a thumb-nail dipped in
     tar);
'Twas his shearing mate who wrote it, and *verbatim* I will quote it:
   "Clancy's gone to Queensland droving, and we don't know
     where he are."

In my wild erratic fancy visions come to me of Clancy
   Gone a-droving "down the Cooper" where the Western drovers
      go;
As the stock are slowly stringing, Clancy rides behind them singing,
   For the drover's life has pleasures that the townsfolk never know.

And the bush has friends to meet him, and their kindly voices greet
   him
   In the murmur of the breezes and the river on its bars,
And he sees the vision splendid of the sunlit plains extended,
   And at night the wondrous glory of the everlasting stars.

I am sitting in my dingy little office, where a stingy
   Ray of sunlight struggles feebly down between the houses tall,
And the foetid air and gritty of the dusty, dirty city,
   Through the open window floating, spreads its foulness over all.

And in place of lowing cattle, I can hear the fiendish rattle
   Of the tramways and the buses making hurry down the street;
And the language uninviting of the gutter children fighting
   Comes fitfully and faintly through the ceaseless tramp of feet.

And the hurrying people daunt me, and their pallid faces haunt me
   As they shoulder one another in their rush and nervous haste,
With their eager eyes and greedy, and their stunted forms and
   weedy,
   For townsfolk have no time to grow, they have no time to waste.

And I somehow rather fancy that I'd like to change with Clancy,
   Like to take a turn at droving where the seasons come and go,
While he faced the round eternal of the cash-book and the journal—
   But I doubt he'd suit the office, Clancy, of The Overflow.

HENRY LAWSON   (1867–1922)

Short story writer, poet. Born in N.S.W., had a rudimentary
education.

THE UNION BURIES ITS DEAD

While out boating one Sunday afternoon on a billabong across the
river, we saw a young man on horse-back driving some horses along
the bank. He said it was a fine day, and asked if the water was deep
there. The joker of our party said it was deep enough to drown him,
and he laughed and rode further up. We didn't take much notice of
him.

Next day a funeral gathered at a corner pub and asked each other in to have a drink while waiting for the hearse. They passed away some of the time dancing jigs to a piano in the bar parlour. They passed away the rest of the time sky-larking and fighting.

The defunct was a young union labourer, about twenty-five, who had been drowned the previous day while trying to swim some horses across a billabong of the Darling.

He was almost a stranger in town, and the fact of his having been a union man accounted for the funeral. The police found some union papers in his swag, and called at the General Labourers' Union Office for information about him. That's how we knew. The secretary had very little information to give. The departed was a 'Roman,' and the majority of the town were otherwise—but unionism is stronger than creed. Drink, however, is stronger than unionism; and, when the hearse presently arrived, more than two-thirds of the funeral were unable to follow. They were too drunk.

The procession numbered fifteen, fourteen souls following the broken shell of a soul. Perhaps not one of the fourteen possessed a soul any more than the corpse did—but that doesn't matter.

Four or five of the funeral, who were boarders at the pub, borrowed a trap which the landlord used to carry passengers to and from the railway station. They were strangers to us who were on foot, and we to them. We were all strangers to the corpse.

A horseman, who looked like a drover just returned from a big trip, dropped into our dusty wake and followed us a few hundred yards, dragging his pack-horse behind him, but a friend made wild and demonstrative signals from a hotel verandah—hooking at the air in front with his right hand and jobbing his left thumb over his shoulder in the direction of the bar—so the drover hauled off and didn't catch up to us any more. He was a stranger to the entire show.

We walked in twos. There were three twos. It was very hot and dusty; the heat rushed in fierce dazzling rays across every iron roof and light coloured wall that was turned to the sun. One or two pubs closed respectfully until we got past. They closed their bar doors and the patrons went in and out through some side or back entrance for a few minutes. Bushmen seldom grumble at an inconvenience of this sort, when it is caused by a funeral. They have too much respect for the dead.

On the way to the cemetery we passed three shearers sitting on the shady side of a fence. One was drunk—very drunk. The other two covered their right ears with their hats, out of respect for the departed—whoever he might have been—and one of them kicked the drunk and muttered something to him.

He straightened himself up, stared, and reached helplessly for his hat, which he shoved half off and then on again. Then he made a great effort to pull himself together—and succeeded. He stood up, braced his back against the fence, knocked off his hat, and remorsefully placed his foot on it—to keep it off his head till the funeral passed.

A tall sentimental drover, who walked by my side, cynically quoted Byronic verses suitable to the occasion—to death—and asked with pathetic humour whether we thought the dead man's ticket would be recognised 'over yonder.' It was a G.L.U. ticket, and the general opinion was that it would be recognised.

Presently my friend said:

'You remember, when we were in the boat yesterday, we saw a man driving some horses along the bank?'

'Yes.'

He nodded at the hearse and said:

'Well, that's him.'

I thought awhile.

'I didn't take any particular notice of him,' I said. 'He said something, didn't he?'

'Yes; said it was a fine day. You'd have taken more notice if you'd known that he was doomed to die in the hour and that those were the last words he would say to any man in this world.'

'To be sure,' said a full voice from the rear. 'If ye'd known that ye'd have prolonged the conversation.'

We plodded on across the railway line and along the hot, dusty road which ran to the cemetery, some of us talking about the accident, and lying about the narrow escapes we had had ourselves. Presently someone said:

'There's the Devil.'

I looked up and saw a priest standing in the shade of the tree by the cemetery gate.

The hearse was drawn up and the tail-boards were opened. The funeral extinguished its right ear with its hat as four men lifted the coffin out and laid it over the grave. The priest—a pale, quiet young fellow—stood under the shade of a sapling which grew at the head of the grave. He took off his hat, dropped it carelessly on the ground, and proceeded to business. I noticed that one or two heathens winced slightly when the holy water was sprinkled on the coffin. The drops quickly evaporated, and the little round black spots they left were soon dusted over; but the spots showed, by contrast, the cheapness and shabbiness of the cloth with which the coffin was covered. It seemed black before;—now it looked a dusky grey.

Just here man's ignorance and vanity made a farce of the funeral. A big bull-necked publican, with heavy, blotchy features, and a supremely ignorant expression, picked up the priest's straw hat and held it about two inches over the head of his reverence during the whole of the service. The father, be it remembered, was standing in the shade. A few shoved their hats on and off uneasily, struggling between their disgust for the living and their respect for the dead.

The hat had a conical crown and a brim sloping down all round like a sunshade, and the publican held it with his great red claw spread over the crown. To do the priest justice, perhaps he didn't notice the incident. A stage priest or parson in the same position might have said, 'Put the hat down, my friend; is not the memory of our departed brother worth more than my complexion?' A wattlebark layman might have expressed himself in stronger language, none the less to the point. But my priest seemed unconscious of what was going on. Besides, the publican was a great and important pillar of the church. He couldn't, as an ignorant and conceited ass, lose such a good opportunity of asserting his faithfulness and importance to his church.

The grave looked very narrow under the coffin, and I drew a breath of relief when the box slid easily down. I saw a coffin get stuck once, at Rookwood, and it had to be yanked out with difficulty, and laid on the sods at the feet of the heart-broken relations, who howled dismally while the grave-diggers widened the hole. But they don't cut contracts so fine in the West. Our grave-digger was not altogether bowelless, and, out of respect for that human quality described as 'feelin's,' he scraped up some light and dusty soil and threw it down to deaden the fall of the clay lumps on the coffin. He also tried to steer the first few shovelsful gently down against the end of the grave with the back of the shovel turned outwards, but the hard dry Darling River clods rebounded and knocked all the same. It didn't matter much—nothing does. The fall of lumps of clay on a stranger's coffin doesn't sound any different from the fall of the same things on an ordinary wooden box—at least I didn't notice anything awesome or unusual in the sound; but, perhaps, one of us—the most sensitive—might have been impressed by being reminded of a burial of long ago, when the thump of every sod jolted his heart.

I have left out the wattle—because it wasn't there. I have also neglected to mention the heart-broken old mate, with his grizzled head bowed and great pearly drops streaming down his rugged cheeks. He was absent—he was probably 'Out Back.' For similar reasons I have omitted reference to the suspicious moisture in the eyes of a bearded bush ruffian named Bill. Bill failed to turn up, and the only moisture was that which was induced by the heat. I left out the 'sad Australian sunset' because the sun was not going down at the time. The burial took place exactly at mid-day.

The dead bushman's name was Jim, apparently; but they found no portraits, nor locks of hair, nor any love letters, nor anything of that kind in his swag—not even a reference to his mother; only some papers relating to union matters. Most of us didn't know the name till we saw it on the coffin; we knew him as 'that poor chap that got drowned yesterday.'

'So his name's James Tyson,' said my drover acquaintance, looking at the plate.

'Why! Didn't you know that before?' I asked.

'No; but I knew he was a union man.'

It turned out, afterwards, that J.T. wasn't his real name—only 'the name he went by.'

Anyhow he was buried by it, and most of the 'Great Australian Dailies' have mentioned in their brevity columns that a young man named James John Tyson was drowned in a billabong of the Darling last Sunday.

We did hear, later on, what his real name was; but if we ever chance to read it in the 'Missing Friends Column,' we shall not be able to give any information to heart-broken Mother or Sister or Wife, nor to anyone who could let him hear something to his advantage—for we have already forgotten the name.

THE BUSH UNDERTAKER

'Five Bob!'

The old man shaded his eyes and peered through the dazzling glow of that broiling Christmas Day. He stood just within the door of a slab-and-bark hut situated upon the bank of a barren creek; sheep-yards lay to the right, and a low line of bare, brown ridges formed a suitable background to the scene.

'Five Bob!' shouted he again; and a dusty sheep-dog rose wearily from the shaded side of the hut and looked inquiringly at his master, who pointed towards some sheep which were straggling from the flock.

'Fetch 'em back,' he said confidently.

The dog went off and his master returned to the interior of the hut.

'We'll yard 'em early,' he said to himself; 'the super won't know. We'll yard 'em early, and have the arternoon to ourselves.'

'We'll get dinner,' he added, glancing at some pots on the fire, 'I cud do a bit of doughboy, an' that theer boggabri'll eat like tater-marrer along of the salt meat.' He moved one of the black buckets from the blaze. 'I likes to keep it jist on the sizzle,' he said in explanation to himself; 'hard bilin' makes it tough—I'll keep it jist-a-simmerin'.'

Here his soliloquy was interrupted by the return of the dog.

'All right, Five Bob,' said the hatter, 'dinner'll be ready dreckly. Jist keep yer eye on the sheep till I calls yer; keep 'em well rounded up, an' we'll yard 'em afterwards and have a holiday.'

This speech was accompanied by a gesture evidently intelligible, for the dog retired as though he understood English, and the cooking proceeded.

'I'll take a pick an' shovel with me an' root up that old black fellow,' mused the shepherd, evidently following up a recent train of thought; 'I reckon it'll do now. I'll put in the spuds.'

The last sentence referred to the cooking, the first to a black fellow's grave about which he was curious.

'The sheep's a-campin',' said the soliloquiser, glancing through the door. 'So me an' Five Bob 'll be able to get our dinner in peace. I wish I had just enough fat to make the pan siss; I'd treat myself to a leather-jacket; but it took three weeks' skimmin' to get enough for them theer doughboys.'

In due time the dinner was dished up; and the old man seated himself on a block, with the lid of a gin-case across his knees for a table. Five Bob squatted opposite with the liveliest interest and appreciation depicted on his intelligent countenance.

Dinner proceeded very quietly, except when the carver paused to ask the dog how some tasty morsel went with him, and Five Bob's tail declared that it went very well indeed.

'Here y'are, try this,' cried the old man, tossing him a large piece of doughboy. A click of Five Bob's jaws and the dough was gone.

'Clean into his liver!' said the old man with a faint smile.

He washed up the tinware in the water the duff had been boiled in, and then, with the assistance of the dog, yarded the sheep.

This accomplished, he took a pick and shovel and an old sack, and started out over the ridge, followed, of course, by his four-legged mate. After tramping some three miles he reached a spur, running out from the main ridge. At the extreme end of this, under some gum-trees, was a little mound of earth, barely defined in the grass and indented in the centre as all blackfellows' graves were.

He set to work to dig it up, and sure enough, in about half an hour he bottomed on payable dirt.

When he had raked up all the bones, he amused himself by putting them together on the grass and by speculating as to whether they had belonged to black or white, male or female. Failing, however, to arrive at any satisfactory conclusion, he dusted them with great care, put them in the bag, and started for home.

He took a short cut this time over the ridge and down a gully which was full of ring-barked trees and long white grass. He had nearly reached its mouth when a great greasy black iguana clambered up a sapling from under his feet and looked fightable.

'Dang the jumpt-up thing!' cried the old man. 'It gin me a start!'

At the foot of the sapling he espied an object which he at first thought was the blackened carcass of a sheep, but on closer examination discovered to be the body of a man; it lay with its forehead resting on its hands, dried to a mummy by the intense heat of the western summer.

'Me luck's in for the day and no mistake!' said the shepherd, scratching the back of his head, while he took stock of the remains. He picked up a stick and tapped the body on the shoulder; the flesh sounded like leather. He turned it over on its side; it fell flat on its back like a board, and the shrivelled eyes seemed to peer up at him from under the blackened wrists.

He stepped back involuntarily, but, recovering himself, leant on his stick and took in all the ghastly details.

There was nothing in the blackened features to tell aught of name or race, but the dress proclaimed the remains to be those of a European. The old man caught sight of a black bottle in the grass, close beside the corpse. This set him thinking. Presently he knelt down and examined the soles of the dead man's Blucher boots, and then, rising with an air of conviction, exclaimed: 'Brummy! by gosh!—busted up at last!'

'I tole yer so, Brummy;' he said impressively, addressing the corpse, 'I allers told yer as how it 'ud be—an' here y'are, you thundering jumpt-up cuss-o'-God fool. Yer cud earn mor'n any man in the colony, but yer'd lush it all away. I allers sed as how it 'ud end, an' now yer kin see fur y'self.'

'I spect yer was a comin' t' me t' get fixt up an' set straight agin; then yer was agoin' to swear off, same as yer allers did; an' here y'are, an' now I expect I'll have t' fix yer up for the last time an' make yer decent, for 'twon't do t' leave yer a-lyin' out here like a dead sheep.'

He picked up the corked bottle and examined it. To his great surprise it was nearly full of rum.

'Well, this gits me,' exclaimed the old man; 'me luck's in, this Christmas, an' no mistake. He must a' got the jams early in his spree, or he wouldn't be a-making for me with near a bottleful left. Howsomenever, here goes.'

Looking round, his eyes lit up with satisfaction as he saw some waste bits of bark which had been left by a party of strippers who had been getting bark there for the stations. He picked up two pieces, one about four and the other six feet long, and each about two feet wide, and brought them over to the body. He laid the longest strip by the side of the corpse, which he proceeded to lift on to it.

'Come on, Brummy,' he said, in a softer tone than usual, 'yer ain't as bad as yer might be, considerin' as it must be three good months since yer slipped yer wind. I spect it was the rum as preserved yer. It was the death of yer when yer was alive, an' now yer dead, it preserves yer like—like a mummy.'

Then he placed the other strip on top, with the hollow side downwards—thus sandwiching the defunct between the two pieces—removed the saddle strap, which he wore for a belt, and buckled it round one end, while he tried to think of something to tie up the other with.

'I can't take any more strips off my shirt,' he said, critically examining the skirts of the old blue overshirt he wore. 'I might get a strip or two more off, but it's short enough already. Let's see; how long have I been awearin' of that shirt; Oh, I remember, I bought it jist two days afore Five Bob was pupped. I can't afford a new shirt jist yet; howsomenever, seein' it's Brummy, I'll jist borrow a couple more strips and sew 'em on agen when I git home.'

He up-ended Brummy, and placing his shoulder against the middle of the lower sheet of bark, lifted the corpse to a horizontal position; then taking the bag of bones in his hand, he started for home.

'I ain't a-spendin' sech a dull Christmas arter all,' he reflected, as he plodded on; but he had not walked above a hundred yards when he saw a black iguana sidling into the grass by the side of the path.

'That's another of them theer dang things!' he exclaimed. 'That's two I've seed this mornin'.'

Presently he remarked: 'Yer don't smell none too sweet, Brummy. It must 'a' been jist about the middle of shearin' when yer pegged out. I wonder who got yer last cheque. Shoo! theer's another black gohanner—theer must be a flock on 'em.'

He rested Brummy on the ground while he had another pull at the bottle, and, before going on, packed the bag of bones on his shoulder under the body, but he soon stopped again.

'The thunderin' jumpt-up bones is all skew-whift,' he said, ''Ole on, Brummy, an' I'll fix 'em;' and he leaned the dead man against a tree while he settled the bones on his shoulder, and took another pull at the bottle.

About a mile further on he heard a rustling in the grass to the right, and, looking round, saw another iguana gliding off sideways, with its long snaky neck turned towards him.

This puzzled the shepherd considerably, the strangest part of it being that Five Bob wouldn't touch the reptile, but slunk off with his tail down when ordered to 'sick 'em.'

'Theer's sothin' comic about them theer gohanners,' said the old man at last. "I've seed swarms of grasshoppers an' big mobs of kangaroos, but dang me if ever I seed a flock of black gohanners afore!'

On reaching the hut the old man dumped the corpse against the wall, wrong end up, and stood scratching his head while he endeavoured to collect his muddled thoughts; but he had not placed Brummy at the correct angle, and, consequently, that individual fell forward amd struck him a violent blow on the shoulder with the iron toes of his Blucher boots.

The shock sobered him. He sprang a good yard, instinctively hitching up his moleskins in preparation for flight; but a backward glance revealed to him the true cause of his supposed attack from the rear. Then he lifted the body, stood it on its feet against the chimney, and ruminated as to where he should lodge his mate for the night, not noticing that the shorter sheet of bark had slipped down on the boots and left the face exposed.

'I spect I'll have ter put yer into the chimney-trough for the night, Brummy,' said he, turning round to confront the corpse. 'Yer can't expect me to take yer into the hut, though I did it when yer was in a worse state than—Lord!'

The shepherd was not prepared for the awful scrutiny that gleamed on him from those empty sockets; his nerves received a shock, and it was some time before he recovered himself sufficiently to speak.

'Now look a-here, Brummy,' said he, shaking his finger severely at the delinquent, 'I don't want to pick a row with yer; I'd do as much for yer an' more than any other man, an' well yer knows it; but if yer starts playin' any of yer jumpt-up pranktical jokes on me, and a scarin' of me after a-humpin' of yer 'ome, by the 'oly frost I'll kick yer to jim-rags, so I will.'

This admonition delivered, he hoisted Brummy into the chimney trough, and with a last glance towards the sheep-yards, he retired to his bunk to have, as he said, a snooze.

He had more than a 'snooze' however, for when he woke, it was dark, and the bushman's instinct told him it must be nearly nine o'clock.

He lit a slush lamp and poured the remainder of the rum into a pannikin; but, just as he was about to lift the draught to his lips he heard a peculiar rustling sound overhead, and put the pot down on the table with a slam that spilled some of the precious liquor.

Five Bob whimpered, and the old shepherd, though used, as one living alone in the bush must necessarily be, to the weird and dismal, felt the icy breath of fear at his heart.

He reached hastily for his old shot-gun, and went out to investigate. He walked round the hut several times and examined the roof on all sides, but saw nothing. Brummy appeared to be in the same position.

At last, persuading himself that the noise was caused by 'possums or the wind, the old man went inside, boiled his billy; and after composing his nerves somewhat with a light supper and a meditative smoke, retired for the night. He was aroused several times before midnight by the same mysterious sound overhead, but, though he rose and examined the roof on each occasion by the light of the rising moon, he discovered nothing.

At last he determined to sit up and watch until daybreak, and for this purpose took up a position on a log a short distance from the hut, with his gun laid in readiness across his knee.

After watching for about an hour, he saw a black object coming over the ridge-pole. He grabbed his gun and fired. The thing disappeared. He ran round to the other side of the hut, and there was a great black iguana in violent convulsions on the ground.

Then the old man saw it all. 'The thunderin' jumpt-up thing has been a-havin' o' me,' he exclaimed. 'The same cuss-o'-God wretch has a-followed me 'ome, an' has been a-havin' its Christmas dinner off of Brummy, an' a-hauntin' o' me into the bargain, the jumpt-up tinker!'

As there was no one by whom he could send a message to the station, and the old man dared not leave the sheep and go himself, he determined to bury the body the next afternoon, reflecting that the authorities could disinter it for inquest if they pleased.

So he brought the sheep home early, and made arrangements for the burial by measuring the outer casing of Brummy and digging a hole according to those dimensions.

'That 'minds me,' he said, 'I never rightly knowed Brummy's religion, blest if ever I did. Howsomenever, there's one thing sartin— none o' them theer pianer-fingered parsons is a-goin' ter take the trouble ter travel out inter this God-forgotten part to hold sarvice over him, seein' as how his last cheque's blued. But, as I've got the fun'ral arrangements all in me own hands, I'll do jestice to it, and see that Brummy has a good comfortable buryin'—and more's unpossible.'

'It's time yer turned in Brum,' he said, lifting the body down.

He carried it to the grave and dropped it into one corner like a post. He arranged the bark so as to cover the face, and, by means of a piece of clothes line, lowered the body to a horizontal position. Then he threw in an armful of gum leaves, and then, very reluctantly, took the shovel and dropped in a few shovelfuls of earth.

'An' this is the last of Brummy,' he said, leaning on his spade and looking away over the tops of the ragged gums on the distant range.

This reflection seemed to engender a flood of memories, in which the old man became absorbed. He leaned heavily upon his spade and thought.

'Arter all,' he murmured sadly. 'Arter all—it were Brummy.'

'Brummy,' he said at last, 'it's all over now; nothin' matters now—nothin' didn't ever matter, nor—nor don't. You uster say as how it 'ud be all right termorrer' (pause); 'termorrer's come, Brummy—come fur you—it ain't come fur me yet, but—it's a-comin'.'

He threw in some more earth.

'Yer don't remember, Brummy, an' mebbe yer don't want to remember—*I* don't want to remember—but—well, but, yer see that's where yer got the pull on me.'

He shovelled in some more earth and paused again.

The dog rose, with ears erect, and looked anxiously first at his master and then into the grave.

'Theer oughter be somethin' sed,' muttered the old man; ''tain't right to put 'im under like a dog. There oughter be some sort o' sarmin.' He sighed heavily in the listening silence that followed this remark and proceeded with his work. He filled the grave to the brim this time, and fashioned the mound carefully with his spade. Once or twice he muttered the words, 'I am the rassaraction.' He was evidently trying to remember, as he laid the tools quietly aside, and stood at the head of the grave, the something that ought to be said. He removed his hat, placed it carefully on the grass, held his hands out from his sides and a little to the front, drew a long deep breath, and said with a solemnity that greatly disturbed Five Bob, 'Hashes ter hashes, dus ter dus, Brummy,—an'—an' in hopes of a great an' gerlorious rassaraction!'

He sat down on a log near by, rested his elbows on his knees and passed his hand wearily over his forehead—but only as one who was tired and felt the heat; and presently he rose, took up the tools and walked back to the hut.

And the sun sank again on the grand Australian bush—the nurse and tutor of eccentric minds, the home of the weird, and of much that is different from things in other lands.

ERNEST FAVENC   (1845–1908)

Novelist, short story writer, journalist, poet. Born in London; educated in England and Germany; came to Australia in 1863.

PREFACE TO VOICES OF THE DESERT

The belief that prevailed so long; and the expression of which belief is still to be found in the text of old geographies and maps, namely, that the interior of Australia is one vast desert, has at last been dispelled, but it died hard and struggled to the last for existence. There was some excuse for this widely distributed belief, inasmuch as certain large areas exist in the interior which, as far as human vision can foresee, must ever remain desolate and uninhabitable, and there are enough of these areas to amply justify the old desert theory. The long-protracted droughts too, at times, turn the best inland country into a desert; but the real desert lands of Australia are the tracts of country whereon nothing but spinifex and a few stunted apologies for trees grow. Spinifex, the detested porcupine-grass of Australia, will thrive in barren sand or on a thin coating of gravel covering a solid rock. It can dispense with all moisture, and the future of this description of country seems utterly hopeless.

There are perhaps no absolutely rainless zones on this continent, but there are some parts of western, central Australia where the rainfall is so insignificant that such areas almost merit the title of rainless. In these districts, wherein even the starved natives of the Great Plain seldom venture, and where—if untouched by fire—the spinifex piles itself up in great banks, as impenetrable as a barbed-wire entanglement, the striking feature is, the absolute and utter stillness that prevails. If there is such a thing as darkness which can be felt, then the Australian desert possesses a silence which can be heard, so much does it oppress the intruder into these solitudes. One might remain there a long day and night and never hear as much sound as would be caused by the rustle of a leaf, for a breathless calm broods, at intervals, over the untrodden wilds, and of life there is none, save and only the ever-pervading ants.

Repellent as this country is, there is a wondrous fascination in it, in its strange loneliness and the hidden mysteries it might contain, that calls to the man who has once known it, as surely as the sea calls to the sailor. To pass a night alone in the desert spinifex country, is to feel as much cut off from the ordinary life of the world as one could feel if transplanted to another sphere. The motionless air, so dry and devoid of moisture that a polished gun-barrel can lie exposed to it and remain untouched by a speck of rust, seems to bring the stars nearer to the earth and enhance the beauty of their rays. The ordinary light of the moon is coarse and garish compared to the pure effulgence of the larger planets. On a moonless night the coming of the morning star is heralded by a breaking light that might well be mistaken for the dawn. Like a cold, white flame the planet rises, and to watch its ascent from the horizon gives a man the feeling that he is watching the birth of a new world.

A land such as this, with its great loneliness, its dearth of life, and its enshrouding atmosphere of awe and mystery, has a voice of its own, distinctly different from that of the ordinary Australian bush. To this voice I have, in some of the following verses, tried to give imperfect expression. That the themes inspired by the desert and its surroundings are more mournful than joyous, and the pessimistic view of life more in evidence than the sanguine, is but natural, for, such as these verses are, they were desert-born, and to look back at the time of the birth of some of them, the circumstances and surroundings that inspired them, is to me a memory-picture of the best days of my life.

ARTHUR HENRY ADAMS   (1872–1936)

Playwright, poet, short story writer, novelist. Born and educated in New Zealand; came to Australia about 1898.

THE AUSTRALIAN

Once more this Autumn-earth is ripe,
Parturient of another type.

While with the Past old nations merge
His foot is on the Future's verge.

They watch him, as they huddle, pent,
Striding a spacious continent,

Above the level desert's marge
Looming in his aloofness large.

No flower with fragile sweetness graced—
A lank weed wrestling with the waste;

Pallid of face and gaunt of limb,
The sweetness withered out of him;

Sombre, indomitable, wan,
The juices dried, the glad youth gone.

A little weary from his birth,
His laugh the spectre of a mirth,

Bitter beneath a bitter sky,
To Nature he has no reply.

Wanton, perhaps, and cruel. Yes,
Is not his sun more merciless?

So drab and neutral is his day,
He finds a splendor in the grey,

And from his life's monotony
He draws a dreary melody.

When earth so poor a banquet makes
His pleasures at a gulp he takes;

The feast is his to the last crumb:
Drink while he can ... the drought will come.

His heart a sudden tropic flower,
He loves and loathes within an hour.

Yet you who by the pools abide,
Judge not the man who swerves aside;

He sees beyond your hazy fears;
He roads the desert of the years;

Rearing his cities in the sand,
He builds where even God has banned;

With green a continent he crowns,
And stars a wilderness with towns;

With paths the distances he snares:
His gyves of steel the great plain wears.

A child who takes a world for toy,
To build a nation or destroy,

His childish features frozen stern,
His manhood's task he has to learn—

From feeble tribes to federate
One white and peace-encompassed State.

But if there be no goal to reach? ...
The track lies open, dawns beseech!

Enough that he lay down his load
A little further on the road.

So, toward undreamt-of destinies
He slouches down the centuries.

GEORGE GORDON McCRAE   (1833–1927)

Poet. Born in Scotland; came to Australia in 1841; privately educated.

IN A BUSH HUT

And here they'd sit a-nights before the blaze,
The fire-light glory on their happy faces
In ever-lambent, gently-flickering rays,
As red the reeling sparks in random races
Flew up the chimney on their aimless ways
To fade and fall in different other places,
And dream some casual happy hour away,
More blest than any in the coming day.

Or, with the half-door open—that's to say,
The upper half flung back against the wall—
They'd listen to such birds, as all the day
Kept silence, waiting for the night to fall.
The moon-faced owl, that loves the twilight grey,
Lone on his perch on yon white gum-tree tall,
Of aspect grave and solemn and official,
And air and bearing of the Bench judicial.

The mope-hawk's melancholy cuckoo-note,
The plaint of plover o'er the dark plain fleeting,
In hurrying rush where overhead afloat,
The swan's broad wings the cool night-air are beating
In homeward flight, wild song in every throat,
The joy of glad return in turn repeating:
While from the far lagoon, 'mid reed and rushes,
Bursts forth the clank of frogs among the hushes.

And, booming through the turf in vibrant din,
The great ground-cricket's braying oboe solo,
With burr and jar, and wandering notes that twin,
Now, down beneath the door in rich tremolo,
And—presto!—far the thicket's belt within
With shrill and strident sound that nigh goes through you,
A sound 'twere hard to shape in phrase colloquial,
A sort of *ignis fatuus* ventriloquial.

There, 'neath a moon adrift in flying scud,
As wails the dingo stealing through the ranges,
With eldritch cries that freeze the very blood
In all their ululant and ugly changes,
And fright the startled echoes of the flood
Where sleepy, sings the creek; surely strange is
To pass one moonlight night here, whose grey glamour
Is not invaded by his long-drawn clamour.

They've closed the door, made fast and all secure,
Shut out the moon and stars; the meteors racing
Across the steely sky, now clear and pure,
Grey drift no more grey drifts across it chasing,
To seek their bourne past where the hills endure
And wind-lulled boughs and branches are embracing;
Shut out with these, Night's voices wild and eerie,
A-wander 'mid the ranges dark and dreary.

The fire's all one red glow; the embers sigh;
The flickering light on floor and wall is dancing
With cheerful glint on knives and gun borne high,
From pistol's steel and brass and silver glancing,
In fitful dalliance glad, 'tween far and nigh,
All joyously retreating and advancing,
What rosier, gentler glow in Cupid's camp is
Than here, where all unused, their radiant lamp is.

THE SILENCE OF THE BUSH

There's that in our lone Bush, I know not what,
Which 'genders silence; I've all that to learn.
Here, there and everywhere, to loose the knot
That binds the sheaf-band of the taciturn;
It may be where it freezes; where 'tis hot,
Or streams lie silent in the nymph's cool urn;
In forest depths, or where the lone plain stretches
Sans other roof than sky, o'er heat-worn wretches.

Or 'mid the gully's fern and sassafras,
Where all is cool green glooms and early dusk,
With silvern foliage in delicious mass
As, sunwards, feel their way, the spires of musk;
Or where those solemn branches crossing, pass
And wave o'er-head their pennon'd fragrant husk;
Or by the river's marge or broad gumbower
With lily-pads a-swim and floating flower.

Here might one read the Silence of Fatigue,
And here again of Rest and Admiration.
Where gentle hands are clasped in wordless league,
And eyes meet eyes in eloquent oration,
Or fingers wreathed, accomplish mute intrigue,
Or tell by signs of ardent adoration,
Or past all these, 'neath burning rocks and bare,
The deep and death-like Silence of Despair.

BARBARA BAYNTON   (1862–1929)

Short story writer, novelist. Born in N.S.W.; educated privately;
after 1902 moved frequently between Australia and England.

THE CHOSEN VESSEL

from BUSH STUDIES

She laid the stick and her baby on the grass while she untied the rope
that tethered the calf. The length of the rope separated them. The
cow was near the calf, and both were lying down. Feed along the
creek was plentiful, and every day she found a fresh place to tether
it, since tether it she must, for if she did not, it would stray with the
cow out on the plain. She had plenty of time to go after it, but then
there was baby; and if the cow turned on her out on the plain, and
she with baby—she had been a town girl and was afraid of the cow,
but she did not want the cow to know it. She used to run at first
when it bellowed its protest against the penning up of its calf. This
satisfied the cow, also the calf, but the woman's husband was angry,
and called her—the noun was cur. It was he who forced her to run
and meet the advancing cow, brandishing a stick, and uttering threatening words till the enemy turned and ran. "That's the way!" the
man said, laughing at her white face. In many things he was worse
than the cow, and she wondered if the same rule would apply to the
man, but she was not one to provoke skirmishes even with the cow.

It was early for the calf to go "to bed"—nearly an hour earlier than usual; but she had felt so restless all day. Partly because it was Monday, and the end of the week that would bring her and baby the companionship of its father, was so far off. He was a shearer, and had gone to his shed before daylight that morning. Fifteen miles as the crow flies separated them.

There was a track in front of the house, for it had once been a wine shanty, and a few travellers passed along at intervals. She was not afraid of horsemen; but swagmen, going to, or worse, coming from the dismal, drunken little township, a day's journey beyond, terrified her. One had called at the house today, and asked for tucker.

Ah! that was why she had penned up the calf so early! She feared more from the look of his eyes, and the gleam of his teeth, as he watched her newly awakened baby beat its impatient fists upon her covered breasts, than from the knife that was sheathed in the belt at his waist.

She had given him bread and meat. Her husband, she told him, was sick. She always said that when she was alone, and a swagman came, and she had gone in from the kitchen to the bedroom, and asked questions and replied to them in the best man's voice she could assume. Then he had asked to go into the kitchen to boil his billy, but she gave him tea, and he drank it on the wood-heap. He had walked round and round the house, and there were cracks in some places, and after the last time he had asked for tobacco. She had none to give him, and he had grinned, because there was a broken clay pipe near the wood-heap where he stood, and if there were a man inside, there ought to have been tobacco. Then he asked for money, but women in the bush never have money.

At last he had gone, and she, watching through the cracks saw him when about a quarter of a mile away, turn and look back at the house. He had stood so for some moments with a pretence of fixing his swag, and then, apparently satisfied, moved to the left towards the creek. The creek made a bow round the house, and when he came to it she lost sight of him. Hours after, watching intently for signs of smoke, she saw the man's dog chasing some sheep that had gone to the creek for water, and saw it slink back suddenly, as if the man had called it.

More than once she thought of taking her baby and going to her husband. But in the past, when she had dared to speak of the dangers to which her loneliness exposed her, he had taunted and sneered at her. She need not flatter herself, he had coarsely told her, that anybody would want to run away with her.

Long before nightfall she placed food on the kitchen table, and beside it laid the big brooch that had been her mother's. It was the only thing of value that she had. And she left the kitchen door wide open.

The doors inside she securely fastened. Beside the bolt in the back one she drove in the steel and scissors; against it she piled the table and the stools. Underneath the lock of the front door she forced the handle of the spade, and the blade between the cracks in the flooring boards. Then the prop-stick, cut into lengths, held the top, as the spade held the middle. The windows were little more than portholes; she had nothing to fear through them.

She ate a few mouthfuls of food and drank a cup of milk. But she lighted no fire, and when night came, no candle, but crept with her baby to bed.

What woke her? The wonder was that she had slept—she had not meant to. But she was young, very young. Perhaps the shrinking of the galvanized roof—yet hardly, since that was so usual. Something had set her heart beating wildly; but she lay quite still, only she put her arm over her baby. Then she had both round it, and she prayed, "Little baby, little baby, don't wake!"

The moon's rays shone on the front of the house, and she saw one of the open cracks, quite close to where she lay, darken with a shadow. Then a protesting growl reached her; and she could fancy she heard the man turn hastily. She plainly heard the thud of something striking the dog's ribs, and the long flying strides of the animal as it howled and ran. Still watching, she saw the shadow darken every crack along the wall. She knew by the sounds that the man was trying every standpoint that might help him to see in; but how much he saw she could not tell. She thought of many things she might do to deceive him into the idea that she was not alone. But the sound of her voice would wake baby, and she dreaded that as though it were the only danger that threatened her. So she prayed, "Little baby, don't wake, don't cry!"

Stealthily the man crept about. She knew he had his boots off, because of the vibration that his feet caused as he walked along the veranda to gauge the width of the little window in her room, and the resistance of the front door.

Then he went to the other end, and the uncertainty of what he was doing became unendurable. She had felt safer, far safer, while he was close, and she could watch and listen. She felt she must watch, but the great fear of wakening baby again assailed her. She suddenly recalled that one of the slabs on that side of the house had shrunk in length as well as in width, and had once fallen out. It was held in position only by a wedge of wood underneath. What if he should discover that! The uncertainty increased her terror. She prayed as she gently raised herself with her little one in her arms, held tightly to her breast.

She thought of the knife, and shielded her child's body with her hands and arms. Even its little feet she covered with its white gown, and baby never murmured—it liked to be held so. Noiselessly she crossed to the other side, and stood where she could see and hear, but not be seen. He was trying every slab, and was very near to that with the wedge under it. Then she saw him find it; and heard the sound of the knife as bit by bit he began to cut away the wooden support.

She waited motionless, with her baby pressed tightly to her, though she knew that in another few minutes this man with the cruel eyes, lascivious mouth, and gleaming knife, would enter. One side of the slab tilted; he had only to cut away the remaining little end, when the slab, unless he held it, would fall outside.

She heard his jerked breathing as it kept time with the cuts of the knife, and the brush of his clothes as he rubbed the wall in his movements, for she was so still and quiet, that she did not even tremble. She knew when he ceased, and wondered why. She stood well concealed; she knew he could not see her, and that he would not fear if he did, yet she heard him move cautiously away. Perhaps he expected the slab to fall. Still his motive puzzled her, and she moved even closer, and bent her body the better to listen. Ah! what sound was that? "Listen! Listen!" she bade her heart—her heart that had kept so still, but now bounded with tumultuous throbs that dulled her ears. Nearer and nearer came the sounds, till the welcome thud of a horse's hoof rang out clearly.

"Oh, God! Oh, God! Oh, God!" she cried, for they were very close before she could make sure. She turned to the door, and with her baby in her arms tore frantically at its bolts and bars.

Out she darted at last, and running madly along, saw the horseman beyond her in the distance. She called to him in Christ's name, in her babe's name, still flying like the wind with the speed that deadly peril gives. But the distance grew greater and greater between them, and when she reached the creek her prayers turned to wild shrieks, for there crouched the man she feared, with outstretched arms that caught her as she fell. She knew he was offering terms if she ceased to struggle and cry for help, though louder and louder did she cry for it, but it was only when the man's hand gripped her throat, that the cry of "Murder" came from her lips. And when she ceased, the startled curlews took up the awful sound, and flew shrieking over the horseman's head.

"By God!" said the boundary rider, "it's been a dingo right enough! Eight killed up here, and there's more down in the creek— a ewe and a lamb, I'll bet; and the lamb's alive!" And he shut out the sky with his hand, and watched the crows that were circling round and round, nearing the earth one moment, and the next shooting skywards. By that he knew the lamb must be alive; even a dingo will spare a lamb sometimes.

Yes, the lamb was alive, and after the manner of lambs of its kind did not know its mother when the light came. It had sucked the still warm breasts, and laid its little head on her bosom, and slept till the morn. Then, when it looked at the swollen disfigured face, it wept and would have crept away, but for the hand that still clutched its little gown. Sleep was nodding its golden head and swaying its small body, and the crows were close, so close, to the mother's wide-open eyes, when the boundary rider galloped down.

"Jesus Christ!" he said, covering his eyes. He told afterwards how the little child held out its arms to him, and how he was forced to cut its gown that the dead hand held.

It was election time, and as usual the priest had selected a candidate. His choice was so obviously in the interests of the squatter, that Peter Hennessy's reason, for once in his life, had over-ridden superstition, and he had dared promise his vote to another. Yet he was uneasy, and every time he woke in the night (and it was often) he heard the murmur of his mother's voice. It came through the partition, or under the door. If through the partition he knew she was praying in her bed; but when the sounds came under the door, she was on her knees before the little altar in the corner that enshrined the statue of the Blessed Virgin and Child.

"Mary, Mother of Christ! save my son! Save him!" prayed she in the dairy as she strained and set the evening's milking. "Sweet Mary! for the love of Christ, save him!" The grief in her old face made the morning meal so bitter, that to avoid her he came late to his dinner. It made him so cowardly, that he could not say goodbye to her, and when night fell on the eve of the election day, he rode off secretly.

He had thirty miles to ride to the township to record his vote. He cantered briskly along the great stretch of plain that had nothing but stunted cottonbush to play shadow to the full moon, which glorified a sky of earliest spring. The bruised incense of the flowering clover rose up to him, and the glory of the night appealed vaguely to his imagination, but he was preoccupied with his present act of revolt.

Vividly he saw his mother's agony when she would find him gone. At that moment, he felt sure, she was praying.

"Mary! Mother of Christ!" He repeated the invocation, half unconsciously. And suddenly, out of the stillness, came Christ's name to him—called loudly in despairing accents.

"For Christ's sake! Christ's sake! Christ's sake!" called the voice. Good Catholic that he had been, he crossed himself before he dared to look back. Gliding across a ghostly patch of pipe-clay, he saw a white-robed figure with a babe clasped to her bosom.

All the superstitious awe of his race and religion swayed his brain. The moonlight on the gleaming clay was a "heavenly light" to him, and he knew the white figure not for flesh and blood, but for the Virgin and Child of his mother's prayers. Then, good Catholic that once more he was, he put spurs to his horse's sides and galloped madly away.

His mother's prayers were answered.

Hennessey was the first to record his vote—for the priest's candidate. Then he sought the priest at home, but found that he was out rallying the voters. Still, under the influence of his blessed vision, Hennessy would not go near the public-houses, but wandered about the outskirts of the town for hours, keeping apart from the townspeople, and fasting as penance. He was subdued and mildly ecstatic, feeling as a repentant chastened child, who awaits only the kiss of peace.

And at last, as he stood in the graveyard crossing himself with reverent awe, he heard in the gathering twilight the roar of many voices crying the name of the victor at the election. It was well with the priest.

Again Hennessey sought him., He sat at home, the housekeeper said, and led him into the dimly-lighted study. His seat was immediately opposite a large picture, and as the housekeeper turned up the lamp, once more the face of the Madonna and Child looked down on him, but this time silently, peacefully. The half-parted lips of the Virgin were smiling with compassionate tenderness; her eyes seemed to beam with the forgiveness of an earthly mother for her erring but beloved child.

He fell on his knees in adoration. Transfixed, the wondering priest stood, for, mingled with the adoration, "My Lord and my God!" was the exaltation, "And hast Thou chosen me?"

"What is it, Peter?" said the priest.

"Father," he answered reverently, and with loosened tongue he poured forth the story of his vision.

"Great God!" shouted the priest, "and you did not stop to save her! Have you not heard?"

Many miles further down the creek a man kept throwing an old cap into a waterhole. The dog would bring it out and lay it on the opposite side to where the man stood, but would not allow the man to catch him, though it was only to wash the blood of the sheep from his mouth and throat, for the sight of blood made the man tremble.

JAMES LISTER CUTHBERTSON   (1851–1910)

Poet. Born in Glasgow; educated at Oxford; came to Australia in 1874.

THE BUSH

Give us from dawn to dark
   Blue of Australian skies,
Let there be none to mark
   Whither our pathway lies.

Give us when noontide comes
   Rest in the woodland free—
Fragrant breath of the gums,
   Cold, sweet scent of the sea.

Give us the wattle's gold
   And the dew-laden air,
And the loveliness bold
   Loneliest landscapes wear.

These are the haunts we love,
   Glad with enchanted hours,
Bright as the heavens above,
   Fresh as the wild bush flowers.

VICTOR DALEY   ('Creeve Roe') (1858–1905)

Poet, journalist. Born in Ireland; educated in England; came to Australia in 1878.

DREAMS

I have been dreaming all a summer day
Of rare and dainty poems I would write;
Love-lyrics delicate as lilac-scent,
Soft idylls woven of wind, and flower, and stream,
And songs and sonnets carven in fine gold.

The day is fading and the dusk is cold;
Out of the skies has gone the opal gleam,
Out of my heart has passed the high intent
Into the shadow of the falling night—
Must all my dreams in darkness pass away?

I have been dreaming all a summer day:
Shall I go dreaming so until Life's light
Fades in Death's dusk, and all my days are spent?
Ah, what am I the dreamer but a dream!
The day is fading and the dusk is cold.

My songs and sonnets carven in fine gold
Have faded from me with the last day-beam
That purple lustre to the sea-line lent,
And flushed the clouds with rose and chrysolite;
So days and dreams in darkness pass away.

I have been dreaming all a summer day
Of songs and sonnets carven in fine gold;
But all my dreams in darkness pass away;
The day is fading, and the dusk is cold.

THE CALL OF THE CITY

There is a saying of renown—
'God made the country, man the town.'
Well, everybody to his trade!
But man likes best the thing he made.
The town has little space to spare;
The country has both space and air;
The town's confined, the country free—
Yet, spite of all, the town for me.

For when the hills are grey and night is falling,
And the winds sigh drearily,
I hear the city calling, calling, calling,
With a voice like the great sea.

I used to think I'd like to be
A hermit living lonesomely,
Apart from human care or ken,
Apart from all the haunts of men:
Then I would read in Nature's book,
And drink clear water from the brook,
And live a life of sweet content,
In hollow tree, or cave, or tent.

This was a dream of callow Youth
Which always overleaps the truth,
And thinks, fond fool, it is the sum
Of things that are and things to come.
But now, when youth has gone from me,
I crave for genial company.

For Nature wild I still have zest,
But human nature I love best.

I know that hayseed in the hair
Than grit and grime is healthier,
And that the scent of gums is far
More sweet than reek of pavement-tar.
I know, too, that the breath of kine
Is safer than the smell of wine;
I know that here my days are free—
But, ah! the city calls to me.

Let Zimmerman and all his brood
Proclaim the charms of Solitude,
I'd rather walk down Hunter-street
And meet a man I like to meet,
And talk with him about old times,
And how the market is for rhymès,
Between two drinks, than hold commune
Upon a mountain with the moon.

A soft wind in the gully deep
Is singing all the trees to sleep;
And in the sweet air there is balm,
And Peace is here, and here is Calm.
God knows how these I yearned to find!
Yet I must leave them all behind,
And rise and go—come sun, come rain—
Back to the Sorceress again.

For at the dawn or when the night is falling,
  Or at noon when shadows flee,
I hear the city calling, calling, calling,
  Through the long lone hours to me.

CORREGGIO JONES

Correggio Jones an artist was
  Of pure Australian race,
But native subjects scorned because
  They were too commonplace.

The Bush with all its secrets grim,
  And solemn mystery,
No fascination had for him:
  He had no eyes to see

The long sad spectral desert-march
  Of brave Explorers dead,
Who perished—while the burning arc
  Of blue laughed overhead;

The Solitary Man who stares
  At the mirage so fair,
While Death steals on him unawares
  And grasps him by the hair;

The Lonely Tree that sadly stands,
  With no green neighbour nigh,
And stretches forth its bleached, dead hands,
  For pity to the sky;

The Grey Prospector, weird of dress,
  And wearied overmuch,
Who dies amidst the wilderness—
  With Fortune in his clutch;

The figures of the heroes gone
  Who stood forth undismayed,
And Freedom's Flag shook forth upon
  Eureka's old stockade.

These subjects to Correggio Jones
  No inspiration brought;
He was an ass (in semitones)
  And painted—as he thought.

'In all these things there's no Romance,'
  He muttered, with a sneer;
'They'd never give C. Jones a chance
  To make his genius clear!'

'Grey gums,' he cried, 'and box-woods pale
  They give my genius cramp—
But let me paint some Knights in Mail,
  Or robbers in a camp.

Now, look at those Old Masters—they
  Had all the chances fine,
With churches dim, and ruins grey,
  And castles on the Rhine,

And Lady Gay in miniver,
  And hairy-shirted saint,
And Doges in apparel fair—
  And things a man might paint!

And barons bold and pilgrims pale,
  And battling Knight and King—

The blood-spots on their golden mail—
  And all that sort of thing.

Your Raphael and your Angelo
  And Rubens, and such men,
They simply had a splendid show.
  Give me the same—and then!'

So speaks Correggio Jones—yet sees,
  When past is Night's eclipse,
The dawn come like Harpocrates,
  A rose held to her lips.

The wondrous dawn that is so fair,
  So young and bright and strong,
That e'en the rocks and stones to her
  Sing a Memnonic song.

He will not see that our sky-hue
  Old Italy's outvies,
But still goes yearning for the blue
  Of far Ausonian skies ...

He yet is painting at full bat—
  You'll say, if him you see,
'His body dwells on Gander Flat,
  His soul's in Italy.'

GEORGE ESSEX EVANS   (1863–1909)

Poet. Born in London; came to Australia in 1881.

THE WOMEN OF THE WEST

They left the vine-wreathed cottage and the mansion on the hill,
The houses in the busy streets where life is never still,
The pleasures of the city, and the friends they cherished best:
For love they faced the wilderness—the Women of the West.

The roar, and rush, and fever of the city died away,
And the old-time joys and faces—they were gone for many a day;
In their place the lurching coach-wheel, or the creaking bullock
    chains,
O'er the everlasting sameness of the never-ending plains.

In the slab-built, zinc-roofed homestead of some lately-taken run,
In the tent beside the bankment of a railway just begun,
In the huts on new selections, in the camps of man's unrest,
On the frontiers of the Nation, live the Women of the West.

The red sun robs their beauty, and, in weariness and pain,
The slow years steal the nameless grace that never comes again;
And there are hours men cannot soothe, and words men cannot
    say—
The nearest woman's face may be a hundred miles away.

The wide Bush holds the secrets of their longings and desires,
When the white stars in reverence light their holy altar-fires,
And silence, like the touch of God, sinks deep into the breast—
Perchance He hears and understands the Women of the West.

For them no trumpet sounds the call, no poet plies his arts—
They only hear the beating of their gallant, loving hearts.
But they have sung with silent lives the song all songs above—
The holiness of sacrifice, the dignity of love.

Well have we held our fathers' creed. No call has passed us by.
We faced and fought the wilderness, we sent our sons to die.
And we have hearts to do and dare, and yet, o'er all the rest,
The hearts that made the Nation were the Women of the West.

EDMUND JAMES BANFIELD   (1852–1923)

Journalist. Born in England; came to Australia as a boy.

BEACHCOMBING

from THE CONFESSIONS OF A BEACHCOMBER

"For the Beachcomber, when not a mere ruffian, is the poor relation
of the artist."

In justification of the assumption of the title of "Beachcomber,"
it must be said that, having made good and sufficient provision
against the advent of the wet season (which begins, as a rule, during
the Christmas holidays), the major portion of each week was spent
in first formal and official calls, and then friendly and familiar vists
to the neighbouring islands and the mainland.
    Duty and inclination constrained me to find out what were the
states and moods of all the bays and coves of all the isles; the
location and form of rocks and reefs; the character of shrubs and

trees; the nature of the jungle-covered hilltops; the features of bluffs
and precipices; to understand the style and manner and the conversation of unfamiliar birds; to discover where the turtle most do
congregate; the favourite haunts of fishes. I was in a hurry to partake freely of the novel, and yearned for pleasure of the absolute
freedom of isles uninhabited, shores untrodden; eager to know how
Nature, not under the microscope, behaved; what were her maiden
fancies, what the art with which she allures.

But there was an excuse, rather an imperious command, for all the
apparent waste of time. Before the rains came thundering on the
iron roof of our little hut, the washed-out and enfeebled town-
dweller who gave way to bitter reflections on the first evening of his
new career, could hardly have been recognised, thanks to the robus-
tious, wholesome effects of the free and vitalising life. Fourteen,
frequently sixteen, hours of the twenty-four were spent in the open
air, ashore and afloat.

What a glowing and absolutely authentic testimonial could be
written as to the tonic influence of the misrepresented climate of the
rainy belt of North Queensland on constitutions that have run
down? According to popular opinion, malaria ought to have discovered an exceptionally easy prey. Ague, if the expected had happened, should have gripped and shaken me until my teeth rattled;
and after alternations of raging fever and arctic cold, I ought to have
gone to my long home with the fearful shapes of delirium yelling in
my ears. But there are places other than Judee where they do not
know everything. At the fraction of the fee of a fashionable doctor,
and of the cost of following his fashionable and pleasing advice—a
change to one of the Southern States—in three months one of the
compelling causes for the desertion of town life had been disposed
of by agreeable processes. None of the bitter, after-taste of physic
remained. I knew my island, and was on terms of friendly
admiration—born of knowledge of beauty spots—with all the
others. I had become a citizen of the universe.

During this period of utter abandonment of all serious claims
upon time and exertion came the conviction that the career of the
Beachcomber, the closest possible "return to Nature" now popular-
ly advocated, has charms none other possesses. Then it was that the
lotus-blossom was first eaten.

Unfettered by the laws of society, with the means at hand of ac-
quiring the few necessaries of life that Nature in this generous part
of her domain fails to provide ready-made, a Beachcomber of virtuous instinct, and a due perception of the decency of things, may
enjoy a happy life. Should, however, he be of the type that demands
a wreck or so every month to maintain his supplies of rum or gin,
and other articles of his true religion, and is prepared if wrecks do
not come with regularity to assist tardy Nature by means of false
lights on the shore, he will find no scope whatever among these
orderly isles.

The Beachcomber of tradition parades his coral islet barefooted, bullying guileless natives out of their copra, coco-nut oil and pearl-shell; his chief diet, turtle and turtle eggs and fish; his drink, rum and coco-nut milk—the latter only when the former is impossible. When a wreck happens he becomes a potentate in pyjamas, and with his dusky wives, dressed in bright vestiture, fares sumptuously. And though the ships from the isles do not meet to "pour the wealth of ocean in tribute at his feet," he can still "rush out of his lodgings and eat oysters in regular desperation." A whack on his hardened head from the club of a jealous native is the time-honoured fate of the typical Beachcomber.

Flotsam and jetsam make another class of Beachcomber by stimulating the gaming instincts. Is there a human being, taking part in the rough and tumble of the world, who can honestly make confession and say that he has completely suffocated those inherent instincts of savagedom—joy and patience in the chase, the longing for excitement and surprise, the crude selfishness, the delight in getting something for nothing? Society journals have informed me that titled dames have been known to sit out long and wearisome evenings that they may obtain some paltry favour in a cotillon. And when the sea casts up its gifts on these radiant shores, I boldly and with glee give way to my beachcombing instincts and pick and choose. Never up to the present have I found anything of real value; but am I not buoyed up by pious hopes and sanguine expectations? Is not the game as diverting and as innocent as many others that are played to greater profit? It is a game, too, that cannot be forced, and therefore cannot become demoralising; and having no nice feelings nor fine shades, I rejoice and am glad in it.

And then what strange and varied things one sees! Once a "harness-cask," hostile to every sense, came trundled by waves eager to expel it from the vicinity of these oxless but scented isles. It overcame us as we sailed by, 20 yards off, and the general necessity for temperate diet and restricted dishes came as a sweet and a comforting reflection. No marvel if the ship whence it was ejected was in bad odour among the sailors. Leaving, as it lurched along, a greasy, foul stain on the sea, it may have poisoned multitudes of uncomplaining fishes during its evil course.

Occasionally a case of fruit, washed from the decks of a labouring steamer, drifts ashore. One was the means of introducing a valuable addition to the products of the island. It gave demonstration of how man may unwittingly, and even in opposition to his wit, assist in scattering and multiplying blessings on a smiling land—blessings to last for all time, and perhaps to amend or ameliorate the environment of a budding nation.

Many years ago—in 1878, to speak precisely—a ship laden with fragrant cedar logs from the valley of the Daintree River—140 miles to the north—touched on Kennedy Shoal, 20 miles to the south-east of Dunk Island. Crippled though she was she managed to make

Cardwell, where she was temporarily patched up, and whence she set sail for Melbourne. It was the critical month of March, and the *Merchant*—clumsy and cumbersome, but a good and safe ship given ample sea-room—before sailing many miles on her course, was caught in the coils of a cyclone, the violence of which is well remembered by old residents on the coast to this day, and was lost with all hands. She is supposed to have struck on a reef to the south-ward of the Palm Islands, as the bulk of her cargo was cast ashore in Ramsay Bay, Hinchinbrook Island. Portions of the wreckage were found on the Brook Islands; her figure-head—the spread eagle of the United States—and a seaman's chest were picked up on the beach here. Her windlass, with a child's pinafore entangled with it—for the skipper had taken his wife and two children to bear him company—drifted on the South Franklands, 40 miles to the north, and a large portion of the shattered hulk on a reef eastward of Fitzroy Island, 25 miles still farther up the coast. Fate did her worst for the poor *Merchant*, and not yet content, relentlessly pursued two (if not more) of the vessels which sought to recover her cedar, strewn on the treacherous sands of Ramsay Bay. Some of the logs, how-ever, drifted to our quiet coves, and portions remain sound to this day. One more promising and accessible we beachcombed. It pro-vided planks for a punt, besides various articles of furniture, and gave me some most practical homilies on contentment. Having found and duly salvaged that log, it was necessary to cut it up; and then I began to be thankful that pit-sawing was not forced upon me as a profession in the days of inexperienced youth. Pit-sawing is deceptive. It has the appearance of being easy, though not genteel, when others are the toilers, and in the red dust, torn by the polished steel teeth from out the heart of the dull log, do you not "inhale the balmy smells of nard and cassia which the musky wings of the zephyrs scatter through the cedared groves of the Hesperides?" Is not that fragrance sufficient compensation for your toil, with the clean red planks profit over and above legitimate earnings? Yet that long saw tugs at your very heart-strings, and you know that to get a real, not merely sentimental, liking for the craft of the sawyer, you must take to it very young, before the possibilities of other occupa-tions and pastimes have distorted your genius. This worthy lesson comes from the gentle art of Beachcombing.

Again, a German barque, driven out of its course, found unex-pectedly a detached portion of the Great Barrier Reef 200 miles away to the south. When the south-easters came, they pounded away so vigorously with the heavy guns of the sea that in a brief space nothing was left of the big ship save some distorted fragments of iron jammed in among the nigger-heads of coral and the crevices of the rocks. A few weeks after, portions of the wreck were depos-ited on Dunk Island, and the beach of the mainland for miles was strewn with timber. That wreck was the greatest favour bestowed me in my profession of Beachcomber. Long and heavy pieces of angle-iron came bolted to raft-like sections of the deck; various kinds of timber proved useful in a variety of ways. What? was I to leave it all, unclaimed and unregarded—in excess of morality and modesty—on the beach, to be honey-combed by white ants or to rot? or to honestly own up to that sentiment which is the most human of all? Without affectation or apology, I confess that I was overjoyed—that my instincts, pregnant with original sin, received a most delightful fillip. I wallowed for the time being in the luxury of beachcombing.

Upon sober reflection, I cannot say that I am of one mind with the pastor of the Shetland Isles who never omitted this petition from his long prayer—"Lord, if it be Thy holy will to send shipwrecks, do not forget our island"; nor yet with the Breton fishermen, who to this day are of opinion that wreckage is the gift of God, and who therefore take everything that comes in a reverential spirit, as a Divine favour, whether casks of wine or bales of merchandise. But, after all, who am I that I should claim a finer shade of morality than those, with their sturdy wide-spread hands and perpetual blessing? My inherent powers of resistance to such temptations as the winds and tides of Providence put in their way have never been subject to proof. Does virtue go by default where there is no opportunity to be otherwise than virtuous? The very first pipe of port, or aum of Rhenish, or bale of silk, which comes rolling along may wrestle with my morality and so wrench and twist it as to incapacitate it for ordinary usage for months, or may even permanently disable it. And must not I, venturing to regard myself as a truthful historian, frankly admit a sense allied to disappointment when the white blazing beaches are destitute of the most trivial of temptations?

No, the grating of the battered barque, upon which many a wet and weary steersman had stood, now fulfils placid duty as a front gate. No more to be trampled and stamped upon with shifty, sloppy feet—no more to be scrubbed and scored with sand and holystone; painted white, it creaks gratefully every time it swings—the symbol of security, the first outward and visible sign of home, the guardian of the sacred rights of private property, the embodiment of the exclusive. Better so than lying inert under foot on the deck of the barque thrashing through the cold grey seas of the Baltic, or scudding before the unscrupulous billows of Biscay.

Moreover, what notable and precise information this derelict timber gave as to the strength and direction of ocean currents. The wreck took place on the 26th October 1900, in 18 deg. 43 min. S. lat., 147 deg. 57 min. E. long., 72½ miles in a direct line from the port of Townsville, and about 200 miles from Dunk Island. She broke up, after all the cargo had been salvaged, early in January 1901, and on Tuesday, 5th February, at 10 a.m., the seas landed the first of the broken planks in Brammo Bay. Then for a few days the arrivals were continuous. For over 50 miles along the coast the wreckage was scattered, very little going farther north.

Nothing goes south on this part of the coast. Yes, there is one exception during my experience. A veritable cataclysm coincided with a stiff north-easterly breeze, and hundreds of bunches of bananas from plantations on the banks of the Johnstone River—25 miles away—landing-stages and steps, and the beacons from the mouth of the river, drifted south. Most of the more buoyant débris, however, took the next tide back in the direction whence it came.

When there are eight or ten islands and islets within an ˄fter-noon's sail, and miles of mainland beach to police, variety lends her charms to the pursuit of the Beachcomber. Landing in one of the unfrequented coves, he knows not what the winds and the tides may have spread out for inspection and acceptance. Perhaps only an odd coco-nut from the Solomon Islands, its husk riddled by cobra and zoned with barnacles. The germ of life may yet be there. To plant the nut above high-water mark is an obvious duty. Perhaps there is a paddle, with rude tracery on the handle, from the New Hebrides, part of a Fijian canoe that has been bundled over the Barrier, a wooden spoon such as Kanakas use, or the dusky globe of an in-candescent lamp that has glowed out its life in the state-room of some ocean liner, or a broom of Japanese make, a coal-basket, a "fender," a tiger nautilus shell, an oar or a rudder, a tiller, a bottle cast away far out from land to determine the strength and direction of ocean currents, the spinnaker boom of a yacht, the jib-boom of a staunch cutter. Once there was a goodly hammer cemented by the head fast upright on a flat rock, and again the stand of a grindstone, and a trestle, high and elaborately stayed. Cases, invariably and dis-appointingly empty, come and go, planks of strange timber, blocks from some tall ship. A huge black beacon waddled along, dragging a reluctant mass of iron at the end of its chain cable, followed by a roughly-built "flatty" and a huge log of silkwood. A jolly red buoy, weary of the formality of bowing to the swell, broke loose from a sandbank's apron-strings, bounced off in the ecstasies of liberty, romped in the surf, rolled on the beach, worked a cosy bed in the soft warm sand, and has slumbered ever since to the soothing hum of the wind, indifferent to the perplexities of mariners and the fate of ships. The gilded mast-head truck of a smart yacht, with one of her cabin racks, bespoke of recent disaster, unknown and un-accounted, and a brand new oar, finished and fitted with the natti-ness of a man-o'-war's man, told of some wave-swept deck.

That which at the time was the most eloquent message from the sea came close to our door, cast up on the snowy-white coral drift of a little cove, where it immediately attracted notice. Nothing but an untrimmed bamboo staff nearly 30 feet long, carrying an oblong strip of soiled white calico between two such strips of red turkey twill. Tattered and frayed, the flags seemed to tell of the desperate appeal for help of some forlorn castaway; of a human being, marooned on a lonely sandbank on the Barrier, without shelter, food or water, but not altogether bereft of hope. *Bêche-de-mer* fishers have in times past been marooned on the Reef by mutinous blacks, and left to die by slow degrees, or to be drowned by the implacable yet merciful tide. A makeshift rudder well worn bespoke strenuous efforts to steer a troubled boat to shelter, but this crude signal staff, deftly arranged, told of present agony and stress. It might have been the emblem of a tragic event that the Beachcomber single-handed was not able to investigate. As a matter of fact, it was only a temporary datum of one of His Majesty's surveying ships engaged in attempting to set the bounds of the Barrier.

Rarely do we sail about without enjoying the zest of the chance of getting something for nothing. Not yet has the seaman's chest, brass-bound, with its secret compartments full of "fair rose-nobles and bright moidores," been lighted upon; but who can say? Perhaps it has come ashore but now, after leagues of aimless wanderings, and awaits in some cosy cove the next Beachcombing expedition. That from the ill-fated *Merchant* came hither years before my time, and was, in any case, pathetically unromantic.

Peradventure there are many who deem this solitary existence dull? Why, it is brimful of interest and sensation. There are the tragedies of the bush to observe and elucidate; all cannot be foreseen and prevented, or even avenged. A bold falcon the other day swooped down upon a wood-swallow that was imitating the falcon's flight just above my head, and bore it bleeding to a treetop, while I stood shocked at the audacity of the cannibal. A bullet dropped the murderous bird with its dead victim fast in the talons. There are comedies, too, and you have the wit to see them, and in these Beachcombing expeditions expectation fairly effervesces.

One lucky individual—a mere amateur—casually picked up a black-lip mother-of-pearl shell on an island some little distance away. It contained a blue pearl, the price of which gave him such a start in life, that he is now an owner of ships. May not other tides cast up on other shores. other oysters whose lives have been rendered miserable by the presence of pearls?

Byron says—"Even an oyster may be crossed in love." Science, more precise and frank than the frankest of poets, tells us that oysters are afflicted with tapeworms, and to kill the germ of these indecent pests, enclose them in untimely tombs, which from the human standpoint are among the most lovely and precious of gems. The assertions of the scientific are often the reverse of poetical. We are constrained to believe them, but like our poetical delusions better, and for the origin of the pearl prefer the quaint fable of the Persians to the unpleasant fact of the zoologist. A drop of water of ineffable purity falls from heaven to the sea, an oyster gapes and swallows it, the drop hardens and ripens, and becomes a pearl; and who is so devoid of the perception of purity, beauty and worth as to despise a pearl?

Here about, pearls were found. We delight in them, though they prove the previous existence of a filthy ailment. Any oyster may contain a pearl, a pearl of great price—a thing of beauty, a joy for ever. Every gold-lip, every black-lip oyster, is a chance in a lottery. Was there ever a Beachcomber so pure and elevated of soul as to refuse the chances that Nature proffers gratuitously? My meagre horde includes pearls of several tints, black, pink, and white. They represent the paltriest prizes in the lottery that no Government, however paternal, may prohibit, being mere "baroque," fit only to be pounded up as medicine for some Chinaman luxuriously sick. Yet there is a chance. Some day the great prize may be drawn. And then, "Canst thou draw out leviathan with an hook?" The Beachcomber may be perverted into—well, the next best on the list. Yet they say in pitiful tones, those who rake among the muck of the streets, "What a dull life! What a hopeless existence! He is out of it all!" Yes, with a gladsome mind, and all its sounds, if not forgotten, at least muffled by music, soft as dawn, profound as the very sea.

Kennedy Shoal has been mentioned incidentally. Some miles further north are two bare sandbanks. Prior to the year 1890 they were occupied by a *bêche-de-mer* fisherman, whose headquarters were on the chief of the South Barnard Islands—some 12 or 14 miles to the north. In fateful March of that year a cyclone swooped down on this part of the coast with the pent-up fury of a century's restraint. The enormous bloodwood-trees torn out by the roots on Dunk Island testified to the force and ferocity of the storm. The sandbanks, are isolated, dreary spots, the highest portion but 2 or 3 feet above the level reached by spring tides. A cutter—*The Dolphin*—with a crew of aboriginals, in charge of a couple of Kanakas, was anchored at the shoal, and as the cyclone worked up, the Kanakas decided that the one and only bid for life was to run before it to the mainland. It was a forlorn hope—so forlorn that four or five of the aboriginals declined to take part in it, deeming it safer to trust to the sandbank, which they imagined could never be entirely swept by the besoms of the sea. The cutter fled before the storm, only to capsize in the breakers off the mouth of the Johnstone River. Clinging to the wreck until it drifted a few miles south, the Kanakas and crew battled through the waves and eventually reached the shore. Of those who placed their faith on the sandbank not one was spared. The seas raced over it, pounded and flattened it. The men upon it were unconsidered trifles.

The tall and handsome Scandinavian whose fortune was thus assailed was at his home with his wife and children and brother. His yacht—*The Maud*—in the height of the storm, began to drag her anchor. He and his brother went out in a dinghy to secure her. At dusk the wife, young, petite and pretty, with strained anxiety watched the efforts of the men to beat back to shelter. Darkness came, blotting out the scene and its climax. Never after was anything seen or heard of the brothers or the yacht. And for nearly a fortnight the disconsolate wife and her little ones were alone on the island.

Ten years later, on one of the two bare patches of sand, another *bêche-de-mer* smoke-house was built. While the owner, a swarthy Arabian, was out on the reef miles away, a phenomenally high tide occurred. His wife—a comely girl of British descent—was alone on the shoal. She watched the rising water apprehensively, until all the sand was covered save the few feet on which the frail shelter stood. One more ripple and the floor was swamped. Then, wading and swimming, she managed to reach a punt, and so saved her life. Since then these patches of sand have not been regarded as a safe outpost even by those most venturesome of people—*bêche-de-mer* fishers.

This is not an apology, but a confession; not a plea of defence, but a justification—a fair and free chronicle, a frank acknowledgment of the tributes of impartial Neptune—Neptune who gives and who takes away—who stealthily filches with tireless fingers, and who, when in the mood, robs so remorselessly, and with such awful, such majestic violence, that it were impious to whimper. Who beachcombed my three rudders, the one toilfully adzed out in one piece from the beautiful heart of a bean-tree log, another cunningly fitted with a sliding fin, and that of red cedar with famous brass mountings? Who owns the pair of ballast tanks once mine? Who the buoy deemed securely moored? Who the paddles and the rowlocks and the signal halyards, lost because of Neptune's whims and violence? Beachcombing is a nicely adjusted, if not quite an exact art. Not once but several times has the libertine Neptune scandalously seduced punts and dinghies from the respectable precincts of Brammo Bay, and having philandered with them for a while, cynically abandoned them with a bump on the mainland beach, and only once has he sent a punt in return—a poor, soiled, tar-besmirched, disorderly waif that was reported to the police and reluctantly claimed.

A mind inclined to casuistry, could it not defend Beachcombing? Does not the law recognise it under the definition of trover? Why bother about the law and the moralities when it is all so pleasing, so engrossing, and so fair?

The Beachcomber wants no extensive establishment. His possessions need never be mortgaged. The cost of living is measurable by a standard adjustable to individual taste, wants and perceptions. The expenditure of a little manual labour supplies the omissions of and compensates for the undirected impulses which prevail, and the pursuit—if not the profession—leads one to ever-varying scenes, to the contemplation of many of the moods of unaffected, unadvertised Nature. Ashore, one dallies luxuriously with time, free from all the restrictions of streets, every precious moment his very own; afloat in these calm and shallow waters there is a never-ending panorama of entertainment. Coral gardens—gardens of the sea nymphs, wherein fancy feigns cool, shy, chaste faces and pliant forms half-revealed among gently swaying robes; a company of porpoise, a herd of dugong; turtle, queer and familiar fish, occasionally the spouting of a great whale, and always the company of swift and graceful birds. Sometimes the whole expansive ocean is as calm as it can only be in the tropics and bordered by the Barrier Reef—a shield of shimmering silver from which the islands stand out as turquoise bosses. Again, it is of cobalt blue, with changing bands of purple and gleaming pink, or of grey blue—the reflection of a sky pallid and tremulous with excess of light. Or myriad hosts of microscopic creatures—the Red Sea owes to the tribe its name— the multitudinous sea dully incarnadine; or the boat rides buoyantly on the shoulders of Neptune's white horses, while funnel-shaped water spouts sway this way and that. Land is always near, and the flotsam and jetsam, do they not supply that smack of excitement—if not the boisterious hope—bereft of which life might seem "always afternoon?"

These chronicles are toned from first to last by perceptions which came to the Beachcomber—perceptions which lead, mayhap, to a subdued and sober estimate of the purpose and bearing of the pilgrimage of life. Doubts become exalted and glorified, hopes all rapture, when long serene days are spent alone in the contemplation of the splendours of sky and sea, and the enchantment of tropic shores.

Dorothea Mackellar   (1885–1968)

Poet. Born in Sydney; educated privately.

MY COUNTRY

The love of field and coppice,
    Of green and shaded lanes,
Of ordered woods and gardens
    Is running in your veins.
Strong love of grey-blue distance
    Brown streams and soft, dim skies—
I know but cannot share it,
    My love is otherwise.

I love a sunburnt country,
    A land of sweeping plains,
Of ragged mountain ranges,
    Of droughts and flooding rains.

I love her far horizons,
    I love her jewel-sea,
Her beauty and her terror—
    The wide brown land for me!

The stark white ring-barked forests,
    All tragic to the moon,
The sapphire-misted mountains,
    The hot gold hush of noon.
Green tangle of the brushes,
    Where lithe lianas coil,
And orchids deck the tree tops
    And ferns the warm dark soil.

Core of my heart, my country!
    Her pitiless blue sky,
When sick at heart, around us,
    We see the cattle die—
But then the grey clouds gather,
    And we can bless again
The drumming of an army,
    The steady, soaking rain.

Core of my heart, my country!
    Land of the Rainbow Gold,
For flood and fire and famine,
    She pays us back three-fold.
Over the thirsty paddocks,
    Watch, after many days,
The filmy veil of greenness
    That thickens as we gaze ...

An opal-hearted country,
    A wilful, lavish land—
All you who have not loved her,
    You will not understand—
Though earth holds many splendours,
    Wherever I may die,
I know to what brown country
    My homing thoughts will fly.

CHARLES EDWIN WOODROW BEAN   (1879–1968)

Journalist. Born in N.S.W.; educated at Oxford; was Australian
official war correspondent and historian 1914–1918.

THE RED COUNTRY

When European writers, and some Australians too, speak of the
monotony of the Australian scrub—gum-trees, and gum-trees, and
gum-trees still beyond that—they doubtless describe conscientiously enough what they have seen, which is usually a strip of Australia
along the coast. But few of them have any right to speak of Australia
as a whole; for the greater part of Australia is the part that most of
them have not seen, and the chief mark of the scrub which grows in
that part is the bewildering variety of trees. Generally, on no two
miles, often on no two acres, are the trees the same. The difficulty
for a stranger is to know what sort of tree he is for the moment
passing; for he may count thirty different sorts in driving through
one paddock. Many Australians do not know them by name, much
less by sight. But they are the most beautiful trees in Australia.

The most graceful tree in Europe is the silver birch. Householders
cram it into their gardens, however small, and artists into their pictures. There's a tree out back which is a close counter-part of the
silver birch. One would have thought it would have been transplanted into every suburban front lawn. But few suburban Australians have ever heard of—much less seen—the leopardwood. And
at the time of our journey the rabbits were slowly ringbarking it out
of the continent.

The truth is that there exists inside coastal Australia a second
Australia—the larger of the two—of which most of our people
know very little more than do the Londoners. It is the land of those
astonishing grasses which spring up, then vanish for twenty years,
and then suddenly flush up again to the delight of the oldest inhabi-
tant, who is the only man that can spin a yarn about them. It is the
land of the delicate scrub, which is as puzzling as the grass and,
mostly, as useful; of the mulga, the best of all for stock, and one of
the prettiest, with its exquisite black tracework of branches against
its "Liberty" grey leaves; of the applebush or rosewood or
bluebush, which, when half-dry, is fairly good for stock; of the
emu-bush, which droops like the bunch of an emu's tail and is very
good fodder—as the rabbits have found; of the native willow,
which is good to make yokes of; of the gidgea, which is good for
fencing, and which drops beans that are good for sheep, and smells
so pestilential after rain that they say at Nyngan they can tell you
when it is raining about Bourke, because the nearest gidgea is there;
of the leopardwood, which is good feed and bad timber, and crops

up again as often as it is cut; of the myall, which is good sheep-feed; of the whitewood, which is fairly good; and the belar, which is very little good; and the wild fuchsia, whose flowers, full of honey, the sheep at any rate think to be good; of the hopbush, which is good for yeast; and the beefwood, which is good for timber; and the deadfinish, which may be food for whip-handles; and the budda, which is good for nothing except to keep the surface on the ground —to stop the wind from blowing the skin of Australia away and leaving her cheek-bones all shiny red and bare and useless.

For out here you have reached the core of Australia, the real red Australia of the ages, which—though the rivers have worn their channels through it, and spewed out their black silt in narrow ribbons across it—still hems in this flat modern river-soil, so that, if you drive only a few miles from the river-bank, you will always come out in the end upon a red land, a slightly higher land, rising sharply from the grey plain; a land which stretches away and away and away across the heart of Australia, with the history of the oldest continent on earth written in interesting little patches—patches of ironstone pebbles, of river-worn quartz, stony deserts, and a thousand other relics of its bygone sufferings—across the whole face of it.

That is the real Australia, and it is as delicate as its own grasses. In parts the sand, which covers it and contains the whole calendar of priceless seeds that have taken a few million years (at a low estimate) to evolve, is not more than one foot thick; so thin and light and delicate a skin that only the delicate Western scrub holds it in place at all.

There, years before "erosion" became a matter of general public concern, a dangerous problem of wind erosion had fully developed. The Western Lands Board had been studying it and already had taken some wise steps in the effort to check it.

In certain parts, where men had come out on to that country and cut down the scrub recklessly, with roughshod, ready-made European methods, the surface of the earth had blown clean away. In some places, where all that exquisite, wonderful plant-life had been gradually developing through all the ages, it took just one bad season to destroy it; and instead, we found there great patches of "scalded" clay, as bare as on the day when the last wavelet of some old receding ocean lapped over them and left them to evolve a covering for their nakedness.

How much even some enlightened Australians knew about this greater half of Australia may be judged from a single instance. Not so very many years previously, at a time when that wonderful native scrub was being used as the great reserve of fodder in the West—and being used, if anything, too fast—and when the one useful thing which the Government could have done would have been to pass a law making it criminal to destroy it, it was found that the

Lands Department had actually inserted a clause into its Western leases, insisting that lessees must improve the country by clearing it of scrub. The Western Lands Board had since changed all that, yet the thing that struck a townsman coming out upon it was that the real Australia was, even to most Australians, to all intents and purposes an unknown and unstudied country.

The people out there had come thither of their own choice to make their living in their own way; and though they were doing a great work for their country by experimenting with immeasurably the most difficult part of it, they could not very well expect favours over and above those of people who were earning their living elsewhere. But they were justified in expecting that the ministers in the Government, who were their ministers just as much as they were the ministers for Sydney, should be able to look at their questions from their point of view; and they had had some horrible shocks.

Just before one big drought broke, the people of Bourke had received a visit from their Premier. A deputation waited on him there to ask for a few more concessions in railway freights or something. It was hardly necessary to put their case to him, because even people on the other side of the world knew by the cables in the papers what the case along the Darling was just then. The grass had long since disappeared; the face of the country was shifting red and grey sand, blowing about wherever the wind carried it. The fences were covered; dead sheep and fallen trunks had become sand-hills. Millions of trees were killed; the birds had been dropping dead. Except where there were trees, the West was literally not different from the Sahara Desert. Some men's nerves had broken down under the conditions, and they had had to flee from the back-country in fear for their sanity. The rest of the world had been watching the fight against that calamity as people in war follow the struggle at the front. All the rest of Australia, and even Europe, had given signs of their sympathy. What little comfort the men and women out there had, they drew from this. So there was really no need to put the case to their Premier.

However, just for form's sake, they put to him for about three-quarters of an hour some of the urgencies which had been filling the newspapers for months, and which presumably had been worrying the Government into white hairs. He seemed to be listening. When they had pretty well finished he suddenly looked up.

"What do you do with the country in these parts?" he said, waving his hand towards the window. "What—er—what use d'yer make of it?"

They were a little surprised. They had just been telling him for three-quarters of an hour.

But they said:

"Oh, well, we put sheep on it—that is, when there is any grass on it...."

"D'jever think of dairyin'?" asked the Premier.

Now if he had gone round amongst the men in that room and had hit each one of them hard upon the chest, he would have produced much the same sort of effect which he succeeded in producing when he blurted out that question. They went away almost sick with disillusionment.

That Premier knew something of dairying. Perhaps, after all, he saw as far as most of us do beyond our noses.

For that reason, before coming to the station hands—the homestead men whose work is the core of the wool industry—one may be excused for explaining a little further what we learnt of that most interesting but little understood country in which lay the "outside" homesteads that we visited.

THE GENIUS OF AUSTRALIA

Between Gunnedah and Boggabri, overlooking the Namoi River, is a handsome modern homestead built of what seems to be rough-hewn stone. In reality the blocks are not stone, but clever imitations in concrete. Every block was moulded, squared, and dried on the station itself. The walls were built by station labour. Floor-joists, roof-beams, wainscots, window-frames, every inch of woodwork was fitted, joined, mortised by the station carpenter; some of it was cut by the station blacksmith at the station sawmill. The plans were designed by the station-owner.

Imagine a country gentleman in any state in Europe sitting down to plan a house; and then calling in the groom, butler, and coachman, with a gamekeeper or two, a gardener, and a lodgeman, and suggesting that they should manufacture and cut and fit the stone walls, floors, roof-beams and ceilings, and then build them together into his baronial mansion. It is probably true that, if he did so, the statement of every man who heard him would be taken as good evidence of his insanity, and could be used as such by anyone who might be interested in proving it. For those men simply could not begin the work; or, if they could, they would think they couldn't—which comes to the same thing. The Australian, too, has his shortcomings, a full round share of them, and one would be blind to deny it. One would be equally blind not to see that he possesses one virtue in an outstanding degree. He can do almost anything. He is aware of it.

At the little centres of industry on ordinary sheep runs we found men accustomed in the course of an ordinary day's work, to be engaged in making wagons, shafts, iron hinges, gates, in steam-sawing, engine-driving, forging iron, sometimes even moulding it. The man who could do most of these things would not stick at a bit of saddling, would make a whip if necessary, or sole a boot. He would turn soap-boxes into furniture, golden-syrup tins into quart pots, kerosene-tins into anything.

It is still a quality of the Australian that he can make something out of nothing. Out on his sheep runs, ever since the time of the shepherds, he has had to do without the best things, because they don't exist there. So he has made the next best do; and, where even these are not to hand, he has manufactured them out of things which one would have thought it impossible to turn to any use at all. He has done it for so long that it has become more than an art. It has long since become a part of his character, the most valuable part of it. And the man who has that virtue in a degree to which no other among his fellow-countrymen approaches, is the station tradesman; after him, probably, the station-hand.

It is not in born Australians alone that this capacity exists. The roots of it seem to go back deep into his Anglo-Saxon stock. The variety of that stock, as well as its achievements, was borne in upon us as we listened to English as she was spoken about the station buildings on a Western run. The Australian language in the town is a more or less uniform modification of Cockney, although the accent and intonation are now distinctly Australian, and easily recognizable by anyone who is accustomed to them. But in the back country, especially in those years of vigorous immigration, you heard many specimens of the widest variety of accents or dialects, imported (with their owners) from oversea, and taken for granted out back. We city men found it difficult to control our smiles until we got used to it.

Here is a specimen:

Scene: A new northern shearing-shed on which they were just fitting the roof-beams.

Dramatis Personae: A fair-haired nuggety ganger with long arms like a gorilla, and with iron nails and a hammer sticking out pirate-fashion round his belt; the station bullocky, Jacob by name, more like a nugget than even the ganger. Half-a-dozen hands of all sorts and sizes, mostly perched like monkeys about the framework of the shed.

The ganger has been explaining to the owner, over a plan, his private notions of the position of certain "possts" and of the architect who planned them, when his gaze gradually concentrates on a greybeard who is hugging the top of one in a vain struggle to fix two beams there at the same time. Phonetically the conversation is something like this:

Ganger: "Noh den, dad—what you doin' darr?"

Dad (breathlessly): "Whhat like teemberr arr ye giein' us? These round pine pawles arr no use tu a man."

Bright youngster (manoeuvring the other end of the pine pole): "Shike it up, Sandy, you daownt want to be there awl dye."

Ganger: "Dat's no dam good." (In a very audible confidence to the owner) "Dat fellow darr in de white trowsies, he never sunk a post in his life. We'll want dem odder posts tomorro', Mister. Got 'ny sported gam?"

Owner (turning to the nuggety bullocky who is sweating under half a dozen battens which he is unloading from the pile on his wagon): "Hi, Jacob! you can fetch a load of spotted gum from White Dog, can't you? How's the creek for crossing?"

Jacob: "I specs I'll find bottom somewhere. I'm thinking dis team'll get thems tru' it."

Ganger: "He can bring 'em op, ye now; we can't do widaowt 'em, ye now" (smudges a beefy finger across the plan). "We'll be wantin' 'em yarr an' yarr an' yarr, and anodder over yarr," etc., etc....

Now that is just an ordinary chunk cut out of an ordinary conversation. The only extraordinary part about it was that it was not extraordinary. The ordinary conversation that we heard in the bush was a hotch-potch of the dialects of half the British counties. The greybeard came probably from Peebles. The iron-grey ganger spoke English with an accent strangely like that of a Norwegian or a Dane. He was a puzzle until one found that his particular brand of the language of Shakespeare came from the Orkney Islands.

But the real puzzle was Jacob. He was just shouldering the last half-dozen battens, staggered with them to their brothers, flung them down, and stood panting.

"Dat's de won we ben lookin' for," he said, taking out a pipe as nuggety as himself; "must have a fill."

The Boss: "I thought you'd be feelin' it. Finished 'em?"

Jacob: "'iss. Dat's de won I ben lookin' for. Dat's de cobbler. I tought we'd get 'im soon, I'll better be loadin' dem odder possts biforr' I forget, I spec. Gee-ee Baldy.... Gee-ee Brown...." And round butt the slow leading bullocks, and round swings the rest of the team, and round creaks the huge wagon squelching the mud aside like soft chocolate, and down the hill trudges the little bullocky flinging his two-handed whip, a trail of blue smoke fluttering over his shoulder, the clink of his spurs gradually dying away.

"He always wears spurs," said the boss, seeing that we noticed them. "I dunno why; I don't suppose he can ride—he's an Englishman."

That remark may be worth a chapter to itself.

THE BULLOCKY

"You prayin' beg-gurr! I'll teach you to pray."

The big roan bullock was down on his knees. He appeared to us to be doing a tremendous lot. This was evidently the impression which the big roan bullock intended to convey. But it did not take in the little bullocky. He flung his clumsy two-handle whip.

"You beg-gurr," he said. "That'll give you an idea."

They did not often get ideas. Ideas must have been painful things to indulge in. The big roan bullock hopped up from his knees like a little dog.

It struck us ordinary city men, looking on, that this bullocky, as a bullocky, had one fault. He did not hit his bullocks enough. He talked a lot about it. "I'll see to you in a minute," he would hiss. "I'll put t' tape on you. I'll give you sometin' to go on wid, by ghost I will."

But he never did. He worked himself unmercifully. When the whole clumsy arrangement lurched, lurched, lur-r-rched, tilted its forty or fifty wool-bales as rakishly as a fashionable hat, and came slow–ly–to–a–stop with a heavy list to port, he creaked and muttered and groaned, in his efforts to get it out, as painfully as the huge axles themselves. But a more merciful man with animals one never saw.

Perhaps the traditional bullock-driver did still exist, somewhere. Australia resounded with stories of them—men who, when their bullocks were stuck, would cut maps of Australia on their backs with a whip, or chop at them with a spade, or even light a fire under them. All one can say is, we never came across even the tracks of that sort of man. The nearest we ever got to him was to find somebody who said he had once seen a fire lit beneath a jibbing horse.

Bullock-drivers may use fiercer language than other people in the bush. The foulest we heard, by a long distance, was from a shearer. We looked on while one bullock-driver managed his team for half an hour without using a single word that even a lay-reader would call a swear-word. It must have been irritating work, too. It was in the mountains in the South, and he was loading tree-trunks— "snigging" them into position (that is, dragging them along by their ends yoked up to some bullocks as if the trunk were a wagon), and "parbuckling" them on to the dray (which means looping a chain round them, making some bullocks pull it, and rolling the trunks up skids on to the wagon top). "You fool" was about the strongest expression that man used in twenty minutes. Some people, on being told this story, have plainly disbelieved it.

And yet the people out West have a story of their own which may serve to support it. A team was working on the Broken Hill road, and a bullock—the Beelzebub of the team—had turned obstinate, and the coach was passing. The whip was swinging; and some apt remarks were just forming on the back of the bullocky's tongue when he caught sight of a clerical hat on the front seat, and just in time thought better of it. He coughed politely. "Ahem— Strawberry," he said, "proceed!" To his obvious astonishment Strawberry proceeded.

We could presumably have obtained evidence that Western bullock-drivers had not forgotten how to express themselves. But it may be doubted if they really did so any more floridly than other people—miners, for instance. Anyway, when the day of pleading comes, a plea of justification will probably serve the bullock-driver. For example:

There was a driver, a big, kindly, bearded man, who brought his load of wool across many days of quivering plain. Towards the end of one crawling afternoon in summer the team, with the load creaking behind it, shuffled up to the white gate of a railway yard. The slip of a porter boy from down-country had seen for the last half-hour a dust-storm approaching through the middle of the paddock, and came down to the gate to inspect. He was not old enough to have lost the official manner, but still he was a nice boy, and he asked if he should open the gate. The bullocky looked up at him for a moment across his bullocks, and then nodded. The boy opened the gate, and, being a town boy and not meaning any harm, stood in the gateway to watch.

The driver from the other side swung the leading bullocks round towards the opening. They started, and then sheered off. He swung them again, and again they sheered away. He was very hot and tired, and very anxious to get the load up to the wool-bank early and step across the road for a drink, which had been in his mind for some hours. But he did not say a word. He put the leaders around again very patiently. Again they sheered off. At last he stepped round to the off-side to see if anything was wrong, and, as he reached that side of the bullocks, he found himself face to face with an innocent infant in railway uniform. He put his hands on his hips, and drew in one long, slow breath. Then he opened.

"You brass-buttoned, blanky, qualified, asterisked Government official," he began—it was five minutes before he drew breath again. The boy did not wait. He gave one cowering, shrivelled, bewildered glance at the big man, and then made for the station-house as fast as his legs could carry him. He was not frightened of being physically hurt—the big man would no more have thought of hitting a boy than of hitting a woman. But the boy shrank and fled under the sheer force of that language. That was how it affected a human being. Bullocks haven't the power to realize that he is not going to hit them; besides, he may be. So the effect of language on them is not really so strange a matter.

There is no bush character so well known or so much talked of as the bullock-driver. One knew all about him long before one ever went into the country. It is sad to lose illusions. But we came back with very grave doubts whether that friend of our youth existed at all in the likeness we imagined.

We found that a "boss bullock-driver" in a country town was not really a scapegrace for fairy-tales, but a very considerable man. Very often he was a steady one. A "boss bullocky" was a man who owned his own team, and perhaps more than one. He might have two or three teams with a paid bullocky driving each. Among the lot of them there was a proportion that were pretty noisy whilst in town. But of what class in the bush could not that be said?

Not so many years before the First World War the "boss bullocky" used to superintend a pretty extensive business—the whole of the transport across a large part of Australia. If a sheep station or a mine or an hotel was started somewhere out near the bottom right-hand corner of the Northern Territory, it was the bullocky who had to take out to it the sugar, tea, currants, and whole wagon-loads of drinks, and to bring the bales of wool or the ore back. (It is rather strange that, out there, the tea and sugar and currants counted as the main load, and that the wool came in as back freight.) But, by the time of that war, even in the far interior the bullock-driver was fast disappearing before the encroachment of the automobile. The motor-carrier is an interesting fellow too, and in future books he will deserve a chapter to himself; but, with the last bullock driver, the most picturesque character in the old back-country will have passed away.

We had hardly realized what an immense field these men wandered over in their business until one day, in a small town, at the very last end of the railways, our conversation with one of the leading forwarding agents was interrupted by a woman who happened to be passing. She turned to him for a moment.

"I hear the boss is kept out on one of the rivers," she said.

"I wonder where that'll be," he remarked. "The Paroo or the Warrego, I expect."

"I expect it's the Warrego," she said calmly, and went on.

Probably our conversation was resumed. But if so, one of us, at any rate, was hardly listening. A remark had been made, which was out of perspective. One's mind was trying all at once to scramble into utterly new fields of ideas which it opened up. It took a minute or two to get there.

The remark meant that this woman's husband or father was bringing some wool teams, presumably from a place somewhere near the frontiers of New South Wales and Queensland and South Australia, called Thargomindah. Thargomindah is actually in Queensland, but its wool sometimes came to the railway in New South Wales. In getting there it had to cross 240 miles of white and red country, of which every hundred square miles probably contain one man, but probably not one waterhole. However, at two places there run across it depressions which, hundreds of miles further up in Queensland, have been great rivers. Occasionally, when there is rain in the Queensland hills, the water of these two fine rivers comes down and spills itself through these two depressions and over the plains beyond. The Warrego fairly often trickles into the Darling. The Paroo has been known to.

What had happened on this occasion was that one of these two rivers had come down. The boss had seen the streak of it miles ahead, and when he reached the water he found it—as he had expected for several weeks past that he would find it—too fast or deep or wide, or the bottom too soft, for crossing. So he camped on the bank, and was now waiting three or four weeks till it subsided.

As to which river it was, there did not appear to be any definite information. He was somewhere out there, on one or the other— didn't much matter which. They are only ninety miles or so apart.

That was the sort of life it was. A man has camped three months on the bank of the Namoi waiting for it to fall. You found him right out on the plain, a stretcher of sacking on two poles, slung, as if it were a trough for his horse, under the back wheels of his wagon; the edges of the tarpaulin, which covered the whole bulk of the load, pulled as near as could be down to the ground on either side. And there he slept, night after night very cosily, with his dog curled up just beneath him, and the fag-end of his camp-fire made up for the night, a few yards away.

The profit in the bullocky's business mostly depended on whether there was good grass or not. With luck a man might make three or four trips back to the same shed before the whole clip had left. There was often a race for it, and a good deal of competition between different bullock-drivers to get back in time.

Stories were told of that competition. But, as a matter of fact, the rivalry here, as in other cases in the bush, had always been decent. Not only was there a strong etiquette, which might perhaps not be talked about, though it was well recognized in all callings in the bush, but these men were in practically every case too generous to leave a mate in trouble. Two men might be racing for the railway. But if one got bogged in a creek or a cowal (which is a small tree-grown, swampy depression often met with in the red country), the other would never leave him there. He would not feel well if he left a man wallowing there when he might be lending him his team. Besides, in the West, who knows? It might be his turn tomorrow.

There have been brutes of bullockies, just as there have been brutes of bishops. But most were as fair to their bullocks as to their rivals. They kept the whip going for a certain time after the load got stuck. But as soon as a man was convinced that the job was too heavy for his team, the chances were that he would quietly take them out, and perhaps put them at it again next day. After all, the bullocks were his capital. They were worth anything from £10 each. And they were easily enough lost, in all conscience, without his destroying them by lighting fires under them. It had happened much too often that a man had waked in the morning and found £20 worth of bullock lying on its back amongst the thistles. Many years ago a mob of about 600 on the march from the North camped one evening on Boggabri Common, near Gunnedah. In the morning 585 were dead. As to the cause, there were thistles in the common, and the only guess that could be made was that they came suddenly on to this prickly feed without having had time to get used to it. Accidents like that could happen to a bullock-driver any day. A drought was almost worse. One of the first big landholders at Bathurst used to tell of a forgotten drought in the 1830's during which eight bullock teams died in bringing his wool only 150 miles to Sydney. Perhaps in his heyday the bullocky had plenty of time to sit down and think of it. Anyway, of all the philosophers in Australia, universities included, there was probably not one that gave so much of his time to original thought as the bullocky. The Prime Minister of England would find him worth listening to. We noted that he had quite a different manner from the quick-witted shearer or even the station-hand. He was more deliberate. He would sit on an upturned box of groceries reading the paper—he was a man who always read critically—or filling his pipe in front of the fierce fire. And he talked thoughtfully, almost dreamily, in the intervals. He had a way of looking upon men much as he looked on the animals in his team.

"Terrible fat fellow, that fellow Smith," he would say, looking up over his reading spectacles.

"I didn't notice he was so stout," you remark.

"Oh, he was in wonderful condition when I used to know him. I don't know what he's like when the condition's off him. I've never seen him when he was poor."

The bullocky had the most interesting collection of short stories to be heard in the bush. He had travelled for longer than the shearer, and, not being a city man, he had observed every single thing. He had been to stranger places. He was probably a drover once, and, well—you may still meet, bringing cattle into Bourke, drovers who casually mention that in the earlier stages of the journey they had to keep an eye on the blacks, and that, when nearing its end they had to camp the cattle for the purpose of training them, not to be scared at the sight of a man on foot.

It was not always a master carrier who brought the bales from the woolshed to the railway. Most stations had their own bullocky, and often a horse-team or two as well. Indeed, in the West there was probably more wool brought in by the horses than by the bullocks. There might be 12 horses in a team, against 18 or 26 bullocks. We heard of 36 bullocks being yoked up to a wagon which was in a hole. The horse teams were faster; and it might be taken for granted that an Australian preferred to deal with a horse than with a bullock. By the time of the First World War the automobile was beating them both.

"But in a hole," you were told, "gimme the bullocks. A 'orse is good to go when he's at it, but he hasn't the heart of the bullocks. If 'orses get fixed for twenty minutes they're punctured. They won't pull any more, however long you stay there. But bullocks, they'll go back nex' day an' pull the same as ever." Mules had never really caught on, but some people said they must, for a reason which never fails to appeal to the Australian. "They mus' be good. They're using 'em in America."

The automobile was then already being used even in the very far west. But the people in some of the big cities would have been surprised had they known how many of the bales which they saw being driven from the railway had come to the other end of that railway on camels, one on each side of the hump. A fair quantity used to string in from the centre of Australia, from the very farthest white habitation, like an African caravan. And perhaps in these chapters more should have been made not only of the motor-lorry but of the camels. But it would take both a geography and history of Australia to do justice to the wool industry. And if we have followed the bullocky, with his 40 or 50 bales, to the railway—and, as is probably the case, he has found the railway gates closed upon him, and has turned in till the morning—that for present purposes must suffice.

CHRISTOPHER JOHN BRENNAN   (1870–1932)

Poet. Born and educated in Sydney; and Berlin (1892–4); Professor of German and Comparative Literature 1920–1925 at Sydney University.

SWEET SILENCE AFTER BELLS

Sweet silence after bells!
deep in the enamour'd ear
soft incantation dwells.

Filling the rapt still sphere
a liquid crystal swims,
precarious yet clear.

Those metal quiring hymns
shaped ether so succinct:
a while, or it dislimns,

the silence, wanly prinkt
with forms of lingering notes,
inhabits, close, distinct;

and night, the angel, floats
on wings of blessing spread
o'er all the gather'd cotes

where meditation, wed
with love, in gold-lit cells,
absorbs the heaven that shed

sweet silence after bells.

THE YELLOW GAS

The yellow gas is fired from street to street
past rows of heartless homes and hearths unlit,
dead churches, and the unending pavement beat
by crowds—say rather, haggard shades that flit

round nightly haunts of their delusive dream,
where'er our paradisal instinct starves:—
till on the utmost post, its sinuous gleam
crawls in the oily water of the wharves;

where Homer's sea loses his keen breath, hemm'd
what place rebellious piles were driven down—
the priestlike waters to this task condemn'd
to wash the roots of the inhuman town!—

where fat and strange-eyed fish that never saw
the outer deep, broad halls of sapphire light,
glut in the city's draught each nameless maw:
—and there, wide-eyed unto the soulless night,

methinks a drown'd maid's face might fitly show
what we have slain, a life that had been free,
clean, large, nor thus tormented—even so
as are the skies, the salt winds and the sea.

Ay, we had saved our days and kept them whole,
to whom no part in our old joy remains,
had felt those bright winds sweeping thro' our soul
and all the keen sea tumbling in our veins,

had thrill'd to harps of sunrise, when the height
whitens, and dawn dissolves in virgin tears,
or caught, across the hush'd ambrosial night,
the choral music of the swinging spheres,

or drunk the silence if nought else—But no!
and from each rotting soul distil in dreams
a poison, o'er the old earth creeping slow,
that kills the flowers and curdles the live streams,

that taints the fresh breath of re-risen day
and reeks across the pale bewilder'd moon:
—shall we be cleans'd and how? I only pray,
red flame or deluge, may that end be soon!

FIRE IN THE HEAVENS

Fire in the heavens, and fire along the hills,
and fire made solid in the flinty stone,
thick-mass'd or scatter'd pebble, fire that fills
the breathless hour that lives in fire alone.

This valley, long ago the patient bed
of floods that carv'd its antient amplitude,
in stillness of the Egyptian crypt outspread,
endures to drown in noon-day's tyrant mood.

Behind the veil of burning silence bound,
vast life's innumerous busy littleness
is hush'd in vague-conjectured blur of sound
that dulls the brain with slumbrous weight, unless

some dazzling puncture let the stridence throng
in the cicada's torture-point song.

A GRAY AND DUSTY DAYLIGHT FLOWS

A gray and dusty daylight flows
athwart the shatter'd traceries,
pale absence of the ruin'd rose.

Here once, on labour-harden'd knees,
beneath the kindly vaulted gloom
that gather'd them in quickening ease,

they saw the rose of heaven bloom,
alone, in heights of musky air,
with many an angel's painted plume.

So, shadowing forth their dim-felt prayer,
the dædal glass compell'd to grace
the outer day's indifferent stare,

where now its disenhallow'd face
beholds the petal-ribs enclose
nought, in their web of shatter'd lace,

save this pale absence of the rose.

RODERIC JOSEPH QUINN   (1867–1949)

Poet, editor. Born and educated in Sydney.

NOON ON THE BARRIER RANGES

The saltbush steeped in drowsy stillness lies,
    The mulga seems to swoon,
A hawk hangs poised within the burning skies,
    And it is noon.

The river-gums, their leaf-pores closed, distil
    No fresh and cooling breath;
I stand upon an old hard-bitten hill,
    Wide plains beneath.

Here stood tall mountains when the world was young,
    Their peaks uplifted high;
Here was the song of many waters sung
    In days gone by.

The monarch Change, whose will no power withstands
    Vast lord of might
At work by night and day, with tireless hands
    Planed down their height.

With such to see, and seeing ponder on,
    Such mighty ruin wrought,
Why should we wonder at proud Babylon
    Brought down to nought?

Be not amazed, though princes be displaced
    And kingdoms overcast;
Are empires more than mountains, basalt-based,
    That they should last?

A sense of things unreal, seen in dream,
    Is over plain and heights—
The time-worn rocks, the crumbled earth, the gleam
    Of mirage lights;

The horseman riding with a slackened rein
    Alone, a silent man;
The weird, dust-sprites that whirl across the plain
    A little span;

The earth-hued lizard, on the sun-baked rock
    Stretched out in stirless sleep;
The far-off drover and his dusty flock
    Of travelling sheep;

The hidden birds that break the hush, and call,
    And sink again to rest,
The dust-storm, hanging, like a crimson shawl,
    Within the west;

The white quartz glittering on the umber track,
    The claypans cracked and bare;
The poised hawk, hanging like a menace black
    In middle air;

The wonder of the spacious plain and sky,
    The splendour of it all;
The all that is not I—so wide, so high,
    And I so small!

The sun swings on, and up the western verge
    The great shawl-cloud spreads wide,
Till sky and plain in oneness meet and merge,
    Fierce-lit, red-dyed.

A wind, hell-hot and surged with fury, whips
    The trees upon its path,
And all is sudden turmoil and eclipse,
    And cries of wrath.

A choking darkness draws across the sun
    And clouds his splendour o'er,
And though but half his pilgrimage be done,
    'Tis noon no more.

FREDERIC MANNING   (1882–1935)

Novelist, poet. Born in Sydney; educated privately; went to
England in 1897.

THE TRENCHES

Endless lanes sunken in the clay,
Bays, and traverses, fringed with wasted herbage,
Seed-pods of blue scabious, and some lingering blooms;
And the sky, seen as from a well,
Brilliant with frosty stars.
We stumble, cursing, on the slippery duck-boards,
Goaded like the damned by some invisible wrath,
A will stronger than weariness, stronger than animal fear,
Implacable and monotonous.

Here a shaft, slanting, and below
A dusty and flickering light from one feeble candle
And prone figures sleeping uneasily,
Murmuring,
And men who cannot sleep.
With faces impassive as masks,
Bright, feverish eyes, and drawn lips,
Sad, pitiless, terrible faces,
Each an incarnate curse.

Here in a bay, a helmeted sentry
Silent and motionless, watching while two sleep,
And he sees before him
With indifferent eyes the blasted and torn land
Peopled with stiff prone forms, stupidly rigid,
As tho' they had not been men.

Dead are the lips where love laughed or sang,
The hands of youth eager to lay hold of life,
Eyes that have laughed to eyes,
And these were begotten,
O love, and lived lightly, and burnt
With the lust of a man's first strength: ere they were rent,
Almost at unawares, savagely; and strewn
In bloody fragments, to be the carrion
Of rats and crows.

And the sentry moves not, searching
Night for menace with weary eyes.

LEAVES

A frail and tenuous mist lingers on baffled and intricate branches;
Little gilt leaves are still, for quietness holds every bough;
Pools in the muddy road slumber, reflecting indifferent stars;
Steeped in the loveliness of moonlight is earth, and the valleys,
Brimmed up with quiet shadow, with a mist of sleep.

But afar on the horizon rise great pulses of light,
The hammering of guns, wrestling, locked in conflict
Like brute, stone gods of old struggling confusedly;
Then overhead purrs a shell, and our heavies
Answer, with sudden clapping bruits of sound,
Loosening our shells that stream whining and whimpering
    precipitately,
Hounding through air athirst for blood.

And the little gilt leaves
Flicker in falling, like waifs and flakes of flame.

GROTESQUE

These are the dammed circles Dante trod,
Terrible in hopelessness,
But even skulls have their humour,
An eyeless and sardonic mockery:
And we,
Sitting with streaming eyes in the acrid smoke,
That murks our foul, damp billet,
Chant bitterly, with raucous voices
As a choir of frogs
In hideous irony, our patriotic songs.

II : THE TWENTIES AND THIRTIES

Commentary

"Australian culture is at present in a nebulous stage ..." wrote Rex Ingamells in 1938. He reached this conclusion because he did not consider that Australian writers had arrived at a clear view of the distinctiveness of their country. Evidence for this view is the preoccupation during this period with questions of national identity and culture.

After the achievement of Federation and the experience of the First World War, there is some feeling of anti-climax during the twenties. The post-war malaise which is expressed in cynicism and a brittle gaiety in England and America, in Australia takes the form of a search for definition and, by the thirties, some expression of nostalgia for the simplicities of the past—frequently identified by sentimental affirmation of a rural landscape. A corollary is that this is also a period of marked insularity, in which Australian writers remain almost wholly indifferent to the widespread interest in modernism in Europe and America.

The countervailing local certainties are prominent in the fiction of Katharine Susannah Prichard, Kylie Tennant and others. These writers, deeply concerned at the inequities and hardships of the working lives of ordinary people, use the techniques of social realism to promote faith in the ideals of democratic socialism.

John Shaw Neilson, the poet with whom this section begins, reflects aspects of these attitudes, but his poetry has a fine sensitivity far removed from the comparatively ungainly prose of the period. He is a pure lyricist at his best, delicate in his expression of experience. He has some curious natural affinities with the French Symbolist poets, especially in his attempts to capture the essence of things in metaphor and rhythm. Neilson impressed and influenced later lyricists, notably James McAuley.

Kenneth Slessor stands at the end of this period, but at the beginning of modern Australian poetry. He was, as person and poet, "a man of Sydney"; and while the city was not his only subject, it is the focus of a number of his best poems. Slessor's puzzlement about the ultimate questions led Judith Wright to criticise him for nihilism, but his is a modern voice speaking through vivid images of urban and rural landscapes.

JOHN SHAW NEILSON   (1872–1942)

Poet. Born in South Australia; had a minimal education.

THE ORANGE TREE

The young girl stood beside me. I
　Saw not what her young eyes could see:
—A light, she said, not of the sky
　Lives somewhere in the Orange Tree.

—Is it, I said, of east or west?
　The heartbeat of a luminous boy
Who with his faltering flute confessed
　Only the edges of his joy?

Was he, I said, borne to the blue
　In a mad escapade of Spring
Ere he could make a fond adieu
　To his love in the blossoming?

—Listen! The young girl said. There calls
　No voice, no music beats on me;
But it is almost sound: it falls
　This evening on the Orange Tree.

—Does he, I said, so fear the Spring
　Ere the white sap too far can climb?
See in the full gold evening
　All happenings of the olden time?

Is he so goaded by the green?
　Does the compulsion of the dew
Make him unknowable but keen
　Asking with beauty of the blue?

—Listen! the young girl said. For all
　Your hapless talk you fail to see
There is a light, a step, a call
　This evening on the Orange Tree

—Is it, I said, a waste of love
　Imperishably old in pain,
Moving as an affrighted dove
　Under the sunlight or the rain?

Is it a fluttering heart that gave
　Too willingly and was reviled?
Is it the stammering at a grave,
　The last word of a little child?

—Silence! The young girl said. Oh, why,
   Why will you talk to weary me?
Plague me no longer now, for I
   Am listening like the Orange Tree.

LOVE'S COMING

Quietly as rosebuds
   Talk to the thin air,
Love came so lightly
   I knew not he was there.

Quietly as lovers
   Creep at the middle moon,
Softly as players tremble
   In the tears of a tune;

Quietly as lilies
   Their faint vows declare
Came the shy pilgrim:
   I knew not he was there.

Quietly as tears fall
   On a wild sin,
Softly as griefs call
   In a violin;

Without hail or tempest,
   Blue sword or flame,
Love came so lightly
   I knew not that he came.

SONG BE DELICATE

Let your song be delicate.
   The skies declare
No war—the eyes of lovers
   Wake everywhere.

Let your voice be delicate.
   How faint a thing
Is Love, little Love crying
   Under the Spring.

Let your song be delicate.
   The flowers can hear:
Too well they know the tremble
   Of the hollow year.

Let your voice be delicate.
  The bees are home:
All their day's love is sunken
  Safe in the comb.

Let your song be delicate.
  Sing no loud hymn:
Death is abroad.... Oh, the black season!
  The deep—the dim!

THE CRANE IS MY NEIGHBOUR

The bird is my neighbour, a whimsical fellow and dim;
There is in the lake a nobility falling on him.

The bird is a noble, he turns to the sky for a theme,
And the ripples are thoughts coming out to the edge of a dream.

The bird is both ancient and excellent, sober and wise,
But he never could spend all the love that is sent for his eyes.

He bleats no instruction, he is not an arrogant drummer;
His gown is simplicity—blue as the smoke of the summer.

How patient he is as he puts out his wings for the blue!
His eyes are as old as the twilight, and calm as the dew.

The bird is my neighbour, he leaves not a claim for a sigh,
He moves as the guest of the sunlight—he roams in the sky.

The bird is a noble, he turns to the sky for a theme,
And the ripples are thoughts coming out to the edge of a dream.

THE SUNDOWNER

I know not when this tiresome man
With his shrewd, sable billy-can
And his unwashed Democracy
His boomed-up Pilgrimage began.

Sometimes he wandered far outback
On a precarious Tucker Track;
Sometimes he lacked Necessities
No gentleman would like to lack.

Tall was the grass, I understand,
When the old Squatter ruled the land.
Why were the Conquerors kind to him?
Ah, the Wax Matches in his hand!

Where bullockies with oaths intense
Made of the dragged-up trees a fence,
Gambling with scorpions he rolled
His Swag, conspicuous, immense.

In the full splendour of his power
Rarely he touched one mile an hour,
Dawdling at sunset, History says,
For the Pint Pannikin of flour.

Seldom he worked; he was, I fear,
Unreasonably slow and dear;
Little he earned, and that he spent
Deliberately drinking Beer.

Cheerful, sorefooted child of chance,
Swiftly we knew him at a glance;
Boastful and self-compassionate,
Australia's Interstate Romance.

Shall he not live in Robust Rhyme,
Soliloquies and Odes Sublime?
Strictly between ourselves, he was
A rare old Humbug all the time.

In many a Book of Bushland dim
Mopokes shall give him greeting grim;
The old swans pottering in the reeds
Shall pass the time of day to him.

On many a page our Friend shall take
Small sticks his evening fire to make;
Shedding his waistcoat, he shall mix
On its smooth back his Johnny-Cake.

'Mid the dry leaves and silvery bark
Often at nightfall will he park
Close to a homeless creek, and hear
The Bunyip paddling in the dark.

THE POOR CAN FEED THE BIRDS

Ragged, unheeded, stooping, meanly shod,
The poor pass to the pond; not far away
The spires go up to God.

Shyly they come from the unpainted lane;
Coats have they made of old unhappiness
That keeps in every pain.

The rich have fear, perchance their God is dim;
'Tis with the hope of stored-up happiness
They build the spires to Him.

The rich go out in clattering pomp and dare
In the most holy places to insult
The deep Benevolence there.

But 'tis the poor who make the loving words.
Slowly they stoop; it is a sacrament:
The poor can feed the birds.

Old, it is old, this scattering of the bread,
Deep as forgiveness, or the tears that go
Out somewhere to the dead.

The feast of love, the love that is the cure
For all indignities—it reigns, it calls,
It chains us to the pure.

Seldom they speak of God, He is too dim;
So without thought of after happiness
They feed the birds for Him.

The rich men walk not here on the green sod,
But they have builded towers, the timorous
That still go up to God.

Still will the poor go out with loving words;
In the long need, the need for happiness
The poor can feed the birds.

NETTIE PALMER   (1885–1964)

Critic, journalist. Born in Victoria; educated in Melbourne.

from FOURTEEN YEARS: … A PRIVATE JOURNAL

February 9th, 1927

Lately the idea of editing an 'Australian Story-book' has set me
reading the short stories of the 'nineties. Not that I intend to use
any of them; the new anthology must begin where A. G. Stephens
left off when he made his collection at the end of the century; but I
wanted to refresh my memory of what had already been written.
   It certainly hasn't been a voyage of exciting discoveries. Who invented the legend that a band of brilliant short-story writers existed
in the 'nineties, and that in examining the early files of the *Bulletin*

one would stumble upon masterpieces? There wasn't much basis for it. The names are quickening—Alec Montgomery, Louis Becke, Dorrington, Barbara Baynton, Price Warung, Edward Dyson—but the stories above the names are disappointing. Ironic fragments, brisk little dramas separated into scenes by rows of asterisks, sketches of eccentric character, farcical incidents—and that's all. Not much evidence of the subtle, delicate art that can seize upon some episode and give it shape and significance, so that it remains in the mind like a poem.

A page of Lawson's pulls you up with a delicious shock. This is what you've been looking for. Without apparent effort, Lawson takes you straight into his own intimate world and makes you free of it; his easy, colloquial voice has the incantation of rhythm; even his humorous stories stand out from Edward Dyson's in the same way that poetry differs from verse. Until this re-reading, I had accepted Dyson's 'The Golden Shanty' as a sort of classic, but how crude and insensitive it seems beside one of Lawson's comedies! Quite plainly Lawson's short stories have a quality that makes the current grouping of his stories with the others' absurd.

Yet there must have been something about these writers of the 'nineties that gave their readers the sense of a new world being revealed. You can feel it when you place them against the conventional writers of that time—the three-decker novelists and the people who supplied glossy short stories to the American magazines. Whatever else might be said of it, the work of our short-story writers was not marked by a slick emptiness. They were robust; they did not accept circulating-library values; they tried to get near the core of life. This was particularly true of Barbara Baynton and Price Warung. I remember how R. B. Cunninghame Graham, that very eclectic critic, was attracted by Barbara Baynton's writing and compared it with Gorky's—this was somewhere about 1906, when only Gorky's bitter early sketches had come into English. As for Price Warung, he was limited by some conceived necessity to tie his stories to verifiable fact. He could not free himself from the historical convict records. What a masterpiece of pity and terror 'The Secret History of the Ring' might have been if he had been able to lift it from that world into one more definitely his own!

What might have been, though, is not much use to the anthologist. A short story must have its own perfection, or it is nothing. The element of completeness, of art, must enter into it so that it lives as a whole in the mind. Apart from Lawson's work, there is very little use in looking for this kind of perfection in the stories of the 'nineties. If they have left a tradition, it lies in their habit of seeking their subjects directly from life instead of fabricating plots and situations. But there is a greater mastery in Katharine Prichard's story, 'The Cooboo,' published recently in the *Bulletin*, than in the lot of them. What a world of tragedy and strange beauty she has compressed into a couple of thousand words! It is a marvel of economy as well as of feeling—so little stated directly, so much implied. (How is it that in giving the merest necessary background to her story of the remote cattle-country, her phrase 'the tumbled hills' is enough, where it occurs, to make the heart turn over?)

May 2nd, 1933

A little paragraph in the paper announces that A. G. Stephens has died. Inevitably his name was spelt wrongly. It is one of the ironies of his obscure, significant life that he was known, when he was known at all, by his initials, or as The Bookfellow.

All evening I have been remembering my first meeting with him, in 1918. An exhilarating afternoon in early summer, the exhilaration not merely a matter of weather. The war was over, V. would be coming back, life was opening up again. In the garden at Killenna the children and I were playing under the flowering gum when Hugh McCrae appeared, with his usual boisterous gaiety; he had with him some of his family and A. G. Stephens, who was on a visit to Melbourne.

A downright, hearty man, not stout, but rather like that mature sea-captain of Conrad's who seemed 'extremely full of healthy organs.' A man who hadn't time to be anything but healthy. One noted that he was bald, his short, neat beard white. But these were not limitations—impossible to imagine him otherwise. The silver beard belonged to his remarkably fresh colouring; his baldness made a dome for his fine, candid eyes—childlike eyes, someone has said, but belonging to a child whose eagerness never let up. No one could believe, looking at his face, that he was pursued by petty financial worries.

He was hoping to revive the *Bookfellow* soon; that was the chief reason for his Melbourne visit. Much of its space, he hinted, would be devoted to Shaw Neilson. The reception given to 'Heart of Spring', which he had managed to publish—expensively for himself—a year before, made him feel that Neilson whom he had had to carry on his hands for so long was now able to walk alone— or to fly on his Pegasus. A.G.'s interest in our poets was directed chiefly to the makers of lyrics, and of these he put Neilson first. 'He beats the lot of you,' he had said to V. a few years before, showing him the prepared manuscript and wondering when it could be published. He admired McCrae consistently, but I think associated him rather closely with Norman Lindsay, the same thermometer for both rising and falling in his mind.

It was interesting to see him in the garden watching the children—McCrae's and ours—as if they were new creations to him; yet he was the father of quite a long family. McCrae, of course, was acting the playboy. Stephens enjoyed his grace and fantastic gusto, and responded to it. Afterwards, in my little study, crowded as it was with books mostly concerned with my pupils at the time, he asked for French poetry. I had a rather trifling Verlaine selection, containing nothing new to him, and a few studies of Verlaine in German and Italian. He was attracted by a Versailles book (*Cité des Eaux*, by Henri de Régnier), mainly sonnets, but with a few lyrics added. What caught him was an impression of a young girl asleep:

> *Elle n'a, pour sa tête,*
> *Autre couronne*
> *Que ses deux bras entrelacés...*

And then out it came, the word of comment, the final accolade of the Bookfellow as critic: 'Ah, that is sung, not merely said.'

It was this criterion, applied always, that made him draw away from O'Dowd, whom at first he published and praised on the Red Page, producing 'Dawnward?' as one of the *Bulletin* booklets. Not that O'Dowd had become less musical with the years; the harsh, stabbing quatrains of his early work had been followed by 'The Bush,' with its own organ-music. But by the time 'The Bush' appeared, Stephens had dedicated himself wholly to Neilson whose song was delicate, Neilson whom he himself had trained to make the most of his lyrical talent. So when he caught sight of Shirlow's etching of O'Dowd on my wall, he turned away to another wall, where there was a photograph of Joseph Furphy. Yes, he had seen the new issue of 'Such is Life' eighteen months before. It hadn't sold three hundred copies for the *Bulletin* when he had published it in 1903—but he had known what he was doing.

In fact, he had known what he was doing all through. For all his humour, he never made jokes about his own judgment. There were so many ways of being hopelessly wrong—he had found the only way of being right. I remember keeping myself from reminding him that, long before, young Frank Wilmot, finding his verse consistently refused by the *Bookfellow*, had invented the pen-name Furnley Maurice, purely *ad rem*, and had been accepted as a new poet. Stephens, when he discovered his identity, never forgave him. Yet the episode gave Wilmot himself opportunities of being magnanimous in ways the tyrant would never know. He was continually acknowledging his boyhood's debt to the Red Page, and recommending people to read the *Bookfellow*

On the whole the air, when A.G.S. was speaking, was full of possible lightnings, yet with gracious gleams of wit and learning, too. Most of the contacts I had with him afterwards were by letter, but his letters always kept the sound of his voice, as when arguing some literary point: 'You don't agree? Wait till V. comes back and some day we'll go into it hammer and tongs (tongs are married).' He wrote as he spoke—briskly, musically, magisterially—yet with a charming note of play. When his little book on Chris Brennan appeared lately, it ended with a gentle memorial to bookfellowship, the last pages strewing gumleaves one after another in farewell, to Brennan, to Dowell O'Reilly... Now let one leaf more fall, with Stephens' name on it. Let it be aromatic, broad, and well-shaped. He should have died hereafter.

HUGH MCCRAE   (1876–1958)

Poet. Born and educated in Melbourne.

MEMORIES

I can remember still, and still without one drop
    Of weakness in mine eye,
The brown bark farm-house on the hill, the windmill top
    Slow girding at the sky.

The six-foot water dam, its sides thick-pocked with hoofs
    Of many thirsty sheep,
The clover and the pink-lipped brides, the strutted roofs
    Of other farms asleep;

The stack of rain-stained hay, the stack of hay yet sweet
    The double milking shed,
Its arch sunk inwards, pierced and black with all the heat
    Of fifty summers fled.

And I remember plainly too the she-oak tall,
    Whose fingers in the night,
Whenever sudden zephyrs blew, took hold the wall,
    And shook my heart with fright;

For I was but an infant then, and full of fear
    And weird imaginings,
Long routed since, beyond my ken, to leave me clear
    For manhood's greater things.

And there it was my father died (as good a soul
    As ever trod life's path);
Death took him in his chair, beside the burning bole
    Of wood upon our hearth.

And there my mother heard him speak one evening end—
    Long after he was dead—
Whereat she kissed me on the cheek; then, reverend,
    Lay silent in her bed.

I hate the farm-house on the hill, its windmill top
   Slow girding at the sky;
I think and think upon it still without one drop
   Of weakness in mine eye.

EVENING

How tenderly the evening creeps between
The fading curtain of this apple-bough,
A ghost of rose and grey, mid foliage green
Jewelled with stripes of rain.

Ah, look where now,
Trembling, but joyous, like a challenged bride,
The moon, along a bed of daffodil,
Opens a cloud against her golden side ...
As one expectant of her lord's sweet will.

EARTH

Green grows my grave in the grass,
Somewhere ...? Oh, let it be
Here in the land that I love,
My heart's own Italy.

The bee will hum to the bud,
And the bud will whisper to me
Of the dawn and the dew and the flood
And the season's mystery.

The song of the brook through the stones,
The song of the thrush through the tree,
Will mingle and marry and hush
With the music of moonlight and sea.

And mad with their musical chant
I know that my heaven will be
To go through the wild olden wood
Of earth-sweet memory.

Katharine Susannah Prichard   (1883–1969)

Novelist, short story writer, dramatist, journalist. Born in Levuka, Fiji; came to Australia in infancy; educated privately and in Melbourne.

THE COOBOO

They had been mustering all day on the wide plains of Murndoo station. Over the red earth, black with ironstone pebbles, through mulga and curari bush, across the ridges which make a blue wall along the horizon. And the rosy, garish light of sunset was on plains, hills, moving cattle, men and horses.

Through red dust the bullocks mooched, restless and scary still, a wild mob from the hills. John Gray, in the rear with Arra, the boy who was his shadow; Wongana, on the right with his gin, Rose; Frank, the half-caste, on the left with Minni.

A steer breaking from the mob before Rose, she wheeled and went after him. Faint and wailing, a cry followed her, as though her horse had stepped on and crushed some small creature. But the steer was getting away. Arra went after him, stretched along his horse's neck, rounded the beast and rode him back to the mob, sulky and blethering. The mob swayed; it had broken three times that day, but was settling to the road.

John Gray called: "Yienda (you) damn fool, Rosey. Finish!"

The gin, on her slight, rough-haired horse, pulled up scowling.

"Tell Meetchie, Thirty Mile, to-morrow," John Gray said. "Miah, new moon."

Rose slewed her horse away from the mob of men and cattle. That wailing, thin and hard as hair-string, moved with her.

"Minni!"

John Gray jerked his head towards Rose. Minni's bare heels struck her horse's belly; with a turn of the wrist she swung her horse off from the mob, turned, leaned forward, rising in her stirrups, and came up with Rose.

Thin, dark figures on their wiry station-bred horses, the gins rode into the haze of sunset towards the hills. The dull, dirty blue of trousers wrapped round their legs was torn: their short, fairish hair tousled by the wind. But the glitter and tumult of Rose's eyes— Minni looked away from them.

At a little distance, when men and cattle were a moving cloud of red dust, Rose's anger gushed after them.

"Koo!"

Fierce as the cry of a hawk flew her last note of derision and defiance.

A far-away rattle of laughter drifted back across the plains. The men had heard and were laughing at her.

The women walked their horses across country. Alone they would have been afraid, as darkness coming up behind was hovering near them, secreting itself among the low, writhen trees and bushes. Afraid of the evil spirits who wander over the plains and stony ridges when the light of day is withdrawn. But together they were not so afraid. Twenty miles away, over there, below that dent in the hills where Nyedee Creek made a sandy bed for itself among white-bodied gums, was Murndoo homestead and the *uloo* of their people.

There was no track; and in the first darkness, which would be thick as wool after the glow of sunset faded, only their instinct would keep them moving in the direction of the homestead and their own low, round huts of bagging, rusty tin, and dead boughs.

Both were Wongana's women: Rose, tall, gaunt and masterful; Minni, younger, fat and jolly. Rose had been a good stockman in her day: one of the best. Minni did not ride or track nearly as well as Rose.

And yet, as they rode along, Minni pattered complacently of how well she had worked that day; of how she had flashed, this way and that, heading-off breakaways, dashing after them, turning them back so smartly to the mob that John had said, "Good man, Minni!" There was the white bullock—he had rushed near the yards. Had Rose seen the chestnut mare stumble in a crabhole and send Arra flying? But Minni had chased the white bullock, chased him for a couple of miles, and brought him back to the yards. No doubt there would be *nammery* for her and a new *gina-gina* when the men came in from the muster.

She pulled a pipe from her belt, shook the ashes out, and with reins looped over her arm stuffed the bowl with tobacco from a tin tied to her belt. Stooping down, she struck a match on her stirrup-iron, guarded the flame to the pipe between her short, white teeth, and smoked contentedly.

The scowl on Rose's face deepened, darkened. That thin, fretted wailing came from her breast.

She unslung from her neck the rag rope by which the baby had been held against her body, and gave him a sagging breast to suck. Holding him with one arm, she rode slowly, her horse picking his way over the rough, stony earth.

It had been a hard day. The gins were mustering with the men at sunrise. Camped at Nyedee well the night before, in order to get a good start, they had been riding through timbered ridges all the morning, rounding up wild cows, calves and young bullocks, and driving them down to the yards at Nyedee, where John Gray cut out the fats, left old Jimmy and a couple of boys to brand calves, turn the cows and calves back to the ridge again while he took on the mob for trucking at Meekatharra. The bullocks were as wild as birds—needed watching all day. And all the time that small, whimpering bundle against her breast had hampered Rose's movements.

There was nothing the gins liked better than a muster, riding after cattle. And they could ride, were quicker in their movements, more alert than the men; sharper at picking up tracks. They did not go mustering very often nowadays when there was work to do at the homestead. Since John Gray had married, and there was a woman on Murndoo, she found plenty of washing, scrubbing, sweeping, for the gins to do; would not spare them often to go after cattle. But John was short-handed. He had said he must have Rose and Minni to muster Nyedee. And all day her baby's crying had irritated Rose. The *cooboo* had wailed and wailed as she rode with him tied to her body.

The *cooboo* was responsible for the wrong things she had done that day. Stupid things. Rose was furious. The men had yelled at her. Wongana, her man, blackguarding her before everybody, had called her "a hen who did not know where she had laid her eggs." And John Gray, with his "Yienda, damn fool, Rosey. Finish!" had sent her home like a naughty child.

Now, here was Minni jabbering of the tobacco she would get and the new *gina-gina*. How pleased Wongana would be with her! And the *cooboo* wailing, wailing. He wailed as he chewed Rose's empty breast, squirming against her; wailed and gnawed.

She cried out with hurt and impatience. Rage, irritated to madness, rushed through her; rushed, like waters coming down the dry creek-beds after heavy rain. Rose wrenched the *cooboo* from her breast and flung him from her to the ground. There was a crack as of twigs breaking.

Minni glanced aside. "Wiah!" she gasped with widening eyes. But Rose rode on, gazing ahead over the rosy, garish plains and wall of the hills, darkening from blue to purple and indigo.

When the women came into the station kitchen, earth, hills, and trees were dark; the sky heavy with stars. Minni gave his wife John's message—that he would be home with the new moon, in about a fortnight.

Meetchie, as the blacks called Mrs John Gray, could not make out why the gins were so stiff and quiet—why Rose stalked scowling and sulky-fellow, sombre eyes just glancing, and away again. Meetchie wanted to ask about the muster; what sort of condition the bullocks had on; how many were on the road; if many calves had been branded at Nyedee. But she knew them too well to ask questions when they looked like that.

Only when she had given them bread and a tin of jam, cut off hunks of corned beef for them, filled their billies with strong black tea, put sugar in their empty tins, and they were going off to the *uloo*, she was surprised to see Rose without her baby.

"Why, Rose," she exclaimed, "where's the *cooboo*?"

Rose stalked off into the night. Minni glanced back with scared eyes, and followed Rose.

In the dawn, when a cry, remote and anguished, flew through the clear air, Meetchie wondered who was dead in the camp by the creek. She remembered Rose: how she had looked the night before. And the *cooboo*—where was he?

Then she knew it was Rose wailing for her *cooboo* in the dawn; Rose cutting herself with stones until her body bled; Rose screaming in a fury of unavailing grief.

MARY GILMORE   (1865–1962)

Poet, prose writer, journalist. Born in N.S.W.

OLD BOTANY BAY

I'm old
Botany Bay;
Stiff in the joints,
Little to say.

I am he
Who paved the way,
That you might walk
At your ease to-day;

I was the conscript
Sent to hell
To make in the desert
The living well;

I bore the heat,
I blazed the track—
Furrowed and bloody
Upon my back.

I split the rock;
I felled the tree:
The nation *was*—
Because of me!

Old Botany Bay
Taking the sun
From day to day....
Shame on the mouth
That would deny
The knotted hands
That set us high!

THE WARADGERY TRIBE

Harried we were, and spent,
  Broken and falling,
Ere as the cranes we went,
  Crying and calling.

Summer shall see the bird
  Backward returning;
Never shall there be heard,
  Us, who went yearning.

Emptied of us the land;
  Ghostly our going;
Fallen, like spears the hand
  Dropped in the throwing.

We are the lost who went,
  Like the birds, crying;
Hunted, lonely, and spent;
  Broken and dying.

NURSE NO LONG GRIEF

Oh, could we weep,
And weeping bring relief!
But life asks more than tears
And falling leaf.

Though year by year
Tears fall and leaves are shed,
Spring bids new sap arise,
And blood run red.

Nurse no long grief,
Lest the heart flower no more;
Grief builds no barns; its plough
Rusts at the door.

SHE WAS A SCENTED LAND

from OLD DAYS, OLD WAYS

Even in my own life she was a scented land. In spring the bush used
to be a constant choir of song; wings were everywhere; throughout
the changing years might be heard the continual flying of birds:

curlews, plovers, travelling duck, swans, wandering owls, bitterns, night-jars, and in the swamp the bleat of the snipe. From twenty directions at once you could hear the mopoke; from a hundred the curlew. There were the birds of all seasons, and the birds of the different hours of the day; there were the waders, the runners, the creepers, the carrion-eaters, the killers (kestrels, falcons, eagles), and those like the fantails that caught the fluttering insect on the wing.

In sheltered places where the blue wren was plentiful, he was literally in hundreds, a family flight being like a small jewelled cloud slipping tenuously through the undergrowth. In every bush I dare affirm there was a pigeon or a dove; the grass was a moving mass of parrots and parrakeets; while the trees glistened white with cock-atoo, or were flamingo-pink with the galah. Ants swarmed on the earth and trees; native bees, flies, gnats, beetles, spiders, and butter-flies, burst from egg; rose from larvae, emerged from chrysalis. Everywhere things crept, swarmed, climbed, hummed, chirped, whistled, croaked, sang, and flowered. The air was full of the scent of life and honey, of the warm rich smell of feathers and fur.

The Almighty had poured out for plenty, and the black man had guarded that plenty by his care for balance. The black was indeed the unconscious father both of rationing and of the "Five Year Plan."

There were no bad smells about the bush when the kingdom of the wild was its only kingdom; for the army of the small ate corruption before corruption became malodorous. It was not till the settlement came that the earth stank, and sewers burst. Once Australia smelt like the Spice Islands; the winds stooped as they passed because of her blossom; ships knew her before they came to her.

"We are near Australia," said the seamen. "Can't you smell the flowers?"

And people raised their heads and breathed in perfumes as it were out of heaven, for the land was still invisible, or but a bank low down on the horizon. Now only at the Leeuwin, as ships pass, do people raise their heads and snuff the air for scented winds. And then only for a short time in the year. Soon that, too, will be gone.

"It was a land of flowers!" said my grandmother. "At sea we smelt the rich scent of the country, different from anything we had ever known. We noticed the perfume long before we came to it. Those who had come home from Australia told us of it, and all who went out to Australia looked for it."

So spoke all the grandmothers. But who has said it in the full rich way that makes it live? Has anyone really sung to the world the song of this Scented Land? The thick-nosed and dull-eared derided her, and we accepted their derision. They called her a land of song-less birds and scentless flowers. The world believed them; and we for a century followed in the train of the world, even though on our breath her perfumes hung rich.

Indignantly I used to combat the statement:

"But our flowers *are* scented and our birds *do* sing!" I would counter.

"Oh, but your flowers do not smell like *English* flowers, and there are no *nightingales!*" would be the reply. Well, the rose, the lilac, and the nightingale are all Persian. As for our Australian wattle, London now calls it French mimosa....

"*She was a scented land...*" And we were taught to look otherwise, and looked as taught.

"*She was a scented land...*" And only the exile knew her.

In the days of the first-fleeters, in the years of the forth-farers and the forerunners, the hills and shores of Sydney Cove were sheets of flowers.

"There was nowhere that you could step that you did not walk on them. You would see people trying to avoid treading on the blossoms as they walked just as if they were in a garden," my forerunners of that day used to tell me. They also said that, flower-hungry after the long six months voyage with nothing but sea and sky to lengthen sight, and nothing but the ship by which to contract sight, as soon as people set foot on shore they would drop their baggage and run to gather of the abounding loveliness.

"They would be so eager that when their hands were full they would let fall what they had for fresh ones. *And the scent!... The scent!...*"

Where the streets of Sydney now are, the very stones grew rock-lilies; the flannel flower and the boronia covered every inch that was not just bare rock. I had not seen these lilies when my maternal forbears talked to me of their landing in 1837; I was only a child then. But when at sixteen I came to Sydney I walked all round the Quay, along The Rocks, and back through what is now the Tarpeian Way, a thing hacked out of the earth to make a road trying to see as *they* had seen; trying to reset the Scented Land, the Land of Flowers....

I look back to old kitchens with their sanded floors; I see my elders peeling potatoes, saving the skins cut thick at the "eyes" for planting, and nursing them for more seed; I see them picking over scant bushels of wheat that the best grains might be kept for the sparest of sowings. I hear the glad cry:

"There is *a quart, at least, of fairly good seed!*" as my grandfather, my grandmother, or one of my aunts or uncles would stand up to stretch the tired, down-bent back. I smell the aroma of fire from wood such as we will never cut again in Australia; for the very long-growing are all chopped out and destroyed now. And, as I think, I feel glad that I belonged to those who pioneered and helped set the foundations of this the last of the Wonderful Lands.

In the kitchen that I knew so well hung the bunches of drying and already dry herbs; those whose drying in the air was complete tied in paper or calico bags for winter use; for the habits of older countries, less prodigal and less hospitable than this, still governed the habits of the people who first came here. On the outside walls, under the long veranda, hung the bundles of orchard and vine cuttings; and each kind had its own scent. Even the varieties of vines differed in smell—Isabella, Shiraz, Golden Hamburg, Sweet Water! Old-fashioned kinds? True. But they were old-fashioned times.

They were the years of frontier beginnings even if Sydney and the coast districts had already reached stability, to markets and easy comfort. From the deep, dark wine cellar comes the winey, earthy smell of all such places; the greater garden at the front of the house gleams with its laurels, its standard roses, its veronica, its laurustinus, lilacs, and oleanders; and the smaller, less formal, flower-beds at each side of the house, set under the sheltering high rose hedges, send out perfumes on every wind that blows. There lavender and pinks, Sweet William, and rosemary border the shaped beds in which blaze anemone and ranunculus, petunia, and verbena. But under the quick-set, deep in the shade are love-in-a-mist, periwinkle, balm, and violets.

The peach- and plum- and nectarine-trees run in rows down the front orchard to the lower vineyard; the quince- and apple-trees are by the kitchen, the dairy, and the wine-sheds; and between these and the "old" vineyard the cherries, greengages, and figs, are companioned by more peaches, more plums, and more quinces.

"I put *them* in for shade for the cows on the other side," said Uncle Alfred, but we all knew he did it for the love of flowers and trees. And he put in more that ran between the cow-sheds, stables, workshops, and barns just behind the "new" vineyard.

The old parts near the house I wandered in at will. But the new was forbidden. "You are too small yet," they said, "you might get lost *and not come home to dinner!*" But yet, small as I was, the elders talked to me and told me of the things I have written here; told me because to me it was romance, history, picture, and vision; told it to a mind journeying back into a world where my foot would never go because it was too late a comer. And part of it was even then in the land of things past.

"The Spice Islands—where are they, grandmamma?"

"In the Indies, Borneo, Java, Sumatra, the Celebes. They smelt of nutmeg and allspice, of pepper, oranges, cloves, and cinnamon. Ships put out of their course that they might pass near and smell them."

"And when you came here was Australia like that, grandmamma?"

"Australia was just like that, my child. The very birds carried the perfume of her flowers on their feathers.... Ships smelt her scents on the winds as they passed.... She was a land of flowers."

'HENRY HANDEL RICHARDSON'   (Ethel F. Robertson) (1870–1946)

Novelist, short story writer. Born in Melbourne; educated in Melbourne and in Leipzig; from 1887 lived in Germany and England.

THE BATHE

Stripped of her clothing, the child showed the lovely shape of a six-year-old. Just past the dimpled roundnesses of babyhood, the little body stood slim and straight, legs and knees closely met, the skin white as the sand into which the small feet dug, pink toe faultlessly matched to toe.

She was going to bathe.

The tide was out. The alarming, ferocious surf, which at flood came hurtling over the reef, swallowing up the beach, had withdrawn, baring the flat brown coral rocks: far off against their steep brown edges it sucked and gurgled lazily. In retreating, it had left many lovely pools in the reef, all clear as glass, some deep as rooms, grown round their sides with weeds that swam like drowned hair, and hid strange sea-things.

Not to these pools might the child go; nor did she need to prick her soles on the coral. Her bathing-place was a great sandy-bottomed pool that ran out from the beach, and at its deepest came no higher than her chin.

Naked to sun and air, she skipped and frolicked with the delight of the very young, to whom clothes are still an encumbrance. And one of her runs led her headlong into the sea. No toe-dipping tests were necessary here; this water met the skin like a veil of warm silk. In it she splashed and ducked and floated; her hair, which had been screwed into a tight little knob, loosening and floating with her like a nimbus. Tired of play, she came out, trickling and glistening, and lay down in the sand, which was hot to the touch, first on her stomach, then on her back, till she was coated with sand like a fish bread-crumbed for frying. This, for the sheer pleasure of plunging anew, and letting the silken water wash her clean.

At the sight, the two middle-aged women who sat looking on grew restless. And, the prank being repeated, the sand-caked little body vanishing in the limpid water to bob up shining like ivory, the tips of their tongues shot out and surreptitiously moistened their lips. These were dry, their throats were dry, their skins itched; their seats burned from pressing the hot sand.

And suddenly eyes met and brows were lifted in a silent question. Shall we? Dare we risk it?

"Let's!"

For no living thing but themselves moved on the miles of desolate beach; not a neighbour was within cooee; their own shack lay hid behind a hill.

Straightway they fell to rolling up their work and stabbing it with their needles.

Then they, too, undressed.

Tight, high bodices of countless buttons went first, baring the massy arms and fat-creased necks of a plump maturity. Thereafter bunchy skirts were slid over hips and stepped out of. Several petticoats followed, the undermost of red flannel, with scalloped edges. Tight stiff corsets were next squeezed from their moorings and cast aside: the linen beneath lay hot and damply crushed. Long white drawers unbound and, leg by leg, disengaged, voluminous calico chemises appeared, draped in which the pair sat down to take off their boots—buttoned boots—and stockings, their feet emerging red and tired-looking, the toes misshapen, and horny with callosities. Erect again, they yet coyly hesitated before the casting of the last veil, once more sweeping the distance for a possible spy. Nothing stirring, however, up went their arms, dragging the balloon-like garments with them; and, inch by inch, calves, thighs, trunks and breasts were bared to view.

At the prospect of getting water playmates, the child had clapped her hands, hopping up and down where she stood. But this was the first time she had watched a real grown-up undress; she was always in bed and asleep when they did it. Now, in broad day-light, she looked on unrebuked, wildly curious; and surprise soon damped her joy. So this was what was underneath! Skirts and petticoats down, she saw that laps were really legs; while the soft and cosy place you put your head on, when you were tired...

And suddenly she turned tail and ran back to the pool. She didn't want to see.

But your face was the one bit of you you couldn't put under water. So she had to.

Two fat, stark-naked figures were coming down the beach.

They had joined hands, as if to sustain each other in their nudity ... or as if, in shedding their clothes, they had also shed a portion of their years. Gingerly, yet in haste to reach cover, they applied their soles to the tickly sand: a haste that caused unwieldy breasts to bob and swing, bellies and buttocks to wobble. Splay-legged they were, from the weight of these protuberances. Above their knees, garters had cut fierce red lines in the skin; their bodies were criss-crossed with red furrows, from the variety of strings and bones that had lashed them in. The calves of one showed purple-knotted with veins; across the other's abdomen ran a deep, longitudinal scar. One was patched with red hair, one with black.

In a kind of horrid fascination the child stood and stared ... as at two wild outlandish beasts. But before they reached her she again turned, and, heedless of the prickles, ran seawards, out on the reef. This was forbidden. There were shrill cries of: "Naughty girl! Come back!"

Draggingly the child obeyed.

They were waiting for her, and, blind to her hurt, took her between them and waded into the water. When this was up to their knees, they stooped to damp napes and crowns, and sluice their arms. Then they played. They splashed water at each other's great backsides; they lay down and, propped on their elbows, let their legs float; or, forming a ring, moved heavily round to the tune of: *Ring-a-ring-a-rosy, pop down a posy!* And down the child went, till she all but sat on the sand. Not so they. Even with the support of the water they could bend but a few inches; and wider than ever did their legs splay, to permit of their corpulences being lowered.

But the sun was nearing meridian in a cloudless sky. Its rays burnt and stung. The child was sent running up the beach to the clothes-heaps, and returned, not unlike a depressed Amor, bearing in each hand a wide, flower-trimmed, dolly-varden hat, the ribbons of which trailed the sand.

These they perched on their heads, binding the ribbons under their chins; and thus attired waded out to the deep end of the pool. Here, where the water came a few inches above their waists, they stood to cool off, their breasts seeming to float on the surface like half-inflated toy balloons. And when the sand stirred up by their feet had subsided, their legs could be seen through the translucent water oddly foreshortened, with edges that frayed at each ripple.

But a line of foam had shown its teeth at the edge of the reef. The tide was on the turn; it was time to go.

Waddling up the beach they spread their petticoats, and on these stretched themselves out to dry. And as they lay there on their sides, with the supreme mass of hip and buttock arching in the air, their contours were those of seals—great mother-seals come lolloping out of the water to lie about on the sand.

The child had found a piece of dry cuttlefish, and sat pretending to play with it. But she wasn't really. Something had happened which made her not like any more to play. Something ugly. Oh, never ... never ... no, not ever now did she want to grow up. *She* would always stop a little girl.

Percival Reginald Stephensen   (1901–1965)

Critic, editor. Born in Queensland; educated in Brisbane and at Oxford.

from THE FOUNDATIONS OF CULTURE IN AUSTRALIA

What is a national culture? Is it not the expression, in thought-form or art-form, of the Spirit of a Race and of a Place? The Ancient Greeks were few in number, not more all told than the number of people who nowadays live in North Sydney, but the Greeks evolved, from their environment and historical background, a culture which has remained for 2,000 years after they themselves became subjugated and dispersed. The political, economic, and social forms of a nation are *temporary* forms, expressions of the *zeitgeist*, which changes with every decade, with every vagary of invention, epidemics, wars, migrations. Each decade of history is 'modern' to itself, and every modernism passes with the inexorable march of time. Nothing is permanent in a nation except its culture—its ideas of permanence, which are expressed in art, literature, religion, philosophy; ideas which transcend modernism and ephemerality, ideas which survive political, social, and economic changes.

Race and Place are the two permanent elements in a culture, and Place, I think, is even more important than Race in giving that culture its direction. When Races migrate, taking their culture with them, to a new Place, the culture becomes modified. It is the spirit of a Place which ultimately gives any human culture its distinctiveness.

Consider the differences between Indian Art, Chinese Art, Persian Art, Egyptian Art, Dutch Art, Easter Island Art—expressions of places rather than of epochs. The main art tendency remained in each Place while peoples and epochs changed.

Consider, too, how literature expresses the spirit of Place and Race, and forms the concept of a nation. A simple example is the poetry of Robert Burns, which created Scotland or was created by Scotland—which? For present purposes it is enough to establish that the poetry of Burns *is linked with the idea of Scotland*. When Scotsmen emigrate to another Place, they take with them the Scots Place-poetry of Robert Burns. Literature, even more than graphic art, is profoundly national. As an idea, what would England be without the poetic concept recorded by Chaucer, Shakespeare, Herrick, Dickens, and all the English writers from Beowulf to Rudyard Kipling? England lives as an idea, not mainly through the activities of her merchants and moneylenders and politicians and soldiers, though these also have played their part, but through the writings of her poets and men of letters!

So France, the idea of France, lives in Montaigne, Rabelais, Racine, Voltaire, Rousseau, Victor Hugo, Balzac, de Maupassant, and Baudelaire; and Germany lives in Goethe, Heine, Kant, Hegel and Richard Wagner; Russia lives in Dostoevsky, Tolstoy, Chekhov, Maxim Gorki, *et al.*; Scandinavia in Ibsen, Knut Hamsun ... need I continue the examples? I do not wish to flog the obvious fact that a nation, or the idea of a nation, is inseparable from its literature. A nation, in fact, without a literature, is incomplete. Australia without a literature remains a colony, no nation.

A deeper question arises, perplexities confront me, when I attempt the next step in this logic. If art and literature are nationally created, and linked to a vicinity or a Place of Origin, can there be such a thing as universal art or universal literature?

The question is answered by making a distinction between Creation and Appreciation. *Art and literature are nationally created, but become internationally appreciated.* Culture spreads from nation to nation. Each nation contributes ideas to the culture of every other nation. Shakespeare, Balzac, and Dostoevsky each began to do their work as national writers, but now in appreciation they are universal, and belong to all nations.

Throughout all human history, cultures have developed in vicinities because there was not much communication between the isolated parts of the world. Since the invention of printing and the development of transport and means of communication, national cultures are overlapping, influencing one another, local distinctiveness is disappearing. The whole world is becoming one cultural unit, and tends to become one international economic unit. In the twentieth century nationalism is receding, the world is becoming one Place. What then becomes of any theory of nationalism in culture?

I hold to the thesis that cultures are *created* locally, and that every contribution to world-culture (even in a future world-political-and-economic unit) must be instinct with the colour of its place of origin. Ideas, like men and women, are formed locally, no matter how much they travel. There is a universal concept of humanity and world-culture, but it does not destroy individuality, either of persons or places or nations. Soviet Russia, urged by dreams of world-unification, has energetically encouraged and even revived the various nationalities and languages of the Union of Socialist Soviet Republics. Why? Because the Soviet philosophers realize that the very idea of internationalism implies many separate nationalities—combined for economic and political purposes into economic and political unity, but remaining distinct in local customs, *and cultures.*

Thus, no matter how transport and communications may improve, local cultures will always remain. Art and literature will continue to be created locally, or nationally, even in the internationalized world. The charm of writing is to write of what one knows; the charm of reading is to read of what one does not know. For this reason cultures will remain local in creation, and universal in appreciation.

WALTER MURDOCH   (1874–1970)

Essayist. Born in Scotland; came to Australia in 1884; educated in Melbourne; was Professor of English at University of Western Australia 1912–1939; Chancellor 1943–1947.

ON PIONEERING

Hail, ye faithful, much-enduring readers! ... But perhaps I had better explain. I spent a vacation recently in reading nearly three hundred Odes to Western Australia; and I wonder whether anybody ever spent a vacation in this way before, since the world began. I am now convalescent, thank you; except that I find a certain difficulty in not beginning sentences with "Hail!" the symptoms of odeshock have practically disappeared.

They mostly began with "hail" or "all hail" and many of them threw in an extra "hail" whenever their feelings got the better of them or the metre seemed to call for an extra syllable. They hailed everything and everybody; they hailed the country, they hailed the centenary, they hailed our wool, our wheat, our gold, our pearling industry, our wild-flowers, the men of a century ago and the generations yet unborn. One of them exhorted his readers, at intervals, to "shout a loud hooray," and the variation was so pleasing that I felt inclined to take him at his word. Another invited us all to "shout and sing, and make the welkin blithely ring," but most of them were content with something less noisy than this. They were satisfied with hailing.

Of the earnest patriotism of these poets there can be no question; they have boundless faith in their land. We are a young people— "the debutante of nations," one of our singers calls us; and another, whose grammar is his servant, not his master, says, "the youngest of all thy fair sisters art thee"—and, being young, we are apt to be shy and to have too much respect for our elders. Our poets teach us a truer faith,

> Hail, beauteous land! hail, bonzer West Australia;
> Compared with you, all others are a failure.

That is the kind of thing, and it undoubtedly warms the cockles of the heart, though some may object to the rhyme—but then Western

Australia is a puzzling name to fit into rhyme; one minstrel ingeniously solves the problem by turning it round:

> Hail, Groperland! Australia West!
> Of earth's fair places thou art best.

There is no doubt about the fervour of this; and most of these poems are fervid. We are the salt of the earth; other people are its scum. We inhabit the loveliest of lands; other countries are more or less blots on the landscape. Even the size of our State comes in for its meed of praise:

> Hail to Westralia!
> Hail to its bigness!
> Hail to its motto
> "Cygnis insignis."

We have done wonderful things—especially Lord Forrest, who comes into scores of odes; this, for instance, is the country

> Where the purest water flows up-hill
> In accordance with Lord Forrest's will.

Wonderful man! wonderful country! wonderful poets! Hail, every one of you! All hail, in fact.

But what most of these bards praise most loudly and continuously is the character and achievements of the men of a century ago—the pioneers. So far as I am concerned, the net result is that I never want to hear another word about pioneers as long as I live. That being so, you may object, why write an essay about them?—but I hope this essay will turn out, before it is done, not to be about the pioneers at all, but about a quite different subject. Anyhow, I am tired of them,

> Those souls of priceless rarity,
> Pioneers of our State,

who seem to have been physically almost as remarkable as they were in soul:

> Lean they were, with eyes aflame,
> These strong and sturdy men from hame.

"From hame" does not mean that they came from Scotland; it only means that the bard was bothered for a rhyme. (But what was the matter with "they came?") When I try to discover from the odes what, exactly, these persons with flaming eyes and priceless souls did when they arrived, I get no very adequate account of their achievements. One poet does, indeed, endeavour to describe their doings with some exactness.

> They stopped at Mount Eliza,
> They camped beneath a tree,
> They said to one another,
> "This is good enough for me."

But I rather doubt the accuracy of this; the idiom has a too modern sound. It is wiser, perhaps, to keep to general statements, such as—

> They founded here a mighty State,
> On January 26th, 1828.

I suppose this is substantially true, though the poet seems to have antedated the event; and I suppose it is also true that they came to an inhospitable land, where—

> The native with his waddy, his boomerang and spear,
> Held sway o'er its vast spaces by ignorance and fear.

And they got the better of him. At all events, whatever they did and whatever they were, it is in their honour that most of the odes beat the big drum.

> Then give to them the honour,
> For that they well deserve,
> And do your best endeavour
> To hand on the preserve.

By all means. Give them the honour they deserve; and give others the honour they, in their turn, deserve. The centenary celebrations are not to be arranged, I take it, for the glorification of the passengers on the *Parmelia* or of Thomas Peel's syndicate, but rather for public rejoicing that Western Australia has reached a certain stage in her journey—that she has survived the teething troubles (or weathered the storms, if that seems a more dignified way of putting it) of her first century; and for public thankfulness to whatsoever powers, human or divine, have guided her steps so far. Why anybody should pick out for special gratitude the men and women who happened to be the first on the spot it is a little difficult to see. We might as well go farther back and sing paeans of praise to the Angles and Saxons and Jutes, calling them souls of priceless rarity. Or why not sing hymns in honour of Adam, with eyes aflame, and also Eve, his beauteous dame?

The men and women who first came to settle in Australia were of British stock, and of an honourably adventurous strain. They came here to better their fortunes, lured by fantastic accounts of the country (Fraser's report dwelt on the "superiority of the soil"—and also on its "permanent humidity," a feature not conspicuous in my garden). Captain Stirling described it as "the land, out of all that I have seen in various quarters of the world, that possesses the greatest natural attractions." Vast tracts of this land were to be granted to each settler for next to nothing, and they were to cultivate cotton, tobacco, sugar and flax, to rear horses for the East Indian trade, and to establish large herds of cattle and swine for the supply of salt junk to His Majesty's navy and other shipping. They were to make fortunes easily and quickly. The land did not come up to their expectations, and they had but a thin time of it for many years after their arrival.

I do not wish to say a word against them; only, I do not see why especial praise is due to them. They showed a spirit of adventure which is the common birthright of our race—and of other races. They showed great courage in coming out to a remote and unknown world; courage, thank Heaven, is not an uncommon virtue. Are we not all born of women who have sailed gallantly into the perilous sea of marriage and faced death to bring us into the world? Everywhere in our country to-day, not only in remote and lonely places in the backblocks, but in the heart of our cities, too, men and women are confronting their fate with a high courage worthy of all honour. Those pioneers endured many hardships without whimpering; all praise to them for that; but why not praise also the innumerable persons who in our midst to-day are enduring hardships without whimpering, and who, because they do not whimper, are unhonoured and unsung? To single out the pioneers for special glorification is to libel humanity; it is to imply that virtue has been lost. The world is as full to-day as ever it was of the shining virtues of courage in danger and fortitude in adversity. Did the War show that our nation—or any nation—had lost its ancient hardihood? It is impossible to read the newspapers intelligently without being proud to belong to the indomitable human race; but the best examples do not get into the newspapers. They are to be found in all sorts of odd places; in the lonely bush and in the crowded slum; the heroic is everywhere at home.

Of course if, misled by the glamour of the past, you like to talk nonsense about the pioneers, and represent them as souls of priceless rarity stalking about with eyes aflame, I suppose no great harm is done. They were probably decent people, of average intelligence, fairly industrious and not without grit and resourcefulness; very like the normal Australian of to-day. The mistake made by the writers of some of these odes was to suppose that, to write poetry, you must talk nonsense. It is not so. Poetry and nonsense are incompatible. And this nonsense about pioneers gets, after a time, on one's nerves; hence this protest. The world is young; and we are all pioneers.

MY BUSHFIRE

The other evening I was sitting on the veranda of a little cottage in the hills to which I sometimes retire for the purpose of peaceful meditation—or, as my family prefers to believe, of peaceful sleep; anyhow, I will swear that I was not sleeping on this occasion, but meditating. (Possibly my eyes were closed; but who can really do any serious and sustained thinking without closing his eyes and shutting out the distractions of the visible world?) I was meditating on the essential difference between characters in real life and characters in fiction, even the most realistic fiction. Of course with some characters—like Micawber or Uriah Heep, for instance,—the difference is perfectly obvious. You do not meet, in real life, a man who cannot open his mouth without expressing the hope that something will turn up, or without mentioning that he is 'umble. But even with realistically portrayed characters, like Becky Sharp or Mrs Proudie, or Madame Bovary or Anna Karenina, or one of Hardy's men, or one of Balzac's, the difference remains, and it is vital. We say we have met people just like these in real life, but that is not true; there is an enormous difference. We say, in praise of Thackeray, that we know Becky Sharp almost as well as we know our living friends; but that is quite the opposite of the truth; we really know Becky Sharp far better than we know any of our living friends. We know real people by what they say and do; we can only guess at what they are thinking and feeling. Whereas Thackeray can tell us with certainty what Becky is thinking and feeling; he is her creator, and he knows all about her, and can admit us to her innermost secrets. We know our most intimate friends from the outside only; we know a character in a novel from within; we can see the central workings of her soul. We know exactly what Père Goriot feels about his daughters' conduct; we know, because Balzac told us; and Balzac knew, because he was Père Goriot's creator, and knew all there was to be known about him.

So far it was all quite obvious, but very far from satisfactory; because it did not explain why we call some characters true to life, and others false or fantastic. If their creator has a perfectly free hand—if we must believe that his characters think and feel exactly as he says they think and feel—by what standard do we judge the truth or falsehood of a portrait? Plainly their creator has not a perfectly free hand; but by what is he limited? By the facts of human nature? But how do we know the facts of human nature? We only know the facts of our own particular nature; and when you condemn a character in a novel as untrue to life, all you can mean is that character does not think and feel as you, the reader, think and feel; but that proves nothing. Who are you? You are not the only pebble on the beach; your individual soul does not exhaust the possibilities. And yet, though I must not ask the novelist to make all his characters resemble me—and as a matter of fact I do not feel myself to be a bit like Becky Sharp—I know that he has not a perfectly free hand, but is limited by—what? This was leading me on to a large meditation on the Limits of Imaginative Art; and I dare say I would have found a complete solution of the problem if I had not been interrupted—by a bushfire. Such are the vexations by which the philosopher is beset in this ridiculous world.

"Description," said Byron, "is my forte." It is not mine. Neither have I the slightest turn for narrative art, being, I fancy, about the only scribbler in Australia who has not a manuscript novel up his sleeve. I shall therefore refrain from the vain attempt to tell you, in a piece of rapid and vivid prose, the exciting tale of that interruption. If you have ever been through the experience you know all about it; if not, you may take it from me that when one is fighting a healthy bushfire, with a stiffish wind blowing, at the end of a dry summer, one has no time to think about the Limits of Imaginative Art. If you have not seen a bushfire I suppose you have read an account of one in some Australian novel or other; there must be many such accounts, if our novelists have done their duty by their country— though at this moment I can remember none. When I have finished this I shall hunt through the works of Mr Vance Palmer, the best teller of tales in Australia to-day; if anyone could describe the thing adequately he could. My present impression is that nobody could; that, to one who has not seen it, no language could convey an idea of the wonder and terror and beauty of the spectacle by night, when the valley below you and the hillsides around you are all one red, roaring hell of furious destruction. (I am trying my hand at description after all; and, lo! I have got every single word wrong.) Well, putting all high-flown phrases aside, we euchred the fire; my little bush humpy still stands; and in a month or two, when the rains have come, the black landscape will begin to be green again, and the fallen trees will be our only reminders of that strenuous night.

I say "we"—and here comes the point to which all this while I have been leading up. There were only two of us—myself and one other, who strolled up out of nowhere at the moment when the fire was becoming menacing. He took command of the situation at once; it was immediately obvious to me that he was the professional, I the ignorant amateur; and it was not long before I felt pretty much as the Romans must have felt at Lake Regillus when the great twin brethren appeared in the van of their army.

> The gods who live for ever
> Are on our side to-day.

Not that there was anything god-like in his appearance, or in his manners. I can write about him in this personal way because I am morally certain that he will not read these pages, and that he would not recognize himself if he did. He was lean and long-legged, and, though I have not seen him by daylight, I think he had a cynically humorous face. He was a consummate tactician; knew at a glance where the danger-spots would be; and though he never seemed to hurry, never dashed about, was not in the least fussy, and never had his pipe out of his mouth, he was always on the spot when the danger came.... The sight of his black figure against the fierce scarlet background was extraordinarily tranquillizing. Amid all that turmoil of blazing bush and flying flame, the growling and crackling and blustering, the loose-barked trees on fire from top to toe, and scattering with every gust of wind a shower of burning leaves and bark, burning branches whizzing down, the crashing, at intervals, of a falling giant, he never for a moment lost his presence of mind, but stuck to his job, which was to guide the whirlwind and direct the storm. "The poet extolled the firmness of that mind which, in the midst of confusion, uproar, and slaughter, examined and disposed everything with the serene wisdom of a higher intelligence." .... Towards morning, when the fire had swept away to the westward, and my cottage (also four others, whose owners, being city-dwellers, did not happen to be there that night) needed no further defence, he remarked that he thought it was about time to turn in. When I spoke of payment for the great service he had rendered me he replied that it was all in the day's work and that any bloke would do that for another bloke. I used good arguments; but against certain deep-rooted instincts Immanuel Kant himself would argue in vain. To this man, and to men of his type, it is a kind of religion that, if you would keep your self-respect, there are certain transactions into which money must not be allowed to intrude.

To show that he had not taken offence he consented to fill his pipe from my pouch and sauntered away. He was Australian in everything he said and did. If there is an Australian type he is the type. Long, lean, quiet, humorous, inarticulate, sagacious, easy-going, loyal to his own ethical code, standing on his own feet and facing the world with a good-humoured imperturbability careless about economics—he does not grow rich. He can never afford a trip to England, and so England never sees him, and judges Australia by another type altogether—a "better-educated" type. I see that Miss Rebecca West has a remark in her latest book about "the Australian crawl"—an unpleasant phrase, but there is no use in resenting it; it will be more useful to inquire what she means, and whether the tourists who represent us in England have contrived to convey the impression that snobbishness is an Australian trait. If so—and I believe from my own experience that it is so—I wish Mr Wells and Mr Galsworthy and a few other men of genius who have the ear of the British public could be induced to visit Australia—not our cities, which are mere plagiarisms from the old world, but the real Australia, and meet the real Australian. I should be happy to introduce Miss West to my friend of the bush-fire; she might not find him the fine flower of civilization; but "crawl" would be the very last word she would think of applying to him. If I had been a duke or a king or an emperor he would have spoken to me in exactly the same way, as one bloke to another bloke; if I had been a multi-millionaire he would have treated me just the same, with the same helpfulness and the same kindly scorn for my incompetence. (He, and men of his type, were the salt of our Expeditionary Force, and faced death with the same kind of cool nonchalance.) Failing such an introduction, let our novelists and poets carry his portrait to the other side of the world, and show that Australia can produce something better than snobs. Is he a disappearing type? I hope not. I hope he has come to stay, and that ten centuries hence it will be seen that his ideal—the ideal of mateship—has been Australia's great contribution to civilization.

EDWARD VANCE PALMER   (1885–1959)

Short story writer, novelist, playwright, journalist, critic. Born and educated in Queensland.

THE RAINBOW-BIRD

All afternoon as she bent over her slate, Maggie's mind had been filled with a vision of the bird. Blue-green shot with gold, its tail an arrow. Her hair fell over her intense, grape-dark eyes; she hardly knew what she was writing. It was the same every day now. The hands crawled down the cracked face of the clock with aggravating slowness; the teacher's voice droned on and on like a blowfly against the windowpane; the other children squirmed in their seats and folded paper darts to throw across the room. But all she lived for was the moment when she would again see the coloured shape skim from its cavern in the earth, making her catch her breath as if its wings had brushed across her heart.

As soon as school was out she flashed a look at Don, racing down to the bottom fence and along through the bushes that covered the side of the hill. Don was a little behind, limping because of his sore toe; flushed and breathless Maggie had reached the bottom of the gully before he emerged from the undergrowth. One stocking had fallen over her ankle and her hat was at the back of her neck, held by the elastic around her throat, but she cared for nothing but getting away.

From the bottom of the playground she could hear the other girls calling her.

"Wait on, Maggie! We're coming, too."

She tried to shut their voices from her ears. None of them must find out her secret. She hated their empty faces, their coldly-mocking eyes; they made fun of her because she carried beetles' wings and cowries about in her matchbox to stare at under the desk.

"Come on, Don," she called back impatiently, "they'll all be on us soon."

He growled as he caught up with her.

"It's all right for you—you got boots on. This prickly grass hurts like blazes. Why didn't you go down the road?"

"This is nearly half-a-mile shorter.... Come on."

They panted up the other hill and across a cleared paddock that lay between them and the beach. Before the eyes of both of them was the deep cleft left by the store-truck when it was bogged months before, and the little round hole with a heap of sand in front of it. Such a tiny tunnel in the side of the rut that no one would notice unless he saw the bird fly out. They had come on it together when they were looking for mushrooms; there had been a sudden burr of wings almost beneath their feet, a shimmer of opal in the sunbright air, and then a stillness as the bird settled on the she-oak thirty yards away, making their hearts turn over with the sheer beauty of its bronze and luminous green.

A rainbow-bird! And it had come from that rounded tunnel in the sandy earth where the couch-grass was growing over the old rut. Don had wanted to put his hand in and feel if there were any young ones, but Maggie had caught his arm, her eyes desperate.

"No, don't! She's watching. She'll go away and never come back—never."

She wanted just to stand and let her eyes have their fill. That stretch of cropped turf, with the she-oak on a sandy rise above the beach and the miraculous bird shining out of the greeny-grey branches! It was only rarely they surprised her in the nest, for she usually seemed to feel the pattering vibration of their feet along the ground and slip out unobserved. But they never had to look far for her. There in the she-oak she shone, flame-bright and radiant, as if she had just dropped from the blue sky. And sometimes they saw her mate skimming through the air after flies, taking long, sweeping curves and pausing at the top of the curve, a skater on wings, a maker of jewelled patterns, body light as thistledown, every feather blazing with fire and colour. The vision came back to Maggie each night before she closed her eyes in sleep. It belonged to a different world from the school, the dusty road, the yard behind the store that was filled with rusty tins and broken cases.

"That girl!" her mother said, hearing her mutter on the pillow. "It's a bird now."

They hurried across the road, past the spindle-legged house with no fence around it, past the red-roofed cottage where there were bathing-suits hung out to dry. Surely this afternoon the little birds would be out in front of the nest! The day before when they had laid with their ears close to the ground they had heard something thin but distinct, a cheeping and twittering. It had come to them through the warm earth, thrilling them with intense life. Those bits of living colour down there in the dark—how wonderful it would be when they came out into the light!

Maggie pulled up suddenly in the final run, clutching at Don's arm.

"Wait!.... Someone's there.... Don't go on yet."

Breathing hard, Don stood staring at the big, dark figure on the slope overlooking the sea.

"It's Peter Riley watching if the mullet are coming in."

"No, it isn't. It's Cafferty. I know his hat."

"Cafferty?"

"Yes, Cafferty the Honey Man."

The man was standing almost on the nest, looking down into the she-oak by the beach, his body still as a wooden stump, his eyes intent as their own. He moved slightly to the right; they saw he had a gun at his side. Horror laid an icy hand on the girl's heart. What was he doing with a gun there?

Suddenly she started to run.

"Come on! I believe he's found the nest. I believe...."

Her slim legs twinkled like beams of light over the turf, her print frock blew up over her heated face, and Don found it hard to keep up with her. She was out of breath when she reached Cafferty and her eyes were points of fire. He was too occupied to notice her; he was shifting the gun in his hands and watching the she-oak tree. She saw a lump in the pocket of his shirt, a stain of blood.

Words came thickly from her throat.

"What're you doing with that gun?"

"Eh?" he said, hardly looking round.

"You—you've been shooting something.... What's that in your pocket?"

Cafferty let his eyes rest on her stolidly, a slow grin parting his lips.

"Guess."

"It's not... It's a bird."

"Right. Right, first shot. Most people'd have thought it was a rabbit.... Ever see one of those coloured bee-eaters, little girl? Her mate's somewhere about. I'll get him, too, before long."

He took the crumpled bird from his pocket and dangled it before her proudly. Through a blur she saw the ruffled bronze and emerald of its plumage, the film over its eyes, the drop of blood oozing from its beak. Then she threw herself on the turf.

"Beast! That's what you are.... A b-beast."

Cafferty looked from her small, sobbing figure to that of the boy, a sheepish bewilderment in his eyes. He was a hulking, slow-witted fellow, who lived in a humpy on the other side of the creek, sur-rounded by his hives and a thick growth of tea-tree.

"What's the trouble?" he asked. "That bird is it?"

Don had no reply. He was confused, half-ashamed of his sister.

"Lord, you don't want to worry about vermin like that," said Cafferty. "Death on bees, them things are—hanging round the hives and licking 'em up as they come out. And they're not satisfied with robbing you like that, the little devils; they'll go through a flying swarm and take out the queen. It's a fact. Dinkum.... I'd like to wipe the lot of 'em off the face of the earth."

He went over to the tiny opening of the tunnel and bruised the soft earth down over the face of it with his heavy boot. There was a dull passion in his absorbed eyes, a sense of warring against evil.

"No, you don't want to trouble about the likes of them. Unless it's to go after them with a shanghai. There's sixpence a head waiting for any you fetch me. Tell the other youngsters that—a tanner a head. I'm going to clear the lot of 'em out this winter."

Shouldering his gun he moved off down the beach, a lumbering heaviness in his gait. Maggie was still stretched prone on the turf, her face in her arms, and Don watched her awhile, awkward and ill-at-ease. But the superiority of one who has not given himself away was slowly asserting itself. Picking up the dead bird that Cafferty had thrown on the grass he fingered it clumsily, wondering if there were any bees in its crop. It was still warm, but its plumage was ruffled and streaky, and it didn't look nearly so wonderful as when it had shot into the air, the light on its wings. Death on bees, the Honey Man had said. He began to feel a contempt for it.

"Come on, Mag! He's gone now. And the other kids'll be coming along soon."

She rose from the grass, tossing back her hair and looking at the bird with reddened eyes.

"Chuck it away."

"Why? I'm going to take it home and skin it."

"Chuck it away!" she stormed.

He hesitated a moment, and then obeyed her. They trailed over the grass toward the store, Don swinging his bag and whistling to show he didn't care. There must be a lot of rainbow-birds about, and if the Honey Man kept his promise.... Sixpence a head! He could go out with the other boys on Saturday mornings, looking all along the sandy banks. But he wouldn't use a shanghai—no fear! His new Bayard was three times as good.

Maggie took no more notice of him than if he were merely a shadow behind her. Their father was standing waiting for them at the bowser outside the store, and Don had to go for orders on his pony. Maggie trudged upstairs to the room over the shop and flung herself down on the bed. Darkness had fallen over her life. Whenever she closed her eyes she could see the Honey Man's evil face, the broken, tobacco-stained teeth revealed in a grin through the ragged growth of beard. Hatred welled up in her as she thought of him squatting among the tea-tree on the other side of the creek, his gun between his knees, his eyes watching the leaves above. Devil! Grinning devil! If only forked lightning would leap out of the sky and char him to ashes.

When the evening meal was over she went upstairs again without waiting to do her homework. Her mother's voice followed at a distance, dying behind the closed door:

"What's the matter with Maggie now?.... The way that girl lets herself get worked up."

Lying awake, Maggie tried to imagine herself running down the slope and stopping suddenly to see the rainbow-bird whirling round over three spots of colour on the grass. But no! She could only see the soft earth around the nest, squashed by the Honey Man's boot, and the dead bird lying on the grass with a drop of blood on its beak. Wonder and magic—they had gone out of everything! And Don was swaggering round, pretending he didn't care.

A light rain had begun to fall, making hardly any sound upon the roof, dropping with a faint insistent tinkle into the tanks. There were people coming and going in the store below. Between broken drifts of sleep she heard voices running on and on, the telephone's muffled burring, the occasional hoot of a car. But all noises were muted, coming through a pad of distance, of woolly darkness. A funeral, she thought vaguely. They were burying the rainbow-bird.

Near morning, or so it seemed, she heard someone come upstairs, and there was a blare of light in her eyes. Her mother was bending over her with a candle.

"Not asleep yet, dear? Have those people kept you awake?"

The drowsy aftermath of feeling made Maggie's voice thick.

"N-no; it wasn't that. It was because.... Why do they all come here now?"

Her mother tucked an end of the quilt in.

"They brought Mr Cafferty to the shop to wait for the ambulance. He had a little accident and had to be taken in to the hospital.... Go to sleep now."

Maggie's eyes were wide open.

"He's dead?"

"Good gracious, no! Nothing to worry about. He must have been dragging the gun after him as he climbed through the wire-fence across the creek, but they found him soon after it happened. Only in the thigh the wound was."

Through Maggie's mind flashed a sudden conviction.

"He will die. I know he will.... Serve him right, too."

"You don't understand what you're talking about, child," said her mother in a formal, shocked voice. "Everyone's fond of the Honey Man and hopes he'll be all right soon.... You've been lying awake too long. Go to sleep now."

She faded away, leaving Maggie to stare up at the ceiling in the dark. But the vision of a world oppressed by a heavy, brutal heel had vanished. Her mind was lit up again; everything had come right. She could see the cropped slope by the sea, the overgrown wheel-rut, the small, round tunnel with the heap of sand in front of it. And it was the man with the gun who was lying crumpled on the grass. Above him sailed the rainbow-bird, lustrous, triumphant, her opal body poised at the top of a curve, shimmering in the sunbright air.

Rex Ingamells   (1913–1955)

Poet, editor. Born and educated in South Australia; founder of the Jindyworobak movement.

ENVIRONMENTAL VALUES

from CONDITIONAL CULTURE

The natural distinctiveness of the Australian continent from other lands of the world is too fundamental to vanish in the period of human history. The massive gum trees along the banks of the Murray, the gums and the mallee and the tea-tree that straggle about this vast continent; the empty spaces of our deserts; and the atonal music of the magpie and the good-natured mockery of the kookaburra—these are things that must remain. They belong to the indestructible spirit of the place about which D. H. Lawrence has written in a superb piece of natural description at the beginning of *Kangaroo*. But D. H. Lawrence realized that spirit, however intensely, only in a small part: he did not feel at home in the bush, although its power gripped him. There are thousands of Australians today who, if they have not found eloquent tongue, feel, nevertheless, with childlike devotion, the familiar beauty and utter loveliness of the outback environment in many of its moods.

Our pioneers, or the majority of them, were Englishmen who brought to this country the English manners and customs of the moment of their migration. As long as they lived they were strangers in a strange land. Many of them may have become more or less used to their new environment, but they never could become one with it. The background of their minds was made up of other associations. Yet they were isolated from the current movements of fashion and culture in the old country: in this sense they slipped behind the times. The English manners and customs which they inculcated into their children were bound to be considerably out of date by the time those children reached maturity. Thus the word 'colonial' was justified, in so far as it signified rawness and lack of sophistication.

Although fresh influences were continually coming in, these were neither sufficient nor strong enough to compete with the isolation and environmental resistance, and could work only superficially. Hence any genuine culture that might develop in Australia, however it might be refreshed and inspired by English influences, would have to represent the birth of a new soul. A fundamental break, that is, with the spirit of English culture, is the prerequisite for the development of an Australian culture. Without the fact of ultimate individuality, separate identity, any general sense of culture in any country must be misty and anaemic. However strong and innumerable, however desirable and inevitable, however traditional our cultural ties with Europe may be, it is not in these ties that we must as a people seek our individuality. Its quintessence must lie in the realization of whatever things are distinctive in our environment and their sublimation in art and idea, in culture.

Australian culture is at present in a nebulous stage, because our writers have not come clearly to any such realization. I do not wish to be misunderstood. Some of the greatest Australian literature yet to be may have no local colour at all. Its settings may be in China or Mars. Our best poetry must deal with universal themes; and whether or not the Australian environment forms a background is a matter for individual poets. But all this does not affect the essence of my argument. The real test of a people's culture is the way in which they can express themselves in relation to their environment, and the loftiness and universality of their artistic conceptions raised on that basis. When, for example, someone begins a novel and sets the scene in Australia, he cannot hope to produce great art unless he has a true conception of environmental values. When our writers understand these, they will look at most of what they have written to date and say, 'That is the way not to write about Australia'.

The biggest curse and handicap upon our literature is the incongruous use of metaphors, similes, and adjectives. It is usual to find Australian writers describing the bush with much the same terminology as English writers apply to a countryside of oaks and elms and yews and weeping willows, and of skylarks, cuckoos, and nightingales. We find that dewdrops are spoken of as jewels sparkling on the foliage of gum trees. Jewels? Not amid the stark, contorted, shaggy informality of the Australian bushland. Nothing could be more incongruous. Jewels? I see the pageantry of the Old World, and of the march of history from the time when the Norman ladies came to England to the present day, when glittering cosmopolitan crowds mingle in the casinos of Monte Carlo and the ornate ballrooms of Venice; I see the royal courts of England, and those of France and Spain now forgotten; and I see, if you like, a vice-regal gathering or a theatrical party in Adelaide—but I do not, cannot, see jewels metaphored off on gum trees, which are so far removed from all the things with which jewels are traditionally associated. I cannot deplore too vehemently the dangerous habit of using figures of speech with regard to essentially Australian things which call up such a flood of Old World associations as to gloze over all distinctiveness. It has been a piteous custom to write of Australian things with the English idiom, an idiom which can achieve exactness in England but not here.

GARRAKEEN

Garrakeen, the parakeet, is slim and swift.
Like a spear of green and red he flashes through
the cumbered branches by the river-bank.
Watch him, brighter than the clouds, before the day is done;
watch him in the morning, when the gums are bathed with dew,
rivalling the spears of the sun.

When dawn flamed on the Murray I watched for Garrakeen...
Opaline purple and crimson was the river...
He came from the west with blood on his breast,
and the colours of the water were sluggish in sheen
compared with his fire in the air;

the voice of the water was shattered by one
shrill from the spear-bird hurrying there,
flying with the light of the east in his sight,
rivalling the spears of the sun.

HISTORY

These are the images that make my dreams,
strong images but frail; dimmed-with-glow yet clear:

Pioneer ships lumbering in the sunset,
lumbering along our sombre eastern coastline,
swaying, awkward but beautiful, north to Port Jackson...

The stark hatred and reeking soul-fire of men's faces,
men pent in penitentiaries and chained in road-gangs,
herded as cattle, worked as cattle, fierce in their misery...

Stern-hearted freemen, felling tall trees, building
rough homesteads amid far, unfamiliar places,
hoping, cherishing their preconceived
visions of beauty and propriety...

Herds of cattle, lowing by the fertile banks
of eastern rivers; drowsing under redgums,
where the black-and-white magpie sits calling ecstatically...

Flocks of sheep bleating perpetually on green hillsides,
tired of fine feeding, joyous at life...

Deserted station-houses, quiet in drought.
Bones of cattle, camels, horses, men.
And the despised black who lives through it all,
finding himself water, native plums, yams,
and wild-honey from the honey-ants...

Cities growing up,
towering into the future;
and this land's destined
vast cities of imagination.

KENNETH SLESSOR   (1901–1971)

Poet, journalist. Born in N.S.W.; educated in Sydney; official war
correspondent 1940–1944.

WINTER DAWN

At five I wake, rise, rub on the smoking pane
A port to see—water breathing in the air,
Boughs broken. The sun comes up in a golden stain,
Floats like a glassy sea-fruit. There is mist everywhere,
White and humid, and the Harbour is like plated stone,
Dull flakes of ice. One light drips out alone,
One bead of winter-red, smouldering in the steam,
Quietly over the roof-tops—another window
Touched with a crystal fire in the sun's gullies,
One lonely star of the morning, where no stars gleam.

Far away on the rim of this great misty cup,
The sun gilds the dead suburbs as he rises up,
Diamonds the wind-cocks, makes glitter the crusted spikes
On moss-drowned gables. Now the tiles drip scarlet-wet,
Swim like birds' paving-stones, and sunlight strikes
Their watery mirrors with a moister rivulet,
Acid and cold. Here lie those mummied Kings,
Men sleeping in houses, embalmed in stony coffins,
Till the Last Trumpet calls their galleries up,
And the suburbs rise with distant murmurings.

O buried dolls, O men sleeping invisible there,
I stare above your mounds of stone, lean down,
Marooned and lonely in this bitter air,
And in one moment deny your frozen town,
Renounce your bodies—earth falls in clouds away,
Stones lose their meaning, substance is lost in clay,
Roofs fade, and that small smoking forgotten heap,
The city, dissolves to a shell of bricks and paper,
Empty, without purpose, a thing not comprehended,
A broken tomb, where ghosts unknown sleep.

And the least crystal weed, shaken with frost,
The furred herbs of silver, the daisies round-eyed and tart,
Painted in antic china, the smallest night-flower tossed
Like a bright penny on the lawn, stirs more my heart,
Strikes deeper this morning air, than mortal towers
Dried to a common blindness, fainter than flowers,
Fordone, extinguished, as the vapours break,
And dead in the dawn. O Sun that kills with life,
And brings to breath all silent things—O Dawn,
Waken me with old earth, keep me awake!

THE NIGHT-RIDE

Gas flaring on the yellow platform; voices running up and down;
Milk-tins in cold dented silver; half-awake I stare,
Pull up the blind, blink out—all sounds are drugged;
The slow blowing of passengers asleep;
Engines yawning; water in heavy drips;
Black, sinister travellers, lumbering up the station,
One moment in the window, hooked over bags;
Hurrying, unknown faces—boxes with strange labels—
All groping clumsily to mysterious ends,
Out of the gaslight, dragged by private Fates.
Their echoes die. The dark train shakes and plunges;
Bells cry out; the night-ride starts again.
Soon I shall look out into nothing but blackness,
Pale, windy fields. The old roar and knock of the rails
Melts in dull fury. Pull down the blind. Sleep. Sleep.
Nothing but grey, rushing rivers of bush outside.
Gaslight and milk-cans. Of Rapptown I recall nothing else.

ELEGY IN A BOTANIC GARDENS

The smell of birds' nests faintly burning
Is autumn. In the autumn I came
Where spring had used me better,
To the clear red pebbles and the men of stone
And foundered beetles, to the broken Meleager
And thousands of white circles drifting past,
Cold suns in water; even to the dead grove
Where we had kissed, to the Tristania tree
Where we had kissed so awkwardly,
Noted by swans with damp, accusing eyes,
All gone to-day; only the leaves remain,

Gaunt paddles ribbed with herringbones
Of watermelon-pink. Never before
Had I assented to the hateful name
Meryta Macrophylla, on a tin tag.
That was no time for botany. But now the schools,
The horticulturists, come forth
Triumphantly with Latin. So be it now,
Meryta Macrophylla, and the old house,
Ringed with black stone, no Georgian Headlong Hall
With glass-eye windows winking candles forth,
Stuffed with French horns, globes, air-pumps, telescopes
And Cupid in a wig, playing the flute,
But truly, and without escape,
THE NATIONAL HERBARIUM,
Repeated dryly in Roman capitals,
THE NATIONAL HERBARIUM.

CROW COUNTRY

Gutted of station, noise alone,
The crow's voice trembles down the sky
As if this nitrous flange of stone
Wept suddenly with such a cry;
As if the rock found lips to sigh,
The riven earth a mouth to moan;
But we that hear them, stumbling by,
Confuse their torments with our own.

Over the huge abraded rind,
Crow-countries graped with dung, we go,
Past gullies that no longer flow
And wells that nobody can find,
Lashed by the screaming of the crow,
Stabbed by the needles of the mind.

FIVE BELLS

Time that is moved by little fidget wheels
Is not my Time, the flood that does not flow.
Between the double and the single bell
Of a ship's hour, between a round of bells
From the dark warship riding there below,
I have lived many lives, and this one life
Of Joe, long dead, who lives between five bells.

Deep and dissolving verticals of light
Ferry the falls of moonshine down. Five bells
Coldly rung out in a machine's voice. Night and water
Pour to one rip of darkness, the Harbour floats
In air, the Cross hangs upside-down in water.

Why do I think of you, dead man, why thieve
These profitless lodgings from the flukes of thought
Anchored in Time? You have gone from earth,
Gone even from the meaning of a name;
Yet something's there, yet something forms its lips
And hits and cries against the ports of space,
Beating their sides to make its fury heard.

Are you shouting at me, dead man, squeezing your face
In agonies of speech on speechless panes?
Cry louder, beat the windows, bawl your name!

But I hear nothing, nothing ... only bells,
Five bells, the bumpkin calculus of Time.
Your echoes die, your voice is dowsed by Life,
There's not a mouth can fly the pygmy strait—
Nothing except the memory of some bones
Long shoved away, and sucked away, in mud;
And unimportant things you might have done,
Or once I thought you did; but you forgot,
And all have now forgotten—looks and words
And slops of beer; your coat with buttons off,
Your gaunt chin and pricked eye, and raging tales
Of Irish kings and English perfidy.
And dirtier perfidy of publicans
Groaning to God from Darlinghurst.

Five bells.

Then I saw the road, I heard the thunder
Tumble, and felt the talons of the rain
The night we came to Moorebank in slab-dark,
So dark you bore no body, had no face,
But a sheer voice that rattled out of air
(As now you'd cry if I could break the glass),
A voice that spoke beside me in the bush,
Loud for a breath or bitten off by wind,
Of Milton, melons, and the Rights of Man,
And blowing flutes, and how Tahitian girls
Are brown and angry-tongued, and Sydney girls
Are white and angry-tongued, or so you'd found.
But all I heard was words that didn't join
So Milton became melons, melons girls,

And fifty mouths, it seemed, were out that night,
And in each tree an Ear was bending down,
Or something had just run, gone behind grass,
When, blank and bone-white, like maniac's thought,
The naphtha-flash of lightning slit the sky,
Knifing the dark with deathly photographs.
There's not so many with so poor a purse
Or fierce a need, must fare by night like that,
Five miles in darkness on a country track,
But when you do, that's what you think.

Five bells.

In Melbourne, your appetite had gone,
Your angers too; they had been leeched away
By the soft archery of summer rains
And the sponge-paws of wetness, the slow damp
That stuck the leaves of living, snailed the mind,
And showed your bones, that had been sharp with rage,
The sodden ecstasies of rectitude.
I thought of what you'd written in faint ink,
Your journal with the sawn-off lock, that stayed behind
With other things you left, all without use,
All without meaning now, except a sign
That someone had been living who now was dead:
"At Labassa. Room 6 × 8
On top of the tower; because of this, very dark
And cold in winter. Everything has been stowed
Into this room—500 books all shapes
And colours, dealt across the floor
And over sills and on the laps of chairs;
Guns, photoes of many differant things
And different curioes that I obtained ...."

In Sydney, by the spent aquarium-flare
Of penny gaslight on pink wallpaper,
We argued about blowing up the world,
But you were living backward, so each night
You crept a moment closer to the breast,
And they were living, all of them , those frames
And shapes of flesh that had perplexed your youth,
And most your father, the old man gone blind,
With fingers always round a fiddle's neck,
That graveyard mason whose fair monuments
And tablets cut with dreams of piety
Rest on the bosoms of a thousand men
Staked bone by bone, in quiet astonishment
At cargoes they had never thought to bear,
These funeral-cakes of sweet and sculptured stone.

Where have you gone? The tide is over you,
The turn of midnight water's over you,
As Time is over you, and mystery,
And memory, the flood that does not flow.
You have no suburb, like those easier dead
In private berths of dissolution laid—
The tide goes over, the waves ride over you
And let their shadows down like shining hair,
But they are Water; and the sea-pinks bend
Like lilies in your teeth, but they are Weed;
And you are only part of an Idea.
I felt the wet push its black thumb-balls in,
The night you died, I felt your eardrums crack,
And the short agony, the longer dream,
The Nothing that was neither long nor short;
But I was bound, and could not go that way,
But I was blind, and could not feel your hand.
If I could find an answer, could only find
Your meaning, or could say why you were here
Who now are gone, what purpose gave you breath
Or seized it back, might I not hear your voice?

I looked out of my window in the dark
At waves with diamond quills and combs of light
That arched their mackerel-backs and smacked the sand
In the moon's drench, that straight enormous glaze,
And ships far off asleep, and Harbour-buoys
Tossing their fireballs wearily each to each,
And tried to hear your voice, but all I heard
Was a boat's whistle, and the scraping squeal
Of seabirds' voices far away, and bells,
Five bells. Five bells coldly ringing out.

                                                    Five bells.

Note: the poem 'South Country' appears in the Alec King article
'Contemporary Australian Poetry' on p. 446.

III : THE FORTIES TO THE SIXTIES

Commentary

These three decades comprise a period of remarkable growth in all aspects of Australian life, not least in the accomplishments of a number of talented writers in poetry and prose. Beginning in the late 1930s with the work of writers such as White and Stead, later to win recognition as important novelists, the literature of the period is distinguished by a great diversity of forms and subjects, which, in retrospect, can be seen to have grown out of the experience of the preceding century.

Two complementary strands can be noted in the non-fictional prose represented here. There is welcome self-criticism, evidenced in reflections on the nature and shortcomings of Australian society, especially in its intellectual and artistic life. There is also a feeling of self-confidence which prompts the criticism. The earlier debates about nationalism and identity are replaced by discussions about the qualities and achievements of Australian writers, and by more generous notions of subject matter and method.

A considerable body of accomplished poetry deals only slightly, if at all, with specifically Australian subjects. In itself, this fact is an acknowledgement of the Australian writer's links with European intellectual history. Many long poems are written, taking as their subject various aspects of discovery and exploration, and of personal and national history. It is a time in which to search for an adequate symbolism, as James McAuley observed. The same search can be discerned in Australian painting in the period, particularly by Nolan and Arthur Boyd.

The wealth of poetry is matched in general prose and fiction. Major novelists such as Stead, Stow, Martin Boyd, White, and the short-story writer Hal Porter, establish their reputations, and greatly enrich the range of Australian literary experience, while at the same time preserving continuity with the past.

Themes which were introduced in the earliest writing—such as ambivalent feelings towards the landscape, insight into the difficulties of sustaining intellectual life in a large land with a small population, the sense of isolation and distance—are treated with critical self-awareness and a growing sense of historical perspective, as well as with a just appreciation of the advances made in writing overseas.

JAMES MCAULEY   (1917–1976)

Poet, critic, editor. Born and educated in Sydney; was Professor of English at University of Tasmania.

from THE GRINNING MIRROR

For poetry, the consequences of this fixation of the Australian cultural matrix at a late nineteenth-century level of Progress and Enlightenment have been unfortunate.

Poetry is always closely related to the cultural matrix. Even if the poet does not deliberately set out to exemplify the basic ideas and valuations of his society—and he does sometimes do this—he will without thinking about it reflect those ideas and valuations with greater or less fidelity in his work. Even if he sets himself in opposition to his time, it becomes apparent to later eyes how much he remains nevertheless a child of his time. But there is more to it than this: there is much that is obscure and hard to analyse. The words and images of poetry must have a certain irradiation; they gain their effect by arousing a murmuring echo of response in the audience's minds; they have overtones of significance, an aura of association and suggestion, which they acquire because behind the simple words stands the whole resonant organism of a particular society, with its memories, its beliefs, its values, its habitual sentiments. The greatest poetry is always the result not merely of individual genius but of the interaction between individual genius and a particular culture. I am not suggesting that there has to be a complete harmony or univocity between them; indeed a certain tension seems to be fruitful as well as inevitable. But it is easy to see that if the cultural context is impoverished and unfavourable even the highest individual genius will suffer some impairment and frustration. If, for example, the language has been degraded, devitalized and desecrated by advertising, journalism, ideological propaganda, scientism, including social-scientism, and mass-production schooling, the poet may still, by incredible efforts and austerities, make some of the language work poetically, but he would have been able to do much more if he had a more living language to use, not something that feels like chewed paper or tired chewing-gum in the mouth.

Now I have elsewhere drawn attention to the fact, which is not as widely understood as it should be, though obvious enough, that the mental climate or atmosphere created by Progress, Enlightenment and "modernity" is very unfavourable to poetry. The relationship between poetry and this atmosphere can in fact be stated very simply: it is the same as that between a dog and a gas-chamber. There is no genuine poetry which expresses the mentality of Locke, Hume, Bentham, Comte, Marx, Mill, Spencer, to name a representative few. There is no genuine poetry which celebrates the world as Beatrice Webb, Shaw, Wells, Bertrand Russell, Laski or other gurus of recent times have seen it. To come to Australia: there is no genuine poetry which corresponds to the "modernity" present in our heritage. There are, indeed, varieties of sub-standard verse rhetoric which have been used by the bards of Federation, of Utopia, of Nationalism, and more recently of Latterday Leftism. The value of this mass of material may be judged at once by a glance at the work of the most distinguished of the Austral bards of Progress, Bernard O'Dowd. His work is a *cloaca maxima* into which has flowed all the ideological drivel of the nineteenth century—deism, pantheism, nationalism, socialism, democratism and the rest—and its value as literature is nil.

The reason for this lethal effect of naturalism, secularism, utopianism and so forth on poetry is that genuine poetry is always realistic in the proper sense of the word: it bears some proportion to reality, it does not utterly mistake the nature of man and of the world. Erich Heller put this very well in a broadcast talk on poetry: "It is concerned with the true stature of things. And being concerned with the true stature of things, all great poetry is realistic." People who wear spectacles made from the great sorcerer's looking-glass cannot see things in their true stature. No amount of mental energy or passion, no manipulation of the techniques of poetry, no tall terms of rhetoric, will produce work that has dignity or beauty or depth or joy. These qualities can emerge only when the mind plays false to its official views and somehow gets at least partially into contact with reality.

The question arises whether the orthodox Christian component in our heritage may be regarded as a resource for poetry. In principle, yes; but the cultural limitations of modern Catholicism which have been already pointed out must be taken into account here too. The Australian Catholic shares inevitably in the prevailing mood, tone, sentiment and attitude of the rest of the nation, so that he is to that extent out of touch with poetry. In addition, there are disconcerting features of his own heritage as it has come down to him. Over the last few centuries, under the stress of many difficulties, Catholicism has tended to lose contact with the earlier and better cultural traditions that developed under its influence. In the externals of its life it has accepted styles and idioms of art and language which are really unfit for its purposes; and having accepted them it has clung to them with the conservatism which is normal in religious matters. Thus instead of the grandeur and purity and tenderness of the older authentically Christian modes of expression, Christianity became disguised and deformed by the habitual use of Renascence and post-Renascence modes whose origins lay in naturalism and secularism, culminating in the nineteenth century in the loathsome commercial religious art with which we are still familiar and in the rococo pieties of devotional manuals. An imagination contaminated by these external modes cannot easily purge itself and recover purity of vision. It must also be kept in mind that even if a Catholic is not too greatly hampered by these difficulties, he still has to face the problem of writing against the grain of his society, of creating works of art which cannot be in intimate correspondence with its prevailing sentiments, of using forms and styles that have been developed under alien auspices, of communicating with an audience that hardly knows what he is talking about.

At this point I must let in the buzz of protest that has been waiting to be heard. What is all this about poetry and ideology? Poetry has very little to do with metaphysics and theology and the less the better. True, there are some "intellectual" poets who attempt to put their intellectual interests into verse; but the main tradition of Australian poetry is not of this kind. Australian poetry is, and should be, largely a matter of emotions and sense-perceptions, not of theories. Love of nature; simple human situations involving love and grief; tales of action; the working up of historical associations; individual musings and imaginings—these, surely, are the stuff of our poetry.

The first point I want to make about this is that the ideological framework is important whether the poet is attempting a philosophical work or merely giving a lyrical expression to the feelings roused in him by a particular situation. Poetry in its simplest lyrical forms is still culturally conditioned. It is not merely a deterioration in poetry that has intellectual pretensions that I am talking about; it is a deterioration in all kinds of poetry under the stunting and stultifying influence of the modern frame of mind.

One of the most noticeable consequences of the positivist, antimetaphysical, tendency in modern culture is that people who do not explicitly adopt some systematic allegiance, for example to Marxism or orthodox Christianity, readily fall into a state of nescience about their own intellectual assumptions and allegiances. Other people, they feel, have ideological commitments—they have none; other people are biased or prejudiced—they have no special intellectual interest to defend. Their intellectual life subsides into a fog of agnosticism and neutralism. They feel that the true aim of a sensible person should be, like that of the criminal, to avoid convictions. They envisage the writing of poetry as being the play of an unattached sensibility; the material of poetry as confetti of sense-impressions whirled about by little gusts of feeling.

It is necessary to point out that confused and unconscious assumptions, mere "glimmerings and decays" though they may be of older conscious philosophies, are none the less real assumptions. Everyone approaches his experience with certain basic thought-forms, moulds of sentiment, principles of selection and interpretation which he has acquired from his environment. The simplest lyric presupposes a whole scheme of valuation which rests ultimately on a certain metaphysic and *Weltanschauung*. What I am saying is that the more nearly the *Weltanschauung* of the writer conforms to the

modern frame of mind the more incapable he becomes of genuine
poetry; and this can be verified in the productions of Australian
poets, though I do not propose to pursue the demonstration into
the work of individuals.

I am not, let me add, objecting to the appearance of a distinctively
Australian colouring in our poetry. My own work should make this
evident. It is not the poet's business either to avoid or to seek local
colouring. The problem of being Australian does not exist except
for those who are afflicted with the disease of cultural nationalism,
or who are seeking substitute religious gratifications in the pantheis-
tic embrace of an Australian *Erdgeist*, or who are in other ways
ideologically deranged. It is a mark of the stultifying effect of the
cultural climate that so many of our writers should become obsessed with Australianity as their object, subject and programme, and
show an incapacity to deal with themes of permanent universal importance. It is one thing to deal with these themes in their local
aspect and setting if that is the way they come into the mind; it is
another to set up Australianity as an end in itself, as an aesthetic
quality, a *sine qua non*, a critical principle: in short as an idol to
which sacrifice must be made. This is an intellectual perversion of
which too much of our writing and our literary criticism is guilty. It
holds us back in the confines of *provincialism* instead of letting us
progress to a healthy, normal *regionalism*.

The second point I want to make is that Australian critics too
easily assume that poetry with a philosophical content is a minor
variety to be brushed aside. True, a great deal of European poetry
consists of lyrics springing from sensibility rather than metaphysical
contemplation, and some of it consists of verse tales or other enter-
tainments that are not too heavily charged with metaphysical implications. But equally it is true that the body of European poetry
which is by common consent great is overwhelmingly and passionately intent on the great issues of religion, metaphysics, ethics
and politics. Once again, to set "intellectual" poetry on one side as a
peculiar variety and attempt to build a main tradition on other lines
is to succumb to the anti-intellectualism always present in "modernity", and to reveal that one has lost contact with the real traditions of literature.

The last point I want to make is in some ways the most important
of all and the most difficult to demonstrate. I have implied that "the
modern mind" is suffering from a loss of intellectuality, from which
results a deterioration that spreads out through society and affects
the arts. I believe that this intellectual degeneration and loss of tone
(which begins in a turning away from the springs of metaphysical
and religious life) brings a deterioration not merely in the substance
of poetry but also in its formal organization. Where there is a strong
central intellectual tradition one may expect to find the artistic conventions in a healthy state: a high degree of formality which has not
stiffened into inflexibility. Corresponding to the good breeding,

courtesy, and refinement of the social ideal that is developed under these circumstances, there is a poetic grace, courtesy and controlled vitality which can touch the slightest lyric with a note of distinction and'charm. The poem that springs to my mind as an illustration is Waller's:

> Goe lovely Rose,
> Tell her that wastes her time and me,
> That now she knowes,
> When I resemble her to thee,
> How'sweet and fair she seems to be.

The elegance, the syntactical balance, the ease yet tautness, of this poem is possible only because it has behind it an intellectual culture of a high order. That the poet should individually possess this high culture is less important, perhaps, than that he lives and writes surrounded and permeated by it so that it becomes "instinctive".

It is painfully obvious that this capacity for a fine formal organization has greatly declined. Outside the empirical sciences our intellectual life is slack and disorderly. The modern philosophical systems are not so much intellectual constructions as stages in the abandonment of the philosophical task. And outside the professed philosophers there is hardly even the pretence of coherent thought. The counterpart of this is the slackness and disorder of our poetry. This is not primarily a question of adhering to strict rules and traditional methods, because the mere adherence to these, though it may help, will not give the poet's expression that intellectual energy, muscle tone, balance, fineness, grace and courtesy which it lacks. You may say that what I am asking for is something bound up with an aristocratic society and is not obtainable in a democracy. I do not believe that the price of democracy is necessarily semi-barbarism. What is in question is the order that is possible in all spheres in a metaphysically-oriented society, as contrasted with the disorder that invades all spheres in a society which has become metaphysically disoriented and—in a precise sense—unprincipled.

ENVOI

There the blue-green gums are a fringe of remote disorder
And the brown sheep poke at my dreams along the hillsides;
And there in the soil, in the season, in the shifting airs,
Comes the faint sterility that disheartens and derides.

Where once was a sea is now a salty sunken desert,
A futile heart within a fair periphery;
The people are hard-eyed, kindly, with nothing inside them,
The men are independent but you could not call them free.

And I am fitted to that land as the soul is to the body,
I know its contractions, waste, and sprawling indolence;
They are in me and its triumphs are my own,
Hard-won in the thin and bitter years without pretence.

Beauty is order and good chance in the artesian heart
And does not wholly fail, though we impede;
Though the reluctant and uneasy land resent
The gush of waters, the lean plough, the fretful seed.

PIETÀ

A year ago you came
Early into the light.
You lived a day and night,
Then died; no-one to blame.

Once only, with one hand,
Your mother in farewell
Touched you. I cannot tell,
I cannot understand

A thing so dark and deep,
So physical a loss:
One touch, and that was all

She had of you to keep.
Clean wounds, but terrible,
Are those made with the Cross.

FATHER, MOTHER, SON

From the domed head the defeated eyes peer out,
Furtive with unsaid things of a lifetime, that now
Cannot be said by that stiff half-stricken mouth
Whose words come hoarse and slurred, though the mind is sound.

To have to be washed, and fed by hand, and turned
This way and that way by the cheerful nurses,
Who joke, and are sorry for him, and tired of him:
All that is not the worst paralysis.

For fifty years this one thread—he has held
One gold thread of the vesture: he has said
Hail, holy Queen, slightly wrong, each night in secret.
But his wife, and now a lifetime, stand between:

She guards him from his peace. Her love asks only
That in the end he must not seem to disown
Their terms of plighted troth. So he will make
For ever the same choice that he has made—

Unless that gold thread hold, invisibly.
I stand at the bed's foot, helpless like him;
Thinking of legendary Seth who made
A journey back to Paradise, to gain

The oil of mercy for his dying father.
But here three people smile, and, locked apart,
Prove by relatedness that cannot touch
Our sad geometry of family love.

WISTARIA

Does that wistaria vine still break in flower
Like grape-clusters transformed to lilac light
For bees to hover in? It had a power,
Then, to absorb all feelings into sight.

And the mute aching sweetness of its scent
Stored up the quotient of long afternoons
Where time stretched forward, empty of event,
Drifting with bells, pagodas, pale balloons—

Shapes that changed back to flowers at a touch.
The soul must feed on something for its dreams,
In those brick suburbs, and there wasn't much:
It can make do with little, so it seems.

Its formal home had crossed flags at the back
And reverent doubt up front. In equipoise
Between the brass cross and the Union Jack,
It could still quiver to the cheerful noise

That called upon all things to render praise.
Of all things, I liked best that tough old vine
Roping our side fence, offering my days
Clusters of hope that stirred the sense like wine.

IN THE HUON VALLEY

Propped boughs are heavy with apples,
Springtime quite forgotten.
Pears ripen yellow. The wasp
Knows where windfalls lie rotten.

Juices grow rich with sun.
These autumn days are still:
The glassy river reflects
Elm-gold up the hill,

And big white plumes of rushes.
Life is full of returns;
It isn't true that one never
Profits, never learns:

Something is gathered in,
Worth the lifting and stacking;
Apples roll through the graders,
The sheds are noisy with packing.

ST JOHN'S PARK

The mountain is streaked white, the air is cold.
Under a pure blue sky the players begin.
Thickly-clotted prunus lines the way in,
And wattles put on helmets of heavy gold.

A dark-green gum bursts out in crimson flowers.
Old people slowly rot along the wall.
The young ones hardly notice them at all.
Both live in the same picture-book of hours.

Four-turreted a square tower balks the sky,
Casting a shadow; an organ softly plays.
The afternoon wears out in a gold daze.
On ragged wings, uttering its carking cry

A raven scavenges; a flock of gulls
Flies from the tip. The last teams leave the park.
The old have crept inside to meet the dark.
Loss is what nothing alters or annuls.

At nightfall glaring traffic rushes by
Filling the air with reek and the scream of brakes.
Faint stars prick out a sign. And Vega wakes
Liquid and trembling on the northern sky.

MUSIC LATE AT NIGHT

Black gashes in white bark. The gate
Is clouded with spicy prunus flowers.
The moon sails cold through the small hours.
The helpless heart says, hold and wait.

Wait. The lighted empty street
Waits for the start of a new day,
When cars move, dogs and children play.
But now the rigid silence is complete.

Again that soundless music: a taut string,
Burdened unbearably with grief
That smiles acceptance of despair,

Throbs on the very threshold of spring
In the burst flower, the folded leaf:
Puzzling poor flesh to live and care.

BOOK OF HOURS

The world spread open through the window-frame
Offers a language only known by sight.
Two little girls pass by and one is lame;
Six yachts ride at anchor on broken light.

Moment by moment nothing is the same:
Against a blue with drifting bulks of white
A windblown tree is twisted to green flame;
Birds shift among the branches and take flight.

And all this seems to make a kind of claim,
As if it had been given that one might
Decipher it: if there were such a skill

Which one could learn by looking—get it right,
As children learn to read a word, a name,
Another, until meaning comes at will.

Note: the poem 'Terra Australis' appears in the Harry Heseltine article 'Australian Image: the Literary Heritage' on p. 309.

JOHN STREETER MANIFOLD   (1915–)

Poet, journalist, music editor. Born in Melbourne; educated in Victoria and Cambridge.

THE BUNYIP AND THE WHISTLING KETTLE

I knew a most superior camper
   Whose methods were absurdly wrong;
He did not live on tea and damper
   But took a little stove along.

And every place he came to settle
   He spread with gadgets saving toil;
He even had a whistling kettle
   To warn him it was on the boil.

Beneath the waratahs and wattles,
   Boronia and coolibah,
He scattered paper, cans, and bottles,
   And parked his nasty little car.

He camped, this sacrilegious stranger
   (The moon was at the full that week),
Once in a spot that teemed with danger
   Beside a bunyip-haunted creek.

He spread his junk but did not plunder,
   Hoping to stay the week-end long;
He watched the bloodshot sun go under
   Across the silent billabong.

He ate canned food without demurring,
   He put the kettle on for tea.
He did not see the water stirring
   Far out beside a sunken tree.

Then, for the day had made him swelter
   And night was hot and tense to spring,
He donned a bathing suit in shelter
   And left the firelight's friendly ring.

He felt the water kiss and tingle.
   He heard the silence—none too soon!
A ripple broke against the shingle,
   And dark with blood it met the moon.

Abandoned in the hush, the kettle
   Screamed as it guessed its master's plight,
And loud it screamed, the lifeless metal,
   Far into the malicious night.

THE TOMB OF LIEUT. JOHN LEARMONTH, A.I.F.

'At the end on Crete he took to the hills, and said
he'd fight it out with only a revolver. He was a
great soldier.' ... ONE OF HIS MEN IN A LETTER.

This is not sorrow, this is work: I build
A cairn of words over a silent man,
My friend John Learmonth whom the Germans killed.

There was no word of hero in his plan;
Verse should have been his love and peace his trade,
But history turned him to a partisan.

Far from the battle as his bones are laid
Crete will remember him. Remember well,
Mountains of Crete, the Second Field Brigade!

Say Crete, and there is little more to tell
Of muddle tall as treachery, despair
And black defeat resounding like a bell;

But bring the magnifying focus near
And in contempt of muddle and defeat
The old heroic virtues still appear.

Australian blood where hot and icy meet
(James Hogg and Lermontov were of his kin)
Lie still and fertilize the fields of Crete.

Schoolboy, I watched his ballading begin:
Billy and bullocky and billabong,
Our properties of childhood, all were in.

I heard the air though not the undersong,
The fierceness and resolve; but all the same
They're the tradition, and tradition's strong.

Swagman and bushranger die hard, die game,
Die fighting, like that wild colonial boy—
Jack Dowling, says the ballad, was his name.

He also spun his pistol like a toy,
Turned to the hills like wolf or kangaroo,
And faced destruction with a bitter joy.

His freedom gave him nothing else to do
But set his back against his family tree
And fight the better for the fact he knew

He was as good as dead. Because the sea
Was closed and the air dark and the land lost,
'They'll never capture me alive,' said he.

That's courage chemically pure, uncrossed
With sacrifice or duty or career,
Which counts and pays in ready coin the cost

Of holding course. Armies are not its sphere
Where all's contrived to achieve its counterfeit;
It swears with discipline, it's volunteer.

I could as hardly make a moral fit
Around it as around a lightning flash.
There is no moral, that's the point of it,

No moral. But I'm glad of this panache
That sparkles, as from flint, from us and steel,
True to no crown nor presidential sash

Nor flag nor fame. Let others mourn and feel
He died for nothing: nothings have their place.
While thus the kind and civilised conceal

This spring of unsuspected inward grace
And look on death as equals, I am filled
With queer affection for the human race.

INCOGNITO

Every station in the country keeps a pony that was sent
   Late at night to fetch a doctor or a priest,
And has lived the life of Riley since that faraway event,
   But the stories don't impress me in the least;

For I once owned Incognito—what a jewel of a horse!
   He was vastly better bred than many men!
But they handicapped so savagely on every local course
   I was forced to dye him piebald now and then.

For I needed all the money that a sporting life entails,
   Having found the cost of living rather dear,
And my wife, the very sweetest little girl in New South Wales,
   Was presenting me with children every year.

We were spreading superphosphate one October afternoon
   When the missus said she felt a little sick:
We were not expecting Septimus (or Septima) so soon,
   But I thought I'd better fetch the doctor quick,

So I started for the homestead with the minimum delay,
   Where I changed, and put pomade on my moustache;
But before I reached the sliprails Incognito was away,
   And was heading for the township like a flash.

First he swam a flooded river, then he climbed a craggy range,
    And they tell me, though I haven't any proof,
That he galloped thro' the township to the telephone exchange
    Where he dialled the doctor's number with his hoof.

Yes, he notified the doctor, and the midwife, and the vet,
    And he led them up the mountain to my door
Where he planted, panting, pondering, in a rivulet of sweat,
    Till he plainly recollected something more.

Then he stretched his muzzle towards me. He had something in his
        teeth,
    Which he dropped with circumspection in my hand;
And I recognised his offering as a contraceptive sheath,
    So I shot him. It was more than I could stand.

But I've bitterly repented that rash act of injured pride—
    It was not the way a sportsman should behave!
So I'm making my arrangements to be buried at his side,
    And to share poor Incognito's lonely grave.

JOHN MORRISON   (1904–)

Short story writer, novelist. Born and educated in England; migrated to Australia in 1923.

DOG-BOX

I first became aware of her just before the train pulled in.

Flinders Street Station in the peak-hour is a primitive place. You get pushed at from all sides, and if the pressure from one particular quarter is a bit more persistent than from anywhere else the odds are that you won't even notice it. That is, if you're a regular peak-hour traveller, have a long way to go, and are not as young as you used to be.

I was aware of this particular pressure, though. It turned out afterwards to be the edge of a wicker shopping basket, but it felt more like the lid of a garbage can. However, I held my ground and fought down a temptation to look around, because to have done so would have meant moving more than my head, thereby letting someone else in.

The train came into sight running down from the yards, and a murmur of pleasant anticipation ran along the packed platform. Dog-box! We use to talk of the old dears with contempt, but have changed our attitude since the arrival of the Blue Hussies. It was like seeing the old brown teapot come to light.

It slowed to a stop. Those of us at the front pressed backwards as incoming passengers eased open the swinging doors. I was in a good position, but sensed immediate danger as I felt the lid of the garbage can slide round into my left side. I looked down, frowning, because for all the hurly-burly of the five-to-six rush, there is still a point beyond which most sufferers do not go.

She had Mum written all over her. I was close enough to get even the homely middle-aged smell of her; something of well-preserved clothes, wood-ashes, yellow soap, the stew-pot. Below a comfortable bosom she hugged her garbage can battering ram, a well-filled shopping basket topped with what looked like a folded woollen scarf. Two bright eyes flashed up at me out of a face full of character and rich experience.

'Sorry, mister!'

I gave her a smile, and a few more inches of precious ground, but I knew she wasn't a bit sorry. She was as good as past me, and already digging her basket into the backs of two other women who had moved in from the other side.

Nobody got hurt, but Mum was only fifth in. She was beaten by the two women, a big workman, and a little clerk type of fellow who must have been an old hand at the game, because he seemed to come from nowhere to take fourth place.

When I got in I found the two near window-seats occupied by the clerk and the workman. The three women were on the same side as the clerk, with Mum furthest from the window and apparently none too happy about it. In the fourth corner a tough-looking fellow wearing a black belted raincoat and a cloth cap sat watching us troop in with an expression of sleepy insolence on his unshaven face. On his knees lay what was obviously a bottle wrapped up in brown paper. I sat down next to him before I realized that he was half drunk and that I hadn't noticed him before.

'Flinders Street,' I said amiably. 'This train's going back.'

He turned on me a dull heavy-lidded stare. 'Back where?' he asked with a strong Scottish accent.

'Lilydale.'

'Lilydale.' He gave that a moment's consideration. 'An' supposin' tha's where I want tae go?'

'Sorry. I didn't see you get in.'

'An' supposin' I didna get in?'

Now experience has taught me that the best way to deal with a quarrelsome drunk is to meet him halfway. So I said firmly: 'That's what I was supposing.'

'An' supposin' ye're richt?'

I shrugged my shoulders and looked away from him.

But to my relief he suddenly relaxed and clapped a heavy hand on my knee. 'A'richt, Pop. I been sleepin'. A' the way there an' back. I wanted Nunawading. First thing I know I open ma eyes and there's the bluidy cricket ground flyin' past again, the wrong way.'

'You're all right this time,' I said. 'I'm going to Croydon. I'll have an eye on you at Nunawading.'

In the meantime the compartment had filled up, even with a few standing passengers. During my exchange with Scotty I'd been aware of Mum on the other side taking some interest in the proceedings. But not much. She was preoccupied chiefly with the basket and with the two women on her left. The one in the window seat had lit a cigarette and seemed to want to keep to herself. The other, a stoutish matron in navy-blue overcoat and beret, and laden with parcels, was beaming at all of us, ready to take on anybody who'd give her a fair hearing. She had the air of a woman who has made some bargains and feels she has topped off a good day by getting herself a seat on a peak-hour train going home.

Mum looked as if she were still nursing a grievance over being beaten to a corner seat. Without moving her head she kept darting angry little sideways glances. Her leathery face was grim and anxious as she felt under the woollen scarf to see if everything was still there.

On Mum's right a pale youth in black trousers and pink windcheater had opened up a Superman comic. In the far corner the clerk was reading a paperback. On my side there was Scotty, myself, two mates whose names I soon learned were Bill and Ian, and the workman, of whom all I could see were frayed trouser cuffs and a pair of big blucher boots. The standing passengers were reinforced at Richmond by a man who irritated Mum by flicking her face every now and then with the corner of a *Herald* hanging from a hand hooked on to the luggage-rack.

Bill and Ian were discussing an item in the news: Stanley Yankus, the American farmer who was migrating to Australia because he had been fined for growing too much wheat. Ian, sitting next to me, was doing all the listening, so that I picked up most of what Bill was saying.

'What good will it do him, anyhow? It'll be on here again any tick of the clock. I just heard the other night over the air that hundreds of acres of sugar-cane in Queensland ain't going to be cut this year. My old man told me the best job he ever had in his life was dumping butter during the Depression. He used to work all day carting butter down and tipping it into the Bay. Then go home at night to a feed of snags and fried bread. One of his mates got the sack because they found some butter in his bag ...'

I began to get interested, but at that moment Scotty came to life again. No preliminaries. I thought he was sleeping until he whispered right into my ear:

'How about a whisky, Pop?' He tapped the brown paper parcel on his knees. 'Nane o' your Australian tack. Real Scotch—White Horse. Have a nip?'

I told him quite amiably that it wasn't my medicine. He frowned contemptuously.

'What do ye drink?'

'Beer.'

'Supposin' I havna got beer?' He stared hard, as if I'd been demanding beer and what was I going to do about it now.

'That's my bad luck,' I said.

'An' ye no want a whisky?'

'No, thank you.'

On my left I caught Bill's voice: 'I saw another case like Yankus only a few months ago. Only it was pigs. A bloke raising too many pigs ...'

Ian must have moved, for the voice faded. And Scotty was still at me:

'Any objections tae me havin' a nip?'

'No,' I replied, adding impatiently: 'It's your whisky.'

He knitted his brows, and for a moment I thought I'd gone too far too quickly. I tried to appear interested in Mum, but was acutely aware of him keeping me under observation while he decided what to do about me.

Mum had been captured by Mrs Blue Beret. The latter was obscured by one of the standing passengers and I couldn't make out what she was saying, but for the last few minutes her voice had provided a steady overtone to all the other noises in the compartment. Mum was only pretending to be listening. She kept turning her head and nodding sympathetically, but it was plain to me that her mind was never far from her basket. I began to wonder what was in it. She had it hugged close to her stomach, wrists braced against the arched handle, both hands turned inwards and spread out over the folded scarf as if ready to detect the slightest movement of something hidden beneath it.

Bill was flat out on the question of pigs. I'd stolen a peep at him and found him to be a man of middle age with a worried expression on the kind of face that goes with ulcers or a nagging wife.

'Blokes was getting paid for pigs they didn't raise. Now just you get on to it! Say you're a little bloke, just big enough to raise pigs up to the quota. All nicely organized, prices fixed and guaranteed. You get paid for, say fifty pigs that stink and grunt and make pork. But I'm in it in a bigger way. I've got room for two hundred pigs. And I get paid for two hundred pigs. Only I get told to keep just a hundred and fifty—or else! So I declare a hundred and fifty pigs on the hoof and fifty on paper. And I get paid for them fifty paper pigs just like you get paid for your fifty pork pigs. And people everywhere screaming out for bacon. The game stinks.'

Ian murmured something which was inaudible to me, and nodded his head to agree that the game did indeed stink.

I waited, curious to see where Bill would go from there, but Scotty had returned to the attack on the other side. He must have been brooding, because he took up his grievance exactly where he had left off.

'What ye're tellin' me is: this is a free country, eh?'

I pretended not to grasp his meaning.

'If ye don't want tae drink whisky, ye don't have to. An' if I *do* want tae drink whisky—I drink whisky. That it?'

I smiled. 'That's about it.'

'It's as simple as tha', is it?'

'It was your idea!'

'I didna say it was my idea. I was suggestin' maybe it was your idea.' He tapped the parcel again. 'Supposin' a checker got in just as I cracked this bottle. Ye still say I can drink whisky if I want to?'

'That's a chance you'd have to take, my friend,' I parried, still smiling.

'What ye mean is: this is a free country as long as I'm prepared tae take the odds. Is that it'?

I shrugged my shoulders, and once again he retired into his alcoholic whirligig. A moment later, under the pretence of identifying a station we were pulling into, I stole a glance at him. Chin resting on elbow, he was staring out through the window with an expression of sleepy triumph.

Mum also was watching stations. We were in Auburn, and she'd been checking off every stop as if on her way to an appointment of life or death. Conversation with the woman in blue had become clinical. I caught the sentence: 'Anyhow, he gave me some tablets for him to take...' and guessed that the absent Mr Blue Beret was under discussion.

Mum was showing a little more interest, but still only between stations. Every time we stopped she leaned forward to peer out through the window, remaining like that until we were on the move again. She looked cold. She should have been wearing that scarf. It occurred to me that she had taken it off to protect something in the basket. A kitten? Chicken? Whatever it was she never for an instant removed her sheltering hands. Every now and then I saw the worn fingers spread out, feeling, probing. Next to her the pale youth had been through the comic and was fighting a losing battle with sleep. Mum had had to straighten him up several times with discreet little nudges. But I'm a leftwise subsider myself, and I knew that nothing she could do would make him collapse in the other direction. Motherly type as she was, I believe she'd have let him go to sleep on her shoulder if it hadn't been for the basket. I saw her shift it a little away from him and bring her right elbow forward as a barrier.

Bill was in the full tide of the subject of the paper pigs.

'Them pigs that nobody raises get paid for in real money. The blokes that whistles pigs up say you can't whistle money up—not for pigs, anyway. They say it's got to come from somewhere, and that somewhere always means you and me in the long run. Taxes. Say you're on the basic wage and you got a big family to feed.

You'd give 'em all two cackles and a grunt for breakfast every morning if you could, wouldn't you?'

Ian must have agreed with that.

'But you can't, not on your pay. Eggs maybe, but not bacon as well. But, by jeez, you got to pay for bacon! Them paper pigs get paid for with Government dough. And that's you! Now just work it out. You pay taxes to pay blokes to raise paper pigs so that the bloke who raises pork pigs can get a price you can't afford! Now tell me the game doesn't stink.'

Ian evidently was still not prepared to say that the game didn't stink, and a sulky silence fell on my left.

At Camberwell several passengers, including the woman in the corner seat, got off. Nobody got in. Mrs Blue Beret, in full voice on her husband's clinical history, seemed unaware that the corner seat had been vacated until Mum gave her an urgent push. Both of them moved along, and Mum settled herself one place nearer the window with obvious satisfaction. The pale youth lurched violently, collected himself with great embarrassment, apologized, and promptly moved in close to her again. I think he didn't like the look of the passenger who was ready to drop into the empty seat, and felt that if he was going to subside on to anybody it had still better be Mum.

In the commotion Scotty came to life again. I noticed his hand tighten convulsively on the bottle of whisky in the very moment that sleep left him. He shook his head, peered out for the name of the station, relaxed, and after a few seconds' contemplation to thoroughly digest the fact that I was still there, once again began where he had left off.

'So ye think it's a free country, do ye?'

'Look here, my friend,' I began irritably, 'I've done a hard day's work ...'

'A'richt, a'richt, a'richt.' I'd been prepared for a different reaction, and was rather disconcerted when he bent on me a dry smile. 'Why don't ye go tae sleep then? Ye're sittin' there wi' your eyes wide open ...'

'Any objections?'

'No, no objections. If a man wants tae sleep he's entitled tae sleep. If a man doesna want tae sleep...' he waved his hand in a way that made me want to hit him, 'och weel, it's a free country!' And there he left me again, seething.

I decided to have a piece of him next time, whatever the cost.

Mrs Blue Beret was a foot or two further away from me now, but with the standing passengers gone I could hear more of what Mum had to put up with.

'... little pink ones this time. And do you think I could get him to take them? Not on your life! He said they made everything he ate taste like burned cork. And the doctor had gone out of his way to tell me they didn't have no taste at all. It just goes to show what imagination can do for you.'

Mum, carefully checking the train through Canterbury, nodded shrewdly.

'He was particularly crooked on them spoiling his tea. So he said, anyhow. He's always liked his cuppa. So d'you know what I did? I said to him: if you think they're not doing you any good then you'd better stop taking them. And I started putting them into his tea unbeknown to him! And now he's as happy as Larry. Says he hasn't felt better for years, and that them tablets must have been making him worse. Sometimes I could bust right out laughing at him. He looks at me across the table and winks and smacks his lips. "By God, Sally," he says, "it's good to be able to enjoy a decent cup of tea again!"'

Mum chuckled, nodding vigorously, and, I thought, reminiscently. In other circumstances she might have told a good story back. At the moment she just didn't want to be involved in anything. There was that basket...

Bill was still getting a good hearing on pigs:

'The more you look at it the sillier it gets. If you ain't in the pig business you cop it three ways. You don't eat pork, even under the lap. You pay taxes to pay blokes not to raise pigs. And you pay more taxes to pay more blokes to see that the other blokes *don't* raise pork. Because it's like everything else, it's got to be administered. You got to have an office, clerks, paper for forms to fill in so that blokes can say exactly how many pigs they ain't raising. One time farmers just raised pigs, and there wasn't any office anywhere that had anything to do with pig-raising. They just took the little pigs to market. These paper pigs is different ...'

We had come to a halt somewhere between Mont Albert and Box Hill, and Mum was becoming increasingly worried. I believe she'd have given anything for Mrs Blue Beret's corner seat so that she could open the window and look out to see what was the cause of the hold-up. Mrs Blue Beret rambled on, regardless of the fact that Mum obviously wasn't listening. Mum looked thoroughly angry, as if nothing would suit her better just then than a chance to give the Victorian Railways Commissioners a piece of her mind. For the twentieth time I caught her withdrawing her hand from under the scarf, and had to fight down a temptation to lean over and ask her if it was still breathing. I wasn't sure how she'd take it.

More pigs...

'The trouble is, Ian, sooner or later the big blokes is going to take a wake-up to the lurk and go in for it in a big way. They'll monopolize it, get a corner in them paper pigs. They'll have 'em raising litters. They'll be claiming higher prices for 'em because of the rise in costs of all the tucker they don't give 'em to eat. They'll be going overseas trips, tax-free, to study the latest developments in the paper pig-raising industry. They'll get their mates in Parliament to put a duty on imported pork so as to give the home-produced stuff a fair go—struth, we're at Box Hill! We made a quick run tonight...'

I felt a keen disappointment as the two friends reached for their bags on the luggage-rack. It would have been diverting to see how far Bill would have gone in his dissertation on the controls of private enterprise. I noticed that the moment they were out on the platform he started again.

Some other passengers got out also. More came in. Mostly teen-age schoolboys.

Mum had just ridden out another lurch of the pale youth and informed him with a rather tight little smile: 'You was nearly into me basket that time!' He was sitting stiffly now with a red face, trying desperately to find something in the comic that was worth rereading. Mrs Blue Beret announced that she was getting off at Blackburn, and with a new passenger standing against the door I saw Mum gather herself for the slide into the corner seat. With that in prospect she listened quite sympathetically to the final anecdote about Mr Blue Beret's stomach.

'He's supposed to eat brains, you know, but he says he's never sat down to the dirty things in his life and he ain't going to start now. So I give him fish-paste sandwiches in his lunch every other day. That's what he thinks, anyhow. If he's never tasted brains he can't be any the wiser. Sometimes he'll come in from work and say: 'By jeez, Sally, that was a nice bit of fish!' He thinks it's Japanese flat'ead paste ...'

I'd have liked more on that, but just then the tenacious Scot came in again:

'This free country business ...'

'How about giving it a rest?'

'No offence, Pop. Ye're an Aussie, aren't ye?'

'Yes, I'm an Aussie.'

'An' ye say it's a free country?'

'Yes, I do.'

'You always cast your vote at election time?'

'You bet I do!'

'An' supposin' ye dinna like ony o' the candidates? You still cast your vote?'

'I can always vote for the one I dislike least.'

The corners of his lips drooped. 'Ye ca' tha' an argument? The real point o' the matter is: ye got tae vote, haven't yet?'

'Voting *is* compulsory, yes.'

Again the pontifically waving hand. 'That's jist ma point! A free country—an' compulsion wherever ye turn! In Scotland I never missed ma vote, simply because I was free tae please masel. Oot here the first thing they tell me is: Jock, ye got tae vote! Tha's enough for me. Ma hackles is up. If tha's wha' they ca' democracy they can keep it. I've never used ma vote since I set foot in Australia. I believe in real freedom.'

And with that he retired, supremely confident of having finally flattened me, as indeed he had.

I was still reeling under the blow when we reached Blackburn and Mrs Blue Beret gathered up her parcels and got out. The man in the doorway stepped on to the platform to make way for her, so that Mum had no opposition in taking over the corner seat. I thought for a moment that she was going to open the window, but all she wanted was to make sure that it was in good working order. She just pushed it up a few inches, let it fall again, and immediately had another feel of the mystery under the scarf. If she hadn't looked so homely I'd have assumed then that she had some living thing she wanted to destroy, and was only waiting until the compartment was empty before pitching it out on to the line.

The schoolboys were involved in a lively discussion of TV. It might have been a golden opportunity for me to get an insight into juvenile perversion, but nothing now could divert me from Mum and her basket.

Except Scotty, who couldn't resist a final shot during the last lap to Nunawading. I knew for a good minute that he had turned his head and was watching me. I also knew, I don't know how, that he was smiling.

'Dinna let it worry ye, Pop.'

'Do I look worried?'

'No, I'm no sayin' ye look worried. I'm referrin' tae oor wee dispute.'

I said nothing, but was careful to keep a pleasant expression. In spite of everything he had succeeded in making me feel a bit of a nark. We slowed into Nunawading and he took a firm grip on his bottle of whisky and prepared to depart.

'No hurt feelings, Pop?'

'No hurt feelings, Mac. Good luck to you!' I was beginning to like him, but possibly only because he was going.

He lurched out, and, teetering alongside, gave me an ironic salute before banging the door.

'Never mind, Pop, there'll always be an England—as lang as there's a Scotland!'

On again, with Mum and I exchanging understanding smiles across the compartment. I believe she'd have said something but for the fact that, as I noticed with some excitement, she also was near the end of her journey. She was like a cat on hot bricks, measuring off the miles between Nunawading—Mitcham—Ringwood. She must have been feeling very cold. The pinched little neck, where that scarf should have been, was all gooseflesh. Every now and then a shiver passed over her. Her cheeks and the tip of her nose had turned blue. Her feet, which just reached the floor, kept up a cease-less tapping. But in the keen eyes and on the thin lips there was a smile of joyous anticipation. Both hands vanished under the scarf as if to give added protection over the last mile or two. I must have looked vastly interested, because when she caught me watching her she gave me a you-mind-your-own-business kind of stare plain enough to be embarrassing.

Ringwood. No, she didn't get off. But for all practical purposes it *was* the end of her journey. Everything favoured her.

She must have known every stick and stone of that line, because, sitting with a firm grip on the catch, she shot the window up in the very instant that we hit the end of the platform. Out went her head and a frantically waving hand. A long line of waiting passengers rushed past, slowed down, stopped. Mum was hidden from sight as the door opened, but I heard her urgent piping voice:

'Hi, Bill!'

People were getting off, others crowding around to get in. I got a glimpse of a good-looking young station assistant, his startled face trying to see where the voice was coming from. He stepped forward and was blacked out at the other side of the doorway.

'Spare me days, Mum! Where've you been to?'

'In town. Here, cop this—it's a pie—it'll warm you up ...'

'You beaut!'

'How's Elsie?'

'All right, How's Dad?'

'All right. How's Bubby?'

'Fit as a Mallee bull! Got another tooth ...'

The changing passengers were clearing and I got a full-length view of him. He stood with one hand resting on the window ledge, carrying on the conversation while casting hurried glances right and left along the train. His other hand held a small brown paper bag with a grease stain on it.

As the last doors banged he stepped backwards, one arm uplifted. The guard's whistle blew. The train tooted. We jerked into a start.

Mum's head was still at the open window.

'Ta-ta, Bill—eat it while it's hot!'

I thought I'd never seen a sweeter sight than that little woman sitting there with a happy smile as she wrapped the woollen scarf around her frozen neck.

Dear old Mum! To hell with the railways!—eat it while it's hot.

KENNETH MACKENZIE ('Seaforth Mackenzie') (1913–1954)

Poet, novelist. Born and educated in Perth.

THE BAY

How many moons of cool and noble light
   have risen on this long dark harbour-cove
whose tidal waters touch the velvet night
   ebbing and flowing like the voice of love?

Too many for my heart. It dare not tell
   aeons made splendid by such nights as this,
lest its own love seem small beneath the swell
   of the tide rising to its moon-sweet kiss.

Born of Earth's agony, the bay is old.
   Its wild green sides and flowered and rocky shore
have counted suns and moons and stars untold,
   as they will do when I am here no more.

DROUGHT

I drink to the bitterness of drought,
the drying pool, the dying tree,
the barren flower that cannot fruit,
the sun's embracing anarchy.

Skeleton cattle stand like stone
in a stone landscape, where the shade
is whittled to a blackened bone
etching the fallow and the road.

Poor helpless life! The anarchist
has laid his hand upon my heart;
and yet beneath the gripping fist
the soil, the land cannot be hurt.

All that dies will be renewed.
The leaf will spring as green as god.
The draught that bitter drought has brewed
will sweeten suddenly to good,

and I shall laugh and I shall sing
and bend my back above the soil
in praise of that new burgeoning,
quenched and made fair again by toil.

EDDY

On Eddy, who will not get well
and says he feels as crook as hell,
the hospital has cast a spell.

Neglected by a hurrying nurse
he barely has the strength to curse
and cursing only makes him worse.

Worthless and breathless there he lies
with sucked-in lips and bulging eyes
invoking harsh calamities

on staff and patients and the quack
who in a week has not been back
to hear about his last attack

and give him something for his cough ...
Eddy who used to be so tough
has had enough, has had enough.

He falls into a savage sleep
with lip outthrust and chin sunk deep
into the strenuous and steep

rise of his chest; and still around
his grizzled head the curses sound
ferocious, meaningless, profound

like angry flies against a screen
mysteriously placed between
reality and might-have-been.

Discarded at an early date
by life, he follows on his fate
which is to curse, complain and wait

for nothing, taking what he can
with naught to lose and naught to gain
and giving naught to any man

until, as at a secret call,
he enters in the hospital
unsure if he has lived at all.

ROLAND EDWARD ROBINSON   (1912–)

Poet, prose writer. Born in Ireland; came to Australia in 1921; educated in Sydney.

CASUARINA

The last, the long haired casuarina
stands upon the hillside where,
against the turquoise night of those first
yellow stars, she shakes her hair.

She shakes her hair out in her singing
of cliffs and caves and waterfalls,
and tribes who left the lichened sandstone
carved in gods and animals.

This is her country; honeyeaters
cry out its aboriginal name
where on her ridges still the spear-tall
lilies burn in flame and flame.

I listen, and our legend says not
more than this dark singing tree,
although her golden flowering lover
lies slain beside the winter sea.

BLACK COCKATOOS

Rise then, you screaming flight of black cockatoos,
and spread your red barred tail-feathers out and scream
over the spears of the reeds and the purple lilies,
over the red rock walls of this sun-gashed gorge,
and gather in broken and screaming flight and turn
heading far up this jade-green river's reaches.
So shall I find me harsh and blendless words
of barbarous beauty enough to sing this land.

ROBERT DAVID FITZGERALD (1902–)

Poet. Born and educated in Sydney.

LONG SINCE ...

Long since I heard the muttered anger of the reef;
but it was far off even then, so far indeed
that an imagined murmur, like the ear's belief
and faith of the night, was mingled with a fuller knell
throbbing across the silence, and one could not tell
which sounds were of air stirring, which come at the mind's need.

And that was the old sea, alive beyond the calm
of those wide-reaching waters stifled in the lagoon—
alert, masterful waves summoning beach and palm
to be up and about and moving and ever upon quest
of new desires of the spirit, not sunk in a soft rest
only expectant of some drunkenness of the moon.

I knew it also for my own heart's call to me,
as baffling still as it would seem in the lost time
when it was loveliness on edge with melody,
elusive always and yet eternally to be sought
past any meaning of meaning or any thought of thought
now wistfully heard again in even so dulled a clime.

I turned harshly and strode back to the native town,
watched by the wooden faces, the stolid Fijian eyes,
sought my thatched doorway, entered, mechanically sat down,
wondering what fate was on me or what weakness took toll
that thus I must go scurrying ratwise to my hole
lest some true self should claim me with imperious cries.

THE FACE OF THE WATERS

Once again the scurry of feet—those myriads
crossing the black granite; and again
laughter cruelly in pursuit; and then
the twang like a harpstring or the spring of a trap,
and the swerve on the polished surface: the soft little pads
sidling and skidding and avoiding; but soon caught up
in the hand of laughter and put back....

There is no release from the rack
of darkness for the unformed shape,
the unexisting thought

stretched half-and-half
in the shadow of beginning and that denser black
under the imminence of huge pylons—
the deeper nought;
but neither is there anything to escape,
or to laugh,
or to twang that string which is not a string but silence
plucked at the heart of silence.

Nor can there be a floor to the bottomless;
except in so far as conjecture must arrive,
lungs cracking, at the depth of its dive;
where downward further is further distress
with no change in it; as if a mile and an inch
are equally squeezed into a pinch,
and retreating limits of cold mind
frozen, smoothed, defined.

Out of the tension of silence (the twanged string);
from the agony of not being (that terrible laughter
tortured by darkness); out of it all
once again the tentative migration; once again
a universe on the edge of being born:
feet running fearfully out of nothing
at the core of nothing:
colour, light, fire, fearfully
becoming eyes and understanding: sound becoming ears....

For eternity is not space reaching
on without end to it; not time without end to it,
nor infinity working round in a circle;
but a placeless dot enclosing nothing,
the pre-time pinpoint of impossible beginning,
enclosed by nothing, not even by emptiness—
impossible: so wholly at odds with possibilities
that, always emergent and wrestling and interlinking
they shatter it and return to it, are all of it and part of it.
It is your hand stretched out to touch your neighbour's,
and feet running through the dark, directionless like darkness.

Worlds that were spun adrift re-enter
that intolerable centre;
indeed the widest-looping comet
never departed from it;
it alone exists.
And though, opposing it, there persists
the enormous structure of forces, laws,
as background for other coming and going,
that's but a pattern, a phase, no pause,

of ever-being-erected, ever-growing
ideas unphysically alternative
to nothing, which is the quick. You may say hills live,
or life's the imperfect aspect of a flowing
that sorts itself as hills; much as thoughts wind
selectively through mind.

The egg-shell collapses
in the fist of the eternal instant;
all is what is was before.
Yet is that eternal instant
the pinpoint bursting into reality,
the possibilities and perhapses,
the feet scurrying on the floor.
It is the suspense also
with which the outward thrust
holds the inward surrender—
the stresses in the shell before it buckles under:
the struggle to magpie-morning and all life's clamour and lust;
the part breaking through the whole;
light and the clear day and so simple a goal.

EDGE

Knife's edge, moon's edge, water's edge,
graze the throat of the formed shape
that sense fills where shape vanishes:
air at the ground limit of steel,
the thin disc in the moon's curve,
land gliding out of no land.

The new image, the freed thought,
are carved from that inert bulk
where the known ends and the unknown
is cut down before it—at the mind's edge,
the knife-edge at the throat of darkness.

SONG IN AUTUMN

Though we have put
white breath to its brief caper
in the early air,
and have known elsewhere
stiff fingers, frost underfoot,
sun thin as paper;

cold then was a lens
focussing sight, and showed that riggers' gear,
the spider's cables,
anchored between the immense
steel trusses of built grass. The hills were so near
you could pick up pebbles.

It is different at evening: damp rises
not crisp or definite like frost
but seeping into the blood and brain—
the end of enterprises.
And while, out of many things lost,
courage may remain,

this much is certain
from others' experience
and was indeed foretold:
noon's over; the days shorten.
Let there be no pretence;
none here likes the cold.

THE ALWAYS BEGINNING

Their song tells nothing of the place or nature
of any outsetting. Like ours, departure—
just from each day—was towards what future
holds its destinies undelivered
but still for seeking in territory severed
but the sky's edge from seas discovered.

It was dead calm; and the boat drifted
on sea scattered with the storm's litter—
litter itself, a limping cripple
battered about the bow, dismasted
after the fury of a night which fastened
itself to the wind with teeth of darkness
then bit into daylight hours—a night-time
crunching their world to a gap so finite
that crests of waves were its tumbling skyline,
till a calm, sudden as if it had fallen,
spread like a net on its captured waters.
Sun shone; and the gale halted.

And so, where flung by the tyranny of weather,
near rifts in a reef that must be breasted
they poled their way and to more than shelter—
to a new now of the always beginning
thought not of sail with a prow seen misty
in the slit spray of the cold Pacific.

Others had taken possession early
of islands raised by this ocean journey
and beached their boats while still seaworthy;
but these wrecked few were the last of kinfolk,
and swept overside were their carved bone symbols,
their forefathers' fund of ancient wisdom.
—Surely ourselves? In like lost fashion

have we now sunk in change—wild ocean—
standards, principles, creeds, tradition
(valid or bigotry) which our elders,
tribal civilization builders,
held for the tasks about their shoulders?

We too take part in that journey, bearers
of stamina to new times, seafarers
on ignorance through the dark and terrors
where waves and winds about us topple
rigging we trusted in, who grapple
still with elements, a primitive people,
nothing before us—distance foragers
starting for the may-be; random voyagers
like those long-ago stranded villagers.

WILLIAM HART-SMITH   (1911–)

Poet. Born in England; educated there and in Scotland and New
Zealand; came to Australia in 1936; lives in Perth.

COLUMBUS GOES WEST

Columbus looks towards the New World,
the sea is flat and nothing breaks the rim
of the world's disc;
he takes the sphere with him.

Day into night the same, the only change
the living variation at the core
of this man's universe;
and silent on the silver ship he broods.

Red gouts of weed, and skimming fish, to crack
the stupefying emptiness of sea;
night, and the unimpassioned gaze of stars ...

And God be praised for the compass, oaths
bawled in the fo'c'sle,
broken heads and wine,
song and guitars,

the tramp of boots,
the wash and whip of brine.

WILLY WILLIES

Willy willies are spirit trees
made of dust and sand

Tall trunks they have
without roots

They are always moving
as if searching for somewhere to stand and grow

They spin like the shaft of a firestick
in the palms of a firemaker's hands

but the point skids
on the hardwood surface

unable to bite
to find a groove

overturning stones
sucking up leaves

making the sky
rain pebbles and sticks

They snatch a man's hearth from between his knees
They eat up his wurley and spit out the bits

They fill his mouth with sand
and make of his eyes hot stones

When the women see
a willy willy coming

they run
they hide

for they can hear the spirit children
crying inside them

looking for mothers
in order to be born

HAROLD STEWART   (1916–)

Poet. Born and educated in Sydney; lives in Japan.

THE LEAF-MAKERS

There was an ancient craftsman once, who made
A silken-green semitransparent jade
To imitate a living mulberry-leaf,
So delicately carved in low relief
Its map of veins and lucid arteries
Seemed to flow with the cool green blood of trees.
Three years of patient handicraft, intent
Upon this leaf-like portrait, had he spent
So that intricate cutting could indent
Around its profile every nick and notch,
And even turn to a rain-discoloured blotch
Russet with which the mineral was laced,
So perfectly was imperfection placed.
Before the Prince of Sung he then displayed,
Polished to glossiness, the finished jade;
And when the lapidary's work was laid
Among fresh mulberry-leaves to rival them,
A silk-worm, curious with hunger, picked
The leaf of artifice: its senses tricked,
It tried to bite the jade from tip to stem!
The Prince of Sung unwittingly allowed
Wonder to change his face, and so endowed
The artisan with patronage and praise
For skill that could outwit an insect's gaze.
Hearing of which, Lieh-tzǔ countered: "Now,
If it should take as long as that for Tao
To make a single bud unfurl with care
Its crinkled wing into the spring's harsh air,
Seldom would trees have anything to wear!"

SAILING DOWN THE BAY OF ISE

Astern, I watched the wake unwind
A scroll on which the sunset drew
Molten calligraphy, and signed
The wash that it incarnadined
Along this bay of silken blue.

The oppressive sun had now resigned
Its burning power, and set at last
A seal whose crimson fire declined
On smouldering clouds that overcast
The port dissolving in the past.

I looked to starboard on a view
Where shaded foothills were defined
Against the hazier peaks behind
In serried ranges, dimmer through
Evening veils of lilac hue.

To port the coastline, close at first,
Soon broadened out in cove and cape:
A shoal of islands lay dispersed
Within a bay, whose narrow gape
Had let some fins of rock escape.

Ahead, the topmost sails of white
Against the offing's twilit frieze
Climbed the horizon into sight;
The fishing fleet had caught the breeze
Nearing their haven for the night.

To front the sea, a sheer-cliffed isle,
Conifer-crested, reared its pile,
Ruining down in tumbled blocks
To where a village, roofed with tile,
Twinkled among the leeward rocks.

Passing between the harbour's wide
Headlands and out to open sea,
The eager ship began to ride
The dip and swell of incoming tide,
As space and darkness set it free.

Soon from the bows I could behold
The lunar pearl of pallid gold
Out of nocturnal depths emerge,
Until its radiance had unrolled
Nacreous scriptures on the surge.

Oh, as the Sun burns out and dies
Within my body, may the glow
Of Moon-illumined wonder rise
In my benighted mind and grow
Immortally serene and wise!

Alan Moorehead   (1910–1983)

Prose writer, journalist. Born and educated in Melbourne; lived in England.

BOTANY BAY

from THE FATAL IMPACT

After his first visit to Tahiti in 1769 Cook sailed south to New Zealand and spend six months charting the coastline on the two islands. More than a year and a half had now elapsed since he had left England, and it was time to think of returning home. The obvious route to take was the one across the south Pacific to Cape Horn, since that would have enabled him to continue his search for a southern continent, but the winter was coming on, barely six months' rations remained, and the *Endeavour's* sails and rigging, now badly in need of repair, were hardly likely to stand up to the Antarctic gales in that vast stretch of ocean. Consequently another and more promising plan was decided upon: they would strike westward until they reached the eastern seaboard of the country of New Holland and then follow it to the north or wherever it took them until they reached its extremity. Then they would turn west and sail to the Dutch outpost of civilization at Batavia, where they could refit and revictual the ship.

It was a hazardous proposition. The west coast of New Holland (it was not to be called Australia until half a century later), was known in rough outline, but the east coast was entirely unexplored; no white man had ever been there and the existing maps were merely guesswork. But the *Endeavour's* crew had been restored to health by their six months' stay in New Zealand, and the officers, on being consulted, were all eager for new discoveries; and so on 1 April 1770, they set sail for the unknown. It was a fair voyage; the weather was warm, dolphins leapt about the ship 'like salmons' and *Diomedea exulans*, the Wandering albatross, that largest and strongest of all sea birds, came circling trustingly around the rigging, a wonderful target for Banks's gun. He must have bagged twenty or more of them before the *Endeavour* reached home.

Herman Melville described very well what it was like to sail in these seas:

> The Trades were blowing with a mild, steady strain upon the canvas, and the ship heading right out into the immense blank of the Western Pacific.... Forever advancing we seemed forever in the same place, and every day was the former lived over again.... We saw no ships, expected to see none ... porpoises and other fish sporting under the bows like pups ashore ... at intervals the grey albatross, peculiar in these seas, came flapping his immense wings over us.

Melville arrived in the Pacific seventy years later than Cook and knew where he was headed for; Cook did not. Day after day the dawn disclosed nothing but the empty ocean, and no one knew when he would see land again. Thus it was an event when on the sixteenth day the officer on watch thought—he was not quite certain—that he saw a butterfly, and a little later a small land bird like a sparrow came on board. This was followed by the appearance of a gannet holding a steady course for the west—the *Endeavour's* course—as though it knew that there was land in that direction. Squally weather set in. Then on 19 April Lieutenant Zachary Hicks cried out at first light that land lay ahead. Cook stood towards it for two hours, and at 8 a.m., when he was fifteen miles from the coast, altered course so that he could run beside it. He had sighted the extreme south-eastern corner of the continent, and he named it Point Hicks—a timely gesture since the lieutenant, like so many other young men in the ship, was to die before the next year was out.

Rain and gales continued through the day—this part of the Tasman Sea is notorious for rough weather—and at one time the grey sky joined the sea between them and the shore in three transparent wavering waterspouts. Next day they had a clear view of the land and Banks thought it looked very promising: 'The country this morn rose in gentle sloping hills which had the appearance of the highest fertility, every hill seemed clothed with trees of no mean size; at noon a smoke was seen a little way inland, and in the evening several more.'

Smoke meant inhabitants, and sure enough on 22 April they saw through their glasses five black men standing on the shore. It was impossible, however, to make a landing; heavy waves were beating on the rocks, and a fresh breeze drove them steadily northwards. Soon they came up with chalky cliffs that reminded them of England, and more natives were seen, two of them carrying a canoe. Cook put out a boat, but heavy surf prevented him from landing and they went on again. At last, on 28 April—nine days after they had first sighted the coast—they saw an opening in the cliffs and the *Endeavour* put in for the shore. There were natives about, some of them spearing fish from canoes, others watching from the rocks and along the cliffs.

Now the Australian aborigines were no graceful south sea islanders with golden skins such as the *Endeavour's* crew had encountered at Tahiti. Already they had been given an unflattering reputation. The Dutch who touched on the northwest of the continent in 1606 had described them as 'wild, cruel, black savages ... poor and abject wretches'. William Dampier, who had also been on the north-west coast in 1688, had written his famous account:

> The inhabitants of this country are the miserablest people in the world. The Hodmadods (Hottentots) of Monomatapa, though a nasty

people, yet for wealth are gentlemen to these; who have no houses and skin garments, sheep, poultry and fruits of the earth, ostrich eggs etc. as the Hodmadods have; and setting aside their human shape, they differ but little from brutes. Their eyelids are always half-closed to keep the flies out of their eyes.... They had great bottle noses, pretty full lips, and wide mouths. The two foreteeth of their upper jaw are wanting in all of them, men and women, old and young; whether they draw them out I know not; neither have they any beards. They are long-visaged, and of a very unpleasing aspect, having no one graceful feature in their faces. Their hair is black, short and curled like that of the negroes; and not long and lank like the common Indians. The colour of their skins, both of their faces and the rest of their body, is coal black like that of the negroes of Guinea. They have no sort of clothes, but a piece of rind of a tree like a girdle about their waists and a handful of long grass or 3 or 4 small green boughs full of leaves thrust under their girdle to cover their nakedness.

They have no houses, but lie in the open air, without any covering, the earth being their bed and the heaven their canopy. Whether they cohabit one man to one woman, or promiscuously, I know not but they do live in companies, 20 or 30 men, women and children together. Their only food is a small sort of fish ... for the earth affords them no food at all. There is neither herb, root, pulse nor any sort of grain for them to eat that we saw; nor any sort of bird or beast that they can catch, having no instruments wherewithal to do so. I did not perceive that they did worship anything....

In short, the lowest of the low.

The bay the *Endeavour* was now entering was divided by two thousand miles or more from the north-west coast of Australia, but it was presumed by Cook and Banks (who had both read Dampier) that the inhabitants, if not the landscape, would be pretty much the same all over the continent—if it was a continent. But this was not at all so. The natives they were now observing in a setting of gently rising, wooded hills were a lithe and nimble people, their hair was straight, not woolly like a negro's, the men were bearded and their skins were dark brown rather than black. Moreover they had weapons, spears, shields and throwing sticks, they built canoes, they lived in crude huts made of branches, and there was every evidence that they hunted, not only animals of some strange sort, but also the marvellously coloured birds that were flying through the trees.

In other words, this contact they were making was something entirely new, and one can imagine the excitement with which Cook and his men gazed through their glasses as the *Endeavour*, with one of her boats sounding the way ahead, came quietly through the entrance of the bay and soon after midday found an anchorage on the southern side, abreast of a group of huts.

There is a strange quality in the Australian landscape. To a European and especially an English eye it is, at first, lacking in freshness and greeness; the light is too harsh, the trees too thin and sparse, the ground too hard and there are no soft outlines anywhere. Desiccation seems to be the theme, a pitiless drying-out of all sap and moisture, and monotonous is the favourite adjective for the bush: monotonous and therefore worthless. It is a country for the ants. But then on closer acquaintance one begins to perceive that, very silently and slowly, life is going on here at another level: the embattled young sapling that looks so gnarled and old is full of strength, its tiny flowers are a gay miniature of larger flowers, and its leaves, when burnt or crushed, release a smell as pungent as a lemon's. Dead fallen trees, it is true, give a graveyard appearance to the ground and the prevailing colour of the scrub is greenish grey. But then unexpectedly a flock of pink galahs will perch on the bare branches, or one catches sight of the wattle in flower and it is more gold than gold can ever be, a clear leaping colour in a field of grey. The bell-bird's single note is a small bell sounding against utter silence, and the fungus, pushing up through the cracked brown clay, is a dome of bright scarlet. These things, however, have to be discovered. Nothing is at once revealed. You must walk for miles alone and gradually the feel of the bush begins to seep into the mind, its immense stillness and quietness; and out of that austerity it is a wonderful thing to see a wild animal start up and bound away, or to come on a group of herons fishing in a waterhole. There is nothing menacing in the bush—even the snakes will always avoid you if they can—and nearly always overhead there is the pale blue sky. Like the bush itself it has a kind of implacable indifference but it is not oppressive. One feels very well in this dry air.

The part of the coast on which Cook was now making his first landing is not quite typical of all this dryness. The bush here comes down to the shore and the transparent sea-water froths and sparkles like champagne as it tumbles in long rollers on the beaches of yellow sand. In the estuaries one escapes from the restlessness of the sea into backwaters full of reeds where ducks and wading birds abound, and beyond these the hills, thickly covered with bush, rise up from the sea plain. One glimpses here and there a rocky precipice. It is not a grand or dramatic spectacle, but it is very beautiful and it has that kind of rugged expansiveness that makes the traveller feel alive and free. In Cook's time it must have seemed excessively remote.

Some odd things were happening on the shore as the *Endeavour* approached. One group of natives, about a dozen in all, went up on to a rise to watch, and when the vessel's boat came near they beckoned the sailors to come ashore. On the other hand, no notice at all seemed to be taken of the *Endeavour* herself. There she was, 106 feet long, with her high masts and her great sails, and when she passed within a quarter of a mile of some fishermen in four canoes they did not even bother to look up. Then when she had anchored close to the shore a naked woman carrying wood appeared with three children. 'She often looked at the ship,' Banks tells us, 'but expressed neither surprise nor concern. Soon after this she lighted a fire and the four canoes came in from the fishing: the people landed, hauled up their boats and began to dress their dinner, to all appearance totally unmoved by us....'

The Englishmen ate their midday meal on board and then in two boats set out for the shore, thinking that these strange quiescent people would allow them to make a peaceful landing. They were wrong. Two natives menaced them from the rocks with long spears, and they were not deterred by the fact that there were at least thirty men in the *Endeavour's* boats. No amount of pleading with them by signs had any effect, so Cook took a musket and fired it over their heads. Still they held their ground, and Cook fired a second shot at their legs knowing that he could do them little harm, the distance being forty yards. The only result of this was to make one of the natives run off to his hut for a shield and then, as the sailors came ashore, both men threw their spears. Two more shots had to be fired before they were driven off. Cook and Banks went up to the huts, where they found half a dozen children who showed no interest of any kind when they were given presents of beads and ribbons; they left them lying on the ground.

There were some interesting aspects in all this. The sight of the *Endeavour* had apparently meant nothing to these primitives because it was too strange, too monstrous, to be comprehended. It had appeared out of nowhere like some menacing phenomenon of nature, a waterspout or a roll of thunder, and by ignoring it or pretending to ignore it no doubt they had hoped that it would go away. As Sydney Parkinson wrote, the natives 'were so abashed at first they took little notice of us'. But when the small boats had put out from the ship it had been another thing: the English sailors had been instantly recognized as human, a palpable evil, and despite their clothes and pale faces, despite even their roaring incomprehensible shooting-sticks, they had been courageously opposed.

And so it went on for the next few days while the *Endeavour's* crew came ashore to gather wood and to fill their watercasks. Little groups of blacks would appear through the trees and stand for a moment to shout and throw a spear or two. Then they would vanish again into the bush. Every attempt to parley with them or to offer them presents came to nothing. Had they been wild animals they could not have been more difficult to deal with. 'All they seemed to want,' Cook wrote, 'was for us to be gone.'

(Dampier, on his second voyage to North-west Australia in 1699, had had similar experiences, but had been more drastic. When one of his sailors was speared he fired his gun, he says, and 'frighted them (the blacks) at first, yet they soon learnt to despise it, tossing up their hands, and crying Pooh, Pooh, Pooh; and, coming on afresh with great noise, I thought it high time to charge again, and shoot one of them, which I did.')

For the rest it was an excellent landfall. The crew netted enormous quantities of fish in the bay, and there were giant oysters and other shellfish to be found on the rocks as well. The botanists, wandering ashore, came upon trees and plants that had never been described before; the eucalypt, for example, with its long, thin, scented leaves, and a shrub with large furry nuts which was eventually to become known as the Banksia. The birds were wonderful —great flocks of brightly coloured cockatoos and lorikeets that were entirely strange to European ornithology—and since they had never been shot at before Banks brought down as many as he wished. The skins he preserved, and with the meat the *Endeavour*'s cook made an excellent parrot pie. Sometimes the foraging parties caught glimpses of queer elusive animals: a quadruped about the size of a rabbit, a much larger beast that fed on grass and resembled a stag, another that looked like a wolf, and still another that seemed to be some sort of a polecat or a weasel. But none of these creatures lingered in sight long enough to be described or drawn.

A week went by very pleasantly, and it was marred only by the death of a consumptive seaman named Forby Sutherland, the first white man to be buried on this distant coast.

There was a ceremony on shore before they sailed. The Union Jack was flown, the ship's name and the date were carved on a tree, and the hospitable harbour which had supplied Banks and Solander with so many new plants was named Botany Bay. It seems ironic that so innocent a name was to become a synonym for all that was heartless and cruel, not only in this new country, but in Georgian civilization as well.

So now on 6 May 1770 they sailed on to the north, noting from the sea, but not entering, Port Jackson, which was later to be the site of Sydney, one of the largest cities in the Southern Hemisphere; past Cape Byron which was named after Byron's grandfather, the *Dolphin*'s first captain; past the site of Brisbane and so on into the tropics.

Eve Langley   (1908–1974)

Novelist, poet. Born and educated in N.S.W.

AUSTRALIA

The brown round of the continent tonight
Rises up, shoulder on shoulder, searching for the sun;
And all the white French rains that once took flight
Into the earth, rise slowly, one by one,
Remembering Villon who left a rag on every tree.
Perhaps he walked Australia long ago,
Mourning for all those women white and sad as snow.
Verlaine perhaps enchanted by our seas
Cried in his lyric voice that purple hours
Lay waxen-mitred in our purple flowers ...
The wildflowers of Australia; a thin brown
Veil of lost Autumn is somehow caught around
Their stalks unspeaking, as though Springtime at the core
Was a small child lost in the bush for ever more.

Douglas Stewart   (1913–)

Poet, essayist. Born and educated in New Zealand; came to Sydney
1938.

THE GULLY

If life is here how stealthily
It moves in this green hall of rock
Where mosses flourish soft and thick
And lichens imperceptibly
In wrinkled fans and circles shape
A civilization cold as sleep
On wall of stone and fallen tree.

Only in the deep secrecy
Of bracken-fern and maidenhair
One shaft of pink is glowing here
And poised in tiny ecstasy
With all life's hunger in its look
And arm outflung for the sweet shock
The trigger-flower strikes the bee.

MOSQUITO ORCHID

Such infinitesimal things,
Mosquito orchids flying
Low where the grass-tree parts
And winter's sun lies dying
In a flash of green and bronze
On the dead beetle's wings
Among the broken stones.

Such infinitesimal things
And yet so many, so many,
Little green leaves like hearts,
Bright wings and red antennae
All swarming into the cold,
It seems the whole hillside stings
And glints from the grey leaf-mould.

THE SNOW-GUM

It is the snow-gum silently,
In noon's blue and the silvery
Flowering of light on snow,
Performing its slow miracle
Where upon drift and icicle
Perfect lies its shadow.

Leaf upon leaf's fidelity,
The creamy trunk's solidity,
The full-grown curve of the crown,
It is the tree's perfection
Now shown in clear reflection
Like flakes of soft grey stone.

Out of the granite's eternity,
Out of the winters' long enmity,
Something is done on the snow;
And the silver light like ecstasy
Flows where the green tree perfectly
Curves to its perfect shadow.

THE FIERCE COUNTRY

Three hundred miles to Birdsville from Marree
Man makes his mark across a fierce country
That has no flower but the whitening bone and skull
Of long-dead cattle, no word but "I will kill".

Here the world ends in a shield of purple stone
Naked in its long war against the sun;
The white stones flash, the red stones leap with fire:
It wants no interlopers to come here.

Whatever it is that speaks through softer earth
Still tries to stammer indeed its broken phrases;
Between some crack in the stone mosaic brings forth
Yellow and white like suns the papery daisies;

The cassia drinks the sky in its gold cup,
Straggling on sandhills the dwarf wild-hops lift up
Their tufts of crimson flame; and the first hot wind
Blows out the suns and smothers the flames in sand.

And man too like the earth in the good season
When the Diamantina floods the whole horizon
And the cattle grow fat on wildflowers says his proud word:
Gathers the stones and builds four-square and hard:

Where the mirage still watches with glittering eyes
The ruins of his homestead crumble on the iron rise.
Dust on the waterless plains blows over his track,
The sun glares down on the stones and the stones glare back.

Peter Cowan   (1914–)

Short story writer, novelist. Born and educated in Perth.

THE TRACTOR

She watched him coming back from the gate, walking towards the slightly ornate suburban-style house she felt to be so incongruous set down on the bare rise, behind it the sheds and yards and the thin belt of shade trees. Yet he and his family were proud of it, grateful for its convenience and modernity, and had so clearly not understood her first quizzical remarks that she had never repeated them.

He stood on the edge of the veranda, and she saw in his face the anger that seemed to deepen because he knew the feeling to be impotent.

She said, "What is it?"

"Mackay's two big tractors—that they were going to use for the scrub-clearing—they've been interfered with. Sand put into the oil. The one they started up will cost a few hundred to repair."

"But no one would do that," she said, as if already it were settled, her temporizing without point.

"We know who did it."

"Surely he didn't come right up to the sheds—as close as that to the house—"

"No. They left the tractors down in the bottom paddock. Where they were going to start clearing."

"And now—they can't?"

"Now they can't. Not till the tractor's repaired."

She looked towards the distant line of the low scrub that was deepening in colour as the evening came. She said, "That is what he wanted."

"What he wants is to make as much trouble as he can. We haven't done anything to him."

"You were going to clear the land along the bottom paddock at the back of Mackay's. Where he lives."

"Where he lives?"

"You told me he lived in the bush there."

"He lives anywhere. And he takes the ball floats off the taps in the sheep tanks and the water runs to waste, and he breaks the fences when he feels like it, and leaves the gates open—"

"You think he does this deliberately?"

"How else?"

"Oh," she said, "yet it is all so ruthless."

"You mean what he does?"

"No. You only ever think of what he does."

"Well, I'll admit he's given us a few things to think about."

"Clearing with those tractors and the chain," she said. "Everything in their path goes—kangaroos—all the small things that live in the scrub—all the trees—"

He looked at her as if her words held some relevance that must come to him. He said, "We clear the land. Yes."

"You clear it," she said. "It seems to be what is happening everywhere today."

"I don't know what you mean, Ann," he said.

She got up from the chair by the steps. "Perhaps he feels something should be left."

"Look," he said, "maybe you teach too much nature study at school. Or you read all this stuff about how we shouldn't shoot the bloody 'roos—so that when some crazy swine wrecks our property you think he's some sort of a—"

"Some sort of a what?"

"I don't know," he said, aware she mocked him. "Better than us."

"No," she said. "Perhaps just different."

"Different all right."

"What are you going to do?"

"Get the police," he said. "They don't take much notice most of the time, but they will of this." He looked at her as if he would provoke the calm he felt to be assumed. "We'll burn him out if we can't get him any other way."

She looked up quickly and for a moment he was afraid.

"You wouldn't do that."

"He's gone too far this time," he said stubbornly.

The long thin streamers of cloud above the darkening line of scrub were becoming deep and hard in colour, scarlet against the dying light. He watched her face that seemed now calm, remote, as if their words were erased. She was small, slight, somehow always neat, contained. Her dark hair was drawn straight back, her brows clearly marked, lifting slightly so that they seemed to give humour sometimes to her serious expression, her firm mouth.

"I'd better go, Ken."

"The family expect you for tea."

"It's Sunday night. I've to work in the morning. I have some things to prepare."

"Look," he said. "If it's this business—"

"No, I'm just tired. And I've assignments to mark."

"All right," he said.

As they drove she watched the long shadows that spread across the road and over the paddocks from the few shade trees, the light now with a clarity denied through the heat of the day. She would have liked to make some gesture to break the tension between them, to explain to him why she had been unwilling to stay and listen to the inevitable talk of what had happened. But to tell him that at such times she became afraid, as if she could never become one of them, certain that the disagreements now easily enough brought to a truce must in the end defeat them, would not lessen their dissension.

He said suddenly, "You're worried about it, aren't you?"

She knew he referred to themselves, as if he had been aware of her own thoughts.

"Yes," she said. "Sometimes."

"It could be all right, Ann. You'd come to like it here."

"In so many ways I do."

"It's nothing like it used to be. This light land has come good now. We've done well. We've got everything—you wouldn't be without anything you'd have in the city."

"I know that, Ken," she said.

"But you're not sure of it."

She thought he perhaps did this deliberately, seeking to provoke an issue on material grounds, these at least being demonstrative of some conclusion, that he was lost, unwilling, in the face of their real uncertainty. He was more perceptive, she knew, than he cared to reveal, but he had a stubbornness she felt it was perhaps impossible to defeat. Before it, she relented a little.

"Not sure of some things. You must give me time. After all, I— hadn't thought to live here. It's different for you."

The few high trees stood out darkly above the low thick scrub, and beyond she could see the roofs of the town.

He said, "This other business will probably be over next week, anyhow."

She supposed he deliberately minimized this which perhaps he did not understand, preferring evasion, the pretence that when it was settled it would not matter. As to him it might not. But he was so clearly afraid that she would escape. She reached out quickly and touched his hand.

He stopped the car before the house near the end of the main street, where she boarded. Farther down, near the club, she could see the cars parked, and people moving without haste along the pavements.

There was no wind, and in the darkness the street was hot, as if the endless heat of summer was never to be dissipated. As he closed the door of the car he said, "I have to go out to the paddock on the way back. It won't take long."

She made no comment and he said, as if to prevent her censure, "I've got to take some stuff from the store out there."

"They haven't found him?"

"No. The police think he's moved out. But we know he hasn't. He makes fools of them in the bush. They've been looking since Sunday, but they've given it up now. Anyhow, you could walk right past him at three feet. And there are no tracks."

"To be able to dodge them like that he must know all this country very well."

"I suppose he does."

"Almost—more than that. He must understand it."

"He doesn't seem to do anything else all day."

She smiled. "Well, do you?"

"I'm not sure what you mean by that. You mean we don't understand it?"

"Perhaps in a different way. You're making it something you can understand."

"Here we go again." He banged his hand against the steering wheel. "We never take a trick. Why don't you go and live with this character?"

She laughed suddenly. "I'm sorry, Ken. But how long has he been here? That's a harmless enough question!"

"He's been around here something like ten years. I remember when I was at school. He's mad."

She said, "All those who oppose us are mad."

"Well," he said, "we're going to get him out this time. We're taking shifts down at the tractors, and we've got a watch on a camp of his we found."

"A camp?"

"Made out of boughs." His voice was grudging. "Pretty well made. You could live in it. We flushed him out, because he left some food, and a radio."

"That's not in keeping—a radio."

"It doesn't work. May never have been any good. But it might be only that the batteries are flat. We'll find out. But he could have camps like that all through the bush. We'll be lucky if he comes back to this one."

They turned off through a fence gate, and down along a track that followed a side fence. He switched off the car lights and drove slowly.

"He'll hear the car," he said. "Still, the lights are a give-away."

Suddenly they were close to the dark thick scrub, and then she saw the forms of the tractors, gaunt, high, like grotesque patches of shadow. Two men moved up to the car. One of them started to say something, then saw her, and paused.

He said, "He came back, Ken. Got the food. We never saw him."

They carried rifles, and suddenly she began to laugh. They looked at her with a surprise that had not yet become hostility.

"It—it just seems funny," she said weakly.

"It's not funny," Ken said. She was aware of their anger.

"We'll get him," the man she recognized as Don Mackay said. "We'll get him this time."

She was reminded suddenly of the boys at school in the playground at the lunch period, confronted by some argument that physical force could not immediately solve. Even their voices sound alike, she thought. Perhaps it is not so serious. But when they had taken the box Ken handed out to them, they stepped back from the car and she saw again the guns they carried, and the parallel frightened her.

"How long will they be repairing the tractor?" she asked.

"End of the week." His voice was brusque. She knew she had belittled him before his friends. She moved closer to him as he drove, and he looked briefly at her small, serious face shadowed in the half-light of the car.

"We'll go through there next week. I wish he'd get between the tractors when they're dragging the chain, that's all."

"Is he armed?"

"Yes," he said. "He is. He's lived off the land for years. And by taking food. He might be dangerous now."

She said slowly, "I wonder what made him begin to live like that?"

"No one will know that."

"You'll have to take care."

"There'll be a few of us there to watch for him."

"Actually, he hasn't ever threatened anyone, has he?"

"No. But he's never damaged anything big like this. And the police have never bothered about him before, either. You can see why. He's made fools of them."

"And of you."

"All right. And of us."

"Oh, Ken," she said, "I'm sorry. It's—it's just that I wish somehow you could just let him be."

"And have him do what he likes?"

"Well, he's not done anything much."

"Only wrecked a tractor."

"He would hate the tractors," she said, as if she no longer spoke to him, but was trying to work something out to her own satisfaction.

"Well, it's a reason why we can't leave him there."

"I suppose," she said, "you have to clear that land?"

"Of course. We clear some land every year. It's a tax deduction. And we need it the way taxation is."

"So there can't be anybody who wants things to stay the way they are for a while?"

He looked at her strangely. "Stay the way they are?"

If it was not what she meant she could not perhaps find words that were any more adequate. It was not a simple thing of statement, of definition, this that she felt. She saw with a sudden desolating clarity the grey sprawl of suburbs crossed by the black lines of roads, the clusters of city buildings that clawed up like a sudden focus, the endless tawdry, over-decorated little houses like the one he and his family had placed on the long low rise of land from which almost all else had been erased. As though, she thought painfully, he hated this land she had herself, incongruously enough, come to feel for in the brief time she had been close to it. And it was perhaps worse that he did not see what he was doing, himself a part of some force beyond him. Duped by pride. It was as if she had made some discovery she could not communicate to him and that set them apart.

She said desperately, "Do we have to change everything? Wipe out everything so that everlastingly we can grow things, make things, get tax deductions? You don't even leave a few acres of timber, somewhere for animals and birds—"

"Animals and birds," he said. "You can't stop progress."

"The unanswerable answer," she said. Before them the shade trees showed briefly along the road as it turned near the farm. "So we must all conform."

He slowed the car for the house gate, and in the headlights she saw the facade of the house as if they had turned into a suburban street. As he stopped the motor the silence held them. For a moment they did not move, then he drew her against him, his arm lightly about her shoulders, the gesture token of a security they might both have willed, denying the words with which they had held themselves separate.

"Maybe," he said slowly, "it's because you're so crazy I have to have you. You—you're different—"

"I'm sorry, Ken. Because I'm afraid I do love you—I suppose I have to have you, too."

"And you'd rather you didn't."

"Perhaps," she said, "I would rather I didn't."

"It's a mess, isn't it?"

"It might sort out," she said, and she laughed with him. At the house the front door opened briefly, the light shining across the entrance porch as someone looked out at the car.

At the week-end she had arranged to stay at the farm, and she expected him to call for her soon after breakfast. She put her small case on the veranda, but as he did not come she went back inside. Idly, rather irritated at his lateness, she took out her paints and began to work on the flower illustration she was making. She had begun to paint the native flowers, their grotesque seeds and leaves, to use for her teaching, but the work had begun to absorb her, and she spent whatever time she could searching for new examples. Many, at first, she could not identify. Now, though she told no one, she had begun to hope the paintings might be publishable if she could complete series of different areas.

It was mid-morning when she heard him outside. In the car as they drove he said, "Some of the fences were broken, out by Hadley's boundary. We've been too busy this week to look down there, and the sheep had gone through into the scrub. We got most of them back."

"You lost some?"

"Some."

"I'm sorry," she said, as if somehow it were her fault.

"He knows we're going to clear that land, and he's out to do as much damage as he can first.'

She had no wish to draw him, as if she deliberately sought their disagreement, but it seemed she must form the words, place them before him, his evasion too easy.

"You're sure about it, Ken, aren't you? that he's just getting his own back? That it's as simple as that?"

"It's obvious. He's done pretty well so far."

"And that's the only side there is to it?"

"What else could there be? He can't expect to stop us."

"He might know that."

"Well—that proves it."

"No—perhaps we've all got to make a gesture of some sort. For the things we believe in."

He shook his head. "You put it your way if you like. But what I believe in is using that land."

"Yes, Ken."

"We can't all be dreamers." And then, refusing to be further drawn, he laughed. "It's funny the way I've got caught up with one. Perhaps it will sort out, like you said. You do the dreaming. I'll do the work."

She ran her hands lightly over her arms, smiling at him. "You think we might convert one another?"

"It's a risk we'll have to take."

"Yes. I suppose we're young enough."

"I'll be out a bit this week-end, Ann. We've got to stop this somehow. While we've a few sheep left."

He went out late in the afternoon, and she helped his mother in the kitchen. The older woman had a quietness and a kind of insight that she found attractive, and they had always got on well together, though sometimes Ann was irritated by her acceptance of the men's decisions and views, as if this was something she no longer questioned, or perhaps, Ann thought, she had never questioned.

When Ken came back she heard him talking to his father on the veranda, and then the older man's voice raised in disagreement, though she could distinguish only a few of the words. She went out through the kitchen door and the men stopped talking.

As she came towards them Ken said, "We've found one of his camps. Ted and Don found it, but this time they turned off and kept away. They didn't go near enough for him to realize they'd seen it. We made that mistake last time."

"Where is this?" she said.

"It's new. So he may still be there. It's down in the paddock off the side road to Mackay's. Straight in from the dam. About half a mile north in the scrub."

"There."

"Yes. By the new land. Where we were going to build." He looked at her as if she might have contradicted him. "When we were married."

"What will you do?"

His father said, "I told them to get the police."

"He walked away from the police last time." For a moment his eyes met the girl's. "And us. All right. We were no better. And the reporters came up from town. Photographers all over the place. A seven-day wonder for the suburbanites."

"It's not something that happens every day," she said. "Naturally, it was news."

"They'll make it news again, if we let them. But this time it will be different. We don't do anything until tomorrow night. That way he won't be suspicious if he sees our tracks near the camp. Then Sunday night we'll make a line north of the camp, and if the wind's right we'll burn back towards the firebreak along the paddock. He'll have to break out through the paddock. We'll have a chance that way."

"I think it's too big a risk," his father said. "You'll burn the whole of that country. You can't do it."

"We were going to clear it, anyway."

"You can't start a fire like that."

"If we try to close in on the camp he'll hear us."

"You could still get him. There's enough of you."

"He'd go between us in the bush. No matter how close we were. You know that. No one's been able to get a sight of him in the bush. The police had trackers there last week. They found plenty of tracks. But he kept as far ahead or behind them as he liked. No," he said, "he's made fools of us long enough. I think we've got a chance now."

He turned suddenly towards the girl, and she stood beside him, not moving. His words seemed to her to hold a kind of defiance as if he did not himself believe in them, and she thought that it was not simply that he doubted their ability to carry out the plan, but that he did not really believe in the idea of the fire himself. That if she or his father did not further pursue it he might be glad to drop it. But she could not be certain, and before she could speak, as if he intended to prevent her words, he said, "Let's forget this now, Ann. We'll go over to Harris's after tea. They've got a bit of a show on there for May's birthday."

Almost all those she had come to know seemed to have found their way to the party. And all of them discussed the hermit, as they called him; she realized it was general knowledge that he was expected to be caught soon. She listened to the undercurrent of derision that the police with all their resources had been mocked by this man it seemed none of them had seen, as if in this they were on his side. Some of the older people she spoke to claimed to have caught glimpses of him when, some years earlier, he had taken food quite freely for a time from the farmhouses. Some claimed to know his name. But it seemed to her, as she mixed with them and listened to them, that none of them really cared. She felt they simply accepted the idea that he must be denied, driven from cover and killed if necessary, as they might have accepted the killing of a dingo or a fox, a creature for them without motive or reason. When she tried to turn their words, to question them, they looked at her with a kind of surprise, or the beginning of suspicion, perhaps in doubt of her as a teacher of their children. And she saw that quite quickly they exhausted the topic, turning to the enjoyment of the evening, as if already the whole thing was disposed of. In the end she thought it was their lack of involvement, their bland rejection of responsibility, that irritated her to the point of anger, so that she was forced to hold herself from rudeness.

It was late when they returned, and in her room, after she had changed, she stood for a time by the window in the darkness. There was a small moon that seemed scarcely to break the dark ground shadow, and beyond the paddocks she could not see where the scrub began. Her sense of anger had given place to dejection and a kind of fear. She tried to imagine the man who in the darkness slept in what they had described as his camp, something she could picture only as a kind of child's cubby house in the thick scrub. But she could form no picture of him as a physical being, only that it seemed to her he must possess imagination and sensibility beyond that of his pursuers, that he must be someone not difficult to talk to, someone who would understand her own feeling about these things for which he was persecuted. And who might even, she thought, be glad to know, however briefly, that they were shared. She was aware of a sense of disloyalty, but the image persisted, and it was suddenly monstrous that the darkness of the scrub should be swept by the glare of fire, as she would see it from the window where she stood now, the man stumbling from it in some unimaginable indignity. And though she had doubted the men's intention to carry out their plan, it seemed now in the darkness only too probable that in anger they might do what she, and perhaps they, feared. And it was impossible. Her hands felt the cold of the sill, she was aware of the faint wind that blew in through the window, cool upon her skin, and she could hear it in the boughs of the few shade trees behind the house.

On Sunday, in the afternoon, Ken left to make arrangements with the other men. His parents were resting, but she knew they would not question her going out, they were used to her wandering about the farm, looking for the plants she wished to paint. She went down through the yard gate, across the paddock towards the track that led out to the belt of scrub and timber. It seemed, in the heat, farther than she had expected.

She walked along the side fence, where the brush began, feeling that it would hide her if any of the men were watching. If she met them she would say she had come to look for Ken. She could see the dam ahead, the smooth red banks rising steeply, to one side a few thin trees, motionless in the heat.

At the dam she paused. The side track to Mackay's had turned some distance back to the left. In front of her, facing north, the scrub was thick, untouched, she was suddenly reluctant to go beyond the fence on the far side of the dam.

She pushed the wires down and stepped through. She began to pick her way through the scrub, choosing the small, almost imperceptible pockets where the bushes were thinner. It was only after a time, when she could no longer see the dam or the trees beside it, that she realized her method of walking had led her away from a straight line. She had no clear idea how far she had come. She went on until she was certain she had covered half a mile, but as she stopped it was suddenly clear she could have deviated in any direction.

The bushes grew upward on their thin sparse stems to a rounded umbrella-like top, the leaves tough, elongated and spindly. They stretched away like endless replicas, rising head-high, become too thick for her to go farther. As she looked about it seemed improbable she had come so far. In the heat the scrub was silent. Along the reddish ground, over the thin stalks, the ants moved, in places she had walked round their mud-coloured mounds. She looked down at the ground, at the hard brittle twigs and fallen leaves, some of them already cemented by the ants. In a kind of fear she began to walk.

A short distance to the right a thin patch of trees lifted above the bushes, and though she thought it was the wrong direction she began to push her way towards it. The trees were like some sharp variation in the endless grey pattern of the brush that rose about her.

Beneath them the bark and leaves were thick upon the ground. She stood in the patch of shade, and she tried to reason that she could not have come far, that she could find her way back if she was careful. And in the silence she thought again, as she had the night before, of the man she had come to warn. It had seemed that if she could explain to him, he must understand, and that perhaps he would go. She had relied on there being understanding between them, that at least in these things they must feel alike. So that it had seemed her words would have effect. Now, in the heat and the silence, it was a dream, holding in this place no reality. She could never have thought to do it. And it was here he had spent ten years. It was like nothing she could encompass. She felt a sharp, childish misery, as if she might have allowed herself tears.

It occurred to her that if she could climb one of the trees she might gain an idea of direction. But the trunks were slippery, without foothold, and at the second attempt she fell, twisting her leg. She leant against the trunk, afraid of the pain, trying to deny it, as if she would will herself to be without injury that might imprison her.

She was not aware of any movement or sound, but she looked up, and turned slightly, still holding to the smooth trunk. He was standing just at the edge of the clump of trees. He might have been there all the time. Or been attracted by the noise she had made.

She said weakly, "I—didn't see you—"

His face held no expression she could read. His hair was grey and short, and she was vaguely surprised, as if she had imagined something different, but cut crudely, and streaked across his head by sweat. He was very thin, all the redundant flesh might long ago have been burnt from him, his arms stick-like, knotted and black. His hands held a rifle, and she knew a sudden fear that he would kill her, that somehow she must place words between them before he took her simply as one of his persecutors.

She said quickly, "I came to warn you—they have found your camp—tonight they mean to drive you out towards the paddocks—"

But they were not the words she had planned. His eyes gave her no sign. They were very dark, sharp somehow, and she knew suddenly they were like the eyes of an animal or a bird, watchful, with their own recognition and knowledge which was not hers. The stubble of beard across his face was whitish, his skin dark from the sun.

"I—if only you would go from here," she said. "They only want you to go—they don't understand—"

The words were dead in the heat and the silence. She saw the flies that crawled across his face.

"I wanted to help you," she said, and she despised herself in her terror. Only his hands seemed to move faintly about the rifle. His stillness was insupportable. Abruptly she began to sob, the sound loud, gulping, ridiculous, her hands lifting to her face.

He seemed to step backwards. His movement was somehow liquid, unhuman, and then she thought of the natives she had once seen in the north, not the town natives whose movements had grown like her own. But with a strange inevitability he moved like an animal or the vibration of the thin sparse trees before the wind. She did not see him go. She looked at the boles of the trees where he had stood, and she could hear her own sobbing.

Some time in the afternoon she heard the sudden sound of shots, flat, unreal, soon lost in the silence. But she walked towards where the sound had seemed to be, and after a time, without warning she came on the track that ran towards Mackay's place. She had gone only a short distance when she heard the voices, and called out. The men came through the scrub and she saw them on the track. She began to run towards them but checked herself. Farther down she saw a Landrover and one of the police. Ken said, "We missed you— we've been searching—it was only that Ted saw where you'd walked down the fence—"

She said, "The shots—I heard them—"

"We were looking for you. We didn't see him. He tried to get past us, then shot at Don—we had to shoot."

She did not speak and he said, "We had to do it, Ann. We sent for the police. But where were you? How did you get out here?"

There was nothing she could tell him. She said, "I was looking for you, I think."

The Landrover had drawn up beside them, and the driver opened the door for her. They moved back down the dry rutted track where the thin shade had begun to stretch in from the broken scrub.

JUDITH WRIGHT (1915–)

Poet, critic. Born in northern N.S.W.; educated in Sydney.

BULLOCKY

Beside his heavy-shouldered team,
thirsty with drought and chilled with rain,
he weathered all the striding years
till they ran widdershins in his brain:

Till the long solitary tracks
etched deeper with each lurching load
were populous before his eyes,
and fiends and angels used his road.

All the long straining journey grew
a mad apocalyptic dream,
and he old Moses, and the slaves
his suffering and stubborn team.

Then in his evening camp beneath
the half-light pillars of the trees
he filled the steepled cone of night
with shouted prayers and prophecies.

While past the campfire's crimson ring
the star-struck darkness cupped him round,
and centuries of cattlebells
rang with their sweet uneasy sound.

Grass is across the waggon-tracks,
and plough strikes bone beneath the grass,
and vineyards cover all the slopes
where the dead teams were used to pass.

O vine, grow close upon that bone
and hold it with your rooted hand.
The prophet Moses feeds the grape,
and fruitful is the Promised Land.

WOMAN TO MAN

The eyeless labourer in the night,
the selfless, shapeless seed I hold,
builds for its resurrection day—
silent and swift and deep from sight
foresees the unimagined light.

This is no child with a child's face;
this has no name to name it by:
yet you and I have known it well.
This is our hunter and our chase,
the third who lay in our embrace.

This is the strength that your arm knows,
the arc of flesh that is my breast,
the precise crystals of our eyes.
This is the blood's wild tree that grows
the intricate and folded rose.

This is the maker and the made;
this is the question and reply;
the blind head butting at the dark,
the blaze of light along the blade.
Oh hold me, for I am afraid.

AT COOLOOLA

The blue crane fishing in Cooloola's twilight
has fished there longer than our centuries.
He is the certain heir of lake and evening,
and he will wear their colour till he dies,

but I'm a stranger, come of a conquering people.
I cannot share his calm, who watch his lake,
being unloved by all my eyes delight in,
and made uneasy, for an old murder's sake.

Those dark-skinned people who once named Cooloola
knew that no land is lost or won by wars,
for earth is spirit: the invader's feet will tangle
in nets there and his blood be thinned by fears.

Riding at noon and ninety years ago,
my grandfather was beckoned by a ghost—
a black accoutred warrior armed for fighting,
who sank into bare plain, as now into time past.

White shores of sand, plumed reed and paperbark,
clear heavenly levels frequented by crane and swan—
I know that we are justified only by love,
but oppressed by arrogant guilt, have room for none.

And walking on clean sand among the prints
of bird and animal, I am challenged by a driftwood spear
thrust from the water; and, like my grandfather,
must quiet a heart accused by its own fear.

REQUEST TO A YEAR

If the year is meditating a suitable gift,
I should like it to be the attitude
of my great-great-grandmother,
legendary devotee of the arts,

who, having had eight children
and little opportunity for painting pictures,
sat one day on a high rock
beside a river in Switzerland

and from a difficult distance viewed
her second son, balanced on a small ice-floe,
drift down the current towards a waterfall
that struck rock-bottom eighty feet below,

while her second daughter, impeded,
no doubt, by the petticoats of the day,
stretched out a last-hope alpenstock
(which luckily later caught him on his way).

Nothing, it was evident, could be done;
and with the artist's isolating eye
my great-great-grandmother hastily sketched the scene.
The sketch survives to prove the story by.

Year, if you have no Mother's day present planned;
reach back and bring me the firmness of her hand.

NIGHT HERONS

It was after a day's rain:
the street facing the west
was lit with growing yellow;
the black road gleamed.

First one child looked and saw
and told another.
Face after face, the windows
flowered with eyes.

It was like a long fuse lighted,
the news travelling.
No one called out loudly;
everyone said "Hush."

The light deepened; the wet road
answered in daffodil colours,
and down its centre
walked the two tall herons.

Stranger than wild birds, even,
what happened on those faces:
suddenly believing in something,
they smiled and opened.

Children thought of fountains,
circuses, swans feeding:
women remembered words
spoken when they were young.

Everyone said "Hush;"
no one spoke loudly;
but suddenly the herons
rose and were gone. The light faded.

A DOCUMENT

"Sign there." I signed, but still uneasily.
I sold the coachwood forest in my name.
Both had been given me; but all the same
remember that I signed uneasily.

Ceratopetalum, Scented Satinwood:
a tree attaining seventy feet in height.
Those pale-red calyces like sunset light
burned in my mind. A flesh-pink pliant wood

used in coachbuilding. Difficult of access
(those slopes were steep). But it was World War Two.
Their wood went into bomber-planes. They grew
hundreds of years to meet those hurried axes.

Under our socio-legal dispensation
both name and woodland had been given me.
I was much younger then than any tree
matured for timber. But to help the nation

I signed the document. The stand was pure
(eight hundred trees perhaps). Uneasily
(the bark smells sweetly when you wound the tree)
I set upon this land my signature.

ALEC DERWENT HOPE   (1907–)

Poet, critic. Born in N.S.W.; educated at Sydney and Oxford;
Emeritus Professor of English at Australian National University.

STANDARDS IN AUSTRALIAN LITERATURE

From time to time in the press and on the air we hear discussions of
Australian literature which attempt to assess its place among the
literatures of the world, or simply to discuss what it has achieved in
the century and a half since it started. Sometimes these discussions
lead to acrimonious correspondence, particularly when a writer or
speaker suggests that our literature falls short of the standards or the
achievements of other countries. It usually emerges from such controversy that those who take sides in it are often judging by very
different standards, and that nobody's standards seem to be at all
explicit. Sometimes a book is praised and decried for substantially
the same reasons; the same reason seems sometimes to be given for
praising one book and decrying another; often the reasons given
appear to have very little to do with literature; and the critics often
fail to distinguish between what Australian writing is, and what, on
one ground or another, they would like Australian writing to be. In
other words the combatants are largely wasting their time. If we
want to form any clear idea of Australian literature and its importance to ourselves or anyone else, we ought to begin with as clear an
idea as possible of what we demand of it and why. We should get
our standards clear.

  The confusion that exists about Australian literature today is
partly a reflection of a general confusion about literary standards,
and partly the result of special problems of assessment that face all
colonial literatures, in fact most literatures in their early stages.
There is very little in the way of a coherent body of literary theory
by which we may judge books, and no set of rules by which their
composition may be judged. Such rules as are generally accepted are
so general that a writer may observe them all and still write a very
dull book and a writer of genius may break most of them and produce something like a masterpiece. Literary standards are established by two things: the existence of undoubted and enduring
works of genius and the existence of a body of critical opinion
which can only be vaguely defined as the 'judgment of the best
minds' which in turn constitutes something equally hard to define,
called the 'level of taste'. In order that this body of critical opinion
shall be effective it needs to command respect, have standing and
prestige; and for this there needs to be an educated class or body of
readers—people who not only read books but read criticism and
discuss the opinions of critics.

A literature which has these three can be said to have an established literary tradition and is likely to have a high standard of literary achievement. It will have universities where scholars devote themselves to the continual reassessment and discussion of the classics of native literature and keep the traditions alive by forming the taste of the reading class who come to them to study the masterpieces. It will be able to support serious literary reviews in which the work of new writers receives thorough appraisement. And in this way it will provide an atmosphere in which young writers of promise get the notice they deserve, and the encouragement and the challenge to their powers without which they are apt to wither on the stalk. The existence of a considerable and discriminating reading class is important in another way: there must be enough readers who buy books to enable writers to live by literature, for worthwhile arts cannot be spare-time occupations.

These conditions have rarely all existed together in one country. Since the end of the eighteenth century, roughly speaking, universities in England have taken up the study of English literature, and authors have been able to support themselves by writing. But other conditions have made the maintenance of a single high standard more difficult. In the first place, the Romantic movement tended to set up a rival scale of literary standards to that of the classical tradition; and the Romantic tradition was no sooner established than it gave birth to a number of new theories, each with its own set of standards. Realism, Naturalism, Estheticism, Symbolism, Imagism, Surrealism and Social Realism have all arisen in the last 60 or 70 years, and, as their standards of judgment are often incompatible, criticism is now in a state of great confusion. Australian literature has come into being entirely within this period of divided and conflicting standards.

In the second place, the spread of general education, rising standards of living, and the dilution of the reading class by large numbers of people who were able and willing to read but not educated, has had the curious effect of depressing literary standards and dividing them. Cheap literature which aims at nothing but amusement has an enormous market, and publishers who make fortunes from comics, westerns, thrillers, detective romances, magazine stories, science fiction and the more fatuous sorts of novel are under economic pressure which automatically transmits itself to writers. Gresham's Law, which says that where two grades of currency are in circulation, the debased coinage will drive out the good, also operates in literature. Organized publicity accelerates the process. Moreover, literature, which was once the one form of intellectual entertainment open to everyone, now has to compete with the radio and the cinema which are easier, cheaper and more immediately exciting. Dickens and Thackeray wrote for the whole class of readers. Nowadays there tends to be one group of writers writing 'literary' novels for a limited group of readers and another writing what is sometimes called 'low-brow' fiction for the rest.

It is against this background of divided and depressed standards in general that the question of Australian writing must be considered.

It will be clear why Australian literature, growing up in this period of confusions, should have had special problems in establishing its own standards. Countries like England and France and the United States have been better off because their literary traditions were already established; countries like South Africa, Canada and Australia have been less fortunate. While their literatures were developing, they themselves were at a pioneering stage of development and their civilizations were provincial in their outlook: that is to say, they looked, as provincial cities do to their capital, towards England as a source of ideas and artistic creation. Moreover, they lacked anything that could be called an educated class of readers of sufficient importance to support local writers; and what readers there were naturally felt themselves cut off from the centre of civilization and were anxious to keep up with the best that was being written abroad.

Australian writers have, therefore, always had to compete for the attention of the best sort of readers with contemporary English and American writers, whereas their opposite numbers in England and America have been assured of the attention of the most discriminating part of their home public. As a result they have often had most success with, and perhaps unconsciously aimed at pleasing, a less discriminating class of readers whose tastes were not so 'literary'; and they have tended to avoid competition with overseas writers and have concentrated on being as 'Australian' as possible. This has meant, in effect, the attempt to set up a special and purely Australian standard of writing.

As is natural in a new country, there have been few writers who by the general standards of European literature were at all outstanding. Australians have produced some very good writing, but none of the indubitable and acknowledged masterpieces which form the real basis of a literary tradition. Universities have given scant place to the study of Australian literature, partly for this reason, with the result that among educated Australians few know anything systematically about their own literature and fewer still have considered it as a critical discipline in the way that educated American or English university-trained men and women have been led to consider their own literature.

Lastly, Australia has never been able to support the literary and critical journals, common abroad, in which new writings can be properly analysed and assessed. For this both the public and the writers have had to depend largely on ephemeral newspaper reviews in which the space allowed has meant that no real analysis can be made and the judgment of critics always appears, and often is, arbitrary and perfunctory.

From the beginning Australian writers and their local critics have been extremely conscious of the difference between this country and the home country, which naturally supplied the literary standards with which they started. So there was from the outset a tendency in criticism which one might describe as a sense of colonial uncertainty, an apologetic tone which was plainly caused by a patriotic desire to stand equal with the rest of the world. At an earlier period in criticism this attitude of 'apology' is most marked. H. G. Turner and A. Sutherland in their book *The Development of Australian Literature*, published in 1898, wrote in the following terms:

> To the Australian heart there may be much that is of moving appeal in verses that to others seem only bald and commonplace or rude and colloquial.... So, while we have our Shakespeare societies, our Browning clubs, though men still retain their deepest ardour for their Shelley, their Wordsworth or their Tennyson, still there is something that Gordon and Kendall and Marcus Clarke can say to us which others are unable to hear. An English reader may dip with a certain curiosity into the works of these writers and award them a stinted measure of chill praise, but the Australian, as he reads, has no thought of praise or of criticism. He feels his heart burn within him as he proceeds, and therein is the poet justified, more than in acres of laudatory reviews. (pp. ix–xi)

The obvious tendency in this passage is to argue that, while Australian writers do not, admittedly, reach the standard of contemporary English literature, they have a special appeal to Australians, and that English critics and readers who do not know the country at first-hand cannot appreciate them at their true worth. By the end of the First World War, however, this apologetic note largely disappears. The critics continue to be on the defensive, but now they claim that Australian literature has justified itself and a slightly truculent note appears in much of our critical writing. There is a demand that Australian writing shall be granted an equal place with that of other literatures. For instance, John K. Ewers in his *Creative Writing in Australia* (1945) takes up the cudgels for Henry Kendall:

> C. Hartley Grattan has contemptuously dismissed him as 'a barely respectable minor poet, leaning heavily on Wordsworth and Keats'. But he was something more than that. His interpretation of the Australian bushland as he knew it was original and sincere and it has won the affection of succeeding generations of Australians. He was conscious of his own imperfections. (p. 34)

Part of this new attitude is due, I think, to a lack of comparative standards. There is a tendency to over-estimate, sometimes quite absurdly, the importance of certain Australian writers, simply because they loom large in the local scene. The critics forget how small the scene is. The big frog in the small pond looks bigger than he really is. Part of the attitude is also due to a natural and proper tendency in criticism to erect a Pantheon of writers, to establish a literary canon and to range Australian writers in order of magnitude and importance. Writers like Henry Lawson, Joseph Furphy and Henry Handel Richardson stand near the head of the critic's list and they tend to settle into the position of classics. The next step is to make an unspoken assumption that the classics of any one literature are equal to those of any other.

This tendency has its natural reaction in critics whose motto seems to be 'Can any good thing come out of Nazareth?' An example is Randolph Hughes's criticism of Australian literature in general and of Henry Kendall in particular in his *C. J. Brennan: An Essay in Values* (1934):

> [*The Times*] brings forward Kendall as a star of major magnitude in the Heaven of antipodean verse, just as a historian of English literature might use Milton as a norm of excellence by which to assess the deficiencies of the otherwise incomparable Shakespeare. Kendall was no doubt a thoroughly amiable person, and he wrote some engagingly plaintive poetry of a kind that would merit a page in an anthology that aimed at being comprehensive; but even in the relatively barren or weedy field of Australian literature, he is no more than a minor poet. (p. 82)

It was also after the First World War that a form of over-enthusiastic nationalism began to appear in the form of more organized critical arguments. There were, first of all, those critics, like Miles Franklin in her book on Furphy, who continued the sort of view put forward by Turner and Sutherland. She claimed that because Australian literature is something *sui generis* it cannot be judged by the standards that apply to other literatures. There is at least something in this point of view; for instance, each country develops a language peculiar to itself, having its own special forms and overtones of meaning; each country develops its own way of life; and the techniques of its literature can only be judged in the frame of reference of this language, of this way of life. But the fallacy of the argument is first, that even when this is admitted, there *are* common standards for the whole European literary tradition of which Australian literature forms a part; and secondly, that it is easy to over-estimate the differences between the English way of life and that of other parts of the English-speaking world.

The extreme nationalist point of view has been pushed furthest by a group of writers and critics who arose in the 1930's calling themselves the Jindyworobaks. The argument of this group depended on a mystique of the soil. It was argued that the transplanted Europeans in this country were cut off from the real sources of creative literature because their roots were still in English literature and not in the Australian scene. The extremists of the group regarded the aborigines as the only people in contact with the real Australia and drawing their tradition directly from the soil. They argued that the real creative movement in Australian literature could only arise if writers were prepared to cut their connection with the European literary tradition and to graft themselves on to the traditions and life of the aboriginal inhabitants. One objection to this argument seems to be that a good deal of vital creative writing has arisen in Australia from people who have had no contact with the aborigines at all. To most Australians, in fact, the aborigines and their way of life are more remote and foreign than that of the Redskins of North America, whom they at least know at second-hand through American literature. But the fundamental fallacy of this point of view can be indicated by pointing out that English literature itself is based not in the native Teutonic tradition but on two traditions entirely foreign to the Anglo-Saxons: the Christian-Jewish tradition and the classical Greco-Roman tradition.

It is only fair to point out that this stage of Australian criticism appears to be passing. Books like Vance Palmer's *The Legend of the Nineties* (1954), G. A. Wilkes's *New Perspectives on Brennan's Poetry* (1953), and Leonie J. Gibson's *Henry Handel Richardson and Some of Her Sources* (1954), to mention some of the most outstanding, show a tendency to judge our writers simply as writers and not as specifically Australian writers, and to apply the mature and discriminating standards which are characteristic of the best criticism everywhere.

The standards and the problems of Australian criticism reflect, of course, those of the writers themselves. Something like a real tradition of Australian writing has now been established, and we should consider what the main features of this tradition are, since it is bound to have its effect in determining present and future standards. If one looks at the three fields of prose fiction, poetry and drama, what sort of general pattern emerges?

As a whole Australia has a literature that is largely concerned with life on the land and pays very little attention to life in the cities and larger towns. This is perhaps natural, for the culture of the cities is for the most part cosmopolitan and provincial, whereas that of the country and the country towns has a character quite of its own, parochial perhaps, but genuinely and recognizably Australian, and it has been the ambition of nine-tenths of the poets and novelists of the country to depict and record the typical and authentic Australia in something like its own terms. This is no doubt a character of colonial literatures everywhere. There is the lure of a great mass of unexplored and unexploited material and there is the natural urge to come to terms with one's native surroundings. But Australian writing seems to have deliberately prolonged its adolescence. In essentials the job was done fifty years ago, but Australian poets and novelists are still busy pioneering. There is no problem for the English novelist in being sufficiently 'English' to win acceptance.

But books are still apt to be judged in Australia by the degree to which they are 'Australian' in atmosphere and outlook.

This obsession with the scene rather than with the individual, with what is typical rather than with what is distinctive, and with what is specifically Australian rather than with what is specifically human, comes out in other ways. More than half the novels which have some claim to distinction are historical novels. There seems to be a natural affinity between pioneering a literature and literature about pioneering the land. If one considers only the successful Australian novels written since the turn of the century, most of them are in one sense or another historical or attempt to create a picture of the country through the medium of fiction.

The novelists seem to be perpetually looking over their shoulders, and there is a general feeling that the 'real Australia' for which they are all looking lies somewhere in the past. What in the late nineteenth century and early twentieth century was a genuine attempt to create an image and shape for the country has now degenerated into a dream of an illusory or ideal country, a country of droving and pioneering, of exploration and settlement, of free enterprise and adventure, of a simple and comradely way of life. All are in comforting contrast to the actual present of a highly industrialized modern society, a thoroughly urbanized way of life, even in rural areas, and all the comfortable monotony of a social service state. The other was the 'real Australia', a country of individuals and individualists engaged in a simple and heroic struggle with soil and weather. This is why the writers of fiction so often turn back to the world of Henry Lawson and Joseph Furphy, to the Rum Rebellion, the Eureka Stockade and the bushranging exploits of Ned Kelly and Starlight. What began as an attempt to come to grips with reality has ended in an attempt to impose a dream.

A recent novel which has been applauded both in Australia and in America, Patrick White's *The Tree of Man* (1955) is a case in point. White has lived abroad; his writing shows him to be aware of and able to take his place among novelists of the day; his technique is sophisticated and experimental; he has a powerful conception of character, and his theme, unlike that of many of his contemporaries and predecessors, is centred in exceptional and individual character. Yet he has been unable to resist the 'pattern' that seems imposed on Australian fiction. The story is one of pioneering on the land; the life and humours of a small bush community are arbitrarily added to his central theme; and the dramas of fire, flood, drought, isolation and the struggle to make a living are introduced one by one as stock ingredients. The city is represented as alien territory and the more comfortably off as an alien race. The whole thing is set in the past, though not in the distant past. What makes it the more striking is that all the clichés of Australian fiction are there, and that none of these clichés is really relevant to the theme.

Another curious feature of Australian fiction is its continued pre-
dilection for what Wordsworth called 'humble and rustic life'.
Many Australian writers themselves have been among the under-
privileged and the battlers, but this will not entirely account for the
tendency. Vance Palmer has carefully analysed some of its main
causes in his discussion of the socialism of the 1890's. A lead was
given by that socialist and nationalist weekly, the *Bulletin*, in establishing an Australian school of writers at a time when socialism and
nationalism made common cause. But the odd thing is that this
tradition has persisted, though the structure of Australian society
has altered completely since the turn of the century. The great fortunes of the rich, the predominance of the landed interests, the absence of social services and the lack of political power of the working classes have all been things of the past for a long time. Australia
is now a highly organized social service state, an industrialized state
in which the three major power groups, industry, labour and agriculture, are represented by political parties with only minor differences of policy. Australians now for the most part form a
homogeneous middle class. It has little in the way of a real proletar-
iat or a wealthy leisured class. Yet Australian fiction practically
ignores all except the lower income groups, just as, on the whole, it
ignores the cities and concentrates on the country. The 'real' Australian in fiction more often than not tends to be a drover, a shearer, a small farmer, a wharf labourer, a factory hand, a miner or
prospector, very rarely a businessman, a lawyer, a scholar, an artist,
a station-owner or a civil servant, unless these occupations are made
romantic by an historical setting in the past. In recent years the
left-wing movement in writing which calls itself Social Realism has
been able to exploit this tendency and has attracted many of the
young writers and quite a number of the older ones, so that the
tendency to limit the field of fiction to the 'workers' has shown no
tendency to decrease.

Poetry in Australia has shown a constant tendency to be descriptive. This is partly due to the fact that the tradition began under the
influence of the Romantic movement. The shade of Wordsworth
haunts our poets. From Harpur and Kendall in the early nineteenth
century to Douglas Stewart and Judith Wright at the present day, it
would hardly be unfair to say that nine-tenths of the poems written
in this country deal with its scenery. The poets, however, have a
wider range than the novelists, and have solved the problem of coming to grips with the country rather better. The best Australian
poetry today gives the impression of poets who start *from* the local
scene as something given, whereas the impression the older poetry
gave was that of poets who aimed *at* the local scene as something to
be domesticated in literature. Moreover, in poetry there has always
been another tradition than the 'national' one. Brennan, McCrae
and Neilson, among the older poets, wrote poetry that was simply
poetry and did not try to be 'Australian' poetry. Perhaps the fact

that the traditional subjects of poetry are the primary passions of the heart and the universal facts of human life has protected it. Love, for example, is one of the commonest themes of poetry and even the most enthusiastic nationalist might hesitate to maintain that there is a specifically Australian sort of love.

Poetry is in a healthy state in Australia today. After a period of literary measles in the twenties and thirties, when Imagism, Surrealism, Apocalypse and other experimental diseases took a temporary hold, the poets have now returned to writing in the main stream of the tradition and 'making it new' in the traditional manner. There are at least a dozen poets with a high degree of craftsmanship and all have something to say. Among them I would place Kenneth Slessor, Robert FitzGerald, Judith Wright, Rosemary Dobson, James McAuley, Harold Stewart, Vincent Buckley, David Campbell, Nan McDonald, Douglas Stewart and Dorothy Auchterlonie.

Though many of them are in one sense or another descriptive poets, the best of them avoid the two crippling obsessions of much previous Australian poetry: that to look at scenery is in itself to have a poetic experience, and that not to deal with themes specifically Australian is to be derivative, second-hand or 'academic'. Another advantage the poets enjoy which the writers of fiction do not, is that poetry does not pay and is not expected to, so that there is no pressure from the market, which, in fiction, undoubtedly favours the romantically or highly-coloured Australian themes.

There is not much to say about Australian drama for the very good reason that drama needs actors, a theatre and a lot of capital. There have never been many theatres in Australia, even in the capital cities, and those there were have always preferred to import plays which have been proved successes in England or America. Australian dramatists have therefore largely been limited to writing for the amateur stage, and the standard achieved has necessarily been itself amateur. However, there are signs that what happened in the United States may in time happen here. The repertory theatre movement has gradually improved its standard of acting and production to a point where the public begins to support it as it does the commercial theatre, and local playwrights are beginning to find a real outlet for their talents. The recent acceptance of Ray Lawler's *The Summer of the Seventeenth Doll* (1957) for professional production in England may be the beginning of the next step in the same process as that by which the little theatre movement in America opened the way to a national American drama of professional standard. But so far there has been no real achievement in drama except in the form of radio plays. Douglas Stewart's *Ned Kelly* (1943) and *The Fire on the Snow* (1944) have proved effective and moving in production, though they are not remarkable as literature. In general, the few Australian plays worth reading show the same bias shown by the Australian novel, that is, towards history, the myth of the land, and the depiction of the lives of the toilers.

A short survey of the situation of literature in Australia today leads, then, to the conclusion that in the first hundred and fifty years Australia has not done brilliantly but neither has she done badly. In fiction she can point to a number of competent writers, though she has so far produced none of outstanding genius. The same is true of poetry. She is beginning to move out of the period of provincialism and parochial nationalism, though many of her writers are still bogged down in the view that they must at all costs be as Australian as possible. She has achieved a definite national tradition, even if it is a narrow one and even if the standard of writing is still generally amateurish. It is a tradition that lacks standing, for it is still without the standards that a range of acknowledged masterpieces provides.

Works of genius cannot be produced by planning or by legislation or by goodwill. But the conditions for encouraging writers of genius to make the best use of their powers can in some measure be provided. Among those most lacking in Australia today are the provision of adequate organs of informed literary criticism; the provision for the serious scholarly study and assessment of our national literature in our national universities; the provision of public support for a national theatre; and, last and perhaps most important of all, the provision of means by which young writers of talent can learn and practise their profession and continue to eat and live like their fellow citizens.

There is a further point to raise: if this is the present position, it is natural to ask what the future is likely to be. If we look at the main colonial literatures of the modern world, those of North and South America, South Africa, New Zealand and Canada, we see that they have developed in very different ways, but all have passed through very similar stages of development. Those of the Latin-American republics and of the United States have had the longest period of growth and have reached a stage of development where they are not only autonomous, but for some time have produced writers whose work has influenced the literature of the former mother countries: England, Spain and Portugal.

The most interesting comparisons for us are with Canada and the United States. The 'colonial' period in American writing lasted more than two hundred years, and during that time no writer of genius appeared; indeed, no writer who made his mark on English literature. In the early nineteenth century writers of a different calibre began to appear. Thoreau, Melville, Whitman, Poe, Hawthorne, Longfellow, Lowell, Whittier and Emerson form a list of names of international reputation, whose works were read, discussed, admired or abused by the whole English-speaking world in the nineteenth century. At least five of them are still important influences on contemporary literature. Two of them, Poe and Whitman, have affected the whole course of the European poetic tradition. One of them, Herman Melville, after a long period of neglect, has begun to take his place as one of the writers of outstanding genius. After this, American literature was launched with its own tradition, which has continued to produce writers who easily take a prominent and important place in the field of European letters. It is interesting to notice that all the writers just mentioned were born in the first twenty years of the nineteenth century. The change from colonialism to an independent and autonomous tradition was sudden, brilliant and permanent.

Much the same holds good of the Spanish literature of South and Central America. English literature, after a period of three hundred years of tutelage to French literature, suddenly established itself with Chaucer, and thereafter went its own way. Something similar occurred with Latin literature at the end of the Republic after a long period of dependence on Greek literature, and with the brilliant flowering of Russian literature in the nineteenth century after a period of tutelage to Western Europe, particularly to France. It looks, therefore, as though there is a general pattern in these things and we may expect, perhaps in the near future, that Australian literature, after a period of uncertainty and experiment, will produce a first crop of writers of international reputation and thus stand firmly on its own feet. But we should be cautious about anticipating the change. Critics in general are only too apt to find geniuses under every bush. The emergence of an autonomous literary tradition, able to challenge comparison with others, differs very much in the time it takes. Canada, which has a longer history than Australia, still stands today very much where Australia stands. Brazil, until recently, lagged far behind Spanish South America.

Two things emerge from these remarks on the way in which literatures establish themselves. One is that the vital change usually occurs quite suddenly; the other is that it is very much dependent on the emergence of a work of undoubted and recognizable genius. Australia has so far not produced such a writer and this is not to be wondered at. For genius appears rarely, sporadically, and is quite unpredictable. Once in two or three hundred years is as much as one can expect for the appearance of one of those enduring masterpieces which automatically become the standards by which all other literature is to be judged. Canada, Australia and South Africa have not so far been fortunate. They have produced some writers of the second rank. In Australia, Henry Handel Richardson and Henry Lawson among prose writers, Christopher Brennan among poets, were able and brilliant, but they lacked the range, the imagination, the mastery that put a writer in the first rank.

This distinction between writers of great importance and great writers in the absolute sense deserves some elucidation, because modern psychology has confused the issue. The psychological theory that all human abilities follow what is called 'the normal curve', has led us to believe that genius is simply the extreme upper end of a continuous ladder or scale of ability, such that great capacity merges insensibly into the sort of performance that produces masterpieces. Now, while this may be true of the gifts of writers, it is not true of their performances. There is a distinct and unmistakable gap between the many works of great ability and the few rare masterpieces. There is an absolute difference in kind between them which an analogy may help to make clear.

A few years ago, the present writer was walking in the mountains of eastern Victoria. It was winter time. All around there rose impressive and formidable mountains. Then a turn of the valley brought us in view of Mount Buller. It was only a few hundred feet higher than the surrounding peaks, made of the same material, and of similar shape. In summer one would only have noticed that it stood a little higher than its fellows. But those few hundred feet took the mountain above the snow-line, and at that moment the sun was shining on a magnificent snow-storm. The head of the mountain rose into another and altogether different world and produced an effect of unforgettable majesty and beauty.

Something of this sort marks off the masterpiece from impressive but lesser achievements in literature. The powers that go to the creation of both are the same, the themes are common, the technical skills may be present in much the same degree. But the work of genius is the one that 'surpasses the snow-line' and once it does we have a new synthesis of the powers which all genuine writers have in common. We have passed from the world of values which are relative into the world in which values are absolute, from the historical to the timeless, from the works which criticism assesses to the works by which criticism makes its assessments. Of these we may say, as Matthew Arnold said of Shakespeare:

> Others abide our question. Thou art free.
> We ask and ask—Thou smilest and art still
> Out-topping knowledge.

Contemporaries are apt to make curious mistakes in judging living writers from this point of view. Opinion changes from age to age even about the masterpieces, and even long-term criticism may be confused or mistaken, but on the whole it is on the existence of works such as these that any notion of literary standards must ultimately rely.

Now it may be pointed out that the European literary tradition, in spite of national variations, is still *one* tradition. Australian literature is a part of that tradition and grows directly from it as a branch of English literature. Why, then, should it have to wait for the emergence of masterpieces of its own to establish its own tradition? As far as *criticism* is concerned there would seem to be no reason. You can compare Henry Handel Richardson with Fielding, with Tolstoy or Stendhal, and find where she stands as a novelist. *The reason lies not in the problem of assessment but in the stimulus to creation among the writers themselves.* There is something in a masterpiece—native, indigenous and speaking the untranslatable language of a specific civilization—by which the writers of that country can measure themselves and feel the force of their own talents in a way which they can rarely do with the masterpieces of other lands. It is for *this* reason that Australia must wait for the final requirement in standards on which a fully formed literary tradition is based.

AUSTRALIA

A nation of trees, drab green and desolate grey
In the field uniform of modern wars,
Darkens her hills, those endless, outstretched paws
Of Sphinx demolished or stone lion worn away.

They call her a young country, but they lie:
She is the last of lands, the emptiest,
A woman beyond her change of life, a breast
Still tender but within the womb is dry;

Without songs, architecture, history:
The emotions and superstitions of younger lands.
Her rivers of water drown among inland sands,
The river of her immense stupidity

Floods her monotonous tribes from Cairns to Perth.
In them at last the ultimate men arrive
Whose boast is not "we live" but "we survive",
A type who will inhabit the dying earth.

And her five cities, like five teeming sores,
Each drains her, a vast parasite robber-state
Where second-hand Europeans pullulate
Timidly on the edge of alien shores.

Yet there are some like me turn gladly home
From the lush jungle of modern thought, to find
The Arabian desert of the human mind,
Hoping, if still from the deserts the prophets come,

Such savage and scarlet as no green hills dare
Springs in that waste, some spirit which escapes
The learned doubt, the chatter of cultured apes
Which is called civilization over there.

THE DEATH OF THE BIRD

For every bird there is this last migration:
Once more the cooling year kindles her heart;
With a warm passage to the summer station
Love pricks the course in lights across the chart.

Year after year a speck on the map, divided
By a whole hemisphere, summons her to come;
Season after season, sure and safely guided,
Going away she is also coming home.

And being home, memory becomes a passion
With which she feeds her brood and straws her nest,
Aware of ghosts that haunt the heart's possession
And exiled love mourning within the breast.

The sands are green with a mirage of valleys;
The palm-tree casts a shadow not its own;
Down the long architrave of temple or palace
Blows a cool air from moorland scarps of stone.

And day by day the whisper of love grows stronger;
That delicate voice, more urgent with despair,
Custom and fear constraining her no longer,
Drives her at last on the waste leagues of air.

A vanishing speck in those inane dominions,
Single and frail, uncertain of her place,
Alone in the bright host of her companions,
Lost in the blue unfriendliness of space,

She feels it close now, the appointed season:
The invisible thread is broken as she flies;
Suddenly, without warning, without reason,
The guiding spark of instinct winks and dies.

Try as she will, the trackless world delivers
No way, the wilderness of light no sign,
The immense and complex map of hills and rivers
Mocks her small wisdom with its vast design.

And darkness rises from the eastern valleys,
And the winds buffet her with their hungry breath,
And the great earth, with neither grief nor malice,
Receives the tiny burden of her death.

WILLIAM BUTLER YEATS

To have found at last that noble, candid speech
In which all things worth saying may be said,
Which, whether the mind asks, or the heart bids, to each
Affords its daily bread;

To have been afraid neither of lust nor hate,
To have shown the dance, and when the dancer ceased,
The bloody head of prophecy on a plate
Borne in at Herod's feast;

To have loved the bitter, lucid mind of Swift,
Bred passion against the times, made wisdom strong;
To have sweetened with your pride's instinctive gift
The brutal mouth of song;

To have shared with Blake uncompromising scorn
For art grown smug and clever, shown your age
The virgin leading home the unicorn
And loosed his sacred rage—

But more than all, when from my arms she went
That blessed my body all night, naked and near,
And all was done, and order and content
Closed the Platonic Year,

Was it *not* chance alone that made us look
Into the glass of the Great Memory
And know the eternal moments, in your book,
That we had grown to be?

MEDITATION ON A BONE

A piece of bone, found at Trondhjem in 1901, with the following runic inscription (about A.D. 1050) cut on it:

> *I loved her as a maiden; I will not trouble Erlend's detestable wife; better she should be a widow.*

Words scored upon a bone,
Scratched in despair or rage—
Nine hundred years have gone;
Now, in another age,
They burn with passion on
A scholar's tranquil page.

The scholar takes his pen
And turns the bone about,
And writes those words again.
Once more they seethe and shout,
And through a human brain
Undying hate rings out.

"I loved her when a maid;
I loathe and love the wife
That warms another's bed:
Let him beware his life!"
The scholar's hand is stayed;
His pen becomes a knife

To grave in living bone
The fierce archaic cry.
He sits and reads his own
Dull sum of misery.
A thousand years have flown
Before that ink is dry.

And, in a foreign tongue,
A man, who is not he,
Reads and his heart is wrung
This ancient grief to see,
And thinks: When I am dung,
What bone shall speak for me?

THE WALKER

Who walks round my house all night?
None but lanky Tom.

AN OLD CHILDREN'S GAME

Who walks round my house all night,
Stepping sad and slow,
Ghost or woman, child or sprite?
None that I do know.

Who is she that haunts the dark
When the moon is down,
Street or garden, pale or park,
Through the sleeping town?

When the frost falls thick and chill
And the stars slide by,
In my bed I hear it still,
Hear her walk and sigh.

Sultry midnights when I wake
In the clutch of fear,
Though my bones with fever shake,
Nothing do I hear;

Nothing, nothing can I spy
Through the darkened pane;
Yet, when on my bed I lie,
Come those steps again;

Comes the sound of mortal grief
And the tread of woe—
Is it woman, spirit, thief,
Pacing to and fro?

"Lover, keep your careless bed,
Turn you to the wall.
Not the living, not the dead
Answers here your call;

"But a witness from the void,
Banned with drug and knife,
Whom your coward heart destroyed
In the gates of life."

MOSCHUS MOSCHIFERUS

A Song for St Cecilia's Day

In the high jungle where Assam meets Tibet
The small Kastura, most archaic of deer,
Were driven in herds to cram the hunters' net
And slaughtered for the musk-pods which they bear;

But in those thickets of rhododendron and birch
The tiny creatures now grow hard to find.
Fewer and fewer survive each year. The search
Employs new means, more exquisite and refined:

The hunters now set out by two or three;
Each carries a bow and one a slender flute.
Deep in the forest the archers choose a tree
And climb; the piper squats against the root.

And there they wait until all trace of man
And rumour of his passage dies away.
They melt into the leaves and, while they scan
The glade below, their comrade starts to play.

Through those vast listening woods a tremulous skein
Of melody wavers, delicate and shrill:
Now dancing and now pensive, now a rain
Of pure, bright drops of sound and now the still,

Sad wailing of lament; from tune to tune
It winds and modulates without a pause;
The hunters hold their breath; the trance of noon
Grows tense; with its full power the music draws

A shadow from a juniper's darker shade;
Bright-eyed, with quivering muzzle and pricked ear,
The little musk-deer slips into the glade
Led by an ecstasy that conquers fear.

A wild enchantment lures him, step by step,
Into its net of crystalline sound, until
The leaves stir overhead, the bowstrings snap
And poisoned shafts bite sharp into the kill.

Then, as the victim shudders, leaps and falls,
The music soars to a delicious peak,
And on and on its silvery piping calls
Fresh spoil for the rewards the hunters seek.

But when the woods are emptied and the dusk
Draws in, the men climb down and count their prey,
Cut out the little glands that hold the musk
And leave the carcasses to rot away.

A hundred thousand or so are killed each year;
Cause and effect are very simply linked:
Rich scents demand the musk, and so the deer,
Its source, must soon, they say, become extinct.

Divine Cecilia, there is no more to say!
Of all who praised the power of music, few
Knew of these things. In honour of your day
Accept this song I too have made for you.

FRANCIS WEBB   (1925–1974)

Poet. Born in Adelaide; educated in Sydney.

MORGAN'S COUNTRY

This is Morgan's country: now steady, Bill.
(Stunted and grey, hunted and murderous.)
Squeeze for the first pressure. Shoot to kill.

Five: a star dozing in its cold cavern.
Six: first shuffle of boards in the cold house.
And the sun lagging on seven.

The grey wolf at his breakfast. He cannot think
Why he must make haste, unless because their eyes
Are poison at every well where he might drink.

Unless because their gabbling voices force
The doors of his grandeur—first terror, then only hate.
Now terror again. Dust swarms under the doors.

Ashes drift on the dead-sea shadow of his plate.
Why should he heed them? What to do but kill
When his angel howls, when the sounds reverberate

In the last grey pipe of his brain? At the window sill
A blowfly strums on two strings of air:
Ambush and slaughter tingle against the lull.

But the Cave, his mother, is close beside his chair,
Her sunless face scribbled with cobwebs, bones
Rattling in her throat when she speaks. And there

The stone Look-out, his towering father, leans
Like a splinter from the seamed palm of the plain.
Their counsel of thunder arms him. A threat of rain.

Seven: and a blaze fiercer than the sun.
The wind struggles in the arms of the starved tree,
The temple breaks on a threadbare mat of glass.

Eight: even under the sun's trajectory
This country looks grey, hunted and murderous.

BELLS OF ST PETER MANCROFT

Gay golden volleys of banter
Bombard the clockwork grief;
A frisson of gold at the centre
Of prayer, bright core of life.

Who knew the old lofty tower,
The ancient holy eye,
To come open like a flower,
To roll and wink with joy?

Townspeople, who wear
Shrewd colours and know the move,
Now blunder and wander, I swear,
In a transport of love.

And the belfry, hale and blest:
Picture the jolly hand
Milking each swinging breast
Of its laughing golden sound.

FIVE DAYS OLD

(For Christopher John)

Christmas is in the air.
You are given into my hands
Out of quietest, loneliest lands.
My trembling is all my prayer.
To blown straw was given
All the fullness of Heaven.

The tiny, not the immense,
Will teach our groping eyes.
So the absorbed skies
Bleed stars of innocence.
So cloud-voice in war and trouble
Is at last Christ in the stable.

Now wonderingly engrossed
In your fearless delicacies,
I am launched upon sacred seas,
Humbly and utterly lost
In the mystery of creation,
Bells, bells of ocean.

Too pure for my tongue to praise,
That sober, exquisite yawn
Or the gradual, generous dawn
At an eyelid, maker of days:
To shrive my thought for perfection
I must breathe old tempests of action

For the snowflake and face of love,
Windfall and word of truth,
Honour close to death.

O eternal truthfulness, Dove,
Tell me what I hold—
Myrrh? Frankincense? Gold?

If this is man, then the danger
And fear are as lights of the inn,
Faint and remote as sin
Out here by the manger.
In the sleeping, weeping weather
We shall all kneel down together.

A DEATH AT WINSON GREEN

There is a green spell stolen from Birmingham;
Your peering omnibus overlooks the fence,
Or the grey, bobbing lifelines of a tram.
Here, through the small hours, sings our innocence.
Joists, apathetic pillars plot this ward,
Tired timbers wheeze and settle into dust,
We labour, labour: for the treacherous lord
Of time, the dazed historic sunlight, must
Be wheeled in a seizure towards one gaping bed,
Quake like foam on the lip, or lie still as the dead.

Visitors' Day: the graven perpetual smile,
String-bags agape, and pity's laundered glove.
The last of the heathens shuffles down the aisle,
Dark glass to a beauty which we hate and love.
Our empires rouse against this ancient fear,
Longsufferings, anecdotes, levelled at our doom;
Mine-tracks of old allegiance, prying here,
Perplex the sick man raving in his room.
Outside, a shunting engine hales from bed
The reminiscent feast-day, long since dead.

Noon reddens, trader birds deal cannily
With Winson Green, and the slouch-hatted sun
Gapes at windows netted in wire, and we
Like early kings with book and word cast down
Realities from our squared electric shore.
Two orderlies are whistling-in the spring;
Doors slam; and a man is dying at the core
Of triumph won. As a tattered, powerful wing
The screen bears out his face against the bed,
Silver, derelict, rapt, and almost dead.

Evening gropes out of colour; yet we work
To cleanse our shore from limpet histories;
Traffic and factory-whistle turn berserk;

Inviolate, faithful as a saint he lies.
Twilight itself breaks up, the venal ship,
Upon the silver integrity of his face.
No bread shall tempt that fine, tormented lip.
Let shadow switch to light—he holds his place.
Unmarked, unmoving, from the gaping bed
Towards birth he labours, honour, almost dead.

The wiry cricket moiling at his loom
Debates a themeless project with dour night,
The sick man raves beside me in his room;
I sleep as a child, rouse up as a child might.
I cannot pray; that fine lip prays for me
With every gasp at breath; his burden grows
Heavier as all earth lightens, and all sea.
Time crouches, watching, near his face of snows.
He is all life, thrown on the gaping bed,
Blind, silent, in a trance, and shortly, dead.

HARRY

It's the day for writing that letter, if one is able,
And so the striped institutional shirt is wedged
Between this holy holy chair and table.
He has purloined paper, he has begged and cadged
The bent institutional pen,
The ink. And our droll old men
Are darting constantly where he weaves his sacrament.

Sacrifice? Propitiation? All are blent
In the moron's painstaking fingers—so painstaking.
His vestments our giddy yarns of the firmament,
Women, gods, electric trains, and our remaking
Of all known worlds—but not yet
Has our giddy alphabet
Perplexed his priestcraft and spilled the cruet of innocence.

We have been plucked from the world of commonsense,
Fondling between our hands some shining loot,
Wife, mother, beach, fisticuffs, eloquence,
As the lank tree cherishes every distorted shoot.
What queer shards we could steal
Shaped him, realer than the Real:
But it is no goddess of ours guiding the fingers
    and the thumb.

She cries: *Ab aeterno ordinata sum.*
He writes to the woman, this lad who will never marry.

One vowel and the thousand laborious serifs will come
To this pudgy Christ, and the old shape of Mary.
Before seasonal pelts and the thin
Soft tactile underskin
Of air were stretched across earth, they have sported
   and are one.

Was it then at this altar-stone the mind was begun?
The image besieges our Troy. Consider the sick
Convulsions of movement, and the featureless baldy sun
Insensible—sparing that compulsive nervous tic.
Before life, the fantastic succession,
An imbecile makes his confession,
Is filled with the Word unwritten, has almost genuflected.

Because the wise world has for ever and ever rejected
Him and because your children would scream at the sight
Of his mongol mouth stained with food, he has resurrected
The spontaneous thought retarded and infantile Light.
Transfigured with him we stand
Among walls of the no-man's-land
While he licks the soiled envelope with lover's caress

Directing it to the House of no known address.

DAVID CAMPBELL   (1915–1979)

Poet. Born in N.S.W.; educated at Sydney and Cambridge.

WINTER STOCK ROUTE

Here where red dust rose
To raddle sheep and men
And the kelpie tongued at noon,
Silence has come again.
The great-boled gumtrees bow
Beneath their load of snow.

The drover and his dray
Have gone; and on this hill
I find myself alone
And Time standing still.
Printless the white road lies
Before my quiet skis.

But where my skis trace
Their transient snow furrow,
For generations both
Man and beast will follow.
Now in this winter passage
I cross the deserted stage.

ARIEL

Frost and snow, frost and snow:
The old ram scratches with a frozen toe
At silver tussocks in the payable mist
And stuffs his belly like a treasure chest.

His tracks run green up the mountainside
Where he throws a shadow like a storm-cloud's hide;
He has tossed the sun in a fire of thorns,
And a little bird whistles between his horns.

"Sweet-pretty-creature!" sings the matchstick bird,
And on height and in chasm his voice is heard;
Like a bell of ice or the crack of the frost
It rings in the ears of his grazing host.

"Sweet-pretty-creature!" While all is as still
As the bird on the ram on the frozen hill,
O the wagtail warms to his tiny art
And glaciers move through the great beast's heart.

WHO POINTS THE SWALLOW

Love who points the swallow home
And scarves the russet at his throat,
Dreaming in the needle's eye,
Guide us through the maze of glass
Where the forceful cannot pass,
With your silent clarity.

There where blood and sap are one,
Thrush's heart and daisy's root
Keep the measure of the dance,
Though within their cage of bone
Griefs and tigers stalk alone,
Locked in private arrogance.

Lay the shadow of our fear
With the brilliance of your light,
Naked we can meet the storm,
Travellers who journeyed far
To find you at our own front door,
O love who points the swallow home.

NIGHT SOWING

O gentle, gentle land
Where the green ear shall grow,
Now you are edged with light:
The moon has crisped the fallow,
The furrows run with night.

This is the season's hour:
While couples are in bed,
I sow the paddocks late,
Scatter like sparks the seed
And see the dark ignite.

O gentle land, I sow
The heart's living grain.
Stars draw their harrows over,
Dews send their melting rain:
I meet you as a lover.

PRAYER FOR RAIN

Sweet rain, bless our windy farm,
Stepping round in skirts of storm
While these marble acres lie
Open to an empty sky.

Sown deep, the oaten grain
Awaits, as words wait in the brain,
Your release that out of dew
It may make the world anew.

Sweet rain, bless our windy farm,
Stepping round in skirts of storm:
Amongst the broken clods the hare
Folds his ears like hands in prayer.

KU-RING-GAI ROCK CARVINGS

I

The Lovers

Making love for ten thousand years on a rockledge:
    The boronia springs up purple
  From the stone, and we lay together briefly
  For as long as those two lovers.

Honeyeaters

The gymea and emus wait for the lithe tribesmen
    And the great whales doze, but the fish
  Leap down the flowering sandstone
  Where honeyeater chickens rage.

Fish

Trapped on a blue hill above blue bays
    The stone shoals move one way:
  From rockledge through the blue heads,
  It is light-years to the open sea.

Man and Woman

All night they look at the moon. No ones sees them move,
    Though his arms are raised in praise.
  Delicately their ankles cross
  And her fork is an inch-deep groove.

Whales

They whistled the whales and whales litter the landscape
    Like stranded boulders with calves
  Carved on their backs. And there they blow
  Low banksia scrub, a froth of spiked spring flowers.

Spring

The Chase is mad with sex. Flowered trees sustain
    The act of love a season;
  While from stone loins wild orchids spring
  Whose pleasure is in intercourse with beetles.

Spiny Ant-eaters

Spring comes in gold and purple, and the stone echidnas
    Dawdle across the rockface:
  It may be a prickly business
  But their desire goes on forever.

Fairy Penguins

A fairy penguin dives in rock for cover
    With swept-back wings, as jets
  Pencilling vapour-trails, go over:
  For all I know, the rest may still be under.

II

Lizards

Lizards are kin and can return to stone
    At will. Transfixing a shield
  Like a spear a lizard froze in the sun, a thing
  Of bronze, yet quick. See the dart of his tongue!

Bora Ring

The kangaroo has a spear in his side. It was here
    Young men were initiated,
  Tied to a burning tree. Today
  Where are such cooling pools of water?

Tench, 1791

Flesh carvings: for theft, before the assembled tribes,
    A convict was flogged. Daringa,
  Her nets forgotten, wept: while Barangaroo
  Threatened the lasher. A feckless if tender people.

King Boongarie: Etching by Earle

A convict driving nails in a deal coffin:
    They're burying the tribe's last king
  Beside Queen Gooseberry with naval honours.
    His Commodore's uniform (Brisbane's) is in tatters.

Rain

The waterfalls are real. All night it rained
    On black rock where eels
  Slither and cling for centuries
  Out there in the black hills.

Shields

A shield was the symbol of the tribe rather than the spear
    or boomerang. In caves
  And on tessellated pavements, shields
  Forbid the stranger, but hearth and heart are bare.

Weapons

In "the war to end all wars", an obsolete tank
    Patrolling the blue littoral
  From Gabo to York, pitted the rock
  And unearthed from moss a boomerang.

Fire

Ladyslippers tiptoe to the carved birds
    Where the great fire blazed
  Last summer. After the corroboree of flame,
  Black crows complained of two lyrebirds dancing.

III

The Underground

The underground is stirring. Orchid and bird
    Rise from the ashes, seed
  Spread beetle wings; and August's student tribes
  Step out between the blackened trees.

Charcoal Drawings

We drew in charcoal by the poisoned water
    And you cried, Look, a sunfish!
  Light wrinkled stone but you had gone
  Like a blue crane in blue creekwater.

Lyrebirds

The lyrebird is a de Berg. She records
      The sound of men and of birds.
   The Ku-ring-gal live in their rock carvings
   And a note or two of the lyrebird.

Hands

An artist blew ruddy ochre to outline his hand
      in a cave the water glazed.
   You can shake hands with this dead man.
   It teases the mind like John Keats' hand.

Woolgathering

The white-eared honeyeater is fixed in time
      By the hand of Douglas Stewart,
   Yet today it flew out of the bush, or out of his lines,
   To gather wool from my fair son's sweater.

Thought

The instinct of this olive bird to gather fur
      From wallaby and man,
   Quite free from fear at nesting time,
   Is an instant of free thought as old as stone gods.

Baiame

Baiame, the All-father, is a big fellow with a big dong
      And the rayed crown of a god.
   He looks at his Sunday children who snigger and drive
   Home to their home-units. The god is not surprised.

Sri Ramakrishna on Mount Topham

By the cave of the hands a page blew on the wind
      To catch in thorn-flowers. Its message:
   Only those who see Divinity in all things
   May worship the Deity with advantage or safety.

TREE IN A LANDSCAPE

It came as a complete surprise
After long noons of waiting
The tree seemed to grow of its own volition

Its roots split the rock
Its leaves wove lean shadows
No one believed that I had made it

I put a starling in a hollow
In another a scarlet parrot
Birds woke in the boughs
Insects scribbled their brief histories

The tree stripped its bark
Lives blew about me
I lay down in its shade
A small part of the landscape
That entranced I created.

HARRY P. HESELTINE   (1931–)

Critic. Born in W.A.; educated in Perth and Louisiana, U.S.A.;
Professor of English at Royal Military College, Duntroon.

AUSTRALIAN IMAGE:

The Literary Heritage

> 'So much horror in the clear Australian sunlight!'
> DOUGLAS STEWART: *Ned Kelly*

That Australians have a literary heritage is a proposition which, I
imagine, few critics of our culture would seriously deny. The general function of that heritage, too, would probably be a matter of
common agreement. It is the continuing definition of ourselves to
ourselves through the forms of literature; it is the monuments of the
used and usable past which can still enforce their relevance upon us;
it is that element in our most accomplished literary works which
makes known their Australianness. But the specific forces which
have controlled the development of our literature, the special attitudes which reveal the Australianness of Australian writing—these
are matters on which finality has by no means been reached. It must
be said, indeed, that some of the prevailing interpretations of our

literary heritage are not adequate either to its particular exhibits or
to its accumulated quality.

The view of our literature which has acquired perhaps the widest
authority is that which sees it as a contest between an exclusive and
an inclusive culture, in which the latter has consistently marshalled
the superior forces; it is the democratic theme which is at the heart
of our literature. This very plausible view has been argued powerfully and frequently, nowhere with more critical tact that in A. A.
Phillips's *The Australian Tradition*. 'The Currency Lad,' he writes
in the essay on 'The Democratic Theme', 'could be defined, almost,
as the man who did not touch his hat' (p. 35). And the Currency
Lad stands as the most compelling image of man presented in our
writing. Nobody could deny the enormous force of the drive towards egalitarian democracy in Australian writing, or ignore some
of the concomitant attitudes it has established in our literature—the
suspicion of heroes, for instance, or the tendency towards left-wing
political commitments.

Belief in the primacy of the democratic theme, with all its attendant consequences for personal and public action, naturally enough
places Henry Lawson fairly and squarely at the centre of our literary heritage. It is no accident that Phillips's book is distinguished by
sympathetic and sensitive essays on Lawson and Furphy. The
democratic theme clearly does occupy—and occupy significantly—
the minds of many of our earlier writers. I do not question its importance or value; I do wonder if it is at the very centre of the
Australian imagination. Is it the grain of sand which irritates the
oyster into protective action? Or is it the pearl which makes the
grain of sand bearable and (incidentally for the oyster) beautiful? If,
in the past, the democratic theme has been the secret stimulant to
our artistic creation, then certain quite real difficulties are posed for
us. In an article, 'Winds of Change in the Australian Novel' (*The
Australian Quarterly*, XXXII, no. 4, 1960), Norman Bartlett has
stated quite flatly that 'The national billy tea literary tradition—the
gum leaves make all the difference—no longer satisfies us' (p. 75).
And again: 'Those who still march under that once grand old ban-
ner, "Temper democratic, bias Australian," are merely marching in
circles' (p. 80). With these words Bartlett voices an attitude that is
increasingly felt abroad among writers and critics. If all that Lawson
and his tribe can offer is outback mateship and proletarian protest,
they must regretfully, even painfully, be relegated to the past—
historical monuments from which the life of relevance has departed.
I do not happen to believe that we need so completely to turn our
backs on Lawson: yet the difficulty remains. If our literary heritage
offers us nothing but the simple virtues appropriate to a simple
frontier society, what can we do but reject it? We are left with a
heritage which is an empty inheritance.

The cultural historian will not for long be left at a loss by Lawson's qualities and by Bartlett's rejection of them. He will soon go

to work, fitting them into a larger pattern which will comprehend them both. The sub-title of Phillips's book is 'Studies in a Colonial Culture'. And it requires no great flexibility of the imagination to understand both Lawson and Bartlett as representing inevitable stages in the passage of what was once a colonial culture to national independence and maturity. The American scholars have long since marked out the pattern of the progress of their own civilization and literature; and in its general outlines the pattern seems to be a necessary one in any situation where a European culture has been grafted onto—through colonization and conquest—some less advanced society. First of all there is likely to be a period of imitation of the models provided by the parent civilization; this is likely to be followed by a period of intense and sometimes acrimonious debate between the forces of nationalism and those which continue to pay homage to the imperial source; for a time nationalism will appear to be triumphant; but as pre-condition of full maturity, nationalism must suffer rejection and be replaced by a sense of nationhood which is assured and un-selfconscious.

It is easy enough to translate this pattern to Australian literature. Harpur, Kendall, and Gordon, the imitators, are followed by the nationalists of the 'nineties and the turn of the century—nationalists who did not have things so much their own way as we sometimes think, who had to contest their right to assert their Australianness. The force of nationalism carries it with some abatement through the first World War and into the 'twenties; in the 'thirties it experiences a revival of enthusiasm and vigour through the Jindyworobak movement. More balanced views, evident from the beginning of the century, are progressively given more and more weight; though, that the issue is by no means settled yet is suggested by the curious ambivalence of Ray Lawler's second play, *The Piccadilly Bushman*, and by the even more ambivalent reception it was accorded.

Australia's literary heritage is the record of her gradual liberation from the restraints of a colonial culture: the interpretation has as much validity as the democratic theme, and leaves us with the same uneasy sense of incompleteness. An interpretation which can be so widely applied—to the United States, to Canada, to South Africa, as well as to our own country—has its very considerable uses. It equally has its limitations. It holds out the seductive possibility of viewing the entire literature of the United States, Canada, South Africa and Australia as one single and inseparable mass—or mess. Which they aren't, if for no other reason than that the settlers of each land had to face and overcome enormously different physical environments. So, it might be argued, the finding of a true relation to the land, the very earth, has been the particular concern of every Australian poet from Charles Harpur to David Campbell. Not the bush workers, or the bush virtues, but the bush itself has been their one true subject. The peculiar ancient harshness of the Australian bush has demanded from our writers the exercise of all their most vital energies. The only way Harpur could live with it was to image it forth as the backdrop to the heroic achievements of the pioneers. Lawson accepted its harshness in bitter surrender to its power to hold him. Brennan, so far as he could and as an act of the will, chose to ignore it. Bernard O'Dowd hymned it as the spirit of Australia. The Jindyworobaks gloried in its primeval indifference to the condition of man. Now our younger poets are able to select from among its many features, and treat them for what they are.

Clearly we must include landscape as a component in our literary heritage. But when we have said landscape, have we said all? And if so, is that enough? Is it enough? This seems to be the question students of Australian culture are driven to again and again. Is our tradition, after all, to be summed up in this or that single word— Mateship? Landscape? Nationalism? Is what we have received from our literary past so *thin* that the simple labels do, in fact, suffice? Most of us would find it difficult to believe that the literature of any nation could be reduced to such direct and formulary clarity; most of us would not like to believe that our own literature could be so reduced. Using the same materials which have always been available, is it possible to construct a version of our literary heritage which will do justice to whatever discoverable complexity and force are latent in it, and at the same time will not disavow its Australian-ness?

The means of carrying out such an enterprise are, I believe, at hand. They can be usefully indicated by resorting to another formulation, but a formulation richer in overtones and implications than any thus far invoked. In an article entitled 'The Background of Romantic Thought' (*Quadrant*, II, no. 1), Herbert Piper asserts that 'there are still many Romantic elements in Australian culture, often unrecognised and unquestioned and yet serving to mark Australian literature off from the modern European literature which rejected Romanticism at least a generation ago' (p. 49). Professor Piper is here, I think, half right and half wrong. He is right in stressing the importance of the Romantic sensibility in Australian literature; he is wrong in those aspects of the Romantic sensibility which he selects as particularly important in our culture; and he is wrong in suggesting a kind of backwardness in our Australian engagement with the Romantic response to life. What I wish to propose as a fundamental element in Australia's literary heritage may be stated something like this. Australian literature is historically a Romantic and post-Romantic phenomenon. Due to certain circumstances of history and geography, it came much *earlier* than European literature to deal with a number of key themes of late Romantic awareness. Although these dealings were very much disguised by colonial necessities, Australian literature, in fact, early took as its central subject what is *still* one of the inescapable concerns of all modern literatures. Such a proposition may well seem to be gratuitously grotesque; it certainly requires the kind of defence afforded only by the display of many items of evidence. Some such items, from within the mainstream of Australian writing, I will provide here; many more could readily be assembled. But first I must isolate that peculiarly modern element in modern literature which, it is my contention, Australian literature so early laid hold on.

I can most conveniently do so by referring to an article by an American critic, Lionel Trilling—'On The Modern Element in Modern Literature' (*Partisan Review*, XXVIII, no. 1). Towards the end of his article Trilling is driven to speaking of 'the subversive tendency of modern literature' (p. 31). It subverts not through this or that political action, not through its Leftism or its Fascism, but in its alienation from any kind of politics, men organized into rational communities. Behind much modern literature, Trilling argues, lies the German Nietzsche. And 'Nietzsche's theory of the social order dismisses all ethical impulse from its origins—the basis of society is to be found in the rationalization of cruelty: as simple as that' (p. 28). A rationalized cruelty is perhaps not likely to recommend itself to the creative artist as an object worthy of his sustained attention. So he becomes an outsider. He becomes Diderot's Nephew of Rameau; or, like Dostoevsky, he sends back Notes from the Underground, brutally destroying all our humanist pieties. The writer, then, is likely to reject society because it is founded on cruelty and sustained by petty rationalistic rules: also, because there are kinds of experience which are positively much more interesting to him. Trilling comments: 'Nothing is more characteristic of modern literature than its discovery and canonization of the primal non-ethical energies [p. 25].... I venture to say that the idea of losing oneself up to the point of self-destruction, of surrendering oneself to experience without regard to self-interest or conventional morality, of escaping wholly from the social bonds is an "element" somewhere in the mind of every modern person who dares to think of what Arnold in his unaffected Victorian way called "the fulness of spiritual perfection"' (p. 35). In exploring the primal energies, the artist is likely to discover that they can command horror as well as delight, yet he will continue his exploration with unabated fascination. 'Is this not the essence of the modern belief about the nature of the artist,' asks Trilling, 'the man who goes down into that hell which is the historical beginning of the human soul, a beginning not outgrown but established in humanity as we know it now, preferring the reality of this hell to the bland lies of the civilization that has overlaid it?' (p. 26).

It is my contention that Australian literature is signalized by its early recognition of the nature of the social contract and by its longstanding awareness of the primal energies of mankind, an awareness which has known little of the sweetening and freshness of early Romantic optimism. Australia's literary heritage is based on a unique combination of glances into the pit and the erection of safety fences to prevent any toppling in.

'Australian literature,' writes Norman Bartlett in the article previously cited, 'so far as I have read it, utterly fails to grapple with the life of politics' (p. 82). To be sure, we have not yet produced a C. P. Snow. Yet is it surprising that the creative minds in a country founded in convictism should have early learned to mistrust the political life? What better illustration than the first half century of British occupation of Australia of Nietzsche's notion that the basis of society is the rationalization of cruelty? When our authors turned to the convict system as viable material for their imaginations, its all-pervading sadism is what struck them most forcibly. The dreadfully enforced rules of the Ring, the absolute viciousness of characters like John Price: this is what we carry away most vividly from Price Warung's *Convict Days*. Marcus Clarke's *For the Term of His Natural Life* is crowded with incident, and saturated with pain, which affects all members and both sides of the system. It is small wonder that our literature has little to tell us about the life of politics—except its cruelty. Even comparatively recent novels like Dal Stivens's *Jimmy Brockett* and Frank Hardy's *Power without Glory* are centred in individuals who perceive the essential nature of political power and who achieve it by the imposition of their own cruel will on the lives of others.

Yet Australian literature is not without its genial elements. Indeed, *Such Is Life*, one of the great monuments of our fiction, is not only a major social document; it is downright sociable. Tom Collins, the narrator, is 'a Government official, of the ninth class,' and therefore something of an outcast; but the basis of the book rests in talk—talk for its own sake, talk round the campfire, talk on the track. Yet all the time shaping and controlling the talk, the meandering meditations, is an ironic intelligence, powerfully aware of the importance of artistic form. Arthur Phillips's essay in *The Australian Tradition* is a first-rate demonstration of the carefully designed structure of *Such Is Life*. Yet this brilliant exposition of Furphy's craftsmanship is curiously deficient. The only use to which Phillips can see that craftsmanship being put is 'to present a complete and significant picture of Riverina life' (p. 19): *Such Is Life* as an especially well-organized and thorough historical document. In fairness, it should be said that Phillips goes on to add that below the aim of giving a complete account of the Riverina 'lay another layer of purpose: an impulsion to give the sense of Life, *the feel of how things happen*' (p. 22). But here Phillips stops—he has little or nothing to say on what was Furphy's sense of Life, how he felt things happening to him. In spite of his sure grasp on the conduct of the narrative, Phillips overlooks the important hint offered by the title—*Such Is Life*. Legend has it that these were the last words of Ned Kelly before he swung—a nihilistic summation of the meaning of his existence. And it is worth refreshing our memories as to the last words of Tom Collins' long recollections:

> Now I had to enact the Cynic philosopher to Moriarty and Butler, and the aristocratic man with a 'past' to Mrs. Beaudesart; with the satisfaction of knowing that each of these was acting a part to me. Such is life, my fellow-mummers—just like a poor player, that bluffs and feints his hour upon the stage, and then cheapens down to mere nonentity. But let me not hear any small witticism to the further effect that its story is a tale told by a vulgarian, full of slang and blanky, signifying—nothing.

Such Is Life is, in effect, concerned with the discrepancy between what we are and what we appear to be, and with the futility of human endeavour. Nosey Alf appears to be a boundary rider, and proves in fact to be Warrigal Alf's forsaken love. Tom Collins pretends to a certain cynicism; he is, in truth, overflowing with a kindness (a kindness which can have tragic consequences). Mrs Beaudesart, insisting on her well-bred airs, is for all that a decayed and snobbish gentlewoman. All the characters of the novel are preparing faces for the faces that they meet, and are continually thwarted in the purposes of their lives. And this is the point of the sociability of *Such Is Life*: it enables its characters to escape from the unbearable reality of being themselves. Society is an act, a decent bluff, which makes bearable the final emptiness, the nothingness of the honestly experienced inner life.

'Nothing' is the last word of one of the central classics of our literary heritage; and it is a word which echoes and re-echoes throughout our literature. In the nineteenth century a persistent and single-minded investigation of the horror of primal experience simply could not be tolerated. The first duty of a frontier society is physical survival; hence evolved that most famous of all Australian survival techniques, the concept of mateship. In our literature, mateship is especially the property of Henry Lawson. And one does not have to go far in his *Prose Works* (Angus & Robertson, 1948) to understand its value for him. It was a necessary defence against the kind of experience which most powerfully laid hold on his imagination. If mateship bulks so large in the canon of Lawson's writing (as indeed it does), it was because behind and beneath it was an even more compelling awareness of horror, of panic and emptiness. Here, for instance, is a passage from one of Lawson's best known tales, 'The Union Buries Its Dead', often cited as an example of Lawson's left-wing solidarity. That it may be; it is something else as well. This is Lawson's description of the actual burial of the unidentified corpse:

> The grave looked very narrow under the coffin, and I drew a breath of relief when the box slid easily down. I saw a coffin get stuck once,

at Rookwood, and it had to be yanked out with difficulty, and laid on the sods at the feet of the heartbroken relations, who howled dismally while the grave-diggers widened the hole. But they don't cut contracts so fine in the West. Our grave-digger was not altogether bowelless, and, out of respect for that human quality described as "feelin's," he scraped up some light and dusty soil and threw it down to deaden the fall of the clay lumps on the coffin. He also tried to steer the first few shovelfuls gently down against the end of the grave with the back of the shovel turned outwards, but the hard dry Darling River clods rebounded and knocked all the same. It didn't matter much—nothing does. The fall of the lumps of clay on a stranger's coffin doesn't sound any different from the fall of the same thing on an ordinary wooden box—at least I didn't notice anything awesome or unusual in the sound; but, perhaps, one of us—the most sensitive—might have been impressed by being reminded of a burial long ago, when the thump of every sod jolted his heart (p. 47).

'It didn't matter much—nothing does.' The assertion is shocking in its finality, but it is the (sometimes unacknowledged) burden of much of Lawson's best writing. If some of Lawson's stories seem rather thin, it is not because they were without content. Rather, they could not afford to face up to their true subject—nothing. They had to take refuge in sociability, they had to create some kind of face or personality which would make shift in the world; in short, they had to opt for mateship.

But mateship has its corollary in Lawson's work—madness. His stories do take cognizance of those who choose to live for and into themselves. The typical fate of such characters is suggested in a story called 'Rats'. Some itinerant shearers come across what they take to be two men struggling in the road. It proves to be a mad traveller wrestling with his swag:

They reached the scene of the trouble, and there stood a little withered old man by the track, with his arms folded close up under his chin; he was dressed mostly in calico patches; and half a dozen corks, suspended on bits of string from the brim of his hat, dangled from his bleared optics to scare away the flies. He was scowling malignantly at a stout, dumpy swag which lay in the middle of the track (p. 112).

At the end of the story the old man is still there, but he has taken to fishing in the dust. Though a lonely old figure, he is not alone in Lawson's bush. Indeed, it is peopled by a remarkably high percentage of hatters, of eccentrics, of people who are plain out of their mind.

They have been driven mad partly by their election out of human society, partly by the nature of the Australian outback. It may be, as Phillips maintains in 'The Democratic Theme', that one of the early exaltations experienced by the Australian Common Man was 'the knowledge that life and victory over a harsh nature could be won only by the strength of the individual's quality as a man' (p. 48). But for the Australian Uncommon Man, for the artist, the bush seems to have served from a quite early date a somewhat different function. For many Australian writers there has been an intimate connection between the nature of the Australian landscape and the quality of the inner life which they actually knew or which they embodied in their writing. Kenneth Slessor, in the first section of *Five Visions of Captain Cook*, has a moment of superb insight when he dates this connection from the beginnings of our history; he ascribes the very discovery of Australia and its subsequent cultural development to an act of madness:

> How many mariners had made that choice
> Paused on the brink of mystery! "Choose now!"
> The winds roared, blowing home, blowing home,
> Over the Coral Sea. "Choose now!" the trades
> Cried once to Tasman, throwing him for choice
> Their teeth or shoulders, and the Dutchman chose
> The wind's way, turning north. "Choose, Bougainville!"
> The wind cried once, and Bougainville had heard
> The voice of God, calling him prudently
> Out of the dead lee shore, and chose the north,
> The wind's way. So, too, Cook made choice,
> Over the brink, into the devil's mouth
> With four months' food, and sailors wild with dreams
> Of English beer, the smoking barns of home.
> So Cook made choice, so Cook sailed westabout,
> So men write poems in Australia.
>
> *(Poems, pp. 57–58).*

Cook sailed over the brink to a continent which, for our nineteenth century writers, was literally capable of driving its inhabitants insane. Lawson and the other writers of the 'nineties were aware of the bush as a physical fact, inescapably present to their immediate lives. For them the insane horror of bush life was perhaps most powerfully projected into one of their recurring themes—the child lost in the bush; not the child lost and found dead, but the child lost, simply swallowed up in all that emptiness. With the possibility of such a fate constantly close to them, it is little wonder that our nineteenth century writers skirted round what they instinctively guessed to be their true subject, the individual human being confronting the primal energies at the centre of his being on the stage of the Australian continent. Instead, they took refuge in the defence of sociable yarning with a group of mates. When they did confront the primeval heart of the matter, it was usually in the form of an attempt to physically subdue the bush and so control its power to subvert the mind.

The first Australian poet directly to confront the heart of his own existence without the mediation of landscape was Christopher Brennan. The disintegration of Brennan's personal life is legendary in the Australian literary consciousness. He is our supreme myth figure of the Romantic artist. It is equally important to realize that in his verse he encountered and recorded just as much horror as in his living. More than any other Australian artist, Brennan suffered the paradox of the late-Romantic experience of love. By love possessed, the poet is driven to ever-increasing intensity of passion at the same time as he comes to ever-increasing knowledge of its final emptiness and capacity to destroy. Foreseeing the end, he yet will not, cannot, forsake his loving until it has accomplished its bitter fulfilment. In Brennan's work, this pattern is rendered with all the ambiguous fascination of its darkness. To be sure, Brennan writes with rare felicity of the brief Paradisal happiness at the beginning of love. But this perception soon shifts to the monstrousness of Lilith and her relation to Adam. In the Lilith sequence from 'The Forest of Night', Lilith, the legendary other wife of Adam, representative of dark and powerful sexuality, addresses her final line to Adam with shuddering and characteristic completeness: 'Go forth: be great, O nothing, I have said' (*The Verse of Christopher Brennan*, ed. Chisholm and Quinn, p. 140).

The first Australian novel to deal in depth with the relation between a man and a woman was published at much the same time as Brennan was writing some of his best and most characteristic verse—Henry Handel Richardson's *Maurice Guest* (1908). This fine book might almost serve as a text to Professor Trilling's account of 'The Modern Element in Modern Literature'. There is, for instance, Krafft's impassioned defence of the artist as the man who seeks his realities beneath the bland lies of civilisation, who gains his wisdom through personal suffering. More important and at the centre of the story is Maurice Guest's obsessed and self-destroying love of Louise Dufrayer. At one level, the novel is a splendidly objective and detailed account of the torments of sexual jealousy; at another, it is a fictional rendering of the Romantic myth of destructive passion. Maurice's life ends in suicide, and it is with these words that Richardson brings to a close her account of his existence:

> Then, as suddenly as the flame of a candle is puffed out by the wind, his life went from him. His right hand twitched, made as if to open, closed again, and stiffened round the iron of the handle. His jaw fell, and, like an inner lid, a glazed film rose over his eyes, which for hours afterwards continued to stare, with an expression of horror and amaze, at the naked branches of the tree.

Throughout the course of our literary history, then, Australian writers have had deeply located in their imagination (either consciously or unconsciously) a sense of the horror of sheer existence. In the nineteenth century, writers sought to protect themselves through direct assaults on their physical environment and by erecting a structure of sociability appropriate to the conditions of their time and place. At about the turn of the century, two major writers emerged who were prepared to confront the secret source of their inspiration directly and without flinching. Among our contemporary writers the strength of the basic stimulus remains unabated, but the honest virtues of the Lawson tradition no longer seem entirely adequate for containing its affronts to their civilized integrity. Have our modern writers developed any techniques to make bearable the nihilism of their deepest experience? It seems to me that they have, and that the most important of them have been generated within that range of activity which I have postulated as Australia's literary heritage.

A. D. Hope, for instance, seeks his salvation in valuing for its own sake the intensity of the experience which brings him to his knowledge of emptiness. Hope's love poetry has been described as puritanic in the bitter disgust which is often implied in the very moment of recording love's sensuous splendour. I would not absolutely repudiate such a view, but I would further suggest that the fury of his love poetry also derives from his need to grasp all that love can offer in order to make bearable the horror and disillusion that follow. In 'The Dinner', thus, he imagines love as a cannibalistic feast, whose savage delights are rendered the more savage and delightful because it is themselves the natives consume. This is how the poem ends:

> Talking in deep, soft, grumbling undertones
> They gnaw and crack and suck the marrowy bones.
> The tit-bits and choice meats they pluck and press
> Each on the other, with grave tenderness,
> And touch and laugh; their strange, fierce features move
> With the delight and confidence of love.
> I watch their loves, I see their human feast
> With the doomed comprehension of the beast;
> I feel the sweat creep through my bristling hair;
> Hollow with rage and fear, I crouch and stare,
> And hear their great jaws strip and crunch and chew,
> And know the flesh they rend and tear is you.
>
> (*Poems*, p. 74)

Poetry of this order is among the most intense being written in Australia today. It seeks to cope with the historic dilemma of the Australian writer by insisting on its personalness. But there are other writers who have kept their eyes turned outwards and have developed a means of using the Australian landscape which, while derived from the earlier writers, has taken on a new sophistication. A feature of a good deal of recent Australian writing has been its willingness to use an exploration of the bush as an analogy for the exploration of the individual soul. The bush becomes a metaphor for the self. Just as at the heart of the continent is a burning, insane emptiness, so too at the heart of a man is the horror of his prehistory. James McAuley's poem, 'Terra Australis', for instance, makes quite explicit the analogical uses to which the Australian land can be put:

> Voyage within you, on the fabled ocean,
> And you will find that Southern Continent,
> Quiros' vision—his hidalgo heart
> And mythical Australia, where reside
> All things in their imagined counterpart.
>
> It is your land of similes: the wattle
> Scatters its pollen on the doubting heart;
> The flowers are wide-awake; the air gives ease.
> There you come home; the magpies call you Jack
> And whistle like larrikins at you from the trees.
>
> There too the angophora preaches on the hillsides
> With the gestures of Moses; and the white cockatoo,
> Perched on his limbs, screams with demoniac pain;
> And who shall say on what errand the insolent emu
> Walks between morning and night on the edge of the plain?
>
> But northward in valleys of the fiery Goat
> Where the sun like a centaur vertically shoots
> His raging arrows with unerring aim,
> Stand the ecstatic solitary pyres
> Of unknown lovers, featureless with flame.
>
> (*Under Aldebaran*, p. 51).

Fiction, however, offers more extended opportunities for the landscape to be used in this manner. A novel which accepts such opportunities is Randolph Stow's *To the Islands*. Set in the north-west of Western Australia, it tells of an ageing missionary, Heriot, who abjures his faith, commits what he believes to be murder, and deliberately loses himself in the land in order to find himself. He strikes out 'to the islands', the phrase by which the local natives mean death. In this literal and metaphorical journey of self-discovery the word which recurs more than all others is 'nothing'. In a violent scene, before he flees from the mission, Heriot deliberately breaks a crucifix, symbolically shattering his old faith. 'I believe in nothing,' he says, 'I can pull down the world' (p. 75). And his thoughts are on nothingness until the ending of the book, when, with death approaching, his journey to the islands almost completed, he whispers to himself, 'My soul is a strange country' (p. 204). In the strange emptiness of the land and of his being, Heriot has found a kind of strength.

One of the most celebrated of recent Australian novels uses, like *To the Islands*, the exploration of the continent as an extended metaphor for the exploration of the soul. The richness of *Voss* can be accounted for, in part, by the fact that it fuses almost all those aspects of Australia's literary heritage which define both its modernity and its Australianness. The genuinely subversive drift of

White's thinking is brilliantly indicated in his earlier work, *The Aunt's Story*. The nature of this record of the progress of Theodora Goodman into insanity is set down with shattering clarity in the epigraphs which White appended to Sections II and III of his novel. Section II, 'Jardin Exotique', is preceded by a quotation from the American, Henry Miller, which concludes with the enlightening phrase, 'the great fragmentation of maturity'. Section III, 'Holstius', which chronicles the final and complete collapse of Theodora's reason, is headed by a single sentence from Olive Schreiner: 'When your life is most real, to me you are mad.' It might well stand as a text for many of the greatest achievements of Australian writing.

At the centre of *Voss* is the disturbing figure of the German explorer. White himself has indicated that this character was influenced by Hitler, 'the arch-megalomaniac of the day'. And Voss imposes his will on the small community he leads by exactly that process which Nietzsche diagnosed as the foundation of political life—the rationalization of cruelty. The distance between Patrick White and Price Warung may not be as great as we at first supposed. Voss lurches off into the fearful heart of Australia with his ill-assorted band of followers—lurches off first into contact with the land itself, ultimately with the continent's native race, those living representatives of humanity's pre-history. In the end, Voss is quite literally destroyed by the primal energies which he is obsessed to understand: the native boy Jacky severs his head from his body. With Voss, 'losing oneself to the point of self-destruction' becomes more than an idea, it is an actually achieved destiny. Before he reaches the end of his own life, he is responsible for the death of all his party save Judd, the tough commonsensical ex-convict who returns to civilization with his distorted account of the realities he has encountered beneath its bland surface. Palfreyman, the professional sufferer, perishes by the spears of the blacks; Le Mesurier, who has had faith both kindled and extinguished by Voss, slits his own throat—a curious descendant of Maurice Guest.

So Voss's mad determination to subdue the continent leads him to destruction at its unrelenting heart. He, too, finally comes to nothing. But his journey has not been in vain. As with Heriot in *To the Islands*, the very recognition of his nothingness becomes a means of salvation. It purges him of his burning pride and cruelty. At the moment of Voss's death, Laura Trevelyan, suffering in spiritual sympathy back in Sydney, rises up in her bed and cries:

> How important it is to understand the three stages. Of God into Man. Man. And man returning into God.... When man is truly humbled, when he has learnt that he is not God, then he is nearest to becoming so. In the end, he may ascend (p. 411).

Voss's journey from pride to the final void has taken him through suffering, humility, and love. It has educated him into humanity. It has not been in vain.

If the alien figure of Voss can fuse so many of the deeper forces which have gone to the making of our literature, one might expect that our native myth hero, Ned Kelly, would elicit from Australian writers some of their most profoundly representative work. In Douglas Stewart's treatment of the outlaw, for instance, it is easy to point to many characteristic Australian traits—the hatred of authority, the masculine vigour and toughness, the outback independence, the refusal to admit defeat. Phillips, in his essay in *The Australian Tradition*, has gone beyond these obvious symptoms of nationality. 'Australian Romanticism and Stewart's *Ned Kelly*' (pp. 96-112) represents the play as a contest between the forces of Vitality and Respectability, or, as Phillips symbolizes the struggle, between Ulysses and Telemachus. This is a reading which clearly has much to recommend it; but also embodied in the very essence of the drama are some of those darker elements of Romanticism which, I suggest, have been so consistently present to the Australian literary imagination.

Ned, Joe Byrne, and the rest of the gang may posses the vitality of Ulysses, the willingness to 'give-it-a-go' we traditionally expect of the Australian. But in the end the energies which dominate Ned in particular are not so much vital as mortal. He strives towards death rather than life; and in this enterprise he is closely attended by the self-destructive irony of Joe Byrne. Their path to death leads through the madness of the Australian bush. For all Ned's talk of outback freedom, what emerges most strongly from the play is a sense of hatters baying at the moon, of the subversion that the bush works on those who commit themselves to its primitive keeping. Ned's vision, a distortion of our rational Australian values, becomes the nightmare of madness.

The dreams of freedom and power which bring Ned to death are not presented as a purely personal affair. Throughout the play, the verse works to make him not so much the representative Australian as the representative of Australia. He incarnates the spirit of the land. And in this incarnation he does not stand in direct opposition to the Respectable (the Livings, the Tarletons, and the rest). It is not simply Ulysses *versus* Telemachus. The Kelly gang and the men they rob are complementary, needing each other to complete a single image of the Australian spirit. Ned and his mates are betrayed by those they have loved (Aaron Sherritt) or those who profess to love them (Curnow); they are destroyed by the men to whom they are tied by the indestructible bonds of hate. 'What happens is the people's doing,' says Byrne; 'and if they hang him,/They hang themselves' (*Four Plays*, p. 213). In the wild shouts of the troopers who close in on Ned in the last scene there is the fierce joy of those who are destroying part of themselves. It is the final paradox of *Ned Kelly* that Ned's expansive dreams can be realized only in death; that those who, in self-protection, destroy him extinguish in so doing their own most vital spirit.

And in that paradox lies the clue to our literary tradition. The canon of our writing presents a façade of mateship, egalitarian democracy, landscape, nationalism, realistic toughness. But always behind the façade looms the fundamental concern of the Australian literary imagination. That concern, marked out by our national origins and given direction by geographic necessity, is to acknowledge the terror at the basis of being, to explore its uses, and to build defences against its dangers. It is that concern which gives Australia's literary heritage its special force and distinction, which guarantees its continuing modernity.

RANDOLPH STOW   (1935–)

Poet, novelist. Born and educated in W.A.; lives in England.

RAW MATERIAL

As I remember, what the editors of *Westerly* suggested I should write in this page or two was a personal account of the problems one meets with in attempting to turn the Australian environment into literature. I was in England at that stage, and after listening many times to questions like: "What sort of climate has Australia?" the Australian environment was beginning to seem a pretty neat little entity, that one competent novelist might dispose of for ever, if the painters hadn't done so already.

But when one thinks about it from closer at hand, "environment" as the artist meets it is almost too complex a thing to be written about at all. The boundary between an individual and his environment is not his skin. It is the point where mind verges on the pure essence of him, that unchanging observer that for want of a better term we must call the soul. The external factors, geographical and sociological, are so mingled with his ways of seeing and states of mind that he may find it impossible to say what he means by his environment, except in the most personal and introspective terms. In a work of art, these are the terms the artist will use. But in a straight essay, he may run into difficulties.

Still, there is undoubtedly an Australian environment "out there", outside one's annotating psyche. And there are a number of acute and sensitive students of it (Sydney Baker, Russel Ward, J. D. Pringle, Robin Boyd, to name four) whose work is appearing in print. There is no need for me to summarize their conclusions. We know about our democratic temperament, our love of sport, our depressing tolerance, and even worship, of the second-rate. We also know about our beaches (will they ever stop telling us about our beaches?), and we know that most of us live in the capital cities. This is what a sociologist means by "The Australian Environment".

Admiring and enjoying this sort of anthropological study as I do, when I try to relate it to the work of a writer I have to admit that it is almost irrelevant. A poet may find in it the inspiration for a poem or two, a novelist might get an idea for a chapter, or a couple of characters. But this abstract "Environment" is really nobody's environment. It has no observer. It is like Ronald Knox's tree when there's no-one about in the Quad. And I can't believe that a writer with any sort of self-awareness would be able to say of it: "This is my raw material."

This ought to be obvious. But it seems it's not, if one can judge by some of the exhortations directed at Australian writers. To say to a writer: "Why don't you write about the washing-machine industry?" or: "By neglecting the cities, you are ignoring seventy per cent of the population" is to equate art with sociology and journalism.

The environment of a writer is as much inside him as in what he observes; and if, from a stern sense of duty, he sets out to re-create the environments of a number of others from purely external data he is likely to come to grief. He may, if he is a near-genius, feel himself into those environments (or, more accurately, incorporate them in his own) so completely that they become his for the time being: but this rarely happens, and that is the weakness of social realism. It is also the temptation to which Australian novelists, with so much land to play around in, are most liable, and when they succumb the results show in the characters—"character" being a part of environment in this sense. Where the characters are flat and the author seems bored, we can be pretty sure he has moved out of his territory. But when the author triumphantly succeeds in creating a character which makes his best friends wonder if they have ever known him—when Shakespeare, for instance, creates a Timon, or Milton a Satan, or Emily Bronte a Heathcliff—we can be equally sure that his environment is a much broader and stranger territory than even best friends could guess at.

I conclude, therefore, that no creative artist in this country can talk about "the Australian environment" in relation to his work, and imagine that he has made anything but the most superficial statement about it. It must be "my environment" always, or at most "my environment here in Australia". There is a feeling of Australia in the landscapes of Drysdale and Nolan, but essentially they are mindscapes of the artists. And from there, Albert Tucker has found it a short step to the moon.

The feeling, the sense, what a Spaniard would call the *sentimiento* of Australia: the external forms filtered back through the conscious and unconscious mind; that is what these artists convey, and what I

would hope to convey if I were capable of executing all I can conceive. In that sense, the world out there is raw material. But only
part of it—all the rest is mind.

So—one is obliged to introspect.

There are two sensations, above all, that the land offers me: the
sense of size, and the sense of the past.

Size is obvious. It *is* a huge country, however often the journalists
may say so, and the distances are vast. But size itself is a complex of
feelings. When one is alone with it, one feels in one way very small,
in another gigantic. One expects something. One is a little like
Adam, perhaps. In the cities, personality is fenced in by the personalities of others. But alone in the bush, with maybe a single crow
(and that sound on a still day widens the world by half) a phrase like
"liberation of the spirit" may begin to sound meaningful.

The sense of the past is linked with this vastness. It is a country in
which one can be aware of a tremendous range of time. It is very
easy to feel—even to "remember"—the period when there was no
animal life on earth. And on the hottest days, in the most desolate
places, it is possible to know, almost kinetically, the endurance of
things.

There is too, and naturally in a country that has been changed so
rapidly by man in so few years, a sense of human history, and in a
way that short history is a précis of the whole career of man. I feel
this strongly, and find it an advantage to have been born of two
pioneer families, one of a city and one of the bush, which often
reminisced and sometimes wrote their reminiscences down. Those
men who fought natives and planted orchards and built homesteads
and churches might have been the ancestors of the human race, not
only of Australia. They were the archetypal settlers St John Perse
invokes in *Anabase*:

> Followers of trails, of seasons, breakers of camp in the small wind of
> the dawn; O seekers of waterholes over the bark of the world; O
> seekers, O finders of reasons to be up and be gone....

So that what, in the end, I see in Australia (so far only in the bush,
but that need not be the end of it) is an enormous symbol: a symbol
for the whole earth, at all times, both before and during the history
of man. And because of its bareness, its absolute simplicity, a truer
and broader symbol of the human environment than, I believe, any
European writer could create from the complex material of Europe.

What it means, every observer will interpret for himself, and interpret differently at different times and in different places. In its
skeletal passivity it will haunt and it will endure.

I am conscious of gaping cracks in this attempt to relate "my
environment" to some theoretical Australian literature. It is full of
bias (against social realism, for instance, when it is no more than

that) and probably useless to anyone but myself. But there is a concept behind it: the concept of a literature based on figures in a landscape, more naked and disturbing than a Border ballad or a Spanish *romance*, in which eternal things are observed with, always, the eyes of the newborn.

This will spring partly from the outward, measurable environment. But, for the rest—

"*J'habiterai mon nom....*"

"I will live in my name," says St John Perse's Stranger among the sands. It is inevitable.

DUST

"Enough," she said. But the dust still rained around her:
over her living room (hideous, autumnal)
dropping its small defiance.
                              The clock turned green.
She spurned her broom and took a train. The neighbours
have heard nothing.

Jungles, deserts, stars—the six days of creation—
came floating in, gold on a chute of light.
In May, grudging farmers admired the carpet
and foretold a rich year.

Miraculous August! What shelves of yellow capeweed,
what pouffes of everlastings. We worship nature
in my country.

Never such heath as flowered on the virgin slopes
of the terrible armchairs. Never convolvulus
brighter than that which choked the china dogs.
Bushwalkers' Clubs boiled their billies with humility
in chimneys where orchids and treesnakes
luxuriantly intertwined.

A photographer came from *The West Australian*, and ten
teenage reportresses. Teachers of botany
overflowed to the garden.

Indeed, trains were run from Yalgoo and Oodnadatta.
But the neighbours slept behind sealed doors, with feather
dusters beside their beds.

LANDSCAPES

A crow cries: and the world unrolls like a blanket;
like a worn bush blanket, charred at the horizons.

But the butcherbird draws all in; that voice is a builder
of roofless cathedrals and claustrophobic forests
—and one need not notice walls, so huge is the sky.

In the morning, waking, one is most in love.
It is then that the cool convection of song and echo
wells in the clearings, and all is possible.

It is then you are not there. We meet after noon.
In the wrack of the crow. In a desert of broken quartz.

NAN McDONALD   (1921–1974)

Poet. Born and educated in Sydney.

WET SUMMER: BOTANIC GARDENS

Under the low dark sky and the sodden leaves
Poor Summer bared her shoulder with coy grace,
Her marble flesh streaked with mortality,
Her sheaf of wheat lay mildewed on her arm,
Her eyes stared vacant from her tear-stained face
On paths empty at noon, on glooms beneath
Great fig-trees, where the drop of rotting fruit
Broke the warm, damp hush, or unbelievable green
Of wet grass still unfaded by the sun
In this strange season. Once we laughed to see
That foolish white thing named for the brazen queen
Whose sword we knew, the fierce and splendid one.

But tonight, alone with the steady sound of rain,
I do not smile, seeing her image there
On the haunted edge of sleep—the blackening marble,
The blind and weeping eyes, the ruined grain—
Seeing this season of the world's despair.

DAY OF THE EARTHQUAKE

It is one thing to know with the mind only
All flesh must die, another to see the cold

Skull-shape behind the smile of friend or kin;
One thing to have read how this world shall wax old
As a garment, and its glory pass away,
Another to hear that deep, strange sound begin
In the still morning, rumbling through the hills,
See, unbelieving, your walls lurch and sway,
Run from the house, while startled voices meet:
"Has the mine blown up?" "Or is it—?"
   No man-made ills
But earth itself foundering beneath our feet.

So quickly over, as though it had not been
Again in the soft light the mountains floated
Calm as on any other autumn day,
The eagle cliffs of Keira overhead
And little Nebo, steep and smooth and green
As a hill painted for a fairytale,
And over its shoulder Kembla's dark crest rearing
To watch the blue coast and the drowsy sail.

And all day long I gazed, my eyes not filled,
Printing my heart with their familiar grace
Till the last whip-bird cried, till evening chilled
The highest golden rock and dimmed the sea—
As having seen on a beloved face
The shadow, the spasm of mortality.

Martin Boyd   (1893–1972)

Novelist. Born in Lucerne, Switzerland; educated in Melbourne;
moved between Australia and England until settling in Rome in
later years.

THE LIGHT ON THE SEA

from MUCH ELSE IN ITALY

Santa Margherita-Ligure was like a painting by Dufy. Everything
was blue and fun. We went straight down to bathe where the sea
stretched placid and shimmering towards Africa. The bathers were
nearly naked and a golden brown, but they had little blue enamel
medals of the Madonna round their necks. Before they went into
the water they dipped in their hands and crossed themselves three
times. We thought at first that they must have mistaken the
Mediterranean for a holy water stoup, and then realized that it is the

holy water of our civilization. They live naturally and unconsciously in the two Stories. From near by the water-skiers set out, skimming gloriously over the waves like souls set free, the modern equivalent of the boy on the dolphin.

In the town the baroque churches with their onion spires, and their interiors sparkling with gold and every kind of prettiness, exist in their own right, and have not superimposed themselves on more venerable beauties. There are no 'tormentose nostalgie del divino' and even where the images bleed we feel that they are really Mrs Siddons.

In the evening the town was like a stage set for musical comedy. We dined out of doors, overlooking the harbour, and expected that at any moment a man might appear on a balcony and sing to the accompaniment of an orchestra which was playing in a sort of garden-restaurant. This did not happen, but a religious procession came along the street, carrying a number of large crucifixes ornamented with elaborate gold filigree. The huge swaying figures looked rather dreadful, especially when they had to be lowered under the electric-light wires, but they did not provoke any reaction from the Irish boy, who had declared that for the next ten days he had no intention of using his brains in any way, excepting to order his dinner, and then they would be under the direction of his stomach. The orchestra stopped playing as the procession passed.

Every day we spent in and out of the water, and lunched under ceilings of hanging grapes. Nowhere was anything but pleasure, and yet the people did not seem to have less contact with the noumena than in the holy places of Assisi and Rome. In the gilded churches there was always a handful of people come to place themselves under their protection; every evening the Maddalenas loudly chanted their rosaries; the little girls made their flying curtsies, and the *putti* occupied themselves fussily in the sanctuary. On Sunday at the sung mass the cathedral was packed, but in this gaudy brilliance the congregation was as quiet and reverent as in the austerity of S. Anselmo. The young priest, with a kind and honest face, walked about the town with his crew of children.

On the ninth day of this wise but brainless life, our last in Italy, we climbed the hill above the town to the west, walking up steep and rugged pathways and along narrow tracks between the terraces where the afternoon sun slanted through the olives. We passed little farm-houses, hidden amongst their vines, heavy with purple grapes, and fruit trees laden with pears and apples. Ripe plums squashed under our feet. The little gardens with zinnias and tomatoes were irrigated through bamboo pipes, and the silence was only broken by the trickling water.

'It is like something in the *Odyssey*,' said the Irish boy. 'This is the eternal pattern of life for mankind, each with his own vine and his own fig tree. This is how we should live, in the enclosed garden of the natural world, in scale with our surroundings, worshipping the noumena of the place, giving them occasionally gifts of fruit and putting flowers between the feet of Hermes. This is the paradise that we really long for.'

Soon we came on to the piazza of Nozzarego, and as we did so a procession came out of the church. They carried a statue of the Virgin, surrounded with flowers and candles and banners. They were all enjoying themselves. No one was particularly solemn, and a boy whose cassock was too short for him, showing his comic white socks, turned round to gossip with another behind him. The procession moved away along the track between the sunlit olive trees, and again the afternoon fell into silence.

It was the Feast of the Assumption, which in his periods of over-cerebration had given the Irish boy so much concern. When we reminded him of this he brushed it aside.

'That sort of thing doesn't matter,' he said. 'These people are living in the Story. They are living the best sort of natural life, but illuminated by the noumena. They are the sort of people from whom exhausted humanity always has to renew itself.'

We walked down by a different way, past more Odyssean farms. From the bend of the lane we saw the promontory of Portofino, sleeping on the flat and vivid sea. Below us two water-skiers behind the same boat were weaving ecstatic curves, and in the delight of the flesh seeming to transcend it. We had come into what was surely the most complete paradise possible on this earth, equal to the heights of Ravello, beyond the dreams of Beato Angelico. And somehow it seemed that the Assumption of the Virgin was connected with all this delight, that the material beauty was raised into heaven, in a way which we who do not use our minds could feel but not understand.

In the evening we began to collect our things, ready to leave on the next day, but after dinner the Irish boy went out for a walk. In a short time he returned, his face alight with excitement.

'You must come out,' he said, 'it's marvellous.'

We replied that we wanted to pack, that the afternoon's walk had been a perfect end to our tour, and we did not want to see anything more.

'But this is much better,' he exclaimed. 'The sea! It's a miracle!'

He was so insistent that reluctantly we went with him down to the harbour. Almost as far as we could see, beyond the point of Rapallo and away to the mole on our right, the water was shimmering with the soft golden light of thousands of candles, floating in cardboard holders. Men in boats were rowing about lighting more candles and setting them on the water. The effect was indescribably lovely, the most beautiful form of illumination we have ever known.

The Irish boy said that the boat of the materialistic scientist could not float in that water. We suggested that perhaps it had capsized and he was drowned. The poor man finds his soul in the hands of the powers in which he does not believe. The evil noumena rush like a wind to a vacuum to fill his emptiness, while the good noumena, who do not understand English, and so are only aware of his desire to be honest and not of his intellectual statements, for the sake of this try to rescue him, and he finds himself the very battlefield of the war in heaven. His sufferings are appalling, but he will finally be delivered through our prayers and his own desire for honesty.

There is, however, another boat out there, and one far more menacing. We can just discern amongst those leaning over the side, trying to feel a tingling in their finger-tips, a man in a green jacket against which there is a white dot, which might be a weekly paper. He is, rather oddly, a guest on a millionaire's yacht, but the millionaire is also a Communist who hopes after the revolution to become a supercommissar owing to his great managerial efficiency, and so make little alteration in his way of life. He is at the moment engaged in smashing any small businesses and farms that remain, the units of English freedom and potential mirrors of Bethlehem, a project equally dear to the heart of the man with the *New Statesman.* As neither of them have any conception of the Perfect Drawing, of the divine humanity which should inform our society, they are like a pair of architects with the most up-to-date equipment, a complete knowledge of strains and stresses, but with not the faintest idea of what a house should look like, or what kind of people should live in it.

The yacht pushed its way among the candles, swamping many of them, hiding the light of others from the shore, so that the owner could have a close-up of what only should be seen with worship from afar.

The Irish boy was horrified and distressed. There were angry tears in his eyes.

'I would rather be the poorest fisherman lighting those candles,' he said, 'than the owner of the yacht that is putting them out.'

From this statement it seemed that his search was rewarded. For he had, at the centre of his being, renounced the world; not the natural world, the enclosed garden which is our home, but the evil world which exploits it for the gratification of senseless lusts, of the tingling insulated from the heart, and of power and of pride.

At Paestum in May the earth was covered with flowers around the temple of Ceres, the mother of the fruitful earth and of our bodies. At Santa Margherita in August the sea was covered with light in honour of the Mother of Christ and of our souls. The two Stories, the Greek story and the Gospel story, the first redeemed by the second, had combined to meet his double nature, and in them, in spite of all stumbling-blocks, he will live and move and have his being.

EXPATRIATE

from DAY OF MY DELIGHT

I had vaguely thought that coming to live in Rome, I would be entering a sort of Maurice Baring world of immense culture and distinction; or be like Mrs G. who spent her ten years here talking to princes. I do not know whether this would have been possible, as I did not present the few letters of introduction I had. I do not believe that men over sixty like going to parties. Walter Savage Landor said that it was barbaric for more than two people to dine together. I would increase the number to four, possibly, among old friends, to six. Anyhow, when I may have had the chance of entering a society which thirty years earlier I would have thought dazzling, I no longer had the inclination for it.

My chief human interest was in Luciano and when I wanted the society of my own countrymen I could go to the English Centre, where I met people of every sort, some of whom have in time become my good friends.

But this time in Rome has been unrelated to all that had gone before, which fact slowly and subconsciously has had the effect of enabling me to see that previous life with complete objectivity. The result of that detached vision I hope to give in the final chapter. Here, as the excuse for my autobiography, apart from ordinary human evidence, is the fact that I am a writer, I shall give a short review of myself in that capacity.

Everybody's literary career begins at school, but with the majority of people it ends there. I wrote verses for the school magazine, *The Mitre*, and for my last two years I was its editor. But many other boys also wrote verses as good, or better than mine. Once when we were studying *Pride and Prejudice*, the headmaster pointed out how Jane Austen, instead of describing her characters, conveyed their reality by their actions. I had no idea then of being a novelist or any kind of writer, but this remained in my mind as the essence of good fiction, and I think has influenced the intention of all my novels. This was only brought into my conscious mind two years ago, when I read an essay on my work by Doctor Leonie Kramer of the University of New South Wales. She writes of my "highly original method of depicting" my characters; and of my "chief interest—the description of character in the making".

After the war, disturbed by the loss of and separation from friends, I wrote some poems in the style of Rupert Brooke, but this was chiefly to express my feelings.

Again, when I left Batcombe, I wanted to express my feelings, and this time I did it in a novel, as I have related. When this was accepted by Constables, I naturally wrote another, and when this was also accepted I considered myself a novelist. I was not anything else. Constables accepted yet a third book *The Montforts*. All these books were published under a pseudonym, but lately *the Montforts* was republished under my own name, like the belated recognition of an illegitimate child. The other two and the pseudonym I wish forgotten. Completely unknown as I was, Constables gave me more generous terms for these than I have had for my latest books. I had to deal with Michael Sadlier, who was helpful and courteous, while Otto Kyllman, the then chairman of the firm, came out and gave me encouraging words.

But I am not exclusively, or chiefly a writer. At one time the phrase "life and letters" was often used. With me life comes a long way before letters, and I believe that life is for delight. If some phase of life or some incident gives me this, or if it evokes a sense of its pathos, or a repudiation of cruelty or injustice, I want to perpetuate that in writing as clear and vivid as I can make it. When I have done so, I do not want to go on writing until I have a new impulse, not as a man goes on making wheelbarrows, though if he is a good craftsman he will have some feeling for his wheelbarrows.

I have heard literary people talk about "new ways of using words" as if this was the whole purpose of "contemporary" writing. This is putting the symbol above the reality, like putting money above the goods it represents, which in the Myth is the Idolatry of the Golden Calf. Idolatry is usually thought of as a rather foolish but harmless veneration of images. It is something much more serious, a corrupt attitude of mind, which in public life is almost universal today.

It is the quality of a man's imagination, his sense of values and his powers of observation that make him a good writer, and he must have an adequate command of words to express himself. But the most brilliant ability to arrange words in new patterns, without these three things, will not make him good. The greatness of a novel depends on its content of humanity.

A Melbourne critic not long ago wrote that I was an amateur. She stated this as one of my failings, but as when the young man in Sussex told me I had the face of a mediaeval peasant, I was very pleased at her censure. Some of the greatest novelists have been amateur. Tolstoy was a soldier, a nobleman, and a peasant, not a professional writer. It was his powerful imagination and sense of humanity that made him great. Flaubert struggled for six years to produce *Madame Bovary*, his only real achievement. He did not sit down and write it straight off with professional competence. Proust was obsessed by the society of the Faubourg St Germain. It set his essential self purring creatively. Its rich twilight glows and fades through the pages of his great novel, but it is full of technical faults that a professional writer would have avoided. They do not matter.

The above critic wrote of "the capacity for hard work" as one of the marks of a good writer. It may be of the professional, but not of the truly creative writer. He does not work, he functions. He cannot do this until his essential self, the Holy Ghost in him, begins to purr. He cannot produce by cerebration alone, however hard he tries.

This has a correspondence with the difference between talent and genius. These two things are different in kind not in degree, as Dallas Kenmare has shown in *The Nature of Genius*. The talented writer can turn on the tap of his ability at any moment, the genius has to wait for the spark from heaven, or rather for the dynamo of his essential self to function. The merit of his work depends on the quality of his essential self alone. It is not necessarily better than that of a man of talent. It is possible for it to be worse.

A few days ago I walked into an exhibition of paintings. They were inspired, but they were hideous and depraved. The colours were cold blue-grey and black. A naked woman, her body covered with huge black sores, was getting into bed. Two men, who looked the personifications of intellectual cruelty, filthy torturers, were seated motionless at two tables. One felt one was in hell. They were the work of an evil genius, and they were bad. The critics assume that because works like these I have described provoke a powerful reaction, they have great merit, but it is only the same reaction as when one sees the decaying corpse of a dog in the gutter. It does not need a work of art to produce it. In writing any fool can produce a bad character, and evoke vividly a scene of filth. He is merely stimulating a physical reaction to squalor, and in time giving weak characters a taste for it. It needs far more skill, with sympathy and subtle observation to portray a good character, or to make a scene of beauty vivid.

The truly great work of art of course must have genius. Talent alone cannot produce it. The old saying that genius is the capacity for taking infinite pains is nonsense. The genius lost in creative frenzy is not consciously taking infinite pains. He is merely allowing his essential self to function, which may involve the infinite pains.

However, perhaps it is enough to repeat what is often said, that the novelist must be a poet in his apprehensions. The true critic must also have those apprehensions. Though he lacks the ability to use them creatively, he can recognise them in the work of another, and share in the act of creation by helping the reader to do the same. Such critics are few. The modern idea that literary critics can be "scientifically trained" is resulting in grotesque absurdities. Last week I read in the first paragraph alone of a review in a highbrow weekly the following phrases:

"alienation from modern assumptions";
"The essence of the novelist's art is the quotidian";

"The wound-and-bow psychological theory";
"methodological inferences".

It must be great fun concocting this jargon, but it has no connection with the poetic intuition which is essential to the criticism of works of art. Apart from this pretentious clique, there was up to about ten years ago a large body of conscientious reviewers, competent to deal with the bulk of newly published fiction. I am now coming to how this affects my own story.

Up to about that time I was nearly always treated fairly and sometimes very well by reviewers. If I had an unfavourable review it was a rational judgment, not an outburst of spleen. Since then a large proportion of my reviews have been quite unprincipled. I give some examples:

A reviewer, a Roman Catholic, in a leading London newspaper dismissed my book, *Much Else in Italy*, with an insolent snarl. The book showed much sympathy with Roman Catholicism, but also contained some sharp criticism. I protested to the literary editor, who gave as sufficient excuse that the reviewer "was irritated by something written in the blurb" which I had not written!

Another writer of a malicious review gave as sufficient excuse that he "was temperamentally opposed to me".

While writing a passage in the above book, I thought: "If anyone liked to lift this out of its context, he could make me look a complete fool. But I don't suppose anyone would be so low as that." But a reviewer in a leading Sunday newspaper was so low.

Since then I have had reviews of extraordinary guttersnipe abuse. Other present-day reviewers have developed a technique of supercilious belittlement, which can be applied to any work, great or trivial. Here is how one of these might review, say, *Romeo and Juliet*:

"This is the saccharine tale of a couple of Italian teenagers suffering from erotomania, whose respective parents have had a row, which prevents the pair from getting into bed together. There is every sort of cheap stage device, moonlit balconies and the rest. The play wades drearily through moanings and murders, until we end up practically in a morgue. It has, I suppose, a few lines of lyrical adroitness, which I must admit set my teeth on edge, but which may titillate the palates of those over sixty."

This method can be used on anything, as a typhoid germ can destroy equally a man of the finest intelligence or a half-wit. My last two or three books, whether good or bad, were submitted to a proportion of reviews of this kind.

Many of the reviewers are also publishers' readers, and so are in almost complete control of the literary world. It seems to me that a high proportion of these are intellectual delinquents, while the remainder support the Establishment. To neither kind am I acceptable.

Living in Italy, I did not quite realise what was happening until about five years ago. I had a letter from my agent telling me that "fiction today" must be "violent, outspoken and crudely sexual". To say that fiction today must be anything except what the author chooses to write about, and present with his individual vision, struck me as odd, but to tell an author of established reputation that in his middle sixties he must begin to write filth astonished me. I replied that I preferred to fade out than to trade in pornography and that practically finished my literary career.

I should have realised earlier what was happening. C. P. Snow had said to me, referring to some novelist: "Fiction isn't going that way." I remember a vague feeling of surprise that fiction should be regarded as a mass-produced commodity, and "go" in a certain direction, like the design of motor cars.

While I was at Trumpington, George, who was literary adviser to Murrays, came down for occasional week-ends, bringing me beautiful bottles of *Château Mouton Rothschild*, and suggesting that I should submit my next book to Murrays. C. P. Snow had also told me that when he changed to Macmillans his sales went up by tens of thousands. I thought that Murrays were the same kind of old-established publisher, and would have the same effect on me. I also heard that they were very gentlemanly, and I imagined that they were one of those mythological firms who, having taken an author, would back him up in his characteristic work, even if it brought in little money. So I gave them the manuscript of *Outbreak of Love*. They told me on the day I signed the contract, that it would not be published for a year, and they refused my next book, *Much Else in Italy*. I heard later from an outside source that it was thought to be extremely blasphemous. When it was published by Macmillans, but without the effect enjoyed by C. P. Snow, it was given in the *Church Times* two columns of the highest praise I have ever had. I decided to avoid very gentlemanly firms in future. But I had no future.

My next and last novel *When Blackbirds Sing* had a strange history, due I think to its subject, but I shall leave the reader to judge.

My aim was to show the awakening of a young man, caught in the 1914 war, to the reality of what he was doing, and to spotlight the essential act of murder; but I wrote to appeal to the minds and not to the glands of the reader, which is expected in war fiction today. As this is the most important negative preoccupation of my life, I wrote with all the cold intensity of which I am capable, suppressing any impulse to be witty or irrelevant.

My agent was evidently delighted with the manuscript, and wrote to me enthusiastically, addressing me as "Dear Boyd" dropping the "Mr." which is a sure sign that an agent or publisher thinks a book is going to pay. When *Lucinda* was so successful I had a pink and personal Christmas card from my then agent—the first in fourteen years of association.

When the book at last was published, one of the best critics in England wrote to me that it was the "most real and compelling book I had written" and that it had "the stark necessity of a Sophocles tragedy". A university lecturer, a Litt. D., wrote to me praising it highly, and saying it was my best book. Olivia Manning, reviewing it in the *Sunday Times*, wrote of "my power of conveying emotional profundity" and said that "when time had sorted things out" I would have "an enduring place among the writers of my time." An American reviewer wrote that just as he was beginning to despair of modern fiction, a book would come along to restore his faith, and *When Blackbirds Sing* was one of these. I had several letters of appreciation from friends who had never written to me before about my books. Last year over eighteen months after its publication, I saw it in two public libraries and took it down to see how much it had been read. It had been out steadily every fortnight since it had appeared, while works of the best known authors on the same shelves had only been out half a dozen times.

Very well—it seems odd that a book with these appreciations should be so bad that it could not find a publisher. Yet this is what happened for about five years. It was refused by nearly every leading publisher in London, not one of whom gave a genuine reason for his refusal; and I happen to know that it had had some excellent readers' reports. Finally it was taken by a small American firm, who took four months to give a decision, and a further year to publish it. Their terms were far below those given me by Constables for my first novel.

It seems clear that the theme of the novel was the reason for its rejection. One critic said to me: "No one could go to war again after reading that book."

But on its publication an even more curious phenomenon occurred. I had been used to having sheaves of reviews. My last novel had been praised in every leading paper, and I was recognised in England, if not in Australia, as one of the two major novelists of the latter country. If I had written a very bad book, it was a matter of literary interest and an item of news; but except for the *Sunday Times* review, which somehow slipped through, *When Blackbirds Sing* was received in dead silence. A man in the literary world told me that this must be a deliberate conspiracy, I did not see how this could be possible, though I had other evidence that it might be. Anyhow, I accepted that England was no longer a country where "a man may speak the thing he will". This present book I hope will prove that I am wrong.

Shortly after this, I received my agent's request for pornography and gave up what no longer seemed to me a reputable profession. All this killed the Langton sequence, which I had intended should cover one hundred years.

In 1961 I took to drawing and painting, and last year held an exhibition of my work in Cambridge, risking the accusation hurled at any of my relatives who does this, that I was cashing in on my nephew Arthur's success.

The impulse behind my painting was to show man living untrammelled in delight in the natural world. There were boys riding on dolphins; Europa on the bull; a series of donkey boys escaped to freedom, eating the golden apples of paradise and meeting the goose girls, overcome with hilarity; Spartans dancing; and Children of the Sun.

Friends told me that entering the gallery with all these golden brown bodies in graceful antics round the wall, gave them a feeling of great cheerfulness.

The vicar's wife said they were disgusting.

DOROTHY HEWETT   (1923–)

Poet, playwright, novelist. Born and educated in Perth; lives in Sydney.

IN MIDLAND WHERE THE TRAINS GO BY

In Midland still the trains go by,
The black smoke thunders on the sky,
Still in the grass the lovers lie.
And cheek on cheek and sigh on sigh
They dream and weep as you and I,
In Midland where the trains go by.

Across the bridge, across the town,
The workers hurry up and down.
The pub still stands, the publican
Is still a gross, corrupted man.
And bottles clinking in the park
Make symphonies of summer dark.

Across the bridge the stars go down,
Our two ghosts meet across the town.
Who dared so much must surely creep
Between young lovers lips, asleep,
Who dared so much must surely live
In train-smoke off the Midland bridge.

In Midland, in the railway yards,
They shuffle time like packs of cards
And kings and queens and jacks go down,
But we come up in Midland town.

O factory girls in cotton slips
And men with grease across your lips,
Let kings and queens and jacks go down
But we'll still kiss in Midland town.

An oath, a whisper and a laugh,
Will make our better epitaph.
We'll share a noggin in the park
And whistle songs against the dark.
There is no death that we can die
In Midland, where the trains go by.

ONCE I RODE WITH CLANCY...

Once I rode with Clancy through the wet hills of Wickepin,
By Kunjin and Corrigin with moonlight on the roofs,
And the iron shone faint and ghostly on the lonely moonlit siding
And the salt earth rang like crystal underneath our flying hoofs.

O once I rode with Clancy when my white flesh was tender,
And my hair a golden cloud along the wind,
Among the hills of Wickepin, the dry salt plains of Corrigin,
Where all my Quaker forebears strove and sinned.

Their black hats went bobbing through the Kunjin churchyard,
With great rapacious noses, sombre-eyed,
Ringbarked gums and planted pine trees, built a raw church
In a clearing, made it consecrated ground because they died.

From this seed I spring— the dour and sardonic Quaker men,
The women with hooked noses, baking bread,
Breeding, hymning, sowing, fencing off the stony earth,
That salts their bones for thanksgiving when they're dead.

It's a country full of old men, with thumbscrews on their hunger,
Their crosses leaning sideways in the scrub.
My cousins spit to windward, great noses blue with moonlight,
Their shoulders propping up the Kunjin pub.

O once I rode with Clancy through the wet hills of Wickepin,
By Kunjin and Corrigin with moonlight on the roofs,
And the iron shone faint and ghostly on the lonely, moonlit siding
And the salt earth rang like crystal underneath our flying hoofs.

And the old men rose muttering and cursed us from the graveyard
When they saw our wild white hoofs go flashing by,
For I ride with landless Clancy and their prayers are at my back,
They can shout out strings of curses on the sky.

By Wickepin, by Corrigin, by Kunjin's flinty hills,
On wild white hoofs that kindle into flame,
The river is my mirror, the wattle tree our roof,
Adrift across our bed like golden rain.

Let the old men clack and mutter, let their dead eyes run with rain.
I hear the crack of doom across the scrub,
For though I ride with Clancy there is much of me remains,
In that moonlit dust outside the Kunjin pub.

My golden hair has faded, my tender flesh is dark,
My voice has learned a wet and windy sigh
And I lean above the creekbed, catch my breath upon a ghost,
With a great rapacious nose and sombre eye.

JOHN BLIGHT   (1913–)

Poet. Born in South Australia; lives in Queensland.

THE BEACHCOMBER

I have lit upon the old man's secret, know
the error on his brow is like the error
of the fragile waves whose mirror
after mirror crashing, builds yet its character. So
I know he likes the ocean beach best, will escape
only on Sundays to the lee of the cape.
It is his converse with the breakers, playing ducks
and drakes with our conventions, make him somebody
excusable: one man like a poet, shoddy
in morals, quarrelsome, who bucks
society, and, for his sane rebuke,
is allotted the space-room of the beach;
respected there, given a friendly look
if they can nail him; sought for his fish-tall speech.

SEA LEVEL

Over this flat-pan sea, this mud haven,
This shelf of the sea-floor, sea birds paddle
And the red mud raddles the sea.
You are on creation's level. Proven

Your lowly origin, where, in one puddle,
Sea-snails and your toes agree—
The same spasms and rhythms. Stub
On a rock, or a sharp stab of a beak;
They draw in. Pain is the one language
Spoken to them. You, in the sky, snub
Your feet. Impediments! But can you take
Your brain's cloud and drift, disengage
The body's pawns? Try: disconnect
The thought from their feeling, and soon
The soul is wrecked.

ROSEMARY DOBSON   (1920–)

Poet. Born and educated in Sydney; lives in Canberra.

STILL LIFE

Tall glass, round loaf and tumbled cloth
And leaning flask of smoky brown,
The guttered candle and the cask;
And Time and Silence flowing down,

Welling against the canvas, held
By stroke and feather-touch of paint
As one might build a weir to hold
Some spreading pool in sweet restraint.

Whose was the hand that held the brush?
And who the guest who came to break
The loaf which I, three hundred years
Belated, still reach out to take?

I, who now pour the wine and tilt
The glass, would wish that well you fare,
Good sir, who set out food and drink
That all who see might take and share.

COCK CROW

Wanting to be myself, alone,
Between the lit house and the town
I took the road, and at the bridge
Turned back and walked the way I'd come.

Three times I took that lonely stretch,
Three times the dark trees closed me round,
The night absolved me of my bonds;
Only my footsteps held the ground.

My mother and my daughter slept,
One life behind and one before,
And I that stood between denied
Their needs in shutting-to the door.

And walking up and down the road
Knew myself, separate and alone,
Cut off from human cries, from pain,
And love that grows about the bone.

Too brief illusion! Thrice for me
I heard the cock crow on the hill
And turned the handle of the door
Thinking I knew his meaning well.

ACROSS THE STRAITS

Down from his post in the tower
Of glass, concrete, and steel
When daylight drained from the city
He sank like a stone in a well.

The maiden cries in the lift-well
All night for a severed head,
But the doors like knives behind him
Closed on the air instead.

And seven head-scarfed furies
Began to polish and swill
The murderous marbled flooring
To try for his undipped heel.

Oh, there is peril in cities—
But he gained the outermost door
And paused like a swimmer ready
To try for a fabled shore.

And he cried as he cried ever nightly
Aloud to the deities,
"Safe conduct, gods, to my loved one
Over these battering seas."

As a tumult of waves the traffic
Roared against concrete and steel,
And he cleft through the shoals of impeding
Crowds, and dived under the swell.

She has hung her lit lamp in the window,
She presses her face to the pane,
In a wild commotion of longing
She waits for his coming again.

Oh, there is peril in cities—
He shall not escape as he please,
And Hero shall watch for Leander
In vain on those dark, bitter seas.

TRANSLATIONS UNDER THE TREES

Wine to drink at a plank table,
Poems blowing about,
Some we stalk like Li Po and the moon in the stream,
Some we put under the carafe.

Pollen brushed from the table
Flies off to make forests
In faraway countries;
May change a landscape.

Poems blow away like pollen,
Find distant destinations,
Can seed new songs
In another language.

AT THE COAST

The high wind has stripped the bark from the gum-trees,
Smooth-boled they follow each other down to the water.

From rented houses the daughters of professors
Emerge smooth-limbed in this light summer season,

They step from behind the trees at the edge of the water
As smooth as ochre and as cool as lemon.

And which are girls and which are smooth-limbed saplings?
The light is trembling on them from the water.

They glow and flicker in and out of shadow
Like poetry behind the print on pages.

ALISTER KERSHAW   (1921–)

Poet, journalist. Born and educated in Melbourne; has lived in France since 1947.

THE LAST EXPATRIATE

New Australians—so why not new Europeans? Why are expatriates in one direction virtuous and discerning fellows—in the other, renegades and *ratés*?

This business of expatriation—*towards* Europe—awakens a fanged resentment in the stay-at-homes, a raucous defensiveness in the expatriates. It is very odd.

You're supposed to 'lose your roots'—whatever that may mean—as soon as you overstay a sabbatical year. What *does* it mean—this losing of roots?

Apparently it's only the 'artists' who suffer from this humiliating deprivation, the poor brutes. Soldiers can be posted overseas for most of their careers, engineers can spend ten years on projects in Assam or the Trobriands: when they get home no-one seems to suspect them of being rootless. It's the painters, the musicians, the writers—especially writers—who occasion such concern, such melancholy head-wagging: every tuppenny-halfpenny critic can always fill up his column in the local paper with sage frettings over the rootlessness of his expatriate betters, shedding goanna tears over the sterility, alcoholism and disillusion ahead of them.

Well, well. Perhaps it's no more than envy, envy and gutlessness. It must be a bit depressing to hang abjectly on to your wretched secure little job year after year, inwardly hankering after St Germain and never having quite enough nerve to get further than Eltham.

Only isn't it time that the consolatory legend was looked at a trifle closer? Most modern writers, at any rate, have been expatriates, from Byron to D. H. Lawrence. And after Lawrence, Roy Campbell lived (past tense now, alas) in Provence and Spain for most of his adult life: it would take a Cyril Connolly to detect his rootlessness. The fact is that he was as much at home in Provence or Spain as in his native South Africa. Is that rootlessness? Or the reverse?

Personally, I've always felt that 'nationality'—the quirks and tics and prejudices and, no doubt, virtues which one picks up from one's early environment—must be pretty damned tenuous if it's endangered by going outside territorial waters.

And, equally, there's something suspect about self-identification with one's native land when accompanied by such very vociferous insistence on one's possession of a passport. A while back I was introduced to a gentleman in Paris who, in a turgid German accent, talked about 'us Australians' for several hours on end. Rarely had I heard so many references to billabongs, waratah, the Nullabor Plains and Tasmanian Devils—with U-modified cropping up as regularly as clockwork and the verb at the end of every sentence. I wondered who or what it was he reminded me of: suddenly I remembered: twenty years ago in Australia there was—is there still?—a school of poets which held that good poetry—good Australian poetry—required at least three strictly antipodean allusions per stanza: *Hiawatha* in the pidgin English of Arnhem Land.

> Where poets kiss away the abos' cares
> And dream of wombats and koala bears.

Getting back to the expatriates .... They become 'decadent' along with everything else. This is like rootlessness—ducdame—with nobody caring to be too precise as to what it means: but the decadence of expatriates is an article of faith with all the home-bodies. You become decadent, it seems, by sheer contagion: all foreigners are decadent; if you live among them long enough, you, too ...

An Australian communist stepped off the plane at Orly, the first instant of his visit to France, sniffed deeply and told a waiting compatriot: 'You can smell the decadence, you can smell the decadence!'

This is where all foreigners come together—communists, business men, bureaucrats: they all share the marvellous antique idea of 'the Frenchman' as a bibulous, gesticulating clown, an aura of ornate garters and hurriedly vacated bedrooms always around him. And 'the Italian, 'the Spaniard' of their imaginings not so very different.

Percipient visitors. In France, they drink a few aperitifs in the vicinity of the place de l'Opéra, hustle unhappily through the Louvre, take in Versailles (with a bit of organizing they can manage both in the same day), spend an evening at the Moulin Rouge and take off for the Côte d'Azur. By the time they're back from Nice or Cannes, they know France like an open book. And, by God, it's decadent—take it from me, Mac, I've *been* there.

As a matter of fact, the expatriates, most of them, don't run much risk of infection. It's a mystery, if you come right down to it, why the hell they live outside their native lands, they're so careful to insulate themselves. They are registered at their ridiculous embassies and wait palpitatingly for the big day each year when they'll be invited to drink a glass of cheap 'sparkling wine' with the bureaucrats. They patronize one particular cafe where the entire clientele is English, Australian, or American, and where even the barman has an Australian accent. They have never set foot in La Roquette, say, or Villejuif, but they tell each other that they've just found a wonderful place 'where the foreigners don't go.' It usually turns out to be the Dôme.

And after a few years, suddenly, in spite of all their precautions, it breaks sickeningly in on them—the unfamiliar language all around, the bizarre food, the unaccustomed drinking hours, the menacing *foreignness* of it all; and hurriedly drawing their cash from the bank—for these daredevils have always got a bit tucked away for an emergency—they tear round to Thomas Cook and buy a one-way ticket home.

Once there, what luxury to drop casual allusions to 'one evening in the Deux Magots ...' or to 'an amusing little boîte in the rue de Seine ...' But, all the same, what a comfort to be back, what a relief, nuzzling once more at the benevolent teats of the mother country!

Within six months they're writing sombrely about the dangers of rootlessness.

What about the few who really go native? It's not easy to generalize since, obviously, they tend to avoid each other; but one can make a reasonable guess or two. I'd imagine that one reason why certain people prefer living in France, for instance, rather than Australia is quite simply that France feels as though it were *meant* to be lived in. Whereas in Australia it was somehow as if one were hanging precariously to a cliff edge, with the Genius Loci stamping on one's finger tips.

There's a point of contact with the mass of Frenchmen, maybe with all Europeans; so that the chances are you—a poet, a painter, or whatever—can pass a pleasant hour or so with a truck-driver, the local cop, the greengrocer. In Australia, I seem to recall, artists huddled uneasily together, only leaving their garrets in order to visit friends at the university.

> No! None can break the umbilical cords
> Which join these poets to their mortar boards.

But what the devil does it matter why this one or that may choose to live in France or Spain or Germany or Greece? What is of much more interest is why there should be such ardent opposition to their doing so. Envy, I've suggested; but that can only apply in specific individual cases. Then there may be those who genuinely believe that a writer who produces great prose in Mildura will go to hell if he sets foot in the Carmargue.

Only is it really so simple? There is a grisly consistency in the cult of stay-at-homism and a sinister vehemence. What does it signify? But what else? It fits in with the ugly slavery of our epoch. Governments like to keep their property close at hand where they can watch it and control it. Only the bureaucratic trusties and the business men on safari after profits can safely be permitted to roam the world. The rest must be subtly (and not too subtly) discouraged from travelling until the happy time when they can be *compelled* to stay put. Hence the grotesque currency restrictions, passports, visas, clearances, and the other impudent impediments to free movement. And hence the propaganda whereby the artists—traditionally suspected of rebellious tendencies although, these days, how unfairly!—are to be convinced that their paint will flake and their lines no longer scan if they ever cross a frontier.

It's gloomily diverting to see so many of them yelping for their own final enslavement.

PATRICK WHITE (1912–)

Novelist, short story writer, playwright. Born in London; educated at Cambridge; settled in Australia after the war.

THE PRODIGAL SON

This is by way of being an answer to Alister Kershaw's recent article *The Last Expatriate*, but as I cannot hope to equal the slash and dash of Kershaw's journalistic weapons, I shall not attempt to answer him point by point. In any case, the reasons why anybody is an expatriate, or why another chooses to return home, are such personal ones that the question can only be answered in a personal way.

At the age of 46 I have spent just on twenty of those years overseas. During the last ten, I have hardly stirred from the six acres of 'Dogwoods,' Castle Hill. It sounds odd, and is perhaps worth trying to explain.

Brought up to believe in the maxim: Only the British can be right, I did accept this during the earlier part of my life. Ironed out in an English public school, and finished off at King's, Cambridge, it was not until 1939, after wandering by myself through most of Western Europe, and finally most of the United States, that I began to grow up and think my own thoughts. The War did the rest. What had seemed a brilliant, intellectual, highly desirable existence, became distressingly parasitic and pointless. There is nothing like a rain of bombs to start one trying to assess one's own achievement. Sitting at night in his London bed-sitting room during the first months of the Blitz, this chromium-plated Australian with two fairly successful novels to his credit came to the conclusion that his achievement was practically nil. Perhaps significantly, he was reading at that time Eyre's *Journal*. Perhaps also he had the wind up; certainly he reached rather often for the bottle of Calvados in the wardrobe. Anyway, he experienced those first sensations of rootlessness which Alister Kershaw has deplored and explained as the 'desire to nuzzle once more at the benevolent teats of the mother country.'

All through the War in the Middle East there persisted a longing to return to the scenes of childhood, which is, after all, the purest well from which the creative artist draws. Aggravated further by the terrible nostalgia of the desert landscapes, this desire was almost quenched by the year I spent stationed in Greece, where perfection presents itself on every hand, not only the perfection of antiquity, but that of nature, and the warmth of human relationships expressed in daily living. Why didn't I stay in Greece? I was tempted to. Perhaps it was the realization that even the most genuine resident Hellenophile accepts automatically the vaguely comic role of Levantine beachcomber. He does not belong, the natives seem to say, not without affection; it is sad for him, but he is nothing. While the Hellenophile continues humbly to hope.

So I did not stay in my elective Greece. Demobilization in England left me with the alternative of remaining in what I then felt to be an actual and spiritual graveyard, with the prospect of ceasing to be an artist and turning instead into that most sterile of beings, a London intellectual, or of returning home, to the stimulus of time remembered. Quite honestly, the thought of a full belly influenced me as well, after toying with the soft, sweet awfulness of horsemeat stew in the London restaurants that I could afford. So I came home. I bought a farm at Castle Hill, and with a Greek friend and partner, Manoly Lascaris, started to grow flowers and vegetables, and to breed Schnauzers and Saanen goats.

The first years I was content with these activities, and to soak myself in landscape. If anybody mentioned Writing, I would reply: 'Oh, one day, perhaps.' But I had no real intention of giving the matter sufficient thought. *The Aunt's Story*, written immediately after the War, before returning to Australia, had succeeded with overseas critics, failed as usual with the local ones, remained half-read, it was obvious from the state of the pages, in the lending libraries. Nothing seemed important, beyond living and eating, with a roof of one's own over one's head.

Then, suddenly, I began to grow discontented. Perhaps, in spite of Australian critics, writing novels was the only thing I could do with any degree of success; even my half-failures were some justification of an otherwise meaningless life. Returning sentimentally to a country I had left in my youth, what had I really found? Was there anything to prevent me packing my bag and leaving like Alister Kershaw and so many other artists? Bitterly I had to admit, no. In all directions stretched the Great Australian Emptiness, in which the mind is the least of possessions, in which the rich man is the important man, in which the schoolmaster and journalist rule what intellectual roost there is, in which beautiful youths and girls stare at life through blind blue eyes, in which human teeth fall like autumn leaves, the buttocks of cars grow hourly glassier, food means cake and steak, muscles prevail, and the march of material ugliness does not raise a quiver from the average nerves.

It was the exaltation of the 'average' that made me panic most, and in this frame of mind, in spite of myself, I began to conceive another novel. Because the void I had to fill was so immense, I wanted to try to suggest in this book every possible aspect of life, through the lives of an ordinary man and woman. But at the same time I wanted to discover the extraordinary behind the ordinary, the mystery and the poetry which alone could make bearable the lives of such people, and incidentally, my own life since my return.

So I began to write *The Tree of Man*. How it was received by the more important Australian critics is now ancient history. Afterwards I wrote *Voss*, possibly conceived during the early days of the Blitz, when I sat reading Eyre's *Journal* in a London bed-setting room. Nourished by months spent trapesing backwards and forwards across the Egyptian and Cyrenaican deserts, influenced by the arch-megalomaniac of the day, the idea finally matured after reading contemporary accounts of Leichhardt's expeditions and A.H. Chisholm's *Strange New World* on returning to Australia.

It would be irrelevant to discuss here the literary aspects of the novel. More important are those intentions of the author which have pleased some readers without their knowing exactly why, and helped to increase the rage of those who found the book meaningless. Always something of a frustrated painter, and a composer *manqué*, I wanted to give my book the textures of music, the sensuousness of paint, to convey through the theme and characters of *Voss* what Delacroix and Blake might have seen, what Mahler and Liszt might have heard. Above all I was determined to prove that the Australian novel is not necessarily the dreary, dun-coloured offspring of journalistic realism. On the whole, the world has been convinced, only here, at the present moment, the dingoes are howling unmercifully.

What, then, have been the rewards of this returned expatriate? I remember when, in the flush of success after my first novel, an old and wise Australian journalist called Guy Innes came to interview me in my London flat. He asked me whether I wanted to go back. I had just 'arrived'; who was I to want to go back? 'Ah, but when you do,' he persisted, 'the colours will come flooding back onto your palette.' This gentle criticism of my first novel only occurred to me as such in recent years. But I think perhaps Guy Innes has been right.

So, amongst the rewards, there is the refreshed landscape, which even in its shabbier, remembered versions has always made a background to my life. The worlds of plants and music may never have revealed themselves had I sat talking brilliantly to Alister Kershaw over a Pernod on the Left Bank. Possibly all art flowers more readily in silence. Certainly the state of simplicity and humility is the only desirable one for artist or for man. While to reach it may be impossible, to attempt to do so is imperative. Stripped of almost everything that I had considered desirable and necessary, I began to try. Writing, which had meant the practice of an art by a polished mind in civilized surroundings, became a struggle to create completely fresh forms out of the rocks and sticks of words. I began to see things for the first time. Even the boredom and frustration presented avenues for endless exploration; even the ugliness, the bags and iron of Australian life, acquired a meaning. As for the cat's cradle of human intercourse, this was necessarily simplified, often bungled, sometimes touching. Its very tentativeness can be a reward. There is always the possibility that the book lent, the record played, may lead to communication between human beings. There is the possibility that one may be helping to people a barely inhabited country with a race possessed of understanding.

These, then, are some of the reasons why an expatriate has stayed, in the face of those disappointments which follow inevitably upon his return. Abstract and unconvincing, the Alister Kershaws will probably answer, but such reasons, as I have already suggested, are a personal matter. More concrete, and most rewarding of all, are the many letters I have received from unknown Australians, for whom my writing seems to have opened a window. To me, the letters alone are reason enough for staying.

WILLY-WAGTAILS BY MOONLIGHT

The Wheelers drove up to the Mackenzies' punctually at six-thirty. It was the hour for which they had been asked. My God, thought Jum Wheeler. It had been raining a little, and the tyres sounded blander on the wet gravel.

In front of the Mackenzies', which was what is known as a Lovely Old Home—colonial style—amongst some carefully natural-looking gums, there stood a taxi.

'Never knew Arch and Nora ask us with anyone else,' Eileen Wheeler said.

'Maybe they didn't. Even now. Maybe it's someone they couldn't get rid of.'

'Or an urgent prescription from the chemist's.'

Eileen Wheeler yawned. She must remember to show sympathy, because Nora Mackenzie was going through a particularly difficult one.

Anyway, they were there, and the door stood open on the lights inside. Even the lives of the people you know, even the lives of Nora and Arch look interesting for a split second, when you drive up and glimpse them through a lit doorway.

'It's that Miss Cullen,' Eileen said.

For there was Miss Cullen, doing something with a brief-case in the hall.

'Ugly bitch,' Jum said.

'Plain is the word,' corrected Eileen.

'Arch couldn't do without her. Practically runs the business.'

Certainly that Miss Cullen looked most methodical, shuffling the immaculate papers, and slipping them into a new pigskin brief-case in Arch and Nora's hall.

'Got a figure,' Eileen conceded.

'But not a chin.'

'Oh, hello, Miss Cullen. It's stopped raining.'

It was too bright stepping suddenly into the hall. The Wheelers brightly blinked. They looked newly made.

'Keeping well, Miss Cullen, I hope?'

'I have nothing to complain about, Mr Wheeler,' Miss Cullen replied.

She snapped the catch. Small, rather pointed breasts under the rain-coat. But, definitely, no chin.

Eileen Wheeler was fixing her hair in the reproduction Sheraton mirror.

She had been to the hairdresser's recently, and the do was still set too tight.

'Well, good-bye now,' Miss Cullen said.

When she smiled there was a hint of gold, but discreet, no more than a bridge. Then she would draw her lips together, and lick them ever so sweetly, as if she had been sucking a not unpleasantly acid sweetie.

Miss Cullen went out the door, closing it firmly but quietly behind her.

'That was Miss Cullen,' said Nora Mackenzie coming down. 'She's Arch's secretary.'

'He couldn't do without her,' she added, as though they did not know.

Nora was like that. Eileen wondered how she and Nora had tagged along together, ever since Goulburn, all those years.

'God, she's plain!' Jum said.

Nora did not exactly frown, but pleated her forehead the way she did when other people's virtues were assailed. Such attacks seemed to affect her personally, causing her almost physical pain.

'But Mildred is so kind,' she insisted.

Nora Mackenzie made a point of calling her husband's employees by first names, trying to make them part of a family which she alone, perhaps, would have liked to exist.

'She brought me some giblet soup, all the way from Balgowlah, that time I had virus 'flu.'

'Was it good, darling?' Eileen asked.

She was going through the routine, rubbing Nora's cheek with her own. Nora was pale. She must remember to be kind.

Nora did not answer, but led the way into the lounge-room.

Nora said:

'I don't think I'll turn on the lights for the present. They hurt my eyes, and it's so restful sitting in the dusk.'

Nora *was* pale. She had, in fact, just taken a couple of Disprin.

'Out of sorts, dear?' Eileen asked.

Nora did not answer, but offered some dry martinis.

Very watery, Jum knew from experience, but drink of a kind.

'Arch will be down presently,' Nora said. 'He had to attend to some business, some letters Miss Cullen brought. Then he went in to have a shower.'

Nora's hands were trembling as she offered the dry martinis, but Eileen remembered they always had.

The Wheelers sat down. It was all so familiar, they did not have to be asked, which was fortunate, as Nora Mackenzie always experienced difficulty in settling guests into chairs. Now she sat down herself, far more diffidently than her friends. The cushions were standing on their points.

Eileen sighed. Old friendships and the first scent of gin always made her nostagic.

'It's stopped raining,' she said, and sighed.

'Arch well?' Jum asked.

As if he cared. She had let the ice get into the cocktail, turning it almost to pure water.

'He has his trouble,' Nora said. 'You know, his back.'

Daring them to have forgotten.

Nora loved Arch. It made Eileen feel ashamed.

So fortunate for them to have discovered each other. Nora Leadbeatter and Arch Mackenzie. Two such bores. And with birdwatching in common. Though Eileen Wheeler had never believed Nora did not make herself learn to like watching birds.

At Goulburn, in the early days, Nora would come out to Glen Davie sometimes to be with Eileen at week-ends. Mr Leadbeatter had been manager at the Wales for a while. He always saw that his daughter had the cleanest notes. Nora was shy, but better than nothing, and the two girls would sit about on the veranda those summer evenings, buffing their nails, and listening to the sheep cough in the home paddock. Eileen gave Nora lessons in making-up. Nora had protested, but was pleased.

'Mother well, darling?' Eileen asked, sipping that sad, watery gin.

'Not exactly *well*,' Nora replied, painfully.

Because she had been to Orange, to visit her widowed mother, who suffered from Parkinson's disease.

'You know what I mean, dear,' said Eileen.

Jum was dropping his ash on the carpet. It might be better when poor bloody Arch came down.

'I have an idea that woman, that Mrs Galloway, is unkind to her,' Nora said.

'Get another,' Eileen advised. 'It isn't like after the War.'

'One can never be sure,' Nora debated. 'One would hate to hurt the woman's feelings.'

Seated in the dusk Nora Mackenzie was of a moth colour. Her face looked as though she had been rubbing it with chalk. Might have, too, in spite of those lessons in make-up. She sat and twisted her hands together.

How very red Nora's hands had been, at Goulburn, at the convent, to which the two girls had gone. Not that they belonged to *those*. It was only convenient. Nora's hands had been red and trembly after practising a tarantella, early, in the frost. So very early all of that. Eileen had learnt about life shortly after puberty. She had tried to tell Nora one or two things, but Nora did not want to hear. Oh, no, no, *please*, Eileen, Nora cried. As though a boy had been twisting her arm. She had those long, entreating, sensitive hands.

And there they were still. Twisting together, making their excuses. For what they had never done.

Arch came in then. He turned on the lights, which made Nora wince, even those lights which barely existed in all the neutrality of Nora's room. Nora did not comment, but smiled, because it was Arch who had committed the crime.

Arch said:

'You two toping hard as usual.'

He poured himself the rest of the cocktail.

Eileen laughed her laugh which people found amusing at parties.

Jum said, and bent his leg, if it hadn't been for Arch and the shower, they wouldn't have had the one too many.

'A little alcohol releases the vitality,' Nora remarked ever so gently.

She always grew anxious at the point where jokes became personal.

Arch composed his mouth under the handle-bars moustache, and Jum knew what they were in for.

'Miss Cullen came out with one or two letters,' Arch was taking pains to explain. 'Something she thought should go off tonight. I take a shower most evenings. Summer, at least.'

'Such humidity,' Nora helped.

Arch looked down into his glass. He might have been composing further remarks, but did not come out with them.

That silly, bloody English-air-force-officer's moustache. It was the only thing Arch had ever dared. War had given him the courage to pinch a detail which did not belong to him.

'That Miss Cullen, useful girl,' Jum suggested.

'Runs the office.'

'Forty, if a day,' Eileen said, whose figure was beginning to slacken off.

Arch said he would not know, and Jum made a joke about Miss Cullen's *cul-de-sac*.

The little pleats had appeared again in Nora Mackenzie's chalky brow. 'Well,' jumping up, quite girlish, she cried, 'I do hope the dinner will be a success.'

And laughed.

Nora was half-way through her second course with that woman at the Chanticleer. Eileen suspected there would be avocadoes stuffed with prawns, chicken *Mornay*, and *crêpes Suzette*.

Eileen was right.

Arch seemed to gain in authority sitting at the head of his table.

'I'd like you to taste this wine,' he said. 'It's very light.'

'Oh, yes?' said Jum.

The wine was corked, but nobody remarked. The second bottle, later on, was somewhat better. The Mackenzies were spreading themselves tonight.

Arch flipped his napkin once or twice, emphasizing a point. He smoothed the handle-bars moustache, which should have concealed a harelip, only there wasn't one. Jum dated from before the moustache, long, long, very long.

Arch said:

'There was a story Armitage told me at lunch. There was a man who bought a mower. Who suffered from indigestion. Now, how, exactly, did it ... go?'

Jum had begun to make those little pellets out of bread. It always fascinated him how grubby the little pellets turned out. And himself not by any means dirty.

Arch failed to remember the point of the story Armitage had told.

It was difficult to understand how Arch had made a success of his business. Perhaps it was that Miss Cullen, breasts and all, under the rain-coat. For a long time Arch had messed around. Travelled in something. Separator parts. Got the agency for some sort of phoney machine for supplying *ozone* to public buildings. The Mackenzies lived at Burwood then. Arch continued to mess around. The War was quite a godsend. Arch was a real adje type. Did a conscientious job. Careful with his allowances, too.

Then, suddenly, after the War, Arch Mackenzie had launched out, started the import-export business. Funny the way a man will suddenly hit on the idea to which his particular brand of stupidity can respond.

The Mackenzies had moved to the North Shore, to the house which still occasionally embarrassed Nora. She felt as though she ought to apologize for success. But there was the bird-watching. Most week-ends they went off to the bush, to the Mountains or somewhere. She felt happier in humbler circumstances. In time she had got used to the tape recorder which they took along. She made herself look upon it as a necessity rather than ostentation.

Eileen was dying for a cigarette.

'May I smoke, Arch?'

'We're amongst friends, aren't we?'

Eileen did not answer that. And Arch fetched the ash-tray they kept handy for those who needed it.

Nora in the kitchen dropped the beans. Everybody heard, but Arch asked Jum for a few tips on investments, as he always did when Nora happened to be out of the room. Nora had some idea that the Stock Exchange was immoral.

Then Nora brought the dish of little, pale tinned peas.

'Ah! *Pet—ty pwah!*' said Jum.

He formed his full, and rather greasy lips into a funnel through which the little rounded syllables poured most impressively.

Nora forgot her embarrassment. She envied Jum his courage in foreign languages. Although there were her lessons in Italian, she would never have dared utter in public.

'Can you bear *crêpes Suzette*?' Nora had to apologize.

'Lovely, darling.' Eileen smiled.

She would have swallowed a tiger. But was, *au fond*, at her gloomiest.

What was the betting Nora would drop the *crêpes Suzette*? It was those long, trembly hands, on which the turquoise ring looked too small and innocent. The Mackenzies were still in the semi-precious bracket in the days when they became engaged.

'How's the old bird-watching?'

Jum had to force himself, but after all he had drunk their wine.

Arch Mackenzie sat deeper in his chair, almost completely at his ease.

'Got some new tapes,' he said. 'We'll play them later. Went up to Kurrajong on Sunday, and got the bell-birds. I'll play you the lyre-bird, too. That was Mount Wilson.'

'Didn't we hear the lyre-bird last time?' Eileen asked.

Arch said:

'Yes.'

Deliberately.

'But wouldn't you like to hear it again? It's something of a collector's piece.'

Nora said they'd be more comfortable drinking their coffee in the lounge.

Then Arch fetched the tape recorder. He set it up on the Queen Anne walnut piecrust. It certainly was an impressive machine.

'I'll play you the lyre-bird.'

'The *pièce de résistance*? Don't you think we should keep it?'

'He can never wait for the lyre-bird.'

Nora had grown almost complacent. She sat holding her coffee, smiling faintly through the steam. The children she had never had with Arch were about to enter.

'Delicious coffee,' Eileen said.

She had finished her filter-tips. She had never felt drearier.

The tape machine had begun to snuffle. There was quite an unusual amount of crackle. Perhaps it was the bush. Yes, that was it. The bush!

'Well, it's really quite remarkable how you people have the patience,' Eileen Wheeler had to say.

'Ssh!'

Arch Mackenzie was frowning. He had sat forward in the period chair.

'This is where it comes in.'

His face was tragic in the shaded light.

'Get it?' he whispered.

His hand was helping. Or commanding.

'Quite remarkable,' Eileen repeated.

Jum was shocked to realize he had only two days left in which to take up the ICI rights for old Thingummy.

Nora sat looking at her empty cup. But lovingly.

Nora could have been beautiful, Eileen saw. And suddenly felt old, she who had stripped once or twice at amusing parties. Nora Mackenzie did not know about that.

Somewhere in the depths of the bush Nora was calling that it had just turned four o'clock, but she had forgotten to pack the thermos.

The machine snuffled.

Arch Mackenzie was listening. He was biting his moustache.

'There's another passage soon.' He frowned.

'Darling,' Nora whispered, 'after the lyre-bird you might slip into the kitchen and change the bulb. It went while I was making the coffee.'

Arch Mackenzie's frown deepened. Even Nora was letting him down.

But she did not see. She was so in love.

It might have been funny if it was not also pathetic. People were horribly pathetic, Eileen Wheeler decided, who had her intellectual moments. She was also feeling sick. It was Nora's *crêpes Suzette*, lying like blankets.

'You'll realize there are one or two rough passages,' Arch said, coming forward when the tape had ended. 'I might cut it.'

'It could do with a little trimming,' Eileen agreed. 'But perhaps it's more natural without.'

Am I a what's-this, a masochist, she asked.

'Don't forget the kitchen bulb,' Nora prompted.

Very gently. Very dreamy.

Her hair had strayed, in full dowdiness, down along her white cheek.

'I'll give you the bell-birds for while I'm gone.'

Jum's throat had begun to rattle. He sat up in time, though, and saved his cup in the same movement.

'I remember the bell-birds', he said.

'Not these ones, you don't. These are new. These are the very latest. The best bell-birds,'

Arch had started the tape, and stalked out of the room, as if to let the bell-birds themselves prove his point.

'It is one of our loveliest recordings,' Nora promised.

They all listened or appeared to.

When Nora said:

'Oh, dear'–getting up–'I do believe'–panting almost–'the bell-bird tape'–trembling–'is damaged.'

Certainly the crackle was more intense.

'Arch will be so terribly upset.'

She had switched off the horrifying machine. With surprising skill for one so helpless. For a moment it seemed to Eileen Wheeler that Nora Mackenzie was going to hide the offending tape somewhere in her bosom. But she thought better of it, and put it aside on one of those little superfluous tables.

'Perhaps it's the machine that's broken,' suggested Jum.

'Oh, no,' said Nora, 'it's the tape. I know. We'll have to give you something else.'

'I can't understand,'–Eileen grinned–'how you ever got around, Nora, to being mechanical.'

'If you're determined,' Nora said.

Her head was lowered in concentration.

'If you want a thing enough.'

She was fixing a fresh tape.

'And we do love our birds. Our Sundays together in the bush.'

The machine had begun its snuffling and shuffling again. Nora Mackenzie raised her head, as if launched on an invocation.

Two or three notes of bird-song fell surprisingly pure and clear, out of the crackle, into the beige and string-coloured room.

'This is one,' Nora said, 'I don't think I've ever heard before.'

She smiled, however, and listened to identify.

'Willy-Wagtails,' Nora said.

Willy-Wagtails were suited to tape. The song tumbled and exulted.

'It must be something,' Nora said, 'that Arch made while I was with Mother. There were a couple of Sundays when he did a little field-work on his own.'

Nora might have given way to a gentle melancholy for all she had foregone if circumstances had not heightened the pitch. There was Arch standing the doorway. Blood streaming.

'Blasted bulb collapsed in my hand!'

'Oh, darling! Oh *dear*!' Nora cried.

The Wheelers were both fascinated. There was the blood dripping on the beige wall-to-wall.

How the willy-wagtails chortled.

Nora Mackenzie literally staggered at her husband, to take upon herself, if possible, the whole ghastly business.

'Come along, Arch,' she moaned. 'We'll fix. In just a minute,' Nora panted.

And simply by closing the door, she succeeded in blotting the situation, all but the drops of blood that were left behind on the carpet.

'Poor old Arch! Bleeding like a pig!' Jum Wheeler said, and laughed.

Eileen added:

'We shall suffer the willy-wags alone.'

Perhaps it was better like that. You could relax. Eileen began to pull. Her step-ins had eaten into her.

The willy-wagtails were at it again.

'Am I going crackers?' asked Jum. 'Listening to those bloody birds!'

When somebody laughed. Out of the tape. The Wheelers sat. Still.

Three-quarters of the bottle! Snuffle crackle. *Arch Mackenzie, you're a fair trimmer!* Again that rather brassy laughter.

'Well, I'll be blowed!' said Jum Wheeler.

'But it's that Miss Cullen,' Eileen said.

The Wheeler spirits soared as surely as plummets dragged the notes of the wagtail down.

But it's far too rocky, and far too late. Besides, it's willy-wagtails we're after. How Miss Cullen laughed. *Willy-wagtails by moon-light!* Arch was less intelligible, as if he had listened to too many birds, and caught the habit. Snuffle crackle went the machine ... *the buttons are not made to undo* ... Miss Cullen informed. *Oh, stop it. Arch!* ARCH! *You're* TEARING *me!*

So that the merciless machine took possession of the room. There in the crackle of twigs, the stench of ants, the two Wheelers sat. There was that long, thin Harry Edwards, Eileen remembered, with bony wrists, had got her down behind the barn. She had hated it at first. All mirth had been exorcized from Miss Cullen's recorded laughter. Grinding out. Grinding out. So much of life was re-corded by now. Returning late from a country dance, the Wheelers had fallen down amongst the sticks and stones, and made what is called love, and risen in the grey hours, to find themselves numb and bulging.

If only the tape, if you knew the trick with the wretched switch.

Jum Wheeler decided not to look at his wife. Little guilty pockets were turning themselves out in his mind. That woman at the Locomotive Hotel. Pockets and pockets of putrefying trash. Down along the creek, amongst the tussocks and the sheep pellets, the sun burning his boy's skin, he played his overture to sex. Alone.

This sort of thing's all very well, Miss Cullen decided. *It's time we turned practical. Are you sure we can find our way back to the car?*

Always trundling. Crackling. But there were the blessed wagtails again.

'Wonder if they forgot the machine?'

'Oh, God! Hasn't the tape bobbed up in Pymble?'

A single willy-wagtail sprinkled its grace-notes through the stuffy room.

'Everything's all right,' Nora announced. 'He's calmer now. I persuaded him to take a drop of brandy.'

'That should fix him,' Jum said.

But Nora was listening to the lone wagtail. She was standing in the bush. Listening. The notes of bird-song falling like mountain water, when they were not chiselled in moonlight.

'There is nothing purer,' Nora said, 'than the song of the wagtail. Excepting Schubert,' she added, 'some of Schubert.'

She was so shyly glad it had occurred to her.

But the Wheelers just sat.

And again Nora Mackenzie was standing alone amongst the inexorable moonlit gums. She thought perhaps she had always felt alone, even with Arch, while grateful even for her loneliness.

'Ah, there you are!' Nora said.

It was Arch. He stood holding out his bandaged wound. Rather rigid. He could have been up for court martial.

'I've missed the willy-wagtails,' Nora said, raising her face to him, exposing her distress, like a girl. 'Some day you'll have to play it to me. When you've the time. And we can concentrate.'

The Wheelers might not have existed.

As for the tape it had discovered silence.

Arch mumbled they'd all better have something to drink.

Jum agreed it was a good idea.

'Positively brilliant,' Eileen said.

Vincent Buckley   (1925–)

Poet, critic. Born in Victoria; educated at Melbourne and Cambridge; Professor of English, University of Melbourne.

ELECTION SPEECH

Mottoes: words blown through a skull,
Programmes unwinding like a chain.
We listen, prurient and dull,
Each one bound by fear or gain
To the last ranting syllable.

Invented perils bring the sweat
Onto his practised lip. No doubt,
However, we shall live to eat
The meals that spin tomorrow out;
No doubt we'll lie in comfort yet

And drive each other to the polls.
Present and future weigh on us
Not as this glib voice recalls
But like a headless incubus,
Deaths, terrors that no vote controls.

He goes in quickly for the kill:
A fact, a promise, and a jibe.
I think of nothing; nothings fill
The image that his words inscribe,
My skull intoning from the hill.

NO NEW THING

No new thing under the sun:
The virtuous who prefer the dark;
Fools knighted; the brave undone;
The athletes at their killing work;
The tender-hearts who step in blood;
The sensitive paralysed in a mood;
The clerks who rubber-stamp our deaths,
Executors of death's estate;
Poets who count their dying breaths;
Lovers who pledge undying hate;
The self-made and self-ruined men;
The envious with the strength of ten.

They crowd in nightmares to my side,
Enlisting even private pain
In some world-plan of suicide:
Man, gutted and obedient man,
Who turns his coat when he is told,
Faithless to our shining world.
And hard-faced men, who beat the drum
To call me to this Cause or that,
Those heirs of someone else's tomb,
Can't see the sweeter work I'm at,
The building of the honeycomb.

STROKE

I

In the faint blue light
We are both strangers; so I'm forced to note
His stare that comes moulded from deep bone,
The full mouth pinched in too far, one hand
Climbing an aluminium bar.
Put, as though for the first time,
In a cot from which only a hand escapes,
He grasps at opposites, knowing
This room's a caricature of childhood.
'I'm done for.'

'They're treating you all right?'
We talk from the corners of our mouths
Like old lags, while his body strains
To notice me, before he goes on watching
At the bed's foot
His flickering familiars,
Skehan, Wilson, Ellis, dead men, faces,
Bodies, paused in the aluminium light,
Submits his answer to his memories,
'Yes, I'm all right. But still it's terrible.'

Words like a fever bring
The pillar of cloud, pillar of fire
Travelling the desert of the mind and face.
The deep-set, momentarily cunning eyes
Keep trying for a way to come
Through the bed's bars to his first home.
And almost find it. Going out I hear
Voices calling requiem, where the cars
Search out the fog and gritty snow,
Hushing its breathing under steady wheels.
Night shakes the seasonable ground.

II

Decorous for the dying's sake
The living talk with eyes and hands
Of football, operations, work;
The pussyfooting nurses take
Their ritual peep; the rule demands

I stand there with a stiff face
Ready, at a word or gleam,
To conjure off the drops of sweat.
So small a licit breathing-space
Brings each inside the other's dream.

Across the bright unechoing floors
The trolleys and attendants rove;
On tiptoe shine, by scoured walls,
The nearly speechless visitors
Skirt the precipice of love.

III

Oaks, pines, the willows with their quiet
Terror; the quiet terror of my age;
The seven-year-old bookworm sitting out
At night, in the intense cold, the horse
Tethered, the stars almost moving,
The cows encroaching on the night grass.
The frost stung my lips; my knees burned;
Darkness alone was homely. The hawthorn tree
Glimmered as though frost had turned to language
And language into sharp massy blossoms.
Once, I even scraped my father's hand
And glimpsed the white underside of poplars
That, moving, almost touched the flashing stars.
Squat, steep-browed, the Methodist Church nestled
Halfway between the distant police station
And the near barn; a whole world
Gave neither words nor heat, but merely
A geometry of the awakening sight.
I had forgotten that night, or nights;
And if I think back, there's nothing mythical:
A cross-legged kid with a brooding nose
His hands were too chilled to wipe,
A book whose pages he could hardly turn.
A silent father he had hardly learned
To touch; cold he could bear,
Though chill-blooded; the dark heat of words.
A life neither calm nor animal.
Now, in the deeper quiet of my age,

I feel thirty years
Turning my blood inwards; neither trees nor stars,
But a hush and start of traffic; spasms of sound
Loosening tram rails, bluestone foundations,
Manuscripts, memories; too many tasks;
A body shrinking round its own
Corruption, though a long way from dying.
We suit our memories to our sufferings.

IV

Every clod reveals an ancestor.
They, the spirit hot in their bodies,
Burned to ash in their own thoughts; could not
Find enough water; rode in a straight line
Twenty miles across country
For hatred jumping every wire fence;
With uillean pipes taunted the air
Ferociously that taunted them;
Spoke with rancour, but with double meanings;
Proud of muscle, hated the bone beneath;
Married to gain forty acres
And a family of bond servants; died bound.
I, their grandson, do not love straight lines,
And talk with a measured voice—in double meanings—
Remembering always, when I think of death,
The grandfather, small, loveless, sinister,
['The most terrible man I ever seen',
Said Joe, who died thin as rice paper]
Horse-breaker, heart-breaker, whose foot scorches,
Fifty years after, the green earth of Kilmore.
It's his heat that lifts my father's frame
Crazily from the wheel-chair, fumbles knots,
Twists in the bed at night,
Considers every help a cruelty.

V

Indoors and out, weather and winds keep up
Time's passion: paddocks white for burning.
As usual, by his bed, I spend my time
Not in talk, but restless noticing:
If pain dulls, grief coarsens.
Each night we come and, voyeurs of decay,
Stare for minutes over the bed's foot,
Imagining, if we think at all,
The body turning ash, the near insane

Knowledge when, in the small hours,
Alone under the cold ceiling, above
The floor where the heating system keeps its pulse,
He grows accustomed to his own sweat
And sweats with helplessness, remembering
How, every day, at eight o'clock
The Polish nurse kisses him goodnight.
His arms are bent like twigs; his eyes
Are blown to the door after her; his tears
Are squeezed out not even for himself.
Where is the green that swells against the blade
Or sways in sap to the high boughs? To the root
He is dry wood, and in his sideways
Falling brings down lights. Our breath
Mingles,
Stirs the green air of the laurel tree.

VI

The roofs are lit with rain.
Winter. In that dark glow,
Now, as three months ago,
I pray that he'll die sane.

On tiles or concrete path
The old wheeling the old,
For whom, in this last world,
Hope is an aftermath,

And the damp trees extend
Branch and thorn. We live
As much as we believe.
All things covet an end.

Once, on the Kerrie road,
I drove with him through fire.
Now, in the burnt cold year,
He drains off piss and blood.

His wounded face tube-fed,
His arm strapped to a bed.

VII

At the merest handshake I feel his blood
Move with the ebb-tide chill. Who can revive
A body settled in its final mood?
To whom, on what tide, can we move, and live?

Later I wheel him out to see the trees:
Willows and oaks, the small plants he mistakes
For rose bushes; and there
In front, looming, light green, cypresses.
His pulse no stronger than the pulse of air.

Dying, he grows more tender, learns to teach
Himself the mysteries I am left to trace.
As I bend to say 'Till next time', I search
For signs of resurrection in his face.

ORIGINS

Down the unreasonably humped
and winding back road, patriarch, he would carry
the week's supplies: whiskey,
bread, tea, jam,
the bushels of feed, the picture calendar,
maybe something to read
for the children: not the mother: not himself

Through the two gates, with their old rusty
tin plaques, he was cut off
as in a highrock wilderness.

He kept no line to us; he never left
his name written; he rode, or walked,
the brown hills like a severed body.

So let you ease your mind back
inch by inch, as if prying
through the tiers of a history, back
to the closed soft place, with its must
of dark orderings, and dried rot,
from which, by a peculiar effort,
you might see, behind, pre-Celtic,
the clear air-shape of mountains.

Home   where your father gulped
the water and sugar
of a mother's love, and the whole house
kept is nap of smell
against the outdoors cold winds
and the earth-centred heat.

Rustle of sacks, the straw-ends
crushed in, the seasoned leather,
mice, spittle, bread, dung, oats,
whiskey, old papers, the sunsmell beating down

onto the halfdoor, from between round hills,
till it took a mushroom or a tuberous
density; smell of sapling in the ash.
In these smells we were begotten.

HAL PORTER   (1911–1984)

Short story writer, poet, novelist, playwright. Born and educated in
Victoria.

COUNTRY TOWN

This, you must know, is less a story of people than of a country
town. Australian? Unmistakably. Plot? Life? Yes. Love? Well—
y-e-e-s. For example, I am put out to know that, in some windy part
of my mind, *I* love this home town as one might inescapably love a
hypocrite uncle as boring as immortality and with the points of
view of a blowfly, or a recurring sweet dream one knows too well is
a dream, or a cocktail that has a terrific lift though it tastes like the
inside of a coffin. Love, you think? Eh?

I left the place thirty years ago. Absence did no more than qualify
me to dispassion about *Before* and *After*, make me see more clearly
what happened next, the new make-up and changed lighting after
Intermission. All I learnt while out smoking the cigarettes too
gaudily labelled *Experience* is—a safe cynicism—that civilization
makes anything no less accidental, anything at all: living, lusting,
dying and so on.

I return one sunset, accidental (you see!)—accidental nice
timing—the town seems, for a thin slice of time, to be not one sker-
rick changed. It has the *High Noon* frontier town look Australian
country towns have when horizontal rays stress that two storeys is
the limit and in Main Street only, that the rest of the town is on one
floor and mostly weatherboard. Those ridge-and-gulch acres of
corrugated iron roofs! Those chimneys!—a functioning museum of
bricklayer fashions: 1873, 1885, 1902, 1919, 1926, 1938, 1959....

My nostalgic, just tearless eye strains to unfade on upper-floor
brick side-walls words still there from my boyhood and earlier:
*Bush's Family Grocer, Kyle's Cash Bakery, Mantles and Robes,
Horse Bazaar—Omnibus Depôt—Wedding Carriages for Hire.*
The tide of falsifying plastic paint, peg-board, and plate glass canted
off the vertical does not rise to the first floor; above is the past; as
well, in Main Street back-yards Chic Sale privies loll spastically
against tors of packing-cases. The two poplars still domineer, dead-
centre of the town, like nervous Azraels; the aluminium-painted

penny-farthing sits as ever on the roof-line of the bicycle shop. Well, well! Are there, beneath these tongue-and-groove false fronts, still fruit-shops unaware of sweet-corn, canteloupes, milk-bars and juke-boxes but which display, as of old, their decay-velveted Valencias, flaccid rhubarb and firkin-sized ironbark pumpkins under fretwork arches and dusty witch-balls? Does artificial rain meander down the butcher's plate-glass in front of the parsley-eyed pig's head on its fly-corpse-curranted marble? Is the arc of enamelled letters BOURNVILLE COCOA (two letters always missing) stuck yet on grocers' shop-windows?

No; and for ever, no.

No the monumental mason's urns and scrolls poking through horehound and fennel; no the smithy, the saddler's, the doctors' red lamps, the Show Day procession, the elm avenues, the hitching-rings on shop-veranda posts; no the hickory golf clubs mashie and cleek, washerwomen, bullockies, knicker-bockered boys in boots, girls in ribbed stockings, the hat on every outdoor head, the immodestly defining cotton bathers from which inky dye seeped into the white-edged sleevelets, and no no no the sound of hoofs on gravel roads. Gone cabby, rabbit-oh and fish-oh, John Chinaman green-grocer, the dago ice-cream cart and its bell, the Hindu old-iron man, the scissors-grinder, the Afghan pedlar, and all their clockwork nags which wore in midsummer their earholed equine millinery above wowserish William S. Hart faces; gone the medieval pageantry of hearse-horses, Black Prince plumes, the top-hatted undertakers in cutaway coats. Gone what was called the night-cart though it came, two-horsed, also in daylight, a zeppelin-grey tank-like machine, two storeys high, back to back terraces of dunnican cubicles that clanged shut as jails must clang. *That* was one of the town's sounds.

Early in December, one found a card on the lavatory seat:

> *Enjoy Christmas as best you can,*
> *And don't forget the dunny man.*

Did parents leave a Christian half-crown near the egg-shaped hole? Or, not breathing, waylay the burly untouchable with the top of his felt hat squashed so horizontal from reeking burdens that he appeared mathematically scalped, and present some gift with a gracious clause? I don't remember. One should know, but....

I knew lies, carnality, happiness, despair, even viciousness and *ennui*. I had heard of Rembrandt, Bach, Pavlova, Tutankhamen and Jack-the Ripper but never of fish and chips, spaghetti or grape-fruit. Oh, a local, a yokel, a hick, a peasant, a simple boy from Woop Woop! Had I heard of wireless? There must have been crystal sets in the shire, but as I prowled back streets, criminally over-nonchalant, to steal quinces or blood-filled Satsumas, I heard only the melancholy of old-maid uprights behind fringed holland blinds.

Fingers of unseen pale hands tinkling "... *I loved beside the Shali-mar ...*" where, indeed, are you now? Piano or pianola, just around the next picket-fence corner overhung by cassias lay—had I known it—the opening of Canberra, *The Jazz Singer*, the Depression, miniature golf, Club Sandwiches, and, for me, long pants, silk socks, Melbourne (The City!) and what I thought was Life. It took years, that last one.

So with Life dwindled to life, kings and kingdoms foundered, bombs dropped as frequently as bricks, the moon to be colonized by scientific dogs or mad Crusoes, I return, middle-aged and less *dégagé* than I thought, to another chain-store town. Fluorescent street-lights glare on the metallic venetians and desperately garish doors. Neons display their *tics* above all the pubs, the cinema, the drive-in, the ice-block automat, the auto-port, the self-service pet-rol bowser, the motel, the transport drivers' steak-and-egg road-houses, and the caravan park whose machicolated public lavatories like Disney castles have been built with municipal delicacy on the top of pioneer graves. Neons utter *Hamburgers, Fish and Chips, Milk Bar, All Night Café, Smokes, Snacks, Eats*—God-knows-what-else—and *Espresso*.

The shingled virgins in berets who tormented my adolescence, and Black-Bottomed or Parma-Waltzed in the Mechanics' Hall—chocolate stencilled dado, tangerine *crêpe* paper streamers looped into gas-less gasoliers under the pitch-pine ceiling—now sit beneath the Wandering Jew and other pendulant weeds of *Maxim's Espresso* smoking king-sized filter-tips, continentally rapping out, "Cappuc-cino!" and tempting the Providence of matronly zippers as they stretch to choose with plastic tongs another musty Jewish-Viennese cake from under the plastic cover. Forsworn the pottery teapot, the toasted ham sandwich and cheese cakes!

Coronetted sewer-poles pierce up in every direction but hoisted high above them like the Euclid problems of *ex-avant-garde* wire-sculpture or Woolworth potato-mashers are the symbols of a sinis-ter craze—the H.P. T.V. aerials.

Had I foreseen all these? Nearly all, for they are everywhere else, the production-belt contrumpery, the wrought-iron knick-knackery, the Yankeefied barbecue furniture, cheap-jack self-service stores, cellophaned rubbish, grubbed-out street elms, mu-nicipal vandalism, pre-fab. schoolrooms, jerry-built Commission houses, "1984" public address systems, the arc-lit pennants and tubbed privets of the used car dealers, the labour-pains of a second Industrial Revolution—how could I not have foreseen? I had not foreseen that I should spend my first night in what, to me, was Mrs Topper's bedroom.

In days when tracks in the river-bank grass or across home-stead paddocks were triple, two for wheels plus one for hoofs, and are now merely car-wheel double, in days when Christmas meant eucalypt saplings glorifying every veranda post of every shop, when Jew's Harps and German transfers could be bought, and cigarette cards were silk-covered, Topper was a schoolboy friend and what I considered rich. His parents' house with slate roof, wide tiled verandas, stables, orchard, tennis court, septic tank, even its palm lawn, arbutus and monkey puzzle had, for me, then, much elegance. Lorraine Lee roses sum it up: they were just in; Toppers had them. We played Mah Jongg, listened to *Horsy, Keep Your Tail Up* and *O, Katharina* on a Victrola inside, a portable Decca outside, ate the non-alcoholic almond-porcupined trifles left over from Mrs Topper's parties and, to make the bosomy housemaid bounce about screeching like a cockatoo, chewed mouthfuls of walnuts which we regurgitated in front of her, pretending we vomited.

One Saturday a charitable bazaar called a Garden Fête was held there. All I remember is one stall, lattice hung with home-made wistaria, and run by the cinema pianist, a fluting spinster beaked as, and now as dead as, Virginia Woolf. A blue paper chrysanthemum at each temple, and hung with a kimono, she sold heart-shaped velveteen pin-cushions, shirt-flannel pen-wipers, gilded wheels made of matchbox drawers (what were they *for?*) and the first Turkish Delight I had tasted.

And once, as though destiny were showing me the other side of the medal first ... the ornamental side, the side for romantic little boys, a side to remember ... I was taken into Mrs Topper's bedroom when she had some *malaise* to say "Hullo", or even "Hello". Since my own bed was rather shame-makingly like the brass and enamelled iron death-bed of Pius XII at Castel Gondolfo her wagon-sized one of fumed oak had a Cecil B. de Mille quality, and Mrs Topper, fragile and *eau-de-Cologned*, rather the air of Gloria Swanson. The room seemed to me enormous and was large; its lavender wallpaper was panelled with strips of what formed the terribly dainty black-and-silver frieze. Through the lace curtains of the bay window could be seen, far off behind the pergola of Dorothy Perkins roses, the morass where I waded for swans' and plovers' eggs, and learnt to smoke, having stolen three Britannia-embossed pennies for the packet from my mother's kitchen-purse, the shabby morocco one with the steel catch.

Now, here I was, more years later than seemed possible even to me who had enthusiastically used up or outrageously thrown away every hour of them, in Mrs Topper's bedroom for the second time—to sleep there for one night.

Topper's is now a boarding-house for men run as scrupulously as a hospital by Hungarians called New Australians; a hoarding under the monkey puzzle shouts Something-or-other Guest House. The property has been subdivided; women's magazine houses, architectural illiteracies of built-in plywood and man-made fibres, share out such Topper trees as remain. The house is also subdivided, partitions bisecting rooms, fibro-plaster sleep-outs lining the verandas. Some garage hand or gas-works stoker is always removing Al Jolson under the shower; ironstone china clashes in the pantry; transistor wirelesses play constantly and from every direction, and—oh, that other side of the medal—Mrs Topper's bedroom, with aseptically white walls, contains four monk-cell beds, four gents' wardrobes, four bedside cupboards and reading-lamps, four vacuumed hideous scatter rugs. Cheek by jowl the men live like well-behaved butch dolls.

Since I was to sleep once only in this room—there was some one-day hitch about a promised bungalow outside—I was unpacking just enough to make a homing perch, and getting my eye in before going out to get anaesthetically drunk, for in no other way would I be able to sleep in this dormitory with three unknowns whose paraphernalia disposed strictly in each quarter-room advertised variously addicted men but undeniable young ones, young *blokes* and to be eluded: middle-aged men of my sort relish young men far less than old men do.

I was, however, not quickly enough unpacked to escape young men for, in acrobat vees, patently dewy from a shower, enter, *vigoroso*, on peanut-shaped toes, one of them. Say, rather, a young man made an entrance: chest out, belly in, a *pas seul* seemed imminent. Instantly, though it was impossible, I felt I knew him, had met him. He was somewhat above short, flaxen, pretty as a pretty ape with little electric-blue eyes which, in a crackle, assessed my suit and shoes and condoned his tooth-paste smile and knuckle-deforming handshake. My mind said, "Ouch!" He was pleased to meet me, man. I how-d'-y'-do'ed. He was Kurt Schmidt, man. He was now—ha, ha—a dinkum Aussie, man. He flexed.

Now he would examine *my* silver-mark.

His torso and arms were physical culture magazine, Mr Universe; he kept on wincing these upper wonders which tapered to skinny legs bandy as Rupert Brooke's and feet small as a girl's. Decidedly better kit-cat than full.

He strutted, he prattled, reluctant to obscure his top-heavy form, to enclose it in whatever usually contained it; he juggled two cut-in dimples as Sonja Henie used to—oh, he turned it on. His English was good though larded with bodgie-isms and low camp patter that were not *quite* right. Self-possessed as a musical comedy child he dealt questions like a Five Hundred hand. How long was I sojourning in this weirdsville burg, huh? What did I do for a crust? How had I got here? Did I have a car? Did I have a car, huh? When I told him that I could not drive one and had no desire to own one, it was as though I had stabbed him. "Oh, no!" he cried in agony. *So I was a weird-o! Really rat! Did I have any bread?* I saw him think that. I saw him jettison his first assessment, sensed his interest change direction; he became as busy and charming as a cat when the refrigerator is opened. But I *must* have a car, man, just for hacking round, like. For cruising, huh? He became fanatic as a missionary; his voice went off key with zeal. Daddy-O, a car was the *most*. A car had protein.

Behind the dimples, the stomach muscles like an active anatomical chart and the heliographing teeth I was aware of dead-pan evaluation: Daddy-O, oh, Daddy-O, how I could send you up! You're a double freak, a squarehead square, a fossil with your dullsville old hand-made brogues, but I dig you—I dig you, creep.

He could, he raved on, *he* could drive a car, but any, and neat-o. Cars fractured him, like. He was a car cat, yes, *man*. Drive! Z-e-e-o-o-oom! Here he unconsciously mimed, trance took him: hands and forearm on a steering-wheel, dimples flattened, he slitted eyes at some roadway flaring under at seventy, eighty, ninety.... Then he came to, lit up, moved in selling hard, saying that a flip ... a *gentleman* like me *should* have a car; I was a grool not to; listen, Daddy-O, he had a gasser of an idea, like—he'd drive for me, with pleasure, but definite *pleasure*. I must must must get a car. Next, intensifying his dimples and so suddenly so very offhandedly that I heard the gears grind, "What you doing tonight, Mac? Dolls, huh?"

It was a try-out subtle as evisceration. A naughty monkey, he looked slyer than he thought he looked wistful and charming.

"No," I said, "no—er—women."

He registered. He rippled muscles at me, smiled and smiled, tacked over me again with miss-nothing eyes. I exchanged jargons, "No dolls. I'm going to get full as a State School, whittled as a penguin, cacko, blind sleeping drunk."

"A booze cat, man!" He looked at nothing on the ceiling, and "By yourself, Jim?" he said.

"By myself." He waited bridally for the unless he'd like to join me. Background hi-fi should have been doing muted dog tunes for ickies—*Moonlight and Roses? Shine on, Harvest Moon?*

I let him ask. I let him thrust himself on me. Since I had long ago learnt to by-pass the eccentricities of the innocent, to be beware of, to flee the naked heart, I was safe dallying here, for this was no simon-pure innocent, this was a shandy one, a pony-shandy and no trouble at all. So, I said, I'd be pleased to have a ... but he was already at his dressing.

I waited while he got into a nylon singlet, a drip-dry non-iron nylo-poplin shirt, while he knotted in a manner new to me a lean strap of tinsel-threaded tie; I waited for the nylon-neon sockettes, the velvety royal blue shoon (they were scarcely shoes); I watched him tease his gilt pompadour with a pink plastic comb and breath on and polish his antiqued signet ring. Now—*now*—the suit!

Therefore, the first night back and out in the home town I had never drunk in was spent drinking in vinyl chairs on laminex table-tops with a suit of a colour and cut I had never drunk with before, sprayed by the dimples, and arch and ancient boyishness of a quarter-bodgie from a Berlin slum, a camp-fringee, New Australian railway fireman who thought that the answer at the end of the book was *The End Justifies the Means*, and that the use of a car to lure fiffies, chickies and sorts was worth Time Out from normality, was worth whatever might occur—the off-beat, the sordid, a gamut of distaste, recrimination, bitterness, any-bloody-thing. He was too young and tainted and foreign to know that my indifference to some conventions was boredom and vanity, and not the colour he thought; he mistook it for tolerance, *laisser-faire* and anything-goes. As we bumped shoulders back to the dormitory that night alternately singing *Die Dör Musik* and wrangling patiently as father and son about cars, it came to me why he had seemed familiar—he was a later but other Otto Nowak from Isherwood's "Good-bye to Berlin". He was a boy of the Friedrichstrasse amusement-joints, corruption and simplicity pathetically balanced, his trained-animal tricks too orchidaceous for an Australian country town, his judgments impaired from a past in which he had sat nibbling sugar wafers, a *Puppenjunge* playing a pick-up in a Hallesches Tor *lokal*. Although a Beautiful Friendship blessed by a scarlet M.G.'ish sort of opentopped and souped-up car did not develop, Kurt Schmidt and I moved from Mister to Christian- to nick-names. I liked him because I did not like him enough to be moved by his desires and frustrations. There was not even a scrap-heap 1929 Chevrolet in sight for him. He could not imagine that I could see through his automobile bowings and scrapings which familiarity bred to nagging; he could not see that I might have pitied him because, to him, I was a rockhead he couldn't drive ape, I was as square as a butter-box and practically a primate. Nevertheless, from time to time, I for catharsis, he to employ doll-less desolation, we went on the scoot together. What he got from these outings except hangovers and grog-blossoms I do not know; I learnt the last verse of *Die Lorelei*.

The town is indeed more changed, or rather is changing more rapidly, than I first thought. It is also less changed, much less changeable. One hand of the clock races on, the other slackens, drags, is reluctant.

The unpainted virgins of my adolescence who handed Conversation Lollies—*Meet me at the Corner, Do you like kisses?*—in High School geography lessons now play the mother's part in the Drama Society's *Quiet Weekend*, rule the roost at Red Cross meetings, support hefty backsides on shooting-sticks at country race meetings, are avid Solo players, make Shepherd's Pie on Tuesday, sell for offshoot Christianity and too much on market-day street-stalls their no-egg Swiss Rolls, their sugar-bag peg-aprons, their jars of unsuccessful jams from which the mould has been skimmed, unbelievable jams—Green-Tomato-and-Passion-Fruit, Carrot-and-Grape. The Angelus rings the same pattern of threes on the same bell I heard as a boy but Pioneer buses now pull up outside St Pat's to let Protestant women holding gesture handkerchiefs on unsure heads and men stiff-legged as Don Juan's Commendatore go staring at the Heaven-and-Hell painted ceiling, while, aloft outside, the Virgin with daddies-long-legs up her marble sleeves holds dusty hands towards the neon-eiffel-scaffolding of Rash's Tyre Service. Seventy-year-old hawthorns still hedge the river-flat paddocks but the hop-kilns have gone, and it is not an Australian navvy or bank clerk who showily swallow-dives and jack-knives from the willows by the Rowing Club but a Berliner, brute-shouldered and maiden-footed, looking younger than he is, peacocking without hope in the minimum of baby-blue satin trunks, spying among the lunch-time shop-girls and Shire Hall typists for a sort, a bint, a woman, a wife, even a talkie-teener sweetheart. Changed, you see, yet unchanged: the Technical School and High School adolescents wear grey *mélange*, school-striped ties, crested caps; only a scattering of these acned androgynes become bejeaned and rug-headed Coca Cola boys when the lawn has been mowed and the morning-wood cut.

The gasometer is rustier; the water-tower is grubbier; the back-streets are blanker now the elms are torn out; but gasometer and water-tower yet, streets yet. And in those back-streets, their Coolgardies replaced by refrigerators, their outdoor coppers by washing machines, their supper-cloths embroidered with crinolined women by aboriginal *motif* ashtrays, those I knew years ago still live among saddle bag suites, music canterburies, Maxfield Parrish reproductions, Congoleum squares, and sideboards as elaborate as reredoses. They are those whose undeveloped beauties of being, whose immature cruelties, nobilities and magnanimities are scarcely used, rarely seen. All the powers of language and pleasures of communication are nil and nix-nought-nothing. Theirs the servile but deadly gestures of animals, the slogans of popular science, the monosyllables of news-items; when it is 103° in the shade, "Hot, eh?" they tender. Much besides charm is truant. Resignation veils all, or self-abnegation reeking of conceit, or the egotism, savagery and delusions of motherhood. My once-friends, those Oxford-Bags-and-Fair-Isle-Sweater youths are R.S.L. men bewitched to Brickhill fans, Masons with ulcers, Rotarians with moustached wives and clean-shaven sons, budgerigar- or delphinium-cranks, committee-men, vestrymen, aitchless speechmakers, Rechabites, beer-goitre boys, scout-masters with the morals of Lamas, saints in an air-lock, mute inglorious Casanovas, filleted Satans, half-cold or flyblown morsels on the plate of Time. I—haunted by such important unimportances as when to write *spirt* and when *spurt*—am irrevocably one of this mob. My once-friends? Perhaps friends yet, whom death will change to nothing but the dead, who see the lost sections of their and my boyhood town shining with false but blinding seduction through the overlayings of thirty years. There, we think, was the pine avenue, *that* garage was the joss-house for the settlement of Amoy Chinese from the gold-fields, there were the pioneer vineyards, the wharves for the river-steamers, the old convent, the row of giant mulberry-trees. Cook's Corner, we say, Balmer's Hill, the Tannies, the Cut, Russo's, the School of Mines—names that will go when we all go. Now is for them and me the transparencies *Now* and *Then* superimposed one on another. We walk two streets when we walk the one.

Not so the foreigners, the New Australians walking in the very heart now of our barbarians' luxury, rubbing shoulders with those who carry like a useless breviary the magic rubbish of *How to Win Friends and Influence People*; not the black-stockinged women all in black and their podgy, sullen daughters, their Latin male-children who switch from raucous boy to raucous Tennessee Williams man between one Saturday morning's Main Street gossiping and the next; not the Sicilians or Albanians or Greeks under 1911 street verandas and the click of changing neons, short-legged, rings on their dirty fingers, womanlessly engaged in melancholy or professional carping, their eyes meantime racing about like crickets to covet in side-glances the *cinemaromanzi* breasts of paper-back platinum blondes; not the Fire Brigade Dance refusee, purple-suited, smelling of Californian Poppy hair-oil, stale sweat and Latvian loneliness; not the gangling Dutchman chewing unwanted lips before the display, like circus machinery, of orange-coloured bale loaders and rotary hoes; not the side-burned pair, in tight trousers of nameless cloth and pointed shoes polka-dotted with punctures, dawdling, as through the mazes of homesickness, among the little girls' games drawn like aboriginal totems on the footpaths. One street only these walk; they inhabit an Ionesco stage-set, a province without memories, or memories only of the day before yesterday: the hysterical misunderstanding at the employment office, the fight behind the Greek Café, the night-out with drunken aborigines under the Wy Yung Bridge, the voice crying, "You bloody dago bastard, you!" the male tears and threatening knife in the shadow of the tannery.

Until my flat was ready, and flats are still as rare in country towns as ants' holidays, I stayed on at the Something-or-other Guest House occupying what the Hungarian proprietors called a bungalow, Kurt Schmidt *die Hütte* and I my cardboard box. It was a seven-foot cube of plaster-board and masonite under a Topper loquat-tree I had often climbed as a child. I fitted into it, just, Laika in Sputnik; a visitor meant a physical relationship. Entering the back gate, near the cave of shadow under the peppercorn, to reach this toy dwelling was, night after night, like turning to yet another illustration in a work by Goya or Hogarth. It was here, outside the gate, that boarders returning home went through a kind of ritual purification. It was partly the result of the stern commercial motherlinesses of the Hungarians, partly unwritten etiquette, to complete pre-sleep dirty work under the peppercorn, to remove all make-up before bedding down; once the gate slammed behind, the night was formally over. Consequently someone was always emptying himself of too much Ruby Port or bottled beer, or maudlinly mopping up the blood-nose he had given his bubbling china, or hooking arms for a surrealistic half an hour over the fence-top to auto-suggest legs strong and biddable for the walk across the yard, up the steps and down the dangerous corridor. Presently, night after night, it was obvious that the snowy-haired one of two bodies wrestling, mumbling and mewling amorously in the cavern of shadow was Kurt Schmidt. The other was the new kitchenmaid-waitress who occupied a cell simmering with cheap scent somewhere in the hive of the boarding-house. After Football Dance, Old Time Ball or cinema, this nightly rehearsal for the activity of consummation boiled down to merely male and female, Kurt Schmidt and Vi'let Smith, saying good night at the front gate, the same gate for both, and a back gate. Vi'let Smith, indeed, may never have had a front gate. For her, the kitchenmaid who was a pantrymaid's daughter, Kurt Schmidt might well be Cinderella's handsome foreigner from a Mills and Boon romance; for the German who had been exposed to more thousands of miles, more sharpening and hardening experiences, this too ordinary relationship was possibly a treachery of his own flesh—or was he astute enough to accept that no grazier's golfing daughter in a Humber would fall for his cute fireman's face, film-star-smutted, at the railway crossing? no doctor's widow (1958 Chrysler Royal) turn her hot eye himwards some enchanted morning outside the barber's? no crumb of country town woman fall to a New Australian from any table the subtlest class higher?

How time blows by gustily as the breaths of passion!

How time blew by!—mopping and mowing like a willy-willy past the plastic bracken in the butcher's Sunday shop-window, past the gravestone of my mother who died ten years younger than I am now, past the Gothic Boer War monument (imported marble), the towering 1914–18 Cenotaph (local granite) with its footnote for the dead of World War II (cracked cement troughs of gazanias), past all sorts of lovers who thought they loved, past Vi'let Smith and her chewed finger-nails and engagement ring of three pin-head diamonds. Kurt Schmidt no longer deepened dimples to excite me to buy an M.G., a jinker or even pawnshop roller-skates. He asked my advice, stern and dedicated, on the fundamentals of setting up house, on radiograms, wall-plaques, musical beer-steins and plastic salad-servers. He austerely dropped tailor-mades for the makings, drank porter-gaffs, put threepences in a milk-bottle, and finished mauling Vi'let good night at the first whistle of the midnight train.

Most evocative, most haunting of night noises is that cry of the late train—wearily exultant journey's-ending, a telescope of sound through which the eye in the ear sees the acres of moonlit paddocks surrounding the town, the never-ending net of post-and-rail, the golgothic slaughter-yards, the cemetery over-run with sparaxis, the rams or ghosts of rams, the mopoke-haunted wind-breaks, the windmills, the messmate hills and bell-bird gullies, the smaller towns beyond—tin and boards and silence broken only by a baby crying like a ewe, the suburbs half-country, the suburbs half-city, and, dirty as a potato, the faraway youth-luring city itself. Ah, the midnight train!—the train awash with fatigue, with abandoned magazines, crushed paper cups, lolling bodies, faces wearing eyes looped in shadows. It is bringing Auntie Ettie the common-as-dirt old age penisoner or Aunt Margaret the well-heeled whinger with her beloved papilloma, it is bringing the end-of-term school-girl boarder, grandpa with the shark's tooth on his watch-chain, Bruce from the Melbourne Show, mother and the new city-born baby, bringing Australians home again. Now it brings too the smell-of-an-oilrag escapees from tourist countries littered with the fabulous wreckage of pasts, the shrewd, the defeated, the go-getting, the horizon-chasing, the under-cutting, from Athens, Bethnal Green, Hamburg, Haarlem, Mammola and Vysoke Myto, the women in black with fate-like faces and dandruffy madonna coiffures, the runtish men reeking with garlic and grappa, the cockney with rotten teeth. Here come the sly eyes, the bare doggy eyes, the lips hemmed together, the cheeks twitching still from a life of unfulfilled ventures, the spiv hands, the beast hands with grimy knuckles, the foreign garments buttoned on savings folded as tightly in purses as fear is in the kernel of being.

In this story of a country town I must, reluctantly, imagine one scene only. One sentence, then, of invention: Kurt Schmidt sits, decorously disposed on the green leather of a second-class smoker, dimples in abeyance, suitcases Teutonically buckled, his tiny cheap-brooch eyes glinting in appraisement of the miles of rich weeds and butter-factories and timber-mills through which he is in a few years to drive a train, perhaps the very one he is now driven in. You see him? ... blond, clean as veal, exercising those emotions that work in pairs, ambition and self-distrust, curiosity and uneasiness, hope and alarms.

Do the sleepless, the wide-awake dying, the woman in labour, the telephone girl on night-duty, the late reader, the insomniac debtor, the youth entangled in prayer, the adulterers under the river-bank horse-chestnuts, the High School teacher correcting algebra, the saxophone player limping homewards, do they all really know, when they hear the whistle that bores the night like an enchanted gimlet, what travels in with their returning flesh-and-blood, with Auntie Ettie or the fourth generation Australian baby brother? Or what else tomorrow might bring besides an aunt's coarse gossip, and new nappies on the rotary-clothes-line by the unsatisfactory lemon-tree in the backyard?

Tomorrow is still, of course, the fancy dress football match,

Thatcher's Summer Sale of Men's Wear, the C.W.A. raffiawork display, the Legacy dinner, the Chess Club final, the Buffaloes' booze-up, the Library Committee meeting, the C.A.E. Mozart evening at the Prince Regent, the rock-'n'-roll in the Mechanics' ... tomorrow is still tomorrow and a repetition of customary yesterdays. The kilties sackdoodle, the band practises *Poet and Peasant* Overture, the trout-fishing opens, the duck-shooting closes, blackberrying is on, mushrooms are everywhere, there are frost, and thunderstorms, and north winds like Magog's breath ... why not? Tomorrow has gone on thus for years.

Thus?

Have you seen the papers on the notice-board outside the police station headed FISCHEREI UND WILDEHOERDE and UFFICIO DELLA PESCA E DELLA CACCIAGIONE? Have you looked in the delicatessens that no longer call themselves Small Goods but sometimes Delikatessen and seen the tins of olive oil, the packets of poppy-seed and noodles, the tinned Dutch strawberries and spinach, the salami, the twenty kinds of cheeses, the sauerkraut, the spaghettini, vermicellini, sopracapellini, fettucce, ziti and calzoni? Who are the once foreign, still foreign-looking, men with greased hair, *café noir* eyes, and sores on the corners of their mouths, whose photographs fill the photographer's display cases? And look!—in the cemetery where a headstone of Welsh slate under an actual yew ninety years old states *Sophia Ellen Knight, 1863*, there are now photographs behind glass cemented into the grave-edgings: this molten-eyed tot with the prissy half-smile and frizzy hair appears to have died here in 1956 somewhere in one of the streets named after pioneers, explorers or Great War brigadiers, *Mariarosa Serafina Tocchi, born 1951, Casalbuono, Italia.*

As country town people do, I know a lot about my country town in a common-or-garden way; eyes and ears get information *gratis*, one breathes in facts, lies or legends effortlessly without needing to nosey-parker—to use the jargon—writer-wise.

I know that, tomorrow, if I am or you are by chance near St John's Church of England which looks over the river-willows, across the lucerne flats to the Old People's Village on the hill, it will amuse to cast a glance at the Rectory oposite. The front door will be hurled open. The Canon's fox-terrier will nimble about Grockishly, yapping like a heathen. The Canon will shoot, jet-propelled, out of the ecclesiastical front gate and come sprinting ex-athletically across the road, back just in time from blessing the fishing-fleet ... just in time, for here comes the bridegroom's taxi containing Kurt Schmidt, the blond fireman from the gnawed core of Berlin, the up-and-coming engine-driver, in a black suit with, thank God, horizontal pockets. His face is brightly silly with nervousness. Now, just femininely late enough, here comes the bride in a nearly charming gown she can wear later at the Hospital Ball, here comes

Vi'let Smith the waitress with Woolworth flowers in her hair and a Marilyn Monroe mouth painted over her mouse-trap one, the waitress-kitchenmaid whose mother was a pantrymaid and whose daughter will be, whose son will be, whose children will be ... will be....

I wrote that I knew much, but that is really all I know about my home town, a country town I am startled to discover that I love as one loves an ageing mother with dyed hair, slapdash lacquered finger-nails, and skirts too short for her varicose-veined legs. Or do I love it as one shudderingly does a cocktail tasting like the inside of a coffin but with a terrific life? Anyway, some sort of cocktail is poured—whew!—and I, you, we, they must drink it. Not pronto, of course, for me ... but certainly later. Oh, cer–tain–ly!

BRETT

When Benito Mussolini was Il Duce the Milan railway station was built.

Architecture without much conscience, it is edificial, colossal, and not unfittingly dictatorial. It is also very dreary: an intention to grandeur of the sublime kind doesn't at all come off. A façade of would-be triumphal arches leads into a succession of vast, austere lobbies, seemingly limitless, and far too lofty. Here, misshapen echoes vault cumbrously and forlornly about like headaches with nowhere to settle.

Once through the first dolorous arcade the traveller is confronted and affronted by a cyclopean alp of stairs which suggests by its mathematical cruelty the incline of an Aztec ziggurat. This scarp of livid stone depresses rather than overawes: it must be toiled up to attain the platforms from one of which *l'accelerato* starts south to run through Lombardy towards Parma, Bologna, Florence, and the ever-flowing, ever-cold fountains of Rome.

On a bleak afternoon in late November, a day of drizzle from a steel-grey sky onto a seal-grey city, Jean D. and I were being farewelled at the station by the Australian Consul-General's wife with whom we had lunched. Afterwards she had come with us to a refrigerated Santa Maria della Grazie while, as our planned last sight-seeing in Milan, we looked again at Leonardo da Vinci's *The Last Supper*.

We were both wary again-lookers drifting through the Old World in the direction of the equator, and back to Australia. Middle-aged, unpassionate but firm friends, hard-bitten tourists, we were revisiting together what we had, when younger, separately visited before. To sum up our itinerary—a Harry's Bar or a Trader Vic's was as much part of it as any Gothic polyptych, Byzantine mosaic or Bernini triton.

Somewhat chastened by *The Last Supper*, we were to catch the two-fifty for Florence.

The three of us stood flinching in the maelstrom of draughts at the foot of the grim cliff of stairs while Mario the consular chauffeur unloaded our baggage from the consular Fiat.

It was I perhaps who first noticed the young woman: her face. It was the Consul-General's wife who first spoke of her.

"Now *that*," she said, "is what I should be wearing." She added, "With my impossible legs."

Jean D. and I, prudent cowards, looked neither at each other nor the legs we'd already noted as misproportionately strapping beneath the Consul-General's wife's svelte upper, and her delicately hollow face. We gave instead the keenest attention to what the young woman wore, the back-view as she ascended with much grace the Teotihuacán-like steep.

It was the year when the pitiless fashion of the mini-skirt was just giving way to a more humane one; freakish legs were returning to the seductive obscurity of longer skirts. In England, Germany, and France we had already seen numbers of women wearing the new style. The one before our eyes was the first we'd seen in Italy. A maxi-coat recalling a Ukrainian Cossack's, and worn with Russian boots, it was not only fitting wear for the untender wintriness of the day but strikingly set off its wearer's tallness and litheness. The flared skirt and its border of fur lilted romantically as she mounted the steps with all the stylish bravado of a *jeune premier* in a Graustarkian operetta. The two women with me went into analytical raptures which I did not interrupt with:

"But did you see her face?"

Useless to interrupt: had they seen it they would by then have forgotten: the Cossackian coat had become headless to them.

It was clear that what had caught my eye had not caught theirs: a face so like Eleanor da Toledo's in the Angelo Bronzino portrait that I felt myself go actually open-mouthed with amazement. It was, in effect, double amazement. There I was, about to board *l'accelerato* for Florence where one of the reasons for a proposed trek through the endless little salons of the Uffizi Gallery was to moon yet again, for the fifth or sixth time, in front of that very portrait with its sealed, cool countenance, its eyes depthless with indifference. Extraordinarily alike, portrait and passer-by: for an absurd moment it seemed reasonable to accept that Eleanor da Toledo could be a sixteenth-century ancestress of the supple stranger whose face was not only also impassive and impenetrable, a courtly mask, but whose hatless black hair was arranged much as the woman in the painting had arranged hers—was that looking-glass still alive?—more than three centuries ago.

Reason alone, I knew, is too fallible. That glimpse of her, fleeting yet charged, was no more than one from which a poem might be

made, taut with regret because both the world and the Milan railway station were boundless enough for me and Eleanor da Toledo's
reincarnation never to be breathing again at the same time the same
freezing air with its odour of damp metal.

Jean D. and I said good-bye to the Consul-General's wife at the
bottom of the steps, and climbed—how much less buoyantly than
the tall girl with the still face and swashbuckling coat!—up and up
into the skirmish of echoes, and the arctic cross-currents of inex-
plicable little indoor winds.

It would have matched my mood of Baudelairean spleen to find
every seat in the train taken, and the corridor jammed with a rain-
soaked herd of pilgrims on their way to Rome. The train was far
from crowded. In the eight-seater *seconda classe* compartment
where we settled five minutes before departure there were only
three passengers.

In one window-seat was a very fat Italian woman, fiftyish, high-
bosomed, with an adolescent moustache.

Opposite her sat a stocky young man brutally handsome as a
brigand.

Their attire announced that they were possibly of the lower middle class, in any country the most conventional, and therefore the
most easily identified. They wore the sort of clothes seen behind the
plate-glass of smaller department stores, the uniform of the hide-
bound and frugal, unemphatic wear, factory-made of artificial materials. The one thing about them not ersatz was their behaviour; but
even that, taking into consideration the melodramatic country we
were in, was orthodox enough.

They were patently mother and son: a family profile jutted out of
her blubber and his sullenness, and they were so engrossed in a
generation tiff that they neither spared us a side-glance nor lost an
impassioned syllable when we came in. They were both holding
forth at the one time; her soprano railing went volubly on above his
fierce baritone declaiming over and over again:

"*Non è stata colpa mia!*"—whatever it was it wasn't his fault—
"*Non è stata colpa mia, mamma! Non ... è ... stata ... colpa ...
mia!*"

On the badgered son's side of the compartment, plumb in the
middle, the half-clock-face of the airconditioning switch directly
above his hair which was like goffered iron, sat another Italian,
perhaps seventy, perhaps only sixty: it was hard to tell. Not once in
the two-and-a-half hours he was with us did we hear him speak, or
catch his eye.

He sat monolithically upright as a stone Rameses, contentedly
withdrawn, his scoured, sun-darkened hands inactively set on his
hams. The contours and rich rustic colouring of his face reminded
me of an Arcimboldi one, a composition of corn-cobs, pomegran-
ates, chestnuts, and onions. He seemed so much of the earth that

we'd have to be, one felt, famished oxen or ailing vines, before his attention would turn to us, and his unreflective eyes come to life. He could, of course, have been a rugged solitary who despised the vile world, and played Ravel exquisitely.

I sat on the so-to-speak masculine side of the compartment, in the corner next to the corridor. Jean arranged herself opposite and, as we usually did on train journeys, we began the process of retracting somewhat from each other. She opened her guide-book at, I had no doubt, the chapter on Florence. A loud-speaker voice gabbling truculently against its own several echoes announced that our train was about to leave. I experienced that sensation of feline well-being mingled with here-we-go-again boredom the experienced traveller is apt to experience at such times.

Then, at the last moment, mere seconds before the wheels turned, the young woman in the Cossack coat flashed radiantly into sight at the doorway, scanned the compartment with lustrous heartless eyes, and appeared to find it worthy of her. From where she stood, and deftly as a basketball player throwing a goal, she tossed her valise onto the rack.

This *coup de théâtre* accomplished, she moved in, and sat with decisive aplomb between Jean D. and the fat mother who, at a climax of son-baiting, her wattles aquiver, spat out a scalding babble of insult. The victim had had enough. Harshly crying, *"Non l'ho fatto apposta!"*—I didn't do it on purpose!—he folded his arms as though barricading himself behind them, set his jaws, and closed his eyes. A door had been slammed in a face.

Furtively, as if sidling from an unhallowed cathedral, the train slipped between the soaring nave piers, through a rood screen of grimy girders, over the no-altar, and out into the Milanese rain so like all other rains, the dejected industrial outskirts that could have been anywhere.

All this, and a funereal burden of smoke lowering above a palisade of chimney-stacks, I took in from the corner of my senses. For the rest I was covertly but wholly taking in the unbelievable late arrival.

She was, I saw, years younger than Bronzino's Eleanor, but twentieth-century experiences had given her an additional gloss of age in a dimension beyond years. Self-possession's self, she lit a cigarette, and opened a Penguin. The nails of the ringless, long long Renaissance fingers were bitten. That was a touch jarringly too human and modern, and stopped me in my tracks on the poetic by-path I'd taken. The Penguin was Elizabeth Bowen's *To the North*.

So, as well as being a nail-biter, she wasn't a Latin after all! This reversed sign-post was more than intriguing: I contemplated a remark about Elizabeth Bowen. Jean D. was ahead of me.

The proximity of the fur-trimmed Cossack sleeve to her Scotch tweed one generated some electricity of intuition. My friend closed the guidebook in a final way and, with the certainty that the animal in the cage she was entering was of a familiar species, spoke to the young woman. The species certainly was familiar; the animal ready to play, and without reserve. She was also Australian. She had been working for three months, *au pair* but with a small salary, as nurse-maid to the baby twins of a Signor and Signora Russo, at Parma. Oh, she was absolutely without reserve. She abhorred Parma, she said, loathed the Signor who was, like all Dago men, sly and a sex maniac; scorned the Signora; and couldn't stand babies. And the meals! *Pasta*, no matter what shape or colour, she hated. Veal too, and sausages containing God knows what. As for the continental breakfast, that was hardly food at all, or at most:

"*Slum* food, actually. Bread-and-jam and cocoa—and I *detest* crusts!"

She was twenty going on twenty-one. Her name was Brett Something-or-Other. Had her mother been reading Hemingway when she was pregnant? I didn't ask although dying to. Maybe, as people do to lighten the hard work of travel, she would come to telling.

Travellers, imprisoned with strangers in foreign trains, ships' bars, air-terminal waiting-rooms, chartered tourist buses lunging through Turkey or Afghanistan, are inclined to foil *ennui* by being as unreticent about themselves as characters in a Chekhov play.

About themselves: how else keep their identity in places they do not belong to?

About themselves: even though the impression they more often than not create is of eccentricity, recklessness, animal cunning, of an incredible toughness shot through with peculiar snobberies and almost-idiot simplicities. Perhaps Brett would later clear up why she had been named Brett. As I listened to her talking to Jean D. in an educated, extrovert voice, it was manifest she had no thought of hiding anything.

I am, her manner said, what I am: lump it or leave it.

While exchanging *dragées* and peppermints and cigarettes, the women exchanged more and more of themselves, admitting me to their confidences but off-handedly, as though I were scarcely human, a dummy on the side-line. For all her poise (the panache, for example, with which she'd entered the compartment) she seemed to live in perpetual suspense. Her version of herself was hounded and harassed, a chronic Victim of Fate. It was done humorously, yet, as I laughed, I felt alarm at what catastrophe might be just ahead: some of the past catastrophes, however hilariously she presented them, seemed to me hair-raising, rape or murder an inch off.

She was always losing things, her passport, traveller's cheques, a camera, or leaving her purse with the last of her money in it at some place so disreputable that there was no hope of its being returned. She missed trains or buses to find herself stranded among near-cutthroats at unhealthy hours, drifted solo into the back-alley haunts of criminals and prostitutes; found herself fighting off inflamed lechers in places so out-of-the-way that no Good Samaritan would have heard her scream. Once she and an Australian girlfriend, speeding through Germany in a rented car had run down a deer on the outskirts of East Berlin at three o'clock in the morning, and had spent three days and nights in a lock-up.

"The food," she said, "was miraculous—*Kaffee mit Sahne*, yet!"

She was, she said, in trouble at the moment, with not a brass razoo to her name, down to her last unbroached packet of cigarettes, and nearly three days late in getting back from the weekend she had nagged Signora Russo into letting her spend in Milan.

"Everything, but everything, happens to poor Brett," she said complacently.

Meantime, outside, a landscape like a rain-botched *grisaille*, sodden Lombardy slid murkily by between the profiles of mother and son. He had been permitted a length of sanctuary behind the barrier of his folded arms and shuttered eyes while she dipped at mechanic intervals into a black plastic carry-all for titbits she chewed with the engrossed mien of a plot-hatcher. A moment arrived when she was sated, and had ruminated her next move into shape. She attacked again, sharply: "Carlo!"

No response so, more sharply, louder: "Car-lo, Car-lo!"

Once more, no response.

The jelly of her face stiffened: she knew he heard within the fort. From among the chattels banked up around her she groped out a chubby umbrella, and tapped his knee with the blunt ferrule. He still kept to his asylum; one felt he had his back to the door, hard. A muscle flickered on his cheek.

"Car-*lo!*"

This time she tapped viciously enough to hurt. He didn't wince but his eyes, as inexpressive as all brown eyes are, shot wide open, then immediately became slits. Politely enough, yet gratingly, threateningly, he asked what she wanted, "*Che cosa desidera?*"

She beat on the seat beside her with a fat little hand, and trilled: "*È troppo duro; è troppo duro.*"

It wasn't hard at all; on this tourist-ridden line even the second class catered for spoiled foreigners. Anyway, had it been brown sienna marble instead of brown leatherette padded with foam rubber, Carlo's mother was her own luxurious cushions. Marble, fakir's spikes, fire-walker's coals, what could her child have done? Nurse her? Advise her to stand, or swing like a larger marmoset from the luggage-rack? He didn't even bother to answer, shut his eyes, and contemptuously, as though to exclude someone crazy.

Unbearable! Unfilial! Humiliating!—the ferrule prodding maliciously at his entwined fore-arms expressed these for her. He came to angry life, and grabbed the ferrule, far from playfully.

"Carlo, ma no!"

She squealed as if we other four were not there, tug-of-warring frantically as with a real snatch-thief, both hands in use. A new line, femininity, was jolted into being.

"Fa freddo," she wailed, piping, frail and helpless.

"Fa freddo, Car-lo mi-o!" and pounded her patent-leather trotters girlishly on the floor to indicate their being violet with cold. Suddenly he let go and, as she bounced back with a squeak, stretched out for the air-conditioner switch above the hair of the Rameses man who didn't even slope his head automatically to one side but remained static and sequestered as a private image. Carlo pushed the pointer to its heat limit, *Caldo*, and, as one saying, "There, boil to death, dear mother, and leave me in peace", again immured himself behind his arms and eyelids.

Brett said very clearly, "The perverse old bitch! What that over-weight madam needs is a back-hander across the chops!"

It was fascinating. Edged with indictment as her voice was, her face remained serene. She might have been praising or blessing the brawlers. They had, however, aroused a sleeping dog. She began again to denigrate Signora Russo and all living Italians. Because of the crystal pitch of her voice, she was as embarrassing as a cruel child. It disordered me. How could she know that the Italians didn't understand English, that she wasn't committing a social atrocity? I suppose, in fact, that she didn't care if every word were intelligible, and that she looked on them as being as culpable as the next Italian.

She hadn't come to Italy to dislike it; its inhabitants had taught her to. She felt blameless: she'd earned her fare over; was paying her way, working her way, conning her way when all else failed, through an Old World she'd been lured into visiting by gilded legends, propaganda ablaze with seductive adjectives. She'd been taken in by a mirage of civilizations accounted superior to her own country's, of breath-taking landscapes strewn with gorgeous cities and enchanting villages alive with diverting and decorative people.

She had been too ingenuous to believe, had not lived long enough to learn, that the Utopias of the pamphlet are what one does one's best to avoid. Now, behind her happy-go-lucky cynicism and auda-cious front, disillusion stirred like Polonius behind the arras. She spared nothing: Italy was a fifth-rate vaudeville show, the Italians cheap and nasty buffoons. She was revolted by the showy clothes hiding the dismal secrets of uncleanliness; sick of the untrustworthi-ness, the emotionalism, and jealous pride; infuriated by the sensual, over-confident faces of those who accosted her.

"Brett's *virgo intacta*, and proud of it," she said almost ringingly. "But a wise virgin, and not a timid one."

The terrors of the flesh she held at bay: she had, it seemed, learnt well the perilous lessons of modesty and love but didn't think them shield enough.

"See here!"

She took from her hand-bag a pair of wickedly pointed little scissors.

"They're silver. My great-grandmother used them for embroidery. She'd die again if she knew, poor lamb, what I use them for."

In queues, crowded trains and trams, cinemas, and public gardens, she carried them in her hand ready to stab into men who touched her. Her intolerance was flawless. Cheek by jowl with Italians in the compartment of *l'accelerato* she was separated from them by an abyss of the spirit. The Italian woman and her son shocked her: she *hated* them, she said, her face as expressionless as a camellia—yet it might have been a serpent speaking.

Curiously, despite a force and stringency in her conversation, one became also aware of odd slacknesses, bewildering non sequiturs. The link between thought and thought seemed especially to dissolve at a direct question. At first I thought she was letting down a safety-curtain on some of Jean D's feelers, but her whole-hearted candour made that unlikely. It was just that, with one foot in sophistication, the other in naïveté, dislocations occurred. She was, for example, denouncing Signora Russo for always being underfoot, always hanging over her own babies:

"I don't know why she bothers with a nanny. I might just as well be in Saudi-Arabia. Sometimes I'd like to hit her."

Jean D., who thinks kindly of most Italians and all babies, said, "Oh, you can't mean that, Brett. She treats you very well. You have plenty of time off. After all, why shouldn't she dote on her own babies?"

"Because she'll ruin them. Besotted woman—tying and untying their ribbons all the time as if they were dolls."

"But she's their *mother*," Jean D., childless, was becoming fervent and stubborn.

"Yes, I suppose the creature is." To my surprise she spoke mildly, as if she had of a sudden seen the Signora in a new light, a kind of Crivelli Madonna dandling two Holy Children in front of an oriel window-sill crowded with porcelain-like fruit, enamelled-looking flowers, and highly glazed cucumbers.

"Then, surely," asked Jean D. more in the manner of a sentimental deaconess than I'd have believed possible, "she can be forgiven, or at least understood?"

"I ... don't ... think ... so." Brett answered lingeringly, apparently in thought. It couldn't have been thought, for she added, "No, I *don't* think so. She's far too pretty, and has varicose veins." She paused. "Anyway, she's a bank-manager's wife."

Jean D. was flummoxed enough to say, "What difference does that make?"

"My father's one, too."

On the subject of returning to Parma three days later after racketing about Milan with wanderer Australian friends on their way to

Venice her thoughts were equally random and unmarried to each other.

"What on earth," Jean D. had asked, "will your Signora say?"

"I don't care a damn what she says. Or does. She can rave on like that obese dolly in the window-seat if it gives her a kick. I'll make up some taradiddle or other—tell her I ran out of lire."

While I was still trying to spot what was askew about this, Jean D. said, "Heavens, girl, *that's* hardly a convincing lie. If you'd no money how could you afford three extra days?"

"It's not a lie." How calm she was. From the hand-bag containing scissors but no money she languidly took her last packet of cigarettes. "I told you I hadn't a brass razoo." Finically as a good little girl, she began opening the packet. "But this morning I had lashings of lucre."

"You haven't lost your purse again?" Jean D. was getting motherly.

"No. I can't imagine why—but no, the money's not lost this time. I lent it to two blokes who were skint."

"You *lent* it!" Jean D. was maternally severe. "So now you're skint. Who were they?" She doubtless pictured a brace of confidence men from Naples pretending to be Veronese counts who'd left their wallets in other suits.

"One was an Australian."

"I see." Jean D. was now absolute mother. "And the other?"

Brett languidly lit a cigarette, languidly exhaled. "Oh, he was an Australian."

A silence had to fall. There was nothing to say. Jean D. look at me, I at her, our eyes as it were shrugging. There was nothing else to do.

At that moment the mother in her discreet production-belt hat animated herself, and intoned with tragic intensity, "*Carlo mio, fa troppo caldo.*"

The son, perhaps truly, like a disciple at Gethsemane, slept on.

"*Io sudo,*" she whined, dabbing a pink handkerchief on her moustache which was indeed beaded with sweat. "*Io sudo, Carlo. Non posso sopportare il calda.*"

"She can't bear the bloody heat!"

Brett rose up, breathing authentic cigarette smoke, and metaphorical flame. "Neither can I. Excuse me, talkative," she said down in the coiffure of the living idol whose self-absorption remained unruffled as she abruptly turned the air-conditioning pointer right back to *Freddo*. "And I sincerely hope, Mother Macree, that you freeze to death."

Whatever the words conveyed to us Australians, the tone cannot have conveyed anything to the Italians, particularly as she uttered without a side-glance at them, and had moved to perform her ostensibly gracious act like a well-bred and mobile caryatid on whose carven tresses an invisible burden of marble acanthus leaves and a ton of architrave were being perfectly balanced. Reseating herself, her visage politely neutral, "God, I *hate* them," she said.

Beyond the windows a drenched Lombardy was running out; before many minutes *l'accelerato* would be in drenched Emilia.

Sky-scraper crags, bottomless primeval lakes, cascades frothing soapily down gorges, leagues of blue-and-white snow-dunes, unemployed nature in any guise is not to my taste. It would have pleased me, however, had the plains docile from centuries of cultivation not been veiled in vertical water, to look out at them, at the tamed rivers, the food-bearing trees and drink-bearing vines, the wounded towers and castles far-off on their hill-top aeries, the farther-off mountains like penitentiary walls still keeping in something mediaeval and feudal, the fumes of vendetta and foray and, in the veins of the last of the vine-leaves, the blood of battle-axed mercenaries, of war-horses and lords, which had long ago extravagantly irrigated the soil. Since I was unable to see what lay outside, the beauty that is feud's aftermath, I had to make do with the feud in the compartment, and await its aftermath.

It wasn't a situation about which to be flinty. Brett's naïveté was too engaging for that, and her fearlessness rather moving because-what was callous in it was not inborn but a culture: necessity its spore. Her fury was, I felt, only that of the displaced and disappointed, transient enough for air to have wafted it into her mind. The faintest movement of the weather-vane, and a breath would puff it out.

Perhaps, now, she could never cry, "Open, sesame!" with the old wide-eyed expectation—she had learnt too much to want to, but she could still cry, "Open, wheat!", "Open, barley!" and not be let down. The consequences of her impercipience meant nothing to her, nothing: it proved nothing except the immeasurable distance between two national minds. She had arrived at the point where civilization (as she recognized it) was seen, by its absence, to have existed where she came from, not where she had come to. Homesickness can calcify the heart and buckle the vision as quickly and easily as vice.

The train advanced into Emilia and the melancholy border-land of twilight. Perhaps because abhorred Parma, amorous Signor Russo, the doting Signora and her beribboned twins, tomorrow and tomorrow, all swam nearer and nearer through the darkening rain, she fell silent, closed her eyes, and did not sleep.

Her face!—behind its composure an engagement with emotion could be guessed at, but the ivory surface, the Goddess of Mercy blankness admitted nothing: her hands with their bitten nails now and then shifted restlessly on her fashionable lap.

Jean D. opened her guidebook. Would it inform her that for nearly five centuries Florence had been, like Rome and Vienna, Madrid and Paris, a centre of fake antiquities and forged masterpieces?

Night's tide was in when Brett opened her eyes.

"Forgive me, Jean. I was out on business. Really! I've been desperately trying to think of something heart-breaking. Hopeless!"

She gave no explanation, but went on, "I must have some money. Must. *Must*."

She was talking to Jean D. rather than to both of us but her wantonly clear voice could no doubt be heard in the next compartment if not farther off.

"Oh, dear, it's maddening. In three weeks' time I want to be out of Parma. You see, there's a promise I've got to keep. Two girlfriends are coming down from Norway. We'll join up at Milan, go down to Rome and Naples, then to Brindisi where we'll get a ship across the Adriatic to Greece. I've been there before, and *loathed* it, but a promise is a promise. Even if I have to sleep in the Parthenon, and get my Victamin C from those sour oranges that grow on the street-trees in Athens, I'll need *real* money to get there. I was certain I'd have it by now, but everything's gone wrong. Me all over, of course. Time's running out. Poor little Brett's on the horns of a whatsis. No matter how much I try and try, I can't get my suit-case stolen. What would you do?"

"To ... to get my suit-case stolen?" Jean D. spoke of a fog. Suddenly it cleared: "Oh, I see. For the insurance, you mean?"

"Yes. Its money for jam. Or so I thought."

She had heavily insured everything she'd brought with her from Australia, and losing her expensive camera at a time when she was on the rocks had found the insurance money a god-send. The camera's loss had been an accident; the loss she was now set on was to be deliberate. The case she hoped to collect on was, she said, a costly monster so large that it had to be wheeled on an also-costly fold-up trolley. For the sort of bread-line travelling she and her young friends now did, invaders' skimpily-accoutred Blitzkriegs, the monster, with its attendant contraption, was a hindrance. It was also potential capital.

Her account of attempts to abandon it was very funny, illegal though her intentions. She'd done everything possible to contrive situations in which her head was morally above water, even if only just. Usually she left it on railway platforms next to the most criminal-looking people in sight while she walked conspicuously away, not looking back, to dally in station bars or waiting-rooms or buffets. Time after time she returned to find it, despised loot, exactly as she'd left it. Twice she had deserted it on buses. Once a group of men who resembled the denizens of a thieves' kitchen had yelled and whistled her back; once a wizened old man with a squint had scorched after her on a new-fangled bicycle.

"I suppose," she said, "the costly bloody monster *and* its costly trolley are too conspicuous to steal. And—" She smiled faintly.— "I'm too conspicuous to be stolen from. It bugs me. Either they're all daft, or I'm fated, or both."

In a Europe she regarded as an elaborate piece of machinery set up to bilk and pillage the tourist, an honesty she regarded as perverse dogged her.

"I'd contemplated defying the fates, and trying again in Milan, but decided no-no-*no*: better to enjoy myself than have the worry of not losing it again. I've got a better plan. When I get off at Parma ... *hell*, where are we?"

The train was decelerating, running over points. She recognized, through the streaming panes, some reassuring combination of lights and outlines.

"Ah, thank God this isn't for me."

It was for Signor Rameses-Arcimboldi who unfolded into an unexpectedly squat man, took an old-fashioned kit-bag from the rack, slid open the door, and wordlessly, on his too-short legs, went out to wait in the corridor.

"*Carlo! Che ora è? Quanto ci fermiano qui? Ho sete, Carlo. Ho appetito!*" keened the mother.

Carlo, eyes balefully open, said cruelly that he wasn't thirsty or hungry: "*Non ho sete. Non ho appetito.*" Outraged, detonated, she released a torrent of melodious abuse. Like a lip-reader, or someone at a *film muto*, he watched, one felt, rather than heard.

The train stopped. The full-dress tirade didn't. The little platform was bare except for the silent man and his kit-bag jogging through the rain. A dog committing a dire aria could be heard. The train started.

"Oh, do shut up, you neurotic old sow," said Brett looking at the palm of one hand. "You know, it's a wonder he doesn't knife the whingeing hag. I'd like to see Signora Giovanni Russo try to bully me like that."

Right then, it came to me that for all the mother's malicious caterwauling and the son's churlishness, all the domestic discord, the two Italians with their passion-afflicted faces had quieter nerves than Brett with her unmarked brow and tender mouth. Theirs might well have been a happy partnership of hate, for hate had as many allegiances as love, and far less fallible ones. If their faces were, so to speak, chewed, their finger-nails weren't.

"You were saying," said Jean D., the orchestra-conductor tapping with the baton, "that when you get off at Parma...."

"I'll show them."

Brett flicked her compact open, reviewed her lips and eyes in the glass, did nothing to them.

"I used to have lovely nails until I took to feasting on them."

She put away the compact, and gazed tranquilly at her fingers.

"They really are repulsive. It makes me shudder to look at them."

"Show whom what?" Jean D. was pedantic but persistent. Curiosity gnawed at her like the Spartan youth's fox: she had no intention of letting Brett's riven mind remain unwelded.

"The insurance people, of course. When I get to Parma my new plan goes straight into action." She inhaled a sighing breath. "I'm going to report to the Dago station-master that I've lost the monster."

We said nothing.

"Have I shocked you? Everyone does it. *Have* I?"

Neither of us answered. I saw Jean D.'s face—and felt mine—congeal at non-committal. I said, "Will they believe you?"

"Oh, don't say that! They'll *have* to believe me. I'll make them. I used to be quite an actress at school; Portia, you know—'it droppeth as the gentle rain', and so on."

She went into a kind of trance, enacting what she'd devised, running over her pathetic script.

"I'll tell them that the case was so enormous it couldn't fit on the mingy little second-class rack, so I left it in the corridor. What else could I do? Why didn't I book it through in the luggage-van? Because, poor maiden, I didn't get to the station in time." She dropped the mediumistic manner, and absurdly pleaded, "You saw that, didn't you, Jean, my leaping on just as the train was moving out?" Then she returned to her other fiction. "I was desperate. I'd been lost for *hours* in Milan, all all alone, and was worried frantic about getting back to the dear, sweet, lovely *bambini*. In the train I was so exhausted from trailing around Milan in the downpour that I fell asleep, and didn't wake up until we arrived at Parma. When I went out into the corridor to get my case—*mamma mia! il mio bello, bello bagaglio*—gone! I'll burst into tears. '*Mamma mia, mamma mia*,' I'll sob, '*Oh, mamma mia, il mio bagaglio!*'"

The snatches of Italian interrupted the bickering in the window-seats; mother and son turned their simmering, feral eyes on the elegant foreigner. She sensed their attention. Without deigning to look at them, she said, "Stare, stare, monkey bear! Mind your own bloody business, slobs!"

I think Jean D. and I thought that, surely this time, some Mediterranean extra-sensory gift might have been at last brought into play, and the rudeness understood, for we both quickly spoke.

"Will it work?" was hers; "It won't work," was mine.

"It has to. I promised the girls I'd meet them outside the Milan cathedral at midday on the fifteenth of next month, traveller's cheques and all. I couldn't let them down. I've got to be a get-rich-quick maiden this time. All this mess wouldn't have happened if one of the nit-wits had had the nous to pinch the case instead of trying to pinch my you-know-what. Imagine poor Brett weeping and wailing in front of a lecherous gang of porters! '*Ah, poverina, poverina*,' they'll croon, and pat me, and I won't be able to use my scissors. And then there'll be the police, and I'll have to repeat the entire *mamma mia* performance."

She inhaled another, deeper sighing breath.

"One must martyr oneself for oneself," she said blandly.

Jean D. was near tears. It wouldn't have surprised me if she'd drawn the regal head down to her bosom.

"But aren't you worried, Brett?"

Did she really mean morally worried? Did she mean, on a lower plane, worried about attempting blatant perjury without any of the technique of the Duse it would require to make it work? Did she, on the lowest plane, mean worried at the possibility of being not believed? Which sort of worried did she mean?

"Worried! Of course. I spent my last lire in that clinical buffet on the Milan station to mop up a few fortifying vinos. I'm worried *stiff*."

She—which sort of worried did she mean? She consulted the compact again, this time using a lipstick, wiping powder on, fussing with her scarf, touching up the leading lady or preparing the victim. Worried? The touched-up face was as pacific as a tarn nothing is reflected in.

She put a cigarette between her lips, and struck a match. The quivering of the tiny flame made it clear that her hand was unsteady.

"Oh dear," she said, "poor Brett."

She blew out the match without lighting the cigarette, and admonished herself: "Stop that instantly, you silly maiden. Stop, right now."

The aristocratic hands with their gnawed nails, held out before her, became still.

"Anyway," she said, putting the cigarette back in the packet, "there's no time."

She stood, reached for her valise, put it on the seat, and sat again, tilting her head back, closing her eyes. She kept them closed for five minutes, ten minutes, until the train, jerking over points, passing through a lighted suburb, came to Parma, and stopped.

She opened her eyes. "Yes, Jean," she said, rising, and taking up her valise. "I'm *very* worried. I've been trying to think of something sad so that I can cry for those galoots out there. Good-bye."

At the door she spoke once again, and then went. The train started. We passed her, pliant and untouchable in the Cossack coat, moving over the brilliant reflections on the wet platform. The rain had gone. Her last words had not: we kept on hearing them.

"I'm terrified. What's going to happen now? All I need is tears, and I can't think of a single unhappy incident in my whole life."

John Russell Rowland   (1925–)

Poet. Born in northern N.S.W.; educated at Sydney.

LAKE GEORGE

Violet-blue and white
As fragile china cups
Tree-freckled hills in distance
Suggest a scene of dreams:
A stretch of white water,
Condensed mist, as foreground
Small waves tripping
Each after each ashore,
A sky of silk over
Birds in the shallows.

Being of conventional
Mind, though one reaches
Stretches to seize some
Meaning or essence
Beyond flat description
Nothing will come; this cold
Half-unearthly country still
Sends back no echo,
Dumb, remains obstinate
Rock, grass, and water.

MADAME BUTTERFLY IN A CHINESE THEATRE

When Pinkerton returned to Butterfly
Their faces were marked equally with tears.
No one at that moment could have told
Which was to die, or was to blame, or which
Had waited emptyhearted through the years

As the stage shows us: see how she stands
With stony mask uplifted to the spotlight
Watching the swallows build their nests again
Against the backcloth, her eyes streaming
Brilliant tears and face unnatural white

While stagehands in singlets change the seasons
Round her, and children wander in the wings,
Gongs resound, and the crackle of the knackers
Accompanies her grief. She stands unmoving
Then, highpitched and heartbroken, she sings.

He meanwhile is in America
Behaving, no doubt, much as he did here
With his elastic grin and unlit pipe
His cheeks as rouged as ever, and his habits
Of upsetting tables and slicking back his hair

Taking medicines to increase virility
And pills for constipation and long life.
Now he returns: an interval of joy
Then final departure. O fearful agony
Terrible deathscene! with collapsible knife

Deep in her stomach, and floods of scarlet
Bursting through her fingers. Who was to blame?
Faithfulness is always innocent
Heart and convention answer. But may one not remark
A too obstinate insistence on her claim?

CAIRO HOTEL

A room the size of a warehouse
With chairs like stick-insects sheltering in corners
And a wide rhetorical bed.

Like a fruit display from the ceiling
The chandelier gleamed; four candelabra
Trophies, stags' heads, stared from the crimson walls.

An airless odour of camphor and fine dust
In the blank wardrobe; and in the topmost drawer
A flimsy envelope addressed in French.

The light-switch fell to pieces under my hand
There were three bells, for Waiter, Maid and Valet
And the traffic trembled all night under the bed

To which, unfortunately, no sequined countess
Mysteriously came, having perhaps mistaken
The door, or by an impulse. The great room

Smelling of dryness and impermanence
Withheld its opportunities: yet I felt
That, given time there, something would have happened.

FREMANTLE

New wide clean bright
Temporary: a collocation of shacks.
Avenues of branched poles, earthscars,
Skeins of wires, roofs and shining asphalt
Tremble together in the brilliant light.

Here Australia begins; see
How luminous the blue air and water,
How dark the hills, the trees with a dry sparkle—
Pass the Moderne Gifte Shoppe, Reg. MacPherson
Ern Jones for Bicycles, Kinkara Tea,

Avoid the rolling barrel, pause
For the sour smell of beer, distinctive
As the tigerish footballers framed against green tiles.
Here is a newspaper; read in its many pages
About Shark Tragedy, Dave Sands and cricket scores.

Rejoice in butchers' shops, and fruit
In pyramid and phalanx on the barrows;
Observe the Capitol and Niagara cafés,
The men's squareshouldered coats, the elder women's
Amazing hats, the children as remote

And delicate as birds; the tone
Of voices, and the cadence of their walk.
Great clouds like deities sail an enormous sky
In which it seems the breath of Europe, dense
With time and wars, humanity and stone

Must instantly dissolve. But see
The riding moon, which here seems so transparent
And is shining now on the countries of your sojourn
Remember the shadow, that appears unmoving
Yet joins all continents in a single day.

Now you are home, and soon
Perhaps, you will feel you have never been away.
Faintly uneasy, a familiar stranger,
Look while you can through this clear glass of arrival:
You will never have quite the same vision again.

CHRISTINA STEAD (1902–1983)

Novelist, short story writer. Born and educated in Sydney; lived abroad from 1928; returned to Australia in 1974.

THE BOY

Her name is Fifi, Fifi Mercier, but she says she is called La Grande Fifi; and that is what we call her among ourselves. If you meet her on the hill, on the street, out shopping, you see in the distance a stout active little lady, in her middle fifties, with a broad pretty face, untidy white hair, dark eyes, a ready smile. She wears an old blue dress, with a peep of petticoat behind, cotton stockings and canvas shoes.

This is what she looks like; but you don't know her. She is a romantic figure. She runs a students' boarding-house on the stiff Lausanne slopes, in a decent middle-class house, where there are some quiet families. But on the ground floor is a retired postman in poor health, who thinks everyone is a German; and on the top floor is a woman who causes traffic congestion on the stairs, especially on market days. She is a witch-doctor, who cures farm animals at a distance, if the farmers bring her a knot of hair or bit of hide; she cures and protects from sickness and evil by swinging a watch. She makes good money and the farmers swear by her: 'If we did not have her, all the animals would die of foot-rot.' The witch makes better money than La Grande Fifi, who is so worried about taxes and rent that she has bad dreams. She dreams that her lodgers are sick and go to the kitchen to heat some milk and barley-sugar (a cure for coughs). She dreams she sees them there and says, 'You must pack, I have to go, I am turned out for not paying the rent; I am sorry for you when you are so sick.' This is her worry. She has four students, and a married couple who do their own cooking on a picnic stove in the handsome large washroom. The students eat with her in the dining-room; their payments are irregular but they do their best.

There is one other boarder, not a student, whom she calls The Boy, *le petit*. His name is Mr Bernard, 'a very young man,' she says; and then she adds that he is thirty-three years of age. He has a pleasant room, a girl-friend who visits him; and he has a mini-piano—he plays well. On Sundays he plays the organ at church. His girl-friend, Miss Corelli, does not visit him often and then only at lunch-time. 'Really I can't tolerate that —have you ever seen the like, a girl visiting a man in his rooms? I must watch the morals of my house,' says La Grande.

The Boy does not seem troubled about it himself. He has been in Fifi's boarding-house eight years and has been engaged five years. His fiancée is a tired-looking blonde who works in his office; he is an accountant. Last year Fifi had to show her landlord that her accounts were in order. They were in order, because Mr Bernard takes care of them. Now the landlord writes to Fifi, 'You did not answer my letter asking for certain information.' What does that mean? It means he is trying to evict Fifi; that is why, for one thing, she has to be strict about morals. So she tells Mr Bernard and the students.

The Boy is tall, dark, good-looking, languid; and in winter he has a cough. She turns off the heating at the end of winter, as soon as she can, to save; and then the Boy stays in bed, partly sick, partly malingering, in protest.

'I shall call the polyclinic doctor,' she says.

'Oh, no, I must have a private physician.'

'I must tell you I called the polyclinic doctor anyway. Who is going to pay for the private physician? I, you think? My dear, you are crafty, the son of a peasant and you are crafty like all peasants. The fact is, you must go to the polyclinic and ask for an X-ray.'

Le petit stayed in bed with a pain in his side and then got up and went for a motor-ride all the afternoon. When he returned she said, 'Now you must go back to work, you are not serious;' and as soon as she said this he went back to bed.

'I don't know what to do with the boy,' she complained to the married couple. 'He has been sick for two years; and he has such habits. He drinks whisky and gin in his room and goes out at night playing poker for money. Sometimes I drink with him in the dining-room, to keep him in. Some days he will say he is cleaned out, he hasn't a cent; and the next day he comes back with money. He is an accountant, a man in a position of trust. Where does the money come from? I know it is a stage in life, and he lives alone in a room; but perhaps it won't get better, it may get worse.'

She worries for another reason. People who have lodgers must have a bedroom for each one in the house; to sleep in the living-rooms is against the law. But La Grande Fifi has no room of her own and sleeps in the dining-room on a couch. When the last meal is finished and the students have gone to their rooms, and the kitchen settled, she makes up her bed there, with sheets and a blanket; and there she goes to bed. But she does not lock the door.

The Boy takes her out once a week to the movies and comes to her room every night. He cannot sleep unless he has told her everything that happened during the day. There's no harm in the others hearing voices there, for it is the dining-room, not her bedroom; and she is not undressed, only resting her legs.

She is often so tired that she wishes he would not. Sometimes you can see her, sitting up on the couch, in her white hair and white

high-necked flannel nightgown, a shawl around her shoulders, waiting for him. She hears him come in the front door: 'Paul!' 'Yes,
Mamma!' 'Come in here, darling: I'm sitting up for you.'

'Poor Mr Bernard, you are a mother to him!' people would sometimes say, and she would reply: 'Oh, I am better than that. His
mother is a very strange person, eccentric, a queer type; she would
not listen to him nor understand what he needs. One must be sympathetic with young people. He left home and came to me—eight
years he's been with me. We have grown used to each other.'

The Boy is her lover. He goes to her room three or four times a
week and stays there, only returning to his own room in the early
hours. Still, while being frank about their relation, for the sake of
decorum they also pretend that it is not so. La Grande Fifi is happy
about it and proud of it. At other times there is trouble. Mr Bernard
on occasion breaks with her; he even leaves the *pension* and goes on
a business trip—that is, he goes to another *pension*. But he returns.
The fact is, Fifi's son, who has a room in the *pension*, makes trouble
about Mr Bernard. Michel is a dark thin self-contained man of
twenty-eight. He has her name, Mercier, a common name; and at
first no one thinks he is her son. They even suspect he may be her
lover. He sits in the kitchen very early, in his pyjamas and gown,
making his own breakfast; he leaves before the others are up. He
often eats his dinner at home, but not always, and he is often away.

Eventually she may say: 'This is my son, Michel,' and it is clear
she is proud of him. Michel sometimes nods and moves away with
an odd gait—soft, and as it were clinging to the floor. After the
introduction he acknowledges no one.

Sometimes she talks about Michel. 'I have relatives in Paris, they
are rich and because I am poor they do not want to see me. I was
there once and they wanted to marry me off; they brought along a
middle-aged man. "I am not in Paris to marry," I said, "I am here
for a holiday." Now they don't want to see me, *ils ne causent pas!*'

She explains that once she spoke French very well; Paris French,
not Swiss French, which is called *français fédéral* for a joke.

'I once had many books,' she says. 'I don't read much now, only
when I'm lying down resting my legs. I know it isn't a good thing.
You see I once lived lower down on the lake side. I gave all my
books and my son's prizes to a bookbinder there; he was my fiancé.
I had a room to let and he lived in it. I quarrelled with him, I put
him out the door and he took away all the books and my son's
prizes. Now it is as if my son never had any prizes. My son was
learning bookbinding with him and then he gave it up. But he does
not care much; he is always on the mountain.'

Once she had a quarrel with her son very early on Friday morning. 'You *must* stay,' she said. 'I am not staying. I'm going on the
mountain.' 'But what shall I do? They are coming to see you,

Michel.' 'I have no interest in it. They are wasting their time. I shall be on the mountain. I want to try the rope.' On this one occasion he hangs about the front door for a few moments and talks to the boarders. Mountaineering is expensive. He has saved up and bought a new nylon rope, very light and thin. He shows the rope to Mr Bernard and other boarders before he goes; and he smiles slightly, quite pleased.

But La Grande Fifi is very sad in the evening and in a low voice confides in Mr Bernard; she cries too. 'The poor girl telephoned from Geneva and wanted to speak to him, but he was away. I said to her, "Claire, he is on the mountain, he is not here." She is Michel's girl and I am very willing for them to marry, I like her; but he doesn't want her any more. He thinks of only one thing. He is obsessed.'

The next day, Saturday, the parents arrived from Geneva with their daughter Claire. They sat in the kitchen for a long time talking. Fifi was not against her son, particularly; nor very much for him. 'I ask him, I keep asking him about the marriage. He says, "It's a nuisance," and goes off. He does not want anything but the mountain. I am very sorry.' 'Oh, we know how it is, Madame.' 'I am really very sorry.' 'Oh, we know it isn't you, Madame.'

It is a dry, acid, restrained scene, with helpless people; without passion, unfortunate. 'Nothing can be done, he won't change. And what sort of a husband would he be, always on the mountain?' 'Yes, yes, but just the same, it's trying. She was promised marriage.' 'He will never marry. He told me so. "I have another interest," he said.'

The Boy is away on holiday; that is, at another *pension*. But after two or three days he begins to telephone her, in the evenings. Once he even telephoned her at lunch-time, when she was busy serving a meal to the young men who had to return to work and classes.

In the evening the Boy again telephoned and they had a long talk. She, too, had things to tell him. 'Really, Paul, I don't know what you're doing there! I don't ask where you are. It is your own choice. Paul, you know my two old men, with the farm and the big vineyard? Yes, I told you, my darling. It is a really big country place, away out; they are wine-growers, really big with an extensive vineyard. Ah, I could have been there myself. I was there every summer. One of them is eighty years old, but hale, active; and the other has been in bed for a year. He's paralysed and can't even eat or drink by himself. He stammers. I could have married the healthy one if I had wanted to. What do you think has happened? It is the hearty one who has died! It is a shock to me, Paul. He died suddenly with pneumonia and with winter coming on. The other one is in his bed, still alive.'

She listened to *le petit* on the 'phone and said, 'But, my son, they were—well, they were brothers—you might say, of a sort. Now, he will dismiss the housekeeper and sell the vineyards. Of course he inherits. You see the kind of thing that happens to me? At one time the healthy one had the reins and if I had married him I would have had my share.... Well, Paul, you must do as you wish. I am not one to give advice. People must work out their own fate.'

'Ah,' she says today to the students at lunch, 'in the next room, the room now rented to the married couple, was once a professor. I think perhaps he was a little mad. He was forty years old and gave lessons at home; he did not go out much. He got up every night at two o'clock and walked up and down, pulled out his trunks, arranged things, made noises, and then went out to the railway station. "What do you do at the station?" I asked. "I enjoy going to the station," he replied.'

'But he didn't like it here. He used to complain, "What kind of town is this? All roofs. Wherever you look, you see a roof." He pushed a table against the window, so that he would not look down at the roofs. I was afraid to go in there. He made passes at me. I found him here—in my dining-room at eleven at night. You know I come in here to rest my legs, until everyone is in, and sometimes I fall asleep. I had not bolted the door—why? I was just waiting to go to bed.'

The fiction is that she sleeps in what is really her son's room.

'"What do you want here?" I said. He made certain proposals to me. I said, "Go away! This is a house full of young people; we must think of their morals." Sometimes I found him here when I came in from the kitchen to rest my legs. He went to Paris in the end and sent me a letter asking me to go there, too. I'm not a young girl to do unconventional things. Think! But I could have been in Paris.'

The Boy came back to her presently and there was bustling and buffeting at night in the dining-room. There was talk, laughter, weeping, expostulation, night-life. Later on, Mr Bernard went back to his room. For a while he seemed to be punishing La Grande Fifi. He invited his girl to come to his room, and when Fifi scolded him he threatened to go back 'There'. Where he had been was never mentioned. He, too, was scrupulous not to hurt her feelings about it. He would say, 'When I was—somewhere, recently...' and 'Naturally, in some other places conditions are different!'

They spent long evenings together. She was glad of him. Her lease was nearly up and she was afraid the landlord would ask a higher rent or find some excuse for putting her out. Michel, her son, was seldom home, usually just to eat and sleep, and in the weekend he would again be on the mountain. If his mother talked to him, he said nothing.

But Fifi and Paul talked of nothing else. 'What will I do if they put me out? Where will I live? And you, too, Paul—where will you live? Will you go back to your mother?' 'No, never'. 'You'll get married, I suppose; you'll marry that girl who comes here? It's high time isn't it? You've been engaged six years,' and Fifi would laugh. 'No, no; she wants to get married, but I haven't the money.' 'Will you go back—over there—where you were?' 'No. I don't know what I'll do.' One evening Paul came in very much excited. He talked all through dinner to all the other lodgers. He went to his room, played the piano a little while Fifi washed the dishes and then she came to his room and they sat there talking it over.

'I can make money, Fifi, we'll have money. You won't have to leave, even if he does raise the rent.' 'But supposing he finds out about my sleeping in the dining-room?' 'No, no, you say you sleep in your son's room.' 'But supposing Michel is here? You know they sent someone already, unexpectedly; and there were Michel's mountain things. They are my son's, I said: he keeps them with me for convenience, but he lives up the mountain. So I got away with it. But people talk. I can't sleep, my darling. I dream we haven't any of us a roof over our heads. The others, too. It is a responsibility. I offer people a roof; I try to make a family life for them.'

'Leave it to me, my dear,' said *le petit*. 'This scheme of mine will make money. I'm a businessman, aren't I? I know the inside of business. I am an income-tax accountant, I know all their secrets; nothing is hidden from me. Now you know, Fifi, my brother is still living at home. He has no go in him. But I left my mother ten years ago and after two years in—another place—I came here and I liked you as soon as I saw you. So leave it to me; your fate is my fate.'

They had a warm eager talk and he told her what he had not been able to tell at the dining-table.

'I met this Italian in a café; I knew him from living over there. He came to me and said that astrakhan skins are being sold dirt cheap because the boom is almost over and astrakhan is going off the market, with all the nylon furs coming in; and then they are going to sell coloured astrakhan, the black skins won't be salable. There's a chance now to make a big profit, people will be greedy for the skins; they'll pay any amount because there are plenty of women who want just that, an astrakhan coat and can't afford it.

'So you see, though the smart markets won't want them, everyone else will and I can unload them in some country, say, Canada or England, where they are not very fashionable, or even Italy and Spain and Greece, where the winters are cool enough. My friend has friends and they will help; and it doesn't matter about the export licences, because we will smuggle them in.'

'Smuggle? can he do that?'

'Well, my friend can't smuggle them, but he thinks what we can do is smuggle them in in automobile tyres. It is something he heard of. We will have to make some connections.'

'But Paul,' she said, worried. 'You know people were picked up last Christmas for smuggling all sorts of things in tyres and now they examine all the tyres at the frontier.'

'We must manage it somehow. Tyres are one of the few things large enough for smuggling skins. Well, if that doesn't work, we must try some other way.'

'Couldn't you try a legal way?' asked Fifi.

'The difficulty is, I am not a registered business. I have no permit and there are the exchange regulations. We must bypass them all. But a businessman can find a way. The first step is to get rid of the skins. Legally, my dear Fifi, you can only export merchandise actually made in the country—for example, Swiss watches; and astrakhan is not of course a Swiss product. And then you could export by exchange, import from Italy some Italian product of the same value. This question of bills and values can be fixed up through friends. Yes, I have been thinking it all out. It will be done and then I'll be in business on my own. You cannot make real money as an accountant. I work hard, I have a good position, but those businessmen make more with a hand's turn than I make in a year. It's the ingenuity which is rewarded, you see. And rightly, I hold.'

'Can't you get on the business register?'

'No, they poke their noses into everything. Later, yes, when I have money to set up business. Then Fifi, you won't have to worry. I'll look after you; I'll set you up in a *pension*—anything you like. I'll buy you a farm. But *you're* in business; you have a business permit. Why can't you do it?'

'My dear child, I have a permit for a boarding-house; and then they're always inspecting me. Look at those people I allow to make meals in their room; I'm not sure that it's legal. It worries me at night. And you must not use your room as a business office, it's not allowed.'

'What will I do? I mustn't lose this opportunity. Well, I had better tell you—I have already bought those skins. I used up all my savings and I borrowed money at work and from a moneylender, because I'll get the return. But they're valuable; I must have somewhere to store them. He's delivering them today. I told him to bring them here.'

'Oh, no. You'll get me into trouble.'

'I have no money to rent a store-room. I haven't a penny. I've mortgaged my salary in advance. What am I to do?'

He began to weep. La Grande Fifi, a soft creature, took him in her arms. He looked worn, his persistent cough became worse; he caught cold in the corridor at night; and every evening he sat begging and cajoling her in the dining-room until time for bed. The Italian, he said, was anxious to get rid of the skins and insisted upon his receiving them.

So she agreed. One lunchtime he came up the stairs three or four times carrying long heavy cardboard boxes which he deposited in his bedroom. They gave out a strong smell of dead skin and preservative. This led to two weeks' hysterical talk between Fifi and Paul. Everyone in the *pension* knew about the proposed deal, the smuggling, not to mention the self-advertisement by the skins in the bedroom.

But the Boy arranged to barter the skins for Italian ceramics. He now received regular business letters at the *pension*, to Fifi's constant worry, and spent two or three Sundays typing his replies. He explained everything to calm her and said, craftily 'My mother would never allow me to make money; she does not understand life, she is, as you know, an eccentric. And though she is your age' (a fact admitted between them) 'she has no experience of life at all. She doesn't understand a plain commercial undertaking.' Fifi was pleased—but her *pension* was her livelihood. His business letters were simple, his telephone conversations naïve; and what with the foolishness of poor Fifi, who related her troubles, and poor Paul, everyone—the satirical and incredulous students and the lodgers—knew all that went on.

One weekend Paul spent sewing the skins up in gunny-sacks; he threw away the cardboard boxes. On another weekend he was mysteriously absent; a doomful quiet hung over the *pension*.

When Paul returned on the Monday it was to mourn. He had tried to cross the frontier to Italy with a gunny-sack full of skins. He was with his sister, who had already lent him all her savings, about 500 Swiss francs. On top of the skins they had placed a few ski-clothes; but how strange it was to take ski-clothes across in a gunny-sack! And then the smell! At any rate the skins were at the frontier waiting to be redeemed.

This being so, *le petit* wrote to the man in Italy: 'I find it impossible to export the skins straight out, so we must agree to a barter. Please let me have a list of the ceramics you intend to send me. I enclose the valuation of the goods I want to send you.'

The value of the skins was given, of course, at much below market value. The importer at once replied: 'Your merchandise is shown to be not enough; it is not what I expected. You have not shown a proper valuation.' (But *le petit* had been told that Signor Gino 'would understand'.) 'To transact this deal you must send more merchandise.'

Paul now borrowed another thousand francs from a moneylender and bought more skins.

La Grande Fifi was deeply disturbed. One of her lodgers had developed a winter cough; she gave him her recipe, barley sugar in hot milk, and this did quieten him for a while; but then another lodger developed signs of heart-strain. Running up and down the steep streets of Lausanne four times a day does not suit all bodies. She did her best for all; and when the long day was over, she had to sit up every night with Paul talking over the tangle he had got into. Sometimes he cried and sometimes he exclaimed, 'But that is business, my dear Fifi; business is a headache. If you haven't the stamina for a little obstacle like this, you can't make money.'

'But supposing they find out, with all these letters and telephone calls, that you are using one of my bedrooms for a business office? I shall get into trouble.' 'What am I to do then? Do you want me put out in the street? Are you going to be like my mother, just criticizing and never helping? See what happened to my elder brother—he is still at home, under her thumb; he will never marry now. He lost his girl. He did everything Mother said. Get rid of the girl she said, and he did. He wanted to go into business, too. She wouldn't let him; she told him he was just a routine brain, a mere clerk. He never got away. Are you going to be like that? I thought you understood me and were on my side.'

Then he would weep and she would comfort him. She did not know what to do. She did not want to lose him; she loved him, half as lover, half as mother.

At last permission was received. He was allowed to exchange the astrakhans for Italian ceramics, which would be coming in as barter, in twenty cases. In the meantime he had written to Berne, to Washington, D.C., and Montreal, about selling the astrakhans and about import licences. He found that he could not take any risk himself nor sign any bills of lading or undertakings, having no business permit, but that the Italian merchant had the necessary authority.

'It is all right,' he said, taking a leap as he came into her room that night. 'All will be well. The Italian will of course take the risk. He is a friend of my friend here, the Italian in the cafe, and they are very anxious to get hold of those skins.'

'If the skins are so good why not sell them here?' said she.

'Try to sell furs in Switzerland!' said he. 'It can't be done. Besides, I have this information privately. It's a quiet little deal. It's very simple, Fifi. You see, you don't understand business. I am not in business, that is why they won't allow me to do it, but they are willing to treat with me: they see I have a business mind.'

The month ran out. Paul obtained a further renewal of his option by assigning the furs. Another month passed. He then tried to resell the furs, as Fifi advised. But the furs he bought for 1200 francs, the dealer now said, could not be resold for even 200 francs—they were rubbish; and overseas, the fad had passed. Paul was excited by all this activity; he was still in business. He kept carbon copies of his letters and at night read them to Fifi. Sometimes he said he was dealing in private matters which could not be breathed even to her. He was self-important, she tender, indulgent, anxious. She no longer believed in his deal, it would bring trouble to the house, but was afraid of his returning to his mother.

Paul's manner is becoming lighter, his tone of voice more singsong. This tall strong man runs in and out of the house at all hours, sings to himself, speaks in a childish pouting voice. When Fifi begins to speak to him he runs into his room, turns on the gramophone, plays a trifle on the piano, leaves his door open, humming and tapping with his heel. Because of the increasing protests of the alarmed landlady he sleeps with her three nights out of four; and when this is not enough to bring her into line, to punish her he invites his enduring girl-friend. She is a young creature of a lower class, an office worker he has been going out with for years. He tells her that he cannot marry until his two sisters marry or his mother dies.

La Grande Fifi is curt with the young girl, who comes at lunch-time and goes to Paul's room. He leaves the door open, shows her his sacks of astrakhan, tells her about his business transactions and plays the gramophone. On the day of her second visit they lie on an old horsehair sofa which stands in the hall under the cloak-pegs; they lie there obstinately with the coat-tails and scarves tickling their faces until the other boarders, returning to class or office, come to get their coats and hats, making rude but not insulting remarks about the progress of their love-affair.

The landlady with dignity tells them to get up off the sofa. 'I shall lose my licence. It that what you want? They will say I am running a disorderly house.' The other lodgers joke and soothe her. But she is outraged and Paul is satisfied. In the evening, when the dining-room is cleared, he goes in to talk to her; she protests, cries, he cries too; and again they are friends.

The second month comes when he cannot pay for his room and board. 'You cannot turn me out,' he says, weeping. 'We have been together for nearly nine years now, ever since I left home, almost.' After a while she says, 'Paul, you must do something. I am very short of funds. You know my son does not always pay for his room. Now I have two boys with me, two sons, you and Michel, who don't pay for their rooms, nor for food. I am only a poor woman. I might seem rich to you, but if they turned me out I haven't a home to go to. If he is forced to, Michel can marry the girl in Geneva, so that he can have a bed from which to start out for the mountain. He would marry for that. My old friend on the farm has just died. I always thought I could, if necessary, go there as housekeeper. But not now.'

'Do not bother with such fantasies,' he cries. 'It won't happen. Think about me. My poor sister has got to go on working as a shop-assistant. She is doing if for me. She believes in me. Besides, if you are so insistent, I can give you twenty francs.'

'But that isn't enough, my dear little one.'

'No, but it will help you get through the month and next payday I can give you something. My position is very difflcult. The man who lent me 1,000 francs is taking back 1,500 francs' worth of furs on the fourth of next month. I can't escape. I've been dodging him for days; but they know I'm here at lunchtime. Where else can I eat? I can't afford to buy a sausage. Is that a way for a man of my age and position to be?'

The students are moderately entertained. 'Will you take the four sacks of astrakhan into eternity with you?' one asks with concern. 'We are really quite worried about it, for they say St. Peter will never allow the skins of dead animals inside the pearly gates.' 'Nonsense, he is a far-seeing man,' says another. 'They are for his grandchildren. He is provident.' Paul listens, muses, laughs; and in a few days he explains to them at table, 'In business we say converted, not exchanged.'

The next month his salary is gone; he owes several thousand francs, his sister and his friend have no savings and La Grande Fifi is behind with her bills. She now talks about the couple in the next room where the professor once lived. 'I should never have allowed it. They live high, spend money like water, they eat large meals in there. That money should be coming into my pocket. It is my house. They don't sleep well at night because they have eaten too much. I should never allow myself to be taken in by foreigners. But then I have a soft nature.' And in a moment she is telling them a wellworn tale about the officer who loved her. She dreamed of him on a white horse, in a blue coat and a gold képi; and within three days of the dream she had a letter from him from Le Havre where he had been on manoeuvres, on a white horse in a blue cloak with a gold képi. He said he had dreamed of her. 'How I miss you, Fifi. I am coming back to get you.' All this happened ten years earlier—twelve, perhaps. But she would not be surprised at any time to see that French officer return to fetch her. Her good humour is restored. She is affectionate towards the lodgers in the big room; and she goes out in the evening to a show with *le petit*. They come home, they have a little drink of cordial, and sit for a long time talking. They are happy making each other promises for the future, when he will have money and free her from worry. Both believers in white horses and képis of gold, they have their moments of joy.

One of the jokes at table—for all are interested in the Italian ceramics—is that they will be able to buy some cheap Christmas presents for their sweethearts and families; or even for themselves, since some of them will eventually set up house.

One day Paul receives advice that a large consignment of Italian chinaware is awaiting him. He must present his papers, pay Customs duty, and remove the goods. He returns home depressed. He cannot dispose of the goods and he has nowhere to store them. His sister and brother live at home; so he must press Fifi to take them into her house. The ceramics are, of course, much bulkier than the skins.

'I could do with some new china here', says Fifi. 'Some of my plates are burned, others are chipped. You really ought to make me a present because of what I have done for you.'

Paul is silent. One of the students says suddenly 'They're bedroom services, jugs and basins and—chamberpots!' Silence.

In the evening: 'I *must* bring them here, Fifi.' 'No, you will not.' 'I must—I have no money for a warehouse.' 'What things are they?' 'Chamberpots.' 'You might as well chop them up into little pieces.'

But he comes back the next day. 'Fifi, my friend in the café tells me something really interesting. You never know, do you? One must keep one's ears open. I have found out that you can export them to America. The Americans are buying all kinds of antiques.' 'Antiques?' 'Yes, they are using nineteenth century wash-basins for saladbowls and chamberpots for ferns. They stand them on a pedestal in the living-room; and they serve sweets in them. I'll go to the Consul and get the addresses of some American buyers.'

He tossed at night, feverish. 'Paul, accept it as a dead loss. You'll be ill. You won't be able to go to the office and I'll have an invalid on my hands.' She tells him to go to the polyclinic for an X-ray; no, he must have a private doctor. 'We mustn't live on the level of people who go to the public hospital, Fifi.' The doctor comes. Paul must stay in bed.

She tells her troubles to the lodgers at table. 'Send him home,' one of them says. 'He has a good home, sister and mother and brother to look after him. Why should you do it?' 'Ah, my dear, you don't understand. His mother is impossible, a medusa, a gorgon. She is as hard as rocks and doesn't understand him. What would he do up there among all those hard hearts? He would die of loneliness.'

His sweetheart visits him. She is admitted unwillingly; and when she leaves Fifi says to her, 'Now you have seen him, you may stay away. This excitement is not good for him. Why do you come? He will never marry. He is an honourable man. He wants to make money first, and that is going to take years. That is what has laid him on his back. I don't want to see you here again.'

When Miss Corelli leaves, Fifi talks to Paul a long time, soothing and insinuating. 'This is very bad for you, don't you see? She has only marriage in mind. These sentimental situations are very unhealthy. Now with me you have a home, a tender heart that loves you and asks nothing.'

And so it is. He stays with Fifi.

GRACE PERRY   (1927–)

Poet, editor. Born in Melbourne; educated in Sydney.

GIRL AT THE PIANO

Swinging thin legs, the child bends to the keyboard,
head tilted sideways looking at the sea,
while fingers follow the familiar patterns
with assumed precision and agility.

Incessant crests ride tirelessly to meet her
and spill themselves in long irregular runs
until her mind is full to overflowing
with unbridled oceans leaping to the sun.

Immersed in summer through the open window,
she will go out along the beach, alone.
She will not see that dark turbulence building
to break in spray against high walls of stone.

ROUTE 31

Route 31
divides the droughtland southward
skimming the surface
                              never part of it
voices submerged in the round-the-clock rumble
language reduced to painted signs
                              hooded lights
                              few handsignals
embankment and cutaway
                              shrink the world
windscreens frame
                              traffic patterns in perspective
pushing from Picton to the Bargo Bush
the wheel rubs hot under the hand
comes a rainfresh wind
                              a touch of summer
unblemished by dust and diesel fumes
suddenly
            the other
                        open country
away out there
how big it is

HOUSE AT BEECROFT

Protected by red roofs and mullioned windows,
three Swiss welcome bells on guard behind oak doors,
the blue chair, wood-carved lovingly like a lyre bird,
waits to dance on black-and-white tiled floors.

A snow of plumblossom applauds in sunlit windows
where divided panels dislocate the air;
ghost gums float through gardens underwater;
thin bones of jacaranda swing at anchor above stairs.

A coral tree releases drowning birds
to bleed among azaleas. Swimming over grass,
a girl wreathed in white muslin, hands full of flowers,
circles slowly in the old rippled glass.

ELIZABETH HARROWER   (1928–)

Novelist, short story writer. Born and educated in Sydney.

THE BEAUTIFUL CLIMATE

The Shaws went down to the cottage on Scotland Island every
week-end for two years. Hector Shaw bought the place from some
hotel-keeper he knew, never having so much as hinted at his intention till the contract was signed. Then he announced to his wife and
daughter the name of a certain house, his ownership of it, its location, and the fact that they would all go down every Friday night to
put it in order.

It was about an hour's drive from Sydney. At the Church Point
wharf they would park the car, lock it up, and wait for the ferry to
take them across to the island.

Five or six families made a living locally, tinkering with boats and
fishing, but most of the houses round about were week-enders, like
the Shaws' place. Usually these cottages were sold complete with a
strip of waterfront and a jetty. In the Shaws' case the jetty was a
long spindly affair of grey wooden palings on rickety stilts, with a
perpendicular ladder that had to be climbed getting in and out of the
boat. Some of the others were handsome constructions equipped
with special flags and lights to summon the ferry-man when it was
time to return to civilisation.

As Mr Shaw had foretold, they were constantly occupied putting
the house in order, but now and then he would buy some green

prawns, collect the lines from the spare-bedroom cupboard, and take his family into the middle of the bay to fish. While he made it obligatory to assume that this was a treat, he performed every action with his customary air of silent, smouldering violence, as if to punish misdemeanours, alarming his wife and daughter greatly.

Mrs Shaw put on her big straw sun-hat, tied it solemnly under her chin, and went behind him down the seventy rough rock steps from the house. She said nothing. The glare from the water gave her migraine. Since a day years before when she was a schoolgirl learning to swim, and had almost drowned, she had had a horror of deep water. Her husband knew it. He was a difficult man, for what reason no one had been able to discover, least of all Hector Shaw himself.

Del followed her mother down the steep bushy track, not speaking, her nerves raw, her soundless protests battering the air about her. She did not *want* to go, nor, of course, could she want to stay when her absence would be used against her mother.

They were not free. Either the hostage, or the one over whom a hostage was held, they seemed destined to play for ever if they meant to preserve the peace. And peace had to be preserved. Everything had always been subordinated to this task. As a child, Del had been taught that happiness was nothing but the absence of unpleasantness. For all she knew, it was true. Unpleasantness, she knew, could be extremely disagreeable. She knew that what was irrational had to be borne, and she knew she and her mother longed for peace and quiet—since she had been told so so often. But still she did not want to go.

Yet that they should not accompany her father was unthinkable. That they should all three be clamped together was, in a way, the whole purpose of the thing. Though Del and her mother were aware that he might one day sink the boat deliberately. It wasn't *likely*, because he was terrified of death, whereas his wife would welcome oblivion, and his daughter had a stony capacity for endurance (so regarding death, at least, they had the upper hand): but it was *possible*. Just as he might crash the car some day on purpose if all three were secure together in it.

"Why do we *do* it?" Del asked her mother relentlessly. "You'd think we were mental defectives the way we troop behind him and do what we're told just to save any trouble. And it never does. Nothing we do makes sure of anything. When I go out to work every day it's as if I'm out on parole. You'd think we were hypnotised."

Her mother sighed and failed to look up, and continued to butter the scones.

"*You're* his wife, so maybe you think you have to do it, but I don't. I'm eighteen."

However, till quite recently she had been a good deal younger, and most accustomed to being used in the cause of peace. Now her

acquiescence gnawed at and baffled her, but though she made isolated stands, in essence she always did submit. Her few rebellions
were carefully gauged to remain within the permitted limits, the
complaints of a prisoner-of-war to the camp-commandant.

This constant nagging from the girl exhausted Mrs Shaw. Exa-
speration penetrated even her alarming headaches. She asked desperately, "What would you do if you *didn't* come? You're too
nervous to stay in town by yourself. And if you did, what would
you do?"

"*Here.* I have to come *here*, but why do we have to go in the
boat?" On a lower note, Del muttered, "I wish I worked at the
kindergarten seven days a week, I dread the night and week-ends."

She could *think* a thing like that, but never say it without a deep
feeling of shame. Something about her situation made her feel not
only, passively, abused, but actively, surprisingly, guilty.

All her analysis notwithstanding, the fishing expeditions took
place whenever the man of the family signified his desire for some
sport. Stationed in the dead centre of the glittering bay, within sight
of their empty house, they sat in the open boat, grasping cork rollers, feeling minute and interesting tugs on their lines from time to
time, losing bait and catching three-inch fish.

Low hills densely covered with thin gums and scrub sloped down
on all sides to the rocky shore. They formed silent walls of a dark
subdued green, without shine. Occasional painted roofs showed
through. Small boats puttered past and disappeared.

As the inevitable pain began to saturate Mrs Shaw's head, she
turned gradually paler. She leaned against the side of the boat with
her eyes closed, her hands obediently clasping the fishing-line she
had been told to hold.

The dazzle of the heavy summer sun sucked up colour till the
scene looked black. Her light skin began to burn. The straw sun-hat
was like a neat little oven in which her hair, her head and all its
contents, were being cooked.

Without expression, head lowered, Del looked at her hands,
fingernails, legs, at the composition of the cork round which her
line was rolled. She glanced sometimes at her mother, and sometimes, by accident, she caught sight of her father's bare feet or his
arm flinging out a newly-baited line, or angling some small silver
fish off the hook and throwing it back, and her eyes sheered away.

The wooden interior of the boat was dry and burning. The three
fishers were seared, beaten down by the sun. The bait smelled. The
water lapped and twinkled blackly but could not be approached:
sharks abounded in the bay.

The cottage was fairly dilapidated. The walls needed painting inside
and out, and parts of the veranda at the front and both sides had to
be re-floored. In the bedrooms, sitting-room and kitchen, most of

the furniture was old and crudely-made. They burned the worst of it, replacing it with new stuff, and what was worth salvaging Mrs Shaw and Del gradually scrubbed, sanded and painted.

Mr Shaw did carpentering jobs, and cleared the ground nearby of some of the thick growth of eucalyptus gums that had made the rooms dark. He installed a generating plant, too, so that they could have electric light instead of relying on kerosene lamps at night.

Now and then his mood changed inexplicably, for reasons so unconnected with events that no study and perpetuation of these external circumstances could ensure a similar result again. Nevertheless, knowing it could not last, believing it might, Mrs Shaw and Del responded shyly, then enthusiastically, but always with respect and circumspection, as if a friendly lion had come to tea.

These hours or days of amazing good humour were passed, as it were, a few feet off the ground, in an atmosphere of slightly hysterical gaiety. They sang, pumping water to the tanks; they joked at either end of the saw, cutting logs for winter fires; they ran, jumped, slithered, and laughed till they had to lean against the trees for support. They reminded each other of all the incidents of other days like these, at other times when his nature was in eclipse.

"We'll fix up a nice shark-proof pool for ourselves," he said. "We own the water-frontage. It's crazy not to be able to cool off when we come down. If you can't have a dip here, surrounded by water, what's the sense? We'd be better to stay home and go to the beach, this weather."

"Three cheers!" Del said. "When do we start?"

The seasons changed. When the nights grew colder, Mr Shaw built huge log-fires in the sitting-room. If his mood permitted, these fires were the cause of his being teased, and he liked very much to be teased.

Charmed by his own idiosyncrasy, he would pile the wood higher and higher, so that the walls and ceiling shone and flickered with the flames, and the whole room crackled like a furnace on the point of explosion. Faces scorching, they would rush to throw open the windows, then they'd fling open the doors, dying for air. Soon the chairs nearest the fire would begin to smoke and then everyone would leap outside to the dark veranda, crimson and choking. Mr Shaw laughed and coughed till he was hoarse, wiping his eyes.

For the first few months, visitors were non-existent, but one night on the ferry the Shaws struck up a friendship with some people called Rivers, who had just bought a cottage next door. They came round one Saturday night to play poker and have supper, and in no time weekly visits to each other's house were established as routine. Grace and Jack Rivers were relaxed and entertaining company. Their easy good-nature fascinated the Shaws, who looked forward to these meetings seriously, as if the Rivers were a sort of rest-cure ordered by a specialist, from which they might pick up some health.

"It was too good to last," Mrs Shaw said later. "People are so funny."

The Rivers' son, Martin, completed his army training and went down to stay on the island for a month before returning to his marine-engineering course at a technical college in town. He and Del met sometimes and talked, but she had not gone sailing with him when he asked her, nor was she tempted to walk across the island to visit his friends who had a pool.

"Why not?" he asked.

"Oh, well..." She looked down at the dusty garden from the veranda where they stood. "I have to paint those chairs this afternoon."

"*Have* to?" Martin had a young, open, slightly-freckled face.

Del looked at him, feeling old, not knowing how to explain how complicated it would be to extricate herself from the house, and her mother and father. He would never understand the drama, the astonishment, that would accompany her statement to them. Even if, eventually, they said, "Go, go!" recovering from their shock, her own joylessness and fatigue were so clear to her in anticipation that she had no desire even to test her strength in the matter.

But one Saturday night over a game of cards, Martin asked her parents if he might take her the next night to a party across the bay. A friend of his, Noel Stacey, had a birthday to celebrate.

Del looked at him with mild surprise. He had asked her. She had refused.

Her father laughed a lot at this request as though it were very funny, or silly, or misguided, or simply impossible. It turned out that it *was* impossible. They had to get back to Sydney early on Sunday night.

If they *did* have to, it was unprecedented, and news to Del. But she looked at her father with no surprise at all.

Martin said, "Well, it'll be a good party," and gave her a quizzical grin. But his mother turned quite pink, and his father cleared his throat gruffly several times. The game broke up a little earlier than usual, and, as it happened, was the last one they ever had together.

Not knowing that it was to be so, however, Mrs Shaw was pleased that the matter had been dealt with so kindly and firmly. "What a funny boy!" she said later, a little coyly, to Del.

"Is he?" she said indifferently.

"One of the new generation," said Mr Shaw, shaking his head, and eyeing her with caution.

"Oh?" she said, and went to bed.

"She didn't really want to go to that party at all," her mother said.

"No, but we won't have him over again, do you think? He's got his own friends. Let him stick to them. There's no need for this. These fellows who've been in army camps—I know what they're like."

"She hardly looked at him. She didn't care." Mrs Shaw collected the six pale-blue cups, saucers and plates on the wooden tray, together with the remnants of supper.

With his back to the fire, hands clasped behind him, Mr Shaw brooded. "He had a nerve though, when you come to think of it. I mean—he's a complete stranger."

Mrs Shaw sighed anxiously, and her eyes went from one side of the room to the other. "I'm sure she didn't like him. She doesn't take much interest in boys. You're the only one."

Mr Shaw laughed reluctantly, looking down at his shoes.

As more and more of the property was duly painted and repaired, the Shaws tended to stop work earlier in the day, perhaps with the unspoken intention of making the remaining tasks last longer. Anyway, the pressure was off, and Mrs Shaw knitted sweaters, and her husband played patience, while Del was invariably glued to some book or other.

No one in the district could remember the original owner-builder of their cottage, or what he was like. But whether it was this first man, or a later owner, *someone* had left a surprisingly good library behind. It seemed likely that the builder had lived and died there, and that his collection had simply been passed on with the property from buyer to buyer, over the years.

Books seemed peculiarly irrelevant on this remote hillside smelling of damp earth and wood-smoke and gums. The island had an ancient, prehistoric, undiscovered air. The alphabet had yet to be invented.

However, the books *had* been transported here by someone, and Del was pleased to find them, particularly the many leather-bound volumes of verse. Normally, in an effort to find out why people were so peculiar, she read nothing but psychology. Even after she knew psychologists did not know, she kept reading it from force of habit, in the hope that she might come across a formula for survival directed specifically at her: *Del Shaw, follow these instructions to the letter!* ...Poetry was a change.

She lay in a deck-chair on the deserted side-veranda and read in the mellow three o'clock, four o'clock, sunshine. There was, eternally, the smell of grass and burning bush, and the homely noise of dishes floating up from someone's kitchen along the path of yellow earth, hidden by trees. And she hated the chair, the mould-spotted book, the sun, the smells, the sounds, her supine self.

And they came on a land where it was always afternoon.

"It's like us, exactly like us and this place," she said to her mother, fiercely brushing her long brown hair in front of the dressing-table's wavy mirror. "Always afternoon. Everyone lolling about. Nobody *doing* anything."

"My goodness!" Her mother stripped the sheets off the bed to take home to the laundry. "I thought we'd all been active enough this week-end to please anyone. And I don't see much afternoon about Monday morning."

"Active! That isn't what I mean. Anyway, I don't mean here or this week-end. I mean everyone, everywhere, all the time. Ambling round till they die." Oh, but that wasn't what she meant, either.

Mrs Shaw's headache look appeared. "It's off to the doctor with you tonight, Miss!"

Del set her teeth together. When her mother had left the room with her arms full of linen, still darting sharp glances at her daughter, Del closed her eyes and raised her face to the ceiling.

Let me *die*.

The words seemed to be ground from her voiceless body, to be ground, powdered stone, from her heart.

She breathed very slowly; she slowly righted her head, carefully balancing its weight on her neck. Then she pulled on her suede jacket, lifted her bag, and clattered down the uneven stone steps to the jetty. It always swayed when anyone set foot on it.

When the cottage had been so patched and cleaned that, short of a great expenditure of capital, no further improvement was possible, Hector Shaw ceased to find any purpose in his visits to it. True, there was still the pool to be tackled, but the summer had gone by without any very active persuasion, any pleading, any teasing, from his wife and daughter. And if *they* were indifferent, far be it from him....

Then there was another thing. Not that it had any connexion with the place, with being on Scotland Island, but it had the side-effect of making the island seem less—safe, salubrious, desirable. Jack Rivers died from a heart-attack one Sunday morning. Only fifty-five he was, and a healthier-looking fellow, you couldn't have wished to meet.

Since the night young Martin Rivers had ruined their poker parties, they had seen very little of Jack and Grace. Sometimes on the ferry they had bumped into each other, and when they had the Shaws, at least, were sorry that it had all worked out so badly. Jack and Grace were good company. It was hard not to feel bitter about the boy having spoiled their nice neighbourly friendship so soon before his father died. Perhaps if Jack had spent more time playing poker and less doing whatever he did do after the Saturdays stopped....

On a mild mid-winter night, a few weeks after Jack Rivers's funeral, the Shaw family sat by the fire. Del was gazing along her corduroy slacks into the flames, away from her book. Her parents were silent over a game of cards.

Mr Shaw took a handful of cashew nuts from a glass dish at his side and started to chew. Then leaning back in his chair, his eyes still fixed on his cards, he said, "By the way, the place's up for sale."

His wife stared at him. "What place?"

"*This* place." He gave her his sour, patient look. "It's been on Dalgety's books for three weeks."

"What for?" Del asked, conveying by the gentleness of her tone, her total absence of criticism. It was dangerous to question him, but then it was dangerous not to, too.

"Well, there isn't much to do round here now. And old Jack's popped off—" (He hadn't meant to say that!) Crunching the cashew nuts, he slid down in his chair expansively, every supra-casual movement premeditated as though he were playing *Hamlet* at Stratford.

The women breathed deeply, not with regret, merely accepting this new fact in their lives. Mrs Shaw said, "Oh! ..." and Del nodded her comprehension. Changing their positions imperceptibly, they prepared to take up their occupations again in the most natural and least offensive ways they could conceive. There was enormous potential danger in any radical change of this sort.

"Ye–es," said Mr Shaw, drawing the small word out to an extraordinary length. "Dalgety's telling them all to come any Saturday or Sunday afternoon." Still he gazed at his handful of cards, then he laid them face down on the table, and with a thumb, thoughtfully rubbed the salt from the cashews into the palm of his other hand. It crumbled onto his knees, and he dusted it down to the rug, seeming agreeably occupied in its distribution.

"Ye–es," he said again, while his wife and daughter gazed at him painfully. "When and if anyone takes the place, I think we'd better use the cash to go for a trip overseas. What do you say? See the Old Country.... Even the boat trip's pretty good, they tell me. You go right round the coast here (that takes about a week), then up to Colombo, Bombay, Aden, through the Suez, then up through the Mediterranean, through the Straits of Messina past some volcano, and past Gibraltar to Marseilles, then London."

There was a silence.

Mr Shaw turned away from the table and his game, and looked straight into his wife's grey eyes—a thing he rarely did. Strangers were all right, he could look at them, but with relations, old acquaintances, his spirit, unconscious, was ashamed and uneasy.

"Go away?" his wife repeated, turning a dreadful colour.

He said, "Life's short. I've earned a holiday. Most of my typists've been abroad. We'll have a year. We'll need a year. *If* someone turns up on the ferry one day and *wants* the place, that is. There's a bit of a slump in real estate just now, but I guess we'll be okay."

And they looked at each other, the three of them, with unfamiliar awe. They were about to leave this dull pretty city where they were all so hard to live with, and go to places they had read about, where the world was, where things happened, where the photographs of famous people came from, where history was, and snow in cities, and works of art, and splendour....

Poetry and patience were discarded from that night, while everyone did extra jobs about the cottage to added to its attractiveness and value. Mrs Shaw and Del planted tea-trees and hibiscus bushes covered with flowers of palest apricot, and pink streaked with red. Mr Shaw cemented the open space under the house (it was propped up on columns on its steep hillside) and the area underneath was like a large extra room, shady and cool. They put some long bamboo chairs down there, fitted with cushions.

Most week-end afternoons, jobs notwithstanding, Del went to the side-veranda to lean over the railing out of sight and watch the ferry go from jetty to jetty and return to Church Point. She watched and willed, but no one ever came to see the house.

It was summer again, and the heatwave broke records. Soon it was six months since the night they had talked about the trip.

Always the island was the same. It was scented, self-sufficient; the earth was warm underfoot, and the air warm to breathe. The hillside sat there, quietly, rustling quietly, a smug curving hillside that had existed for a long time. The water was blue and sparkled with meaningless beauty. Smoke stood in the sunny sky above the bush here and there across the bay, where other week-end visitors were cooking chops, or making coffee on fuel stoves.

Del watched the ferries and bargained with fate, denying herself small pleasures, which was very easy for her to do. She waited. Ferries came and went round the point, but never called at their place.

They lost heart. In the end it would have been impossible even to mention the trip. But they all grieved with a secret enduring grief as if at the death of the one person they had loved. Indeed, they grieved for their own deaths. Each so unknown and un-understood, who else could feel the right regret? From being eaten by the hillside, from eating one another, there had been the chance of a reprieve. Now it was evidently cancelled, and in the meantime irretrievable admissions had been made....

At the kindergarten one Tuesday afternoon Miss Lewis, who was in charge, called Del to the telephone. She sat down, leaning her forehead on her hand before lifting the receiver.

"Hullo?"

"Del, your father's sold the cottage to a pilot. Somebody Barnes. He's bought the tickets. We've just been in to get our cabins. We're leaving in two months."

"What?... A pilot?"

"Yes. We're going on the *Arcadia* on the 28th of November. The cabins are lovely. Ours has got a porthole. We'll have to go shopping, and get injections and passports—"

"We're *going*?"

"Of course we are, you funny girl! We'll tell you all about it when you get home tonight. I've started making lists."

They were going. She was going away. Out in the world she would escape from them. There would be room to run, outside this prison.

"So we're off," her mother said.

Del leaned sideways against the wall, looking out at the eternal afternoon, shining with all its homey peace and glory. "Oh, that's good," she said. "That's good."

PETER PORTER   (1929–)

Poet. Born and educated in Brisbane; since 1951 has lived in London.

PHAR LAP IN THE MELBOURNE MUSEUM

A masterpiece of the taxidermist's art,
Australia's top patrician stares
Gravely ahead at crowded emptiness.
As if alive, the lustre of dead hairs,
Lozenged liquid eyes, black nostrils
Gently flared, otter-satin coat declares
That death cannot visit in this thin perfection.

The democratic hero full of guile,
Noble, handsome, gentle Houyhnhnm
(In both Paddock and St Leger difference is
Lost in the welter of money)—to see him win
Men sold farms, rode miles in floods,
Stole money, locked up wives, somehow got in:
First away, he led the field and easily won.

It was his simple excellence to be best.
Tough men owned him, their minds beset
By stakes, bookies' doubles, crooked jocks.
He soon became a byword, public asset,
A horse with a nation's soul upon his back—
Australia's Ark of the Covenant, set
Before the people, perfect, loved like God.

And like God to be betrayed by friends.
Sent to America, he died of poisoned food.
In Australia children cried to hear the news
(This Prince of Orange knew no bad or good).

It was, as people knew, a plot of life:
To live in strength, to excel and die too soon,
So they drained his body and they stuffed his skin.

Twenty years later on Sunday afternoons
You still can't see him for the rubbing crowds.
He shares with Bradman and Ned Kelly some
Of the dirty jokes you still can't say out loud.
It is Australian innocence to love
The naturally excessive and be proud
Of a thoroughbred bay gelding who ran fast.

ON FIRST LOOKING INTO CHAPMAN'S HESIOD

For 5p at a village fête I bought
Old Homer-Lucan who popped Keats's eyes,
Print smaller than the Book of Common Prayer
But Swinburne at the front, whose judgement is
Always immaculate. I'll never read a tenth
Of it in what life I have left to me
But I did look at *The Georgics*, as he calls
The Works and Days, and there I saw, not quite
The view from Darien but something strange
And balking—Australia, my own country
And its edgy managers—in the picture of
Euboeaen husbandry, terse family feuds
And the minds of gods tangential to the earth.

Like a Taree smallholder splitting logs
And philosophizing on his dangling billies,
The poet mixes hard agrarian instances
With sour sucks to his brother. Chapman, too,
That perpetual motion poetry machine,
Grinds up the classics like bone meal from
The abbatoirs. And the same blunt patriotism,
A long-winded, emphatic, kelpie yapping
About our land, our time, our fate, our strange
And singular way of moons and showers, lakes
Filling oddly—yes, Australians are Boeotians,
Hard as headlands, and, to be fair, with days
As robust as the Scythian wind on stone.

To teach your grandmother to suck eggs
Is a textbook possibility in New South Wales
Or outside Ascra. And such a genealogy too!
The Age of Iron is here, but oh the memories
Of Gold—pioneers preaching to the stringybarks,
Boring the land to death with verses and with

Mental Homes. 'Care-flying ease' and 'Gift-
devouring kings' become the Sonata of the Shotgun
And Europe's Entropy; for 'the axle-tree, the quern,
The hard, fate-fostered man' you choose among
The hand castrator, kerosene in honey tins
And mystic cattlemen: the Land of City States
Greets Australia in a farmer's gods.

Hesiod's father, caught in a miserable village,
Not helped by magic names like Helicon,
Sailed to improve his fortunes, and so did
All our fathers—in turn, their descendants
Lacked initiative, other than the doctors' daughters
Who tripped to England. Rough-nosed Hesiod
Was sure of his property to a slip-rail—
Had there been grants, he'd have farmed all
Summer and spent winter in Corinth
At the Creative Writing Class. Chapman, too,
Would vie with Steiner for the Pentecostal
Silver Tongue. Some of us feel at home nowhere,
Others in one generation fuse with the land.

I salute him then, the blunt old Greek whose way
Of life was as cunning as organic. His poet
Followers still make me feel déraciné
Within myself. One day they're on the campus,
The next in wide hats at a branding or
Sheep drenching, not actually performing
But looking the part and getting instances
For odes that bruise the blood. And history,
So interior a science it almost seems
Like true religion—who would have thought
Australia was the point of all that craft
Of politics in Europe? The apogee, it seems,
Is where your audience and its aspirations are.

'The colt, and mule, and horn-retorted steer'—
A good iambic line to paraphrase.
Long storms have blanched the million bones
Of the Aegean, and as many hurricanes
Will abrade the headstones of my native land:
Sparrows acclimatize but I still seek
The permanently upright city where
Speech is nature and plants conceive in pots,
Where one escapes from what one is and who
One was, where home is just a postmark
And country wisdom clings to calendars,
The opposite of a sunburned truth-teller's
World, haunted by precepts and the Pleiades.

AN AUSTRALIAN GARDEN

For Sally Lehmann

Here we enact the opening of the world
And everything that lives shall have a name
To show its heart; there shall be Migrants,
Old Believers, Sure Retainers; the cold rose
Exclaim perfection to the gangling weeds,
The path lead nowhere—this is like entering
One's self, to find the map of death
Laid out untidily, a satyr's grin
Signalling 'You are here': tomorrow
They are replanting the old court,
Puss may be banished from the sun-warmed stone.

See how our once-lived lives stay on to haunt us,
The flayed beautiful limbs of childhood
In the bole and branches of a great angophora—
Here we can climb and sit on memory
And hear the words which death was making ready
From the start. Such talking as the trees attempt
Is a lesson in perfectability. It stuns
The currawongs along the breaks of blue—
Their lookout cries have guarded Paradise
Since the expulsion of the heart, when man,
Bereft of joy, turned his red hand to gardens.

Spoiled Refugees nestle near Great Natives;
A chorus of winds stirs the pagoda'd stamens:
In this hierarchy of miniatures
Someone is always leaving for the mountains,
Civil servant ants are sure the universe
Stops at the hard hibiscus; the sun is drying
A beleaguered snail and the hydra-headed
Sunflowers wave like lights. If God were to plant
Out all His hopes, He'd have to make two more
Unknown Lovers, ready to find themselves
In innocence, under the weight of His green ban.

In the afternoon we change—an afterthought,
Those deeper greens which join the stalking shadows—
The lighter wattles look like men of taste
With a few well-tied leaves to brummel-up
Their poise. Berries dance in a southerly wind
And the garden tide has turned. Dark on dark.
Janus leaves are opening to the moon
Which makes its own grave roses. Old Man
Camellias root down to keep the sun intact,

The act is canopied with stars. A green sea
Rages through the landscape all the night.

We will not die at once. Nondescript pinks
Survive the death of light and over-refined
Japanese petals bear the weight of dawn's first
Insect. An eye makes damask on the dew.
Time for strangers to accustom themselves
To habitat. What should it be but love?
The transformations have been all to help
Unmagical creatures find their proper skins,
The virgin and the leonine. The past's a warning
That the force of joy is quite unswervable—
'Out of this wood do not desire to go.'

In the sun, which is the garden's moon, the barefoot
Girl espies her monster, all his lovely specialty
Like hairs about his heart. The dream is always
Midday and the two inheritors are made
Proprietors. They have multiplied the sky.
Where is the water, where the terraces, the Tritons
And the cataracts of moss? This is Australia
And the villas are laid out inside their eyes:
It would be easy to unimagine everything,
Only the pressure made by love and death
Holds up the bodies which this Eden grows.

ROBERT HUGHES   (1938–)

Art critic. Born and educated in Sydney; lives in New York.

THE INTELLECTUAL IN AUSTRALIA

Australia is a 'young country'. This cliché opens the board to others, about new-minted sensibility, pioneer spirit, you-have-an-ethos-to-make, and so forth. Some people who have never experienced the climate of intellectual life here assume it is at the stage Harold Rosenberg called Coonskinism: their image of the Australian intellectual is a lusty young Crockett, who knows his terrain like the back of his hand, picking off Redcoats for the challenging sake of his own identity.

The Redcoats, by contrast, march forward in unsuitably serried ranks and perish, defeated by their dream of the final, open, rolling sward where the textbook battles are fought. But the Coonskinner behind the tree wins. He is an idealist—he wants independence. He senses an identity with other Cookskinners elsewhere, because he is essentially a rebel. But he wins because he is pragmatic and faces real issues: where the rocks and trees are, how to fight and when to run, where the foe sits.

In fact, it is idle to describe Australian intellectuals in terms of their pragmatism, mobility, sense of destiny, purpose of identity, or even rebelliousness. There are no Coonskinners here. Yet this vision of a cultural élite has affected the Australians themselves, not only outside watchers. The old sons-of-Australia cultural nationalism of the thirties has given way to a creepier illusion, the mystique of the local boy whose vitality can show those jaded Europeans a thing or two. We see ourselves, romantically, as the Barbarians at the Gates; not, it is true, trying to break them down, but manoeuvring with the doorman for admission.

This only holds true in the arts, where it is virtually restricted to painting. Nobody in Australia imagines that his country has produced any critics or philosophers fit, like Nolan, to have tea with the Queen. For there is no tradition of intellect in Australia. There are only intelligent men.

Why-asking, the habit of inquiry without which intellect loses itself, is not and never has been an Australian trait. The Australian rebel, especially the social rebel, says 'No', not 'Why?' Intellectuals, as we will see later, obsessively cloak their role behind their 'job', as if embarrassed. If the Press wants to denigrate someone, it calls him a pseudo-intellectual. But the converse does not hold; I have never heard anyone praise someone else with the word 'intellectual'. The conclusion is not that the word has lost its meaning for Australians; rather, it has never found one, because the intellectual as such has never found a place in Australian society. To do so, he must change.

Last week, I took an American writer to lunch at the Ozone, a fish restaurant on Sydney Harbour. On the terrace under an awning, you sit at iron tables and eat lobster, *moules marinières* and bouillabaisse from copper stewpans. Behind the Ozone, cottages cluster up to the cliffs on the ocean side, from which suicides regularly jump. In front, there is a narrow concrete esplanade. Glistening, salady chicks wander along it with the odd sexless wiggle Australian girls put on with their bikinis. Next, a line of varnished boats, keel-up on the beach; the harsh white sand; and the smooth harbour water. In the slant glare, your bottle of white rapidly warms. Another is bought. You sit all afternoon, glutted with sun and sweating with food, and sink into that agreeable torpor where talk, or communication of any kind, becomes a pastime. The summer would make an Orwell into a beach bum. Everything is plausible. If a Negro walked by, he would certainly be a night-club performer from America; if a bomber flew over, it would be one of our Canberras, obsolete but friendly; if a warship appeared amid the red spinnakers on the harbour, it would be one of the mothball fleet on its way to some Japanese scrapyard, from its anchorage near the Zoo.

The Ozone is a microcosm of Australia, a place where nothing that happens beyond the terrace seems altogether real and where all things conspire to be comforting. Australia is the only continent which has never suffered invasion by a foreign power. Its smallest capital city, Darwin, was bombed once; a Jap midget submarine sank a ferry in Sydney Harbour and shelled Royal Sydney Golf Club, thinking it was an ammunition dump; these have been the sole enemy actions against the Australian mainland since 1788. Tyranny, pogroms, starvation, civil war, Vichy governments, resistance movements and secret police are simply political abstractions, and to all Australians of my generation they are scarcely even words. Even the local CND concentrates on fallout, since it is assumed that nobody would waste a rocket on Sydney. When a French flagship steamed into Darwin last year, it was found that our northern defences did not have enough guns to fire the requisite salute.

The womb-like ambience of political stability is complete. When your basic freedoms are not menaced you cease to think about them, and finally stop looking to see if they're still there. Thus Australian intellectuals tend to ignore small erosions of their liberty. Australia, in this sense, is the Land of Cockayne, where roast pigs walk, tarts fly into the mouth, and the sleek body becomes insensible to what is happening round the corner. Intellectuals are among the first to go—no friction, no thought—and, as a result, few of them in Australia have even a rudimentary political conscience. I don't mean that they are politically amoral, since this would suggest that they were politically sophisticated, which they are not: they shy away from any kind of engagement. An Australian Camus or an Orwell would be unimaginable: such a man would end waddling like a Strasbourg goose, stuffed with prosperity and dragging his vote around like a diseased liver.

This amalgam of timidity and naiveté cuts both Left and Right. Australia has no Communist intellectuals, only fatigued Clydesdales like Judah Waten, who once told me that 'Khrushchev is infinitely more a revolutionary in art than Herbert Read'. The typical posture of the Australian intellecutal is, Vincent Buckley pointed out in *Australian Civilisation*, vaguely left, but it is a posture rather than a position. That is to say, his political allegiances consist of snap reactions to isolated events, but he does not habitually think in terms of ideologies or broad policy. Buckley, however, failed to note that this stems from the general illusion of political stability: all issues look rather piddling when nothing threatens. Even the snap reactions are coloured by the liberal's fear of losing his small 'l'. Otherwise intelligent men will call a right-winger a Fascist or (if he opposes communism) a McCarthyite; the Right hits back by ascribing pro-communist sympathies to what is really no more than a diffident liberalism. The spiral of semantic blunders unnerves clear political thought. Australian intellectuals, with all exceptions granted, have not had their noses rubbed hard enough into politics to make them think accurately about political terms. They see the façade of politics as a screen of sliding catchwords (Commo, Fascist, 'Ming', confrontation, Liberal, Tory, too soft on Peking), behind which the real manipulation of power is carried out by men in closed rooms (the Labor Caucus, Ash Street, or Press magnates like Sir Frank Packer or Rupert Henderson), and they conclude that they have no possible rôle in such a shadow-world.

In this roundabout way, non-engagement becomes the proof of political integrity. Local intellectuals are sceptical of pre-cut answers to big issues—rightly so, since Australian politicians are famed for the cloudiness of their rhetoric, and Australian politics have the general appearance of a pygmies' dance—but the lack of moral urgency about politics deters them from thinking out their *own* answers.

Thus issues get shoved away, or juggled out of focus. One may have a vicarious yen for past issues ('Take Spain. Now's that's a war I *could* have fought in') but present ones, like the invasions of Tibet or Vietnam, or the conflict between Sukarno and Malaysia, which don't have their Hemingways and Audens to make them real, demand less commitment. 'You can't really discern the issues at stake yet. There's so much propaganda on both sides.' Of course there is; but traditionally, that is the exact point where intellectuals can step in and be useful. The intellectual is not a power man—except when institutionalized; I will come to that presently—but he can provide politics with a conscience by dispelling comfort, illusion and hot air. The tragedy of Australian politics is its lack of intelligent radicals, but the intellectuals have been defeated by the party system.

If the irritants that lead to thought are soothed by the political cocoon and the rich economy, they are further greased by social homogeneity. 'You've got the nigger problem licked,' said Bull Connor, 'you don't let the bastards in.' The keystone of our immigration laws is racial prejudice, the White Australia policy, which states in essence that nobody with a brown, yellow or black skin may take up permanent residence in Australia. No intellectual here seeks to defend White Australia on moral grounds, yet they are oddly slow to attack it publicly. The reason is that race has never become an irritant that puts ideas into action and forces a sense of moral urgency. Race can be safely ignored, until, presumably, the Indonesian marines take Bondi. It is easy to vaguely approve of the Chinese if you don't know any. To most Australian intellectuals the Chinese are either a statistic somewhere north, or the people you buy spring rolls from. The fact that Oriental students are selectively admitted to Australian universities mollifies Australian intellectuals; non-whites can, after all, get in for a while if they are potential intellectuals—that is, if they prove their worth on our terms.

The death, or rather non-birth, of radical thought in Australia has had a second result: the job-consciousness of intellectuals.

The intellectuals' crisis in today's society stems from the fact that radicalism is no longer instinctive. We are so well-off that dissent looks like a faintly silly posture. This affects the older men, for, as the American political commentator William Newman wrote, 'It is tempting *not* to be a radical today as a simple means by which the intellectual firebrand of the 1930s can rid himself of a past which clutters up the present.' But the younger men, the after-1945s, haven't even the irritant of a radical past. The radicalism of Australian thought typified by *The Bulletin* in the nineties became the grotesque conservatism of the thirties and forties; no new interpretations of radicalism have appeared in Australian thought since. And so the dissenter's outlines waver soggily into those of the pundit, the professional know-how man and the academic-with-a-field. Culture as good taste (don't shout, you might wake the baby) is the virtuous hobby of a rich society, so that the popular *Gestalt,* like some huge oyster, at once coats any irritant mind with the nacre of celebrityship, turning the dissenter into one more cultural gem.

In this way, the dissenting intellectual becomes 'a passive spectator, explaining to other passive spectators what is happening'. In Australia we are witnessing what is already a *fait accompli* in America: the inexorable process by which intellectuals are institutionalized. This is greeted as a triumph of pragmatic intellect, a menacing and cloudy phrase which implies that pure speculation is not a fit vocation for thinkers; like the Chinese peasant's dung, every particle of thought has to be ploughed back into the soil of the common *Geist.* There is, as Buckley remarked, 'no nonsense about an intellectual's existing to think and to make other people think'. He has a consultant's job to do, as a teacher, an industrial adviser and ABC man, a university lecturer , or a professional reviewer. (Editors, by the way, prefer 'reviewer' to the word critic, and this is significant: criticism implies something snarky and un-Australian, so that literary 'reviewing' in this country consists mainly of Saturday-page potted summaries of novels.)

The intellectual-as-technician is, by necessity, job conscious, since he tends to restrict his intellectual life to the limits within which it is employable. This has two effects. The first is that he narrows his 'field'. Anyone who has been to America knows the mad end of this splitting and boxing-up of knowledge: the Ph.D theses on the comma-patterns in Dylan Thomas, the visiting lecturer on Marvell who cannot be bothered to read the Augustans, the faculties of Basket Design and Television Administration. The idea that culture is divided into watertight 'fields' is accepted by most intellectuals in Australia; this narrowed myopia damages their understanding of a possible place in a worldwide intellectual community. It is perhaps significant that the only intellectuals here who insist that culture *is* a continuum are on the Right—notably the prominent Catholic critic, James McAuley. If they emanated from the Left, such ideas would suffer from institutionalized distrust of their radical sources. The Australian intellectual, faced with the problem of a fragmented culture, sidles his way round it muttering '*Il nous faut cultiver notre jardin*'.

This fragmentation weakens the intellectual's resistance to the second effect of institutions: pressure. Take, for instance, the Australian Broadcasting Commission, which absorbs a fair number of Australian intellectuals. It is not possible to air radical views on the ABC and stay on the payroll. Programmes which are likely to cause controversy are bluntly discouraged. It is hard to produce anything but pap about significant issues when you know that Brigadier Spry, the head of the Security Service, has the last word on ABC policy. The ABC's record discloses endless censorship from Security, the RSL and the churches. Every intellectual in Australia knows about this, and they all resent it; but too often the cure is a mental reservation, then on with the job. So, too, with the supine attitude intellectuals have towards literary censorship in Australia. In doltish severity, it is surpassed only by the censorship in Ireland, Spain and Portugal, yet protest against it is mostly confined to *sotto-voce* grumbles in clique. And recently we saw the ignoble end of the Orr case, where the framed professor of philosophy from Hobart University, after seven years' protest against wrongful dismissal, was encouraged by his fellow academics to accept a sum of money from the University Senate, *without reinstatement*, as the price of his silence and withdrawal. Such are the convulsions of conscience that we unblinkingly accept. 'Independent thought in Australia,' wrote Douglas MacCullum, 'is so weak that it cannot be said that freedom of thought and speech is generally a living question.' It is not suppressed; it's simply that not enough people are passionately concerned with freedom. One picks one's ideas from the bin of some handy orthodoxy. An emollient materialism does the rest.

A man in an institution cannot think in terms of values, only techniques. The alternative to the institutionalized egghead is the freewheeling one, who has no obligations to anything except ideas. Buckley relates our lack of freewheelers to the absence of a café-culture—more generally, to the lack of informal meeting places for minds. But *any* free cell, to the man-in-the-pub, looks like a cancer, and our conformist instincts ensure the hold of institutions over intellectuals. Nonetheless, despite the conformity and we're-all-right-Jack cant, there is a wellspring of tremendous energy in Australian sensibility. It has shown itself, not in a vital intelligentsia, but in the arts, among novelists, performers, poets and especially artists. This is another sign of fragmentation, but at least Australia is finding its identity, albeit lopsidedly, through the arts. We have seen split-level cultures of this kind before. Identity can only be asserted by action. For artists, the act is creation. For intellectuals in a bourgeois society, where tolerance erodes what opposition can't destroy, this act must embody itself in a tough-minded radicalism. But no pressures, no apparent threats compel Australian conscience to make choices. When choosing one's values does become something more than the existential hobby Australian eggheads think it is, the intellectuals may find their identity, and, with that, a place in the world community of ideas.

R. A. SIMPSON   (1929–)

Poet, editor. Born and educated in Melbourne.

THE BOTANIST

It is an aim to excite a due interest in the general study and ample utilisation of any living forms of vegetation or of important substances derived therefrom. All other objects are secondary, or the institution ceases to be a real garden of science.

Baron Ferdinand von Mueller
Director of the Botanical Gardens, Melbourne
(1857–73)

1

Because of Latin tags and citizens
He left with books, was banished from his garden.

Denied the Eden of his work and choice,
With labels on those trees to tell the world,
He only sulked in dreams when flowers grew
With nameless stems.
                              For years he'd moved alone
In search of life to catalogue—but soon
He learnt the quaint extent of flowers, shrubs
Which only he could name.

2

He saw Australia as a paradox:
His vision found an Eden where the plants
Might kill, the sun might melt his waxy frame
And leave his arrogance to waste in dust.

His clothes were symbols fools could wear to mock
The ignorant, and yet he did not care:
He saw an Eden to be plucked from darkness,
That all those citizens would never see
For this was never "home".

> He had no home
Except an innocence which tantalised,
Which hung and said it must return one day:
Now Sunday crowds walk through the public gardens,
Flutter like paper across the ageing lawns.

3

Speculation and conjecture move each mind
To seek, to plant a "garden of science" where
Life's personal and fixed, though foolish
To citizens who have no eyes at all.

4

Now failures meet his ghost at every turn
And so he labels them with love, and grins.
Here is a drought he did not understand
When he was made to live alone with flesh
And facts.

> Men are judged by acts and words
They'd inter, forget within some soil
That's out of sight and mind to citizens.
He never thought he might become a ghost
Held by a tree whose label fades.

THE DEPARTURE OF GOVERNOR MACQUARIE

Sydney, 1822

Waiting to leave, not wanting to leave like this,
His wife and son beside him in the boat,
The Governor is still imperious.
Oars are upright.

> Across the harbour, masts
As thin as needles, sway, provoke the sky,
Recall for him the pin-pricks he has known:
Hating their exile, men have hated him,
A Scot as humourless as depths in stone.

The future is words. The work is left back there—
Each name left tenderly on what was once
Rubble and rock, trees lacking distinction.
If he was kind to convicts (perhaps unwise)
The rulings have all waxed to order now.

Surrender meant blending with the dolts,
Making corruption his friend, and so he planned
Apart—an exile day by day preserving
Pride and courage for his last eclipse
And that applause heard only in himself.

The continent he leaves remains with him
Like so much of the self that stays unknown.
Over all regret prevails and burns;
It melts convictions and it will not set.

LANDSCAPE

The river is a thought that pours slowly
Down from nowhere, and soon it disappears
Beyond my view and apprehension.
This landscape also has its moving fears.

Here is a mind, and though I look at it
I cannot tell just what it thinks or knows,
Believe it calm as sunlight wakes through clouds,
But feel uncertain as a cloud-thought grows.

Although the rocks are firm, here nothing lasts
Because a text-book tells me that the hills
Were monolithic like a faith, then rain
And servitude, the days of finer wills

Attacked all strength and left pebbles and weeds
To waste. But if a landscape had a voice
And nihilistic words, it might explain
How much is accident and how much choice.

WILLIAM GRONO (1934–)

Poet. Born in W.A.; educated in Perth and New York.

THE WAY WE LIVE NOW

> "... at the end of the earth
> *where existence is most easy.*
> *Snow never falls there and no wild storms*
> *disturb the sweetly flowing days;*
> *only the soothing breezes of the West Wind*
> *drift in each day from Ocean, bearing*
> *constant refreshment for the inhabitants ..."*
>
> (*The Odyssey*, Book IV)

1

Here the talk's of flowering annuals,
investments.

Ah, the *richness* of our soil!

Each morning automatic sprinklers bless
all that's governable and nice;
sleek insects fatten on our ceaseless flowers;
glistening motors roam the land.

In our desirable brick-and-tiles
we dream of real estate.

2

Pursued by industrial suburbs—
"the concrete evidence of our progress"—
the bush has fled to the hills. Those hills are alive
with machines, developers, dust. Beyond,
our country lies, wide
and open.

We are, we often feel, living
on the edge of something good.

3

Nothing disturbs us.

Winds from Africa and Indian waves
bear each day to our long white shore
only what we most admire: fashions,

technology, and rich strangers as neat as
beetles who smile at our
simple friendliness.

4

Yes, we like it here.

Sometimes the shrewdest of us find the time,
after the gardening, before television,
sipping beer on enclosed verandahs,
to speculate on the future.

BRUCE BEAVER   (1928–)

Poet. Born and educated in Sydney.

SITTINGS BY APPOINTMENT ONLY

Some days I feel like a not-so-big
Nest of chairs.
People take me apart just to sit
On top of me
The easier to listen and look at others
Or rest themselves.
Then when the recital's over
I'm left fragmented
For something like a janitor to stack
Me back in my place,
One structure of many pieces.
One day I swear
I'll lock myself together or learn
The knack of collecting
My self in mid-performance and sandwich them:
Captives of the tower,
Cuckoo-guests of my nest of chairs.

FLYING

from AS IT WAS

We had a problem in our family now, actually it was my father's
problem but as he was a living presence once again among us it
became a family problem. Simply he drank too much at weekends
and was inclined to be irascible sometimes during the week. He

knew my mother and I neither loved nor respected him despite his attractive appearance or popularity at the Saturday pubs. This was before I had to bail him regularly out of gaol each week on Sunday mornings with a ten shilling note a regular "part of the pattern", as practising sociologists, psychologists, advertising executives and other collectors of such phrases are inclined to say.

He was invalided from the army to live with us when I was still thirteen and attending Sydney High on something like false pretences (I was quite incapable of learning anything but French phrases and passages of music by heart). I would leave in a year in disgrace, in relief. But my benighted father who was an essentially kind man could not come home to the shared asperities of insecure wife and upstart critic child so was driven on to argue almost interminably with us both, singly or together—"a classical case" as the sociologists etcetera would probably say. Of what? Of obvious incompatibility—of an innate fear of life borne with bravely enough—of an Australasian male's incontrovertible right to seek companionship verging on all but oblivion with and among his own sex as sad and sexless boys in the reiterated ceremony of mateship; all the golden hours relived of golden youth and golden beer—the iron pyrites of hangover and worse: the slow corroding ulcer, the fat-congested heart, the starved, cirrhotic liver, the self-encouraged cancer. Among these stricken boys who had behaved like men in bed, on battlefield, before the sleek or gaunt employer, yet never once within their heart of hearts; who knew the world so well, yet no jot of themselves, my father moved and had his being, and was loved.

And so it seemed my mother had no husband and I no father "to relate to" as the sociologists etcetera and newspapers uphold glibly. Without a doubt I did not want to assume the role of manhood (hairs within my armpits and about my genitals). I unhesitantly shaved the latter's first growth clean, "simulating emasculation" according to all the sociologists etcetera who seemed to live most of my life for the next unlucky seven years. But the prickly then luxuriant growth soon reasserted itself and I forbore merely to strip in front of younger boys. Just as preoccupied with sex as any other satyr of a similar age no exhibitionist tendencies existed for me then or now. But music. And the reading of countless books and comics. These became obsessional. And falling long and faithfully in love with certain film stars seemed to be quite apart from sex, though all were "inter-related" as the etceteras would say.

Early on one particular mid-week evening I was sprawling on my kitchen bed which served also as a couch, placed beneath the big window. The procedure on all weekends was simple, my mother and I took flight on Saturday afternoons to my aunt's house a mile away at Balgowlah. We'd return the next morning but my father would spend the day in bed and not get up until Monday. Perhaps this night he'd skipped the evening meal. For some reason he'd begun to harangue my mother and me, but this time I refused to listen, burrowing my nose into a Buck Rogers comic in which something rather horrible had just occurred. Buck had investigated a melted rocket ship and looked down in horror and pity upon the luckless pilot whose slumped back was facing the inventive reader. I could imagine without much effort the pilot's face resembling a Christmas ham overlaid with glazed crackling, or maybe a distorted charcoal mask, the ship's instruments had dripped into stalagmites of steel and bubble shapes. I was really consciously ignoring my father's berating but was hypnotically drawn to the comic's happenings.

My father strode across the room to my bed and seizing the comic book from me, hurled it through the open window into the night outside. Without a thought I leaped after it through the window and onto the lavatory roof a foot or two below then jumped about another eight feet into the backyard, rolling on grass and clay and grabbing at my comic.

Almost immediately my father had launched himself out of the window and bounced off the roof to land beside me and inspect me for breaks or bruises, the while warning me never to do such a thing again while he, the rentpayer, was talking to me.

I wept and groaned a bit and he accompanied me up the wooden stairs and back into the kitchen where my mother made a pot of tea for us all, shaking bewilderedly her dark head at the peculiar misfortune that had landed her with a brace of aerobatic madmen.

Remembering those moments I think the mantel radio was playing a then quite popular version of the "Spinning Chorus" from the *Flying Dutchman*. I'd learnt that year a fourth part ("Round and round my wheel goes whirling ...") but I'd envied the firsts who'd had the attractive melody. When we re-entered the room my mother had switched off the set. She wanted no background music for further melodramatics. I think the jump had shaken up my middle-aged father more than myself for he quietened down for the rest of the evening but I tucked Buck Rogers beneath the cover of the couch and drank my tea and listened attentively to my parents drinking theirs in silence.

When they went to bed I lay under the window in star-winking and moon-lightened darkness. My heart raced on at the thought of my unthinking leap into "outer space" without a flying-belt, and of how gently the grass and cushioning clay received me, and also of how not one of our neighbours had noticed the flying father and son from their seasonably opened yellow and amber lit windows. And how I had felt more protection than threat from my father's descended figure crouching above me, which no doubt was just another example of a rather predictable "love-hate ploy" in action, as the etceteras would probably say of similar launchings and landings on that calm night in a suburb of the murderous Forties. When I slept I dreamed of melted metal and calcined faces and of flying away from it all, that is, to another ship on a flying-belt quite alone and unafraid of that future.

DESMOND O'GRADY   (1929–)

Short story writer, novelist, journalist. Born in Melbourne; lives in Rome.

THE IMPORTANCE OF BEING HENRY

"I met a bloody fantastic character last night in the Marble bar."

Clyde Burton propped himself on his elbow, looking down on Melinda who he had been caressing while recouping his forces.

"Bewdy. Straight out of Lawson—the hat, the cavalry twill trousers, the far-away eyes. Must find the description of him."

He rummaged in the bookcase beneath a long window. Outside, the blue of Sirius Cove heightened that of the garden's hydrangea heads. Clyde's pubic hair gleamed red in the sunlight lapping his slack stomach.

The one sheet on the bed was as rucked as the harbour. Melinda punched her pillow into shape and rolled on her side away from Clyde. He was often irritatingly randy of a morning. But Sundays were worst of all as neither had to go to university where Clyde lectured on literature and Melinda was completing her arts degree.

She suspected his Sunday morning performances were dictated only by a desire to prove a point. His breaking away to seek Lawson when the surf of her feeling was rising rankled. She wanted to dump him, splinter his surfboard. She guessed he had an opportunity to do something he preferred: dazzle her with his pedantry.

"Here it is," exulted Clyde, falling on the bed with the thick Lawson volume, "this is him—listen: tall and straight yet—rather straighter than he had been—dressed in a comfortable, serviceable sac suit of 'saddle-tweed', and wearing a new sugar-loaf, cabbage-tree hat, he looked over the hurrying street people calmly as though they were sheep of which he was not in charge, and which were not likely to get 'boxed' with his. Not the worst way in which to regard the world."

"There's no mention of cavalry twill pants," objected Melinda, unwilling to play along with Clyde. "You must have been duped by the Marble bar decor—or had a vision when you tottered past the Lawson bookshop there."

"You're awake early this morning Fatso—even if it sounds you slept badly." Fatso, Clyde's surrogate for an endearment, underlined her slimness. "It's him to a T—uncanny. You'll have to believe it."

"Who the hell is he?"

"Lawson calls him Joe Wilson."

"Didn't you ask him his name?"

"You wouldn't expect it to be Joe Wilson would you? I've taught you the XYZ but I see we'll have to go back to the ABC. Writers pinch characteristics not names—if it's the same name, it must be another person, if you savvy. He gave me his card. Got it somewhere—I wasn't tanked enough to lose that."

He fumbled among his clothes draped over a bedside chair, stirring an earth-acidy smell, his.

"Joseph Burgess," he read from the card, "halfway there—if you pull that cracker, Wilson could well topple out. You'll see for yourself Mel," he promised, "at the farewell party."

"You going somewhere?" Melinda asked dryly.

"*He's* sailing for England—I might have missed him altogether."

That afternoon Melinda, who had not touched Lawson since secondary school, read the Joe Wilson stories for the first time. She realized then that they had been completed in 1901.

"Are you having me on?" she challenged Clyde as she dressed for the farewell party, "Lawson's Joe Wilson already had grey hairs."

"He's got a whole head of them now," Clyde replied as if it proved his point. As his student, and when she had first moved in with him, she had accepted such statements as appropriate for a genius.

Melinda confessed she liked the way Lawson talked about Joe's relations with his wife Mary. It was the sort of thing she would like to experience and write herself whereas the models Clyde admired had always seemed unattainable. She read a passage: "Then we sat, side by side, on the edge of the verandah, and talked more than we'd done for years—and there was a good deal of 'Do you remember' in it—and I think we got to understand each other better that night. "And at last Mary said, 'Do you know, Joe, why, I feel tonight just—just like I did the day we were married!' And somehow I had that strange, shy sort of feeling too."

"Now you're having *me* on," Clyde protested. "Didn't know you went for sentimental ratshit."

"It's sweet," said Melinda and he could not tell whether she was serious, "like this other ending: 'You've got the scar on the bridge of your nose still' said Mary, kissing it, 'and'—as if she'd just noticed it for the first time—'why! your hair is greyer than ever', and she pulled down my head, and her fingers began to go through my hair as in the days of old. And when we got to the hotel in Cudgegong, she made me have a bath and lie down on the bed and go to sleep. And when I awoke, late in the afternoon, she was sitting by my side, smoothing my hair."

"The sickest thing about Henry," said Clyde as if dictating a definitive statement, "is his fear of women—most of his characters have been done down by women. You've got those tough bushmen huddled around campfires congratulating each other on escaping from womanly wiles. Pussy fear stalks the bush."

"I don't know," Melinda responded lightly, "Joe Wilson always regrets he didn't treat Mary better."

"That's the other side of the medal—castrating guilt complex. Should've known *you'd* like it. A born castrator."

Melinda asked why, if Clyde destested Lawson, he was so excited by the previous night's meeting.

"The point about a minor writer like Lawson," Clyde answered, "is that we know more about his characters than he does. We can see Lawson's characters are alienated but he can't. Burgess proves what I always suspected about Joe Wilson."

Melinda knew Clyde saw through everyone, regularly. Laser eyes. Right through and out the other side with never a pause. His pub discovery, she guessed, would be a source of anecdotes, briefly holding boredom at bay. But it had stirred her imagination, even if she was wary of letting Clyde know.

"Did you ask his wife's name?"

"Didn't get a chance. That'll be a test though, won't it?"

They both had it in mind when they arrived, in the most conventional clothes they could muster, at the farewell party. But Burgess's wife was Anna, a Singapore Chinese. On meeting her, Clyde gave Melinda a so-much-for-my-theory look. For Melinda, Burgess was almost as big a surprise as Anna. His manner was so English, he was a straightbacked, Alec Guinness-type who would keep up a brave front even while silently crumbling. Melinda guessed hardening of the arteries caused the beyond-the-sheep look of his celluloid-blue eyes.

The venerable, well-heeled guests seemed impervious to the broken mirror sky, the well of harbour directly below the cliff-like apartment building. It reminded Clyde of Venice where baskets were lowered from apartments directly to boats to be filled with fish.

"Why didn't you tell me he comes on like a Pom?" Melinda challenged Clyde as they helped themselves to the buffet.

"Wanted to ignore contrary evidence," admitted Clyde, tired now of his short flight of imagination, bored by the company of old fogeys.

"Complicating, not contrary," corrected Melinda, "Joe Wilson shifted to London and admired the Poms. I can just see him blending with the background."

"That's fancy not imagination—don't let it seduce you," advised

Clyde as he drifted back to the group around Burgess.

Melinda attached herself to Anna who, excluded from the men's conversation, showed her the rest of the apartment.

Clyde, for a last scruple, wanted to pose Burgess the question he had not asked in the Marble bar: "Did you know a writerman named Lawson?"

But it was difficult to corner Burgess. From his conversation, Clyde understood that Burgess had returned to his native land to inspect country property but was happy to be sailing from brassy Sydney. When Clyde finally posed his question, Burgess was drunk on gin and tonic. His chalk white cheeks were flushed and he was fighting a stiff-upper-lipped battle for control of his speech.

"Lawson? Of course." His gaze shifted from the far horizon only he discerned to Clyde who could have been one of the sheep with whom he preferred not to be boxed. "Was at his funeral—never seen anything like it, not a dry eye in Sydney."

Again he looked beyond Clyde who suspected Burgess was a compulsive liar whose fixed stare was calculated to discountenance facts.

Clyde's voice became querulous: "But did you know him, earlier, in the outback?"

"Small selector wasn't he?" said Burgess loftily, "can't remember he was ever on my property—but you never know."

He resumed reminiscing about Slim, a bosom mate of his Burma days, and the necessity of constant quinine supplies.

Should have his pith helmet on out here in the colonies, thought Clyde as he sought Melinda. He calculated they could still make it to a writers' rort in Balmain. Together, they farewelled Burgess.

"Young man, I'd like to present you with this," said Burgess, tipsily, offering Clyde his plate on which a monogram was visible beneath lobster shell and mayonnaise debris.

Clyde, embarrassed, said he would not know what to do with it.

"Nor do I," responded Burgess who seemed to discover then the plate between his hands. "You could inscribe on it, young lady," he added with an effort, "'ware of the demon drink."

"Total loss," was Clyde's comment as they descended from the top floor apartment. Melinda stroked the night air as they walked the harbourfront towards Clyde's car. She looked over her shoulder, then pulled Clyde around just in time to see Burgess, from his apartment window, pensively cast a plate into the dark. It arched fulsomely before slicing the moon-slimed water.

Melinda moaned.

"During the Renaissance, a Roman family used to do that with gold plates," Clyde lectured. "Throw them into the Tiber—they had nets underwater to catch them. Designed to impress the guests. You impressed?"

"Must be the last plate of the set he used with Mary," Melinda drawled.

"Come off it, Fatso. The name's Burgess not Borges."

"No, it *could* be, Clyde." A little girl being wilful.

"Ho-hum. Wishing won't make it so. 'O'Grady says' must be your favourite game—you work by opposites."

He backed the car, wondering why she persisted. She noticed how his powerful shoulders were hunched as if he wore a thick sweater although he had only a light jacket. His body was thickening fast just as his attitudes were jelling hard.

"So Joe Wilson became a Pom."

"He even liked the climate," she insisted, "stood up for the English—there's that line in 'Joe Wilson in England': 'The only solid help I ever got was from an Englishman'. Can't you see Joe'd fit in? Distinguished: they couldn't label him as a rough Aussie. He's acquired the real English touch: he looks through you without seeing you."

Clyde was surprised by Melinda but seemed prepared to humour her.

"How did Joe Wilson get to Burma though? I should have asked him if he'd run into Eric Blair. Or how it was by the old Moulmein pagoda? That's more his period."

"That's easy—once you make the transfer to England, one colony resembles another. All good masculine company."

Suddenly Clyde was irritated by Melinda's febrile talk. He teased her for her freeflow fancy at his friend's in Balmain but she did not rise to the bait. For the first time she felt immune to his sallies.

The following day Clyde exhumed a wide-ranging essay which he believed would, if ever completed, unlock Patrick White. And wrote. But feared at times that he was lost in a desert without contact with either the living or the dead.

As he presumed Lawson had been left behind, he was testy when the subject surfaced again on Tuesday morning. His nerves were frayed by the scorching nor'westerly.

"Jesus!" Clyde had exploded, exasperated by Melinda's recalcitrance in a discussion about Aborigines, "with the best will in the world, it still seems to me women keep their brains between their legs."

Melinda was accustomed to such pleasantries but this time leapt on it as an updated version of Joe Wilson's "I often think it's a great pity that women haven't brains."

"Next you'll prove I'm Joe Wilson."

"Never. Joe Burgess is enough."

"Or too much. You're not going to keep that up, are you?"

"I'm going to write a story about it."

Clyde swung his legs off the bed and sat, sensing he had to stop

Melinda before she went further. It was getting beyond a joke.

"And have him living in the outback with his Chink wife—that's how the Bully got its pink page, I bet: saw red."

"But she came after Mary, of course: Mary couldn't get used to England or the English. Didn't you even take that trick?"

Clyde looked narrow-eyed at Melinda. He suspected she was becoming a Burgess-like liar and it made him insecure.

"Cool it Mel" was his advice, "I was excited about him as a talking point—not to be taken seriously."

"She *told* me, Cylde," Melinda insisted, "Burgess's first wife was Mary."

"It's a fine old name," Clyde responded although he was shaken, "Joe Wilson's wife didn't patent it."

"And whatsmore," she sat and he felt her breasts were bald heads about to butt him," she showed me things he's kept from that first marriage."

"A doubly buggy in the bedroom?"

"No," she said more calmly, like a marksman with his victim's low forehead in his sights, "but a little Wilcox and Gibbs sewing machine."

Clyde was at a loss.

"You don't even remember the stories—what he gave her as a wedding present in 'Water Them Geraniums'."

"How do you know it was the same model?" He knew he was dead but would not lie down. "And you want to begin your brilliant career writing that story? A cock and bull," he said and then repeated it to himself as if listening for a giant coda, "a cock and bull ..." He rose and returned the Lawson volume to the bookcase. He would take a close look at it as soon as Melinda left for the university.

"Sure," said Melinda, "why not? I can start, can't I?" And knew, at last, that she could. The story was shaping itself swiftly now, it had enough kick to reassure her it was alive.

"No one's stopping you Fatso, but you'll go bung. You need not only female fancy but a plausible story—oh yes, oh dear yes, you must tell a story. You'll have to believe me."

The only time he's used "dear" with me, Melinda realized and recognized it was an echo. Nevertheless, she sprang buoyantly from the bed. Before leaving for university she would water the blue hydrangeas by the front gate. Otherwise, in the searing wind, the delicate plants would wilt.

THEA ASTLEY   (1925–)

Novelist, short story writer. Born and educated in Brisbane; lives in North Queensland.

HUNTING THE WILD PINEAPPLE

After all, the house was nothing but an enormous barn, one gigantic living-room sixty by forty which was entered through the garage. Everything about the place groaned with bad taste.

Mr Pasmore ushered his guests—somehow his presence made us third person—from car to garage with the flair and pride of a talented lush, past rows of spigots labelled 'strawberries 7', 'pineapples 12', 'bananas 4'.

'It's simple,' he says twirling a pink gin, and he and his gin lean sideways with film-star lop-sided charm. 'But I'm so bloody lazy. Muscle-blood-bone-marrow-lazy.' His torpid eyes manage a practised twinkle. 'It's all mechanised now. Turn a knob and off race the nutrients. Saves a hell of a lot of trouble and the casuals do all the rough stuff. Weeding. Pinegrubs and so on. And I don't have to pause between drinks.'

He eases us into the living-room, which is split across one end by a twenty-foot curved tank of tropical fish, and twitches at a shoji screen. 'Bedrooms back there. Expand or contract a little according to taste. Makes the john a bit public, but then you can't have everything.'

Who has? But if I can horn in a bit on another's mummery ...

I always seem to be explaining how I got where.

In a town like Mango social movements are amoebic—you'd better believe it, as they say in the US of A. I have dying memories of a middle-aged red-head on a bus to Florida: I want a meaningful relationship, she said. I mean I want to relate, she said. How do I get to express my total self? she asked. Baby, I say mentally, don't ask me, and dumped her in Jacksonville. Here there are these mercurial, spontaneous and apparently directionless surges to north and east; a lively fusion, a parting. The fusing can take eater and eaten by surprise: 'My *goo*'ness!' the little blonde had said in a bar somewhere off Madison, 'I didn't expect *this*!' It's not all carnal, I swear. Mere temporary interpretations, if you like, of what appears to be a strange new language which, despite the sameness of the semantic signals, is strange and new because the signals are given by a stranger. ('I've just changed guards!' Doc. Tripp commented bleakly after his third corrupt marriage.)

That's the fallibility of us. The new inflexion! Ah, *mamma mia*! A new meaning. This body, this face, these fingers, talk *diff*runt! But they don't, of course; and reason asserts itself and the same dull old drone of the expected vision intrudes in those boardroom, bar-room, bedroom clichés I've heard, oh, I've heard, before.

I had moved, one translucent April, into a brief congruence that had originated as business and became shortly but intensely an ardent pattern of mutual succour. Mrs Crystal Bellamy, a calmly widowed South Georgian, impossibly researching the human geography of the north for a nonsense thesis, established a two months' base within the sticky filaments of my bed-and-breakfast web.

We passed swiftly from the manager-client nod to pleasant weather syllables to interrogatory clauses that contained all the primary fervour of two Vasco da Gamas colliding as they rounded the Horn. I'm interested in the violence of quick friendships. Snap up a pal! She was an articulate, golden-bunned lady with a certain piquancy of profile that was, at first encounter, blandly misleading. Be misled, I tell myself (and others, viciously), if only for the colour of expectancy. I am bearded now (arty or distinguished according to company), wooden-legged (the limp is captivating), and with a fringe of hang-ups, monstrous puritan-liberal growths like gall-wasp. No nodes on the skin, mark you: merely a flicker of epidermic sun-spotting—I call it bagassing—where the north has bitten me.

She wrestled me from Crusader Rabbit. My car became her car.

In a kind of tour-captain fever I distributed the country for her in hunks. We pursued lakes, craters, dams, limestone caves, ghost towns, abandoned mining camps, mission settlements, crocodile farms, hippie communes, sugar mills, prawn fleets, rich American marlin fishers, tin fossickers. We ranged north, south, west and, as far as weather would allow us, east. Her bun became sweetly loosened, my sun-spots increased, her note-book thickened. That's the how of it; and the specifics? Well, track them back to a well-intentioned buddy who wanted to prove we're not all grubbing away at the soil up here, that we're smooth, polished, and have swung quite nicely, ta ever so, into the sophisticated seventies.

So smooth that outside the house we are left gawking at a whopping heart-shaped swimming-pool filled with blue tears that blinked as a woman (his wife?) plunged from sight.

Mr Pasmore smiles at us.

'When Tubs emerges, if she does of course, she'll toss up some food. It's a pity in a way you didn't get here while there was more light. I could have shown you a bit more action. Muh-heen-while, I'll stiffen you a couple of stingers. You like that?'

We like that.

The sun took three drinks to go down. Mrs Bellamy gave an elegant paraphrase of academic purpose, and Tubs returned dripping from the pool and vanished behind a screen. Mr Pasmore did not seem to notice her.

'My, my!' he says, to Mrs Bellamy, 'we don't often get visitors of your calibre here.' Snapping the ice tongs. 'Another?'

We have another. Tubs emerges from the screen in a half-buttoned house-gown and heads straight for the bar where Mr Pasmore intercepts her with in-front-of-the-guests *bonhomie* and tells her she must meet these delightful people.

'Call me Crystal,' instructs Mrs Bellamy.

'Crystal,' Mrs Pasmore says obligingly and swigs a triple Scotch.

There are ice noises and Mr Pasmore puts heartbreak music on the tape-deck. Outside the world has gone black.

'What's for dinner, darling?' Mr Pasmore asks.

Tubs is a massive woman hewn from the one stone block. She stares vaguely at her handsome lug of a husband and momentarily her eyes cross with effort.

'There's a lobster somewhere.'

'Somewhere?'

'God knows.' She helps herself to another Scotch.

'Well, well,' Mr Pasmore says, smiling on us brightly, 'we'll just have to see if we can find it, won't we?'

The rummaging sounds from the screened-off kitchen section are terrible to hear. Tubs finishes off her drink and pours another.

'Crystal,' she says.

'Yes?' My bunned blonde registers polite guest stuff.

'Just musing,' Mrs Pasmore says.

We fight the conversation along for a bit, but it is only working two ways as our hostess sits with the lonely hootings of endless distances about her. From behind the screen it sounds as if a whole deep-freeze has been emptied onto the floor.

'My God!' Mr Pasmore cries flinging the screen to one side—and it's true: he's islanded on twenty square feet of frozen goodies. 'Got the damn thing! Afraid you'll have to wait a bit though. I need a drink after that.'

He comes back to us and bends spousily over his wife. 'I could kill you, my dear,' he says with frightful sweetness.

'Not now,' his wife says, regarding him for the first time. 'Not till after the guests go.'

'Certainly not till after the guests go,' Mr Pasmore says.

Beside me Mrs Bellamy quivers with hunter's instinct.

Mr Pasmore is savaging the gin bottle. 'Fuel stop! Just the briefest of fuel stops and we'll do it together. Well, we three will. I think Tubs has opted out, haven't you, Tubs?'

'In,' Tubs says. 'I've opted in.'

There's nothing like doing things together my dad, my mum, my teachers all, all unblinkingly, blindly told me. Oh, my God, there's not! Eventually we got ourselves sorted out with lobster pieces and salad balanced on our laps. ('Tubs gets the small! She didn't help one bit, did dear old Tubs!') The tape-deck changed its mood and

Mr Pasmore sat as closely as possible to Mrs Bellamy and became highly technical as he thanked the good God for all growing things: which appeared to include her.

'Moonrise at nine. If you want,' he suggests, 'if you like, we'll go in search of the wild pineapple.'

'My!' Mrs Pasmore made her first conversational gambit in half an hour. Crystal smiled at me, him, even Tubs, uncertainly.

'Yes, oh yes! We'll do it by car'—he chucked ice into vodkas— 'and take a flash. Bring those. We'll need sustenance for the perils of the journey. Tubs won't come, will you, Tubs? She's rather had hunting the wild pineapple.'

But the moon was behind cloud as he backed his cumbersome elderly Ford from the garage and took it on full beam down the tracks to the paddocks. Our drinks slopped, but Mr Pasmore settled the car into low gear, steered with one arm curved affectionately round the wheel, and sipped elegantly. He was full of whimsy.

'No noise now,' he cautioned, disc-jockey style, as we bumped into the third plantation a mile from the house. 'Some of these big buggers might hear you. We'll go on foot from now on.'

Sitting in the swell of the noisy dark we finished our vodkas. Mr Pasmore's manly and chipper handsomeness should have reassured, but he was just sufficiently not quite like a well-known actor to appear not valid. The car was parked below a crest in the road with sea visible now on our right, its blanched acres distantly alive.

'You right, old man?' he inquires, doing the wrong thing as I stumble getting from the car. 'It's not much of a walk.' I hobble my answer. 'Just keep those flashes down, eh? I always like the element of surprise.' He lopes ahead with ball-toe bounce.

If I say that at this precise moment Mrs Bellamy unloosed her bun and the moon came out, you will charge me with the wretchedness of symbol. She did and it did and under the sudden blaze of both I barely noticed the whisper of her fingers on my arm. 'Don't worry ,' she hummed with musical southern acccent in my ear. 'He's what we call slightly off-centre.'

And why should I care? It's these half-way, middle-term, middling, mean hucksters who demean my spirit. I've always had a taste for the circumferential.

'He'll want you to douse that hair!' And the half-smile from under it.

We caught up with him at the bottom of the slope where he stood, finger-lipping a warning as we came up. He was doing cautionary peerings at the stickle-backed fields, a hunter's ear cocked to the grainy night. Suddenly he lunged sideways, football-tackle mode, and in the prancing beam of his flash his distorted shadow heaved and buckled at the base of the paddock-line 'Lights!' he roared. 'Lights!' The paddock-line was racketing with movement. His body reeled and dived in the quaking air: a shambles of convulsed half-tone.

'Got you!' The voice was cracking at check-mate. 'Goh-hot you!'

'Oh, my God!' Mrs Bellamy whispers beside me, beginning to laugh, to laugh and run forward. His lank shape banked against moonlight. From his hand dangled a huge humped fruit.

Mrs Bellamy was catching on, astute Mrs Bellamy. 'Did it put up much fight?'

Mr Pasmore grinned and I am aware of teeth, the wet curve of lip.

'A flick of the wrist. A mere flick of the wrist,' he says, 'and it was all over. I am,' he says, 'in pretty fair condition. Here. It's for you.' On the word, he tattooed her arms with spikes; the head spears stabbed her chin. He lit, post-coitally I think nastily, a cigarette.

'Why, thank you!' Mrs Bellamy cries. 'You've given me the ears and the tail. But, my God, it's like a barb-wire melon!'

'Now, I like that,' Mr Pasmore murmurs. He turns down his flash and drops a pally arm on each of us. 'I like that very much. In fact, I like that like I like the two.'

'The two?' she asks. I don't. We are limping to the car. Yes. All of us. I'll transfer any disaffection, muddled as I am by hair and pineapples and the clear indifference of hot moonlight.

He's suave again, opening car doors with busy elegant flourishes.

'Two—um—two casuals. Two pickers. We do seem to get a funny crowd round here. Not, mark you, that I carp. No, no. I do not cuh-harp.' He lets in the clutch. 'In fact, it makes a break in a dull life. We have, you might have noticed, a very dull life. It's not often we get visitors like you. Style. Articulateness. The world, as it were, come to the pines.'

Despite the hair-flow Mrs Bellamy says rather tartly, 'You're making fun of us.'

'Mrs Bellamy—Crystal,' he says. 'As if. As very *if*. In a moment,' he adds catching my eye, 'I'll have to make love to this delightful lady simply to prove her wrong. Wrong wrong wrong. No seriously—'Oh, you're a no-but-seriously man, I think sourly. But he isn't. There's no 'but'. 'Nothing happens. That's our problem. Nothing happens.'

He went gloomy on us for half a mile.

'You wouldn't care, would you,' he asks as the house lights shoot between the trees, 'to take a little excursion? It will give Tubs time to achieve her coma. We can visit the—er—two.'

'More human geography,' I whisper. Mrs Bellamy's tanned fingers wre rolling her hair into a sausage, but the profile was still bemusing.

He didn't wait for an answer but reversed the car suddenly with millimetric genius, swinging on rutty tracks to grind back between 'strawberries 1' and 'bananas 3' to an eastern fork. Another half mile—I am counting the death blows to my stump!—and a second house squatting on its moonlit hunkers, a half-veranda'd timber box watching through narrowed eyes like Jason's (there's culture for you!) the grey metal spikes of millions of pineaples.

Mr Pasmore drummed a neat riff on the wall beside the open front door, the over-familiar, paternalistic-presumptuous tat-a-tat, tat-tat, and emitted hearty cries of boss-lure down a passage blazing with unshaded electricity. Space goggled back at us. He rapped again and after another blazing empty minute a lardy perspiring Greek, a cliché of a Greek, hands clasped somewhere where his heart should be, waddled his smiles towards us. I thought he was smiling, I say now.

'Georgy,' Mr Pasmore asks, 'may we come in?' He was already in. 'I've brought you two delightful visitors. They have been exploring the possibility of the pineapple. Do you like that? The possibility of? I mean we all know the positivity of, don't we? What we want, oh, what we all so want want want is the possibility of? Georgy, do you believe in the possibility of the pineapple?'

Georgy giggled and the giggle made ripples on his flesh. So what else could the poor bastard do?. He giggled and his eyes stayed dark as our names were offered and instantly forgotten. The introductions fluttered away like blank paper and came to rest in the mauve cube of a sitting-room which, too, was blazing like a bonfire of snappy magazine cut-outs tacked straight to the walls: glaciers, bad-lands, Alpine staccatos, palm-fringed nirvanas (they lie!—the motel complex has been chopped off by the fraudulent eye of the lens!)—all the clap-trap of plausible fable, while outside, outside, the grey lines of the armed fruit formed a desert of succulence.

There is a rhythm-bodied male of brunette intensity (even I can pick it!) shuffling cards by the window.

Mr Pasmore is saying with relish. 'And this is Tom. In fact, these are the tuh-who!'

Mr Pasmore can smile and smile and be, I am beginning to think, somewhat of a shit; but the young man's smile matches up to his, and his height matches and his accent is what I call all haggis and kilt.

'It's a bonnie sound,' Mr Pasmore says with whimsy. 'I come here to practise m'Scots.' He practised it a bit. 'Y' no theenk ah bung eet on a beet?'

'Two what?' Tom asks, shuffling cards and smiling tensely. He is superbly good-looking and muscular and Georgy watches him with a moist and jealous eye.

'Two? Why, most interesting, most remarkable, most most....' Voice-trail for hand-bafflement gestures. 'They are without a doubt'—turning to us—'the best couple of workers I've had in years. Yes, years. So many, so many bums hit the coast this time of year and all they want to pick is the pay. But with Tom and Georgy, now, it's different. They've been with me—how long is it, Tam?'

'Three years.'

'Three. Well, thruh-hee is a long time. A long time in these parts. Most of them move on after one season and you never see them again. But Georgy and Tom, now, are part of the place. When the pines are finished they stay on for the replants. Georgy and Tom. They solace my evenings. They will even, if asked nicely, make us coffee. And, if asked really nicely, make music.'

'Are you asking nicely?' Tom inquires.

'Very. Oh, very.'

Indifferently, Tom fishes a mouth-organ from his pocket, teases us with an insolent jig during coffee noises. The coffee waddles back, Tom does bravura stuff to Mrs Bellamy's entranced delight, and Mr Pasmore, clasping hands round his mug and surveying the room, appears to be consuming us, not it. I always know when I'm being eaten, even the most delicate of nibbles. But do the others? Somehow being punched in the privacy, not the privates, gives such stunning pain I'm reduced even below whimper-level to shiver.

Tom shakes the saliva out of his mouth-organ, takes a gulp of coffee, and inspects Mrs Bellamy's quince and cream with rapid glances that our host easily nets.

She fills the void. Fatuously. 'Have you always done this?'

'Done what?'

'Well, casual work? Farming?'

'I don't know about thens. Only nows.'

Mr Pasmore is delighted.

'How about a song, Tom? He's a great ballad man, you know.'

And instantly, with an abruptness that was offensive, Tom launched into virile tenor that rang and roared across the room, out the open window and over the acres of pines. ' "Och, Jock, where are y' trewsis?"' he sang, aggressively comic for six verses of *double entendre* hammered home with professional poise and eye-twinkles at each of us in turn: while Georgy poured more coffee and smiled possessively and watched enviously as Mrs Bellamy finally hooked the singer's eye for an entire verse.

The fat happiness of his possession is shaken.

'A good boy, eh? Good voice, eh?' Nodding and observing. Mr Pasmore is beating time with a playful spoon; but Tom drowns the taps with flourishes, to wind up with a smasher of a bow to the lady whose corruptibility he is testing with mock hand on bogus heart.

'Oh yes oh yes! Only the most talented of puh-hickers!' Mr Pasmore cries. 'Only. I told you this is a show farm, my friends, my dear friends, and you are seeing the *spécialité de la muh-haison*!'

'You're surely quite an artist,' Mrs Bellamy says, reluctant to release that hand on the heart. At least she's got his eyes! 'I suppose you've done a bit of singing professionally, have you?'

'A wee bit. Here and there.'

'Oh, it was so good! Very, very good. Could we beg another?'

She's fusing. Relating. She's on the Florida bus. She's giving him the Martini eye in a singles bar. Her orbs glut on his hip-moves as he swings into a chair and rides it back to front.

'I....' Georgy appeared to be gulping. 'I ... I....' His sausage fingers are plucking at her arm. 'I, too.'

I've seen it. You've seen it. We've seen it. Want me to conjugate all the forms of envy? It's rather nice, this, turning into a cipher recorder in the middle years, slapping my wooden-leg for comfort while I note—note, mark you—the gobbledy-gook of sad little human rivalries setting flesh aquake. Oh, I'm sad for them all right. Sad sad sad.

Crystal (the moment calls for intimacy) releases her eyes unwillingly to turn and stare, not resentfully—interestedly, at the fingers on her arm.

'I, too,' Georgy repeats.

'You sing?'

'No, no. An artist. I am an artist.' His eyes are on Tom with love and loathing. 'I paint. I am an artist.'

'An artist?'

Georgy nods and beams.

'Aye, he is that,' Tom agrees. I am the only one to catch the wink. 'Gie us a wee glance at same, Georgy.'

Mr Pasmore, raree-show proprietor, becomes golden with pride. 'Come on, Georgy. Bruh-hing out those etchings, those fabled canvases. If you won't come and see mine,' he adds in a whisper to Mrs Bellamy. 'Eh?'

Georgy's eagerness, all gulps and agreement and smirks of tumid promise, is frightful. Bloated and puffy with his moment, he waddles off to the bedroom and we nurse our discomfort—I nurse mine; Mr Pasmore is asimmer with something—until he limps back with a shabby grocery carton that he heaves onto the table.

'There!' he says. And beams.

We wait.

He smiles before his backdrop of deadly cut-outs, centre-stage at last, clutching his moment.

'Go on, Georgy,' Mr Pasmore says lightly. 'Open up!'

Georgy folded back the cardboard flaps, did an all-thumbs fumble at a protective layer of brown paper, and scooped out half a dozen sketches that he spread on the table before us as if he were fanning a royal flush.

Spanking girls they were, big-thighed, vilely luscious cartoons of comic-strip emptiness, copies of an archetype sex goddess that came with the first fifty lessons. Kid-stuff. Clumsy. Crude.

What to say?'

'Why, Georgy,' Mrs Bellamy says, not daring to look at his eager and waiting face, 'they're really good. Really.' She doesn't look at anyone but keeps shifting her fingers' desperate interest from one sketch to the next, a shade too enthusiastic. 'I'd really love to have one. May I?'

Does Georgy's delighted vanity then do to the others what it's doing to me? Does it?

He puts the sketches aside and purses his mouth critically.

'But that is before,' he says, 'before I am enrolled. These I have sent them. They are trials, you understand.' He is engrossed with explanations. 'To see if I can be an artist perhaps. And they take me, you know. They take me.,' He can hardly contain his joy. 'Oh, very expensive. A lot of money. But you send away, you see, and they send you...there are fifty lessons. They say I have....' He can't find the word and sausage hands wave helplessly.

'Promise, Georgy,' Tom says, helping him. 'They say you have promise. Lots o' promise.'

'That's it. That is what I have. Promise.'

He sucks the word with his head on one side. 'I am enrolled since two years now.'

He dives into the carton again, his pudgy arms milling around, and drags out another box. The two unused brushes lie beautifully beside unsqueezed tubes, three rows of them. The palette is unstained. Georgy runs his fingers lovingly over it.

'Fifty lessons.'

Below the paint-box is a great stack of gleaming knot paper. Reverently Georgy lifts the paper block out and places it carefully, gently, and perfectly square beside his other things. His fingertips keep stroking the paper.

'And all this,' he says. 'I am an artist.'

We all looked at the untouched, well-loved objects.

'How's about more coffee, Thomas?' Mr Pasmore asks. 'Or prithee a Scotch?'

But Georgy it is who hauls himself up. 'I,' he says, 'I make you more coffee. I make you beautiful coffee this time.' He is radiant with possession.

'And when are you sending in that first lesson, Georgy?' Mr Pasmore asks spitefully. 'When are you sending in the fuh-hirst, eh?'

I see Tom flash at him and catch the hate before the laugh.

But Georgy turns back to us from the kitchen door and he is still doped with the dream, wagging, smiling benignly, benignly, at the lunatic acres beyond the open window.

'Soon,' he says. 'Soon now.'

Gwen Harwood   (1920–)

Poet. Born and educated in Brisbane; lives in Hobart.

EARLY LIGHT

Light's planet-leaping shafts go home
    at last between closed lids that keep
knowledge of day's advancing tide
    from the uneasy house of sleep.

Professor Eisenbart looks up
    to see his mistress half awake
smoothing her sleep-indented skin.
    He hears the crested minutes break

into a bleak expanse of hours,
    and through the ruined palisade
of dream-horizoned arms and thighs
    strides time with heartbreak on his blade.

A painting from the Lascaux caves
    hangs reproduced above their bed:
bird-masked beside his wounded prey
    an ithyphallic hunter dead.

ESTUARY

To Rex Hobcroft

Wind crosshatches shallow water.
Paddocks rest in the sea's arm.
Swamphens race through spiky grass.
A wire fence leans, a crazy stave
with sticks for barlines, wind for song.
Over us, interweaving light
with air and substance, ride the gulls.

Words in our undemanding speech
hover and blend with things observed.
Syllables flow in the tide's pulse.
My earliest memory turns in air:
Eclipse. Cocks crow, as if at sunset;
Grandmother, holding a smoked glass,
says to me, *"Look. Remember this."*

Over the goldbrown sand my children
run in the wind. The sky's immense
with spring's new radiance. Far from here,
lying close to the final darkness,
a great-grandmother lives and suffers,
still praising life: another morning
on earth, cockcrow and changing light.

Over the skeleton of thought
mind builds a skin of human texture.
The eye's part of another eye
that guides it through the maze of light.
A line becomes a firm horizon.
All's as it was in the beginning.
Obscuring symbols melt away.

"*Remember this.*" I will remember
this quiet in which the questioning mind
allows reality to enter
its gateway as a friend, unchallenged,
to rest as a friend may, without speaking;
light falling like a benediction
on moments that renew the world.

IRIS

Three years with our three sons you worked to build her,
    named for the rainbow, late and lively child
whom the sea fondles. A fresh breeze has filled her.
    Tension and buoyant ease are reconciled

as she puts off the heavy yoke of land
    and takes the wind's light burden in her sails.
Ship-shape; an even keel: we understand
    old clichés truly—sixty pounds of nails

gripping her ribs, six hundredweight of lead
    flourishing water's frail cascading lace.
Age after age the same, still tenanted
    with earth's first creatures, water bears no trace

of time or history on its shining skin.
    Far from the shore where small crabs trim the rotten
scraps from a city's fringes, we begin
    (husband and wife so long we have forgotten

all singularity), our day of rest
    above that element where none sit hand
in hand, salt glitter tossed from crest to crest
    lights nothing of those gulfs where none can stand

upright; here nothing smiles; pity's unknown.
    A crippled gull I found helplessly dying
used its last life to stab me to the bone.
    Some old, lost self strikes from time's shallows, crying

"Beyond habit, household, children, I am I.
    Who knows my original estate, my name?
Give me my atmosphere, or let me die."
    —Give me your hand. The same pure wind, the same

light-cradling sea shall comfort us, who have
    built our ark faithfully. In fugitive
rainbows of spray she lifts, wave after wave,
    her promise: those the waters bear shall live.

DAVID'S HARP

Saturday morning. I rehearse
the Sunday hymns, fortissimo,
in the cool twilight of the church,
adding new stops at every verse.
Someone creaks the west door. I know
I am the object of his search,
gazed at, as though from far away.
He must be thirty, if a day.

I turn my seventeen-year-old
profile a trifle heavenwards,
and hastily reduce the sound,
accommodating to his bold
descant on *David's Harp*. The Lord's
house might as well be Circe's ground.
"With thee all night I mean to stay,
and wrestle till the break of day."

"With thee all night." So Wesley wrote,
though not with secular intent.
What flourishes that tune will bear!
My tenor wreathes it note by note
in rich Handelian ornament.
Faint burnt-out incense on the air
offends his Presbyterian nose.
He sneezes, stares across the rows
of empty pews between us; still

singing, walks to the organ; stands
beside me; puts his arms around
my waist and squeezes me until
I gasp, then gently lifts my hands
to his, and kisses me. He's sound
of wind. His kiss is long. We share
at last a common need for air.

"Give me one kiss, my bonny lass!"
Vain as a cat, I frown and toss
my head. He watches Brisbane's hot
sunshine, strained through Victorian glass,
lacquer a Station of the Cross.
He scowls and thunders: "Thou shalt not
make any graven images."
But as he bends his head to kiss

the image of his hope, the door
moves with its useful warning creak.
He steps aside. I start to play.
He fills his lungs, and sings once more,
    "Speak to me now, in blessings speak."
A death-pale curate come to pray
kneels, and is forced to find his Lord
through a loud F sharp major chord.

NIGHT THOUGHTS: BABY & DEMON

Baby I'm sick. I need
nursing. Give me your breast.
My orifices bleed.
I cannot sleep. My chest
shakes like a window. Light
guts me. My head's not right.

Demon, we're old, old chap.
Born under the same sign
after some classic rape.
Gemini. Yours is mine.
Sickness and health. We'll share
the end of this affair.

Baby, I'm sick to death.
But I can't die. You do
the songs, you've got the breath.
Give them the old soft shoe.
Put on a lovely show.
Put on your wig, and go.

The service station flags, denticulate
plastic, snap in the wind. Hunched seabirds wait

for light to quench the unmeaning lights of town.
This day will bring the fabulous summer down.

Weather no memory can match will fade
to memory, leaf-drift in the pines' thick shade.

All night salt water stroked and shaped the sand.
All night I heard it. Your bravura hand

chimed me to shores beyond time's rocking swell.
The last cars leave the shabby beach motel.

Lovers and drunks unroofed in sobering air
disperse, ghost-coloured in the streetlight-glare.

Rock-a-bye Baby
   in the motel
Baby will kiss
   and Demon will tell.

One candle lights us. Night's cool airs begin
to lick the luminous edges of our skin.

When the bough bends
   the apple will fall
Baby knows nothing
   Demon knows all.

Draw up the voluptuously crumpled sheet.
In rose-dark silence gentle tongues repeat
the body's triumph through its grand eclipse.
I feel your pulsebeat through my fingertips.

Baby's a rocker
   lost on the shore.
Demon's a mocker.
   Baby's a whore.

World of the happy, innocent and whole:
the body's the best picture of the soul
couched like an animal in savage grace.
Ghost after ghost obscures your sleeping face.

My baby's like a bird of day
   that flutters from my side,
my baby's like an empty beach
   that's ravished by the tide.

So fair are you, my bonny lass,
   so sick and strange am I,

that I must lie with all your loves
   and suck your sweetness dry.

And drink your juices dry, my dear,
   and grind your bones to sand,
then I will walk the empty shore
   and sift you through my hand.

And sift you through my hand, my dear,
   and find you grain by grain
and build your body bone by bone
   and flesh those bones again,

with flesh from all your loves, my love,
   while tides and seasons stream,
until you wake by candle-light
   from your midsummer dream,

and like some gentle creature meet
   the huntsman's murderous eye,
and know you never shall escape
   however fast you fly.

Unhoused I'll shout my drunken songs
   and through the the streets I'll go
compelling all I meet to toast
   the bride they do not know.

Till all your tears are dry, my love,
   and your ghosts fade in the sun.
Be sure I'll have your heart, my love,
   when all your loving's done.

THOUGHTS BEFORE SUNRISE

The season for philosophy draws on.
Pentameters flow smoothly from the pen.
The crops are in, the autumn work is done.
Earth settles down to die and rise again.

The last of the year's sweetness: time to write
long letters home, says Rilke. (This is home.)
The Chinese claim to know the pitch of night,
the mixture of all sound, earth's general hum,

F above middle C. I can't respond.
The house creaks, possums chatter, plover scream,
the geese scream back. Such croaking in the pond!
Hector crows for the sun to colour him

"Ab-so-LUTE-ly! Ab-so-LUTE-ly!"—that bird
never sings Cock-a-doodle. Once he caught
a whipsnake in his beak. Well, there's a word
he offers, very suitable for thought.

The Absolute, the unlimited perfect Being.
In Hector's case, the sun, which gilds his ruff
and sets his green and russet feathers glowing,
absolutely. His life is long enough.

I think of those for whom there'll be no letter
now or in any season, whom no sound
will reach, however pitched. I think of water
frozen to grassblades. Wheatgrains underground.

ALEC KING   (1904–1970)

Critic. Born and educated in England; came to Australia in 1929;
was Professor of English at Monash University.

CONTEMPORARY AUSTRALIAN POETRY

'Australian poetry' as a term for poetry written in Australia is misleading. Australia is an independent nation within the Commonwealth, and we long to be recognized, in Australia, as having a special spirit of our own; but our language is English, and our poetry is
essentially English poetry. It is poetry made out of 'English' with all
its inherited genius, not out of some offspring-language called 'Australian.' The only really authentic Australian poetry is the poetry
of our Aboriginals, totally unintelligible to all but a handful of
white Australians.

This may seem obvious and trivial. But, in fact, it has troubled
both writers and readers in Australia.... We want, in Australia, to
write 'our own literature', and this has sometimes meant a willingness to turn our backs on the mastery of language which alone
makes literature possible, for a 'mastery of English' seems almost an
un-Australian activity.

Our writers of ballad-poetry at the turn of the century filled their
poems with stockriders, runaway cattle, sundowners, lonely settlers
in humpies, gold-diggers, squatters, heat, flies, drought; they filled
their poems with images of things unique to Australia, and with
words specifically Australian because new-minted and unintelligible
to outsiders. Because of this our ballad poetry is thought of by
many as the most genuinely Australian poetry. This would be all
right if it were not assumed that it is also the best Australian poetry.

And a further absurdity is sometimes added: the ballad style is rigorous and rough, and it has been suggested that a certain slapdash pell-mell spontaneity is the mark of true Australian poetry.

Australian poets have, in the last fifty years or so, been coming to understand more deeply the problems of a transplanted culture, and one of the marks of contemporary poetry is, ironically, but inevitably, that is has for many become less 'Australian' simply by being better written. Moreover, partly because we are in Australia less and less cut off from the rest of the world, partly because the majority of Australians are now city bred and very many are almost as ignorant of our own outback country as visitors are, and partly because our poets are interested primarily, as true poets, in the 'mankind of our going' and not in the mass of local customs and habits which are part of any isolated community; because of this the themes of contemporary poetry in Australia tend to be more universal. And again this has meant for many that Australian poetry is becoming less 'Australian'.

Out of the thirty-four poems collected in *Australian Poetry 1963* (a yearly publication), four or possibly five poems only deal with specifically Australian themes; and I doubt whether many readers could tell, from the vocabulary, idiom, or imagery, whether most of the poems had been written in Australia or not.

One of the disservices to Australian literature comes, in fact, from readers in other countries who seem often to want Australian poets to keep on describing Australian landscapes, or the life in the outback, or the Aboriginals, or concentrating on the problem of being an Australian, or doing anything which makes the poetry obviously different from non-Australian poetry. One of the good things to say about our contemporary poetry is that it refuses to satisfy readers who want a guide-book in verse, a tourist's superficial glance of wonder at Australian peculiarities, or a sociological survey bundled up in verse. The 'haunt and main region' of his poetry was for Wordsworth the 'mind of man', not the manners of Cumberland people, or the lay-out of the Lake District. When Keats wrote his 'Autumn Ode', his theme was the old anguish of mutability; he was not concentrating on writing a vividly 'English' poem by describing the peculiarities of an English autumn scene. The maturing of poetry in this country partly shows itself in the fact that poets have ceased to be self-consciously Australian. Like Wordsworth they know where the haunt and main region of their poetry lies; and like Keats they may give a vivid imaginative experience of an Australian scene precisely because it is the vehicle for some insight more universal and more important.

I am suggesting, in saying this, that from one point of view, there is in Australian poetry today no greater difference from poetry written in England than a regional difference. It is not essentially a greater difference than that which we find contrasted in the poetry of Wordsworth and Keats regarded simply as regional poetry. Wordsworth used as his reservoir of images the mountainous north of England, Keats the pastoral south. This is purely incidental and unimportant. Australian poets used as their reservoir of images Australia, American poets America, English poets England. The tendency to overemphasize this regional difference of flavour is strong; but it is stupid. Some of the worst poetry today has the strongest Australian flavour; some of the best has no Australian flavour at all.

Of more importance is the question whether Australian poetry today expresses, as a whole, what any emergent nation longs to find, the presence of a new spirit and temperament, a new kind of vision, tone, character—a something that is as visible as the quality we see as we look back over the achievements of a nation that has emerged some centuries back, as visible as the 'spirit' of the French people.

We are becoming accustomed to visitors who tell us excitedly of the freshness, vigour, 'youth' of our country. We tend to repeat these words to ourselves, because they suggest pleasant qualities. The words, however, as applied to a community of transplanted people, are highly metaphorical and in many ways inept, especially in relation to the arts, to poetry. Might not 'youth', 'freshness', suggest a willingness in poets to experiment boldly in their craft? In fact Australian poetry (except for one burst of wild *avant-garde* freedom in the thirties which was European and unoriginal) has been less experimental than most. This is no weakness. Poets learn their craft from other poets, not from some source of spontaneous inspiration set in motion, for instance, by the consciousness of being 'young and fresh'. If our poetry is worth reading it is partly because our poets are as 'old' as the traditions of poetry-making which they have transplanted from the old countries to the new. In the same way, the first worthwhile painters of Australia were trained in their craft, not by some indigenous Australian flair, but by patient study of the great school of French nineteenth-century Impressionist painting.

Does Australian poetry, today, however, show the qualities of a 'young' nation in some other way? I would like to consider this in relation to the poetry of Kenneth Slessor, one of our living poets. He is a loving citizen of Sydney and is not much given to writing about Australian country scenes; but I would like to quote a poem of his called 'South Country', which deals with the Australian landscape, because it will help me to make a point about our poetry more easily.

South Country

After the whey-faced anonymity
Of river-gums and scribbly-gums and bush,
After the rubbing and the hit of brush,
You come to the South Country.

As if the arguments of trees were done,
The doubts and quarrelling, the plots and pains,
All ended by these clear and gliding planes
Like an abrupt solution.

And over the flat earth of empty farms
The monstrous continent of air floats back
Coloured with rotting sunlight and the black,
Bruised flesh of thunderstorms:

Air arched, enormous, pounding the bony ridge,
Ditches and hutches, with a drench of light,
So huge, from such infinities of height,
You walk on the sky's beach.

While even the dwindled hills are small and bare,
As if, rebellious, buried, pitiful,
Something below pushed up a knob of skull,
Feeling its way to air.

This poem shows something of a quality very visible in Slessor's poetry, a physical rather than a sensuous imagination, a sense of objective things vividly present but not deeply imagined in feeling. It is a quality not only found in the images he gives us but in the obvious need to give, in sound and texture and rhythm, the rub and bruise of solids that are in contact with us. Even the thunderstorm is 'flesh'; and Slessor's fondness here, and all over his poetry, for the echoing of vowel and consonantal sounds within a muscular rather abrupt rhythm emphasizes the sense of physique.

I think it is easy to find this physical imagination in much contemporary Australian poetry. Another short illustration from a poem by J. R. Rowland (in *Australian Poetry 1963*) will help to define the tone:

All day the house blooms like a sail
    With air and light
Trembling at anchor on its gaptoothed piles
In a seawind soft as talc that touches and again touches
    Like a sweet mother. Spade and pail
Trip us by open doors, pennies and shells
Scatter on ledges and on windowsills

With combs, my thongs, your lipstick, saftey pins.
    Sand in the shower,
Salty towels on the verandah rail.

It is fun to begin working out the theory that this kind of imagination is expressive of a genuine and special quality of Australian life today. The theory would run like this: we are materially a well-to-do nation, we are well fed, housed, and are generally full of physical well-being; we love a physical life, are addicted to sports and games; our country is especially kind and rewarding to the young and vigorous: what more natural than that one of our national qualities should be a vivid physical imagination? I do not think this theory is anything more than amusing fun; but before I discuss it further, I want to return to Slessor's poem to pick up another characteristic which is singled out by many critics as specially Australian—its irony.

H. M. Green, the critic and historian of Australian literature, has said: 'It would be as hard for any representative of a young and vigorous and on the whole extremely lucky and prosperous country to be thoroughly disillusioned, as it would be for him to be entirely lacking in the national characteristic of irony'. And Mr Max Harris, who quotes this remark in his pamphlet on Kenneth Slessor, adds, 'An ironic quality of mind is as native to modern Australian poetry as a mythopoeia is natural to modern Australian art'.

There is irony in the poem, 'South Country', an emotion which is obviously not taking itself too seriously, a sense of slightly mocking emphasis and exaggeration. The landscape in the poem is experienced as something verging on the absurd, the portentous, unmanageable by the imagination, something which mocks any feelings one may start to have about it. I think this is a genuine Australian irony, allied to our fondness for 'tall stories' of a wildly exaggerated improbability, our easy going slang, our *ad hoc* attitudes, our liking to cope with immediate physical problems, our lack of passion and violent engagement. It is a kind of defence, obviously, and inevitable perhaps in a transplanted people face to face with the unhomely enormity of our oversize and intemperate continent.

This irony is the lesser irony, however, the defence-irony which moves too easily from the strength of not taking oneself too solemnly to the weakness of not taking anything seriously. The greater irony is not defence but exposure: it knows how feelings passionately believed in are opposed by others equally valid; it exposes one to the irony of existence. I think it is necessary to say this, because if the physical imagination of Australian poets and their share of Australian irony is claimed to make them representative and especially interesting, it is a dubious honour. They are qualities which give a kind of bounce, humour, sturdiness to poetry which is endearing, immediately relished, but quickly exhausted as poetic pleasure.

In any case, I do not like this kind of argument. I think critics in our country and readers from outside are dangerously inclined to seize qualities in Australian literature which can be most successfully thought of as special to this country, only to find, if they are honest, that they are qualities of a minor kind. This is unfair to our writers. Moreover I would have thought the two characteristics I have discussed, a physical imagination and a defensive irony, are found in much western poetry today, in England and America as well as in Australia. They seem to me compulsive qualities in poetry written within a civilization so metaphysically uncertain of its ground, so caught up in the machine of material expansion. Things, bits and pieces of planetary material, natural or man-made, surround us with their peremptory presence asking what we with our ever-ready know-how, are going to do to them; and we are happy to do it. But our feeling for them, our imaginative grasp of their existence, their being, is uncertain, wavering, perplexed. An ironic admission of this disbelief in our feelings seems to me western rather than Australian, though I think we have developed a rather specially visible variety of it in our own country.

Irony, however, is not the only defence or way of coping with it. Another is a rapid fingering of intellectual language through which we may evade emotional commitment, showing itself in brittle rhythms and a cagey tone. And this brings me to the final point I want to make about our contemporary poetry. It seems to me that a good deal of our best poetry reveals qualities that are the very opposite of those one might expect from a superficial grasp of our national characteristics. The poetry is not brash, young, self-consciously vital: it is not ironic, nor specially physical; it is not full of carefully emphasized regional flavours. It is, on the contrary, a poetry that, remaining thoughtful, is surprisingly more simple, sensuous, and passionate than a great deal of modern English verse, showing an involved symbolism or a brittle intellectual verve. Here, for instance, is a poem of Judith Wright who is probably our most widely read contemporary poet:

Midnight

Darkness where I find my sight,
shadowless and burning night,
here where death and life are met
is the fire of Being set.

Watchman eye and workman hand
are spun of water, air, and sand.
These will crumble and be gone—
still that darkness rages on.

As a plant in winter dies
down into the germ, and lies
leafless, tongueless, lost in earth,
imaging its fierce rebirth;

and with the whirling rays of the sun
and shuttle-stroke of living rain
weaves that image from its heart
and like a god is born again—

so let my blood reshape its dream,
drawn into that tideless stream;
that shadowless and burning night
of darkness where I find my sight.

And here is a recent poem of James McAuley, another of our best and most widely read poets:

Pietà

A year ago you came
Early into the light,
You lived a day and night,
Then died; no one to blame.

Once only, with one hand
Your mother in farewell
Touched you. I cannot tell,
I cannot understand

A thing so dark and deep,
So physical a loss:
One touch, and that was all

She had of you to keep.
Clean wounds, but terrible,
Are those made with the Cross.

I have chosen these two poems, full of quiet passion, unspectacular, finely made, because they show, I think, how in an unexpected way contemporary Australian poetry may express the experience of being Australian. These poems have universal not local themes; they are English poems made from the resources of English words; they do not represent any 'Australian outlook' at all; but perhaps they do represent the isolation and loneliness of Australia in an indirect way. We experience a kind of willing seclusion in Australia today, not an enforced isolation as heretofore as far as the world of ideas and imagination is concerned. Communication is so quick that we can be as much citizens of the world as any community anywhere. But our physical isolation gives us a kind of freedom, not to be naïve and ignorant, but to be unfashionable—to be unaffected by the pressure of schools and allegiances that are sophisticated and temporary. I think that this 'unaffectedness' is a genuine quality of contemporary Australian poetry.

I would be wrong if I suggested that the two poems quoted above are examples of a predominating style. Our poetry is as varied in kind and inner life as any western poetry in a world of fringe dwellers round a unanimity we have all lost. I want these two poems to illustrate the fact that Australian poetry today, while being essentially English poetry, does often express the experience of being a poet in this country, far from the sophisticated centres of the 'old world'.

I have not tried to write any systematic account of modern poetry, or chosen to discuss the five or six best contemporary poets, because I think it is more useful and more interesting to hold out a warm but warning invitation to intending readers. We have no major poets; but we have good poets. And the best of our poetry is probably the least obviously Australian. This, of course, is immediately unattractive to an outside reader, for why should he explore Australian poetry merely to find some more English poetry; he is looking rather for special, unusual qualities in poetry that is written in so un-English a place as Australia. This cannot be helped.

Intending readers who want our poetry always full of local colour are wanting the superficial. And those who would like our poetry to express our most visible national qualities, our happy materialism, our egalitarian *bonhomie*, our defensive irony, our impatience with ceremony, are wanting the poetically inferior. Our best poetry is written by poets who know they are human beings by necessity and Australians by accident.

IV: CONTEMPORARY WRITING

Commentary

This section represents the work of the last decade. It would be rash to propose anything definitive about writers who are still writing, and many of whom have only just begun their careers. Patrick White remains the most substantial novelist of the decade, while Thomas Keneally and David Ireland consolidate their reputations. The expatriate Shirley Hazzard has in recent years earned international recognition. Stow and Koch resume their careers as novelists, while David Malouf proves to be just as talented in fiction as in poetry.

In this period drama too becomes significant in interpreting the nature of Australian cultural experience. Whereas in earlier times the Australian theatre depended heavily on imported plays and companies, it is now sustained by Australian dramatists such as White, Williamson, Buzo and Hibberd. In a climate of awakened political consciousness, many of the plays written and performed in this period have dealt with topical social issues, and while some have kinship with the social realist novels of the thirties and forties, the emergence of the drama may be seen in terms of its escape from realism. Much the same applies to the resurgence of Australian film-making.

There is now a very large number of poets contributing to small magazines. Nevertheless the indications are that, while there is a large quantity of writing, stimulated in part by a generous system of government patronage, there might not be as many substantial poets as there were between 1940 and 1970.

It appears in retrospect that over the last forty years modernist tendencies in European and American writing have been assimilated into Australian literature in various ways. But one cannot point to writers of either fiction or poetry who are experimental in the sense of having originated forms and techniques. While they have absorbed the best of modernist methods, their originality is a matter of individual perception rather than formal innovation.

SHIRLEY HAZZARD (1931–)

Short story writer, novelist. Born and educated in Sydney; worked abroad from 1947; full-time writer since 1962; lives in New York.

NOTHING IN EXCESS

'The aim of the Organization,' Mr Bekkus dictated, leaning back in his chair and casting up his eyes to the perforations of the sound-proof ceiling; 'The *aim* of the Organization,' he repeated with emphasis, as though he were directing a firing-squad—and then, 'the *long-range* aim,' narrowing his eyes to this more distant target, 'is to fully utilize the resources of the staff and hopefully by the end of the fiscal year to have laid stress—'

Mr Bekkus frequently misused the word 'hopefully'. He also made a point of saying 'locate' instead of 'find', 'utilize' instead of 'use', and never lost an opportunity to indicate or communicate; and would slip in a 'basically' when he felt unsure of his ground.

'—to have laid greater stress upon the capacities of certain members of the staff at present in junior positions. Since this bears heavily'—Mr Bekkus now leant forward and rested his elbows firmly on his frayed blue blotter—'on the nature of our future work force, attention is drawn to the Director-General's directive set out in (give the document symbol here, Germaine), asking that Personnel Officers communicate the names of staff members having— what was the wording there?' He reached for a mimeographed paper in his tray.

'Imagination,' Germaine supplied.

'—imagination and abilities which could be utilized in more responsible posts.' Mr Bekkus stopped again. 'Where's Swoboda?'

'He went to deposit your pay-cheque, Mr Bekkus.'

'Well, when he comes in tell him I need the figures he's been preparing. Better leave a space at the end, then, for numbers of vacant posts. New paragraph. Candidates should be recommended solely on the basis of outstanding personal attributes, bearing in mind the basic qualifications of an international civil servant as set forth in Part II (that's roman, Germaine) of the Staff Regulations with due regard to education, years of service, age, and administrative ability. Read that back.... All right. We'll set up the breakdown when Swoboda comes across with the figures. Just bang that out, then—copies all round.' Mr Bekkus was always saying 'Bang this out' or 'Dash that off' in a way that somehow minimized Germaine's role and suggested that her job was not only unexacting but even jolly.

'Yes, Mr Bekkus.' Germaine had closed her book and was searching for her extra pencil among the papers on the desk.

'You see how it is, Germaine,' said Mr Bekkus, again leaning back in the tiny office as if he owned it all. 'The Director-General is loosening things up, wants people who have ideas, individuality, not the run-of-the-mill civil servants we've been getting round here.' His gesture was apparently directed towards the outer office, which Germaine shared with Swoboda, the clerk. 'Not just people who fit in with the requirements. And he's prepared to *relax* the requirements in order to get them.'

Germaine wrinkled her forehead. 'But you did say.' She turned up her notes again.

'What did I say?' asked Mr Bekkus, turning faintly hostile.

'Here. Where it says about due regard.'

'Ah—the necessary qualifications. My dear girl, we have to talk in terms of suitable candidates. You can't take on just anybody. You wouldn't suggest that we promote people merely to be kind to them?' Since Germaine looked for a moment as if she might conceivably make such a suggestion, he added belligerently, 'Would you?'

'Oh—no.' And, having found her pencil under the Daily List of Official Documents, she added, 'Here it is.'

'Why, these are the elementary qualifications in any organization today.' Holding up one hand, he enumerated them on his outstretched fingers. 'University education'—Mr Bekkus would have been the last to minimize the importance of this in view of the years it had taken him to wrest his own degree in business administration from a reluctant provincial college. 'Administrative ability. Output. Responsibility. And leadership potential.' Having come to the end of his fingers, he appeared to dismiss the possibility of additional requirements; he had in some way contrived to make them all sound like the same thing.

'I'll leave a blank then,' said Germaine. 'At the end of the page.' She tucked her pencil in the flap of her book and left the room.

Stupid little thing, Mr Bekkus thought indulgently—even, perhaps, companionably. Germaine at any rate need not disturb herself about the new directive: she was lucky to be in the Organization at all. This was the way Mr Bekkus felt about any number of his colleagues.

'Yes, come in, Swoboda. Good. Sit down, will you, and we'll go over these. I've drafted a memo for the Section Chief to sign.'

Swoboda pulled up a chair to the corner of the desk. Swoboda was in his late thirties, slender, Slavic, with a nervous manner but quiet eyes and still hands. Having emerged from Europe after the war as a displaced person, Swoboda had no national standing and had been hired as a clerk by the Organization in its earliest days. As a local recruit he had a lower salary, fewer privileges, and a less interesting occupation than the internationally recruited members of the staff, but in 1947 he had counted himself fortunate to get a job at all. This sense of good fortune had sustained him for some time; it is possible, however, that after more than twenty years at approximately the same rank it was at last beginning to desert him.

Bekkus wanted to be fair. Swoboda made him uneasy, but Bekkus would have admitted that Swoboda could turn in good work under proper supervision. Mr Bekkus flattered himself (as he correctly expressed it) that he had supervised Swoboda pretty thoroughly during the time he had had him in his office—had organized him, in fact, for the maximum potential. Still, Swoboda made him uneasy, for there was something withdrawn about him, something that could not be brought out under proper supervision or even at the Christmas party. Bekkus would have said that Swoboda did not fully communicate.

But Bekkus wanted to be fair. Swoboda was a conscientious staff member, and the calculations he now laid on the corner of the desk represented a great deal of disagreeable work—work which Bekkus freely, though silently, admitted he would not have cared to do himself.

Bekkus lifted the first page. 'All right. And did you break down the turn-over?'

'Here, sir. The number of posts vacated each year in various grades.'

Bekkus glanced down a list headed Resignations and Retirement. 'Good God, is that all? Is this the total? How can we fit new people in if hardly anyone leaves?'

'You're looking at the sub-total. If you'll allow me.' Swoboda turned the page to another heading: Deaths and Dismissals.

'That's more like it,' said Bekkus with relief. 'This means that we can move about fifty people up each year from the Subsidiary into the Specialized grades.' (The staff was divided into these two categories, and there had been little advancement from the Subsidiary to the Specialized. Those few who had in fact managed to get promoted from the lower category were viewed by their new colleagues much as an emancipated slave must have been regarded in ancient Rome by those born free.)

'The trouble, of course,' went on Bekkus, 'is to find capable people on the existing staff. You know what the plan is, Swoboda. The D.-G. wants us to comb the Organization, to comb it thoroughly'—Bekkus made a gesture of grooming some immense shaggy animal—'for staff members of real ability in both categories who've been passed over, keep an eye open for initiative, that kind of thing. These people—these staff members, that is—have resources which have not been fully utilized, and which *can* be utilized, Swoboda....' Mr Bekkus paused, for Swoboda was looking at him with more interest and feeling than usual, then pulled himself together and added, 'within the existing framework.' The feeling and interest passed from Swoboda's expression and left no trace.

Bekkus handed back the tables. 'If you'll get Germaine to stick this in at the foot of the memo, I think we're all set. And then bring me the file on Wyatt, will you? That's A. Wyatt, in the Translation Section. I have to take it to the Board. It's a case for compulsory retirement.'

'Got one,' Algie Wyatt underlined a phrase on the page before him.

'What?' asked Lidia Korabetski, looking up from the passage she was translating.

'Contradiction in terms.' Algie was collecting contradictions in terms: to a nucleus of 'military intelligence' and 'competent authorities' he had added such discoveries as the soul of efficiency, easy virtue, enlightened self-interest, Bankers Trust, and Christian Scientist.

'What?' Lidia asked again.

'*Cultural mission*,' replied Algie, turning the page and looking encouraged, as if he studied the document solely for such rewards as this.

Lidia and Algia were translators at the Organization. That is to say that they sat all day—with an hour off for lunch and breaks for tea—at their desks translating Organization documents out of one of the five official languages and into another. Lidia, who had been brought up in France of Russian and English parentage, translated into French from English and Russian; Algie, who was British and had lived much abroad, translated into English from French and Spanish. They made written translations only, the greater drama of the oral interpretation of debates being reserved for the Organization's simultaneous interpreters. The documents Algie and Lidia translated contained the records of meetings, the recommendations of councils, the reports of committees, the minutes of working groups, and were not all noted for economy or felicity of phrase. However, both Algie and Lidia were resourceful with words and sought to convey the purport of these documents in a faithful and unpretentious manner.

In the several years during which Lidia and Algie had shared an office at the Organization, it had often been remarked that they made an odd pair. This is frequently said of two people whose personalities are ideally complementary, as was the case in this instance. It was also commonly agreed that there was no romance between them—as is often said where there is nothing but romance, pure romance, romance only, with no distracting facts of any kind.

When Lidia first came to share his office, Algie was about fifty-five years old. He was an immense man, of great height and bulky body, whose scarlet face and slightly bloodshot blue eyes proclaimed him something of a drinker. His health having suffered in the exercise of a great capacity for life, he shifted himself about with a heaving, shambling walk and was breathless after the least exertion. When he entered the office in the morning he would stand for some seconds over his desk, apparently exhausted by the efforts, physical and mental, involved in his having arrived there. He would then let himself down, first bulging outwards like a gutted building, then folding in the middle before collapsing into his grey Organization chair. For a while he would sit there, speechless and crimson-faced and heaving like a gong-tormented sea.

Although education and upbringing had prepared him for everything except the necessity of earning his own living, this was by no means Algie's first job. During the thirties he had worked for the Foreign Office in the Balkans, but resigned in order to go to Spain as a correspondent during the Civil War. He spent most of the Second World War as an intelligence officer with the British Army in North Africa and during this time produced a creditable study on Roman remains in Libya and a highly useful Arabic phrase-book for British soldiers. After the war, his private income having dwindled to almost nothing, he entered the Organization in a dramatic escape from a possible career in the world of commerce.

It was not known how Algie came to apply to the Organization; still less how the Organization came to admit him. (It was said that his dossier had become confused with that of an eligible Malayan named Wai-lat, whose application had been unaccountably rejected.) Once in, Algie did the work required of him, overcoming a natural indolence that would have crushed other men. But he and the Organization were incompatible, and should never have been mated.

The Organization had bred, out of a staff recruited from its hundred member nations, a peculiarly anonymous variety of public official, of recognizable aspect and manner. It is a type to be seen to this very day, anxiously carrying a full briefcase or fumbling for a *laissez-passer* in airports throughout the world. In tribute to the levelling powers of Organization life, it may be said that a staff member wearing a sari or *kente* was as recognizable as one in a dark suit, and that the face below the fez was as nervously, as conscientiously Organizational as that beneath the Borsalino. The nature— what Mr Bekkus would have called the 'aim'—of the Organization was such as to attract people of character; having attracted them, it found it could not afford them, that there was no room for personalities, and that its hope for survival lay, like that of all organizations, in the subordination of individual gifts to general procedures. No new country, no new language or way of life, no marriage or involvement in war could have so effectively altered and unified the way in which these people presented themselves to the world. It was this process of subordination that was to be seen going on beneath the homburg or turban. And it was Algie's inability to submit to this process that had delivered his dossier into the hands of Mr Bekkus at the Terminations Board.

To Algie it seemed that he was constantly being asked to take leave of those senses of humour, proportion, and the ridiculous that he had carefully nurtured and refined throughout his life. He could not get used to giving, with a straight face, a continual account of himself; nor could he regard as valid a system of judging a person's usefulness by the extent of his passion for detail. He found himself in a world that required laborious explanation of matters whose very meaning, in his view, depended on their being tacitly understood. His idiosyncrasy, his unpunctuality, his persistence in crediting his superiors with precisely that intuition they lacked and envied, were almost as unwelcome at the Organization as they would have been in the commercial world. He was, in short, an exception: that very thing for which organizations make so little allowance.

Sometimes as Algie sat there in the mornings getting back his breath, Lidia would tell him where she had been the previous evening, what she had been reading or listening to, some detail that would fill the gap since they had left the office the night before. When she did not provide these clues, it usually meant that she had been seeing a lover. She would never have mentioned such a thing to Algie, because of the romance between them.

Like many of the women who worked at the Organization, Lidia was unmarried. Unlike them, she remained so by her own choice. Years before, she had been married to an official of the Organization who had died on his way to a regional meeting of the Global Health Commission in La Paz. (His car overturned on a mountain road, and it was thought that he, like many of the delegates to the Commission, had been affected by the altitude.) Lidia had loved this husband. For some time after his death she kept to herself, and, even when this ceased to be the case, showed no inclination to remarry. She was admired by her male colleagues and much in demand as a companion, being fair-haired, slender, and not given to discussing her work out of office hours.

'Mustn't forget,' Algie now said. 'Got an appointment at two-thirty. Chap called Bekkus in Personnel.'

Lidia gave an absent-minded groan. 'Bekkus. Dreary man.'

'A bit boring.' This was the strongest criticism Algie had ever been known to make of any of his colleagues.

'Boring isn't the word,' said Lidia, although it was. She became more attentive. 'Isn't he on the Appointments and Terminations Board?'

'What's that?'

'Committee for improving our calibre.'

Algie quoted:

> 'Improvement too, the idol of the age,
> Is fed with many a victim.'

There was nothing Algie enjoyed more than the apt quotation, whether delivered by himself or another. It gave him a momentary sensation that the world had come right; that some instant of perfect harmony had been achieved by two minds meeting, possibly across centuries. His own sources, fed by fifty years of wide and joyous reading, were in this respect inexhaustible. He had an unfashionable affection, too, for those poets whom he regarded as his contemporaries—Belloc, Chesterton, de la Mare—and would occasionally look up from his work (the reader will have gathered that looking up from his work was one of Algie's most pronounced mannerisms) to announce that 'Don John of Austria is gone by Alcalar,' or to ask 'Do you remember an Inn, Miranda?'

From all of which it will readily be seen why Algie's file was in the hands of Mr Bekkus and why Algie was not considered suitable for continued employment at the Organization. It may also be seen, however, that Algie's resources were of the kind never yet fully utilized by organization or mankind.

'Yes, here it is.' Lidia had unearthed a printed list from a yellowing stack of papers on the heating equipment beside her. 'R. Bekkus. Appointments and Terminations Board.'

'Well, I've *been* appointed,' Algie remarked, pushing his work away completely and preparing to rise to his feet, 'so perhaps it's the other thing.' He pressed his hands on the desk, heaved himself up and presently shambled off into the corridor.

Lidia went on with her work, and for fifteen minutes there was silence in the office she shared with Algie. It was a room typical of offices throughout the Organization—grey-walled, like that of Mr Bekkus, and floored with rubber tiles of a darker grey. Panels of fluorescent lighting were let into the white soundproofing that covered the ceiling. A wide low window-sill was formed by the metal covers of the radiators, and along this ledge at various intervals were stacked small sheaves of papers—the lower ones yellowing, the upper ones filmed with the grit that found its way through the aluminium window frames. (In each office the heating could be adjusted to some extent, so that in all the rooms of the Organization its international character was manifest in temperatures that ranged from nostalgic approximations of the North Sea to torrid renderings of conditions along the Zambesi.) Algie's and Lidia's desks were pushed together, facing one another, and each had a grey chair upholstered in dark blue. Blue blotters were centred on the desks and surrounded by trays of papers, black desk-sets, stapling machines, and dishes of paper clips—and, in Lidia's case, a philodendron in a cracked ceramic *cache-pot*. On each desk there was also a telephone and a small engagement pad on a metal fixture. There was a typewriter in one corner of the room, and a bookcase—into whose upper shelves dictionaries and bound documents had been crammed—stood with its back to the wall. On the lowest shelf of this bookcase were a pair of galoshes, a watering-can, an unwashed glass vase, a Wedgwood cup and saucer, three cafeteria spoons, and a single black glove.

On one wall, a calendar—the gift of a Japanese travel concern—
was turned to the appropriate month (this was not always the case
in Organization offices), displaying a colourful plate which bore, to
Algie's delight, the legend 'Gorgeous bunch of blooming peonies'.

From the windows, which were vast and clean, one looked on to
a wide river and to its industrial banks beyond. The presence of the
river was refreshing, although it carried almost continuously the
water traffic—coal and railway barges, tugs, tankers, and cargo
vessels—of the great city in which the Organization was laid.
Oceans and rivers with their simple and traditional associations of
purification and continuity are excellent things to have outside
office windows, and in this case helped in some measure to express
that much misrepresented, highly commendable and largely un-
achieved thing—the aim of the Organization.

'Some bad news, I'm afraid.' Tong put his head round Lidia
Korabetski's door—this was literally true, since Tong's small neat
head and long neck were all of him that showed. Tong was beaming.
'Some bad news, yes.' Not naturally malicious, he had developed
rapidly since entering bureaucracy.

Lidia, lifting her head, could not help asking, 'What is it?'

'Wyatt at lunch?' Tong nodded towards Algie's empty desk.

'He's been back from lunch for ages,' said Lidia defensively.
Lunch at the Organization was officially one hour, and Algie was
often overdue.

'They're not renewing his contract.'

'What contract?'

'His Permanent Contract, of course.' Permanence, at the Organization, was viewed in blocks of five years, and a Permanent
Contract was subject to quinquennial review. 'The Terminations
Board decided against renewing. They're going to let him retire early instead.'

'But he doesn't want to retire early. How unfair.'

'Another sort of place would have fired him.'

'And *another* sort of place would have promoted him.'

'Look—I like him too—everyone likes him—but there's a limit.'
Limits were often proudly cited at the Organization.

Lidia took up her pencil again. 'He's a good translator.'

'Well—that's an opinion I never went along with. We worked
together once, you know—on the Preliminary Survey of Intolerance. I had to correct him repeatedly.'

Lidia raised her eyebrows, but merely asked, 'Do you get full
pension if you're retired before time?'

'Wouldn't be a bit surprised if he ends up better off than we do.'

'Oh come.'

'Well, at least they're not firing him. They're being decent. That's
one thing you can say for the Organization. They're decent about
this sort of thing. They wouldn't fire him.'

'He'd get more money if they did.' (Certain indemnities were involved in the rupture of Permanence.) Lidia put her head back down to her work. 'I've got to get on with this.'

Tong, passing Algie coming from the elevators, raised his hand in cordial greeting. 'All O.K. with you, I hope, Wyatt?' (Tong was a man who could reverse himself in this way.)

'Splendid,' grunted Algie. (Algie was a man who could grunt such a word.) He went slowly along the corridor to the office he shared with Lidia.

An odd pair, Tong thought. He still had not told the news about Algie to his friend Pike in Inland Waterways on the floor below. Rather than wait for the elevator, he opened a dangerously heavy door marked 'Sortie de Secours' and ran down the emergency stairs.

'Tong was here,' Lidia said.

'Saw him in the corridor.' Algie let himself into his chair. 'Tong,' he mused. 'The very word is like a bell.'

Lidia had no way of telling whether Algie had been informed that he was to be retired early. She would have liked to make him some show of solidarity but could only offer him a peppermint, which he refused.

'You free for lunch tomorrow?' she asked—Algie's telegraphic manner of communication having rubbed off on her to some extent.

'Tomorrow—what's tomorrow?' Algie turned several pages of his desk calendar. 'Sorry, no. Lunching with Jaspersen. Could change it, perhaps?'

'No, no,' said Lidia hastily, for Jaspersen was the one friend of Algie's who held an influential position in the Organization. 'Some other day.'

'Better make it soon,' remarked Algie—from which Lidia realized that he knew his fate.

They went on with their work in silence for some moments. Then Algie let out a snort of laughter. 'Listen to this. Chap here got it in a nutshell: "*In the year under review, assistance was rendered to sixty differing countries.*"'

Olaf Jaspersen was a year younger than Algie Wyatt and had been at Cambridge with him. People found this hard to believe, for Jaspersen was lean and fleet, his eye was clear, his features youthful. He wore dark, well-cut clothes during the week, and tweeds on Saturday mornings—which he invariably spent at the office. He had joined the Organization shortly after Algie. From the first he had been given important responsibilities, which he handled with efficiency and charm. He now held one of the most senior posts in the Organization and had established a reputation for common sense, justice, and rather more style than was usual. Things seemed to go right with Jaspersen. His career was prospering, his wife was beautiful, his children intelligent; he had even come into a small inheritance lately.

But something had happened to Olaf Jaspersen in recent years. He had fallen in love.

He had fallen in love with the Organization. Like someone who for a long time enjoys the friendship of a beautiful woman but boasts that he would not dream of having an affair with her, he had been conquered all the more completely in the end. During his early years on the staff, he had maintained his outside interests, his social pleasures—the books he read for nothing but enjoyment, the conversations he had that bore no apparent relation to his Organization duties. This state of affairs had flagged, diminished, then altogether ceased to be the case. He was still an able man, but his concept of ability had been coloured by Organization requirements; he found it harder to believe in the existence of abilities that did not directly contribute to the aim of the Organization. He was still, on occasion, gay—but his wit now sprang exclusively from Organization sources and could only be enjoyed by those in the Organizational know (of whom, fortunately for this purpose, his acquaintance had come to be principally composed). He had joined the staff because he believed sincerely, even passionately, in the importance of the Organization; that importance had latterly become indistinguishable from his own. He held, no doubt correctly, that the dissolution of the Organization would be calamitous for the human race; but one felt that the survival of the human race, should the Organization fail, would be regarded by him as a piece of downright impertinence.

Algie liked Olaf Jaspersen. He admired his many good qualities, including those gifts of energy and application which had not been bestowed upon himself. Algie's youthful memories of a lighter, livelier Jaspersen contributed to the place of the present Jaspersen in his affections. Jaspersen, in turn, had recollections of an Algie full of fun and promise, and regretted that the fun had increased in inverse ratio to the promise.

If his loyalty to Algie was in part due to Algie's never having rivalled him professionally, this was a common human weakness and need not be held against him. Jaspersen was genuinely grieved when he learned that Algie was to be retired before time, and genuinely wished to assist him. He therefore came to their lunch appointment prepared to give good advice.

The staff of the Organization took their meals in either of two places: a large and noisy cafeteria where they stood in line, or a large and noisy dining-room where they could—at additional cost—be served. The food, which was plain and good, was substantially the same in both places, although it may be said that in the dining-room the plates were slightly lighter and the forks slightly heavier. It was to the dining-room that Olaf Jaspersen took Algie for lunch this day.

Jaspersen, a man of too much taste to adopt the line of 'Well now, what's this I hear?', found it difficult to raise with Algie the delicate question of enforced resignation. In Jaspersen's view, expulsion from the Organization was a very serious matter—more serious, one might even have said, than it was to Algie himself. When Algie and he were settled with their Scotches and had ordered their respective portions of codfish cakes and chicken à la king, he bent towards Algie. 'A bad development,' he said. 'Can't tell you how sorry.'

'Ah well,' said Algie, 'not to worry.' He gave Jaspersen an appreciative nod, and went on with his drink, which he had already gone on with quite a bit.

'Rolls?' asked the waitress, wheeling up a portable oven.

'Er—one of those,' Jaspersen said.

Putting it on his plate, she identified it with the words, 'Corn muffin.'

'Mistake,' said Algie. 'Nothing but crumbs.'

'Look here, Algie, I know these fellows—on the Board, I mean. Not bad chaps—not villainous, nothing like that—but slow. Not overloaded with ideas. Only understand what's put in front of 'em. Got to be played their way or they can't grasp, you know.'

'Ah well,' said Algie again, briskly setting down his glass as if to herald a change of subject.

'Let me get you another one of those. My point is—in order to handle these chaps, you've got to get inside their minds. Talk their language.' He fished a pamphlet out of his pocket. 'I brought this for you. It's the Procedure of Appeal.' He began to hand it across the table, but at that moment the waitress came up with their lunch.

'Codfish cakes?'

'Here,' said Algie, making room. He took the pamphlet from Jaspersen and laid it on the table beside his plate. His second drink arrived, and Jaspersen ordered half a bottle of white wine.

'The Board', Jaspersen went on, spearing a cube of chicken, 'is not the ultimate authority. That Bekkus is just a glorified clerk.'

'Point is,' Algie observed, 'he *has* been glorified.'

I've been thinking about your case,' said Jaspersen, 'and I don't see how you could lose an appeal. I honestly don't. But get moving on it immediately—you don't have a moment to waste.'

'What year is this?' inquired Algie, turning the bottle round. 'Not at all bad.' When he had demolished the first codfish cake, he said, 'It's good of you, Olaf. But I'm not going to appeal.'

Jaspersen looked less surprised than might have been expected. 'Think it over,' was all he said.

'No,' Algie said. 'Really. Better this way.'

After a pause, Jaspersen went on kindly. 'You have, of course, exactly the sort of qualities the Organization can't cope with. With the Organization it has to be—moderation in all things. I some-times think we should put up in the main lobby that inscription the Greeks used in their temple: "Nothing in Excess".' Jaspersen was pleased to have hit on this reconciliation of Algie's virtues with those of the Organization, for Algie was generally a pushover for the Greeks.

Algie finished another codfish cake and drank his wine, but when he replied Jaspersen was startled by the energy in his voice.

'Nothing in excess,' Algie repeated. 'But one has to understand the meaning of excess. Why should it be taken, as it seems to be these days, to refer simply to self-indulgence, or violence—or en-joyment? Wasn't it intended, don't you think, to refer to all excesses—excess of pettiness, of timorousness, of officiousness, of sententiousness, of censoriousness? Excess of stinginess or rancour? Excess of bores?' Algie went back to his vegetables for a while, and Jaspersen was again surprised when he continued. 'At the other end of that temple, there was a second inscription—"Know Thyself". Didn't mean—d'you think—that we should be mesmerized by every pettifogging detail of our composition. Meant we should understand ourselves in order to be free.' Algie laid down his knife and fork and pushed away his plate. He handed back to Jaspersen the Procedure of Appeal. 'No thanks old boy, really. Fact is, I'm not suited to it here, and from that point of view these chaps are right. You tell me to get inside their minds—but if I did that I might never find my way out again.'

'But Algie, what about your pension? Think of the risk, at your age.'

'I do get something, you know—a reduced pension, or a lump sum. And then—for someone like me, the real risk is to stay.'

After that, they talked of other things. But Jaspersen felt dis-turbed and sad, and his sadness was greater than he could reason-ably account for.

Lidia was coming down in the elevator when Millicent Bass got in. Lidia, on her way to the cafeteria, was pressed between a saintly Indian from Political Settlements (a department high on Algie's list of contradictions in terms) and Swoboda from Personnel, who greeted her in Russian. Behind her were two young Africans, speak-ing French and dressed in Italian suits, a genial roly-poly Iranian, and a Paraguayan called Martinez-MacIntosh with a ginger mous-tache. In front of her was a young girl from the Filing Room who stood in silence with her head bowed. Her pale hair, inefficiently swept upwards, was secured by a plastic clip, so that Lidia had a close view of her slender, somewhat pathetic neck and the topmost ridges of her spinal column. The zipper of her orange wool-jersey dress had been incompletely closed, and the single hook above it was undone. Lidia was toying with the idea of drawing this to the girl's attention when the elevator doors opened at the sixteenth floor to admit Millicent Bass.

Miss Bass was a large lady with a certain presence. One felt that she was about to say 'This way please'—an impression that was fortified, when the elevator doors disclosed her, by the fact that she was standing, upright and expectant, with a document in her hand. She got in, raking the car as she did so with a hostile stare. Her mouth was firmly set, as if to keep back warmer words than those she habitually spoke, and her protuberant eyes were slightly belligerent, as if repressing tears.

Lidia knew her well, having once worked on a report for which Miss Bass was responsible. This was a Report on the Horizontal Coordination of Community Programmes, for Miss Bass was a member of the Department of Social and Anthropological Questions.

'Hello Millicent.'

'Haven't seen you for a while, Lidia.' Miss Bass squeezed in next to the girl in orange and, as far as she was able to do so, looked Lidia up and down. 'You're far too thin,' she announced. (She had the unreflective drawl of her profession, a voice loud yet exhausted.)

When the elevator disgorged them at the cafeteria, Miss Bass completed her scrutiny of Lidia. 'You spend too much money on clothes.'

Lidia was pondering the interesting fact that these two remarks, when reversed ('You are far too fat' and 'You should spend more money on clothes'), are socially impermissible, when Millicent took her off guard by suggesting they lunch together. Rather than betray herself by that fractional hesitation which bespeaks dismay, she accepted heartily. Oh God how ghastly, she said to herself, dropping a selection of forks, knives, and spoons loudly on to a tray.

As they pushed their trays along, Millicent Bass inquired, 'How much does a dress like that cost?' When Lidia was silent, she went on handsomely, 'You don't have to tell me if you don't want to.'

I know that, thought Lidia. It's being *asked* that annoys me.

'This all right for you?' Millicent asked her as they seated themselves near the windows. Lidia nodded, looking around and seeing Bekkus deep in conversation with a colleague at the adjacent table. They transferred their dishes from the tray and placed their handbags on a spare chair. Millicent also had her document, much annotated about the margins, which she pushed to the vacant side of the table. 'I was going to run through that,' she said regretfully. She unfolded a paper napkin in her lap and passed Lidia the salt. 'Those codfish cakes look good.'

Lidia began her lunch, and they exchanged casual remarks in high voices across the cafeteria din. (While talking with Miss Bass of things one did not particularly care about, one had the sensation of constantly attempting to allay her suspicions of one's true ideas and quite different interests.) Miss Bass then spoke in some detail of a new report she was working on, a survey of drainage in Polynesia. Conditions were distressing. There was much to be done. She gave examples.

'Poor things,' Lidia murmured, stoically finishing her meal.

'It's no use saying "poor things", Lidia.' Miss Bass often took it on herself to dictate the responses of others. 'Sentiment doesn't help. What's needed is know-how.'

Lidia was silent, believing that even drains cannot supplant human feeling.

'The trouble with you, Lidia, is that you respond emotionally, not pragmatically. It's a device to retain the sense of patronage. Unconscious, of course. You don't think of people like these as your *brothers*.' Miss Bass was one of those who find it easy and even gratifying to direct fraternal feelings towards large numbers of people living at great distances. Her own brother—who was shiftless and sometimes tried to borrow money from her—she had not seen for over a year. 'You don't relate to them as individuals'. In Miss Bass's mouth the very word 'individuals' denoted legions.

Lidia, casting about for a diversion, was softened to see that Mr Bekkus had brought out photographs of what appeared to be a small child and was showing them to his companion.

'Who *is* that man?' Millicent asked. 'I've seen him around for years.'

'Bekkus, from Personnel.' Lidia lowered her voice. 'He's on the Appointments and Terminations Board.'

'My baby verbalizes,' Bekkus was saying to his colleague. 'Just learning to verbalize.'

'Speaking of which,' Millicent went on, 'I hear you're losing your friend.'

Lidia hesitated, then dug her spoon into her *crème caramel.* 'You mean Algie.'

'Well, there's a limit after all,' Miss Bass said, sensing resistance.

'I'll miss him.'

Miss Bass was not to be repulsed. 'He is impossible.'

Lidia laughed. 'When people say that about Algie, it always reminds me of Bakunin.'

'One of the new translators?' asked Miss Bass, running through the names of the Russian Section in her mind.

'No, no. I mean the Russian revolutionary.'

'He's a friend of Algie's?' Millicent inquired—sharply, for politics were forbidden to the Organization staff, and a direct affiliation with them was one of the few infallible means of obtaining summary dismissal.

'He died a century ago.'

'What's he got to do with Algie?' Miss Bass was still suspicious.

'Oh—he was a big untidy man, and he once said—when some-one told him he was impossible—"I shall continue to be impossible so long as those who are now possible remain possible." '

Millicent was not amused. 'The Organization cannot afford Algie Wyatt.'

'He's a luxury,' Lidia admitted.

'Pleasure-loving,' said Miss Bass, as if this were something un-natural.

'Yes,' Lidia agreed.

'And always trying to be clever.'

'That's right,' said Lidia.

'I'd prefer a more serious attitude,' said Miss Bass. And it was true; she actually would.

Lidia held her spoon poised for a moment and said seriously, 'Millicent, please don't go on about Algie. I don't like it.'

Millicent's only idea of dignity was standing on it, and she did this for some minutes. Soon, however, she forgot what had been said and inquired about the terms of Algie's retirement.

'I really don't know anything about it.' Lidia dropped her crum-pled napkin on her plate.

'He has a choice, I believe—a reduced pension or a lump sum. That's the arrangement for enforced resignation.'

'I don't *know*,' said Lidia. 'Shall we go?'

When they left the cafeteria, they walked along together to the elevators.

'Now I hope you won't think me hard, Miss Bass was beginning, when the elevator arrived—fortunately, perhaps, for her aspiration.

Algie was sitting at his desk when Lidia entered the office. They smiled at each other, and when she was seated at her desk, Lidia asked, 'Did you have a nice time with Jaspersen?'

'Splendid,' grunted Algie, going on with his work. He added, for once without looking up, 'Wanted me to appeal my case. Shan't do it, though.'

'Perhaps you ought to think about it?'

Algie shook his head, still writing. A little later he murmured aloud, 'Never more, Miranda. Never more.'

'Algie,' Lidia said, putting down her pencil. 'What do you think you'll do, then? Take a reduced pension?'

Now Algie did look up, but kept his pencil in his hand. 'No. No. Take my lump sum and look for a small house somewhere along the Mediterranean. In the south of Spain, perhaps. Màlaga, or Torremo-linos. Good climate, some things still fairly cheap.'

'Do you know anyone there?'

'Someone sure to turn up.' He went on with his work for a mo-ment. 'Only thing is—it's very dangerous to die in Spain.'

'How do you mean?'

'Law insists you be buried within twenty-four hours. Doctors not allowed to open your veins. If you should happen still to be alive, you wake up and find yourself in your coffin. When my time comes, I'm going down to Gibraltar and die in safety. Very dangerous to die in Spain.'

'But what if one's really dead?'

Algie looked solemn. 'That's a risk you have to take.'

Algie died the following year at Torremolinos. He died very suddenly, of a stroke, and had no time to reach safety in Gibraltar. An obituary paragraph of some length appeared in the London *Times*, and a brief notice in the Organization's staff gazette, which misspelt his name. For so large a man, he left few material traces in the world. The slim remnants of his lump sum went to a sixteen-year-old nephew. His book on Roman remains in Libya is being reissued by an English publisher with private means.

Just about the time of Algie's death, Lidia became engaged to a handsome Scotsman in the Political Settlements Department. Although they have since been married, Lidia has kept her job and now shares her office with a Luxembourgeois who seldom looks up from his work and confesses to having no memory for verse. No one mourned the death of Algie more than Olaf Jaspersen, who remarked that he felt as if he had lost a part of himself. Jaspersen has recently attended important conferences abroad, and has taken to coming in to the office on Sundays. Millicent Bass is being sent to Africa, and regards this as a challenge; her arrival there is being accepted in the same spirit.

Swoboda has been put forward for a promotion, but has been warned that there may be some delay. Mr Bekkus has received *his* promotion, though over some objections. He is still combing the Organization, with little success, for unutilized sources of ability and imagination. He continues to dictate letters in his characteristic style, and his baby is now verbalizing fluently along much the same lines.

Algie's last letter to Lidia was written only a few days before he died, but reached her some weeks later, as he had neglected to mark it '*Correo Aéreo*'. In this letter he reported the discovery of several new contradictions in terms and mentioned, among other things, that Piero della Francesca died on the same day that Columbus discovered America, and that there is in Mexico a rat poison called The Last Supper. Such information is hard to come by these days; now that Algie was gone, Lidia could not readily think of another source.

VIVIAN SMITH   (1933–)

Poet, critic. Born and educated in Hobart; and at Sydney; Reader in
English at Sydney University.

AT AN EXHIBITION OF HISTORICAL PAINTINGS, HOBART

The sadness in the human visage stares
out of these frames, out of these distant eyes;
the static bodies painted without love
that only lack of talent could disguise.

Those bland receding hills are too remote
where the quaint natives squat with awkward calm.
One carries a kangaroo like a worn toy;
his axe alert with emphasised alarm.

Those nearer woollen hills are now all streets;
even the water in the harbor's changed.
Much is alike and yet a slight precise
disparity seems intended and arranged—

as in that late pink terrace's facade.
How neat the houses look. How clean each brick.
One cannot say they look much older now,
but somehow more themselves, less accurate.

And see the pride in this expansive view:
churches, houses, farms, a prison tower:
a grand gesture like wide-open arms
showing the artist's trust, his clumsy power.

And this much later vision, grander still:
the main street sedate carriages unroll
towards the inappropriate, tentative mountain:
a flow of lines the artist can't control—

the foreground nearly breaks out of its frame
the streets end so abruptly in the water...
But how some themes return. A whaling ship.
The last natives. Here that silent slaughter

is really not prefigured or avoided.
One merely sees a profile, a full face,
a body sitting stiffly in a chair:
the soon-forgotten absence of a race...

Album pieces: bowls of brown glazed fruit...
I'm drawn back yet again to those few studies
of native women whose long floral dresses
made them first aware of their own bodies.

History has made artists of all these
painters without energy or feature.
But how some gazes cling. Around the hall
the pathos of the past, the human creature.

THE MAN FERN NEAR THE BUS STOP

The man fern near the bus stop waves at me
one scaly feather swaying out of the dark,
slightly drunk with rain and freckled with old spores
it touches me with its slow question mark.

Something in the shadows catches at the throat,
smelling like old slippers, drying like a skin,
scraped like an emu or a gumboot stuck with fur,
straining all the time to take me in.

Cellophane crinkles in the fern's pineapple heart.
The fur parts slowly showing a crumpled horn.
A ruffled sea horse stands in swaying weed,
And held in cotton wool, a mouse unborn.

I look down at it now, a tiny toe, a crook,
remembering voices and growing without choice—
the buds of fingers breaking into power
and long fibres breaking in the voice.

TWENTY YEARS OF SYDNEY

It's twenty years of Sydney to the month
I came here first out of my fog-bound south
to frangipani trees in old backyards,
and late at night the moon distorting palms.

Even then the Cross was crumby, out of touch.
I was too timid for Bohemia as a style
or living long in rooms in dark Rose Bay hotels.
All one night a storm flogged herds of Moreton Bays,
for days the esplanade was stuck with purple figs.
The flying boat circled for hours and couldn't land.

That was the week I met Slessor alone
walking down Phillip Street smoking his cigar,
his pink scrubbed skin never touched by the sun.
Fastidious, bow tie, he smiled like the Cheshire cat:
"If you change your city you are sure to change your style."
A kind man, he always praised the young.

STILL LIFE

This still life is still life after all.
These massed hydrangeas standing near the wall
as big as cushions puffed up on a chair
loll their heads like pink clowns in the air
who just perform and do not need to know.
They bloom with blue like heaped up mountain snow.

These flowers bring such fullness to the room
they stand like resurrections from the tomb.
Now at season's end with tarnished golds
the year rots like a mirror which still holds
blue and silver merging with the frame.
These are colours with a flower's name.

We sit and watch their clouds of pink, their sheen,
the way they look both savage and serene
drawing the light and holding it at bay:
a storm inside a storm that has been stilled
with something finished, something unfulfilled.

CHRISTOPHER KOCH (1932–)

Novelist, poet. Born and educated in Hobart; lives in Sydney.

THE RADIO MEN

from THE DOUBLEMAN

The studios of a big broadcasting organisation at night have the hush of a deserted church. But underneath this is a low, thrilling hum, like that of a ship at sea: there is little sign of life in the corridors, but you know the organism is alive.

On the night of the production that launched Richard Miller's career in Sydney, the dim little foyer of the ABS building in King's Cross was entirely deserted. The commissionaire was away from his desk, on which he had left his girlie magazine and a packet of cigarettes. Miller waited, having pressed the lift button, with a sense of trespassing. Someone had thrown a cigar butt into the metal ash tray by the lift doors, and the smell lingered. Down a pine-panelled corridor opening off the foyer, an illuminated globe of red glass glowed above a door, lettered: ON AIR. But that wasn't the studio he wanted: the big Drama studio was on the second floor.

The lift was ancient: he could hear it groaning and wheezing down to get him like a peevish old man. His hands were sweating, and he wiped one on his trousers, his script clutched in the other. He was nervous, he told me; but his governing mood seems to have been that of a prizefighter going into the ring: one of ruthless cunning. It would have been nice, he said, to recall that night as one which rewarded him with success after years of struggle. Instead, it was coloured with someone else's pain: that of our Phil Desmond, who would die, some two years later, of the overdose of sleeping pills so clearly in his destiny.

There was no mirror in the coffin-like lift; as it laboured upwards, he pushed his hair into place as best he could, and straightened his tie. Wearing this tie, in the height of the Sydney summer, was helping to make him sweat; but when in doubt in those days it was best to be formal. He didn't know what the prejudices of the ABS Drama Producer might be, but ABS had a reputation for formality. He wore a navy Bermuda jacket as well—a present to himself to celebrate his arrival in Sydney, and to achieve an image of affluence: Elizabeth Bay playboy, dependent on no-one. If you looked too hungry, no-one wanted to use you, and so you sank further. But the coat had reduced his savings to a dangerous level; and he was still living on these savings, having been in the city for over two months.

There was no other way to break in, he said. The first step on the road to failure was to take a part-time job. An actor had to be available, day after empty day, waiting for the 'phone, making unsolicited visits to all the broadcasting producers to remind them of his existence. Each day, he had gone in to Metro Casting in Pitt Street, to be told by the secretary that there were no calls for him. She had always been hopeful for him, though.

A middle-aged woman with greying, upswept brown hair, up-swept spectacles, and a motherly veneer that totally disappeared during certain steely 'phone calls she made, she seemed to Miller like a Fate, seated in her cubby-hole over the three 'phones and the huge typewriter, surrounded by casting lists on clip-boards and publicity shots of Sydney's famous and half-famous actors.

'You mustn't get down-*cast*, dear, I've known young actors to take months to get their first jobs, here. There's so many hammering at the doors, in this town. But your audition impressed ABS Drama, that's for sure. Martin Gadsby really said nice things about it.' Her voice became confidential. 'Most of them hate him, of course, he can be such an old swine. But you'll just have to get on the right side of him.' Mouth pursed as though sucking back a smile, she looked at him sideways. 'I'm sure you'll manage that, Richard—you're a smart young chap.'

He had listened carefully. She was right, he said. Radio, as the catch-phrase had it, was still king, and old Martin Gadsby, who had hired him now, was king of radio drama. Radio was still the only medium that could give an actor a living; and Sydney was the only city in Australia where enough radio was produced to keep a legion of such actors fully employed.

The king was dying, of course. Television had been here for seven years, and crude local drama series and variety shows were on the increase. He had plans about that; but meanwhile, the dying king must be his patron.

The lift jerked to a halt, and he yanked at the heavy steel door.

He sat quietly studying his script on one of the tubular-steel chairs against the far wall of Studio 250, keeping an eye on the window of the control room opposite. The Drama studio was large, and there were more than enough chairs to accommodate the eight or so actors here, so that Miller had empty places on either side of him. The place smelled of stale cigarette smoke and clean carpet. Screens stood about, and the odd equipment of the Sound Effects man: an electric buzzer; plates to rattle; odd pieces of ironmongery whose purposes couldn't be guessed, and a door in a frame, on wheels. They were doing Rattigan's 'Ross', so the cast was all-male; and none of the other actors seemed particularly disposed to be friendly. Having introduced themselves, and found out which agency he was from, they ignored him—except for Archie Breen, a man with a bitter upper lip, who asked him suspiciously if he belonged to Actor's Equity. On finding that Miller did, Archie resumed the study of his script. Looking up, Miller would now and then catch a pair of speculative eyes on him. Their talk and laughter was muted and flat, in this sound-proofed chamber.

He was glad not to be drawn into the talk, since he wanted to study the faces around him, and simply to listen to these famous voices, most of which had come from the Bakelite radios of childhood. They brought back infantile excitements, and he took a simple pleasure in the fact that he had joined their owners at last. That pleasure, touched with the savour of childhood's obedient wonder, must seem quaint now, Miller said; but I understood, as anyone would have who grew up in the lost era of books and radio.

There, leaning on the grand piano, was Dr Fu Manchu, who had laughed maniacally from behind the glowing radio dial when Miller was ten years old, to thrill him with terror: greying, lanky old Eric Mawby, with arched black eyebrows and avuncular glasses, whose rich, melodramatic bass he recognised instantly. But what Eric was saying now, instead of uttering frenzied Oriental curses, was: 'Beatrice? Beatrice was pissed out of her mind. Someone had to get her outside and give her three black coffees before she could go on. Afterwards, she had no idea whether she'd played Lady Macbeth or Little Red Riding Hood. She did it beautifully, of course.'

A plump man standing at the piano bent slightly at the waist, going pink with laughter. He was about forty-five, and had wrinkled, thinning red hair and a snubby, bulldog face. 'But of course,' he said. 'Poor Beatrice. Eventually she *will* play Little Red Riding Hood, I'm afraid. Only Children's Session will hire her.'

Where had Miller heard before this cool, beautifully modulated, hero's voice? It took only a few moments to realise that he was looking at boyhood's lean-jawed leader with the steel-blue eyes. He was Bulldog Drummond, and the Saint, and every Nick and Simon and Ralph who had ever mastered danger: Miller's own beloved shadow, whose real name turned out to be Ronald Porter.

The voices and the laughter began to become spasmodic, in the private, motionless air. There was no air-conditioning in this aged studio; instead two giant electric fans, on standards as tall as men, revolved full blast at either end of the room, and as the silence took over, he became conscious of their humming. People were glancing at watches; rustling scripts. It was now nearly fifteen minutes over starting time for the rehearsal, and obviously this was not usual. '... hell's he doing?' someone muttered. Since the stand mike in the centre of the floor was open, such mutterings could be picked up in the control room; and the actors were unusually cautious, it seemed to Miller. Many glances were cast at the control room window.

In there, motionless at the producer's desk, Martin Gadsby sat bulkily hunched, a cigarette between his lips, surveying them with a sulky expression, as though they were to blame for something. He was somewhere in his late fifties, with a clipped moustache that made him resemble a British Army officer: an effect that was partially negated by dyed blond hair worn in an artistic fringe. He turned to speak to the Sound Effects operator, a cadaverous man in a grey cardigan who stood stooped over a line of turntables like a chef preparing sauces, while the glassy-eyed panel operator sprawled motionless in his chair, staring at nothing. Because of the sound-proofing, it was all in dumb-show; under the fluorescent lights of their cabinet of command, the three looked super-real: wax figures in a showcase. But it was the actors, really, who were in the showcase, since the control room could hear them on the stand mike, while they couldn't eavesdrop on the control room. That was one of the ways in which Gadsby's power was defined.

'Who's not here?' Eric Mawby asked suddenly. His perfectly-produced, hammy old voice had the authority of special eminence. '*Someone* isn't here,' he said, 'obviously. Martin would never be this late starting, otherwise. What part's not spoken for?'

They all began to compare scripts and talk at once.

'I'm Dickinson.'

'Who's doubling as Parsons? You, Fred?'

'I'm Allenby,' Eric Mawby said. 'And you've got the plum of course, Phil.' He was looking at a sad-faced man of about forty, who sat by himself against the wall opposite Miller, a few places down from the control-room window, and who looked up at Mawby with pale eyes that appeared to have been drained of colour by some sort of tragic excess. Miller guessed at a nervous breakdown, or alcoholism.

'That's right Eric,' he said. 'That's if you call a masochistic queer who gets buggered by Turks a plum part.'

There was a burst of laughter around the studio, but the sad-faced man didn't smile. He had a beautiful voice, and now Miller knew who he was; he had been trying to remember. Philip Desmond was the closest thing Australia then had to a star; he had done two films and a good deal of stage work, and his Shakespearean performances were revered. But theatre made no-one a living in Australia: like everyone else, Desmond made his living in ABS radio plays like this one, and in the big commercial soap operas ('When a Girl Marries'; 'Reflections in a Wine Glass'.) He still had the remnants of those matinee-idol's good looks that had been fashionable in Britain, and therefore here, in the 1930's: dark blond hair parted on one side; wide-set eyes whose straight top lids made them look dauntingly steady. But the mouth had a petulant softness; all the lines of the face were drawn down by a weary melancholy, and there were unusually emphatic pouches under his eyes. Tonight he would play the clinically-depressed Lawrence of Arabia: type-casting, Miller thought. He was young, happy and cruel, then.

'What about you, young man?'

Eric Mawby was addressing him, and he started. He didn't much care for being called 'young man' at twenty-six, but he knew he looked younger than his age, and decided to assume an air of boyish modesty. Mawby was wondering if he had a part of any size. He didn't, of course.

'I'm Franks,' he said. 'The lecturer.'

'Ah yes,' Mawby said, in his most avuncular voice. 'Nice little part, first time out, eh?'

Miller smiled with hypocritical appreciation. Old and respected actors like Mawby, high on the Sydney pecking order, took it on themselves to approve or disapprove of young climbers: it was very important to get on with them.

'So no-one seems to be missing,' said the voice of Bulldog Drummond, and Ronald Porter looked about him in puzzlement. As he did so, a huge, hollow voice sounded from a monitor the size of a packing case, over by the door. It was Martin Gadsby from the control-room; he had been listening, and had now put the key of his mike down.

'What we're waiting for, *mes amis*, is a bloody man who has simply not turned up, and who *was* to have played the Turkish General.' His key went up again and he was seen to be on the telephone, the cigarette wagging in his mouth as he spoke.

A few seconds later the hushed double doors of the studio opened, and he was moving across the carpet towards them, script in hand: shorter and stockier than he had seemed through the glass, well-pressed and immaculate, in a navy Bermuda jacket like Miller's and an old-fashioned red bow tie. Miller now regretted his own Bermuda jacket.

'Mr Simon Harrington has simply not turned up,' Gadsby said. 'His agency knows nothing.' He had an actor's voice, resonant, almost booming, with the standard Southern English accent that was then obligatory, in broadcasting and the theatre: only a few fugitive diphthongs gave away his Australian origins. He took the cigarette from his mouth, holding it away from himself as though it were about to explode. 'Unreliability's becoming a *disease*," he said. 'I'll give him five minutes more, and if he doesn't come, we have no choice but to go home.'

Various murmurs began.

'I agree, Martin, it's bloody poor,' Eric Mawby said, in an official voice. 'But it's not such a big part. I'd be happy to double for you.'

Gadsby looked at him with an almost tragic expression. His elderly eyes were an unusual forget-me-not blue: the eyes of an ageing beauty queen. Like the startling blond hair, they were in blatant contrast with his grey moustache and sagging, disciplinarian's face. 'Thank you, Eric,' he said, 'but no. Allenby, which you have, is important—but so is this part. It's one of the most controversial in the play, and whoever does it must develop it from this first rehearsal. So for now, we'll cancel.'

Their regretful expressions were false; they would have to be paid for the call anyway. There was a silence. Then Ronald Porter asked: 'Isn't there a small enough part anywhere to double with this one? Or someone with a small part who could change over?'

'I think I could do it,' Miller said.

All the faces around the walls looked at him; Gadsby, the cigarette back in his mouth, pivoted slightly; raised his eyebrows. 'Ah. The new young man. Showing commendable ambition, eh, dear boy?'

There were small chuckles—some of them malicious.

'I appreciate the offer,' Gadsby said, with disconcerting politeness. 'However, I think it may be premature. We've yet to see what you can do.'

'I believe I could do this,' Miller said. 'It's a very interesting role. It needs a balance between erotic sadism and sympathy. I've read it carefully.'

'Well well,' Gadsby said. 'You have indeed.' The beauty queen's eyes studied him, while Miller kept his own gaze firm yet pleasantly deferential. Gadsby turned the pages of his script, squinting through smoke. 'You're doing the lecturer,' he said musingly. 'Only one scene. But you couldn't double it with the General; he comes into that scene too. I think someone else will have to double as the lecturer—leaving you to make what you can of the General. But if you can't give me what I want, we abandon rehearsal.'

He padded over to the wall, picked up a chair, carried it back to the middle of the floor, and straddled it, folding back his script to give cues for the first read through. Silence returned, during which eyes hovered about Miller like mosquitos. An unknown had no business asking for such a part in the studio; but he had won, and this was a play that would attract attention. The homosexual rape of Lawrence of Arabia was a shocking theme in that year, and the play had only recently had its run on the London stage.

They halted for a coffee break at the end of the first act, at a point where Miller had appeared in two scenes, but not yet in the key scene where Lawrence was tortured. Gadsby spoke briefly to most of the figures on their chairs around the walls, his criticisms peremptory, without much detail. 'The General is interesting,' he said to Miller. 'But let's wait and see what you do with his big scene.' Then he turned to Phil Desmond. 'Phil, your Lawrence is too camp.'

Phil Desmond raised weary eyebrows. 'Well, he *is* camp, Martin, isn't he?'

'That doesn't mean you play him as a trissy little queen, dear boy.'

'I believe that's how Guinness played him.'

Gadsby took the cigarette from his mouth and stared as though he had been affronted; in the silence, his breathing could distinctly be heard. 'I doubt that,' he said. 'I really do. But whatever the case may be, would you mind playing it my way?'

Phil Desmond now had the expression of a small boy being rebuked by a cruel teacher. 'Which way is that, Martin?' he asked. 'You haven't told me.'

'Some things surely don't need pointing out,' Gadsby said. 'Lawrence, whatever his sexual proclivities, was a man of action and a hero. Would it be too much to bear that in mind, Phil, or beyond your powers to convey it?'

Desmond's mouth twisted; but his eyes dropped to his script, and he said nothing. Gadsby stood up; and with an air of relief, the others began to get up too, and to straggle out through the double doors for coffee. Miller followed, passing Gadsby, whom he heard say: 'Just hang on a moment, Phil—I'd like to talk to you.'

Phil Desmond's face looked hunted.

Coffee was bought in paper cups from a milk-bar in Darlinghurst Road. Going down in the lift, nobody spoke for a moment. Then Eric Mawby said to Miller: '*You* know how to jump in, don't you, young man? You're lucky—Martin doesn't often take a punt on unknowns.'

Kevin Murphy took attention away from Miller, perhaps out of kindness. Handsome in the dark Irish way, with a neat moustache, he often played World War Two Air Force officers—which was what he had been. 'Too true, Eric,' he said. 'Martin's the greatest hand at casting in the business—he only backs certainties. That makes it easy.' There was knowing laughter at this.

On the way back to the studio, Miller went along to the washroom. It was large, blue-tiled, brightly-lit and empty, except for a man who stood at the row of washbasins, hunched over, his back to Miller. When Miller came back from the urinal to the basins, the man was still there, still stooped in the same attitude; and something about his stillness made Miller curious. He looked up at the reflection in the big mirror above the basins.

It was Philip Desmond, and he was crying. The reflected face looking back at the reflection of Miller's was crumpled into a mask of tragedy, tears running down the cheeks.

Miller let liquid soap trickle slowly from his hands, and gazed at this unbelievable image. He was too horrified to look away, and the pale, red-rimmed eyes didn't seem to expect him to do so: seemed, on the contrary, to expect attention to their woe. Miller swung sideways to take in the real face, half-hoping that the mirror had misrepresented it, and that Desmond merely had grit in his eye.

But no; he was silently crying, and looked more than ever like a schoolboy who had just been caned—or would have done, had it not been for the heavy bags under the eyes, and the deep lines from the nose to the corners of the mouth. The tears ran into these furrows. He drew in breath and sobbed softly, leaning with both hands on the basin, his head turning now to look into Miller's actual face. Then he spoke.

'If–Mr–Martin–Gadsby,' he said, spacing the words, 'is-rude to me–again, I shall bloody well–walk out.'

Miller could find no answer to this, but tried to look sympathetic. He felt infinitely sorry for Phil, he told me, yet infinitely contemptuous. Desmond was the best actor in Australia: was this all he could do with his success? The crying man swayed a little, straightening from the basin, and Miller caught the smell of liquor; he was half drunk.

Desmond blew his nose; the sobbing had abated, and he wiped his eyes, which were no longer looking at Miller and scarcely seemed aware of him. In a small, reasonable voice, apparently to himself, he said: 'I really don't have to take this. No.' Then he looked up again. 'You're just starting,' he said. 'And you're pushy enough to make it, that's obvious. You might even be good, I don't know. Take some advice.' He paused.

'What's that?' Miller asked.

'Get out.' He smiled: a falsely winsome smile. 'Get out, sonny, or spend your bloody life recording commercials for toilet paper, and being insulted by talentless old shits like Martin Gadsby.' His voice rose now, booming in the echo-chamber of the washroom: no longer the small voice of suffering, but the huge, effortlessly-projected voice of the stage professional, heavily and bitterly hammy. 'Do you re-ally want to be an *ac*-tor?'

He burst into a fit of laughter, staring at Miller expectantly; then he lapsed into falsetto giggling, and his eyes filled with tears again. From the laughter? Grief? Miller couldn't tell. It became apparent that it wasn't really Miller he looked at, but at something in his mind; and Miller walked towards the door.

As he did so, the voice rang out strongly again. 'Oh, *General*! You're going to arrange for me to be *broken*, when we go back in there, aren't you? "Bodily integrity violated, will broken"—isn't that how it goes? Will you enjoy that? Martin will. He's looking forward to this scene. Oh, by the way, he *likes* young actors. It's just the old ones he gets sick of.' He began to laugh again, and Miller let the door swing shut.

Lawrence, it may be recalled, doesn't actually speak to the Turkish General in Rattigan's play; so Miller didn't at any stage exchange dialogue with Philip Desmond. Lawrence was tortured and sodomised in an outer room, while the General, within earshot, discussed it with a young Captain. Then Lawrence was dragged in; he lay on the floor semi-conscious, and the General spoke to him; but he couldn't respond.

The only actors at the stand mike now were the cheerful Murphy, who played the Captain, and Miller. Phil Desmond sat on his chair by the control room window, his eyes, still pinkish from crying, seeming to ask for mercy; and it was probably Miller's private knowledge of Desmond's suffering that enabled him to play the scene as well as he did. He worked very close on mike, giving the General a soft but penetrating voice, with a suggestion of sibilance. It helped to make him sound obscene, under a perfectly civilized and intelligent surface.

At the moment when Lawrence was dragged in and flung on the floor; at the moment when the General leaned over and pulled Lawrence's head up by the hair, Miller could not resist a quick glance at Phil Desmond.

'"You must understand that I *know*,"' he said. He was telling him that he knew what had been revealed by the rape: in the General's words: 'Bodily integrity violated, will broken.'

The silence in the studio had deepened two layers. As Miller looked up from his script, he caught a glimpse of Gadsby through the glass. He was sitting very still, watching as though trying to work out a puzzle. The smoke from his cigarette went straight upwards.

LES A. MURRAY   (1938–)

Poet. Born in northern N.S.W.; educated in Sydney.

AN ABSOLUTELY ORDINARY RAINBOW

The word goes round Repins,
the murmur goes round Lorenzinis,
at Tattersalls, men look up from sheets of numbers,
the Stock Exchange scribblers forget the chalk in their hands
and men with bread in their pockets leave the Greek Club:
There's a fellow crying in Martin Place. They can't stop him.

The traffic in George Street is banked up for half a mile
and drained of motion. The crowds are edgy with talk
and more crowds come hurrying. Many run in the back streets
which minutes ago were busy main streets, pointing:
There's a fellow weeping down there. No one can stop him.

The man we surround, the man no one approaches
simply weeps, and does not cover it, weeps
not like a child, not like the wind, like a man
and does not declaim it, nor beat his breast, nor even
sob very loudly—yet the dignity of his weeping

holds us back from his space, the hollow he makes about him
in the midday light, in his pentagram of sorrow,
and uniforms back in the crowd who tried to seize him
stare out at him, and feel, with amazement, their minds
longing for tears as children for a rainbow.

Some will say, in the years to come, a halo
or force stood around him. There is no such thing.
Some will say they were shocked and would have stopped him
but they will not have been there. The fiercest manhood,
the toughest reserve, the slickest wit amongst us

trembles with silence, and burns with unexpected
judgements of peace. Some in the concourse scream
who thought themselves happy. Only the smallest children
and such as look out of Paradise come near him
and sit at his feet, with dogs and dusty pigeons.

Ridiculous, says a man near me, and stops
his mouth with his hands, as if it uttered vomit—
and I see a woman, shining, stretch her hand
and shake as she receives the gift of weeping;
as many as follow her also receive it

and many weep for sheer acceptance, and more
refuse to weep for fear of all acceptance,
but the weeping man, like the earth, requires nothing,
the man who weeps ignores us, and cries out
of his writhen face and ordinary body

not words, but grief, not messages, but sorrow
hard as the earth, sheer, present as the sea—
and when he stops, he simply walks between us
mopping his face with the dignity of one
man who has wept, and now has finished weeping.

Evading believers, he hurries off down Pitt Street.

THE BROAD BEAN SERMON

Beanstalks, in any breeze, are a slack church parade
without belief, saying *trepass against us* in unison,
recruits in mint Air Force dacron, with unbuttoned leaves.

Upright with water like men, square in stem-section
they grow to great lengths, drink rain, keel over all ways,
kink down and grow up afresh, with proffered new greenstuff.

Above the cat-and-mouse floor of a thin bean forest
snails hang rapt in their food, ants hurry through Escher's three
    worlds,
spiders tense and sag like little black flags in their cordage.

Going out to pick beans with the sun high as fence-tops, you find
plenty, and fetch them. An hour or a cloud later
you find shirtfulls more. At every hour of daylight

appear more that you missed: ripe, knobbly ones, fleshy-sided,
thin-straight, thin-crescent, frown-shaped, bird-shouldered,
    boat-keeled ones,
beans knuckled and single-bulged, minute green dolphins at suck,

beans upright like lecturing, outstretched like blessing fingers
in the incident light, and more still, oblique to your notice
that the noon glare or cloud-light or afternoon slants will uncover

till you ask yourself Could I have overlooked so many, or
do they form in an hour? unfolding into reality
like templates for subtly broad grins, like unique caught expressions,

like edible meanings, each sealed around with a string
and affixed to its moment, an unceasing colloquial assembly,
the portly, the stiff, and those lolling in pointed green slippers....

Wondering who'll like the spare bagfulls, you grin with happiness
—it is your health—you vow to pick them all
even the last few, weeks off yet, misshapen as toes.

THE CONQUEST

Phillip was a kindly, rational man:
Friendship and Trust will win the natives, Sir.
Such was the deck the Governor walked upon.

One deck below, lieutenants hawked and spat.
One level lower, and dank nightmares grew.
Small floating Englands where our world began.

And what was trust when the harsh dead swarmed ashore
and warriors, trembling, watched the utterly strange
hard clouds, dawn beings, down there where time began,

so alien the eye could barely fix
blue parrot-figures wrecking the light with change,
man-shapes digging where no yam roots were?

The Governor proffers cloth and English words,
the tribesmen defy him in good Dhuruwal.
Marines stand firm, known warriors bite their beards.

Glass beads are scattered in that gulf of style
but pickpockets squeal, clubbed in imagination
as naked Indians circle them like birds.

They won't Respond. They threaten us. Drive them off.
In genuine grief, the Governor turns away.
Blowflies form trinkets for a harsher grief.

As the sickness of the earth bites into flesh
trees moan like women, striplings collapse like trees—
fever of Portsmouth hulks, the Deptford cough.

It makes dogs furtive,what they find to eat
but the noonday forest will not feed white men.
Capture some Natives, quick. Much may be learned

indeed, on both Sides. Sir! And Phillip smiles.
Two live to tell the back lanes of his smile
and the food ships come, and the barracks rise as planned.

And once again the Governor goes around
with his Amity. The yeasts of reason work,
triangle screams confirm the widening ground.

No one records what month the first striped men
mounted a clawing child, then slit her throat
but the spear hits Phillip with a desperate sound.

The thoughtful savage with Athenian flanks
fades from the old books here. The sketchers draw
pipe-smoking cretins jigging on thin shanks

poor for the first time, learning the Crown Lands tune.
The age of unnoticed languages begins
and Phillip, recovering, gives a nodded thanks.

McEntire speared! My personal huntsman, Speared!
Ten Heads for this, and two alive to hang!
A brave lieutenant cools it, bid by bid,

to a decent six. The punitive squads march off
without result, but this quandong of wrath
ferments in slaughters for a hundred years.

They couldn't tell us how to farm their skin.
They camped with dogs in the rift glens of our mind
till their old men mumbled who the stars had been.

They had the noon trees' spiritual walk.
Pathetic with sores, they could be suddenly not,
the low horizon strangely concealing them.

A few still hunt way out beyond philosophy
where nothing is sacred till it is your flesh
and the leaves, the creeks shine through their poverty

or so we hope. We make our conquests, too.
The ruins at our feet are hard to see.
For all the generous Governor tried to do

the planet he had touched began to melt
though he used much Reason, and foreshadowed more
before he recoiled into his century.

THE MITCHELLS

I am seeing this: two men are sitting on a pole
they have dug a hole for and will, after dinner, raise
I think for wires. Water boils in a prune tin.
Bees hum their shift in unthinning mists of white

bursaria blossom, under the noon of wattles.
The men eat big meat sandwiches out of a styrofoam

box with a handle. One is overheard saying:
drought that year. Yes. Like trying to farm the road.

The first man, if asked, would say *I'm one of the Mitchells.*
The other would gaze for a while, dried leaves in his palm,
and looking up, with pain and subtle amusement,

say *I'm one of the Mitchells.* Of the pair, one has been rich
but never stopped wearing his oil-stained felt hat. Nearly everything
they say is ritual. Sometimes the scene is an avenue.

SYDNEY AND THE BUSH

When Sydney and the Bush first met
there was no open ground
and men and girls, in chains and not,
all made an urgent sound.

Then convicts bled and warders bred,
the bush went back and back,
the men of Fire and of Earth
became White men and Black.

When Sydney ordered lavish books
and warmed her feet with coal
the bush came skylarking to town
and gave poor folk a soul.

Then bushmen sank and factories rose
and warders set the tone—
the Bush, in quarter-acre blocks,
helped families hold their own.

When Sydney and the Bush meet now
there is antipathy
and fashionable suburbs float
at night, far out to sea.

When Sydney rules without the Bush
she is a warders' shop
with heavy dancing overhead,
the music will not stop

and when the drummers want a laugh
Australians are sent up.
When Sydney and the Bush meet now
there is no common ground.

CHRIS WALLACE-CRABBE   (1934–)

Poet, critic. Born and educated in Melbourne; Reader in English at Melbourne University.

MELBOURNE

Not on the ocean, on a muted bay
Where the broad rays drift slowly over mud
And flathead loll on sand, a city bloats
Between the plains of water and of loam,
If surf beats, it is faint and far away;
If slogans blow around, we stay at home.

And, like the bay, our blood flows easily,
Not warm, not cold (in all things moderate),
Following our familiar tides. Elsewhere
Victims are bleeding, sun is beating down
On patriot, guerrilla, refugee.
We see the newsreels when we dine in town.

Ideas are grown in other gardens while
This chocolate soil throws up its harvest of
Imported and deciduous platitudes,
None of them flowering boldly or for long;
And we, the gardeners, securely smile
Humming a bar or two of rusty song.

Old tunes are good enough if sing we must;
Old images, re-vamped *ad nauseam*,
Will sate the burgher's eye and keep him quiet
As the great wheels run on, and should he seek
Variety, there's wind, there's heat, there's frost
To feed his conversation all the week.

Highway by highway the remorseless cars
Strangle the city, put it out of pain,
Its limbs still kicking feebly on the hills.
Nobody cares. The artists sail at dawn
For brisker ports, or not in public bars.
Though much has died here, little has been born.

TERRA AUSTRALIS

Here, and here only in an age of iron,
    The dreamers are proved right;
No armies underlie these rolling fields,

No lost loves haunt the night,
Nor can the farmer, turning with his spade,
  Bring shard or helm to light.

Innocence clad in brown and faded gold
  Walks up and down these hills
Where unobtrusive flickering flowers rebuke
  The show of daffodils:
With sombre colours and with sparse designs
  Acre on acre fills.

Paradise lingers like a tapestry;
  The web has not been torn,
Luther and Cromwell, Socrates and Marx
  Have never yet been born,
Nor did a glowing Florence rise to shape
  The European dawn.

We are the final children of the earth
  Whom knowledge has not scarred,
Delighting still in sunlight and green grass
  Back in our own backyard:
Gaping, we hear the tales of adulthood
  Where life is dour and hard,
Far, far away, beyond some wicked wood.

THE WILD COLONIAL PUZZLER

Padding through the grounds of a great house,
meaning to make sense
of all this landed equanimity,
lawn, gazebos, coaltits, wagtails
and garlicky water, I want to tell you
beware of Australians bearing gifts.
I bring along the stink of restlessness
like an infection, like a second skin;
but to say this, friends, would be to patronize,
assuming you don't know what you know.

Hopkins lived here.
I can't pretend to equal his unrest
nor his quick marvellous inwardness
with spray, pod, quoin, penumbra, ripple,
everything unresting in creation,
but cross the garden, quiet as a fieldmouse
to that waterlily-splintered pond
where a bent classical figure, Prometheus maybe,
looks up to make sure
promised Lancastrian thunderstorms haven't broken.

DAVID MALOUF (1934–)

Poet, novelist. Born and educated in Brisbane; lives in Italy.

ON REFUSING AN ALL RISK INSURANCE POLICY

Blue slate on the roof where pigeons
walk. Between walls
dust and the furious nightlife
of spiders. In the room
under the roof, we climb
together towards sleep.

The middle floor is open
to callers; cigar-ash,
and the small surf of excitement
that froths on beer; rainbow
colours of conversation
that flash on the air.

Below, the light of dented
saucepans, an onion
sprouting on the sill;
dull metal and dishwater;
the sun in a knifebox;
the dolour of soup spoons.

All safe as houses: fire
kennelled in a matchbox,
the water of drowned valleys
dammed behind taps.
Barring accidents—or malice.
Nothing's disaster-proof.

Fat tongues may lick at doorknobs
and drowned fish rot
in mud-cracks, behind doors.
These are the minor hazards
we live with, climbing
to sleep in the giant's mouth.

READING HORACE OUTSIDE SYDNEY, 1970

The distance is deceptive: Sydney glitters invisible
in its holocaust of air, just thirty miles away, in Rome
two thousand years from here, a goosequill scrapes, two crack
    divisions
are hurled against a furclad, barbarous northern people pushing

south into history; small throats are cut at committee-tables,
a marriage dies in bed; bald officials like old pennies
worn smooth by time and trade were once my copper-keen
    school-fellows,
who studied Cicero and shook their heads over the fall

of virtue in high places; now on pills twelve storeys high
in air, they shake their heads and fall and pause and walk again.
Somewhere across a border shabby barefoot warriors
stumble into grass, an empire mourns, in small wars seeking

safe boundaries against death. Over the traffic, over the harbour,
    lions
roar, schoolboys scramble out of nightmares, mineral stocks
fall with a noiseless crash, the sight of millions; cicadas
are heard, shrill under stones, in the long suspension of our breath.

Out here wheat breathes and surges, poplars flare. On the highway
    lorries
throb towards city squares. High in the blue a Cessna bi-plane
cropdusting lucerne turns to catch the sun. The brilliant granule
of dust climbs out of sight. Its shadow dances in my palm.

FOR TWO CHILDREN:

Lelo and Alex Tesei

Across the lake the small houses appear
to be real, or to imagine themselves somehow
painted on the view and leaning toward
their shaky selves in water, taking the sun
for granted, stretching their timbers, half asleep
in a dream of such apparent permanence
that we hire a boat and would row across to visit,
or walk there if we could, watching fishes
snap their tails beside us and the mirror
scales reflect us tiny on their backs.

Instead we trail our hands under a jetty
and stay close in to shore. The water is clear,
metallic, deep, with an edge so keen our hands
are struck off at the wrist, set in Peru, say,
or Alaska, in a reliquary of solid
rock crystal. No longer ours, they seek
adventures. In the houses opposite, across
the blue-black glassy lake they stroke a cat
or crumble cup-cakes, saying we should have come there
too. And indeed we should, in a hired dinghy

and a swirl of smoke over icy pebbles, trailing
our oars and flicking crumbs of rainbowed sunlight
at fishtails in our wake. But the houses seem
no nearer. At arm's distance our hands give up
a career of pins-and-needles and drift back
to a warm, a known continent. Only the fish
rise to the surface and their round mouths gape.
We lean to where the boat tugs at its shadow
down there, blue-black and deep. Where have you been
all day? they ask at the boatshed on the beach.

REPORT FROM CHAMPAGNE COUNTRY

Such green-gold days: old vines knot in the sun, and Pol de
    Limbourg's
Tres Riches Heures unwind their gothic tendrils. The vinestock
    knows
what's here. Black-pudding land, the sluice where an artery was
    drained,

a whole generation in the field, two armies deadlocked
still. They push an inch this way that way as earth resettles
under them, and silence; shinbone, brain-pan, clavicle

parting in the shambles. A cartwheel splinters; crossbow, rifle
move off from the hand; the wars go on. From random shots
in May 1940 through richer strata, chivalry

and tribal skirmishes in woods ploughed under. Chantry chapels
ride over their bones, the land is thick with minerals,
an intelligence still active as chins tilt upwards, lower ranks

spring to the alert. Dispersed in wheatfields, a platoon
spreads out, trailing as old-man's-beard from fenceposts—early
    runners
of the green revolution. I've an uncle under here;

another uncle coughed all through my childhood the corrosive
airs of La Belle France, its gold light tickled in his chest.
Good years and heady for some, the bubbling 'Twenties. He
    choked at last

on his bawdy anecdotes, went back to the regiment; another
gold-leaf hero sunk in the minds of boys pissed off with honour
-boards and manhood's rare, impulsive gift. I come to judge

for myself. Hell's under here. I stoop and scrabble at the earth.
Our century is topsoil inches thick, a cover of herbage,
and suddenly I'm there: messtins, webbing, a howitzer-shell

hard-packed with char and powdery red dust, the heat of battle
cooling. Metal burns to slow extinction. Not to be softened
yet or for decades yet, or gathered back. Launching free

of its course round the earth's true magnet, it becomes mere space-
    trash, debris
of a happening not of its own dimension, war economies
unloading here their surplus, thirty million factory-hands,

grey ghostly legions clubbed with sleep, sleepwalking. Ground-fog
    rolls
towards them. At trench-rat level on their bellies or balanced over
a quagmire of bones, they dream their lifetime on the duckboards

in the jobless years, the dole and breadqueue cities, lose their nerve
and slip. Regulation boots, belt, helmet, tins of bully take them
down with the other faces. They sink through battles, weeks of mud

to a green place out of war. At ease and easy, big hands loosen,
fill with earth. Under autumn's oak-leaf cluster, out of range
of field-glass scrutiny, they shift to a softer focus, growing

used to such neighbours now as snail-shell fossils, woodlice, tongues
that lick their brows for salt. They make their separate peace: for
    this one
warm rain and nettle soup, for that one shell-shock, a steel splinter

that climbs six feet to settle in the brain; and death that faltered
once in no-man's-land surprises them in the no-man's-land
of suburban Sunday morning; they find their slow way back to earth.

It is quiet now, out here. Though the mind wears thin at this point,
    even
at midday; cattle stare into dead men's eyes, slow jaws mull over
enigmas, energies at work down there, brutal illusions

we are not done with yet, the good years go on happening.
Two uncles lost, no firm ground won on either side. The iron
hedges sprout new barbs and will not be grubbed out in my lifetime,

the peace is illusory. From the earth dark bubbles climb, invade
the bloodstream, burst and flood our consciousness. There are
    manoeuvres
in all these fields. And a mustering in streets of the old divisions,

the flash of savage creeds, a longing—wilful, absolute—
to be finished with all this, a passion for certitude, to enter
the pure state of the Future, unique and terrible citizenship

for which nothing, not flesh, not blood, is pure enough, and the
    earth too deeply
stained with humanity to be our place of resurrection.
And still the dead climb back. From battlefields, ghettos of ash

in the blacksoil lands the *Untermenschen* stir, all energy
in a free state finding eyes in tubers, limbs in pale birch saplings.
The plump fruit swells to bursting-point. An excitement not our
   own

too long held back, bursts through us, green-gold summers on a
   time-fuse
exploding in our flesh. In the glare and over-heat of wheatfields
grain crowds towards a fence, the cry of more than insects wavers,

ascendant on the breeze. Their lives, our lives too deeply mingled
to speak with a voice that is not theirs, who find in our drunken
   shambling
the first steps of a dance. At the threshing even dust is gold.

FAY ZWICKY   (1933–)

Poet, short story writer. Born and educated in Melbourne; lives in
Perth.

IDENTITY

'Our greatest joys to mark an outline truly
And know the piece of earth on which we stand.'
So you may say, and I in part accept the newly
Taken exploration of a whispering land,

But voices in the country of the mind
Tame the crueller aspect of my days.
Irresolute as fine weather, I am blind
With memories. Nature was never friendly, her ways

Severed me and serious poets should never be severed,
Should lovers be, namers of colours, shapes, plants.
Not urban neurotics from frustrate armchairs levered
To stare through glass at bird-forsaken haunts.

Nature poets are rarely as tranquil or composed
As they sound. Wordsworth fussed around, man
Speaking to God, not men—delight imposed
On distraction. John Clare ate weeds. Cowper ran

Mad from the world's disease. Their city hell
My heaven, their order my darkness. 'One vast mill'
Can compass rival landscapes. So I'll sell
The poet's soul for memory's Eden, whirl

The glass above the ravenous soil split
Wide in veined caverns, shaped by affliction.
Seeded in flame, hatched to withstand, I'll pit
Double-tongued desert winds against my conviction.

SUMMER POGROM

Spade-bearded Grandfather, squat Lenin
In the snows of Donna Buang.
Your bicycle a wiry crutch, nomadic homburg
Alien, black, correct. Beneath, the curt defiant
Filamented eye. Does it count the dead
Between the Cossack horses' legs in Kovno?

Those dead who sleep in me, me dry
In a garden veiled with myrtle and oleander,
Desert snows that powder memory's track
Scoured by burning winds from eastern rocks,
Flushing the lobes of mind,
Fat white dormant flowrets.

Aggressive under dappled shade, girl in a glove;
Collins Street in autumn,
Mirage of clattering crowds: Why don't you speak English?
I don't understand, *I don't understand!*
Sei nicht so ein Dummerchen, nobody cares.
Not for you the upreared hooves of Nikolai,
Eat your icecream, Kleine, *may his soul rot*,
These are good days.

Flared candles; the gift of children; love,
Need fulfilled, a name it has to have—how else to feel?
A radiance in the garden, the Electrolux man chats,
Cosy spectre of the afternoon's decay.
My eye his eye, the snows of Kovno cover us.
Is that my son bloodied against Isaac the Baker's door?

The tepid river's edge, reeds creak, rats' nests fold and quiver,
My feet sink in sand; the children splash and call, sleek
Little satyrs diamond-eyed reined to summer's roundabout,
Hiding from me. Must I excavate you,
Agents of my death? Hushed snows are deep, the
Dead lie deep in me.

MORRIS LURIE   (1938–)

Short story writer, novelist, journalist. Born and educated in Melbourne.

RAPPAPORT LAYS AN EGG

Business is brisk. All week the shop has been cluttered with people, people coming and going, inquiring, expressing interest, reaching, taking, at times so many it's been positively dangerous, valuable items in perilous sway, the magic eye front door buzzer (which upsets the canary in the room at the back) providing ceaseless musical accompaniment, an electronic French farce, buzz buzz, buzz buzz, goodbye to lamps and urns and brass beds and frolicsome garden statuary and even that hideous Victorian overmantle ten feet long at least with every available inch between and around the spotted inset mirrors knobbly with rudely-carved angels and lions and clusters of fruit, the whole business jet black with either age or grime (surely that wasn't the original finish), yes, even that's gone, sold, a little lady saw it and fell in love with it and had to have it and paid instant cash, likewise the hatstand with the three broken knobs and the alarming list, what a week it's been, seven thousand taken, maybe more, and now it's six o'clock, Friday, the week over and done, the CLOSED sign up on the door and on the road outside all Melbourne streaming home, cars, schoolgirls, a jangling green tram, in and out of the samovars and the art nouveau table decorations and the Staffordshire dogs in the window they rush and slip, while inside, Rappaport, sole proprietor of Rappaport Antiques, unmarried, thirty-three, stands with his friend Friedlander, who is two years older and looking for a job, Friedlander expressing amazement at the volume of trade, but on Rappaport's face, where there should be satisfaction, prosperity, glee, is indecision, gloom, possibly even (but it's a bit dark in here, Rappaport hasn't yet switched on the lights) a scowl.

A scowl?

"That lamp," says Rappaport. "You know that lamp I sold on Tuesday? You know the one. With the *spikes*. Sold it for two hundred and fifty and you know what? An absolutely identical one down the road, except the spikes weren't even as spikey, went this morning for—guess? *Four hundred.*"

"Gee." says Friedlander. "But listen, what'd you *pay* for your lamp?"

"I don't know," Rappaport mumbles. "Twenty, twenty-five."

"Twenty-five and you got two fifty? A million per cent profit! What are you complaining about, for God's sake?"

"What I'm complaining about is … *inflation.*" Rappaport hisses out the word. "*Galloping inflation.* Inflation is suddenly galloping so much it's practically insane to let anything go, at any price. Sell it tomorrow and you get double. *Triple* even."

And Rappaport gives his moustache a mournful chew, his shoulders slumped, true misery in his eyes.

"Ah, stop grumbling, Rappie," Friedlander says. "Wow, you've just taken in seven thousand and—"

"Big deal," Rappaport rumbles. "And what about my *stock?* What about my *name?* Friedlander," he confides, his voice down to a whisper, "you know what this galloping inflation is doing to me? *I am no longer the biggest thief in town.*"

What a pronouncement! Friedlander has to take a step back. Is the man joking? Is this some new kind of antique dealer humour? Friedlander doesn't know whether to laugh or cry, Rappaport standing slumped before him in his baggy Yves St Laurent jeans, his Turnbull and Asser shirt, his Jaeger knitwear, his Bally boots, begging for sympathy. He laughs.

"Take me home, Rappie," he says. "Take me home to my wife and children. It's lentils for dinner again tonight, but I don't care, we'll put the children to bed and then afterwards Kerry and I will take up the lino in the kitchen and who knows, maybe we'll find some old newspapers we can read, and when we've read them we can burn them to keep warm, and then we'll draw our thin coats over our pale bodies and go to sleep."

"Wait in the car, Friedlander," Rappaport says, his manner suddenly icy. "And don't slam the door! There's valuable stuff in there and I'm not in the mood for disasters."

These drives in Rappaport's car. This year it's a Peugeot station wagon, bright green, a mighty console of heating and demisting knobs in the front, it's like flying a plane, also the latest in stereophonic push-button cassette players, the speakers set in the doors and on the floor a fine litter of Rappaport's musical tastes, Al Bowley and Noel Coward and the complete *oeuvre* of Frankie Laine, plus, to lend a little tone, a selection of Beethoven done on the moog. Friedlander eases himself in very carefully, not disturbing a thing, and a minute later in comes Rappaport, crashing and crunching and muttering oaths. Something falls over in the back. Rappaport's door won't close. A newspaper is sent to the boot, pages fluttering like a bird. Another oath. Another door slam. Friedlander sits very quietly, not saying a word. Rappaport slams the car into gear and off they go.

"That lamp," Rappaport growls.

They have been driving together like this for more than a dozen years, the cars each year getting posher as Rapppaport's fortune grows, but inside always the same, the same junk, the same newspapers and magazines, the same lightshades and vases and mirrors and prints (a fortune, a fortune!) placed so recklessly it's dangerous to sit, the same flotsam of vital addresses and messages and phone numbers and business cards, Rappaport's hurricane-struck filing system, impossible to actually put your hand on one that you want but nothing ever thrown out. And, for more than a dozen years, the same dialogue too. Anyhow, the same recurring themes.

"Real estate," Rappaport breathes.

Friedlander doesn't say anything. If he walked, he'd be home in five minutes, but that's not the form. Over the years he's learnt, come to understand, that these drives are necessary, Rappaport the restless modern man needs to be in motion, behind the wheel, needs to have buildings floating past, tree-lined streets, bridges, traffic, the soft rumble of tyres beneath him, life in flux, before he can confide his heart's most secret woes. And Friedlander's role is to listen. Rappaport is the patient. Friedlander is Dr Freud.

"My father," Rappaport mutters.

They turn right, then left, then right again, Rappaport doing no more than twenty miles an hour, eyes narrowed, his face hard, focused dead ahead. Friedlander, still silent, takes out his cigarettes, quietly, sneaks one to his lips, out of the corner of his eye watching Rappaport for some display of emotion. And ah, here it comes.

"Half a million!" Rappaport explodes. "The place went for half a million and I could have got it for twenty-seven. My father."

And looking out of his window Friedlander sees that this is where Rappaport has brought him, they are cruising past the lumpy grey building where Rappaport, as he has told Friedlander many times, could have made his pile.

"'It's not a proposition,' he said," Rappaport is rumbling. "A proposition? The best part of town! Property's going up here a thousand a week!"

"Is that so?" says Friedlander.

Mr Rappaport is not enamoured of this son. The other, the doctor, can do no wrong, but for Rappaport his father has just one word. "*Doopeh.*"

The lumpy grey building slides slowly past, Rappaport grieving after it with his eyes. Half a million! And still going up! This is the building where Rappaport ran to his father, begged him on bended knees to help him out, swore by all that was sacred that here was the guaranteed sure-fire red-hot real-estate bargain such as comes up once in a lifetime, maybe less, and his father listened, thought, stroked his chin, and finally proclaimed, "It's not a proposition." And then added, just to make things crystal clear between them, "*Doopeh.*" And now it's worth a fortune.

But Friedlander doesn't feel sad. Truth to tell, all this money talk bores him slightly. This isn't the old Rappaport. He remembers how they used to rush to movies together, followed by gargantuan Chinese meals. Ah, those were the days! What's happened to that Rappaport? They haven't done a movie together for years.

"Hey, where are we going?" Friedlander asks. "I'm supposed to be home."

But Rappaport doesn't reply, and really Friedlander shouldn't have asked, because he knows where they're going. They're doing what Friedlander calls (but secretly) "The Tour," that slow, mournful drive past all the properties that Rappaport at one time or another asked his father to help him with, and some of which he even put deposits on himself they were so good, and then had to sell, sustaining losses, shops, houses, building sites, every single one of which has at least quadrupled in value, but from Rappaport's father always the same word. *"Doopeh."*

And as the buildings float past Rappaport grieves and moans and chews his moustache, the car filling with misery, until Friedlander can't stand it a second longer and says, "Rappie, I think you should have special T-shirts made up, you know, those printed ones, with your business philosophy written out on the chest."

And he digs out a ballpoint pen, and on the back cover of a handy magazine carefully letters the legend:

BUY CHEAP
SELL CHEAPER
LIVE IN ETERNAL REGRET

"Friedlander," says Rappaport, his voice barely audible, "I can't tell you how nice it is to have you around," and neither of them says another word until Rappaport pulls up, as he does so often after one of his mournful tours, in the driveway of his parents' comfortable suburban home.

Mrs Rappaport is on the telephone. She is gossiping. Smoke from her menthol cigarette veils the room. Also steam from her cup of tea, which is by her left hand, and from which she takes small excited sips when she gets the chance. She is always on the telephone when Friedlander comes, a round, pleasant woman without a real care in the world. Friedlander gives her a polite smile as he goes past with Rappaport to the kitchen, where Mr Rappaport sits at the table, chewing bread.

"Dad," says Rappaport.

They sit.

Mr Rappaport has always seemed to Friedlander a surly man, but this is probably not true. He's a serious man. Wide-shouldered. Feet on the ground. Bald. Also a scoffing anti-smoker so Friedlander doesn't take out his cigarettes.

"I sold that lamp," Rappaport says. "You know the one I told you about. The one I bought for twenty dollars. Sold it for two hundred and fifty. Business has been very good."

Mr Rappaport doesn't say a word.

"And that hatstand," says Rappaport. "I sold that too. Five hundred. Cash."

And in the quiet of the kitchen Rappaport runs through his week's dealings, explaining, adding, outlining future plans, his voice somehow a little high, a little slow, a little modest, even when the sums, to Friedlander at least, seem astronomical. Twenty minutes tick slowly past. Friedlander looks down at his hands. Mr Rappaport reaches for another piece of bread.

"Well," says Rappaport. A silence falls. "I'd better go," Rappaport says. Friedlander starts to stand up. "I'll see you, dad," Rappaport says. Rappaport and Friedlander move towards the door. Rappaport gives his father a small wave. "We're off," Rappaport says. Mr Rappaport remains at the kitchen table, possibly nodding, it's hard to tell.

Back in the car, Rappaport speaks. "Hey, my father was in a good mood today," he says. "He didn't call me *doopeh.*"

A week passes. Business remains brisk. Calling in on Friday around six Friedlander notes the absence of many large items, including the solid lead fountain with the three dolphins and the urchin on top which Friedlander had sworn no one in his right mind would ever buy, gone, carted away, and what's this? Where's the gloom, where's the depression, where's the talk of what galloping inflation is doing to the antique trade? Not a word. In fact, Rappaport is the opposite. He seems positively buoyant.

"My dad's helping me," Rappaport says.

"What do you mean?" Friedlander asks.

"A shop," Rappaport says. "I've found this absolutely beautiful shop. My dad's going to help me buy it. I'm sick and tired of paying rent for this foul dump, and anyhow it's not big enough. I haven't got any room to move."

"How much?" Friedlander asks.

"Auction," Rappaport says. "But don't worry, I know the area like the back of my hand, I know what things round there are worth, what they're fetching, it'll go for seventy, maybe seventy-five, absolute tops, and my dad's agreed to help me to eighty."

"What do you mean, help?"

"Well," says Rappaport, "I'll put in five, he'll put up the rest. It's a tremendous investment for him. A beautiful shop. Just wait till you see it."

Friedlander takes a step back and looks at his friend. The excitement, the joy! He's going to buy a shop. Look at him, Friedlander thinks. When did I last see him excited like this? Not for years. Not since we used to go to those movies together, rushing like lunatics to be first in. Or that time at the fancy dress ball, putting beer into champagne bottles and leaping onto tables with a single bound.

"Don't do it," Friedlander says.

"What do you mean?"

"Don't go to your father," Friedlander says. "Look, how many times have you gone to him? And how many times has he turned you down? You know how it is. Listen, you've been in business— what? Ten years? Twelve? Have you ever been hungry, have you ever had to sleep out in the rain? So what do you want your father for, all of a sudden? Rappie, you're selling him your *individuality*, your *soul*, and all for a lousy shop. Don't do it."

Rappaport doesn't say a word. Nor does he look at Friedlander. He drops his eyes, looks down at his Bally boots, begins to chew his moustache. A lengthy silence falls over Rappaport Antiques.

"Well, that's my opinion," Friedlander says. "You do what you want to do."

Further silence. Further looking down.

"Look, I think I might walk home tonight," Friedlander says. "I need the exercise. See you, Rappie."

And he tries for a smile but it doesn't somehow come off, and he goes out quickly, doesn't look back.

Hey, why the lecture, why did I explode like that? Friedlander asks himself, walking slowly home, and he goes over it all again, this way and that, and when he gets home he starts to tell Kerry about it all and halfway through he is suddenly struck by a completely different thought.

"Hey, I've made a big mistake," he says. "I got it all wrong. He's not selling his *soul*, for God's sake. Look, all these years Rappie's been after just one thing. His father's respect. That's what he wants, that's what's important to him. Not the shop, what's a shop? What he wants is for his father to say, 'You're not a *doopeh*, you're a bright boy, and just to show you how much I think of you, here's seventy thousand.' And I told him not to do it. I lectured him. I carried on like an idiot."

"Phone him up," Kerry says. "Phone him up and tell him what you've just told me."

"Ah, I can't," Friedlander says. "Not now."

"Well, if you don't, I think you're a rat."

"I know," Friedlander says. "Do you think I feel good? I just can't though, that's all. Hey, the auction! I'll go to the auction! Rappaport and his father, side by side! I must find out exactly when it is. That's one auction I wouldn't miss for the world."

The auction. Father and son. Mr Rappaport stands stiff and straight in a dove-coloured raincoat, Rappaport has chosen a jacket featuring a muted check, both of them very serious, silent, Friedlander a few steps behind not daring to approach. It's three o'clock on a Thursday afternoon and not a bad crowd here. Seventy people? Eighty? But how many are serious bidders, how many have just come for a look?

It used to be a butcher shop, these premises that Rappaport desires, you can still see some sawdust around on the floor. Also the old tiled walls, bleak and white, here and there one dropped off making a crossword puzzle pattern. Ssh, the auctioneer is holding up his hand.

The terms of sale are lengthy and then there follows a description of the premises, of the locality, of the business potential, of all Australia, it seems to Friedlander, who is nervous beyond words, and why? He's not a bidder. He looks across at Rappaport and his father and sees that both of them are white-faced, doubly serious, ramrod stiff, and he can't help feeling—what's this?—a certain pride.

Good luck, Friedlander whispers to himself.

A silence. A vacuum. God, it's horrible, Friedlander can't breathe, and then bang, it's away.

The bidding stats at forty thousand, in seconds is at eighty, then a leapfrog up to a hundred, a hundred and ten. There's a pause here, but not for long, up to a hundred and thirty it goes, and a minute it's all over. Sold for a hundred and forty-eight thousand dollars, neither Rappaport nor his father having got a bid in, the pair of them as white-faced and ramrod stiff as before, but Friedlander can see that they're thunderstruck, crushed. He doesn't know whether he should go over to them or not. He does. He is ignored.

"Sorry, dad," Rappaport is saying. "I forgot to calculate for galloping inflation."

Mr Rappaport at first says nothing. His face is blank. Serious. Bald. He looks slowly at Friedlander and then at his son. Friedlander steels himself for the word and finally out it comes.

"*Doopeh*," says Mr Rappaport and walks slowly away.

Friedlander stands with Rappaport. What is there to say?

"Come on, Friedy," says Rappaport. "I'll drive you home."

Thomas Shapcott (1935–)

Poet. Born and educated in Queensland.

SHABBYTOWN FUGUE

1.

The little oxenfaced girls bump down together
over the hill into the shoppingcentre.
The neighbours' clump of oleander leans over
dusty and pink and nobody bothers.
Sun shines through the dust like pollen.

2.

The sky tightens open the hollow.
Blistered streetsigns squint
they rub the abrasive air

back to parched countrytown to
pitsawn shanty to
spindly trees a plain
dry shade that
splits

3.

Foursquare Tiptop GoldenFleece
hygienic plasticwrap with enzymes
give us this day our daily frootloops
start the day well with colds smog carbonmonoxide
weather forecast
      A WESTERLY CHANGE
          blow away powerhouse
          blow away foundrysmoke
          factory incinerator
          crematorium
      a westerly dust, sandpaper heart
      to settle in lungs
      scar eyes nose throat
and the chemists stay in business
the doctors extend credit.

4.

Boys like young unbroken animals
                the little oxfaced girls
morning dance with shadows
             blown away with morning
let them trample over
          let them be rough with affection
they shake the flowers of their heads
              they break the oleander
and every street is home
          they are not lost
where all the world spins
          our children laugh full and defenceless
they will not believe they shall be cursed
            they shall be cursed.

BARRY OAKLEY   (1931–)

Novelist, short story writer, playwright. Born and educated in Melbourne.

SCANLAN

A monologue in one act

The set should suggest a seminar situation; a long table, surrounded by empty chairs. Flask of water and glass. At each side of the head of the table, at a moderate distance, large potted ferns. Above the head of the table hangs a large picture of the nineteenth century Australian poet Henry Kendall.

Enter Scanlan, a middle-aged academic in a middle-aged academic suit. He's obviously late, and looks somewhat disoriented and hard-pressed. He carries a bulging briefcase, which he puts on the table and unpacks as he starts his lecture.

Scanlan:

Permit me to apologise ladies and gentlemen for my late arrival. I missed my plane by a matter of minutes, dashing into the airport just as it was preparing for take-off. It's a rhetorical question, but I'm still going to ask it—is there anything so irrevocable as an air-craft narrowly missed? But miss it I did, and the next hour was spent cooling my heels in the terminal building. Terminal. As in illness. The air overheated, the music piped, the lights fluorescent, the ears harried by public announcements, the thirst slaked by li-quor excessively priced. The road to hell, paved with vinyl tile and fruit-fly inspectors.

But now the journey is over, and what an honor it is to stand before such a distinguished assemblage, amongst whom I note some old friends—(bowing to each) Professor McGiff, still hearty and hale at eighty, Dr. Williams making light of her calipers, Mr. Gelly obviously recovered from his stroke—and my old colleague Dr. Grigsby, whom apparently we have to thank for organising this seminar, and (looking at Grigsby's chair with guarded suspicion) who was responsible, I have only just discovered, for my receiving an invitation, though it is not his signature that appears at the base of the letter ... (trailing off mysteriously, as if suspecting a plot)

And now, I can delay no longer. I can put off no more the moment when I must leave my burrow and show my ears above the grass. Prime your fowling pieces ladies and gentlemen, release the hounds, send the beaters forward—Scanlan is out and running!... Henry

Kendall And The Poetry of Possibility. Or, Henry Kendall And The Forests Of The Heart ... or, Henry Kendall And The Metrics of Ambiguity ... or the Prosody Of Pain ... or The Dactyls Of Defeat ... or, Henry Kendall, Bo Diddley Or Baudelaire ... (muttering) that should just about please everyone.... Of those among you who are wondering why my subject is a nineteenth century poet, delivered at a seminar devoted to twentieth century Australian literary issues, I request patience. I must ask you to (making odd paw-and-claw gestures with the hands) bear with me ... despite the conventional wisdom to the contrary, despite Doctor Grigsby's printed opinion that our poet is no more than Wordsworth and water, I propose to show that, far from being a mere Victorian versifier, Henry Kendall is in fact a harbinger of our present age.

First, a speedy background sketch (suddenly standing and plucking)—a date, from the palmtrees of history! 1813—the crossing of the—? (looking around, schoolmasterish, for suggestions) yes, over there—Blue Mountains! Correct. And the men who did it, who sound collectively like a firm of solicitors, were as you know Blaxland Lawson and Wentworth ... a firm of solicitors (musing) ... surely there is a more appropriate collective noun ... a weakness of solicitors ... a pride of lions and a humilitation of barristers—I'm sorry. Lecturing to students is one thing. Performing before one's peers is another. The result is nervousness, dryness of the throat, attempts to retrieve the situation with whimsy. I take sedatives on medical advice ... (producing suspicious-looking flask and drinking from it with odd furtive movement while trying to distract his audience by gesturing toward the Kendall portrait with blackboard pointer) Handsome fellow, very handsome. (refreshed, lubricated and unwittingly making it apparent that it's not the first drink he's had that day). 1813, and the Blue Mountains crossed and the limitless vistas beyond ... if I could quote from one authority on the subject ... (ferreting amongst his papers).... 'What was the cause of this expansion? The thirst of British manufacturers for wool (sucking at his coatsleeve uncontrollably then quickly getting a grip on himself) and the hunger of Australian farmers for land (brief biting and snapping with the jaws), very soon outran (jogging on the spot) the narrow hinterland of Sydney....' And what do we descry, as we cross those blue peaks? (still jogging) To the west, the eternal horizontals of the plains ... to the north and south, the ageless verticals of the rain forests! Forests where the new generation were also to take root and rise up, straight and tall as the gums!

It must be remembered that up until this time Australian verse did no more than (strange simian arm-movements) ape English models ... as the natives delighted in cast-off top hats and jackets, so too did our earliest versifiers make themselves foolish by dressing themselves in the trappings of a Pope or a Johnson.... Listen for example to W. C. Wentworth's *Australasia*—note the relentlessly heavy Augustan hand (as he reads, his hands become heavier, forcing the page down, pressing harder and harder against the tabletop)–

> *And oh Britannia! Shoulds't thou cease to ride*
> *Despotic Empress of Old Ocean's tide*
> *May this, thy last-born infant then arise*
> (ironical fortissimo)
> *To glad thy heart and greet thy parent's eyes*
> *And Australasia Float With Flag Unfurled*
> *A New Britannia in Another World!*

It was this conventional sensibility that the new breed of Currency-lad poets, Charles Harpur and Henry Kendall, decisively rejected. They set themselves the daunting task of re-interpreting the continent in the light of the new romantic temper—it was they who pioneered that long struggle to absorb and render the alien Australian landscape (reaching out to whack at the fern fronds with the pointer)—a struggle that continues to the present day!

And so—pace Dr. Grigsby and his recent opinion that Henry Kendall is (ferreting, then quoting with contempt) 'confined by diction, prosody and self-pity in a petit-bourgeois velvet cell of his own making'—the truth of the matter is that Kendall opens windows rather than closes them ... it is Kendall that alerts our eyes and ears to the majesty and mystery of Nature—antipodean nature, that vegetation dense and dark, those rain forests that edge ever closer, prowling, stalking (approaching the ferns with his pointer as if about to impale a wild animal, then attacking and becoming entangled)—they're not called creeper for nothing—breathing, alive, luxuriant, moving closer, ever closer—while we sit here fiddling with abstractions!... (picking himself up from unsuccessful encounter with ferns)—it's all right for the English—they've communed with their landscape for centuries—tamed, smoothed, shaped, polished it till they can see their faces in it—while for us—within an arm's length—the wilds! (regaining thread and drinking from flask) If my conduct appears excessive ladies and gentlemen I apologise—I've been under strain these last few months—an overwhelming sense of loss, of loneliness—as if my inner being had been extracted one evening when I lay asleep and I am now left with life in two dimensions, as if I'm participating in a shadow play, a repetitive and meaningless ritual, as if some central part of me has wasted away and I wake each morning trapped inside the increasingly shapeless sack of my own body—and that deprived of this shaping spirit this body decays not by the year but by the hour, the hair greying as I look at it, the face pouching and wrinkling as I stare ... the only person who still believes in my existence is my wife, who conducts an endless war of attrition against me, in the mistaken belief that I am not already vanquished, attenuated, a shade, a shrug,

a tone of voice, an opinion, a striped tie ... (regaining thread) So—
let us hear no more about Kendall the sentimental nineteenth century painter and decorator ... it must be understood that his relationship with nature is a symbolic one, that he is in fact a poet of
Baudelairean correspondences, that his art engages in a two-way
movement, (miming an outward movement) projecting his emotions onto nature in an *outward* thrust, while (miming an inward
movement) *internalising* that landscape at the same time ... it is in
the light of this (trying to do both at once and threshing about)
symbiotic rhythm that his art should be considered.... You want
chapter and verse? I give you chapter and verse. (turning round and
looking up at portrait as if it's a god that has to be placated)—

> From the runs of the Narran wide-dotted with sheep
> And loud with the lowing of cattle
> We speed for a land where the strange forests sleep
> And the hidden creeks bubble and—brattle!

(looking round quickly) Dr. Grigsby? I'd know that laugh anywhere. You find the last word amusing? You feel no pity for the
luckless versifier, who, having had the misfortune to require the
word cattle in an abab quatrain, finds himself apparently in difficulties in line four? Yes—the hidden creeks bubble and brattle. And
why not? There are other rhymes at his disposal—prattle, rattle,
battle, tattle—but spurning these easy solutions, the poet opts to
invent a word, an alliterative neologism that is highly effective—
listen! (pouring a drink and holding it up to his ear)—brattling!
(drinks)
But what do we care about the cant and pedantry of academics? To
our horses! (reading with galloping fervour, and becoming increasingly equestrian as he does so)

> Now call on the horses and leave the blind courses
> And sources of rivers that all of us know—

—Three rimes Grigsby, in a line and a half!—

> For crossing the ridges and passing the ledges
> And running up gorges we'll come to the verges
> Of gullies where waters eternally flow—

—halfrimes and eyerimes and blindrimes! And you say this man is a
nobody—you who have never even ridden a horse, never dared
anything, never felt the wind in your face—(reading and riding
faster)

> The leagues we may travel down beds of hot gravel
> The clay-crusted reaches where moisture bath been
> While searching for waters may vex us and thwart us
> Yet who would be quailing or fainting or failing?
> Not you who are sons of the Narran I—ween

—Yes, ween. Chuckle away. It wasn't considered so funny a hundred years ago my friend, I assure you—Wordsworth used it—Shelley—Keats—in those days *everybody* was weening.

(pause, drinks) My throat's so dry—my nerves—I know your game—I know what you're up to (to Grigsby) it's not Kendall you're mocking, it's me. You find it amusing that I have devoted my life to a nonentity, is that it? Well my good friend and ladies and gentlemen, I see it otherwise—it is I, not you, that have the task, the challenge—I've been called, required, obligated—to defend the gentle garden of Henry Kendall—I keep the lines straight, the plots weeded, the colours and images well watered—I weed, delve, prune—but every so often a herbivore escapes from the herd, pushes in the gate and gets inside, grunting, tossing, trampling (pointing the pointer at Grigsby, and flourishing an imaginary cape matador-fashion)—but I'll have you out of here before the hour's up—you and all the other snorters and bellowers—one day my faith in Henry Kendall will be—(extending his arms, assuming a crucified posture) redeemed! He will be recognised for the poet that he is—apologies will be made—revaluations, pilgrimages, bouquets of flowers, articles in the Saturday pages—he will be raised up on high, and I, like the good thief, will accompany him into his kingdom! (pause) And the Grigsbys of this world will come pleading for a drop of water! (drinks) I'm sorry, I speak excessively, wax vehement ... I'm tired, if you want the truth of the matter ... I slept badly, haunted by the thought that upon my performance here today my reputation, for what it is worth, stands or falls ... and yet my wife has conceived the remarkable notion that seminars such as these are pretexts, that once the preliminaries are disposed of, middle-aged academics such as myself home in on the nearest attractive woman in the gathering, follow her scent, stalk her behind the tea urn, and fall upon her in a shower of sugar cubes and biscuits ... accordingly ... my wife—my wife Margaret, took measures to prevent my departure. I found, on dressing this morning, I had no belt for my trousers, but this proved a disguised blessing, helping as it did to conceal the fact that she'd hidden away virtually every sock I had to my name....

It is a disservice nevertheless to any artist to praise him over and beyond his due merits. And since we find ourselves fallen amongst Kendall's bush ballads, some discriminations are therefore in order ... if these poems, lively as they are, are compared with the rough popular songs that precede them, or the work of Gordon and Paterson that comes after, it will be seen that our poet (weary after a bout of peripatetic lecturing, he goes to sit down, misses the chair, almost falls to floor)—falls between two stools ... failing as he does to recapture the crude earthy vigour of the former, while at the same time too poetical to attain the lively narrative drive of the latter...

Kendall indeed was an intensely self-conscious and literary writer—
not for him the easy familiarity of (bursting into song)

> *'Tis of a wild colonial boy, Jack Doolan was his name*
> *Of poor but honest parents, he was born in Castlemaine*
> *He was his father's only hope, his mother's only joy,*
> *And dearly did his parents love their wild colonial boy*

—with its rough-hewn hearty spontaneities and rollicking
choruses—(sings again, louder)

> *Come all me hearties, we'll roam the mountains high*
> *Together we will plunder, together we will die*
> *We'll wander over valleys and gallop over plains*
> *But we'll scorn to live in slavery—*

(breaking off) Phew. The heat. (takes off jacket, revealing ragged
shirt. Regards it ruefully) So determined was my dear wife that I
should be spared the carnal delights of the seminar that my shirts
were left unwashed, which is why I appear before you in a garment
usually reserved for weekend gardening...

It is Kendall's love of description, his fondness for figure and trope
that lead him to overlay his ballads with an elaboration that makes
them hybrids—neither (momentary swimming movements) the fish
of ballad nor (flapping movements) the fair lyric fowl—thus: (reciting)

> *When the thunder ceases pealing and the stars up*
> *heaven are stealing*
> *And the moon above us wheeling throws her*
> *pleasant glances round—*

(flapping again) not quite lyrical fowl—and this (reciting, fishily)

> *From our home we boldly sally 'neath the trysting*
> *tree to rally*
> *For a night hunt up the valley, with our brothers*
> *and the hound!*

—not quite the authentic piscian article either ... Phew. So hot!
(loosens tie, undoes some shirt buttons, exposing a Puffing Billy
Preservation Society tee shirt, which again he inspects ruefully before proceeding) What a strange little family—husband, wife and
one introverted adolescent son, a loner, a brooder, whose one passion in life is railways. Trains all over his walls, speeding, shunting,
steaming ... timetables, brochures and esoteric books on forgotten
narrow-gauges deep in the timberlands ... last summer I painted the
ceiling of his room. Ignorant as I am of practical matters, I applied
the new paint directly over the old ... every time the door is opened
or closed a strange thing happens ... a tiny shower of white paint-
specks falls, fine as dandruff, on him, his bed, his books...

Kendall always aspired to write a long narrative poem but never succeeded, perhaps because of the difficulties he encountered in his personal life. Plagued by money worries, tempted by the twin demons of self-pity and alcohol, he never seemed to find time for anything other than short lyrical outbursts (bursts uncontrollably into high-pitched song, then checks himself)... Indeed the fact must be faced, in any treatment of his life and work, that Kendall had many weaknesses, and drink was one of them—but this scarcely justifies the following (ferreting about for quote)—'In April 1872 Kendall finally succumbed to the chronic instability and weakness of will that had always plagued him—abandoned by his muse, his wife and his family, he wandered the streets and slept in the gutters of Sydney, saturated in alcohol—a condition for which he had no one to blame but himself'.

This is Dr. Grigsby's final and pitiless conclusion to the article to which I have already referred—an article which dismisses in four pages the labours of two lives—not only the poet's, but also, if I may be permitted to say so, my own ... Dr. Grigsby is seemingly unaware of the difficulties of colonial life for the sensitive person, and the special difficulties it held for the artist ... for the handful of poets who practised their art at the time suicide was the rule rather than the exception—such was the raw hurly-burly of frontier existence ... (musing) remarkable the number of compound words suggesting confusion, all beginning with aitch ... hurly burly ... hocus pocus ... higgledy piggledy.... There were good reasons for Kendall's periodic attempts to seek refuge in drink ... hotch potch, there's another ... though Kendall's volume *Leaves From Australian Forests* was well received, it failed financially—holus bolus, that's a fifth—leaving him in desperate straits—harem scarem, a sixth—then, when his baby daughter took ill and died, he blamed himself—wait, helter skelter, there's dozens of 'em—hugger mugger, hanky panky, hurdy gurdy (starts to wander, as if lost, in circles, getting giddy)—hurdy gurdy—hurdy gurdy—hurdy gurdy—is it any wonder he wandered the Sydney streets lost and ill, eventually succumbing—hurdy gurdy—hurdy-gurdy—to (losing his balance and falling) complete nervous collapse. (dragging himself clear of the table, then dealing briskly, still prone, with an apparent attempt to stop his lecture) No sir, I won't be interrupted—I have the floor. (reciting, with a mixture of sadness and defiance)

> *But sorrow speaks in sighing leaf*
> *And trouble talketh in the ti⟨?⟩*
> *The skirts of a stupendous grief*
> *Are travelling ever at my side*
> *The world is at me with the heat*
> *And toil and cares that tire*
> *I cannot with my feeble feet*
> *Climb after my desire.*

(lifting himself up, wary but determined, and pointing to Grigsby)
You want to bring Kendall down and me with him. That's your
plan. That's why you had me invited here today. Every man has his
time of darkness—knowing that mine was upon me, you lured me
here, hiding behind the signature of a functionary, hoping you had
supplied enough rope for me to hang myself publicly ... you really
think four contemptible pages in an obscure quarterly (pointing to
Kendall photo) will bring us down? Four pages of polemic, ridicule,
rhetoric, innuendo, calumny, detraction, contumely, begging of
questions, a prioris, argumentums ad hominem, pathetic fallacies,
ignoratio elenchis, undistributed middles... (regaining thread) Not
even Kendall's finest lyric achievement is safe from Grigsby's flail-
ing haymakers and knees to the groin. In his headlong jump to his
foolish conclusion, the exquisite Bellbirds is dealt a flurry of kicks
and punches on the way...Kendall is attacked, if you please, for
claiming that the notes of the bellbird are 'softer than slumber' (first
uncontrollable tinkle or trill) when they are allegedly in fact a stac-
cato tinkling (second trill). Dr. Grigsby is up to his usual trick of
lifting a poetic phrase out of context, thus depriving it of symbolic
resonance—let us put his crystalline expression back in the jewelled
setting where it belongs—(recites)

> By channels of coolness the echoes are calling
> And down the dim gorges I hear the creek falling

(another trilling outburst)

> It lives in the mountains where moss and the sedges
> Touch with their beauty the banks and the ledges

(Through the rest of the poem he fights the impulse, managing finally to get it under control)

> Through breaks of the cedar and sycamore bowers
> Struggles the light that is love to the flowers
> —And softer than slumber and sweeter than singing
> The notes of the bellbirds are running and ringing

... a combination of pictures, personal feeling and (final brief trill)
music that taken together represent a pioneering assimilation of the
Australian landscape into poetry.

Yes Dr. Grigsby, he wrote as a Victorian with Wordsworth and
Tennyson as models. Yes, he was often guilty of sentimentality and
even bathos—but he had at his best, rare moments the pure gift of
song—and that is what matters. To hear *Mooni*, one of his finest
lyrics, spoken by one of our finest actors, will I think drive my
point home (switches on tape recorder. Sounds of Scanlan and his
wife in somewhat heated argument. Listens mutely, resignedly for a
few moments before switching it off) I'm sorry. My son, even my
son, is also at odds with me ... he has developed a sado/masochistic

habit of covertly recording our marital disagreements, and has inserted this somehow on the tape ... (presses button, runs tape for a few seconds at high speed, stops, switches it on again. This time, sounds of savage, almost hysterical argument. Turns it off, and faces Grigsby).

Music to your ears. Bliss. Sitting there smug as a pavement artist. All your own work ... the moment you discovered myself and your poor wife red-handed, in flagrante, you told *my* wife, and I've been paying for it ever since. One would have thought that would have been revenge enough for you—but no, not you ... not content with wrecking two—no three—lives, you pursue me, stricken as I am, into the garden of verse. But that was a mistake—you didn't reckon that your victim, trapped, driven to desperation at being tracked down and cornered in this last retreat, would finally turn against his tormentor and show his teeth! (regaining thread) There are indications that Kendall toyed with the idea of a narrative poem set on the mythical island of Tenna. In response to a letter from Henry Halloran in 1878, urging him to write such a poem, he replied (ferreting through his papers, picking up one after the other, and finally settling on one, which he reads as from a diary) *February* Returned this day from bird watching holiday at the Promontory. Fifteen different species in five days. Note-books filled. Photographs taken. Friendship firmed. Confidences exchanged over campfire under a sky smoking and crackling with stars ... poor Grigsby tells me he is unhappily married ... several cans of beer later I tell him I am too... (puts page down, picks up another)—to Halloran's letter, the poet replied—'the long poem you wish me to write would require more leisure than that at present under my command. I have to work very hard, and my labour sometimes runs deep into the night ...' (puts down page, picks up another) *April* Barbecue at Yarra Bend. Chops overcooked, claret raw ... (looking at Grigsby) keen to show your old-public-school skills with the sculls, you suggest we hire a dinghy for a sally down river. Room for five only. You go with the children and Margaret—while your wife and I volunteer to stay behind. As your craft, expertly handled, proceeds vigorously round the bend, Sylvia and I ... Sylvia and I, both deprived, famished, crying out for... (regaining thread)
—In his early years Kendall produced a number of rather conventional love poems. Though their metrication is agreeable and the language never less than apt, these works have a certain mechanical quality ... as the years passed however and his experience deepened, there is a corresponding increase in the passion of his poetry ... *May, June, July* ... happy times. Whenever Dr. Grigsby is lecturing and I happn to be free, I visit my beloved Sylvia, who waits for me, just a short walk away, scented with pomades and lotions ... I leave my room, cross the campus lawns. My blood pumps hard and high with expectation, excitement seems to lift me off the ground, I skim

the grass weightless—I look for an analogue, a co-relative of my desire, and lo it appears, as if I've created it, summoned it up, beyond the trees—the spiked dome of Newman College, something rare, exotic, tropical, from Mexico perhaps or even Byzantium... (regaining thread) An added richness of tone, an intenser passion, is found in Kendall's second volume of verse—and though to us today such poems as *A Spanish Love Song* and *Campaspe* seem harmless enough, to the Victorians they appeared outspoken and bold. George Smithers, reviewing this particular volume in *The Colonial Monthly*, has this to say—'Kendall's love knows nothing of chastity or purity—it is a (gradually becoming affected, meditative, because of the erotic implications of the words) wild hot foaming passion ... libidinous in thought, and preying solely upon physical beauty ... he invests the female form with a sumptuousness of beauty which kindles the pulse as you read it ... he makes his women Cleopatras in the ... impassioned suggestiveness of their physique ... these are not the women of love but of lust ... such women as these are not we hope destined to be the daughters and wives of the future generations of Australians ...'

(slumps in his seat) We—incandesced, every time we touched one another ... she in her bath-robe of crimson towelling ... we rid ourselves of our clothes and then, at certain magical times, of our bodies as well ... the drapes drawn ... loving in noon darkness ... flying blind ... ecstatic levitations ... hawk-like soarings ... sweet, gentle descents.... soft landings on unknown fields ... we sailed, we voyaged, we rounded capes, we beached, climbed hills, leapt off cliffs, swam, sank, swirled—and there, as we lay together at five fathoms, was Dr. Grigsby standing at the door ... he was supposed to be lecturing on the beginnings of the novel and the rising middle classes ... (to Grigsby) you were very strong on the middle classes ... they were always coming up in your lectures ... whenever there was a painting or a play or a novel there they were, rising, rising ... (regaining thread) It is in *Leaves From Australian Forests* that we find Kendall's most sustained love lyric, an elegy, beautifully turned, passionately felt, in memory of his disappointed love for Rose Barnett—

> But Rose Lorraine—oh Rose Lorraine
> I'll whisper now where no one hears
> If you should chance to meet again
> The man you kissed in soft dead years...

(pause. Brief reverie. He wanders the stage a little, as if searching)

> If I that breathe your slow sweet name
> As one breathes low notes on a flute...

—Sylvia? Sylvia? (at Grigsby) You'd bided your time, ducked out of your lecture and slipped back to the house, leaving the rising middle classes suspended twenty feet in the air. You gave me fifteen minutes start then came after me, creeping down the sideway, sneaking in the back door ... insinuating yourself along the hallway, perhaps on all fours ... then you paused and no doubt you listened, you heard our noises as we drowned, then—then—you opened the door—slowly, and saw me trespassing in your garden, entangled on your floral bedspread—I saw you as if through water, you were there for only a second, an apparition, not looking, your eyes lowered as if the submarine light stung them—then you closed the door gently, for all the world like an intruding butler.

(regaining) Despite the efforts of the respectable to suggest the contrary, it was undoubtedly Rose Barnett that was Kendall's great love and not his wife Charlotte, who admittedly had much to contend with in living with so sensitive and wayward a man...

You closed the door quietly and discreetly, as if you'd discovered us both sound asleep ... you walked back to the university, where by now the wretched middle classes lay all over the grass like a crumpled balloon, you went to your office and—you rang my wife ... (as if quelling an interruption from Grigsby) yes—I don't deny it was all very upsetting—but ringing my wife was hardly the action of a person who's upset—it was a cold and calculated action, a cruel and deliberate action—but you calculated badly—it was just what Margaret wanted to hear, it proved once and for all that I was the worthless, faithless, degenerate creature she had always believed me to be ... so your strategy failed ... her contempt for me, your contempt for Sylvia drove us closer together, made us more hopeless, more desperate ... we promised you both that we'd never meet—and went on meeting!

(regaining) Kendall's eldest son wrote of him thus—'all Kendall's petulant excuses for his own lapses and failings, his unfortunate itch to throw upon his nearest and dearest the blame for his own faults, should not be taken as justified. His very action in living so long with his wife should help at least in part to cancel the shame of what he calls his irresponsible moments ...' We met in parks, in cars, in the basements of buildings, the flats of friends ... you tried another tactic. You used the last weapon you had—your children. You got leave from the university and you took them away from her ... she was torn between them and me, she was a woman halved, quartered ... to stop her being pulled apart, I let her go...

—nevertheless, Kendall's love for Rose Barnett was deep and abiding. The depth of his sorrow when his romance with her was finally broken haunts *Farewell*, one of his finest poems—

> *And part we thus? The spell is broken*
> *On thee my thoughts no more may dwell*
> *And all that now remains is spoken*
> *In this sad simple word Farewell.*

We meet no more! And thus shall perish
The dreams, the hopes that once were mine
And memory may not dare to cherish
One gentle look or smile of thine.

The saddest and the tenderest token
Of my despair words may not tell
For all—for all—

I gave her up ... you forced me out of her garden ... wounded, I crept into his (pointing to Kendall's picture) ... green dreams, flowered images ... and you—you pursued me even there—seeking the death-blow, you followed me ... you lured me out with an invitation, knowing that it was my own dark time ... she in another city ... my own now alien to me ... my wife's prickings and kickings ...

darkness descends on me ... attacks of nerves, depression, irritability ... bouts of drinking, incoherence at late afternoon lectures, a fall down the steps of the Arts Building ... to ensure my final humiliation before the academic world, you arrange to have me invited here today ... I take the bait, not realising it was your doing until it was too late ... hoping to regain my footing, longing to retrieve all, to plumb as it were the caverns of the imagination before an admiring audience of my peers ... a speleologist, that's what I'd be, exploring depths no one has yet ventured ... underground lakes, subterranean auroras, iridescent wall paintings ... the water's rising, but I would surface in time to applause, and tell of amazing discoveries ... the water's rising, threatening to cut me off ... the air growing more and more foul, dank, unbreathable ... (lights slowly down) the darkness closing in, my tugs on the rope going unanswered ... harder to breathe—darker—darker... Henry Kendall—his lamp, his lifeline to the real world, his poem entitled Beyond Kerguelen, the remotest island on earth, admired by Oscar Wilde ... extraordinary performance ... never be invited again ... time of darkness—no light and no tunnel ... signed his early works Henry Kendall NAP which stood for Native Australian Poet ... Sylvia? Sylvia?

(darkness)

Bruce Dawe   (1930–)

Poet. Born in Victoria; educated in Victoria and in Queensland where he now lives.

AND A GOOD FRIDAY WAS HAD BY ALL

You men there, keep those women back
and God Almighty he laid down
on the crossed timber and old Silenus
my offsider looked at me as if to say
nice work for soldiers, your mind's not your own
once you sign that dotted line Ave Caesar
and all that malarkey Imperator Rex

well this Nazarene
didn't make it any easier
really—not like the ones
who kick up a fuss so you can
do your block and take it out on them

                                   Silenus
held the spikes steady and I let fly
with the sledge-hammer, not looking
on the downswing trying hard not to hear
over the women's wailing the bones give way
the iron shocking the dumb wood.

Orders is orders, I said after it was over
nothing personal you understand—we had a
drill-sergeant once thought he was God but he wasn't
a patch on you

then we hauled on the ropes
and he rose in the hot air
like a diver just leaving the springboard, arms spread
so it seemed
over the whole damned creation
over the big men who must have had it in for him
and the curious ones who'll watch anything if it's free
with only the usual women caring anywhere
and a blind man in tears.

LIFE-CYCLE

for Big Jim Phelan

When children are born in Victoria
they are wrapped in the club-colours, laid in beribboned cots,
having already begun a lifetime's barracking.

Carn, they cry, Carn ... feebly at first
while parents playfully tussle with them
for possession of a rusk: Ah, he's a little Tiger! (And they are ...)

Hoisted shoulder-high at their first League game
they are like innocent monsters who have been years swimming
towards the daylight's roaring empyrean

Until, now, hearts shrapnelled with rapture,
they break surface and are forever lost,
their minds rippling out like streamers

In the pure flood of sound, they are scarfed with light, a voice
like the voice of God booms from the stands
Ooohh you bludger and the covenant is sealed.

Hot pies and potato-crisps they will eat,
they will forswear the Demons, cling to the Saints
and behold their team going up the ladder into Heaven,

And the tides of life will be the tides of the home-team's fortunes
—the reckless proposal after the one-point win,
the wedding and honeymoon after the grand-final ...

They will not grow old as those from more northern States grow
   old,
for them it will always be three-quarter-time
with the scores level and the wind advantage in the final term,

That passion persisting, like a race-memory, through the welter of
   seasons,
enabling old-timers by boundary-fences to dream of resurgent lions
and centaur-figures from the past to replenish continually the
   present,

So that mythology may be perpetually renewed
and Chicken Smallhorn return like the maize-god
in a thousand shapes, the dancers changing

But the dance forever the same—the elderly still
loyally crying Carn ... Carn ... (if feebly) unto the very end,
having seen in the six-foot recruit from Eaglehawk their hope of
   salvation.

OPEN INVITATION, OR
YOU TOO CAN HAVE A BODY POLITIC LIKE OURS
IF YOU'RE NOT CAREFUL!

Come unto me all ye who protest and are pamphlet-laden
and I will get you arrested why now
we can *all* be communists! No longer
is it necessary to read Marx and inwardly digest
—you too can be a communist-radical-dupe
by courtesy of the Traffic Act of 1949 ... Simplicity
itself! No more night-study of *Das Kapital*
and *On Guerilla Warfare* by their thongs
ye shall know them (not to mention their
ANTI-URANIUM T-shirts!) so don't think you can come here
hot from your Kremlin-sponsored pot-shops
and fill this lawful orderly Palatinate
with articles of dissent we know
your type from way back crawling
from the ubiquitous tertiary slime and the jungles of the Far North
and corrupted South into the light of our tourist-oriented
primeval day *Back back you monsters the Jurassic*
is 500 million years ahead Charles Darwin
you have just been given
a lawful direction and a thousand anti-evolutionists in the columns
                              of provincial newspapers
can't be wrong and as for you Herr Luther
your Ninety-five Theses on that church-door at Wittenberg
are in clear violation of the regulation requiring placards to be
no more than 610 square millimetres *and of cardboard* and I must
                                          warn you
that if you step off any city footpath objecting to
the selling of indulgences or yellow-cake
you will have graduated as fully-qualified
SCUM to appear in court on Monday morning
charged with watever we can think up in the meantime
So take your pick mate, either a quick thump in the ear a night in the
                    cells a fifty-dollar fine
                    and the democratic right to dissent
or a quiet night at home with the wife and kids and
                    watch it all happening to Thomas More
                    and Galileo in Sanyo-Colour
                    on the Six-O'Clock News—the choice
(as always in a democracy)
is YOURS!

Michael Dransfield (1948–1973)

Poet. Born and educated in Sydney.

BUMS' RUSH

Yea, is not even Apollo, with hair and harpstring of gold
A bitter God to follow, a beautiful God to behold.

Swinburne

Becoming an eskimo isnt hard once you must.
You start by going far away, perhaps another landmass,
into the jungle of cold air and make a room a cave a hole
in the surface with your axe. Furnish it simply like devils island
carve a ledge for effigies and another to sleep on.
Land of the midnight sun it keeps you awake turns ice walls blue
   there are blue
ice walls the effigies a bled white silhouette/
wrapt in a fur you try not to remember but its easier just to let go
and be re-tried re-convicted re-crucified after a few years you even
forget to bleed. Blue all year like a duke's veins
like her eyes might have been once
when she had eyes. Freezing to death is the cleanest place on earth.
And identity you need not concern yourself with names you are the
   last of your species.
The worst pain is the morphine blue crevasse and real eskimos
never mind that. Their hallucinations are red-etched norse demons
they etch those on stone make fifty copies and sell them at cape
   dorset.
In the early winter mornings
sometimes you will hear the snow winds blowing in on you
soon then you will become impatient as lost souls do
you will think you hear someone calling
when it comes to that all you need do is
take a last look at the effigy collection
say farewell to friends you may have made among the graven images
then walk as a human lemming would
out across the bay to where the ice is thinnest and let yourself
   vanish.

A DIFFICULT PATRIOTISM

In the gentle hours of night
she moves in the Vivaldi room
arranging cadences.

Candlesoft movements
elegance of a Bourdelle figure,
an Ile de France autumn—fractional
light in a beech spinney.

How well it is managed,
chiaroscuro of laudanum
piccolo lovemaking stonecraft.

"See Australia First"!
Dry Welsh tower at Moonta,
desolate miles, scattered
poems, forgotten heroes.

Europe lures away our idealists with
mythologies. Here to be different is agony
There it is natural. But this greatest country,

Australia, to leave it means
death to the spirit. We cannot
change it with our verses and kisses and years,
nor succumb. Perhaps evolve.

AND NO BIRD SINGS

the music is over
its time now
for silence, for
listening to the wind, the
rain.   say nothing,
that would be wrong, speaking
is words no more, is not poems.
humanity is ghosts and politics,
is hopeless sentiment.

its time now
to say nothing
time for the wind

time for the green pastures
the quiet waters

time for
Cain or a serpent
or a miracle

FRANK MOORHOUSE   (1938–)

Short story writer, script writer. Born in N.S.W.

THE COMMUNE DOES NOT WANT YOU

At the door of the commune I hesitated. What ectoplasmic shapes and indistinguishable bearded denim and mumbling cabalism throbbed here, Oh Lord.

I knocked. Do you knock at a commune door? (too unflowing? does it pre-empt their attention?) Do you just go in, affectionately, pacifically? Or is it by initiation?

A young man as fresh as a constable, no beard, came to the door, opened it and went back in.

'Hey,' I called, 'is this Milton's commune?'

'It's not *Milton's* commune, but he lives here, yes,' he said, over his shoulder.

'Is he in?' I asked the receding back but the man disappeared into a dark hole at the end of the hall.

Don't they have caution? I could be the enemy of the commune.

Any manners, residue of their middle class?

Any guidelines for the handling of callers?

I groped my way into the commune.

There appeared in the dim light, amid the raga music, to be a person in every room or the shape of a person. Were they the residents or were they callers? Or were they too answering the advertisement for the room? In a commune there is always this group sitting around the kitchen table reading or picking at themselves, toes or noses, drinking tea, and you don't know if any of them live there or whether you can sit in that chair or is that Big Paddy's chair or is that where Papa Milton always sits.

I'm too dressed. I reprimand my bow tie with a twist, a yank.

No one looks up when I come in. Nose picking leads to brain damage.

'Hullo there.'

Someone dragged snot a mile along their nasal passage.

They have their heads down, reading upside down newspaper wrapping or the labels on packets, drinking tea from enamel army mugs.

'Is Milton in?'

'I think he's in his room.'

I could not see who said this. I could not, for the life of me, see their lips move.

'Which is his room?'

'Just bang on the wall and shout.'

I was not going to bang on the wall and shout.

'I think he's with some chick,' someone else said, although again I saw no lips move.

I moved into the other room. It was not so much that I moved, more that the unreceptivity poked me out through a huge circular hole in the wall into yet another even darker room. They had knocked this huge circular hole in the wall, leaving rubble. I sat down on a lopsided bean bag chair, keeping one of my legs outriggered so that I wouldn't fall over. The beans always move away from me. A pig squealed out from somewhere in the chair. A pig. From under me.

In the dimness I saw a girl with long suffocating hair about her face—personality concealment—who said, 'Come here Pushkin, did the nasty man sit upon you.'

'It wasn't my intention,' I told her, 'I like ... animals ... pigs.'

'Do you have a pig?' she asked.

'I did have a cat but it decamped. It went away. Greener pastures.'

'Cats only do that to people who ill-treat them.'

'Oh no—it just went away.'

'You must have ill-treated it.'

'No, cats just go sometimes—for personal reasons.'

'That's the only reason they run away—ill-treatment.'

'No, I like animals. I used to talk to the cat. Shaw said cats like a good conversation but you must speak slowly.'

'You hurt Pushkin.'

'I didn't mean to hurt Pushkin. I want to see Milton. About the vacant room. Is he with a chick?'

'Don't use the word "chick" with me if you want a reply.'

But. I was going to say to her that I never use the word but that it had hopped onto my tongue from the other room, from the Kitchen Klatsch, but oh well, I let it go.

'The herbs look good—the watercress is growing well.'

'Anyone can grow watercress.'

I was going to tell her that in the story *The Girl Who Met Simone de Beauvoir in Paris* the male in the story is based on me. That I have, despite my use of the word chick, agonised on the questions of liberation. I am imperfectly liberated, that's true, I wanted to reconstruct but parts were missing. Maybe they could be imported.

I told her instead that I went to a commune once in Phoenix, Arizona, where everyone was smoking dope and I was drinking Lone Star Beer and they had a pet Red Indian who noticed this and came over to me and said, Wow man, you drinking Lone Star Beer, give me some man, I love beer, I can't smoke this shit, where you from. I told him from Australia and he said he'd heard great things about Australia, like everyone drinks. I said yes everyone drinks, almost everyone. He said that sounded like the place for him.

At first she made no comment.

Then she said, 'Do you always talk so much—you're not a very "still" person are you? And I suppose that was meant to be a put down of dope.'

How long, I thought, how long should I give Milton if he's with a girl.

'How is the commune coming along?' I asked, ploughing on with courtesy.

'Look man, this is a house we all share. If you want to call it a commune you call it a commune, but for us it is a simple experiment in shared living with a polyfunctional endospace.'

Ah!! So that explains the knocked down walls, the huge circular holes.

I had been told that, as for sharing, it was Milton who paid.

'Why do you wear a bow tie?'

'Oh that,' I looked down, as if it had grown there unnoticed by me, 'Oh ... a bit of a lark ... a bit of a giggle ... a bit of scream ... a sort of a joke.'

She seemed to be staring at me severely.

I stumbled on, 'Oh, about clothes—I don't give a damn. A lark. Dress never worries me. I've got some jeans at home actually.'

'Pity,' she said, 'I thought for a moment we'd have one male here who presented himself. Men think that caring about clothing is female. And therefore beneath consideration. See, sloppiness is another put down of women. Dress for me is a way of speaking.'

'I like the idea of a sharing experience,' I said, 'learning to share Milton's money.'

'I find that offensive,' she said.

'Oh come now,' I said, 'it was a joke. I lived with Milton before—in the Gatsby House and he paid then. He paid for the jazz bands on the lawn, everything. I mean it wasn't a moral statement. Far be it from me ...'

'I didn't know Milton then,' she said. She was, I could tell, not interested in knowing about anything which happened before her existence. She was not interested.

I don't blame her.

I began to stare at my hands, which an interviewer once said were 'nervous'.

Then I thought of something chatty to say, knowing about brown rice and communes and such, 'In Chinese restaurants it was always sophisticated to order boiled rice instead of fried rice. I always liked fried rice best but ordered boiled to be correct. Now I read Ted Moloney and he says ordering fried rice is quite acceptable and doesn't offend Chinese chefs.'

Again she made no comment. I think she was being 'still'.

She spoke, 'I don't find that in any way interesting—getting hung-up about sophistication and all that.'

'But I thought it showed ... never mind ... have you read the latest *Rolling Stone*?' I asked.

'I don't read newspapers,' she said.

'Oh, I read every newspaper.'

'You must have a very messed up head.'

'I read the manifest content and I read the non-manifest content. I read the archetypes, osmotypes and the leadertypes. I see the ideological meaning and the unintended information.'

'I don't read any newspapers,' she repeated.

'Oh, I guess I really just read the manifest content. I've pretty much given up classifying news into Merry Tales, Fairy Tales, Animal Tales, Migratory Legends, Cosmogonic Legends and such. I don't do that much now.'

'I'm a dancer.'

'Oh yes?'

'I'm learning Theatre of the Noh.'

'It's a rich world—I'm learning Theatre of the Maybe Not.'

'Is that some sort of put down?'

'I wonder if he's finished yet,' I said, nodding upwards, leaning across and stroking the ... pig.

'Do you know Lance Ferguson?' she asked.

'No.'

'Do you know Sheena Petrie?'

'No.'

'Are you Australian?'

'Of course, from Sydney.'

'Strange that you don't know anyone.'

'I know *some* people.'

'Where do you live?'

'Here, here in Balmain.'

'No ...!!'

'Yep—for ten years or more.'

'Incredible, and you don't know Lance Ferguson or Sheena Petrie?'

'Never heard of them.'

'Wow,' she shook her head to herself and made a coughing laugh, 'oh wow—you must live in a hole in the ground or something.'

'I guess,' I said glumly, 'they're Milton's new scene—I'm from his first scene.'

'And you say you know Milton?'

'Yes, of course.'

'You mustn't know him very well if you don't know Lance Ferguson or Sheena Petrie.'

'Ten years—I've known him for ten years. He was my closet friend, I mean closest friend. I haven't seen him for a few months.'

'Are you part of the Balmain Bourgeoisie?'

'No. Not part of the Balmain Bourgeoisie.'

'Who do you know?'

'Adrian Heber.'

'He's a spy. Everyone knows Adrian Heber.'

'He's not a spy.'

'Sheena won't believe this when I tell her.'

'I wonder if Milton's finished yet.'

I heard a lavatory flush. 'Maybe that's him,' I said.

'No, that's Harvey.'

'How do you know?'

'He has a weak bladder.'

I stare at my nervous hands again.

'I have no problems like that,' I reassure her.

Then I said, 'Perhaps I should go up or something.'

She then left the room, without saying where she was going, but she took the pig with her—as if I couldn't be trusted with it.

I fancied that I could still hear the bed squeaking above me.

I looked through the huge circular hole in the wall at the people still sitting around the kitchen table, picking at themselves. Nose picking can lead to brain damage.

I gave up. I went to the wall and banged and shouted, 'Milton!' No one answered.

I went back into the dim endospace and fought my way onto the bean bag chair.

'You!!' an imperious voice came from the ceiling and, looking up, I saw a hitherto unnoticed manhole-sized hole. A girl, not the girl with the pig, but a girl dressed as far as I could see, in only a man's shirt was crouched there.

It occurred to me that I may have been watched the whole time— by the Commune Committee.

'Here's a note from Milton and your book back,' she called, and dropped a note wrapped around a stone, and a book.

The note read: 'Go away. The commune does not want you.'

The book he returned was Oliver Schreiner's *Stories, Dreams and Allegories*.

'Did he like it?' I asked, trying to point attention away from the wounding note.

'He said he didn't open it. If you gave it to him he said, it must have had a malign intent. A way of spooking his equilibrium.'

Scratching his duco.

'He said that applying for the room under the name Buck Fuller was not considered a good joke by the commune and the commune was not fooled.'

And the commune did not laugh.

'Are you Sheena Petrie?'

'No.'

'Do you know her?'

'Of course. Everyone knows Sheena. She's Milton's best friend.'

'Is there a commune for people who do not fit very well into communes? Could you advise me?'

'I was instructed not to talk with you any further. You must go now.'

Antigone Kefala

Poet. Born in Roumania; educated in New Zealand; came to
Sydney in the sixties.

THE PEANUT VENDOR

You see them leaning out of gates
their faces bored on Sunday afternoons
their eyes living past landscapes.
Newcomers from old countries.
The one I see each night catching the 9 o'clock.
Dark, stocky, with two beady eyes; wan now,
spare weathered face, stump of a hand,
a basket full of peanuts.

The ancient quays at home have forged him patiently
for years, so deeply and so well, that as he walks,
bow-legged, the tables sprout around him, and the sea
familiar and deceptive in the glass like silence of
the light, and everywhere, uncoiling in the air,
the plaintive voices of amanedes.

Yet if one spoke to him in parks, of home,
his eyes would flicker for a moment only,
past the accumulated tiredness of years,
refusing to be lured, suspicious.

The owner dead. The one who did possess in his
own youth the secret of the living bird,
and could have made it fly,
breathtakingly, blue nerve and sunlight.

HERAKLION

Silver blue honey
the sea
the man kept dipping his oars
in the silence.

Past the old fort
the fishermen mending their nets
debris of cork on the stone.

The sea, strolled with us
a friend at our elbow
in the evening that
was raining alabaster dust
on the waters.

JUDITH RODRIGUEZ   (1936–   )

Poet, short story writer. Born in Perth; educated in Brisbane.

NU-PLASTIK FANFARE RED

I declare myself:
I am painting my room red.
Because they haven't any
flat red suitable for interiors,
because their acres of colour-card
are snowy with daylight only,
because it will look like Danger! Explosives,
or would you prefer a basement cabaret?
a decent home where Italians moved in,
Como perhaps (yes, I've gilded the mirror)
or simply infernal—

I rejoice to be doing it
with quick-drying plastic,
for small area decoration.
I tear at the wall, brush speeding:
let's expand this limited stuff!
It dries impetuously in patches,
I at edges too late scrub; this is a fight.
I sought the conditions,
and the unbroken wall is yet to come.
Clear stretches screech into clots,
streak into smokiness.
Botched job this, my instant
hell! and no re-sale value, Dad;
cliché too. Well, too bad.

It's satisfying to note
this mix is right for pottery.
(Good glad shock of seeing
that red-figure vases *are*.
Not 4th-edition-earthy, but stab-colour,
new-vine, red-Attis-flower, the full howl.)
My inward amphora!

Even thus shyly to surface:
up we go red, flag-balloon,
broomstick-rocket!
Brandishing blood and fire, pumping
lungs external as leaves!
This is a red land, sour
with blood it has not shed,
money not lost, risks evaded,

blood it has forgotten, dried
in furnace airs that vainly
figure (since mines are doing well)
the fire. Torpor
of a disallowed abortion.

Why not a red room?

FAMILY

In my mother's family
we have no ancestors
only the long silence
between pogroms.

In my father's family
we have little tradition—
lands, legends, powers
passed us by.

In my country
we have no grandparents
no continuing song
no dances. Silence

feeds music,
father's our legend.
Husband and wife, estuary
into a continent,

we open our arms:
touch peaks, touch breakers.
Forest and white water
our children dance.

GEOFFREY LEHMANN   (1940–)

Poet. Born and educated in Sydney.

THE EMPEROR CLAUDIUS

(as Tacitus would have had him speak)

I sometimes wonder if I am a man
Or a good-natured shadow. People think
I do not care that ex-slaves run my empire.

Such things in fact cause me much guilt and worry.
I often brood when in my bath, but mostly
What worries me is that I do not worry.

Some weeks ago, though, when they told me
That Silius and my wife had just got married,
Mind you, with public contract, feast and all,
And that imperial treasures holus bolus
Were used as decorations in his household,
Well that was just too much—even for me!

A glorious gust of anger filled me. Yes!
I raged! My face flushed darkly and I shook—
Or so they tell me—then my fury vanished
After a pleasant dinner and some wine.

Ah, could I feel again that beautiful anger!
I crave some unimaginable infamy
Or foulness, some unspeakable disaster,
So that my rage might last a week or fortnight!

THE SONG OF THE HOUSE

Blue gas-rings burning in the darkened kitchen.
As figures move in doorways, shadows cross
Rectangles of light flung on lawns. Floors creak.
My mother reads in bed, spectacles on nose,
(A brief glimpse through some double glass-paned doors)
And on a couch, lights on, my father dozes,
Hands clasped, face baked with the red glaze of age,
Deeply inert features of fired porcelain.
My desk-lamp spotlights foliage, cricket songs wobble,
Air shifts through windows, barely perceptible,
And an autumn coolness prowls around the house.

This is a song of love for childhood's house,
Galvanized roof crouched low beneath the night
Of bright stars flashing rapid messages,
Dim plankton of remoter galaxies,
Leaves of black glass and yellow juicy moons.

David Lake(1929–)

Poet. Born in India, educated there and at Cambridge; lives in Australia.

TO HORACE

"How sweet and fit, for fatherland to die—"
Your bland official voice,
Horace, charms half-truth to a double lie
That still bemuses boys.

It's not (to start with) pure self-sacrifice
That's laid down in the drill:
In Father Caesar's service that's a vice—
True Virtue means to kill.

And, come to that, it's never sweet to fall
With metal in your guts:
It smells, and hurts—sweeter far from it all
To tumble girls in huts;

For fathering the country, fitter too,
Since Nature made that wound
And tooled the weapon fittingly, as you,
Friend Horace, must have found

After you dropped all causes with your shield
And sensibly kept warm
With loyal odes far from Philippi's field
On your snug Sabine farm

Where you sincerely celebrated wine,
Love, fireside—as to war,
You praised the patriotic death divine
And broached another jar.

Geoff Page   (1940–)

Poet. Born and educated in N.S.W.; lives in Canberra.

SMALLTOWN MEMORIALS

No matter how small
Every town has one;
Maybe just the obelisk,
A few names inlaid;

More often full-scale granite,
Marble digger (arms reversed),
Long descending lists of dead:
Sometimes not even a town,
A thickening of houses
Or a few unlikely trees
Glimpsed on a back road
Will have one.

1919, 1920:
All over the country;
Maybe a band, slow march;
Mayors, shire councils;
Relatives for whom
Print was already
Only print; mates,
Come back, moving
Into unexpected days;

A ring of Fords and sulkies;
The toned-down bit
Of Billy Hughes from an
Ex-recruiting sergeant.
Unveiled;
Then seen each day—
Noticed once a year;
And then not always,
Everywhere.

The next bequeathed us
Parks and pools

But something in that first
Demanded stone.

BONDI AFTERNOON 1915

Elioth Gruner

The wind plays through
the painted weather.

No cloud. The sea
and air, one blue.

A hemisphere
away from gunfire

an artist finds
his image for the year:

a girl in white
blown muslin, walking

in the last
clear afternoon.

STREETON

An afternoon of 1890 summer
shades away through blue—
range haze to
paler smoke, then air.

Closer in, three parasols
pause to someone's call,
smile back, then fall
from view

below a line of grass.
The middle ground is sparse
with trees—light strokes imply
the claims of fences.

River sand slopes down
to pools
that lift away through brown
and back to blue.

Drying in
the studio, the afternoon is thin
with distance—moving out already
two ways into time.

ANDREW TAYLOR   (1940–)

Poet. Born and educated in Victoria; lives in South Australia.

DEVELOPING A WIFE

In the one cool room in the house
he held her face two inches under the water
rocking it ever so gently
ever so gently. Her smile
of two hours earlier came back to him
dimly at first through the water, then with more
boldness and more clarity.

The world is too much with us
on a hot day (he thought); better
this kind of drowning into a new degree,
a fraction of a second infinitely
protracted into purity. Her smile
free now of chemical and the perverse
alchemy of heat dust and destroying wind
free from the irritation, the tears
and the anger that had finally driven him
down to this moment,
was perfect, was
irreversible, a new reality.
Is it, he thought, that there is truth
here which she imperfectly embodies?
Or is it I that I'm developing here—
my dream, my vision of her,
my sleight of hand?
Perhaps, he thought, our marriage is like this?—
flimsy, unreal, but in its own way real:
a moment, a perfection glimpsed, then gone, gone utterly,
yet caught all the same, our axis, stationary,
the other side of drowning?
                              He bore
her smile out in the heat to her, as a gift.

NORWINCH SLEEPING

For reasons known
only to itself
(maybe to Konrad Lorenz)
my cat has described a perfect circle
and is sleeping within it
like an animal scone
like half an orange 11 inches in diameter
like the knitted top of a head

usually when it's sleeping it twitches
stalking birds
down the long slanting
lawns of a dream
or its ears listen to what I say

not today
it's beyond us now
its animal geometry
a feline planet
it can be anything or nothing

not even its name washes ashore
if I touch it
it makes a noise like the sea

PROLOGUE

My new arm measures its season
by the white watch mark at the wrist.
Already, without reason,
the weather like an alchemist
turns into gold the matter of my arm,
tracing the shape of time across the bone.

JOHN GRIFFIN   (1935–)

Poet. Born and educated in South Australia.

THE PASSAGE TO THE CAPE

A voyage equally prosperous. William Brown,
drowned on passage from Exeter to Hell,
would disagree. Nothing remarkable
occurred. So Tench, terse, having with buoy

and boat on human salvage sped,
waited the squally day; with faded quill
he traced delight, like aching whispers,
on his jaw. And wondered for the words

to tell of William Brown's last thresh
of air, his gulp of seeming buckets full
of sea. Nothing remarkable. Then dysentery,
but in no instance mortal; its cause unknown.

THE DARLING JUNCTION

Turbid, the taste of decay; even,
from grassy bank and trees, an English scene,
except the blacks, where the lizard tongue
of land eased the rivers along

to their melting. At first, bundled now
in one channel, they flowed apart.
Thin and clear on sand, the Murray ran.
The Darling, deeper, thrust its turbidity

beside. Two meeting streams must merge.
M'Leay, death with an old tin kettle,
and Sturt, earnest, no comprehension
in terms not born of himself, moved on

in the muddy flow. A mile or so
(or measure in decades) the thin stream,
so clear on its beds of sand, was lost
in the sweet flood with the taste of decay.

Michael Wilding   (1942–)

Short story writer, novelist, critic, editor. Born in England;
educated at Oxford; Reader in English at Sydney University.

ANOTHER DAY ON A SELECTION

The cleaning lady came in today when I was making myself some
toast in the kitchen. I had already thrown away two pieces that had
got burnt when I started trying to do something else. Sometimes
when it is late in the morning and I think I should have got up
earlier and done more things, I try and do everything together and
fuck it all up. And there is no reason why I should have got up
earlier, or at all. The only reasons are those residual guilts about not
getting up early. I try and face them. To get up at dawn is to limit
yourself to the daylight hours and fall asleep at sunset. And then
you miss all the pleasures of the night. The owls and the foxes and
the flying foxes and the hedgehogs. They of course miss the pleasures of the day. I prefer to be an amphibian of day and night; so
you get up around about eleven and you have round about seven or
eight hours of daylight and then you have round about seven or
eight hours of night and then you go to bed round about one or
two. That is my theory. I do not announce it to the cleaning lady.
Suddenly to announce it as I scrape the burnt bits off my toast might
look defensive. Though just her arriving there makes me feel defensive, as if I should have been up and eaten breakfast hours ago.
Perhaps I was, and this is just a mid-morning snack. How is she to
know otherwise? How can I communicate that to her in body lan-

guage that answers the body language of her disapproval? And why do we have a cleaning lady, that makes me feel bad too? Why couldn't we clean our own kitchen?

I could see the processes gone through; there is no reason why women should be expected to do the cleaning; however we do not want to have a roster, we are not living in a military camp; however if the cleaning is left to good will and spontaneous activity and me or Nick or Klip, the women will end up doing it, so to avoid that, since no one enjoys doing it, a cleaning lady is hired. But these problems of consciousness lead us into worse situations; now we are employers and exploiters; and it is still a woman who does the cleaning, and calling her a cleaning person doesn't alter that fact; it just obscures it.

And I feel her different consciousness, she lives by a different system than ours which she probably wouldn't call a system, and I can see why, given all the burnt toast, about which she is already communicating a distaste, for the waste of burnt bread, for the carelessness in burning bread, slice after fucking slice, for still making toast so late in the morning, and making it badly. I sit there spreading honey. I like honey. I am not convinced that it is not especially good for you. Though I wouldn't mind if it wasn't. Most things aren't. And I like it. And many of the other things too.

I feel I am spreading it on too thickly from the way she turns from the sink to watch me spreading it. Why shouldn't I spread it as thick as I like? Why do I have to worry about how I spread it? Why do I have to worry whether it should be thick or thickly? The sink is a disgusting mess. I feel guilty about that. Though why should I, why should I feel guilty just because the sink has all this water in it and plates and pots and pans and glasses just lying in it? What does it matter? It isn't breeding mosquitoes. It is too greasy for that.

But I feel bad about it, I feel this sensation somewhere between nausea and revulsion and despair; I feel like going away and starting a new sink somewhere with new pots and pans and glasses. I think in this aspect I am a natural nomad.

I worry that we should have cleaned it up before she came. Isn't that what you do for cleaning ladies, so as not to disgust and appal them, since everyone else's house they visit to clean has been cleaned up for them before they get there? And who else would leave all that washing up?

'Been having a party?' she says, indicating the empty flagons and the beer cans.

I do not know whether to say No to assure her we are not the sort of noisy disruptive people who have parties and disturb the neighbourhood; or Yes so she won't think we drink that amount normally. The truth is probably both, we are the sort of noisy disruptive people who have parties and we do drink that amount occasionally. Occasionally to both, parties and drinking. Bobbie's homecoming was in a way a party: though we didn't drink that much more than we'd normally drink. What anyway is our normality? Why should it have to be acceptable to her? Maybe the bottles and cans and flagons have just sort of accreted over the course of time and never been cleared away. That wouldn't make her any happier if I told her that either.

'That house on the hill,' she said, 'they seem to have one continual party.'

'Which house is that?' I ask.

Licking my figers and trying to clean up the toast crumbs that have spread out beyond the perimeter of the plate.

She describes it to me. All the wild magnolia growing over it.

'The goings on there,' she says.

'Really.'

Her back to me, her arms in the soapy water sorting out the washing up. She is stout and wears an apron.

I am curious about the goings on. I feel I shouldn't ask, to ask is to betray the people in the house on the hill, to draw them into a gossip circuit, to aid the censuring of them, to validate all the shoulds and shouldn'ts, which are words I prefer to leave in The Oxford English Dictionary on Historical Principles, though wouldn't want eliminated altogether. Those ignorant of their history are condemned to repeat it.

'Drinking and all those drugs and in and out of each other's beds all the time.'

I want to know, I am curious, I am excited, sure I would rather the people in the house on the hill had told us themselves, invited us up maybe, but they haven't so—

They wear flowing dresses and sarongs and beads and sit on their verandah smoking dope. They have an air of sultry, pollen-laden sensuality about them, with the magnolia, and the hibiscus, and the honeysuckle, and the jasmine: draping the gateway, twining up the chimney stack and curling along the roof.

A terrible fire trap.

Clean leaves out of your guttering, cut creepers and dry grass clear of the house.

I have no need to ask her. My feeling of guilt at asking is purely optional, there for me to experience if I need it. She will tell me without any asking, as long as I sit there, eating my toast or licking up crumbs or just playing with the knife, as long as I indicate I am there with ears.

I am.

Maybe I should get up and go away, that way the gossip will be halted. But to get up and go away as soon as she comes in, that would be rude. And the gossip is spreading anyway, I am merely ears that hear it, I am not going to be relaying it. Unless it is very exciting; in which case I'll be telling Lily and Bobbie and Rose and

Nick and Klip and Sky-High. But until I hear it, I will not know whether it is exciting.

'Four at a time, I've seen them, all in the same bed. I suppose they think that was just ordinary, the way they don't worry about someone coming in and seeing them. No doubt at nights there'd be six or eight of them crawling all over each other. It isn't right, you know. It's upsetting for the old folk. And the children. I wouldn't let a child of mine near there. No knowing what might become of them. And the drugs. Growing it in their back yard. And picking mushrooms, as brazen as could be. No shame at all. They walk about naked as the lord created them. Men and women. Touching each other. I've seen it. It's not like they're even nudists and just walk around naked and disregard each other. Touching everything like you wouldn't believe. And the sheets.'

I hear something moving on the verandah. I hope it is not Lily walking through naked. Or Bobbie smoking a joint. I would love to see Lily walk through naked into my arms. But not at this moment. I wouldn't mind a smoke either. But not just now.

And these my joys and pleasures and I am hoping they will not materialise.

'People won't stand for those sorts of goings on,' she said. 'They had all their windows smashed the other night and red paint thrown over that old van they drive.'

'People feel as strongly as that about them?' I said, for some reason, feeling something had to be said.

'Strongly?' she said. 'I should think so and so they should. That isn't anything yet, you mark my words. I wouldn't be surprised if they found themselves burned down one night.'

Like the university regiment.

'Really,' I said. It didn't seem what I was expected to say. Just something I learned over in England. I think she would have liked something stronger. The only other choice was 'Heavens,' and that didn't sound especially right either. So I said 'Really' and then I left the kitchen, trying to indicate by my body stance I was off to do some work, I had merely stopped for a mid-morning snack.

I thought of lying in my hammock on the verandah, but she would be out there eventually and find me. I thought of wandering through the meadow looking for mushrooms, but she would see me through the windows. I walked down to the beach. Lily was making sandcastles with Roo. Bobbie and Nick were reading. Rose was lying on her back with her arm over her eyes to keep the sun out.

Bobbie looked up.

'You finished?' she said. 'We thought we'd all come down here so you could get some work done.'

'I couldn't do anything with the cleaning lady.'

'Oh God,' said Bobbie. Bobbie believes in work more than she believes in God.

'Oh God' from Bobbie wasn't especially right for the occasion. I would have liked something stronger. 'No,' I said, 'it wasn't just that she was there, she was freaking me out telling me about the Goings On in this house up the hill and how the locals had been throwing stones through their windows and paint over their combivan and are going to end up burning it down.'

'Oh God,' said Bobbie.

The country.

Heavy.

'Which house?' Nick said.

'The house wasn't the point, the point was us; like everything was directed at Goings On.'

'Orgies,' said Rose.

'Yes,' I said.

'You just have a guilty conscience,' Rose said.

'What at?' said Bobbie.

'Leaving us out for a start,' Rose said.

'But which was the other house?' Nick said, 'there aren't any other houses.'

'It's an old cottage with magnolia all over its roof and honeysuckle over the gate and it's on the track going up the hill.'

'It sounds beautiful,' said Lily.

'I've never seen it,' said Nick.

'Well she ought to know if she lives here,' said Bobbie.

'Who?' said Lily.

'The cleaning lady.'

'What cleaning lady?'

'The one that stopped me working,' I said.

'What are you talking about?' said Lily, 'we don't have a cleaning lady, do we?'

'I thought you must have got one while I was away,' said Bobbie.

'Why would we want a cleaning lady? How would we pay for one? Where would we get one from?' said Lily.

'Shit,' said Nick.

ROBERT ADAMSON   (1944–)

Poet. Born in Sydney.

THE RIVER

A *step is taken*, and all the world's before me.
Night so clear,

stars hang in the low branches,
small-fires, riding waves of thin atmosphere,

islands parting tide as meteors burn air.

Oysters powder to chalk in my hands.

A flying fox collides against my trunk
as the first memory unfurls.

Rocks on the shoreline milling the star-fire,
and each extinguished star,

an angel set free from the tide's long drive.

The memory shines—its fragments falling into place,
and the heavens revealing themselves

as my roots trail, deep nets
between channel and shoal, gathering in

cosmic spinel, Milky Way, Gemini.

I look all about; God, I search all around me.

She surrounds me here
as the light transfigures light

the butterfly exploding herself, colours thrown over
the nets of lights in transfiguration.

The sea's adrift, tails outspread, the harbour dawn.
A gale in my hair as mountains move in.

I drift over lake, through surf-break
and valley. Shifting before me

another place. *On the edge or place inverted
from Ocean starts another place,*

before me—entangled of trees, unseemly
in this time, this place.

Humming nerves of the tide, the eels
twine themselves round, loop and flick

glow through valleys of silt, rise breaking surface,
twisting light, dislodging

memory from its original lineaments.

Tonight time is its own universe, shining in mangroves
through opaque leaves, bodies, plumage

and hands across tide.
The old fear returns through the monument of a fishbone,

and wings of an ice bird waving from rockface
with hardly an instinct.

A step back and my love's before me,
life shot through with these savage changes.

The memory ash—we face each other alone now
with no God to answer to.

After centuries, almost together now
the threshold in sight.

We turn in the rushing tide again and again to each other,
making fire of this, and setting it

here between swamp-flower and star.

To let love go forth to the world's end,
to set our lives in the Centre.

Though the tide turns the river back on itself,
and at its mouth, Ocean.

MURRAY BAIL   (1941–)

Short story writer, novelist. Born in Adelaide.

THE DROVER'S WIFE

The Drover's Wife (1945)

There has perhaps been a mistake—but of no great importance—made in the denomination of this picture. The woman depicted is not "The Drover's Wife". She is my wife. We have not seen each other now ... it must be getting on thirty years. This portrait was painted shortly after she left—and had joined him. Notice she has very conveniently hidden her wedding hand. It is a canvas 20 × 24 inches, signed 1/r "Russell Drysdale".

I say "shortly after" because she has our small suitcase—Drysdale has made it look like a shopping bag—and she is wearing the sandshoes she normally wore to the beach. Besides, it is dated 1945.

It is Hazel alright.

How much can you tell by a face? That a woman has left a husband and two children? Here, I think the artist has fallen down (though how was he to know?). He has Hazel with a resigned helpless expression—as if it was all my fault. Or, as if she had been a country woman all her ruddy life.

Otherwise the likeness is fair enough.

Hazel was large-boned. Our last argument I remember concerned her weight. She weighed—I have the figures—12st. 4 ozs. And she wasn't exactly tall. I see that she put it back on almost immediately. It doesn't take long. See her legs.

She had a small, pretty face, I'll give her that. I was always surprised by her eyes. How solemn they were. The painting shows that. Overall, a gentle face, one that other women liked. How long it must have lasted up in the drought conditions is anybody's guess.

A drover! Why a drover? It has come as a shock to me.

"I am just going round the corner," she wrote, characteristically. It was a piece of butcher's paper left on the table.

Then, and this sounded odd at the time: "Your tea's in the oven. Don't give Trev any carrots."

Now that sounded as if she wouldn't be back, but after puzzling over it, I dimissed it.

And I think that is what hurt me most. No "Dear" at the top, not even "Gordon". No "love" at the bottom. Hazel left without so much as a goodbye. We could have talked it over.

Adelaide is a small town. People soon got to know. They ... shied away. I was left alone to bring up Trevor and Kay. It took a long time—years—before, if asked, I could say: "She vamoosed. I haven't got a clue to where."

Fancy coming across her in a painting, one reproduced in colour at that. I suppose in a way that makes Hazel famous.

The picture gives little away though. It is the outback—but where exactly? South Australia? It could easily be Queensland, West Australia, the Northern Territory. We don't know. You could never find that spot.

He is bending over (feeding?) the horse, so it is around dusk. This is borne out by the length of Hazel's shadow. It is probably in the region of 5 p.m. Probably still over the hundred mark. What a place to spend the night. The silence would have already begun.

Hazel looks unhappy. I can see she is having second thoughts. Alright, it was soon after she had left me; but she is standing away, in the foreground, as though they're not speaking. See that? Distance = doubts. They've had an argument.

Of course, I want to know all about him. I don't even know his name. In Drysdale's picture he is a silhouette. A completely black figure. He could have been an Aborigine; by the late forties I understand some were employed as drovers.

But I rejected that.

I took a magnifying glass. I wanted to see the expression on his face. What colour is his hair? Magnified, he is nothing but brush strokes. A real mystery man.

It is my opinion, however, that he is a small character. See his size in relation to the horse, to the wheels of the cart. Either that, or it is a ruddy big horse.

It begins to fall into place.

I had an argument with our youngest, Kay, the other day. Both she and Trevor sometimes visit me. I might add, she hasn't married and has her mother's general build. She was blaming me, said people said mum was a good sort.

Right. I nodded.

"Then why did she scoot?"

"Your mother," I said thinking quickly, "had a silly streak."

If looks could kill!

I searched around—"She liked to paddle in water!"

Kay gave a nasty laugh, "What? You're the limit. You really are."

Of course, I hadn't explained properly. And I didn't even know then she had gone off with a drover.

Hazel was basically shy, even with me: quiet, generally non-committal. At the same time, I can imagine her allowing herself to be painted so soon after running off without leaving even a phone number or forwarding address. It fits. It sounds funny, but it does.

This silly streak. Heavy snow covered Mt. Barker for the first time and we took the Austin up on the Sunday. From a visual point of view it was certainly remarkable. Our gum trees and stringy barks somehow do not go with the white stuff, not even the old Ghost Gum. I mentioned this to Hazel but she just ran into it and began chucking snowballs at me. People were laughing. Then she fell in up to her knees, squawking like a schoolgirl. I didn't mean to speak harshly, but I went up to her, "Come on, don't be stupid. Get up." She went very quiet. She didn't speak for hours.

Kay of course wouldn't remember that.

With the benefit of hindsight, and looking at this portrait by Drysdale, I can see Hazel had a soft side. I think I let her clumsiness get me down. The sight of sweat patches under her arms, for example, somehow put me in a bad mood. It irritated me the way she chopped wood. I think she enjoyed chopping wood. There was the time I caught her lugging into the house the ice for the ice chest— this is just after the war. The ice man didn't seem to notice; he was following, working out his change. It somehow made her less attractive in my eyes, I don't know why. And then of course she killed that snake down at the beach shack we took one Christmas. I happened to lift the lid of the incinerator—a black brute, its head bashed in. "It was under the house," she explained.

It was a two-roomed shack, bare floorboards. It had a primus stove, and an asbestos toilet down the back. Hazel didn't mind. Quite the contrary; when it came time to leave she was downcast. I had to be at town for work.

The picture reminds me. It was around then Hazel took to wearing just a slip around the house. And bare feet. The dress in the picture looks like a slip. She even used to burn rubbish in it down the back.

I don't know.

"Hello, missus!" I used to say, entering the kitchen. Not perfect perhaps, especially by today's standards, but that is my way of showing affection. I think Hazel understood. Sometimes I could see she was touched.

I mention that to illustrate our marriage was not all nit-picking and argument. When I realized she had gone I sat for nights in the lounge with the lights out. I am a dentist. You can't have shaking hands and be a dentist. The word passed around. Only now, touch wood, has the practice picked up to any extent.

Does this explain at all why she left?

Not really.

To return to the picture. Drysdale has left out the flies. No doubt he didn't want Hazel waving her hand, or them crawling over her face. Nevertheless, this is a serious omission. It is altering the truth for the sake of a pretty picture, or "composition". I've been up around there—and there are hundreds of flies. Not necessarily germ carriers, "bush flies" I think these are called; and they drive you mad. Hazel of course accepted everything without a song and dance. She didn't mind the heat, or the flies.

It was a camping holiday. We had one of those striped beach tents shaped like a bell. I thought at the time it would prove handy— visible from the air—if we got lost. Now that is a point. Although I will never forget the colours and the assortment of rocks I saw up there I have no desire to return, none. I realized one night. Standing a few yards from the tent, the cavernous sky and the silence all round suddenly made me shudder. I felt lost. It defied logic. And during the day the bush, which is small and prickly, offered no help (I was going to say "sympathy"). It was stinking hot.

Yet Hazel was in her element, so much so she seemed to take no interest in the surroundings. She acted as if she were part of it. I felt ourselves moving apart, as if I didn't belong there, especially with her. I felt left out. My mistake was to believe it was a passing phase, almost a form of indolence on her part.

An unfortunate incident didn't help. We were looking for a camp site. "Not yet. No, not there," I kept saying—mainly to myself, for Hazel let me go on, barely saying a word. At last I found a spot. A tree showed in the dark. We bedded down. Past midnight we were woken by a terrifying noise and lights. The children all began to cry. I had pitched camp alongside the Adelaide-Port Augusta railway line.

Twenty or thirty miles north of Port Augusta I turned back. I had to. We seemed to be losing our senses. We actually met a drover somewhere around there. He was off on the side making tea. When

I asked where were his sheep, or the cattle, he gave a wave of his hand. For some reason this amused Hazel. She squatted down. I can still see her expression, silly girl.

The man didn't say much. He did offer tea though. "Come on," said Hazel, smiling up at me.

Hazel and her silly streak—she knew I wanted to get back. The drover, a diplomat, poked at the fire with a stick.

I said:

"You can if you want. I'll be in the car."

That is all.

I recall the drover as a thin head in a khaki hat, not talkative, with dusty boots. He is indistinct. Is it him? I don't know. Hazel—it is Hazel and the rotten landscape that dominate everything.

ROGER McDONALD   (1941–)

Poet, novelist. Born in N.S.W.; educated in Sydney.

COMPONENTS

Here are
blue teapot,
aluminium air.

A yellow desk,
straw matting,
wheaten lines of dusk.

A mango tree,
light climbing down
from day.

And distant thunder
walking into glass.

Here are
three components
equally clear.

The sound
of a millet broom
on stony ground.

A child's fist
pounding on boards
without rest.

A woman's voice
warping the afternoon
with its one choice.

1915

Up they go, yawning,
the crack of knuckles dropped
to smooth the heaving
in their legs, while some,
ashamed, split bile
between their teeth,
and hum to drown their stomachs.

Others touch their lips
on splintered wood
to reach for home—
'a bloke's a mug'
thinks one (who sees
a ringbarked hill)
another hisses drily
(leaping burrs).

All dreaming,
when the whistle
splits the pea, as up
they scramble, pockets fat
with Champion Flake
in battered tins,
and letters wadded thick
from Mum (who says,
'always keep
some warm clothes on …')

Up from slits in dirt
they rise, and here they stop.
A cold long light swings over.

Hard like ice
it cracks their shins—
they feel a drill and mallet
climb their bones, then cold
then warmth as blood spills out from pockets,
chests, and mouths.
No mother comes to help, although
a metal voice is whining
'boys, relax', as one
by one they totter to their knees.

TWENTY-FOUR HOUR FORECAST

In the east
the sea is expected to run
silver the hour between four and five.
In the west, darkness may brood
a while longer.
Stars are predicted, but will clear
soon after dawn.

Masses of air will glide
from one place to another throughout the day.
Following dawn, the green tops of trees
will be subject to motion.
Under this condition, leaves are inclined
to clot the grass underfoot.

Throughout the day also
light and shade will alternate.
Dappled effects may follow,
elsewhere sharp divisions will be noted
especially between stands of trees
and open ground.

At six in the evening, the darkness
previously observed in the west
will build up in the east.
This will occur more forcefully
in the north than the south.
In the south a scattering of stars
is expected to pursue the sun slowly,
while the north will face a condition
of abrupt darkness, modified by the same stars
arriving earlier, and in greater numbers.

At four or five in the morning
a pale instability is predicted,
influencing the light of the stars
and the colour of the sea, which as previously noted
turns silver at this early hour.

NICHOLAS HASLUCK   (1942–)

Poet, short story writer, novelist. Born in Canberra; educated in
Perth and Oxford; lives in Perth.

MORNING SPRINKLERS

The sprinkler spits
each whisk of water up
in rapid rings.

Soft circles drift
and ripple in the air.

Stoop, touch laughter
and retreat…
children scuttle
to the hunt
with squinting eyes
convulsive in the spray.

Touch, touch laughter
and retreat …
they tame the hoop
of muzzled tides.

Let turbines spin
and valleys overflow—

light feet
come dancing
down the water-wheel,
opening bleary eyes.

YILGARN

Bought petrol at a roadhouse.
The only bowser in the street.
A school-bus standing under
the eucalypts.

The owner wanted out.
He said so and the way he
said it—speaking awkwardly
of a down payment—
told me it was true.

The best way back?
By Peter Dawkins' tractor.
That's the best turning.

Flickerings of roadside scrub.
Splinters of dead timber.
Fence-posts stumbling into salt flats.
A tractor, an iron shell, lop-sided,
one axle deep in the mire.

Peter Dawkins' tractor—
left to rust.

He went to the wall.
After his wife cleared out.
Though what went wrong between them
is anybody's guess.

No other landmarks.
And not much to see.
Not on this road.
A rabbit sometimes ...
a windmill.

JENNIFER J. RANKIN   (1941–1979)

Poet. Born and educated in Sydney.

CLIFFS

Where the cliff cleaves up
clean into the sky
I see my day cut through

and again another cliff

and again

cleaving up.

Then it is the faulting
the falling in folds
the going back into the sea.

And this day and again this day
and again days.

Birds fly in formation.
They jettison space
while at the cliff line
a twigged bush thinly etches away
the hard edge.

Cliffs heave in blue air

heaving and faulting
rising and falling
bird flight, twig etching,

cleaving up and folding back.

PETER CAREY   (1944–)

Short story writer, novelist. Born in Victoria, educated in
Melbourne.

A WINDMILL IN THE WEST

The soldier has been on the line for two weeks. No-one has come.
The electrified fence stretches across the desert, north to south,
south to north, going as far as the eye can see without bending or
altering course. In the heat its distant sections shimmer and float.
Only at dusk do they return to their true positions. With the exception of the break at the soldier's post the ten foot high electrified
fence is uninterrupted. Although, further up the line, perhaps twenty miles along, there may be another post similar or identical to this
one. Perhaps there is not. Perhaps the break at this post is the only
entry point, the only exit point—no-one has told him. No-one has
told him anything except that he must not ask questions. The officer
who briefed him told the soldier only what was considered necessary: that the area to the west could be considered the United States,
although, in fact, it was not; that the area to the east of the line could
be considered to be Australia, which it was; that no-one, with the
exception of U.S. military personnel carrying a special pass from
Southern Command, should be permitted to cross the line at this
point. They gave him a photostat copy of an old pass, dated two
years before, and drove him out to the line in a Ford truck. That was
all.
    No-one in the United States had briefed him about the line—its
existence was never mentioned. No-one anywhere has told him if
the line is part of a large circle, or whether it is straight; no-one has

taken the trouble to mention the actual length of the line. The line may go straight across Australia, for all the soldier knows, from north to south, cutting the country in half. And, even if this were the case, he would not know where, would not be able to point out the line's location on a map. He was flown from the United States, together with two cooks, five jeeps, and various other supplies, directly to the base at Yallamby. After they landed there was no orientation brief, no maps—he waited fifteen hours before someone came to claim him.

So, for all he knows, this line could be anywhere in Australia. It is even possible that there are two parallel lines, or perhaps several hundred, each at thirty-mile intervals. It is even possible that some lines are better than others, that not all of them stretch through this desert with its whining silence and singing in the line.

The road crosses the line, roughly, at a right angle. The fact that it is not exactly a right angle has caused him considerable irritation for two weeks. For the first week he was unable to locate the thing that was irritating him, it was something small and hard, like a stone in his boot.

The bitumen road crosses the line at the slightest angle away from a right angle. He has calculated it to be, approximately, eighty-seven degrees. In another month those missing three degrees could become worse.

The soldier, who is standing on double white lines that run the length of the road, kicks a small red rock back into the desert.

The soldier sits inside the door of the caravan, his eyes focused on the dusty screen of his dark glasses, his long body cradled in his arm chair. He was informed, three weeks ago, that he would be permitted to bring a crate of specified size containing personal effects. From this he gathered some ill-defined idea of what was ahead of him. He is not a young soldier, and remembering other times in other countries he located an arm chair that would fit within the specified dimensions. The remaining space he packed with magazines, thrillers, and a copy of the Bible. The Bible was an afterthought. It puzzled him at the time, but he hasn't thought of it or looked at it since.

He had expected, while he put the crate together, that he would have a fight on his hands, sooner or later, because of that armchair. Because he had envisaged a camp. But there was no camp, merely this caravan on the line.

The soldier polishes and cleans his dark glasses, which were made to prescription in Dallas, Texas, and stands up inside the caravan. As usual he bumps his head. His natural stoop has become more exaggerated, more protective, because of this caravan. He has hit his head so often that he now has a permanent patch that is red and raw, just at the top, just where the crewcut is thin and worn like an old sandy carpet.

But this is not a caravan, not a real caravan. It resembles an aluminium coffin, an aluminium coffin with a peculiar swivelling base constructed like the base of a heavy gun. The soldier has no idea why anyone should design it that way, but he has taken advantage of it, changing the direction of the caravan so that the front door faces away from the wind. Changing the view, is what he calls it, changing the view.

No matter which way you point that door the view doesn't alter. All that changes is the amount of fence you see. Because there is nothing else—no mountains, no grass, nothing but a windmill on the western side of the line. The corporal who drove him out in the Ford said that things grew in the desert if it rained. The corporal said that it rained two years ago. He said small flowers grew all over the desert, flowers and grass.

Once or twice the soldier has set out to walk to the windmill, for no good reason. He is not curious about its purpose—it is like the road, an irritation.

He took plenty of ammunition, two grenades, and his carbine, and while he walked across the hot rocky desert he kept an eye on the caravan and the break in the wire where the road came through. He was overcome with tiredness before he reached the windmill, possibly because it was further away than it appeared to be, possibly because he knew what it would look like when he got there.

The day before yesterday he came close enough to hear it clanking, a peculiar metallic noise that travelled from the windmill to him, across the desert. No-one else in the world could hear that clanking. He spat on the ground and watched his spittle disappear. Then he fired several rounds in the direction of the windmill, just on semi-automatic. Then he turned around and walked slowly back, his neck prickling.

The thermometer recorded 120 degrees inside the caravan when he got back.

The walls are well insulated—about one foot and three inches in thickness. But he has the need to have the door open and the airconditioner became strange and, eventually, stopped. He hasn't reported the breakdown because it is, after all, of his own making. And, even if they came out from Yallamby and fixed it, he would leave the door open again and it would break down again. And there would be arguments about the door.

He needs the air. It is something he has had since he was small, the need for air coming from outside. Without good air he has headaches, and the airconditioner does not give good air. Perhaps the other soldiers at the other posts along the line sit inside and peer at the desert through their thick glass windows, if there are any other soldiers. But it is not possible for him to do that. He likes to have the air.

He has had the need since he was a child and the need has not diminished so that now, in his forty-third year, the fights he has fought to keep windows open have brought him a small degree of fame. He is tall and thin and not born to be a fighter, but his need for air forced him to learn. He is not a straight fighter, and would be called dirty in many places, but he has the ability to win, and that is all he has ever needed.

Soon he will go out and get himself another bucket of scorpions. The method is simple in the extreme. There are holes every two or three inches apart, all the way across the desert. If you pour water down these holes the scorpions come up. It amuses him to think that they come up to drink. He laughs quietly to himself and talks to the scorpions as they emerge. When they come up he scoops them into a coffee mug and tips them into the blue bucket. Later on he pours boiling water from the artesian bore over the lot of them. That is how he fills a bucket with scorpions.

To the north of the road he marked out a rough grid. Each square of this grid (its interstices marked with empty bottles and beer cans) can be calculated to contain approximately one bucket of scorpions. His plan, a new plan, developed only yesterday, is to rid the desert of a bucket full for each day he is here. As of this moment one square can be reckoned to be clear of scorpions.

The soldier, who has been sitting in his armchair, pulls on his heavy boots and goes in search of yeseterday's bucket. The glare outside the caravan is considerable, and, in spite of the sunglasses, he needs to shade his eyes. Most of the glare comes from the aluminium caravan. Everything looks like one of those colour photographs he took in Washington, overexposed and bleached out.

The blue bucket is where he put it last night, beside the generator. Not having to support the airconditioning, the generator has become quiet, almost silent.

He takes the blue bucket which once held strawberry jam and empties a soft black mass of scorpions onto the road, right in the middle, across those double white lines. In another two weeks he will have fifteen neat piles right along the centre of the road. If you could manage two bucketfuls a day there would be thirty. Perhaps, if he became really interested in it and worked hard at it, he could have several hundred buckets of scorpions lined up along those double lines. But sooner or later he will be relieved from duty or be visited by the supply truck, and then he will have to remove the scorpions before the truck reaches the spot.

He walks slowly, his boots scuffing the road, the blue bucket banging softly against his long leg, and enters the caravan where he begins to search for a coffee mug. Soon he will go out and get himself another bucket of scorpions.

The sun is low now and everything is becoming quieter, or perhaps it is only that the wind, the new wind, suggests quietness while being, in fact, louder. The sand which lies on the hard rocky base of the desert is swept in sudden gusts and flurries. Occasionally one of these small storms engulfs him, stinging his face and arms. But for all the noises and sand of wind it appears to him that there is no sound at all.

He stands in the middle of the road, his shoulders drooping, a copy of *Playboy* in his hand, and gazes along the road, as far as he can see. Somewhere up towards the western horizon he can make out an animal of some type crossing the road. It is not a kangaroo. It is something else but he doesn't know exactly what.

He gazes to the west, over past the windmill, watching the slowly darkening sky. Without turning his legs he twists his trunk and head around to watch the sun sinking slowly in the eastern sky.

He squats a little, bending just enough to place the copy of *Playboy* gently on the road. Walking slowly towards the caravan he looks once more at the windmill which is slowly disappearing in the dark western sky.

The carbine is lying on his bunk. He clips a fresh magazine into it, and returns to his place on the road, his long legs moving slowly over the sand, unhurriedly. The noise of his boots on the roadway reminds him of countless parades. He flicks the carbine to automatic and, having raised it gently to his shoulder, pours the whole magazine into the sun which continues to set in the east.

He lies on the bunk in the hot darkness wearing only his shorts and a pair of soft white socks. He has always kept a supply of these socks, a special type purchased from Fish & Degenhardt in Dallas, thick white socks with heavy towelling along the sole to soak up the sweat. He bought a dozen pairs from Fish & Degenhardt three weeks ago. They cost $4.20 a pair.

He lies on the bunk and listens to the wind in the fence.

There are some things he must settle in his mind but he would prefer, for the moment, to forget about them. He would like not to think about east or west. What is east and what is west could be settled quickly and easily. There is an army issue compass on the shelf above his head. He could go outside now, take a flashlight with him, and settle it.

But now he is unsure as to what he has misunderstood. Perhaps the area to the geographical east is to be considered as part of the United States, and the area to the west as Australian. Or perhaps it is as he remembered: the west is the United States and the east Australian; perhaps it is this and he has simply misunderstood which was east and which west. He was sure that the windmill was in the United States. He seems to remember the corporal making some joke about it, but it is possible that he misunderstood the joke.

There is also another possibility concerning the sun setting in the east. It creeps into his mind from time to time and he attempts to prevent it by blocking his ears.

He had been instructed to keep intruders on the outside but he is no longer clear as to what "outside" could mean. If they had taken the trouble to inform him of what lay "inside" he would be able to evaluate the seriousness of his position. He considers telephoning the base to ask, and dismisses it quickly, his neck and ears reddening at the thought of it.

It is hot, very hot. He tries to see the *Playboy* nude in the dark, craning his head up from the pillow. He runs his dry fingers over the shiny paper and thinks about the line. If only they had told him if it was part of a circle, or a square, or whatever shape it was. Somehow that could help. It would not be so bad if he knew the shape.

Now, in the darkness, it is merely a line, stretching across the desert as far as his mind can see. He pulls his knees up to his stomach, clutching his soft socks in his big dry hands, and rolls over on his side.

Outside the wind seems to have stopped. Sometimes he thinks he can hear the windmill clanking.

The alarm goes at 4.30 A.M. and, although he wakes instantly, his head is still filled with unravelled dreams. He does not like to remember those dreams. A long line of silk thread spun out of his navel, and he, the spinner, could not halt the spinning. He can still taste the emptiness in his stomach. It is not the emptiness of hunger but something more, as if the silk has taken something precious from him.

He bumps around the caravan in the dark. He does not like to use the light. He did not use it last night either. He is happier in the dark. He spills a bottle of insect repellent but finds the coffee next to it. With his cigarette lighter he lights the primus.

He could go outside, if he wanted, and take boiling water straight from the artesian bore, but he is happier to boil it. It makes a small happy noise inside the caravan which is normally so dense and quiet, like a room in an expensive hotel.

It will become light soon. The sun will rise but he doesn't think about this, about the sun, about the line, about what the line divides, encircles, or contains, about anything but the sound of boiling water.

The blue flame of the primus casts a flickering light over the pits and hollows of his face. He can see his face in the shaving mirror, like the surface of a planet, a photograph of the surface of the moon in *Life* magazine. It is strange and unknown to him. He rubs his hands over it, more to cover the reflected image than to feel its texture.

The coffee is ready now and he dresses while it cools off. For some reason he puts on his dress uniform. Just for a change, is what he tells himself. The uniform is clean and pressed, lying in the bottom of his duffle bag. It was pressed in Dallas Texas and still smells of American starch and the clean steam of those big hot laundries with their automatic presses.

In the middle of the desert the smell is like an old snapshot. He smiles in soft surprise as he puts it on.

He stands in the middle of the road. It is still cold and he stamps up and down looking at the place where the horizon is. He can make nothing out, nothing but stars, stars he is unfamiliar with. He could never memorise them anyway, never remember which was the bear or the bull, and it had caused him no inconvenience, this lack of knowledge.

He stands in the middle of the road and turns his head slowly around, scanning the soft horizon. Sooner or later there will be a patch, lighter than any other, as if a small city has appeared just over the edge, a city with its lights on. Then it will get bigger and then it will get hot, and before that he will have settled one of the questions concerning east and west.

He turns towards the east. He looks down the road in the direction he has known as "east" for two weeks, for two weeks until he was crazy enough to watch the sun set. He watches now for a long time. He stands still with his hands behind his back, as if bound, and feels a prickling along the back of his neck.

He stands on the road with his feet astride the double white line, in the at-ease position. He remains standing there until an undeniable shadow is cast in front of him. It is his own shadow, long and lean, stretching along the road, cast by the sun which is rising in the "west". He slowly turns to watch the windmill which is silhouetted against the clear morning sky.

It is sometime later, perhaps five minutes, perhaps thirty, when he notices the small aeroplane. It is travelling down from the "north", directly above the wire and very low. It occurs to him that the plane is too low to be picked up by radar, but he is not alarmed. In all likelihood it is an inspection tour, a routine check, or even a supply visit. The plane has been to the other posts up "north", a little further along the line.

Only when the plane is very close does he realize that it is civilian. Then it is over him, over the caravan, and he can see its civilian registration. As it circles and comes in to land on the road he is running hard for the caravan and his carbine. He stuffs his pockets full of clips and emerges as the plane comes to rest some ten yards from the caravan.

What now follows, he experiences distantly. As if he himself were observing his actions. He was once in a car accident in California where his tyre blew on the highway. He still remembers watching himself battle to control the car, he watched quite calmly, without fear.

Now he motions the pilot out of the plane and indicates that he should stand by the wing with his hands above his head. Accustomed to service in foreign countries he has no need of the English language. He grunts in a certain manner, waving and poking with the carbine to add meaning to the sounds. The pilot speaks but the soldier has no need to listen.

The pilot is a middle-aged man with a fat stomach. He is dressed in white: shorts, shirt, and socks. He has the brown shoes and white skin of a city man. He appears concerned. The soldier cannot be worried by this. He asks the pilot what he wants, using simple English, easy words to understand.

The man replies hurriedly, explaining that he was lost and nearly out of petrol. He is on his way to a mission station, at a place that the soldier does not even bother to hear—it would mean nothing.

The soldier then indicates that the pilot may sit in the shade beneath the wing of the aircraft. The pilot appears doubtful, perhaps thinking of his white clothing, but having looked at the soldier he moves awkwardly under the wing, huddling strangely.

The soldier then explains that he will telephone. He also explains that, should the man try to move or escape, he will be shot.

He dials the number he has never dialled before. At the moment of dialling he realizes that he is unsure of what the telephone is connected to: Yallamby base which is on the "outside", or whatever is on the "inside".

The phone is answered. It is an officer, a major he has never heard of. He explains the situation to the major who asks him details about the type of fuel required. The soldier steps outside and obtains the information, then returns to the major on the phone.

Before hanging up the major asks, what side of the wire was he on?

The soldier replies, on the outside.

It is two hours before the truck comes. It is driven by a captain. That is strange, but it does not surprise the soldier. However it disappoints him, for he had hoped to settle a few questions regarding the "outside" and "inside". It will be impossible to settle them now.

There are few words. The captain and the soldier unload several drums and a handpump. The captain reprimands the soldier for his lack of courtesy to the pilot. The soldier salutes.

The captain and the pilot exchange a few words while the soldier fixes the tailboard of the truck—the pilot appears to be asking questions but it is impossible to hear what he asks or how he is answered.

The captain turns the truck around, driving off the road and over the scorpion grid, and returns slowly to wherever he came from.

The pilot waves from his open cockpit. The soldier returns his greeting, waving slowly from his position beside the road. The pilot guns the motor and taxis along the road, then turns, ready for take-off.

At this point it occurs to the soldier that the man may be about to fly across the "inside", across what is the United States. It is his job to prevent this. He tries to wave the man down but he seems to be occupied with other things, or misunderstands the waving. The plane is now accelerating and coming towards the soldier. He runs towards it, waving.

It is impossible to know which is the "inside". It would have been impossible to ask a captain. They could have court-martialled him for that.

He stands beside the road as the small plane comes towards him, already off the road. It is perhaps six feet off the road when he levels his carbine and shoots. The wings tip slightly to the left and then to the right. In the area known as the "west" the small aeroplane tips onto its left wing, rolls, and explodes in a sudden blast of flame and smoke.

The soldier, who is now standing in the middle of the road, watches it burn.

He has a mattock, pick, and shovel. He flattens what he can and breaks those members that can be broken. Then he begins to dig a hole in which to bury the remains of the aeroplane. The ground is hard, composed mostly of rock. He will need a big hole. His uniform, his dress uniform, has become blackened and dirty. He digs continually, his fingers and hands bleeding and blistered. There are many scorpions. He cannot be bothered with them, there is no time. He tells them, there is no time now.

It is hot, very hot.

He digs, weeping slowly with fatigue.

Sometimes, while he digs, he thinks he can hear the windmill clanking. He weeps slowly, wondering if the windmill could possibly hear him.

HAL COLEBATCH   (1945–)

Poet, novelist. Born and educated in Perth.

THE LAST GRAMMARIANS

(For all Sub-editors)

This is a strange altar for this rite:
this kidney-shaped table and bowed, balding men.
But it is all, now, in this strange time when
others can only use tools less hard and bright.

Now when the conventional priests are burning
all inconvenient texts, and in the schools
new manpower needs less serviceable tools,
cotton-wool wrapped. The future is returning.

See these tired men with faulty hearts
who care for words because they must,
moving their shirt-sleeves in a ceaseless dust,
the last who have remained, and whose parts

are to maintain the tools, as sharp and tight
as possible, for small and humble tasks,
who keep last mysteries behind tired masks,
moving their pens in hard fluorescent light.

And if words are all we have, then let us know
who care for them and hold, now poet and scholar are gone,
who at this altar keep a last fire burning on,
because they must, when dusts of midnight blow.

WALKING HOME FROM WORK

Hot summer evening in this quiet land
with cats on low walls and, crunching underfoot,
the mown stems of grass, grass dying at the root
in the hot Summer. The neighbours stand

in every garden, watering shrubs and grass
with beetles and clicking leaves. Hose in hand
each watches the hours. We all understand
property values. The hours pass.

Native plants and woodchips would not be
the same as this moist green that should not grow
here in the red suburban evening's glow
between the sandhills and the sea

but would save water, and for this street
would look well enough. Why do we stand for hours
between Australian boat-trailers and English flowers
to pour water into sand between our feet?

Respect for something? Ancestral memories?
Some need to irrigate? Some need to fill our time?
One could not call it mystic or sublime,
yet it is amiable, under these skies.

ROBERT GRAY   (1945–)

Poet. Born and educated in N.S.W.

CHURCH GROUNDS

Bright Sunday at lunchtime
in the grimy suburb:
the presbytery's at prayers
or eating, and the nuns also—
I shortcut through
their schoolyard, down the steps
beside the church, onto
asphalt marked out
for basketball, in orange,
with the metal goals
swung down by the kids, the nets
torn and hanging like
stranded seaweed.
The garbage cans are tipped over
by them or
the stray dogs. Down here
under brick walls
(the colour of cold baked meat)
a flock of pigeons
walking. Nothing else around.
The pigeons pedal off in all
directions, eyes backwards—they
keep pecking
at the air in front of them
as they go. Tick, tick, tick.
If they're not
stabbing at the ground
for crumbs, they're keeping on
into nothing;
that's their whole life ...

LANDSCAPE 4

The river at its brim—
vast sweep
of ripples, full sailed in morning sun.

Clotted, drip-leafed gums
lean on the red
mud bank. Rickety log jetty
in socks
of oyster shells,
where milk cans stand.

The sawmill, a roof of rusty tin
on posts, over
shadow. The diagonal wooden
crane beam.

And dunes of sawdust lying about;
from somewhere there
a giant cigarette smoke.

The farmer, in felt that, rides
a tractor, rakes up the dust—
lurches
on a wading animal. Huge embossed wheels
roll down.

The exhaust-pipe chimney
beside him: through those clear fumes
and heat, the mountains—
each a half-pitched
Big Top,
blue-black—
as if seen through a window
awash.
That stripe
of lacquered green cane.

Let off on the highway,
I climb down,
heaving a haversack
through smoky green bushes,
sulphur
bladey grass. The thrashing noise
behind. Insects everywhere, on the boil.
Stinking Roger—
hot, sweetish, fermenting smell.

And the river
here, in this mid-morning's
littered
with a whole street of
fallen plate glass,
filled with
light.

J. S. HARRY (1949–)

Poet. Born in Sydney.

BETWEEN THE SAND DUNES AND THE CATTLE

Going
in the direction
of the bending grass-stalks
between the whitesand patches—windblown, driftspread
wide and smooth
across the bones of thirstless cattle
old and soft as ancient wood,

you may walk
across the path
of the one-inch
long red ant
where it forages
translucent
amber-red as if the light
had climbed behind
the bodyjuices   inside the skin—

two hundred million years   of insect
behind its travelling—It is going
in the direction of the wind that bends away
from the ocean spray tossed upward, over dunes.

Five hundred yards inland
small green blowflies fire themselves like buckshot
from the body of the cow we stumble on.
The legless maggots have no distinct head.
Vertebrates in the live stage
being somewhat less   than useful
they do not notice us at all.

A sound or a scent starts the
dull sudden thudding:
the two kangaroos that startle
into noon.

Late a golden whistler
moves across the stillness
putting sound-pegs on his holding.
There are wildflowers on the hills.
Coffee velvet wildflowers
come one hundred times each century.
Roots pin the dustdry twiggy shrubs
to the boneholds between these dunes.

After
the sun has dropped
its compass point—
how far   there'll be no telling
north south east or west   of here or there's
the dark   we'll walk as now
stumbling, over roots and into branches.
In the spaces of the sky, five hundred years
or now
our eyes hunt stars.

TIME IN A PELICAN'S WING

lake george's
pelicans

stationary
as elders or royal relations

immobilized
by an absence of light

stand formal

like knives & forks
stuck upright
in mud for the night

day will have them up
using themselves
differently

spooning mud
water vegetables
& fish

so what

if they've been having
the flavours of the
lakes they fished in changed

as the nameless
brands of water
were formed & disappeared

on this continent

for 30 or 40 million years

they have followed water
scooping fish frogs crabs to live
to here—

today lake george
   is the clearest of soups—

unknowing

as the tide's pollutants move
   on the shore-crabs
as the effluent flows
   down the rivers & creeks

as the agricultural chemicals
   wash   off the land
into streams

what time is left
   in the flight of their wings—

unlike humans or sun
   they are not
big drinkers of lakes

they will dribble back the water
   keep the fish

we are joined to them by ignorance
what time is left in anyone's drink

RICHARD TIPPING   (1949–)

Poet, editor. Born and educated in Adelaide.

DOMESTIC HARDCORE

Three years in any place
is too long—

what you came for
quickly settled

playing on home ground

nest of the taken
for granted
each pathway known
chose this, began

any starting point, here
for instance

habit becomes landscape

the familiar fixed
breakfast a certainty
shelter of the rest
assured, bed

& kitchen functionaries
deadweight of books, personal
artefacts
          you are thingd
finally
in domestic hardcore

but thats not
what has been important
& no reason to go

measuring the force
of circumstance

trying to sort out
reflex from happiness
with a snip snip here
& a snap

ping off by force
of common sense, cultural
twitches nothing less

than all the shit that goes
with just being human

identity bits
unloading surplus baggage
the only necessity is self
possession—

get out of here

AGAINST OR FOR BEAUTY

Peasant women etc
ox paddyfield & so on
plough slush straw hat
child in arms etc etc

delete arms insert on back
child on back—rub out
back insert backwards
child strapped on backwards

Peasant woman etc
screech run fall & so on
bullets napalm shrapnel
child in mud etc etc

delete mud insert broken
child broken—rub out
broken insert blown apart
child mangled blown apart

Peasant woman etc
what can we do & so on
being sickened is a luxury
aesthetics of pain etc etc

delete pain insert revolution
aesthetics of revolution—rub out
aesthetics insert beauty
revolution must be

CHARLES BUCKMASTER   (1951–1972)

Poet. Born in Victoria.

WILPENA POUND

—Where we had stood
at the peak of the mountain
and had first noticed   that we were
inside.

below us, the pass, and about us
a circle of mountains:
red aside orange
the rocks
laced with colour.

and the bushland below
'so dense, in some areas'

—she had said,

'that one can barely pass through it.'

The Pound—originally,
a depressed plateau, the centre
having eroded, leaving a natural enclosure

—a plain
circled by mountains.

Where we had stood
by the groupings of boulders, inside the Pound

spread on the rocks, exhausted
by the climb

facing west, toward the sun, the miles
of forest against mountain

the isolation!

winding track, below,
through the pass

—the way to the Outside.

Mordor—the mountains—
in the 'other world'.

'This is our home, the place
for our people'

she said,
without realizing ...

'to think that we could
climb down that path, into the forest,
to the centre of the Pound

and never
return again.'

(Taking up your axe—the trees
for your home

... at some un-marked spring—bathing your child
in the water of the mountains

... Gardens about your cabin

... Within the voice of the forest ...)

This circle of mountains!—a natural
and an un-natural
isolation.

'The tribes of the Ranges
were exterminated.' (Poisoned flour,
'Aborigine Shoots'—
'near here, a massacre, in the 1880s:'
said John.

　　　And for this!—

The Pound stretches twelve miles
—twelve miles of heavily forested plain
thinning on all sides against the mountains.
About and around the centre—the remains of the lost;
where few men have been.
Twelve miles of complete/the final
isolation.

And I had little else to give you but love:
now, there is that which we shall take from you,
this land, being
our land:

there is reason for many to be bitter—this land,
your pastures
stained with blood from dark-skinned wounds.

Land of clouds; from the heights of mountain
to plain ...
I go down through the forest and pick up the spear
which fell
from the hand of my brother
as he died

a century past.

Though you refuse our offer; understand, father:
My brothers and I are of the forest
and we are aware of its nature more fully than you

—the forest
is our home father:
the battle to be fought is of self-preservation.

… And I take up that weapon and return
to the hunt.

Sunset. To the west, etched
in a sky of all colour—a lone tree against light:

and to the north, the Pound: a circle of fire.

PETER KOCAN   (1947–)

Poet, novelist. Born in N.S.W.; educated in Melbourne.

MORISSET: AFTER TEN YEARS

Perhaps I have gained empathy
In some things. I'm familiar
With this landscape where so much life
Clings for sustenance. I know
This earth in sun and in rain,
The sky's every tint, the way
Of time's subtle alteration.

The trees that I walk beneath
Have nursed ten generations
Of birds since I came. I know which branches
The moon climbs in through the year.
I've learned the vernacular
Of local wind and water,
The grasses' colloquial whisper.

I have felt the hidden clock
Of instinct drawing the swan
And wild duck across the sky,
And waking the possum by night,
The parrot by day. I have seen
The snake and the hawk busy
About their proper business.

And yet the other dimension
Of the place, after ten years,

Remains a mystery—that old
Perversity of human grief
Tearing always at itself
With strange wastings in the flesh
And alien weathers in the head.

COWS

Cows graze across the hill,
Measuring the day
As their shadows tell
Irrelevant time. Their gait is half-way
Between moving and standing still.

The sun is gentle on the green
Of their meadow, their mouths deep
In its heavy warmth.
A watcher could fall asleep
Into the depth
Of that untroubled scene.

From each dewdrop morning
To every day's end
They follow the cycle
Of the rhythm of the world turning
In its season. A miracle
Of normalcy is a cow's mind.

Beyond thought's prickling fever
They dwell in the grace
Of their own true concerns,
And in that place
Know they will live forever
With butterflies around their horns.

LOST CAUSES

I think of nothing now
But lost causes, and how
Many preferred to fall
Fighting, for good or ill.

For some it was a creed,
Or empty bellies, or pride
Stiffened their beaten ranks
Even while their sun sank.

Like the croppy boys, all
Exposed on Vinegar Hill
To shot and cannonade.
By nightfall most were dead.

Or it was loyalty:
When the hacked clansmen lay
Across Culloden Moor
Or bled in the heather

Old men and women chose
To risk an English noose,
Humming Jacobite airs
At the passing soldiers.

They did more than bequeath
A gallant epitaph
And a handful of songs:
Their stubbornness brings

A glass near to focus
On what it is in us
Might still comprehend
The time to make a stand.

KEVIN HART   (1954–)

Poet. Born in London; educated in England, Canberra and
California.

POZIÈRES

The moon shines over the field,
it looks at itself from the bottom of the Somme;
it enters the houses of Pozières
and spills across the tables, white as salt.

Over the church with its burning candles,
over the white-haired man still drinking
the moon looks down.

           This face is pure white,
this face remembers nothing. And the people sleep
and the moon enters their dreams:
a clock that says it is all over now,
a plate that says eat all you wish.

And at the bottom of the old man's glass
the moon sparkles like a coin, but his face remains dark
like the other face of the moon.

EVENING

1

Night slowly expands across the city; a full moon appears, a white
    counter.

In the suburbs it is dusty as torchlight, there are houses on stilts,
    houses brown and heavy as pennies with the face of the
    dead Queen.

And in the sky stormclouds gather, the evening's headache.

In the houses there are dolls with bright fixed eyes kept under beds
    with broken clocks and women's hats with orchids,
    dangling fruit.

In shop windows the dead are assembling, dressed in all the fashions
    of the living.

We try to fathom their faces, squeezing ourselves against the glass,
    bequeathing them our breath.

And everywhere this darkness, as in the corners of Cathedrals.

A breeze brings the smell of rotting cardboard from the docks, and
    smoke from the last ferry casting off, about to cross the
    black river.

A boy stands on board with his father; he looks into the sky and
    sees the moon, he looks into the waters: the moon is there
    also.

2

On Ann Street and Elizabeth Street, on the dead-end roads, and all
    down the river that glitters like a snail's trail,
    the full moon shines.

All night she wanders the streets, with nothing to do, she looks into
    our windows and sees cane furniture like
    stick-insects, a cat lapping milk in a dark kitchen.

She lingers on Roma Street Station, smelling old leather suitcases.

She peers into verandahs and bedrooms, examining the whites of
    eyes, of those who cannot sleep, who pour themselves
    another drink. She cools their glasses.

She is with the ship coming towards the harbour, with those who
    can only just see the city, a string of lights, a rosary.

On the hospitals and churches, on the bamboo that knots in
    overgrown gardens, she shines, accepting everything.

Those still out this night look up; the moon is in the highest point of
    the sky, above each one of them.

She settles on tables and changes them to altars, she sits at the
    bottom of puddles,

While over all the city a steady rain begins to fall, the sound of
    many clocks.

PETER GOLDSWORTHY (1951–)

Poet. Born in Queensland; educated in South Australia and
Northern Territory.

BRICKIE

He slaps each brick
into the palm of the last

—stone fists,
loaves of earth.

His rhythms
are music for good listening

and the two minute poems
of race-callers.

Noon is a sweltering kiln.
He shelters among pallets

with a bottle of lunch,
a pack of tailor-mades.

Some days walls are enough craft.
Some days he's almost one himself,

a worn landscape
slowing into afternoon.

SHANE MCCAULEY   (1954–)

Poet. Born in England; came to Australia in 1959; educated in Perth and Sydney.

BEACHED WHALES

Even those temporarily saved return,
Cruise in, death snug within them.
We say there is no discernible reason,
Talk as if mass suicide were foreign
To us, ponder such inscrutable insanity.
Yet on their beach, filled with
The enigma of the land's calling, they
Sing, and just before their weight
Crushes them, they feel legs grow,
Try to crawl, urge on their great hearts
And die. Those that don't do so quickly
We shoot. We are merciful, and have reasons
For just about everything.

TWO-UP SCHOOL, ANZAC DAY

The atmosphere of the tribal cave, both
Ritual and game, the spinner with beery breath
Coming into the group's centre intent
As javelin-thrower. The coins for a moment
Twinkling planets against the swaying light,
Each bark of result triumphant as bets
Are resolved. Hands scoop up the floundering
Paper, and even the losers are smiling
At the wayward disposition of the fall.
Fortune will ignore blindfold the very next call.

JAMIE GRANT (1949–)

Poet. Born and educated in Melbourne.

FARMER PICKING MUSHROOMS

The idea of emptiness drenches this place
like smoke. Clouds like white slabs of lichen
grip sky's rough hollow bark. I walk in thistle fur
paddocks. Light slices mottled space.

The cold sun smells of snow—white ledges stain
coarse screes. A long way off, some poplars
grow out of our homestead. No people
anywhere. On hills, sheep anchored like stones.

No need for me to be here. For weeks
these unasked dreams have pushed their roots
down through my sleep. I don't think of my wife.
Coming downhill, I step across a creek.

Now those poplars look nearer. The farm's roof
is thatched with shadows, verandahs pulled
round like a hat brim. Behind, the hills
boil up like clouds. I've found no mushrooms.

Footprints ran through my garden. Her lover's
breath breeds in her lungs like a fungus.

GLENDA ADAMS (1940–)

Short story writer, novelist. Born and educated in Sydney; left Australia in 1964 for New York.

A SNAKE DOWN UNDER

We sat in our navy blue serge tunics with white blouses. We sat without moving, our hands on our heads, our feet squarely on the floor under our desks.

The teacher read us a story: A girl got lost in the bush. She wandered all day looking for the way back home. When night fell she took refuge in a cave and fell asleep on the rocky floor. When she awoke she saw to her dismay that a snake had come while she slept and had coiled itself on her warm lap, where it now rested peacefully. The girl did not scream or move lest the snake be aroused and bite her. She stayed still without budging the whole day and the following night, until at last the snake slid away of its own accord. The girl was shocked but unharmed.

We sat on the floor of the gym in our gym uniforms: brown shirts and old-fashioned flared shorts no higher than six inches above the knee, beige ankle socks and brown sneakers. Our mothers had embroidered our initials in gold on the shirt pocket. We sat cross-legged in rows, our backs straight, our hands resting on our knees.

The gym mistress, in ballet slippers, stood before us, her hands clasped before her, her back straight, her stomach muscles firm. She said: If ever a snake should bite you, do not panic. Take a belt or a piece of string and tie a tourniquet around the affected limb between the bite and the heart. Take a sharp knife or razor blade. Make a series of cuts, criss-cross, over the bite. Then, suck at the cuts to remove the poison. Do not swallow. Spit out the blood and the poison. If you have a cut on you gum or lip, get a friend to suck out the poison instead. Then go to the nearest doctor. Try to kill the snake and take it with you. Otherwise, note carefully its distinguishing features.

My friend at school was caught with a copy of *East of Eden*. The headmistress called a special assembly. We stood in rows, at attention, eyes front, half an arm's distance from each other.

The headmistress said: One girl, and I shan't name names, has been reading a book that is highly unsuitable for high school pupils. I shan't name the book, but you know which book I mean. If I find that book inside the school gates again, I will take serious measures. It is hard for some of you to know what is right and what is wrong. Just remember this. If you are thinking of doing something, ask yourself: could I tell my mother about this? If the answer is no, then you can be sure you are doing something wrong.

I know of a girl who went bushwalking and sat on a snake curled up on a rock in the sun. The snake bit her. But since she was with a group that included boys, she was too embarrassed to say anything. So she kept on walking, until the poison overcame her. She fell ill and only then did she admit that a snake had bitten her on a very private part. But it was too late to help her. She died.

When I was sixteen my mother encouraged me to telephone a boy and ask him to be my partner for the school dance. She said: You are old enough to decide who you want to go out with and who you don't want to go out with. I trust you completely.

After that I went out with a Roman Catholic, then an immigrant Dutchman, then an Indonesian.

My mother asked me what I thought I was doing. She said: You can go out with anyone you like as long as it's someone nice.

In the museum were two photographs. In the first, a snake had bitten and killed a young goat. In the second, the snake's jaws were stretched open and the goat was half inside the snake. The outline of the goat's body was visible within the body of the snake. The caption read: Snake trying to eat goat. Once snake begins to eat, it cannot stop. Jaws work like conveyor belt.

A girl on our street suddenly left and went to Queensland for six months. My mother said it was because she had gone too far. She said to me: You know, don't you, that if anything ever happens to you, you can come to me for help. But of course I know you won't ever have to, because you wouldn't ever do anything like that.

Forty minutes of scripture a week was compulsory in all state schools. The Church of England girls sat with hands flat on the desk to preclude fidgeting and note passing. A lay preacher stood before us, his arms upstretched to heaven, his hands and voice shaking. He said: Fornication is a sin and evil. I kissed only one woman, once, before I married. And that was the woman who became my wife. The day I asked her to marry me and she said yes, we sealed our vow with a kiss. I have looked upon no other woman.

I encountered my first snake when I went for an early morning walk beside a wheat field in France. I walked gazing at the sky. When I felt a movement on my leg I looked down. Across my instep rested the tail of a tweedy-skinned snake. The rest of its body was inside the leg of my jeans, resting against my own bare leg. The head was at my knee.
  I broke the rules. I screamed and kicked and stamped. The snake fell out of my jeans in a heap and fled into the wheat. I ran back to the house crying.
  My friend said, "Did it offer you an apple?"

THE MOTHERS HAVE CURLY HAIR

The mothers have curly hair but they are not smiling. One is sitting on the sand hunched under the plastic beach umbrella, sunglasses hiding her eyes and a kerchief tied across the lower half of her face, like a highwayman or a bank robber. The other is burying her son in sand, up to his chin.
  The mothers are dressed identically in navy blue ankle-length robes of brushed cotton, like sweatshirts, with hoods and kangaroo pockets. They bought them the day before and agreed that since they hardly saw each other during the year it did not matter that they had identical outfits. But now on the beach they look as if they are members of a sect, fugitives from The Force of Destiny.
  The mother under the umbrella is called Lesley. Little curls, permed before she left the city for this holiday, poke from under

the hood of the robe. Her seven-year-old daughter Lisa is in the parking lot, confined to the Dodge Dart for having struck little August across the back with a piece of driftwood. Lisa is either slumped in a corner of the back seat reading her second-hand *Millie the Model* comics or has strewn all the tissues from the Scottissue box around the interior of the car. It is possible that she is still sobbing, her fist or the inside of her elbow pressed against her eyes, because of her mother's angry face that had bent down and shouted into hers.

The mothers had watched their children struggling with the driftwood. Lisa tried to wrench it away from August. Lisa had seen it first. It was hers. August would not let go. He had picked it up first. It was his. Lisa twisted it out of August's grasp.

"August sticks up for himself well," said Lesley.

"But Lisa always wins," said Maggie.

August kicked sand at Lisa. Lisa turned around and whacked him across the back with the driftwood. Lesley had to get up. She ran down the beach in her robe and mask, grabbed her child, and yanked her away by the arm, yanked her all the way up from the waves, up the sand dunes to the parking lot and into the Dodge Dart.

Two rather interesting-looking men, searching for a good spot for surf fishing, stopped to watch the spectacle, then picked up their gear and walked on.

"You know why you're being put in the car," Lesley said to Lisa.

"But he kicked at me," said Lisa.

"And did he? Did he actually kick you? Did he?"

"He tried to," said Lisa.

"Oh, for God's sake," said Lesley.

"I saw it first and he kicked me," said Lisa. She was crying hard.

Lesley now lies curled up under the umbrella while Maggie buries August in the sand. It is the last day of their holiday. That morning Maggie had plaited her hair into 40 little pigtails, dreadlocks, and now, unplaited, her hair curls wildly. August looks pleased. Maggie has dug a deep hole for him to sit in, and she has piled sand all over him. She places the piece of driftwood on the sand near his head. But his hands are firmly buried, and he can't move them to break through the sand to hold it.

The day before they had all watched a nuclear family build a sandcastle, a process which involved the careful up-ending of bucketloads of wet sand, one bucket mould on top of the other; all under the supervision of the father. They had built a moat around the whole structure so that when the tide came in the waves would be diverted around the castle and not erode it, at least not for a while.

From her umbrella Lesley had been thinking about the man she is in love with who lives far away and cannot get around to leaving his wife. She had been watching that family build its castle and quoting to herself *The Mistress Addresses the Wife* by Naomi Replansky which begins, "Your castle may be sand, but I am not the sea." It had made her feel justly sad and at the same time pleased to have found for once an apt quotation at the right time.

Maggie had just finished building sand cars for Lisa and August, with bucket seats and dashboards of controls. August made a show of parking his car carefully and getting out with elaborate caution so that the sides would not fall in. Then he rushed across to the family group and hurled himself on top of their castle, destroying the turrets and two wings. Lesley had seen what he was intending to do as soon as he made that show of parking his sand car. Maggie had been fixing Lisa's car. But only after August began his assault, after he had pounced on the castle, could Lesley say anything.

"Oh, Maggie, look what August has done," she said, and she wished she did not sound like a tattle tale. She was pleased when from time to time it was Maggie's child and not hers who performed an anti-social act.

That was yesterday, and August had ended up in the Dart. Now, for a treat, as a reward for having been hit by Lisa with the driftwood, he is buried up to his neck in sand. Then Maggie goes for a swim. A grim swim. Maggie swims grimly every day. It is wrong, she feels, to be at the beach and not swim. Lesley feels that it is wrong to be on holiday and feel that one has to swim, and during their two weeks at the Cape, she has entered the water only four times.

August, having been buried in sand, cannot rush into the water after Maggie and spoil his mother's swim. His head waggles back and forth on top of the sand as he yells to Maggie to dig him out so that he can be near her again. But Maggie does not hear. She is ducking under the water, and her hair has gone straight again.

Lesley wears the kerchief over her face to protect her fair skin from the sun, which is reflected from the sand and the water. Her sensitivity to the sun and her attitude about swimming and exercise in general has caused some problems during this holiday at the seaside. She has a great capacity for sitting still and pondering life and love and drawing the conclusion each time that there is no justice. Maggie, who is in love with no one any more, agrees that there is no justice. She is always on the go, building castles, collecting oysters, digging for clams, swimming, hiking, riding her bicycle and generally not sitting down at all.

At breakfast Maggie asks August if he would like sunflower seeds on his yogurt.

"I don't like sunflower seeds," replies August.

"Yes, you do," says Maggie.

"No, I don't," says August.

"Don't be silly," says Maggie. "You've had them before and you like them." She sprinkles the sunflower seeds on the yogurt.

August cries and says he won't eat it.

"You may not be excused until you eat your breakfast," says Maggie.

August cries more energetically.

Lisa says, "Mmmm," as she eats her yogurt and jam, smacking her lips. "I hate sunflower seeds," she contributes, and August wails afresh, resting his head on the table beside his bowl.

Maggie spends a lot of time either coaxing the right food by the teaspoonful down August's throat or preventing the wrong food from going down. When August tries to eat every bit of his watermelon Maggie tells him to be careful not to eat the green part of the flesh near the skin or he will get sick. When August does indeed eat the green part, Maggie has to take it from him and with her finger extract the mouthful already being chewed.

While August has been either eating the green part of the watermelon flesh or not eating his sunflower seeds, Lesley has been sitting on the sofa reading the *Arabian Nights*, which she bought second-hand when Lisa spent her pocket money on the *Millie the Model* comics. Lisa has left the table without excusing herself and, with her comics tucked in her shorts, is now playing with two beach balls, kicking first her red one and then August's green one against the living room wall.

"Oh, for God's sake, stop that noise," says Lesley.

"That's my ball," says August, trying to escape from the breakfast table.

"Just two more spoonfuls," says Maggie.

August downs the yogurt plus seeds and rushes up to Lisa to reclaim his ball. But Lisa scoops up both balls and holds them above her head, saying she is playing a game that is very special to her and she needs two balls.

August howls. Lesley says, "Oh, for God's sake. I'm about to lose my temper." Maggie says, "Give August his ball." August is screaming and kicks Lisa, who cries, "He kicked me," and runs out of the cottage with both balls. August is on the floor sobbing. Lesley has to put down her book and go after Lisa to instruct her to give August his ball.

Later, on the sand at the edge of the bay in front of their cottage Maggie is playing with August, throwing him his beach ball. Lisa askes if she can play, too, and Maggie says, "Get your own ball and play with it." Lisa runs crying back to the cottage, where Lesley sits indoors out of the sun, reading, and tells on Maggie. Lesley considers returning to the city.

"Just stay here with me and color something," she says.

"I hate staying with you. I want them," says Lisa.

Maggie and Lesley have rented this little cottage on the bay in order to relax after a year's hard work, to enjoy their children, and to meet people.

The sand in front of their cottage is convenient and warm, but the water is shallow with a low tide that produces half a mile of knee-deep water. Few people come to this stretch of sand. Maggie, digging up oysters one low tide at dusk, actually ran into a man about her age digging up oysters with his son, and they smiled at each other. A couple of days later she saw him at the health food store in the village and they smiled at each other again, but that is the last time Maggie sees him, even though she digs up oysters often and goes to the health food store almost every day for supplies. Having bought nuts and fruit and natural hot dogs the second last day of their holiday and not seen the man again, Lesley and Maggie went to a boutique and bought their ankle-length robes while Lisa and August sát on the cannon on the village green preoccupied with their all-natural ice cream cones.

This holiday straddles two weeks, one before the season opens, the other after, and the cottage costs a great deal less for that first week. They visited the ocean beach the second day, but there were no people there, apart from a few teenagers gathered around a transistor radio playing disco. Maggie was building a sand fort and after a while went up to the teenagers and inquired, "Do you really think that everyone wants to listen to your music?"

They looked up at her surprised. "Pardon us for living," a girl replied.

"I don't mind your living," said Maggie. "It's your music I mind."

They turned the music down for a while, but Maggie said that the ocean beach clearly did not attract the kind of people she and Lesley would want to meet, and Lesley said it was just as well, because she could not sit out on the sand all day with her skin.

They go mostly to the freshwater pond, midway between the ocean and the bay, where the water is freezing cold. Lisa and August like the calm water and the pontoons. Lesley likes the trees where she can crouch away from the sun. Maggie likes it because August likes it. And there are no teenagers.

The four of them are there now. It is quite chilly. Nearby two young couples lie on the thin strip of sand. One woman reads *A Man and Two Women*. Her head rests on the stomach of her husband, who, while he reads *The World According to Garp*, caresses her midriff with one hand. The other woman reads a book by James Carroll and from time to time watches her husband who has put down his book and now stands with the chilly water up to the legs of his red swimming trunks.

A little rowboat has pulled in to the shallow of the pond. A couple, a strong, tanned young man and an older woman, is rowing. The woman swings herself over the near side of the boat into the water and steadies it, tilting it a little away from her while the young man swings himself over the far side. He stands there with the water up to his trunks, while she drags the boat onto the beach alone. Then she comes back into the water to the young man. He puts his arm around her shoulder, and they stand there close together for a minute or so, talking quietly. Then they turn toward the beach, he leaning heavily on her, and as they emerge it becomes clear that he has only one leg.

The man in red trunks has come out of the water, too, and his wife puts down James Carroll and dries his legs for him. The two young couples engage in a lively literary discussion.

It is four o'clock, and Lesley can remove her kerchief mask. The sun is lower and there is a breeze.

A man and a woman walk along the pond edge, past Lesley and Maggie sitting shivering on the sand. The man makes a honking sound, which makes Lisa and August look up from the plastic boats they are playing with at the water's edge. Lisa has been swimming, and although she is shivering in her wet bathing costume she has refused to put on her new sweatshirt that reads "Cape Cod Mass" in white letters and "Lisa" in multi-colored glitter letters across the chest. August wears his identical sweatshirt with "Cape Cod Mass" in white letters and "August" also in white letters. They had bought the sweatshirts in Provincetown one day, and Maggie had had August's name ironed on in white letters without giving August a choice. He was too short to see the counter where letters of different colors were displayed. Maggie had thought the multi-colored glitter letters gaudy and cheap. Lisa, when she saw August in his shirt, said, "I want one, too," and Lesley said, "Oh, for God's sake," meaning "all right," and then Lisa, who was much taller, chose the multi-colored glitter letters for her name, and August cried because he wanted glitter, too. The only thing Maggie could say was, "Glitter is for girls," although it went against her principles to make distinctions on the grounds of sex.

Maggie now has to keep calling out to August as he plays at the water's edge to be careful not to get his sweatshirt wet because it is cold and he shall catch cold.

When the children hear the man honking, they look up.

"Come on, Freddy," says the woman with him, "come along." Freddy wears only beige trunks and his skin is mottled pink and blue. He clutches the woman's arm and they stumble a few yards past Lesley and Maggie. The woman leading Freddy throws their towels on the sand and without letting Freddy go takes off her T-shirt and pulls him after her into the water.

Freddy honks and hoots. "It too cold. It too deep." The water is up to his knees, but his companion yanks him further into the water, and once he is in up to his waist, she starts splashing him, and he giggles and shrieks and shivers. "It too cold. It too deep."

Lisa and August have stopped playing and walk along the water's edge to watch this grown woman pulling this grown man into the water. Lisa goes into the water to get a closer look.

"August, come back here," calls Maggie before August can even organise himself to follow Lisa.

Lisa is helping the woman splash and pull Freddy.

"Lisa," calls Lesley, but Lisa takes no notice.

Afterwards, as Maggie primes the charcoal and Lesley makes screwdrivers, they tell the children about mental retardation. Maggie and Lesley explain that Freddy can't help being that way and they ask the children, "Aren't you lucky you are healthy and normal?"

After dinner, Maggie goes for a moonlight hike while Lesley dozes. Maggie meets and talks to a neighbor, a middle-aged woman out walking her cocker spaniel. They comment on the beautiful evening, and the woman tells Maggie, a complete stranger, that she goes for walks as often as she can to get away from her old mother who is in her cottage with a terminal illness.

Two days before the end of their vacation, Maggie and Lesley and the children return to the ocean beach and find that, the season having begun, it is now crowded. They don't want to go to the pond any more because of Freddy, and they are annoyed that they had not known that people had started coming to the ocean beach. This is the day that August destroys the sandcastle, and the next day Lisa hits August with the driftwood.

Throughout the holiday they have gone out to dinner alternate nights, having decided that eating out might be a good way to meet people. They are eating at the Lobster Shanty and it is the last night of their holiday. The Shanty is noisy and crowded. Lesley has dressed in purple drawstring trousers, a mauve shirt and a blue cotton waistcoat, and wears various chains and rings. Maggie wears an off-white sweater she has crocheted and jeans, but no jewellery. They have both washed their hair. Lesley's perm frizzes nicely around her face. Maggie's dreadlocks have been unplaited and her long hair falls in spectacular corrugations to her shoulder. Lisa has even told them both that they look pretty.

Lisa now wants more french fries and so does August, who has been eating his sole happily until Lisa pushes hers away, saying it tastes bad.

"Oh, for God's sake," says Lesley.

"No french fries," says Maggie.

The two children fall to the floor crying and kicking, and the mothers have to drag them out of the restaurant to the Dodge Dart, where they yell and scold their children.

Maggie turns to Lesley and says, "Well, they can't just have what they want, can they?"

"Oh, for God's sake," says little Lisa. "Oh, for God's sake," mimics August. And they are both bundled into the car.

INDEX OF AUTHORS
AND TITLES